To Joan, with love

Augsburg Commentary on the New Testament
ACTS

Gerhard A. Krodel

Augsburg Publishing House
Minneapolis, Minnesota

AUGSBURG COMMENTARY ON THE NEW TESTAMENT
Acts

Copyright © 1986 Augsburg Publishing House

Scripture quotations unless otherwise noted are from the Revised Standard Version of the Bible, copyright 1946, 1952, and 1971 by the Division of Christian Education of the National Council of Churches.

Material from *Acts* by Gerhard Krodel, Proclamation Commentaries (Philadelphia: Fortress Press, 1981), is used by permission of the publisher.

Library of Congress Cataloging-in-Publication Data

Krodel, Gerhard, 1926–
    ACTS.

    (Augsburg commentary on the New Testament)
    Bibliography: p.
    1. Bible. N.T. Acts—Commentaries. I. Title.
II. Series.
BS2625.3.K75   1986   226'.607   86-10796
ISBN 0-8066-8884-X

Manufactured in the U.S.A.   APH 10-9046

1   2   3   4   5   6   7   8   9   0   1   2   3   4   5   6   7   8   9

CONTENTS

FOREWORD

The AUGSBURG COMMENTARY ON THE NEW TESTA-
MENT is written for laypeople, students, and pastors. Laypeople
will use it as a resource for Bible study at home and at church.
Students and instructors will read it to probe the basic message of
the books of the New Testament. And pastors will find it to be a
valuable aid for sermon and lesson preparation.

The plan of each commentary is designed to enhance its useful-
ness. The Introduction presents a topical overview of the biblical
book to be discussed and provides information on the historical
circumstances in which that book was written. It may also contain
a summary of the biblical writer's thought. In the body of the commentary, the interpreter sets forth in brief compass the meaning of
the biblical text. The procedure is to explain the text section by
section. Care has also been taken to avoid the heavy use of technical
terms. Because the readers of the commentary will have their Bibles
at hand, the biblical text itself has not been printed out. In general,
the editors recommend the use of the Revised Standard Version of
the Bible.

The authors of this commentary series are professors at seminaries
and universities and are themselves ordained. They have been selected both because of their expertise and because they worship in
the same congregations as the people for whom they are writing.
In elucidating the text of Scripture, therefore, they attest to their

belief that central to the faith and life of the church of God is the Word of God.

The Editorial Committee

Roy A. Harrisville
Luther Northwestern Theological Seminary
St. Paul, Minnesota

Jack Dean Kingsbury
Union Theological Seminary
Richmond, Virginia

Gerhard A. Krodel
Lutheran Theological Seminary
Gettysburg, Pennsylvania

ABBREVIATIONS

BS	*Bibliotheca Sacra*
BWANT	Beiträge zur Wissenschaft vom Alten und Neuen Testament
BZNW	Beiheft zur *ZNW*
CBQ	*Catholic Biblical Quarterly*
HTR	*Harvard Theological Review*
IDB	*Interpreter's Dictionary of the Bible*
JAAR	*Journal of the American Academy of Religion*
JJS	*Journal of Jewish Studies*
JSNT	*Journal for the Study of the New Testament*
JThS	*Journal of Theological Studies*
KJV	King James Version
LXX	Septuagint (the Greek Old Testament)
NovTest	*Novum Testamentum*
NTS	*New Testament Studies*
PGM	*Papyri graecae magicae*, ed. K. Preisendanz
SBL	Society of Biblical Literature
SBLDS	SBL Dissertation Series
SBLMS	SBL Monograph Series
SBT	Studies in Biblical Theology
SNTSMS	Society of New Testament Studies Monograph Series
StANT	Studien zum Alten und Neuen Testament
TDNT	*Theological Dictionary of the New Testament*, ed. G. Kittel
ThR	*Theologische Rundschau*
TU	Texte und Untersuchungen zur Geschichte der altchristlichen Literatur
WUNT	Wissenschaftliche Untersuchungen zum Neuen Testament
ZNW	*Zeitschrift für die neutestamentlichen Wissenschaft*

ACKNOWLEDGMENTS

I would like to express my gratitude to the Aid Association for Lutherans for their Franklin Clark Fry Fellowship, which helped make the writing of this book possible, and to Mary Miller, our gracious secretary, for her superb typing of my manuscript.

INTRODUCTION

The book of Acts is one of the most exciting books of antiquity. Some 50 years ago, E. J. Goodspeed wrote: "Where, within eighty pages, will be found such a varied series of exciting events—trials, riots, persecutions, escapes, martyrdoms, voyages, shipwrecks, rescues—set in that amazing panorama of the ancient world—Jerusalem, Antioch, Philippi, Corinth, Athens, Ephesus, Rome? And with such scenery and settings—temples, courts, prisons, deserts, ships, barracks, theaters? Has any opera such variety? A bewildering range of scenes and actions (and of speeches) passes before the eye of the historian. And in all of them he sees the providential hand that has made and guided this great movement for the salvation of mankind" (*Introduction to the New Testament*, pp. 187-88).

1. The Author and Setting as Known from Tradition

The person who composed this amazing book did not identify himself by name. The titles *Gospel according to Luke* and *Acts of the Apostles* were added when the two books were incorporated into the New Testament canon. These titles were certainly not part of the original work. According to Irenaeus (died A.D. 202; *Against Heresies* 3.1.14), Tertullian (died A.D. 220; *Against Marcion* 4.2), Eusebius (died A.D. 339; *Church History* 3.4) and others, the author of the Third Gospel and Acts was Luke, the traveling companion of Paul and the "beloved physician" (Col. 4:14; Philemon 24; 2 Tim. 4:11).

Undoubtedly, Paul had a coworker named Luke (Philemon 24). Moreover, some sections in Acts are written in the first person plural ("we" instead of "he" or "they"; see comments on 16:10), suggesting the author's presence among Paul's traveling companions. However, the first person plural narration could be a literary device, and the church fathers probably inferred the author's identity from data found in the New Testament (2 Tim. 4:9-12, esp. v. 11 in conjunction with Acts 28:14, "we").

To be sure, the author of Acts, when he was still very young, could have been a traveling companion of Paul. Writing some 40 years later, he made some errors and produced discrepancies which become obvious when we compare his narrative with data from Paul's letters (e.g., see comments on 11:30). The closer we tie our author to Paul, the more difficult and contrived become the explanations of the discrepancies between Acts and the authentic Pauline letters. We shall continue to call the author by his traditional name, Luke, without identifying him as one of Paul's traveling companions.

He wrote Luke-Acts certainly after the destruction of Jerusalem (Luke 13:35; 19:41-44; 21:20-24), and since he made use of the Gospel of Mark which was composed around A.D. 70, we may assume the decade of A.D. 80–90 for the origin of Luke's two-volume work. The place of writing is unknown. Among the cities and regions suggested by scholars are Macedonia, Achaia, Ephesus, Antioch, Caesarea, and Rome. It would seem that Rome might possibly be the place of origin. Luke wrote about what God accomplished "among us" (Luke 1:1), and God's final accomplishment in Luke's narrative is Paul's coming to Rome (Acts 28:14, 16), bringing the normative traditions with him (cf. B. H. Streeter, *The Four Gospels*, 1925, p. 531).

2. The Author as Known from His Work

We can learn quite a few things about the author from his writing. For one, Luke was the first Christian who intentionally wrote literature and made literary claims (as his preface, Luke 1:1-4, demonstrates). As a person of culture, he was familiar with the literary customs of his day. Moreover, he was the master storyteller of the New Testament. Through him we hear the great parables of the good Samaritan (Luke 10:25-37), the rich fool (Luke 12:16-21), the prodigal son (Luke 15:11-32), and Lazarus and Dives (Luke 16:19-31), as well as the Christmas, Easter, and Pentecost stories (Luke

Introduction

2; 24; Acts 2). With a few strokes of his pen, he could sketch vivid scenes, such as the riot in the theater of Ephesus. "Now some cried one thing, some another; for the assembly was in confusion, and most of them did not know why they had come together" (Acts 19:32). Furthermore, he was able to write in a variety of styles, imitating the style of the Septuagint (= LXX, the Greek translation of the Old Testament) when appropriate, as, for instance, in the infancy narratives or when Jews speak to Jews. But Luke could also employ Greek concepts, ideas, and literary customs, as, for example, when he told of Paul's speech on the Areopagus or of his address to King Agrippa. Luke's knowledge of the Greek Bible is thorough and his use of biblical citations shows a sophistication which surpasses that of the other evangelists.

If Luke was a Gentile, as is generally assumed, then he was an extraordinary Gentile, steeped in the study of the Old Testament and sensitive to the feelings and needs of Jewish believers. Hence, he cited the apostles' decree three times (e.g., 15:20), depicted Paul as a pious Pharisee (23:6; 26:4-8), gave colorful vignettes of Jewish piety throughout his narrative, and, from the first chapter of his Gospel to the last of Acts, he showed that the roots of the church lie embedded in the Old Testament, in God's promises to Abraham and Moses, to David and the people of Israel through the prophets. In the light of the content of his work, it would seem to me that Luke could have been a Hellenistic Jew or a proselyte to Judaism. At the very least he had been a God-fearer. Even the first Gentile Christians are depicted by him as devout Gentiles who feared God. Luke thinks it important to tell us that Cornelius's piety found expression in that he "gave alms liberally to the people," that is, to the Jewish people, and therefore he was "well spoken of by the whole Jewish nation" (10:2, 22; cf. Luke 7:4-5). It is hence not surprising that the theme of many of Luke's stories, as well as the major theme of Luke-Acts is the message of salvation in relation to the Jewish people.

Luke was not just a great storyteller. He was also able to construct a lengthy and coherent narrative. He composed one story out of many different traditions. He claimed that he "investigated all things accurately from the beginning" (Luke 1:3a), and we have no reason to doubt his claim. But what is indeed amazing is that he was able to produce one coherent narrative in two volumes on the basis of a mass of diverse traditions.

In order to accomplish this, Luke had to omit what did not fit his purposes. For instance, he omitted all theological controversies in which the historical Paul was embroiled, except the debate at the apostles' conference. For Luke the continuity of the Christian message which he depicted from Jesus via the apostles to Paul insured the doctrinal purity of the church until Paul's departure (20:29). He also omitted the real reason for sailing past Ephesus (see comments on 20:16), as well as the story of Paul's collection (see comments on 21:17-26).

On occasion, Luke abbreviated the telling of events (cf. 18:22-23) or he compressed a period which may have taken years by selecting a few incidents (Acts 13–14).

He could also create the impression of a lengthy period even when only a few traditions were available to him. By inserting summary statements, speeches, and statements concerning the church's growth, Luke used the meager five traditions that were at his disposal for Acts 2:1—8:4 to great advantage, conveying excitement, movement, growth, and change in the attitude of the people and their leaders.

Luke could idealize the past (cf. Acts 2:43-47; 4:32-35) and he schematized and generalized particular occurrences. Thus, for instance, the Lukan Paul always entered the synagogue first, because the fulfillment of the promise applies first to Jews (cf. 2:39; 3:25-26; 13:26, 32-33).

Occasionally he transposed materials. It was important for him to show that it was Peter, the spokesman of the apostles, who inaugurated the Gentile mission. In reality, this decisive step was taken either by Philip (8:40) or by nameless Hellenists in Antioch. For theological reasons, Luke transposed the note about the work of the Hellenists in Antioch (11:20) to a position after the story of Cornelius's conversion by Peter.

While Luke compressed some material in order to gain space for vivid episodes and speeches, he repeated what he wanted to emphasize. The conversions of Cornelius (10:1—11:17; 15:7-11) and of Saul (9:1-19; 22:1-16; 26:4-18), as well as the apostles' decree (15:20, 29; 21:25; cf. 16:4-5) are narrated three times. The Christological kerygma and proofs from Scripture are presented in all the missionary speeches to Jews either in elaborate (2:22-36) or in summary form (4:10-12; 5:30-32; 28:23b). Jerusalem as the place of origin of the Christian witness and Rome as the destiny of Paul's journey are highlighted by repetition (1:4, 8, 12; 2:5, 14, etc.; 19:21; 23:11; 27:24).

Luke also combined traditions which historically did not belong together. For instance, he introduced the apostles' decree into his account of the decisions of the apostles' conference, even though historically the decree was not part of the conference's deliberations, but constituted a separate tradition (see comments on chap. 15).

He could also separate what historically was in all probability one event, e.g., Paul's arrival at Ephesus (18:19 and 19:1b; see comments on 18:22). It also seems probable that the two arrests of Acts 4 and 5 refer to the same event. Luke apparently had only a handful of Jerusalem traditions, so he made two arrests out of one and heightened the second conflict.

At times Luke overemphasized particular aspects for a variety of reasons. From Paul himself we know that he had been (past tense) a Pharisee, blameless according to the law (Phil. 3:5). The Lukan Paul, however, exclaimed, "I am a Pharisee" (23:6, present tense). The life of the historical Paul as a believer in Christ was grounded in the cross and resurrection of Jesus, not in his Pharisaic piety (Phil. 3:7-11). The Lukan Paul, however, scored a different point. For him the hope of the resurrection is the bridge between Pharisaic Judaism and the church's message of the resurrection. Therefore, Pharisaic Judaism remains a partner in dialog in Acts and can even be a defender of Christians (cf. 5:35-39; 23:7-9), even as Paul's message represents "the hope of Israel" (26:4-8; 28:20, 23).

Finally, the reader of Acts should appreciate Luke's artistry as a writer who created a variety of characters. He portrays distinct groups of Christians, of Jews and pagans, of leaders and common folk and of different types of mobs. Not all unbelieving Jews, for instance, are vicious, but there are noble Jews in Beroea (17:11-12) and the Roman Jews are strikingly different from the mob in Jerusalem that wants Paul out of the way (cf. 21:36; 22:22 with 28:17-22). Nor are all Roman officials fair-minded. The magistrates of Philippi are anti-Semitic (16:20-21) and even fair-minded Gallio shows an anti-Semitic streak (18:16-17). The procurators Felix and Festus knew very well that Paul was innocent, but kept him a prisoner nevertheless, for different and yet fundamentally similar reasons (24:26-27; 25:9,18-21). And Pilate's politics place him in proximity to Herod and the Sanhedrin (4:25-27).

3. The Surface Structure of Stories and Speeches in Acts

Luke's literary ability also becomes apparent in the way he structured individual units of his narrative. An example best illustrates his procedure. In Acts 3:1-10 we hear a typical miracle story which serves as paradigm of Luke's note in 2:43 that many signs were done through the apostles. The miracle story ends with the lame man "praising God," that is, responding positively (cf. Luke 17:11-19), and with the people filled with wondering puzzlement.

In the following speech, Peter interprets the miracle for his audience. Part one of the speech (vv. 12-16) tells how the miracle came about; part two (vv. 17-26) calls the audience to repentance as the only proper response in the face of God's action. The audience consists of "all the people," or "the people." They form an inclusion around the speech (3:11; 4:1). Having witnessed to the people, Luke will tell us next about their witness before the council (4:1-23) that "arrested" (4:3) and at the end "released" them (4:23).

Part one of the speech (3:11-16) has the following surface structure:

(A) The healing miracle was not done by our own power or piety (v. 12);
  (B) (Through the miracle) God glorified his servant (v. 13a);
    (C) You delivered him up. . .and denied him (v. 13b);
    (C′) You denied the Holy and Righteous One. . .and killed the Author of life (vv. 14-15a);
  (B′) God raised him from the dead (v. 15b);
(A′) His name as well as faith, which comes through him, brought about this healing miracle (v. 16).

Part two of the speech (vv. 17-26) draws the conclusion for the hearers who had been responsible for Jesus' death (vv. 13-15) even though they acted in ignorance (v. 17). However, through their action God fulfilled the prophecies concerning the Messiah's death (v.

18

18). The structure of part two, following the transition (vv. 17-18), is:

(A) Repent and turn that your sins may be blotted out (v. 19a);
  (B) (1) That the times of refreshing may come from the presence of the Lord;
  (2) And God may send the Messiah appointed for you;
  (3) Who remains in heaven until the time of establishing all of God's promises (vv. 19b-21);
    (C) (Citation of Scripture, v. 22) Moses said,
      (1) The Lord will raise up for you a prophet;
      (2) You shall listen to him in all that he speaks to you;
      (3) Those who do not listen to him "shall be destroyed from the people" (that is, God shall destroy them, v. 23);
        (D) All the prophets proclaimed "these days" (v. 24)
        (D') You are the sons of the prophets and of the covenant (v. 25a);
    (C') (Citation of Scripture, v. 25b) God said to Abraham, In your (Abraham's) seed all the families of the earth shall be blessed (by God);
  (B') God sent his servant to you first (v. 26a);
(A') To bless you in turning every one of you from your wickedness (v. 26b).

A (v. 19a) and A' (v. 26b) interpret each other and develop the theme. Repentance is a turning from wickedness and to God. Its intended purpose and goal is the forgiveness of sins which is the blessing promised to Abraham. Through the invitation to repentance and the offer of forgiveness God himself is eager to "turn every one of you from your wickedness."

B (vv. 19b-21) and B' (v. 26a) indicate a twofold sending of Jesus, "the Messiah" and "the servant of God." The second sending has not yet occurred, for the Messiah is still in "heaven" (v. 21), but God will send him at his parousia for the glorious consummation of the times of refreshing and for the concluding establishment of all of God's promises. The first sending of God's servant includes not only his earthly ministry, but above all his mission after his resurrection through his apostolic witnesses, who preach first to Jerusalem offering forgiveness of sins.

C (vv. 22-23) and C' (v. 25b) are two citations which contain two unconditional promises of God. One, the promise that God will raise up the prophet like Moses has already been fulfilled in Jesus' resurrection (and prior ministry). The first consequence of the fulfilled promise is "listen to him" in all that he tells you, which includes his call to repentance issued through Peter to the Jerusalemites. A second consequence is that those who do not listen shall be cut off from the people at the parousia and the final judgment, when those who listen now shall experience the fullness of the refreshing "from the presence of the Lord God." The second unconditional promise is made to Abraham and is in the process of realization through repentance, forgiveness, and the blessing of God's gift of the Holy Spirit, who initiates the times of refreshing in the present. Yet also this promise that "all the families of the earth shall be blessed" in the seed of Abraham looks to the future consummation. Then the blessing of healing in body and the forgiveness of sins experienced in the present find their completion in the resurrection of the dead. Then "all" of God's promises shall be established.

D (v. 24) and D' (v. 25a): all the prophets proclaim "these days," namely, the present as the time for repentance and turning to God (vv. 17 and 26), of decision for or against the Author of life (v. 15), of listening to the prophet like Moses (v. 22), and of appropriating the blessing in Abraham's seed (v. 25b). But "these days" may also refer to the future, to the time of consummation (vv. 19b-21) and the time of judgment (v. 23) in which all who do not listen now to the prophet like Moses will be destroyed. What the prophets proclaim is of ultimate concern to you, because "you are the sons of the prophets" and therefore God, through the apostolic witness, has sent his servant "to you first" in order that you may "listen to him," repent, and receive forgiveness of sins and the promised blessing of the Holy Spirit. As sons of the prophets, the people of Jerusalem should be receptive to the fulfillment announced by the prophets of old and realized already in part in these present days. (See also section 3:17-26 of the Commentary.)

The reader of Acts who listens to Luke's voice should be attentive to the surface structure of narratives and speeches. Each story and speech has its own point, but the whole narrative has a broader and deeper meaning than its individual parts.

4. Salvation History

Luke created one narrative out of many stories. His narrative deals with the salvation which God accomplished in history through Jesus the Savior and which God continues to accomplish in history through the message of salvation proclaimed by the church on its way through history. In short, Luke wrote a narrative of salvation history in which he updated biblical history.

In comparison to the other Gospel writers, Luke extended his narrative backward and forward. It does not begin with the ministry of John the Baptist, as in Mark, but with the announcement of the Baptist's birth in Jerusalem. His first volume does not end with the disciples assembled after Easter on a mountain in Galilee or by the Galilean lake (Matt. 28:16-20; John 21), but in Jerusalem. In distinction from Matthew's great commission, we hear only one explicit command at the end of Luke's Gospel, namely, "Stay in the city" between Easter and Pentecost "until you are clothed with power from on high" (Luke 24:49). There in Jerusalem, which was the goal of Jesus' journey (Luke 9:51) and the place of his suffering, death, and resurrection, he announced God's plan of salvation which includes not only his predestined fate but also "that repentance and forgiveness of sins should be preached in his name to all nations, beginning from Jerusalem" (Luke 24:47). God's plan of salvation, marked out in Scripture (Luke 24:44, Greek, *dei,* "it must," it is God's will and plan) extends the history of Jesus into the history of the church and its witness. No one before Luke and no one after him took this daring step and told the story of the church as the continuation of the story of Jesus. Luke's history is his story, God's story, as revealed in the Old Testament, in Jesus' story, and the church's story. Because Luke's history has as its subject the "Savior who is Christ, the Lord" (Luke 2:11) and "the message of this salvation (Acts 13:26), we are justified in calling his work a *History of Salvation,* with the subtitles "From Jesus to Paul," "From Jerusalem to Rome," and "From Jews only to Gentiles also."

In his second volume Luke did not deal with the diverse mission movements of the earliest church, which probably reached into the

Sinai and Egypt, Eastern Syria and Mesopotamia, but he selected one particular strand that led from Peter to Paul and from Jerusalem to Rome. His salvation history has the form of a historical monograph that begins in Jerusalem.

What is the significance of that city? It is the center of the people of God and therefore the center of the church in Acts. Hence every section in Acts is connected with Jerusalem. "Out of Zion shall go forth the law, and the word of the Lord from Jerusalem," Isaiah had proclaimed (2:3), and so it does. In Jerusalem the old prophet Simeon proclaimed that the Christ child will be "a light for revelation to the Gentiles and for glory to thy people Israel" (Luke 2:32). In Jerusalem the spread of the message of salvation beyond Israel to Gentiles is announced prophetically and carried out in the power of the Spirit (Acts 10–28). But Jerusalem is also the place where the people of God "delivered up," "denied," and "killed" Jesus, the Servant of God and "Author of life" (Acts 3:13-15). Yet this act of Jerusalem's people was not the end. In a stunning reversal, God vindicated Jesus by raising him from the dead and offered salvation once more to Jerusalem's people and their leaders (Acts 2–5). At the end of Acts we find on one hand "many ten thousands" of believers in Jerusalem and Judea (21:20) but, on the other hand, we hear of the same kind of repudiation of the Christian message and its messengers (Acts 22:22-23) which Stephen (chaps. 6-7) and Jesus had encountered (Luke 23). The reader of Luke-Acts knows that Jesus' prediction concerning Jerusalem's destruction had been fulfilled, because Jerusalem "did not know" the time of its "visitation" (Luke 19:44). This visitation also included the witness of Jesus' followers after Easter, as Luke 21:12-24 suggests and Acts 1–7 narrates. On the literary level, Jerusalem gives coherence to Luke's two volumes. Both volumes begin in Jerusalem, and with Luke 9:51 the story moves toward Jerusalem while with Acts 8:4 it moves away from it without, however, losing its connection with it (cf. 11:2,22; 15:4-29; 18:22; 20:22; 21:17—23:22; 23:11,17; 28:17,21). On the theological level, Jerusalem represents the great theological problem for Luke. Did God reject his people who rejected his visitation through Jesus and through his servant-witnesses? The commentary will deal with this question in 1:6; 3:19-21; and 28:20,23,28.

If Luke's story is salvation history, then he must show that God's purpose and plan (Greek, *boulē*, Luke 7:30; Acts 2:23; 4:28; cf. 3:18; 5:38-39; 13:36; 20:27) is the force that directs the story of Jesus and of the church in history. How did he do that in his second volume? First, by showing that the church's growth is the work of God (e.g., 2:41, "they were added" means: God added them; 5:14; 6:7; 9:31; etc.). Second, Luke showed that it was not an ecclesiastical program which the apostles carried out on their own initiative, but it was the Holy Spirit, the Lord Jesus, God himself who carried out his plan through his church. The apostles and disciples did not fulfill their own program, but they took one step at a time in agreement with the logic of the gospel. First, they witnessed in Jerusalem and soon encountered opposition. When a persecution which they had not planned scattered the church from Jerusalem, they preached the Word throughout the land of Judea and Samaria and the towns and cities of the coast as far as Antioch (8:1-40; 11:19). Step by step the barrier posed by circumcision was overcome, not by Peter's initiative, but by God's direction. And step by step the Jerusalem community was led to recognize that baptized, but uncircumcised believers were part of the people of God (10:1—11:17). All-important decisions in Acts were reached under the guidance of the Holy Spirit, or of Jesus, decisions such as the commission for the first missionary journey (13:2-4; cf. 14:27), the apostles' decree (15:28); the decision to enter Europe (16:6-10), the resolution to remain in Corinth (18:9-10), to travel to Jerusalem (19:21; 20:22) and to Rome (19:21; 23:11; 27:23). In Luke's narrative of salvation history, the purpose and plan of the faithful God come to the fore.

Third, Luke showed that the events narrated in his updated biblical history were in agreement with God's promise and therefore corresponded to his plan found in Scripture. The fulfillment of Scripture is therefore related by Luke not only to Jesus' birth, ministry, death, and resurrection but also to the ministry of Jesus' apostles and servant-witnesses (e.g., Acts 1:20; 2:16-18; 13:41, 47; 15:15-18; 28:26-28). Even the opponents of Jesus and of his servant-witnesses perversely and without intent fulfilled the Scripture by their action (13:27, 41; 28:26).

Fourth, Luke's narrative also demonstrates fulfillments of predictions by angels (Luke 1:13-21, 26-37; 2:10-12; Acts 27:23-24); by living prophets, such as Zechariah (Luke 1:67-79), Simeon (Luke 2:28-35), and Agabus (Acts 11:27-28; 21:10-11); by Paul (Acts 20:22-23; 27:22); and, last but not least, by Jesus, the prophet like Moses. He predicted not only his passion and resurrection, Peter's denial, and details such as Luke 19:29-31, but he also promised the Holy Spirit (Luke 24:49; Acts 1:8), a promise he fulfilled in Acts 2. He promised protection of Paul in Corinth (Acts 18:9-10), which was fulfilled in 18:12-17. He promised "wisdom" which no one can "withstand" to his followers when they are called to testify under pressure (Luke 21:15), a promise which found fulfillment in Acts 6:10 (same Greek verb). Other examples are given in the commentary.

Among predictions which find fulfillment in the story of Acts, we may note Joel's prophecy, cited by Peter (2:17), which promised "visions" and dreams. Luke told of their occurrence (10:9-16; 16:9; 18:9; 22:17-18; 23:11; 27:23). In 3:23 Peter referred to individuals who "shall be destroyed from the people," and thus it happened that in a proleptic judgment scene Ananias and Sapphira are cut off dead "from the people" (5:1-10). On the other hand, in the same speech Peter had promised "times of refreshing. . .from the presence of the Lord" and Luke narrated the initial fulfillment of this promise in his picture of an alternative society (4:32-34; 9:31). Other examples are pointed out in the commentary.

At the beginning of Luke's first volume, the ancient Simeon prophesied that Jesus "is set for the fall and rising of many in Israel and for a sign that is spoken against" (Luke 2:34-35). Luke's subsequent story narrates the fulfillment of this basic prediction and, at the end of his story in Rome, we hear that among Jews "everywhere" Christianity "is spoken against" (28:22). But we also hear in Acts of the rising of many in Israel to faith, of the rapid growth of the church, of 3000 that were baptized on Pentecost, of a growth that also continues after Stephen's martyrdom (9:31, 35, 42) and eventually reaches "many ten thousands" (21:20) of Jewish believers in Jerusalem and Judea. Moreover, Luke tells of Jews in the diaspora who joined the messianic people of God in Damascus and Antioch, in Asia Minor, Macedonia, Achaia, and also in Rome (28:24). Thus Luke narrated the division caused by Jesus and his messengers within Israel in accordance with Simeon's prediction.

At the beginning of Luke's second volume, Jesus announced the basic promise of the gift of the Holy Spirit (1:4-5, 8) through whom he continues to carry out his ministry in and through his chosen servant-witnesses (cf. 3:22; 26:23). The main characters in Acts are the Twelve, particularly Peter, the Seven, particularly Stephen and Philip, and finally Barnabas and Paul, especially the latter. They are all filled with the Holy Spirit, continue Jesus' prophetic ministry to Israel, preach and heal in his name, cause acceptance and rejection among the people, and advance the plot of Acts.

Finally, the last word of Jesus prior to his ascension (Acts 1:8) predicted and mandated the course of the church's mission and witness and also provided an outline for the story of Acts: Introduction (chap. 1); Witness in Jerusalem, Judea, and Samaria (chaps. 2–9); Witness to the End of the Earth (chaps. 10–28) (this outline corresponds to Luke's first volume: Introduction [Luke 1:1—4:13]; Ministry in Galilee [4:14—9:50]; Journey to and Ministry in Jerusalem [9:51—24:52]).

However, Rome, where Luke's story ends, is not "the end of the earth" (1:8), but the center of the empire. Acts therefore concludes in an open-ended way, and Christ's mandate of 1:8 is still in the process of realization at the end of Luke's story. Hence Paul continued to preach in Rome for two whole years (28:30-31). But the reader can draw assurance that, since Paul reached Rome against incredible odds and in fulfillment of the Spirit's directive (19:21) and the promise of the Lord Jesus (23:11), therefore the Christian witness shall reach the end of the earth, no matter what obstacles it may encounter. The fulfillments narrated in Luke-Acts give assurance (cf. Luke 1:4) that also those promises that have not yet been fulfilled in this narrative shall, in God's own time, come to fulfillment.

In Acts 1:9 Luke narrated the ascension of Jesus, which had been in view since Luke 9:51. The ascension itself functions as promise and pledge of Jesus' future parousia (Acts 1:11) when God will send his Messiah from heaven (3:20-21). Then those promises that have not yet been fulfilled shall be fulfilled (cf. 3:21), such as the resurrection of the dead (24:15; 26:6-8) and with it the restoration of the kingdom to Israel (1:6). Moreover, fulfillment of prophecy indicates that God is at work in history and grants assurance of legitimacy to the church's message of salvation, provided it remains in continuity with that history. It gives assurance for the church's future in history and in the ultimate future when the salvation offered in the present shall be completed in the resurrection of the dead. Finally, fulfillment of prophecy demonstrates the faithfulness of God who keeps his promises.

Of course, Luke was also aware that prophecy can be misunderstood and that fulfillment cannot be seen by eyes that are closed.

In his final scene he has Paul expounding the Scriptures to Jews in Rome from morning till evening "trying to convince them about Jesus both from the law of Moses and from the prophets" (28:23). The result of his efforts was, as always, a division among the Jews. The promise-fulfillment scheme is not without ambiguity, and Luke knew that, just as his contemporary Josephus knew it. Writing about the Jewish war against Rome Josephus stated: "But what more than all else incited them [the Jews] to the war [against Rome in A.D. 66] was an ambiguous oracle, likewise found in their sacred scriptures, to the effect that at that time someone from their country would become ruler of the world. This they understood to mean someone from their own race, and many of their wise men went astray in their interpretation of it" (*War* 6.312-313).

The misinterpretation of prophecy to which Josephus referred had disastrous consequences for Judaism and for Jerusalem: From Luke's perspective the key to the misunderstanding of prophecy by "many of their wise men" lies in the identity and mystery of the Messiah, who according to God's plan "must suffer" (2:23, etc.). God's Messiah is not a glorious warrior-king who engages in a holy war, destroys Israel's enemies, wading in a sea of blood and then ruling the world. He is the suffering servant of God (8:32-33) who was committed to losing himself entirely in the service of God and of his people irrespective of the cost to him. He did not heap suffering on others—including his opponents—but was ready to take it upon himself in accordance with God's will or plan (Luke 22:42).

The identity and mystery of the Messiah was perceived by the disciples only at and after Easter, not before (cf. Luke 9:45; 18:34). When the vindicated servant of God opened their "eyes" and their "mind," then they understood the Scripture and the Messiah's mystery in the light of Jesus' vindication by God (Luke 24:25; 31-32, 45-47). From Luke's point of view the messianic promises of the Old Testament can only be misunderstood unless they are understood in the light of their fulfillment through the suffering and resurrected Messiah Jesus. It was from this perspective that Luke narrated his story and showed that the events in this history from Jesus to Paul and from Jerusalem to Rome corresponded to God's plan and purpose found in Scripture. Luke's work itself is a witness to that plan.

5. Jesus Christ, the Holy Spirit, and Periods of Salvation History

a. Jesus Christ

"There is salvation in no one else, for there is no other name under heaven given among people by which we must be saved" (4:12, author's trans.). "Jesus of Nazareth, a man attested to you by God with mighty works and wonders and signs which God did through him in your midst" (2:22) is the one "whom you [the leaders of the people] crucified, whom God raised from the dead" (4:10). He is "the stone" rejected by the builders, the leaders, "which has become the head of the corner" (4:11), because God exalted him at his right hand (2:33) and offers salvation through him.

Among the many Christological titles in Acts, *Christ, Messiah* (of God), and *Lord* occur most frequently. The title *Christ* is often used in connection with the proof from Scripture and the necessity of his suffering (e.g., 3:18; 17:3; 26:22-23; Luke 24:26,46; cf. Acts 2:22-32).

Jesus is *Lord* also prior to Easter (Luke 2:11; 19:31,34), but the church confesses him as Lord because God raised him from the dead (Luke 24:34; Acts 2:21,36; 4:33; 8:16,25; 9:10-11,13,15,17,27-28,35,42, etc.; 28:31). Therefore he is "Lord of all" and has a legitimate claim on both Jews and Gentiles (10:36). At times it is not easy to decide whether God or Jesus is meant in Acts. It is clear that prayers are addressed not only to the Lord God (4:24), but also to the Lord Jesus (7:59 and probably also 1:24). In Acts 14:3 we hear that the missionaries spoke "boldly for the Lord," which probably means that they preached Jesus as Lord (cf. 9:27-29). Is "the will of the Lord" which Paul wants to be done (21:14) the will of Jesus or of God? Probably of Jesus, because it was Paul's hope to finish the ministry that he had "received from the Lord Jesus" (20:24) and therefore he was ready to die for "the Lord Jesus" (21:13). The instances in Acts where it is difficult to distinguish whether Lord refers to Jesus or to God demonstrate that, according to Luke, since Easter one can no longer talk about the Lord God without talking about the Lord Jesus, who is Lord of all (10:36; cf. 2:34-36).

The title *Son of God* in Acts is found only in words spoken by Paul and probably refers to Jesus' unique relationship to God (9:20: 13:33, quoting Psalm 2; Acts 8:37, which is a later addition to the text; see the footnote of the RSV; for Son of God see below). *Servant* of the Lord is found in Peter's speech (3:13,26), in the prayer of the community (4:27,30), and indirectly in the text read by the eunuch (8:32-33). The servant of God is the humiliated and rejected one (8:32-33; 4:27) whom God raised from the dead (3:26) and whom God glorifies through signs and wonders performed in his name (3:13; 4:30).

The Holy and Righteous One (3:14; the Righteous One, 7:52; 22:14), as well as the *Author of life* (3:15; 5:31), are rare titles bearing an antique patina and expressing Jesus' function in God's design on one hand in contrast to the deed of the Jerusalemites. You "killed the Author of life" eternal reveals the perverse intent of the people (3:15), which is mitigated by their ignorance (3:17).

The title *Savior* (5:31; 13:23) appears for the first time in New Testament writings in Phil. 3:20 and becomes quite common in later writings (Eph. 5:23; 2 Tim. 1:10; Titus 3:6; 2 Peter 1:1,11; 2:20; 3:2; etc.) and could refer not only to Jesus but also to God (Luke 1:47; Jude 25; 1 Tim. 1:1; 2:3; 4:10; Titus 3:4). In Luke-Acts the title is always used in relation to the people of Israel regardless of whether it refers to God (Luke 1:47) or to Jesus (Luke 2:11; Acts 5:31; 13:23). Moreover, this title must be seen in relation to "salvation" (Greek, *sōtēria:* Luke 1:69,71,77; 19:9; Acts 4:12; 7:25, "deliverance"; 13:26,47; 16:17; 27:34, "strength"; and Greek, *sōtērion:* Luke 2:30; 3:6; Acts 28:28) as well as in relation to the verb "to save" which in miracle stories is translated "to heal" or to "be well" (Greek, *sōzō:* e.g., Luke 8:12,36, "heal"; 8:50, "to be well"; 9:24; 17:19, "made you well"; 18:26; 19:10; 23:35; Acts 2:21,40; 4:9, "healed"; 11:14; 14:9, "be made well"; 15:1,11; 16:30-31; 27:20,31, in the sense of "rescued from peril").

To be healed in Luke is to be saved in the sense that healing miracles are signs of present and future salvation, of forgiveness of sins and the gift of the Holy Spirit sealed in Baptism (2:38-40) and of the future resurrection of the dead. Not everyone who experienced physical healing came to faith and was saved (Luke 17:11-19; RSV "made well" instead of "saved you"; cf. Luke 7:50). As Moses wanted to bring deliverance (Greek, *sōtēria*, "salvation") to his people in Egypt, "but they did not understand" (7:25) and therefore he was forced to flee (7:29), so Jesus the Savior rejected hears, "He saved others; let him save himself" (Luke 23:35), and he died.

The title *Son of man* which, apart from 7:56, is found only on the lips of Jesus has caused much consternation among interpreters and will be discussed in the Commentary.

There are three descriptions in Acts which are not used as titles. *Son of David* (2:29-31; 13:23) and *seed of Abraham* (3:26) indicate Jesus' descent and disclose the fulfillment of God's unconditional promise made to Abraham and to David through Jesus. Above all, Jesus is presented as *the prophet like Moses*. After the raising of the widow's son at Nain, the people exclaimed, "A great prophet has arisen among us!" and "God has visited his people" (Luke 7:16). The Emmaus disciples spoke of him as "a prophet mighty in deed and word before God and all the people" (Luke 24:19). At Pentecost Peter said that Jesus was "attested to you by God with mighty works and wonders and signs" (2:22) just like Moses, who "was mighty in his words and deeds" (7:22). Just as miracles and "living oracles," that is, life-giving words (7:38), were the distinguishing mark of Moses, the great prophet, so they were of Jesus, the prophet like Moses. Moreover, God had promised unconditionally that he "will raise up for you a prophet from your brethren as he raised me up" (7:37; 3:22). In this speech the raised-up prophet like Moses to whom Peter's audience should now "listen" refers to the resurrected Jesus, because Peter's audience in Jerusalem had not listened to the earthly Jesus before Easter, but rejected him (Luke 23). If it referred only to the earthly Jesus, then Peter's admonition to the Jerusalemites to "listen to him" would be an exercise in sheer futility. What they had done cannot be undone, but can only be forgiven (3:19). So then, the raised-up prophet like Moses is the resurrected Jesus. But in what sense?

Acts 7:17-41 provides the answer. Moses had been sent to the people two times and he was twice rejected by them. The first time (7:23-29) Moses wanted to "visit" (cf. Luke 7:16) his enslaved brethren, "but they did not understand" that "God was giving them deliverance [Greek, *sōtēria*, "salvation"] by his hand" (7:25). And so he was "thrust aside" (7:27), rejected by his people. In exile he was commissioned by God to come to his people a second time and deliver them (7:34). Moses led the people out of Egypt in the exodus performing "wonders and signs" (7:37). But Israel rejected Moses a second time, now by turning to idolatry (7:39-41). The result was that God sent his people into the exile (7:43).

The first sending of Jesus parallels the first sending of Moses, and Peter's statements about Jesus (2:23-24; 3:13-15) correspond to what Stephen said about Moses. Jesus, like Moses, came to "save the lost" and "set at liberty those who are oppressed" (Luke 19:10; 4:18), but Jerusalem "would not" listen (Luke 13:34) and rejected him (Luke 23). However, just as God through Moses offered Israel a second chance, so he did through Jesus. After Easter Jesus is sent once more to Israel first (3:26) and once more he offers forgiveness and salvation to his people (through his servant-witnesses). Therefore Peter exhorted the people, "Listen to him," and he warned that those who do not listen shall be cut off from the people (3:22-23; the opposite of 2:40). Judgment will fall on them even as it fell on Israel in the exile.

The twofold rejection of Moses corresponds to the twofold rejection of Jesus and to Luke's two volumes. In his Gospel, Luke "dealt with all that Jesus began to do and teach" (Acts 1:1) and he narrated Jesus' first rejection by the people. In his second volume, Acts, Luke told what Jesus continued to do and to teach through his servant-witnesses and Jesus' second rejection by the people. Thus the Moses story with its twofold rejection served as the structure for Luke's entire work in two volumes.

However, God's saving purpose is not thwarted. Simeon's prediction of a division within Israel (Luke 2:34) and of "many" coming to faith in Jesus Christ, the Savior of Israel, is also narrated in each volume. We hear of small beginnings in Galilee and of Jesus choosing new leaders. They would replace the old leaders who rejected the "beloved son." The vineyard which is Israel will be entrusted to the 12 apostles (Luke 20:9-19; 22:28-30). In Acts the apostles function as the leaders of the messianically restored people (Acts 1–15) that in Jerusalem and Judea alone number "many ten thousands" of believers at the end of Luke's story (21:20). Luke-Acts narrates not only the twofold rejection of the Messiah-Servant-Lord, but also the "rising of many in Israel" (Luke 2:34), who "listen" to Jesus, the prophet like Moses.

Jesus is God's eschatological agent of salvation in that God sent him (13:23), anointed him with the Holy Spirit (10:38), proclaimed *shalom* (10:36), did signs and wonders through him (2:22), delivered him up according to his plan (2:23; cf. 3:18), raised him from the dead (2:24, 32; 3:15, 26), exalted him to his right hand (2:33; 5:31), gave the Holy Spirit for transmission to the church through him (2:33), appointed him as judge of the world (17:31; 10:42), and shall "send" him from heaven for his glorious parousia (3:20-21a). We recognize that Luke's Christology offered the building blocks for the Apostles' Creed as well as the creed's use of "Son of God."

While Luke never spoke about the *preexistent* Son of God, he traced Jesus' origin to his miraculous conception by the Holy Spirit in the virgin Mary (Luke 1:35; note the conjunction "therefore"). Jesus is the Son of God because of the action of the Holy Spirit at his conception and at his resurrection (13:33). The virginal conception is never mentioned in Acts, because Luke's second book contains the testimony of eyewitnesses. Yet the virginal conception is the reason why Jesus is the Son of God, just as the resurrection is the reason why he remains the Son of God after Easter (13:33; 9:20). As the earthly Son of God Jesus was the Obedient One or Righteous One, who in obedience submitted to his Father's will and plan (Luke 22:22), while Israel's leaders "rejected the purpose of God for themselves" (Luke 7:30).

b. The Holy Spirit and Periods of Salvation History

According to Conzelmann's interpretation of Luke-Acts, Jesus is "the center of time," which is preceded by "the time of promise" and followed by "the time of the church." There is considerable truth to Conzelmann's conclusion. After all, Luke's two volumes follow this scheme, with the first dealing with the time of Jesus and the second with the time of the church. Yet we should also note that the time of the promise—the time of the Old Testament—also saw fulfillments of specific promises, according to Luke. Thus, for instance, God's promise to Abraham concerning his posterity, their oppression in Egypt, the exodus and the possession of the land (7:5-7,17) came to fulfillment in Old Testament times (7:17-22,36,45). But more important is the fact that Luke connected the time of Jesus with the time of the church in two ways. First, through the idea of the eschatological fulfillment, Luke tied the time of Jesus inseparably to the time of the church and vice versa. "*Today* this scripture has been fulfilled," Jesus announced in his inaugural sermon in Nazareth (Luke 4:21). At Pentecost Peter declared in his keynote address that the coming of the Holy Spirit upon the disciples signals the

31

presence of "the last days" in which Joel's prophecy has come to fulfillment (Acts 2:17). Both periods therefore are the time of salvation, of eschatological fulfillment, in accordance with God's promise.

Second, the exaltation of Jesus means that during the time of the church Jesus does not recede into the past like any other historical figure, but he remains present to and contemporary with the church. The church does not exist "after" him, but "under" him, and he is not absent but active through the Holy Spirit offering salvation in word and deed through his witnesses (cf. 26:23). He appears in visions to Ananias and to Paul (9:10-16; 9:4-6; 18:9; 23:11). He gives specific instructions (e.g., 22:17-21), and grants "signs and wonders" to his servants, thereby undergirding and bearing "witness to the word of his grace" (14:3). Instead of healing "in his name" Peter could say, "Jesus Christ heals you" (9:34). Because Jesus is not an absent Lord who has receded into the past, Paul could commit the elders "to the Lord in whom they believed" (14:23; here and in 14:3 "the Lord" is Jesus, as the context shows). Because Jesus is present and contemporary Stephen could ask him to receive his spirit (7:59), and Peter and Paul could affirm that repentance, faith, forgiveness, and the Holy Spirit are granted by Jesus (5:31; 3:16; 2:33; 13:38-39; etc.).

Therefore, from one perspective the time of Jesus and of the church belong inseparably together because it is the time of the eschatological fulfillment in which Jesus functions as Savior in accordance with God's plan. However, from another perspective we can distinguish three periods. "The law and the prophets were until John" (Luke 16:16). The time of the law and the prophets ended with John the Baptist. Therefore, Luke narrated John's imprisonment prior to Jesus' baptism (Luke 3:20-22). During that period the Holy Spirit was given to specially chosen individuals, the prophets. In their writings, inspired by the Holy Spirit, God revealed his will and plan and the Holy Spirit spoke through them (1:16; 4:25; 28:25).

In the center of time, Jesus is the exclusive bearer of the Spirit. The opening chapters of Luke's Gospel, which present the prophetic, Spirit-filled Zechariah (Luke 1:67-79), Elizabeth (Luke 1:41-45), Simeon (Luke 2:25-35), Anna (Luke 2:36), and John the Baptist (Luke 1:76), serve as transition from the Old Testament time to the center of time which is the time of the fulfillment through Jesus.

The old man Simeon was waiting for the fulfillment, "looking for the consolation of Israel," and the Holy Spirit revealed to him that "he should not see death until he had seen the Lord's Christ" (Luke 2:25-26). With his presentation of Simeon Luke showed us that the time of Christ is linked directly and without a break to the time of the Old Testament.

The center of time begins with Jesus' announcement, "The Spirit of the Lord is upon me . . . today this scripture has been fulfilled" (Luke 4:16-21), and it ends with his ascension (Luke 24:51; Acts 1:9). After a 10-day interim the time of the church begins at Pentecost (2:1-41) and ends at Christ's parousia (1:11).

During the time of the church the Holy Spirit is given by God not just to select individuals, but democratically to the whole people of God. In virtue of Christ's achievement the Holy Spirit is "poured out" by the exalted Christ upon each and every one of his disciples in fulfillment of God's prophecy through Joel (2:17-18,33,38).

Jesus not only promised the gift and power of the Holy Spirit (Luke 24:49; Acts 1:4-5,8), but the exalted Lord is the mediator of the Spirit (2:33). In the same way the Holy Spirit is the presence of God and of Christ (16:7) among God's believing people. Preaching and Baptism are the means by which the Holy Spirit is granted to them. Even when the anomaly occurred that the Holy Spirit fell on the first Gentile converts, on Cornelius and his household, Peter nevertheless had them baptized (10:44-48), because Baptism in the name of Jesus and the Holy Spirit belong together. As Baptism initiated the ministry of the Spirit-filled Jesus, so it initiates and empowers his followers to their ministry, to witness and prophecy, to mission and endurance under pressure (1:8; 2:17; 4:29-31; Luke 12:12; Acts 6:10; 19:21; 20:22-23). The Holy Spirit placed elders into their office to nurture and guard the church (20:28). He commissioned Barnabas and Paul for mission (13:2,4) and gave consolation and exhortation to the church (9:31). Through his Spirit God cleanses hearts by faith (15:8-9). Miracles performed by apostles are the Spirit's witness to Christ's resurrection (5:31-32) and undergird the witness spoken by them (4:30). Last but not least, just as Jesus Christ continues to be active in and through the proclamation of his servant-witnesses (26:23; 3:22) during the time of the church, so likewise the Holy Spirit is active in their proclamation. Therefore, to reject the Christian proclamation is to "resist the Holy Spirit" which is the mark of a "stiff-necked people" (7:51). In conclusion, the time of the church is the time of eschatological fulfillment, a time of continuing activity by the exalted Lord, a time of the Spirit's presence, a time of witness and mission to Jews and Gentiles (1:8), of endurance and trials, and also a time of rejection and division.

6. Speeches

In his preface Luke claimed that he "investigated all things accurately from the beginning" and he referred to sources for his information, to "eyewitnesses and ministers of the word" who had delivered traditions and to predecessors who had written narratives (Luke 1:1-4).

Of the 1000 verses in Acts, the speeches make up about 300. If one were to read Acts and skip over the speeches, one would have a barren book. It is the speeches, located at strategic points, that give substance and depth to Luke's story, interpret events, proclaim the good news, denounce disobedience, exhort believers, defend against false charges, and reveal God's power behind events.

Are these speeches verbatim reports of what was actually said in particular situations? Some ancient Greeks practiced not only speed writing, but committed to memory all of Homer, 48 books with about 600 lines per book. We modern Western people with our shrunken capacity for memorization can hardly imagine what people at Luke's time were able to memorize, remember, and recite, if they wanted to. Paul taught for two years in "the hall of Tyrannus" in Ephesus (19:9), and his teaching certainly included memorization similar to the method used in rabbinic schools. As a Jew and a student educated "at the feet of Gamaliel" (22:3), Paul was not only aware of this type of instruction by repetition and memorization, but also of the importance of memory for community life. Thus, theoretically, it would not be impossible to imagine that the speeches in Acts are more or less verbatim reports of what was spoken on particular occasions.

Looking at the speeches in Acts, we see several reasons why the theoretical possibility just mentioned is in fact most improbable. In the first place, one can hardly imagine anyone taking notes during events such as Pentecost, or the riots in Ephesus and Jerusalem (Acts 2; 19; 21–22). No disciples were present when Gamaliel made his speech (5:34-39) or when the Sanhedrin deliberated privately (4:16-17), or when Jewish plotters talked to the chief priests (23:14-15), or when Festus and Agrippa talked to each other (25:14-22; 26:31-32). Therefore, these speeches are not a record of what was actually said, but at best a recollection of what might have been said. Moreover, if one compares the three accounts of Paul's conversion (chaps. 9; 22; 26), one notices that Luke was not concerned with a word-for-word account of what Jesus said to Paul or Ananias. The same is true when we compare the four versions of the angel's message to Cornelius (chaps. 10–11). In short, as far as Luke is concerned, the speeches in Acts are not meant to be verbatim reports.

Second, the speeches by Peter, Paul, and James are literary compositions. They are much too short to be real speeches. They are not outlines of real speeches either, but written compositions produced for Luke's readers. The style and content of Peter's and Paul's speeches to Jews is identical and the speeches of Acts 2 and 13 are even interdependent. The use of Psalm 16 in Acts 13:35-37 presupposes a knowledge of the detailed argumentation of Acts 2:25-32, but Luke can assume that the reader of Acts 13 has also read the second chapter. In short, Peter speaks like Paul and both speak like Luke. Particular speeches are composed by someone who knows what is said in others.

In the third place, speeches have a function in Greek and Hellenistic historical writings that differs from the function of a newspaper report of a particular speech. The latter should be as accurate as possible, quoting verbatim the speech, or its important parts. In historical writings of the Hellenistic age, speeches are inserted in order to show a person's important thoughts, interpret the meaning of events, give moral lessons, or simply entertain. The speeches have to be appropriate to the individual who speaks and to the occasion (Lucian, *On How to Write History* 58). No Greek or Hellenistic historian gave a verbatim report of a speech in his historical writing. He may not even have known if a particular person made a speech on a particular occasion. But that would not stop a historian from placing one in the mouth of a hero or a heel. Even when the text of a speech was known, a historian would not feel constrained to incorporate it. There is the famous example of an actual speech by the Emperor Claudius (cf. 11:28; 18:2) which has survived because it was inscribed on bronze tablets that were found in Lyons. The speech is published in *Corpus Inscriptionum Latinarum* (vol. 13, Berlin, 1907, no. 1668). Yet Tacitus did not reproduce it in his *Annals* 11:24. The Jewish historian Josephus, who regarded the Bible as divinely inspired Word of God, nevertheless felt compelled to put a lengthy speech to Isaac into Abraham's mouth which is without basis in the Old Testament (*Ant.* 1.228-231). Moreover, Josephus twice reproduced the same speech, by the same person, given on the same occasion. It was a speech by Herod to his troops found in Josephus's *War* 1:373-379 as well as in his *Ant.* 15.127-146. But the versions of the same speech are strikingly different because Josephus pursued different aims in each case. If Luke wrote as a historian within the context of his time, then modern readers may not expect verbatim reports in the speeches of Acts. Rather, we must ask what Luke was trying to tell his readers by means of a particular speech. This contribution by Martin Dibelius in his splendid article "The Speeches in Acts and Ancient Historiography" (*Studies in Acts*, 1951, pp. 138-185) has withstood the test of time.

Finally, by recognizing that these speeches are Lukan compositions directed to the reader of Acts rather than to the historical audience and expressing a variety of aims which Luke sought to attain, we have not yet answered the question whether the author of Acts also incorporated prior traditions into his speeches. The missionary speeches to Jews (Acts 2–5; 13), Dibelius believed, were patterned according to sermons "customary in the author's day. This is how the gospel is preached and ought to be preached" ("The Speeches," p. 165). However, other scholars have rightly pointed out that the missionary speeches to Jews do not represent preaching which is contemporary to Luke, because they are literary constructions, thoroughly permeated by Lukan theology. True enough.

However, Luke did incorporate prior traditions such as Christological titles (e.g., the Servant), formulas (e.g., God raised him from the dead), and at least some traditional fragments (e.g., the times of refreshing . . . the times of establishing; 3:19-21). Moreover, the two speeches to Gentiles (14:15-17 and 17:22-31) follow a traditional pre-Lukan pattern recognizable in 1 Thess. 1:9-10 and Heb. 6:1-2. Furthermore, the speeches to Jews in all probability are also based on a pre-Lukan pattern which contrasted (1) the deed of the Jews (they rejected him) with (2) the deed of the faithful God (he raised him from the dead) and concluded (3) with a call to turn to God by Baptism in the name of Jesus. Unfortunately, we have no clear examples of pre-Lukan preaching to Jews in the New Testament. But one may ask, What would a Christian Jew have said to non-Christian Jews whom he wanted to bring into the messianic community? For reaching Jews the idea of an atonement and forgiveness connected with the death and blood of the Messiah (cf. Luke 22:20; Acts 20:29; 1 Cor. 15:3) was not of paramount importance, because Jews already had a variety of means of atonement. However, the decisive question was whether Israel together with God rejected Jesus in his crucifixion. The pattern suggested above draws a contrast between Israel and its deed, on the one hand, and, on the other, the faithful God who raised Jesus from the dead— thereby vindicating him—and who now invited Jews to respond to God's deed with repentance and Baptism before the imminent coming of the End. This contrast pattern is present at least partially in Stephen's speech (and in Q, Luke 11:47-48, 49-51; 13:34-35), where the denial and rejection of Jesus is the climax of a history characterized by disobedience toward God. If we add to it the pre-Lukan resurrection formula and the invitation to repentance resulting from God's resurrection action, then we would arrive at the pre-Lukan pattern postulated above. Such a pattern is basic to all the speeches to Jews in Acts and it seems improbable that Luke invented it. This pattern probably represents one form of the earliest preaching to Jews (another is found in Q) and from it developed traditions such as Rom. 4:25 and 1 Cor. 15:3-5.

Luke added elements to this pattern, namely, the significance of Jesus' ministry (2:22), the idea of God's plan (2:23), the proof from Scripture and the importance of eyewitnesses. He omitted any reference to the imminent End as a motivation for the call to repentance and Baptism. In its place Luke spoke of the gift of the Holy Spirit through the Exalted One, a gift received by baptized believers in the present (2:38).

In addition to missionary speeches to Jews and Gentiles we also find in Acts different types of speeches to Christians by Peter (1:16-22; 11:5-17; 15:7-11), by James (15:13-21), and by Paul (his farewell to the elders of Ephesus in Miletus, 20:18-35). Also in these the presence of pre-Lukan material can be recognized (e.g., the apostles'

37

decree in James's speech of Acts 15). Moreover, in chaps. 22–28 we find several major and minor defense speeches by Paul in which he defended not only himself but Christianity. The presence of pre-Lukan traditions can be recognized in these speeches also, e.g., the curriculum vitae of Paul in Acts 22:1-21 and 26:2-23. Luke used a tradition which told (1) of an orthodox Pharisee, Saul (2) who persecuted Christians, (3) and was confronted by the resurrected Lord (4) who commissioned him. This pattern "can be traced back to Paul's own defense of his missionary activity" (Jervell [see Bibliography], p. 162) and it is most improbable that Luke himself created it on the basis of Paul's letters (e.g., Phil. 3:3-5). It is generally agreed that if Luke knew of the existence of Paul's letters, he did *not* use them. In his defense speeches he used Pauline traditions. Other traditional material that appears in them is Paul's place of birth, Tarsus in Cilicia (22:3), his education in Jerusalem under Gamaliel (22:3), his Roman citizenship (22:29), his father's status as a Pharisee, etc.

Finally, there are short speeches by Jews and Gentiles, by Gamaliel (5:35-39), Demetrius (19:25-27), the city clerk of Ephesus (19:35-40), Tertullus (24:2-8), the Roman procurators Felix (24:22, 25) and Festus (25:14-21, 24-27), and short replies by minor characters (e.g., 16:15, 20-21; 19:3; etc.). Not to be ignored are brief questions, exhortations, commands, and consolations by angels, the Holy Spirit, and the resurrected and exalted Lord (e.g., 1:4-5, 7-8; 10:4-6; 12:7-8; 13:2; 18:9-10; 23:11; 27:23-24). Acts also contains letters by Christians to Christians (15:23-29) and by one Roman official to another (23:25-30; cf. 25:26). All speeches, short or (relatively) long, express Luke's point of view. Some certainly incorporate traditions, while others may also do so even though we cannot recognize pre-Lukan traditions in them.

The speeches in Acts are aimed primarily at the reader rather than at the specific historical situation. This can be seen most easily in Stephen's speech (Acts 7), which does not directly address the charges against him. It also applies to other speeches. Calling Christians "the saints" (26:10) would be as inappropriate in the historical situation of Acts 26 as giving a curriculum vitae in answer to the charges against Paul. Also note the device of an interruption to a speech when all that is necessary has been said. In agreement with Hellenistic historians, Luke placed speeches into the mouth of his main characters, but Luke's purpose differed from theirs. He sought neither to entertain nor to give moral lessons nor merely to illuminate the significance of a situation, but to proclaim the word and way of the Lord that begins in the Old Testament, finds an eschatological fulfillment in the history of Jesus and continues through the present to the End of time.

7. Sources

The quest for sources which Luke may have used in constructing his second volume has always been guided by the desire to support the historical trustworthiness of Acts for a reconstruction of earliest Christianity. And indeed without Acts we could not reconstruct the course of Paul's ministry. Jervel debunked the notion that earliest Christianity in view of its belief in the imminent End had no interest in preserving traditions about the apostles. Yet the search for written sources behind Acts has produced a multitude of diverse hypotheses with no agreement among interpreters. (For a summary see J. Dupont, *The Sources of Acts*, 1964, and W. G. Kümmel, *Introduction.*) Luke may have used written sources for the first 15 chapters but we can no longer reconstruct them because the style is uniformly Lukan and thus we lack criteria for distinguishing between source and redaction. But the author certainly used *traditions* about Peter's imprisonment, Stephen's martyrdom, Ananias and Sapphira, etc., lists of names (1:13; 6:5; 13:1), as well as traditional material in composing his speeches (see above).

Dibelius, Kümmel, and many other scholars think that for chapters 16 to 28 the author of Acts had one or more itineraries available in which the first person plural narration was used. We will deal with this hypothesis in comments on 16:10. Even if the availability of such a diary seems improbable to me (it would have perished in the storm at sea anyway, chap. 27), Luke nevertheless had recourse to traditions and reports and for some parts (e.g., 20:13-15) perhaps even to eyewitness accounts.

8. Luke the Historian and Theologian

The effort to locate Luke-Acts among the types (genres) of Hellenistic literature has produced a variety of options. Among the suggestions that have been advanced the one that places Luke-Acts within the genre of religious romances of antiquity can safely be discarded. The apocryphal Acts belong in this category, which offers religious entertainment and has no concern for what actually happened. More intriguing is the proposal by C. H. Talbert that Luke-Acts belongs to the genre of cultic biography. The biography of the founder of a cult or of a philosophical school was followed by narratives or lists about his successors. As a prime example of this genre Talbert points to Diogenes Laertius, *Lives of Eminent Philosophers*. One purpose of this kind of biography was to establish a line of legitimate tradition. In the case of Luke-Acts the legitimate tradition came from the founder, Jesus (vol. 1), via the Twelve to Paul, and from him it was passed on to the elders of Ephesus (vol. 2; cf. Acts 20:18-35). We would readily agree that the continuity of the Christian tradition was one of Luke's concerns and that a biographical interest and even features of religious romances are present in Luke's work. But one can also recognize that all the major characters in Acts are portrayed in identical terms (except for minor individuality). They are all filled with the Holy Spirit, speak with boldness, perform signs and wonders, and create acceptance or rejection of their message. In short, they are depicted as Christian prophets.

Moreover, the term *succession* (Greek, *diadochē*), which is prominent not only in Diogenes Laertius's work but also in Jewish accounts of rabbinic succession, is conspicuous by its absence in Acts. Luke knew the word *successor* (see Acts 24:27), but he did not apply it to a Christian line of succession. Why not? Because it is God or the Holy Spirit who calls persons into the ministerial office (20:28) and neither the office as such nor ministerial succession as such guarantees that the Word of God is preached in truth and purity. Finally, with Talbert's proposal one would expect that the names of the Ephesian elders would be given. They, however, remain nameless, even though more than 100 names appear in Acts. Undoubtedly, Paul's mantle fell on the Ephesian elders who were challenged to watch out for their own integrity and to protect their flock from dangers from without and within (20:28-31), but ministerial succession was not a concern of Luke, otherwise he would have been obliged to give the names of the Ephesian elders.

In agreement with most interpreters, we hold that Luke was and endeavored to be a biblical historian intent on updating biblical history through his history from Jesus to Paul, from Jerusalem to Rome, and from witness exclusively to Jews to witness primarily to Gentiles (cf. 28:28), a history which is in accordance with God's plans found in sacred Scripture.

For Luke historiography serves his theological purposes, but this insight may not diminish the fact that Luke the historian wanted to write history and not fiction. For him, history was the story of God, Christ, and the Holy Spirit with Jews and Gentiles through chosen servant-witnesses on their way from Jerusalem to Rome. As a historian, Luke deserves a place among the great historians of antiquity. After all, to Greek and Latin historians of Luke's time the Christian movement was a matter that could either be ignored or else be ridiculed as an abominable "superstition" (e.g., Tacitus, *Annals* 15.44; cf. Acts 25:19). By recognizing the invincible rise of Christianity, Luke was a better historian than anyone else among his contemporaries.

Luke's theological aim may not detract from the mass of accurate historical detail which he provided in Acts. Even when he rewrote historical data in the interest of his theological aim (see comments on 6:1-6), we are dependent on Luke for knowing about the Hellenists around the Seven who played the decisive role in the development of Christianity from a Jewish sect to a world religion (see Hengel, *Between Jesus and Paul*, 1983, pp. 1-29).

As a historian, Luke can be evaluated to some extent by data contained in Paul's letters. Both Acts and Paul's letters agree that Paul had persecuted Christians prior to his conversion and call and that he had been a Pharisee, "zealous for the traditions of my fathers" (Gal. 1:14; Acts 22:3; 26:5). He came from the tribe of Benjamin (Rom. 11:1), hence his Hebrew name, Saul, the name of the first Israelite king from that tribe. He became a Christian through a special revelation (Gal. 1:15-16; Acts 9:4-5, 15-16; 26:14-18), and was smuggled out in a basket lowered over the city walls of Damascus (Acts 9:23-25; 2 Cor. 11:32-33). After his first visit to Jerusalem as a Christian he went into "the regions of Syria and Cilicia" (Gal. 1:21; Acts 9:30); he joined Barnabas in his work in Antioch (Acts 11:26; Gal. 2:1), endured persecution in Antioch, Iconium, and Lystra—in that order (Acts 13–14; 2 Tim. 3:11; cf. 2 Cor. 11:25 and Acts 14:19). At the apostles' conference Gentiles were not required to be circumcised (Acts 15; Gal. 2:1-10). Paul and Barnabas subsequently separated and Paul took Silas and Timothy along on his next missionary journey (Acts 15:39-40; 16:3; 1 Thess. 1:1). Paul established congregations in Philippi, Thessalonica, Corinth, and Ephesus (Acts 16–19; 1 Thess. 1:1; 2:2; 3:1; and other Pauline letters). The shameful treatment in Philippi and Thessalonica mentioned in Acts 16:22; 17:5 is alluded to in 1 Thess. 2:2 and 1:6. He worked for his own support (Acts 18:3; cf. 1 Thess. 2:9; 1 Cor. 4:12; 9:18). In Corinth and Ephesus he met Aquila and Priscilla (18:1-3, 18; 1 Cor. 16:19; 2 Tim. 4:19). Apollos was in Ephesus and Corinth (Acts 18:24-28; 1 Cor. 16:12; 3:5). Paul experienced persecution by synagogue authorities (2 Cor. 11:24) and James became ever more influential in Jerusalem (Acts 15:19-21; 21:17-26; Gal. 2:9, 12; Paul mentioned James first among the three "pillars" of the Jerusalem community).

Agreements between Acts and Paul's letters suggest that also other data of Acts may be on firm historical foundation. Conversely, Luke did not arbitrarily invent persons when his traditions were silent. We are not told the names of the persons who first preached the gospel in Damascus or in Antioch, Syria. No names of persons converted are given for the mission in Antioch, Pisidia, Iconium, Lystra, and Derbe (13:14—14:28) in contrast to Athens, Corinth, and Ephesus (17:34; 18:7-8; 19:29). The incidental reference to the edict of the emperor Claudius (18:2) can be substantiated from Suetonius, just as the mention of Gallio, Felix, Festus, Drusilla, Bernice, and Agrippa II is verifiable from an inscription and from Josephus. Luke gave no time references in the first 15 chapters of Acts because his tradition did not contain them (cf. Acts 13–14). Therefore the chronological data in subsequent chapters become all the more important (cf. 17:2; 18:11; 19:8, 10; 20:3, 6, 13-15). The travel summary of 20:1-3 can be verified from 1 Cor. 16:5 and 2 Cor. 2:12-13, which state that on his way from Ephesus to Macedonia Paul had worked successfully in Troas. Detailed information about time and place continues in Acts for Paul's travel to Jerusalem, transfer to Caesarea, and his journey to Rome. To be sure, in this instance we cannot demonstrate the accuracy of Luke's details, but there is no prior basis for discarding them as Lukan inventions.

Sherwin-White has pointed out that Luke correctly distinguished between imperial and senatorial provinces and designated officials by their proper titles, even though in the case of Cyprus the province had changed its status from the time of Acts 13 to Luke's own time. The magistrates of the Roman colony of Philippi were designated as "praetors" while those of Thessalonica are correctly called "politarchs," a rare word, but found in inscriptions referring to Thessalonian magistrates. The executive officer of Ephesus was correctly identified by Luke as "city clerk" (better, "chancellor") and he also knew that "Asiarchs" resided there (19:31,35). In contrast to them, the chief officer of Malta was rightly identified as "the first [chief] man of the island," also attested to by an inscription (28:7). We may therefore be confident that his name, Publius, was not invented by Luke, nor the circumstances surrounding his hospitality. In conclusion, two false alternatives concerning the historical reliability of the data found in Acts should be avoided. A radical skepticism toward Acts as a source for understanding the history of earliest Christianity is as uncalled-for as a militant fundamentalism which indulges in harmonizing the discrepancies between Acts and the Pauline letters. The latter have precedence for us in making historical judgments, not because the Pauline letters are free from bias, but because they arose out of a situation of immediacy that is absent in Acts (cf. Acts 17:14; 18:5 with 1 Thess. 3:1-2).

9. The Text of Acts

The book of Acts circulated in two distinct types of text within the early church. They are commonly called the *Western* text and the *Alexandrian* text. In Acts the differences between the two text types are so great that some scholars suggested that Luke himself produced two editions. One, represented by the Western text type of Acts, is about 9% longer than the other edition represented by the Alexandrian text type.

Even though scholars and Bible societies prefer "more often than not the shorter Alexandrian text" (Metzger), still the Western text is interesting because it represents the effort of an early Christian scholar to improve and thereby interpret the text of Acts. We are fortunate to have *A Textual Commentary on the Greek New Testament* (1971) by Bruce Metzger, in which all significant variant readings are judiciously discussed by chapter and verse.

As a beginning one should read Metzger's introduction to the text of Acts and his comments on a few variant readings, such as 1:2, 4; 2:17-21; 8:37; 15:20, 29 (apostles' decree). Some Western readings may deserve a better hearing than what is found in his commentary, e.g., 12:10; 19:9; 20:4, 15; 27:5.

10. Listening, Asking Questions, and Seeing Differences

Ernst Käsemann once said, "Exegesis is the craft of listening to a text, of asking questions, and of seeing differences." As a craft, exegesis combines technical skills with artistic appreciation and subtlety. In the following commentary we shall now and then raise historical questions and recognize differences, for instance, between the Lukan Paul and the historical Paul who speaks to us through his (authentic) letters, or between Luke's story of the apostles' conference and Paul's story. Since Luke was writing a historical monograph, historical questions are legitimate. But primarily we shall listen to Luke's own voice as he tells his story, entering the narrative world of his story, listening to what Acts has to say about God, Christ, and the Holy Spirit; Peter, Stephen, and Paul; Jews and Gentiles, conflicts and triumphs. We will always keep in mind that Acts is Luke's own sequel and in some ways his commentary on his Gospel story. By listening to his story and asking questions, we seek to discover Luke's theological point of view. We shall listen to *what* Luke tells us and to *how* he tells his story.

How does Luke tell his story (see §§ 2–6 above)? First, he aligns himself completely with the apostles and the other servants of Jesus. He has no interest in giving a neutral report of a disinterested bystander, even though he assumes the position of a detached observer. Moreover, Luke is "omniscient." Within the confines of his story world he knows what goes on in the hearts of people (e.g., 5:17), is privy to private and secret conversations (e.g., 23:13-15; 25:13-22) and to personal revelations (e.g., 23:11).

Second, at irregular intervals Luke gives summary statements (e.g., 2:42-47) and progress reports (e.g., the word of God increased, 6:7; cf. Luke 8:4-15). He changes pace, telling an exciting story in great detail (e.g., 10:1—11:17), followed by a generalized report. He introduces new directions in his story in 6:1 and 15:36 by telling us of conflicts among Christians which nevertheless resulted in further growth (6:7) or in two missionary journeys instead of one (15:39-41). In 19:21 Luke tells us that Paul "resolved in the Spirit" to travel to Jerusalem and afterward, "I must also see Rome." Paul's resolution introduces Rome for the first time in Luke's story provides the structure for the last two sections of Acts.

Luke used most space (10:1—11:17) to signal the incorporation of the first Gentile into the people of God and he referred to Cornelius's conversion twice more in Acts 15 to underline its pivotal importance. We are therefore justified in regarding it as the beginning of Luke's second part, in which the gospel is preached not only to Jews but also to Gentiles. Luke used the device of repetition (of the kerygma, of the invitation to repent, of the apostles' decree, of Paul's conversion, and of Jewish rejection) to signal what is of paramount importance in his story.

He provides a geographic outline for his story in the final word of Jesus before his ascension (1:8) so that the reader can understand individual events in relation to the whole story as it progresses from Jerusalem to Rome. Yet that progress is not told as a simple straightforward movement. As progress is made beyond Jerusalem the story always reverts back there, only to reach out ever farther beyond the center of Judaism, yet again and again returning to Jerusalem.

Third, Luke not only gave an overall structure to his narrative which is determined by people, Jews and Gentiles, and places, from Jerusalem to Rome, he also structured individual stories and speeches as we have already seen (Introduction, § 3).

Fourth, Luke tells his story of Acts by drawing extensive parallels among Jesus, Peter, Stephen, and Paul, as we shall see in the commentary. These parallels indicate that the story of Jesus continues in Acts through the work and word of his apostles and servant-witnesses.

Fifth, Luke does not tell us everything at once; rather he tells his story through his sequential plot, episode by episode. His plot is open-ended as we shall argue in the comments on chap. 28, because the End does not come in Rome.

Luke placed his Acts story within the history of salvation that begins with Abraham and ends with the consummation. We can distinguish between the time sequence in which Luke tells his story and the time in which events occur. The times when promises or threats are made are distinguished from the times in which partial fulfillments are brought about and also from the time of an ultimate fulfillment which, from Luke's viewpoint, may lie either in the past or in the future (cf. Acts 7). God's unconditional promises determine salvation history. In spite of rejections of his prophets, of his Messiah, and of the prophetic servant-witnesses of Jesus by the people, God's unconditional promises are in the process of realization in Luke's updated biblical history. His story narrates and thereby interprets the fulfillment of conditional and of unconditional promises in history and it narrates the responses of believers and unbelievers, of Jews and Gentiles, of prophetic witnesses and diverse authorities. By interpreting the church's course on its way from Jerusalem to Rome as the story of divine fulfillments, Luke gave encouragement and consolation in the face of perceived threats or real danger arising from conflicts with Jews, pagan neighbors, and Roman authorities. Last, but not least, Luke gathered the normative tradition for his church in the first Christian canon.

Finally, this commentary is indebted to prior scholarly works. Their insights have been incorporated without giving credit beyond the bibliography. I have profited most from the works of Dibelius, Haenchen, Conzelmann, Danker, Jervell, Johnson, Karris, Moessner, O'Toole, Praeder, Talbert, and Tiede. My debt to them is great, even when I disagree with some of their conclusions. A mass of footnotes could not be incorporated into this commentary, because its intended readers have only limited access to scholarly debate and literature.

OUTLINE OF ACTS

I.   Introduction: Easter to Pentecost (1:1-26)

II. Part 1: The Witness in Jerusalem, Judea, and Samaria (2:1—9:43)
   A. Witness in Jerusalem (2:1—5:42)
      1. Pentecost (2:1-47)
         a. The Miracle of Pentecost (2:1-13)
         b. Peter's Pentecost Witness (2:14-41) (Speech)
         c. Summary Statement: The Life of the Pentecost Community (2:42-47)
      2. Apostolic Benefaction and Sadducean Opposition (3:1—4:31) (Speech)
      3. The Life of the Community and Threats from Within and Without (4:32—5:42) (Summary Statements: 4:32-35; 5:12-16; 5:42)

   B. The Hellenists, Stephen's Witness, and Martyrdom (6:1—8:3)
      1. The Appointment of the Seven (6:1-7)
      2. Arrest of Stephen (6:8—7:1)
      3. Stephen's Defense (7:2-53) (Speech)
      4. Martyrdom and Persecution (7:54—8:3)

   C. Witness beyond Jerusalem (8:4—9:43)
      1. The Mission of Philip (8:4-40)
         a. Philip in Samaria (8:4-25)

47

COMMENTARY

Introduction: Easter to Pentecost (1:1-26)

This chapter, together with Luke 24, forms the center of Luke's two-volume work and is, if for this reason alone, important. It marks the end of the era of Jesus on earth and introduces the era of the coming church and its witness in the power of the Spirit. Both chapters underscore the continuity that exists between Jesus and his church. In Luke 24:46-47 we hear that salvation centers on three events: the death of the Messiah, his resurrection, *and* the proclamation of salvation "in his name" to Jews and Gentiles. The phrase "in his name" unites the proclamation to Jews and Gentiles inseparably with the events of Jesus' death and resurrection and makes it clear that Jesus' saving activity did not end in the past with his cross and resurrection. It continues into the present in the form of proclamation "in his name" (Luke 24:47) "to the end of the earth" (Acts 1:8).

The continuity between Jesus and the church is also implied in the proem of Acts (1:1-2) which states that in the Third Gospel our author dealt with all that Jesus **began to do and teach,** implying that in his second volume he will deal with the continuation of Jesus' word and work. Jesus "proclaims light" to Jews and Gentiles through his chosen witnesses (26:23), performs signs and wonders through his servants (9:34), and identifies with them in their suffering and tribulations (9:4). Jesus acts, speaks, and suffers in his messengers who represent him and continue his cause. "He who hears you hears me, and he who rejects you rejects me" (Luke 10:16).

This first chapter of Acts brings out the continuity between Jesus and the church in several other ways. First, prominence is given to

51

the apostles, mentioned at the beginning, the middle, and the end of the chapter (1:2, 13, 26). They had accompanied Jesus from his baptism to his ascension (1:21) and they are therefore qualified to function as the link between Jesus and his church. Second, the Holy Spirit (1:2, 5, 8, 16) is the divine power which effects the continuity of biblical history from the Old Testament (1:16) via Jesus (1:2) to the church (1:5, 8). The Spirit who had spoken through David and the prophets was present in Jesus when he chose the apostles, and is the same Spirit promised by Jesus to his church. Third, the theme of promise and fulfillment (1:4, 8, 11, 16) gives unity to Luke's two volumes and connects both of them with the Old Testament on one hand and the future consummation on the other. Fulfillments that have already occurred, such as the death, resurrection, and ascension of the Messiah are the ground for the church's assurance of the fulfillment that is yet to come (cf. v. 11). Fourth, the place where the Spirit would come is Jerusalem (1:4, 8, 12). For Luke Jerusalem symbolizes the continuity of biblical history in terms of space. It was the geographic goal of Jesus' journey (Luke 9:51) and the place of his passion and his Easter appearances. Within the immediate environs of Jerusalem (1:12), Jesus ascended into heaven, and in Jerusalem, the Holy Spirit came upon the church. From there the witness began "to the end of the earth" (1:8). Note that each section in Acts is connected with Jerusalem (cf. Acts 2–7; 8:1, 14, 25, 26; 9:2, 20, 26, 28; 11:2, 27; 13:31; 15:2, 4; 18:22; 19:21; 20:22; 21:12-13, 17; 23:11; 28:17). Fifth, the continuity between Jesus and the church consists in the message. The pre- and post-Easter Jesus, as well as Peter, Philip, and Paul, preached "the kingdom of God" (Luke 4:43; Acts 1:3; 8:12; 28:23, 31). The "kingdom of God" in Luke-Acts means that God's sovereign, saving reign is already present in Jesus. The content of the church's preaching is therefore in continuity with the message of Jesus (cf. Luke 24:44, 48 with Acts 26:22-23). For Luke proclamation to Jews and Gentiles is part of the salvation of God through Jesus and constitutes Luke's rationale for writing Acts. The continuity between Christ and the post-Pentecost church is grounded in the Holy Spirit as the heavenly force, in Jerusalem as the earthly place, in the promise-fulfillment pattern, in the apostles as Christ's chosen representatives and primary witnesses, and in the identical message which Jesus and his apostles proclaimed.

The structure of chapter 1 is rather difficult to discern. The following is a tentative proposal.

I. The Proem (vv. 1-2)
II. Introduction (vv. 3-26)
    A. From Easter to the Ascension (vv. 3-5)
    B. The Ascension (vv. 6-14)
        1. The Disciples' Question (v. 6)
        2. Jesus' Promise and Mandate (vv. 7-8)
        3. The Ascension (v. 9)
        4. Interpretation of the Ascension (vv. 10-11)
        5. The Pre-Pentecost Community in Jerusalem (vv. 12-14)
    C. The By-Election (vv. 15-26)
        1. The Fate of Judas (vv. 15-20)
        2. The Election of Matthias (vv. 21-26)

The Proem (1:1-2)

Following the literary custom of ancient authors, Luke began his second volume with a proem, a preface, in which he recapitulated the content of his first book and named the person, Theophilus, to whom this volume is dedicated. Theophilus means "friend of God," and undoubtedly refers to an individual whom Luke wished to honor and who would see to the book's distribution. We know nothing about the identity of Theophilus, but we can gather from the proem to the Third Gospel that he needed assurance, certainty (*asphaleia*), concerning the content of the Christian instruction. In short, Theophilus was a Christian, not some pagan sympathizer of equestrian or senatorial rank. The omission of the honorific address "most excellent" (Luke 1:3) in the proem of Acts does not indicate that Theophilus had become a Christian since Luke wrote his Gospel, but merely follows the literary convention in proems of subsequent volumes.

Luke's first book covered Jesus' earthly ministry from his baptism **until the day when he was taken up** into heaven. The annunciation and birth narratives of the first two chapters of Luke's Gospel are not included in the verb "began" (v. 1); those chapters (Luke 1–2) are merely an introduction, a prelude, to **all that Jesus began to do and teach.** His ministry started with his baptism, not with his conception. Hence, the virginal conception is not part of the kerygma of Acts, in contrast to Jesus' baptism (cf. 1:22; 10:37; 11:16; 13:24-

25). Moreover, Luke claimed completeness in his narrative about Jesus' ministry. His Gospel included **all that Jesus began to do and teach** (cf. Luke 1:3, "all things"). **To do and teach** characterizes Jesus' total ministry in contrast to that of his disciples. In the Third Gospel the disciples never teach. Their teaching ministry began only after the resurrected Jesus had "opened their minds to understand the scriptures" (Luke 24:45-47). Hence, they teach only after Pentecost (4:2, 18, etc.).

Frequently, interpreters have rejected the translation "all that Jesus *began* to do and teach." This translation implies that Jesus' ministry up to the ascension was only the beginning of a work that was to be extended and continued as narrated in Acts. Instead, some have proposed that in accordance with the usage of the LXX, the Greek verb "began" is superfluous and should not be translated at all. In contrast to the RSV text of 1:1, we would then read, "all that Jesus did and taught." Still others suggest that the verb should be translated adverbially: "All that Jesus did and taught from the beginning" (cf. Luke 1:2, 3; Acts 1:22). None of these alternative translations would imply that Acts contains the continuation of Jesus' ministry through his apostles and servants. However, a pleonastic use of this verb in imitation of the style of the LXX is out of place in a proem and an adverbial use has no parallel in Acts. Above all, Paul's concluding defense speech in Acts clearly indicates that Jesus, after his death and resurrection, continues to proclaim salvation through his witnesses (26:23). Therefore, the carefully worded proem of Acts 1:1-2 views Jesus' ministry up to the ascension as the beginning of a ministry which finds its continuation in the ministry of his apostles and witnesses.

In summarizing Luke's first volume, the proem refers to the ascension (the goal of Jesus' ministry, cf. Luke 9:51), to his miracles and teachings, and to the election of the 12 apostles, who were chosen from a larger group of disciples (Luke 6:12-16) and appointed to be the true leaders of Israel (Luke 22:30). Moreover, the proem refers to the mandate of Christ to his disciples prior to his ascension, namely, that they remain in Jerusalem and be witnesses (Luke 24:48-49). Lastly, the proem refers to the Holy Spirit. The phrase **through the Holy Spirit** should not be connected with Jesus' commandment to the apostles, as in the RSV, but with their election. Luke inverted the word order for the sake of emphasis on other occasions also (e.g.,

20:18). In Luke 6:12-14, we read that Jesus continued in prayer all night long prior to the election of the apostles. The proem interprets this scene by stating that their election came about under the Spirit's direction.

After the recapitulation of Luke's first book, one would expect to find a brief summary of his second, but none follows. Several ancient historians likewise omitted a summary of the content of subsequent volumes of their work. Luke was able to adopt this practice especially since he had implied the content of Acts by using the verb *began* (v. 1) and since he summarized his second book in the final saying of Jesus (v. 8).

From Easter to the Ascension (1:3-5)

A general characterization of the period (v. 3) is followed by a particular event (vv. 4-5). The apostles are witnesses not *of* the resurrection, since no one saw Jesus become alive in the tomb, but *to* the resurrection, because Jesus appeared to them **many** times, not just once or twice on Easter day or on the day of his ascension. Yet he was not with them continuously during this period. In Luke 24, Jesus appeared not only to the 11 apostles, but also to a larger group of disciples who were with them (Luke 24:33-43). In Acts 1:2-3 the **apostles** are singled out because, chosen by Jesus through the Spirit (v. 2), they will function as the normative witnesses to Jesus and as the true leaders of Israel.

However, Jesus' appearances to other disciples are presupposed also in Acts 1 (cf. vv. 21, 23). His appearances constitute **many proofs** in that they overcame the unbelief and despondency caused by **his passion** (cf. Luke 24), which is a Lukan expression for his death (Acts 17:3). Faith in Christ is the work of the risen living Christ. The phrase **many proofs** refers specifically to incidents such as the breaking of the bread (Luke 24:30-31), the showing of his hands and feet (24:39), and the eating of broiled fish (24:42-43)—all of which demonstrate the reality of his bodily resurrection (cf. the emphasis on Jesus' body in Luke 23:52,55; 24:3,39—an emphasis absent in Mark). During this period the resurrected Jesus did not introduce a new or secret teaching, but taught the same as he had done in his ministry prior to Easter, namely (literally), "the things that pertain to the **kingdom of God**" (cf. Luke 4:43). In Luke this means that God's future reign is already present in Jesus' ministry, his death, resurrection, and subsequent proclamation (Luke 11:20; 24:46-47). The subject of the teaching about the kingdom also prepares for the question of the disciples concerning the time of the coming of the kingdom in v. 6. In the epilog of Acts, Paul preaches "the kingdom of God" in Rome. This subject which Jesus taught the apostles also during the interim between the resurrection and the ascension forms brackets around the book of Acts.

The statement that the Easter appearances took place **during forty days** comes as a surprise to the reader of Luke 24:33-52. There the ascension would seem to take place on Easter evening; early copyists therefore sought to harmonize Acts 1:3 with Luke 24 by omitting the reference to the ascension in Luke 24:51 (see Metzger).

Four additional comments

1. A 40-day period between Easter and the ascension is, apart from this verse, unknown in the New Testament and in early Christian literature. It reappears in Tertullian (*Apology* 21.29) around A.D. 200, when the book of Acts had entered the canon. In Barn. 15:9 the ascension takes place on a Sunday, while gnostic writings refer to 18 months, 545 or 550 days, or even 11 years (Irenaeus, *Ag. Her.*, 1.3.2; 1.30.14; *Asc. Isa.* 9:12; *Apoc. James; Pistis Sophia,* chap. 1).

2. According to Luke, it is not the resurrected Jesus but the Lord exalted to the right hand of God who bestows the Spirit (in distinction from John 20:22). Our author created a unique, holy interim by using the round number of 40 days. This number lends itself because of its symbolic significance in the Old Testament as well as in the synoptic tradition (e.g., Exod. 34:28; 1 Kings 19:8; Luke 4:1-2). The 40-day period gave Luke the opportunity to fill the time between the ascension and Pentecost by narrating the election of Matthias. This narrative presupposes the absence of Jesus.

3. Luke limited the period of Christ's appearances in time to **forty days.** This holy interim between Easter and the ascension is unrepeatable and contains the church-founding resurrection appearances of Jesus. Luke limited these also in space to **Jerusalem,** as the following verse shows. In doing so, he deliberately excluded Galilean appearances of which he was aware (Matt. 28:16; John 21:1-7; compare Mark 16:7 with Luke 24:6,49). Luke's limitations of res-

urrection appearances in time and space automatically placed Paul's vision on the Damascus road (9:1-9) on a different level.

Paul's vision of Jesus occurred *after* the ascension and apart from Jerusalem, while the church-founding appearances took place *during* the 40-day period prior to the ascension, in and around Jerusalem. Paul therefore based his Easter kerygma on these, rather than his own Damascus experience (13:31). It is only when Luke narrated Paul's vita in his defense speeches that an appeal is made to Paul's vision and the resulting break in his biography. Luke's limitation automatically undercut all heretical Christians who might claim that their teaching was legitimate because they, too, had seen the resurrected Jesus.

4. The discrepancy concerning the date of the ascension in Luke 24 and Acts 1 should sensitize us to what kind of a historian Luke actually was. He certainly was not a pedant for whom factual accuracy was the ultimate goal. Rather, he was fond of variations and could picture the same event from different perspectives. In Luke 24:50-52, the ascension functions as the conclusion of the earthly ministry of Jesus, who is carried into heaven as he blesses his disciples. In Acts 1 the ascension functions as the presupposition for the Spirit's coming upon the church, which remains forever dependent upon the apostolic resurrection witness. This witness is based on Jesus' appearances during 40 days, not just during one day nor during an indefinite period of some years.

Verse 4 recounts a particular incident within the 40-day interim. Instead of translating, **while staying with them** (RSV), we should probably translate: "while eating with them" in agreement with many early translations (see Metzger, 278-279). Luke knew that with whom one eats is important (e.g., Luke 5:30; 7:36; 10:7; 14:12-15; 19:5-10; 22:30; Acts 2:46; 11:3). The risen Lord had eaten with his disciples and in their presence (Luke 24:20-31; 24:41-43; Acts 10:41). In this verse Luke probably sketched the scene of a meal of the resurrected Jesus with his disciples during which he gave instruction and made a promise. As in meals prior to Easter, so now the meal becomes the occasion for specific teaching. His instruction consists in a prohibition. The apostles are required **not to depart from Jerusalem** (cf. Luke 24:49b). The holy interim is tied to the holy city. The prohibition is followed by a promise. They are **to wait for the promise of the Father,** which means to wait for the Spirit that the

Father had promised in the Old Testament (Joel 2:28). **You heard from me** concerning this promise refers to Luke 24:49 and perhaps Luke 11:13. The promise will find fulfillment **before many days,** that is, shortly, on Pentecost.

Verse 5 gives the reason for waiting, in direct speech. A traditional word of John the Baptist is placed on Jesus' mouth (cf. Mark 1:8) and John's water baptism is contrasted with being **baptized with the Holy Spirit.** Jesus does not say here "*I* will baptize you," but uses the passive voice as a circumlocution for an activity of God. He, the Father, will baptize them. Jesus himself is the mediator of this Spirit baptism (2:33). This verse does not deal explicitly with Christian water Baptism in Jesus' name, which begins at Pentecost and which mediates the Spirit (cf. 2:38). Rather, it deals with the outpouring of the Spirit itself. To be "baptized with the Holy Spirit" is a metaphor for receiving the Spirit. John's water baptism expressed the repentance of the baptized and promised forgiveness (Luke 3:3), but it did not and could not mediate the Holy Spirit. Baptism with the Holy Spirit will occur when the Spirit "falls" or is "poured out" over Jesus' followers on Pentecost. The coming of the Spirit will fulfill not only **the Father's** promise, but also Jesus' promise made during a meal in the holy interim (cf. 11:16).

The Ascension (1:6-14)

A question of the apostles (v. 6) and disciples is followed by the final mandate of Jesus (vv. 7-8). The ascension (v. 9) is not narrated from Jesus' perspective, but from the perspective of the eyewitnesses. It is interpreted as pledge and promise of his future parousia (vv. 10-11). The ascension day community returns to Jerusalem, and their return marks the transition to the next scene (vv. 12-14).

6—The persons who had **come together** are not specified. The context makes it clear that not only the 11 apostles but also other disciples are thought to be present (cf. vv. 12-14, 23; cf. Luke 24:33). Their question, **Will you at this time restore the kingdom to Israel?** can be understood in different ways. (1) It may express that either historically or in Luke's opinion the disciples had not yet shed their Jewish nationalistic expectations and still hoped for Israel's messianic restoration. But is it probable that Luke would place a false question into the mouth of the disciples after Jesus had "opened their minds" and "opened . . . the scriptures" for them (Luke 24:32, 45)? Luke was hardly telling his readers that even on ascension day a nation-alistic misconception prevailed among the apostles and disciples. (2) Other interpreters therefore hold that the disciples' question is merely a foil for reminding the reader that the eschaton is not im-minent, that the kingdom of God does not appear at once with finality, that the end of "the times of the Gentiles" is not at hand (Luke 21:24). But we should note that the disciples asked not just about the time of the End, but about the restoration of **the kingdom to Israel.** (3) The question is primarily a literary device that enables Luke to bring some important teaching forward. Such questions abound in Luke-Acts (e.g., Luke 1:34; 13:23-24; 17:20; 19:11-27; Acts 2:37; 22:10). At any rate the latter alternative should be the starting point for interpreting this verse. The disciples' question is prompted by Jesus' promise of the Spirit (v. 5) and deals with the problem of time, whether **at this time,** that is, in a short time, when the Spirit comes, **the kingdom** will be restored to Israel. Moreover, the question deals with the extension of the kingdom. Does it in-clude **Israel** only? And finally, what is the role of the resurrected Lord? How does he relate to Israel and the kingdom? In short, the question, when, for whom, and through whom the kingdom will be established with finality receives an answer in the last word of Jesus before his ascension.

7-8—Jesus' answer has two parts. He first rejects all speculations concerning the time when the kingdom will come with finality. Such speculations, no matter how popular in Luke's environment or in ours, are an intrusion on the sovereignty of God. In his Gospel, Luke had omitted the text of Mark 13:32 (cf. Luke 21:33ff.). He now introduced and recast this saying as part of Jesus' last word. If Chris-tians at Luke's time felt that their hopes for an imminent end had been disappointed, this last word of Jesus told them that their dis-appointment is fully justified because they were not to know the **times or seasons** of the future coming of the kingdom in the first place. Moreover, **at this time,** when the Spirit comes (v. 5), Jesus will not **restore the kingdom to Israel** with finality. How he will do so at the **times and seasons** of the End is left open-ended—and for good reason. The God of Israel is full of surprises and faithful to "all" his promises made to Israel (cf. 3:21). What God and his Mes-siah will do to Israel at the End lies beyond the scope of Acts. However, according to Luke, Israel's restoration already begins at

Pentecost and continues in the church's mission (15:16-17). Yet only the End will complete the restoration of the kingdom to Israel and bring the fulfillment of "all" of God's promises (3:21).

The second part of Jesus' answer repeats the promise of the Spirit's coming and contains the mandate to be his witnesses. Jesus' own role is indicated only indirectly: **You shall receive power** (cf. Luke 24:49). Later, in Acts 2:33, it will become clear that God grants the Holy Spirit through the exalted Lord. His disciples receive the fulfillment of his promise of the Spirit through Jesus himself. Thus he will enable them to take up the new task of being his **witnesses** "at this time" between Pentecost and parousia. His mandate to witness also deals with the question of the kingdom's extension and its relation to Israel. The apostles and disciples shall witness **in Jerusalem and in all Judea and Samaria and to the end of the earth** (cf. Luke 24:47). The people of the kingdom will not be limited to Israel (cf. Luke 13:23-29). Rather, the establishment and restoration of Israel before the End takes place through the inclusion of Gentiles into the people of God (15:16-18). Such inclusion is also in agreement with the Old Testament. The phrase **to the end of the earth** is borrowed from Isa. 49:6, where Yahweh's servant is told to be a light to the nations, the instrument through which salvation reaches "to the end of the earth." This universal servant-witness task is now mandated to the apostles and disciples, even as in 13:47 it is mandated to Paul.

The last word and mandate of Jesus also summarizes and structures the narrative of Acts. For Luke, Jerusalem, Judea, and Samaria comprise one geographic unit, namely, the land of Jews and half-Jews (cf. 9:31 where three regions comprise one geographic unit). The first part of Luke's story of the witness in Jerusalem, Judea, and Samaria concludes with 9:43. Chapter 10 begins his second part which narrates the movement "to the end of the earth" and the inclusion of Gentiles into the restored people of God (cf. 15:16-17). The book of Acts concludes with Paul witnessing in Rome. In Luke's narrative, none of those addressed by Jesus on ascension day reached Rome. But it was the same message concerning the kingdom of God and its restoration to Israel that Paul proclaimed in the capital of the Gentile empire (cf. 28:20, 23, 31). Rome is not the end of the earth, but the center of the empire from which all roads lead to the end of the earth. Paul's proclamation in Rome guaranteed that the normative witness enshrined in Luke-Acts *will* reach the end of the earth. Therefore Acts concludes in an open-ended way, and the final mandate of Jesus of 1:8 calls the church of Luke to continue the task of carrying the apostolic witness to the end of the earth, even as Paul had carried it to Asia Minor, Greece, and Rome.

9 (The ascension)—Luke is the only New Testament writer who gives a brief description of the ascension. He differentiated between the resurrection and the exaltation of Christ (cf. John 20:17) and connected the latter with the ascension. The ascension concludes the 40-day period of Jesus' appearances. Paul also thought that the time of the resurrection appearances was limited, though of course not to 40 days. When he called himself "the last" of all the apostles, and one "untimely born" as an apostle (1 Cor. 15:5-8), he apparently believed that the Easter appearances had come to a conclusion with Christ's appearance to him. However, for Luke the vision of Jesus which Paul had on the road to Damascus occurred after the ascension and therefore it is not on the same level as the church-founding appearances of Jesus to his disciples before the ascension.

After Christ's final words which the apostles and disciples heard (vv. 7-8), Luke narrates a final scene which they see with their own eyes and which concluded the unique period after Easter when Jesus was still on earth, appearing, eating, and speaking with his followers. In this final scene Jesus is removed from earth and enters the realm of God by ascending into heaven. Verse 9 is structured according to an *a-b-b-a* pattern, whereby the beginning and the end of the sentence (a) refer to the disciples' "seeing," or to their "sight," and the middle (b) refers to Jesus' ascension on a cloud. The emphasis on "seeing" is repeated three times in the following two verses (vv. 10-11). The apostles and disciples are eyewitnesses of the ascension and their witness is the ground of the church's exaltation kerygma. Luke narrated in v. 9 why a Christian is able to say that Jesus has been exalted to God's right hand (2:33; 5:31).

The **cloud** is not only a symbol of a divine epiphany (a sign and veil of God's presence; cf. Luke 9:34; Exod. 24:15-18); it is here the vehicle by means of which Jesus is taken up into the presence of God. The singular, **a cloud,** corresponds to Luke 21:27 where Luke had changed the plural "clouds" of Mark 13:26 into a singular. This means that the cloud of his ascension will be the vehicle on which he comes at his parousia (see v. 11).

10-11 (Interpretation of the ascension)—At the empty tomb (Luke 24:1-12) and after the ascension Luke presented *two* divine messengers. Otherwise angels appear singly (e.g., Luke 1:11; Acts 27:23; etc.) At the empty tomb our author had changed the single Markan angel into two angels (cf. Luke 24:4 = Mark 16:5). His reason probably was to underscore the importance of the divine interpretation of a pivotal event in God's story. At the tomb and after the ascension the angels first utter a reproach (v. 11a; cf. Luke 24:5) which is introduced with **why**. The reproach is followed by an interpretation in both episodes. In v. 11 the ascension is interpreted as guarantee of Jesus' future parousia. The theme of the future parousia of **this Jesus** had not been stated in Luke 24 and constitutes the first new theme in Acts. Now the reader knows that "the Son of man" who comes "in a cloud with power and great glory" and completes Israel's "redemption" (Luke 21:27-28) is none other than **this Jesus.** His parousia will fulfill the hope expressed in the disciples' question of v. 6 and conclude the time of witnessing to the end of the earth (vv. 7-8). Jesus in his last word had rejected the question concerning the date of the kingdom's coming and its limitation to Israel. He had indicated indirectly that his role in the restoration of the kingdom to Israel would begin through their witness in the power of the Spirit. Now the interpreting angels point out not when, but *that* he will come and how he will come. The consummation and restoration of the kingdom to Israel in the parousia of Christ is as certain as is the ascension to which the eyewitnesses can testify. Moreover, Luke connected not only the ascension but also the parousia with **Jerusalem** (cf. v. 12). Because the climax of the kingdom's restoration to Israel comes at the parousia, therefore the parousia will take place at Jerusalem. In the meantime, instead of **gazing into heaven** and speculating about the times and seasons of the parousia, there is work to be done and the disciples must get ready for it.

The ascension was important to Luke for several reasons. (1) It assured the church that its Lord will triumph in the end, no matter how many tribulations (14:22) it must undergo in its witness and mission between Pentecost and parousia. (2) The ascension is the presupposition of the Spirit's coming, because it is the ascended Christ (not the Jesus of Easter day, as in John 20:19-23) who mediates the Spirit (2:33). (3) The resurrection appearances are completed with the ascension. Subsequent visions of Jesus appearing from heaven (9:1-9) are not as normative for the church as his appearances between Easter and the ascension, because that 40-day period, when Jesus was still on earth and spoke and ate with his disciples, is unrepeatable. (4) Jesus has changed his place and is no longer accessible as he was when he walked the dusty roads from Galilee to Jerusalem. He is now in heaven at the right hand of God (2:33-34). Therefore when Christians speak of God, they must also speak of Jesus. (5) Jesus does not recede into the past and become a figure of past history, but as the ascended Lord he is always contemporary with his church. The church exists not merely after him, but primarily under him. (6) Jesus now operates through his witnesses (cf. 26:23). (7) As the Lord at God's right hand, he has a legitimate claim on Israel and on the world. He shall return and restore the kingdom to Israel with finality.

12-14 (The ascension day community)—This summary statement is closely tied to the preceding verses by its introduction, **then they returned to Jerusalem,** in obedience with the command of v. 4. We now hear that the ascension took place on **the mount called Olivet** which is **a sabbath day's journey** from Jerusalem, that is, less than three-fourths of a mile. However, in Luke 24:50-52 the ascension took place at Bethany, which is three miles from Jerusalem. The reason for this discrepancy probably lies in Luke's imperfect knowledge of the geography around Jerusalem which made him think that Bethany and Mount Olivet are in the same locale (cf. Luke 19:29 with Mark 11:1; Luke 22:39 with Mark 14:26, 32; Luke 21:37-38 with Mark 11:11-12). The core of the community of about 120 people (v. 15) was the apostles whose names had appeared at the beginning of Jesus' ministry (Luke 6:14) and which are repeated once more after its conclusion. They are not the only eyewitnesses, but they are the normative eyewitnesses because they had been "chosen" by Jesus from a larger group of disciples (cf. v. 2). John now appears in second place, and together with Peter, he will be the only apostle mentioned by name in subsequent stories. The absence of Judas shows that the circle of the Twelve is no longer complete, and so the list of names serves also as transition to the following narrative (vv. 15-26). The ascension day community consists of Galileans only (cf. Acts 1:11; 13:30). **Women** play a prominent role in it (cf. Luke 8:2-3; 23:49, 55; 24:1-11, 33). Among them is **Mary,** his mother (Luke 1:26-56; 8:19-21). Also **his brothers** belonged to it (cf. Mark 3:31, omitted by

Luke; cf. Mark 6:3 with Luke 8:19). One of them, James, will be a leader in the Jerusalem community (15:13-21; 21:18). The community **with one accord** expressed its unanimity in **prayer** as it waited for the fulfillment of Jesus' promise to them (cf. v. 8).

The By-election (1:15-26)

In addition to prayer and expectant waiting, the election of Matthias, necessitated by Judas's betrayal, took place in the 10-day period between the ascension and Pentecost. The two parts of the narrative are connected by two quotations (v. 20). The first (LXX Ps. 68:26 = Ps. 69:25) shows that Judas's fate was determined by God, the second (LXX Ps. 108:8 = Ps. 109:8) shows that the vacated apostolic office must be filled. The structure of this section is: *(a)* narrative (vv. 15-19), *(b)* proof text (v. 20a, b), *(b)* proof text (v. 20c), *(a)* narrative (vv. 21-26).

15-20 (The fate of Judas)—In those days, between the ascension and Pentecost, Peter took up his assignment to "strengthen his brothers" (Luke 22:32) by addressing the community on the issue of Judas's betrayal. He interpreted it not psychologically in terms of motives, but theologically in terms of fulfillment of Scripture. Through David **the Holy Spirit** predicted the betrayal and fate of **Judas** (v. 16).

Peter did not suggest that God's predestination erased or diminished Judas's guilt. No one can argue "God made me do it." Human guilt and God's design cannot be played off one against the other. But by stating that his deed was part of God's design, Judas's treachery loses its scandal for the community.

Verses 17-19 give not only the reasons why the Psalms, quoted in v. 20, apply to Judas, but also provide background information for Luke's readers. In an actual speech by Peter to the 120 Galileans one would hardly expect to hear about Judas's fate, as though his audience did not know about it already. But Luke's reader needs the information. In short, the speech is Luke's literary work, and the reference to **their language** (v. 19) indicates the same. This almost commonly accepted conclusion concerning the speeches in Acts is in this case strengthened by the use of the text of the LXX in v. 20. One would hardly suppose that Peter would quote the Greek Bible to an Aramaic-speaking audience.

With **the reward** for **his wickedness** (Luke 22:3-6, 47) Judas bought a farm (v. 18, rather than a **field,** RSV), because the quotation speaks of **his habitation** (v. 20). Moreover **he burst open** when he fell, that is, he must have fallen from a roof rather than tripped in a field. The Greek word can mean either field or farmstead. As a consequence of his ghastly death his farm became known as **Akeldama, that is, Field of Blood** (v. 19). Matthew gives a different version of how this field received its name (Matt. 27:3-10). In Luke, however, it is Judas's blood that gave rise to the name and the **Field of Blood** was bought by him, not the priests. Both evangelists indicate fulfillment of Scripture, but in different ways (cf. Matt. 27:9-10; Acts 1:19-20). In short, it would seem that a field called **Akeldama** was already known by that name when Christian traditions connected that name in different ways with Judas's fate.

The first citation (v. 20a and b) which predicted that Judas's **habitation** would **become desolate** has already been fulfilled. The second citation (v. 20c), **his office let another take** (Ps. 109:8), constitutes not a prediction but a command which is yet to be fulfilled. It requires the appointment of someone to take Judas's place among the apostles. The following narrative of Matthias's election shows that this directive was carried out. But in order to have a command in the second citation, Luke had to change the Greek optative form (which in the Psalm expressed a human wish) into an imperative. He had made some changes in the first citation also, where the LXX reads "their habitation" and "in it" instead of the Hebrew text which has "camp" and "in their tents." The Hebrew text would not have been suitable to score the point of Luke's text and connect Judas's fate with this psalm. Even so, Luke had to change the plural of the LXX "their habitation" into the singular "his habitation" to make the quotation fit the occasion.

Modern readers have difficulty with the New Testament writers' use of the Old Testament. But we should remember that their method of interpreting Old Testament texts corresponded to the way biblical texts were interpreted at that time. There was little or no regard for the original meaning of a text or even for the wider context of a particular verse. However, the New Testament writers read the Old Testament from a new perspective, the Christ event. They not only found in the Old Testament a source from which they drew much of their vocabulary to express their faith in Christ but they also made new connections between promises and predictions on one hand and the Christ event on the other. Thus when Christians read Psalm 69, which was the lament of a pious person praying for deliverance from his enemies, and when they came across v. 9, "zeal for thy house hast consumed me," they connected it with Jesus (cf. John 2:17), who was content to lose himself entirely in the service of God. Whom does this verse fit better than him? Coming across v. 25 Luke saw a connection with Jesus' betrayer and his fate. The basic conviction which is expressed in the use of the Old Testament by New Testament writers is that the same God who speaks in the Old Testament has acted decisively in Christ.

Before Luke will narrate the opposition to the Christian witness from Jews and Gentiles he reminds his readers that even an apostle, chosen by Jesus, had been a total failure. His diabolical betrayal of Jesus was connected with money (Luke 22:5; cf. Luke 16:13). With the reward for his unrighteous act, he sought to buy security for himself (Acts 1:18; cf. Luke 12:15) and met his judgment. Our possessions and the use we make of them are inseparably intertwined with our relationship to God, Christ, and the Holy Spirit. This Lukan theme will reappear in Acts more than once. But Judas's betrayal for money offers a warning to Luke's church. At the same time Luke tells his church that God is in control even in the devil's and the traitor's hour (cf. Luke 22:53).

21-26 (Election of Matthias)—The conclusion is drawn from the divine command (v. 20c) that the "office" abandoned by Judas **must** be filled by someone else. The qualifications for an apostle are spelled out. He must have been a disciple of Jesus and have **accompanied us** throughout his ministry **beginning from the baptism of John until the day when he was taken up.** In Luke's Gospel the Twelve did not forsake Jesus and flee at the time of his arrest (in contrast to Mark; cf. Luke 22:47-53 = Mark 14:43-50). They continued with Jesus in his trials (Luke 22:28) and they were present at his crucifixion among "all his acquaintances" (Luke 23:49). Thus they are eyewitnesses **during all the time** of his ministry up to and including the ascension. The function of the new apostle is to **become with us a witness to his resurrection** (v. 22). One might ask whether the candidate is not already a witness to the resurrection if he fulfills the qualifications for apostleship (vv. 21-22). How can he then **become** one? Two brief answers: First, even though the apostles are eyewitnesses who encountered the resurrected Lord they begin to give their witness about him only at Pentecost (cf. 1:8). Second, the witness of the apostles is normative witness because they have been chosen by Christ for this purpose. Prior to his election Matthias was merely an eyewitness. Luke presupposes that Christ had appeared not only to the eleven, but also to a larger group of disciples (e.g., 1:23; Luke 24:13, 18, 33-52). They too become witnesses to his resurrection—on Pentecost. The apostolic witness, however, is the normative witness which Luke brings in Acts.

Two persons were presented, **Joseph called Barsabbas** whose Latin surname was **Justus,** and **Matthias.** It is not clear whether the prayer of the community is addressed to God or to Jesus, since the address **Lord** can refer to either. If the act of choosing an apostle in v. 25 corresponds to the act of choosing performed by Jesus (v. 2), we may conclude that the prayer of the community (vv. 24-25) was directed to Jesus. He is addressed in prayer also in 7:59-60. Here he is asked to make his choice between the two candidates known. After the prayer **they cast lots** on behalf of the two. We are not certain how this was done. Perhaps two sticks bearing the names of the candidates were placed in a container which was shaken until one fell out (Lev. 16:8; Num 26:55; 1QS 5:3 refer to decisions by lot but do not describe how it was done; in Prov. 16:33 the lot "is cast into the lap"). **The lot fell on Matthias** which means that the Lord had chosen him to be one of the 12 apostles. The community is now ready for Pentecost, where it will appear as the true Israel with the Twelve as its leaders witnessing to and pleading with Israel. Luke's story of the election of Matthias does not advocate the idea of an apostolic succession. New elections of apostles will not be necessary later on because the apostles will leave their ministry not by betrayal but by death (cf. 12:2). In this particular case an election became necessary, because there should be 12 apostles who represent the 12 tribes of Israel and symbolically express Jesus' claim on Israel as a whole. Through this by-election the circle of the Twelve is reconstituted.

Luke generally equated the *apostles* with the Twelve, following a tradition present also in Matt. 10:2 and Rev. 21:14 (and perhaps Mark 6:30). This tradition differs from 1 Cor. 15:3-8, in which the Twelve are clearly not equated with the apostles but rather distinguished from them. However, even though Peter was one of the

Twelve, still Paul called him an apostle (Gal. 1:18-19). Historically, the circle of the Twelve residing in Jerusalem apparently disappeared when individual members departed from Jerusalem (cf. 12:17) and engaged in missionary work. Then, as Paul's language in Gal. 1:18-19 shows, individual members of the Twelve became known as apostles, because they too did the work of apostles, of persons who had encountered the resurrected Jesus and been sent by him to do missionary work. The group of apostles which also included women (cf. Rom. 16:7) was of course originally larger than the Twelve. Luke limited the apostles to the Twelve, except in Acts 14:4, 14 (see comments there), just as he had limited the resurrection appearances in time and in space.

Part 1: The Witness in Jerusalem, Judea, and Samaria (2:1—9:43)

Part 1 of Acts begins with the foundational narrative of Pentecost followed by Peter's inaugural sermon which sets forth what God has "accomplished among us" (Luke 1:1) after the resurrection of Jesus. The story of Pentecost determines the narrative of Acts and especially its first part in which the Spirit-filled community confronts Israel as a whole in word and deed. A summary statement of the life of the community (2:42-47) contains themes that are being unfolded in Part 1 and are connected with external and internal threats. The apostolic "doctrine" (2:41) is heard in speeches by Peter and John, by the apostles and Stephen. "Wonders and signs" (2:43) are narrated in detail (3:1-10) or in summary fashion (5:12, 15-16; 6:8). But opposition to miracles and teaching "in the name of Jesus" arose and grew in intensity from arrests and threats (4:1-22), to arrests and beatings (5:17-42), and finally to arrest ending in martyrdom (6:12—7:60). Stephen's martyrdom in turn is followed by a general persecution which shatters the close "fellowship" of the Jerusalem community (8:1, 4). Yet in spite of and even through persecution the church experiences growth. One reason why opposition and persecution did not diminish the community is found in Gamaliel's advice (5:38-39) and another reason in the community's "prayer" (4:24-31). Ultimately it is God and his Messiah who direct the church and even redirect the church's persecutor into a witness of Christ. Woven into Luke's narrative of the growth of the church through opposition are stories about internal threats that endanger the fellowship from within.

We shall now look at the sequential plot. The Pentecost story is followed by a miraculous healing (3:1-10) which leads to Peter's speech (3:11-26); the speech in turn leads to his and John's arrest (4:1-22). Having been warned not to speak anymore "in the name of Jesus" (4:18) the apostles joined the community which prayed to

69

God that he would grant them to speak his word in "boldness" (4:29) even as God undergirds and witnesses to their preaching through "signs and wonders" (4:30). This first arrest and release was the beginning of an ever-sharpening confrontation with the Jewish leaders. A second summary statement on the community's life (4:32-35; cf. 2:42-47) is followed by a positive example toward possessions (4:36) and by a threat to the integrity of the community (5:1-11) arising from within. A third summary statement highlights apostolic miracles and the community's growth (5:12-16). A second confrontation between all the apostles and the Jewish leaders ends on the one hand with Gamaliel's advice (5:33-39) and on the other with the beating of the apostles and their continued defiance of the Sanhedrin's authority (5:40-42). A new internal danger threatened the unity of the community. It again dealt with material things, namely, the neglect of the widows of the Hellenists in the daily distribution (6:1-6). To avoid a breakdown of the unity, "the Twelve" summoned all disciples and divided the responsibilities in order to meet the threat of discord. Further growth resulted from dealing imaginatively with this internal crisis (6:7). However, Stephen also did "signs and wonders" (6:8) just like the apostles, and aggressively preached the Word which led to his arrest, his speech, and his martyrdom (6:8—7:60). A general persecution against the church in Jerusalem followed Stephen's martyrdom, a persecution which "scattered" the fellowship of the community (8:1, 4) and resulted surprisingly in further growth among the Samaritans (8:4-25). But new internal dangers also became apparent. Would there be one church or would there be a Samaritan church separate from and unequal to the Jerusalem church? Moreover, is the power to bestow the Holy Spirit for sale (8:18-19)? Luke had clearly shown that our use of material possessions is related to and determined by the gift of the Holy Spirit. Just so, why should we not use material possessions to acquire the gift of the Holy Spirit? In the final section the worst opponent of the church, Saul, is turned into a servant-witness of Jesus (9:1-30) and thus, at the end of Part 1, "the church throughout all Judea and Galilee and Samaria had peace" and experienced further growth (9:31), just as it was at its beginning at Pentecost (2:47-48). Two stories about Peter connect Part 1 with Part 2 and bring him from Jerusalem to the vicinity of Caesarea (9:32-43), thus setting the stage for the story of the Pentecost of the Gentiles (10:1—11:18).

◼ Witness in Jerusalem (2:1—5:42)

Pentecost (2:1-47)

The Pentecost story introduces the first part of Acts. It initiates the apostolic witness and mission in Jerusalem, Judea, and Samaria (2:1—9:43). Simultaneously, it summarizes the content of Luke's second volume. Just as the Third Article of the Apostles' Creed follows the Second, so the book of Acts which narrates the story of the Holy Spirit, creating, filling, and sustaining the church and directing it on its way from Jerusalem to Rome follows Luke's Gospel which tells the story of Jesus Christ. Moreover, just as Jesus' inaugural sermon at Nazareth (Luke 4:16-30) signaled the beginning of his public ministry and summarized the content of Luke's Gospel, so Peter's speech inaugurated the church's witness to Israel and summarizes the message of Acts.

Luke told the Pentecost story in three parts: (1) The miracle of Pentecost (2:1-13) caused consternation and ridicule (vv. 12-13) which gave an opportunity for (2) Peter's keynote address, which interpreted the dazzling display of Pentecost and witnessed to the mighty acts of God (2:14-40); (3) a summary statement announces the result of Pentecost and presents a sketch of the life of the messianically restored, Spirit-filled church, that is, the true Israel (2:41-47). The structure of Luke's story shows that its focus lies in Peter's address. Through the outpouring of the Holy Spirit the Lukan apostles and disciples became what they had not yet been, **witnesses** of Jesus and of his resurrection (cf. 1:8, 21-22). The time of waiting and praying in seclusion had come to an end (cf. 1:13-14) as the day of fulfillment arrived, in agreement with Jesus' promise (Luke 24:49; Acts 1:4-8). A new phase in the story of God and his people was being inaugurated. But the new phase does not break the story's continuity, because the pattern of promise and fulfillment, the presence of apostles and disciples who had accompanied Jesus from Galilee to Jerusalem, and above all the gift of the Holy Spirit guarantee the continuity of the story.

The Miracle of Pentecost (2:1-13)

An introduction (v. 1) is followed by miraculous external events which are audible (v. 2) and visual (v. 3) and which have an internal

71

effect on the disciples in that **they were all filled with the Holy Spirit** (v. 4a). In turn, this experience manifested itself in miraculous speech (v. 4b). The **sound** and the **tongues** from heaven brought about the sound of proclamation and praise **in other tongues** (4b). The center of this *a-b-a* structure lies in the statement **they were all filled with the Holy Spirit** (v. 4a). With this picture Luke emphatically underscored the externality of the Holy Spirit (vv. 1-4). The Holy Spirit is not an innate divine quality which merely needs to be awakened, but it is God's power that enters believers from outside. The storm and the fire (vv. 2-3) indicate the origin from whence the Spirit comes; the distribution and resting of the fire show to whom the Spirit comes. The primary effect was that all disciples were **filled with the Holy Spirit.** A secondary external effect consisted in their speech in **other tongues.**

The focus shifts in v. 5 from the disciples to the public. As in miracle stories, so here, a crowd testifies to the reality of this startling occurrence. Simple Galileans proclaim God's mighty acts in various languages (vv. 5-11). Here, as well as in subsequent missionary speeches, the reaction of the crowd is divided (vv. 12-13). Astonishment and inquiry on one hand, rejection and ridicule on the other, mark the division within Israel. Jesus' ministry resulted in "the fall and rising of many in Israel" and he became "a sign that is spoken against" (Luke 2:34). Likewise, the Spirit-filled church caused division within Israel from the second to the very last chapter of Acts (cf. 28:22-24).

The interpreter should be aware that Luke did not narrate a historically realistic account. For instance, where in Jerusalem could such a mass of people have gathered? Three thousand of them were converted (v. 41)! **The house where they were sitting** (v. 2) refers neither to the court of the Gentiles, nor to the temple building proper (where one did not sit), but to the "upper room" (1:13). How was it possible that neither the Romans nor the Jewish authorities intervened in the face of such a challenge? How could Peter address such a multitude without a loudspeaker system? How could the diaspora Jews know that the speakers were Galileans? Is it realistic to suppose that these Jews from the diaspora would, in direct discourse, enumerate the list of nations (vv. 8-11)? In short, the interpreter should take Luke's hints seriously and refrain from treating this narrative as if it were a newsreel. Rather, we should inquire into possible traditions used by Luke and the theological message he intended.

It would seem that a pre-Lukan tradition consisting of vv. 2, 3, 4b (minus "other"), 6a, and perhaps 12 told of the first manifestation of glossolalia, of uttering unintelligible syllables in a state of ecstasy (cf. 1 Corinthians 14). Since Hellenistic Christians valued this phenomenon highly, it would seem probable that the pre-Lukan tradition arose in Antioch, Syria. Luke, however, reinterpreted this tradition by making it a unique miracle involving foreign languages. He added "other" before tongues in v. 4b and identified them as native languages of different nations and regions (*dialektos*, vv. 6 and 8). He also used a second tradition consisting of a list of nations and regions in order to underline the magnitude of the foreign-language miracle. Finally, he dated the Spirit's coming on Pentecost and located the event in Jerusalem. He could locate it there because he knew that the preeminent church of "the Way" (24:14) had experienced the Spirit's presence and proclaimed Christ boldly (cf. 4:29-31). Jerusalem had been the goal of Jesus' itinerant ministry (cf. Luke 9:51; 13:33), the place of his passion, resurrection, and ascension. Contrary to Matthew, Mark, and John 21, our evangelist has no room for Galilean resurrection appearances, because the resurrected Christ commanded his disciples to remain in Jerusalem and "not to depart" until Pentecost (Luke 24:49; Acts 1:4). Therefore, the last great eschatological event prior to the parousia also had to take place in Jerusalem, in accordance with Jesus' promise (Acts 1:4-8). Also, Jerusalem guarantees the historical continuity of salvation history and the priority of Israel and it indicates the place where the authentic Christian tradition had its origin.

Why did Luke choose the Jewish festival of Pentecost as the date for the Spirit's coming? The answer probably lies in Luke's Christology. For him it was the Messiah and Lord, exalted to the right hand of God, who bestowed the Spirit on the church (v. 33). Therefore, the Spirit could come only after the ascension-exaltation which he located 40 days after Easter. Hence Luke chose the next Jewish festival after the ascension, namely, Pentecost. Its very name, "the 50th day" (after the Passover) related it directly to Easter and to the resurrection of him who is the mediator of the Holy Spirit (vv. 32-33). At any rate, the language of v. 1 is thoroughly Lukan. The date of Pentecost as the time of the first coming of the Spirit is unknown not only in the New Testament, apart from v. 1, but also in second-century Christian literature. According to John's Gospel, the gift of the Spirit was imparted on Easter evening and not 50 days later (John 20:19-23).

1—Luke used biblical language to introduce the narrative and mark the beginning of a new phase in the story of God with his people. The Greek text is similar to the language of Luke 9:51. The fulfillment of the promise of Jesus is about to take place (cf. 1:4-8). The members of the community **were all together in one place,** not just the apostles (cf. 1:14, 15). In the next verse we hear that it was a **house** in which they had gathered. The reader would think of the upper room (cf. 1:13) rather than of the temple or of the court of the Gentiles, in which people would not be **sitting.** Luke does not bother to tell us how all 120 members of the community could find space in that **house** (cf. 1:15). **Pentecost,** the 50th day after Passover, was also known as the Feast of Weeks because it was celebrated seven weeks after the beginning of the wheat harvest (Exod. 23:16; 34:22; Lev. 23:15-21; Deut. 16:9-10). When the firstfruits of the wheat harvest could no longer be offered to God in Jerusalem after the destruction of the temple in A.D. 70, Pentecost became the festival which commemorated the giving of the Torah and the making of the covenant at Mount Sinai. This new content of Pentecost resulted from the tradition that about 50 days after the Passover Moses received the Torah from God on Mount Sinai (cf. Exod. 19:1). Thus Luke chose Pentecost as the date of the Spirit's coming upon the church. The experience of the Holy Spirit preceded Luke's theological interpretation of the Spirit. His interpretation, given in Peter's speech, did not relate the Holy Spirit to the Sinai covenant and its renewal nor to the Torah of Moses, be it in terms of abrogation, supplementation, or vindication of the Torah by the Spirit. Peter's speech does not refer to the Torah.

Only Luke and John narrate and thereby interpret the gift of the Spirit and, while they disagree concerning the date, they are in basic agreement with each other and with Paul's declaration, "If a person does not possess the Spirit of Christ, he or she is not a Christian" (Rom. 8:9, author's trans.).

2-3—A miraculous event occurs **suddenly. A sound . . . like the rush of a mighty wind** came **from heaven.** In Greek and Hebrew the same word can mean both "Spirit" and "wind" (cf. John 3:8).

Here it is not the Spirit which **filled all the house,** but the sound. Luke's use of analogy shows that we are not dealing with natural phenomena but with the inbreaking of the powers of heaven. The storm symbolizes the audible presence of the Spirit of God. In addition visual **tongues as of fire** appeared, **distributed and resting on each one of them,** not just on the Twelve. The sound like a storm and the tongues like fire signify from where the Spirit comes, from heaven. The distribution of the tongues and their resting signify to whom the Spirit comes, to **each** believer. Storm and fire are motifs found in Old Testament theophany stories (cf. 1 Kings 19:11). Yahweh "descended" upon Mount Sinai "in fire" (Exod. 19:18) and Isaiah proclaimed, "Behold the Lord shall come like fire . . . in the flame of fire. . . . I come to gather all nations and tongues" (Isa. 66:15,18, LXX). From Philo we hear that on Mount Sinai there were "claps of thunder . . ., flashes of lightning, the rush of a heaven-sent fire. . . . From the midst of the fire . . . there sounded forth . . . a voice, for the flame became articulate speech in the language familiar to the audience" (*The Decalog,* 32–35). Luke used traditional theophany motifs, but he did not connect Pentecost with the Sinai covenant. Through the theophany motifs he made the uniqueness of the Spirit's coming upon the church visible and audible. This first outpouring of the Spirit on Pentecost is unrepeatable, like the virginal conception, and it came about not as a consequence of preaching (as in 10:44 and 19:6), but directly and without mediation. Therefore it was accompanied by miraculous occurrences from heaven, in agreement with the Baptist's promise that the Messiah "shall baptize you with the Holy Spirit [the wind from heaven] and with fire" (Luke 3:16).

4—The effect of the miraculous occurrence was an internal one in that the disciples were **all filled with the Holy Spirit.** No one was excluded; they **all** received the same gift. This gift manifested itself externally in that all **began to speak in other tongues.** Note the play on words: **tongues as of fire** are related to **other tongues.** Later on these **other tongues** are identified as foreign languages (vv. 6 and 8; Greek, *dialektos*). This first outpouring of the Spirit upon the church is unique not only because of the theophany motifs which accompanied it but also because of the language miracle in which it manifested itself. The language miracle of Pentecost does not mean the end of the confusion of languages, a sort of Babel in reverse

(Gen. 11:1-9). The idea that one language, namely, Hebrew, will be established at the end of time just as it was in the beginning is clearly absent in this story as well as in Peter's subsequent speech. On the contrary, Luke assumed that the disciples spoke in a multitude of languages. Nor should we think of a miracle of audition (cf. v. 8) rather than of speaking in foreign intelligible languages. A miracle of audition would mean that the audience merely thought they heard the disciples speak in their native languages, when in fact the disciples did not. Such a miracle of audition would presuppose that also the audience had already received the Holy Spirit directly and without mediation. This, however, is clearly not the case in Luke's story, for in vv. 38-39 the audience is exhorted to repent and be baptized in order to receive the gift of the Holy Spirit. Luke was well aware that proclamation creates faith, and the miracle of preaching in different languages constituted the first effect of the Spirit's coming upon the church at Pentecost. Nor may we identify the speaking **in other tongues** with the glossolalia about which Paul wrote in 1 Corinthians 12–14. There he referred to incomprehensible utterances which require a translator before they can be understood. At Pentecost, however, the disciples speak in the native vernacular of diverse peoples. Nor are merely two or three languages involved, but rather a dozen or so, as the list of nations shows. The fact that we cannot imagine such a language miracle may not become the hermeneutical key with which we seek to understand this story. Miracles like the virginal conception or the Pentecost miracle are beyond our comprehension, from Luke's point of view.

If some modern Christians claim that their glossolalia is a repetition of the Pentecost experience, they ignore the theophanic phenomena and the foreign-language miracle of Luke's story. And should they claim that their glossolalia is actually speech in foreign languages like the native languages of the Parthians, Medes, or Elamites, they still would not repeat the miracle of Pentecost, because when they perform their glossolalia no Jews speaking ancient Parthian are present. Thus even if their claim were correct it would amount to a total waste of God's power.

For Luke, the language miracle of Pentecost is unrepeatable. Yet that which is central in his Pentecost story, namely, that the believers **were all filled with the Holy Spirit** is not limited to Pentecost but constitutes the mark of the church until the parousia. Instead of being **filled with,** Luke can refer to being "baptized with" the Holy Spirit (1:5; 11:16), to be "full of" the Spirit (6:3), or say that God "pours out" the Spirit (2:17, 33), "gives" it (5:32; 8:18), or that believers "receive" the Spirit (2:38; 10:47) which "falls on" them (8:16; 10:44) or "comes" upon them (1:8; 19:6). All these phrases indicate that the Holy Spirit is the gift and the empowerment granted by God to his believing people. This gift cannot be produced by them through "spiritual" exercises. Later on in his narrative Luke will tell us of the coming of the Holy Spirit upon Samaritans and Gentiles and the Ephesian disciples, but then the theophanic motifs of vv. 2-3 will be absent and the speaking "in tongues" (10:46; 19:6) is not identified as speaking in foreign languages (Greek, *dialektos,* vv. 6, 8, or **other** tongues, v. 4, or **our own tongues,** v. 11). On those two occasions (10:46; 19:6) Luke presented the type of ecstatic praise, the glossolalia, to which Paul referred in 1 Corinthians 14. (For Paul's own assessment of this phenomenon see 1 Cor. 14:19, 39.)

5-11—The scene changes as the public appears and testifies to the miracle of Pentecost. One should not ask how the crowd knew that the disciples were Galileans. Luke's readers know it (cf. 1:11). Nor should one ask whether each member of the audience heard all the disciples speak in his native language. If so, how could he know that others in the crowd heard different languages? Luke did not say that each heard many languages, among them his own native tongue. He did not reflect on these aspects of his narrative. Only one point was important to him. God's mighty acts must be praised and proclaimed in understandable languages, and such proclamation was the first manifestation of the Spirit-filled community.

The audience which appears quite suddenly and unexpectedly consisted of **Jews and proselytes.** The latter were Gentiles who had converted to Judaism. The good news of God's fulfilled promise is directed to Jews first, not to humanity as such (cf. 2:39; 3:26; 13:32-33). Yet the list of nations anticipates the worldwide scope of the gospel to which Peter, at the end of his speech, referred when he spoke of "all that are far off" (v. 39). Moreover, the presence of these Jews **from every nation under heaven** symbolized the beginning of the gathering of the scattered tribes of Israel (cf. Isa. 66:18) and thus of the restoration of the kingdom to Israel before the parousia (1:6). Above all, the list of nations underlines the scope of the language miracle of Pentecost.

There is general agreement that Luke incorporated a traditional list of nations and regions. Its traditional nature becomes apparent when we recognize that it omits many regions of the Pauline mission to which Acts refers (such as Syria, Galatia, Macedonia, and Achaia) and it mentions names which do not reappear in Acts (such as Parthians, Medes, Elamites, Mesopotamia, Cappadocia, Pontus, Egypt, and Libya). The presence of **Judea** (v. 9) has frequently been regarded as a textual corruption for Lydia, India, or some other name. Interpreters asked why the people residing in **Jerusalem** and hence in **Judea** should be amazed to hear the disciples speak in their own tongue. But Luke may have thought that the disciples, being Galileans (1:11; Luke 22:59), spoke with a peculiar accent. At any rate, the textual support for **Judea** is total. The pre-Lukan form of the list can no longer be determined with certainty. Luke probably added **visitors from Rome,** in order to indicate how Christianity reached Rome prior to Paul's arrival. Some **visitors** were converted and returned home and therefore could greet Paul at the Forum of Appius and Three Taverns (28:15). The other Jews named by regions or nations were not visitors but returnees who had permanently settled in Jerusalem and **were dwelling** there (v. 5). Luke probably also added **Jews and proselytes, Cretans and Arabians,** which summarize the make-up of the audience, the last pair probably referring to inhabitants of islands and of the mainland. The list apparently originated in Judaism (cf. Billerbeck, 2:606-614) and enumerated the major regions and nations in which Jews lived. If we omit **Rome** we have 12 (or 2 x 6) names which are listed in the form of two S curves. If the list originated in the Jewish community of Antioch, Syria, it would be understandable why Syria is omitted and why Judea is in it. From the perspective of Syria the nations and regions where Jewish communities existed may have been enumerated in the pre-Lukan list. Luke bracketed the list with references to speaking in diverse foreign languages (vv. 8 and 11) and thus he used the list to bring out the magnitude of the language miracle and to hint at the eschatological gathering of Israel.

12-13—The reaction of the audience was twofold. **All were amazed and perplexed,** and asked, **What does this mean? Others,** however, already knew the answer and said that the disciples were drunk, **filled with new wine.** Both reactions are Luke's literary devices, paving the way for Peter's speech. Such a speech became necessary because Luke had merely summarized the language miracle by stating that the disciples had proclaimed **the mighty works of God** (v. 11). He could hardly relay what each of the 20 or 120 disciples had said, especially since they had spoken simultaneously. Therefore, the content of their proclamation and praise of God's mighty acts must now be unfolded. This Peter did in his Pentecost speech. His audience is not humanity as such, nor mere individuals but Israel as a whole, representatively gathered **from every nation under heaven.**

Peter's Pentecost Witness (2:14-41)

An introduction (vv. 14-16) connects the speech with the situation. Peter quickly refuted the scoffers who supposed that the Spirit-filled disciples were filled with wine and therefore drunk by pointing out that 9 o'clock in the morning is not the time for drunkenness. His following speech is a prophetic interpretation and proclamation. Just as Jesus after his baptism inaugurated and summarized his own ministry (Luke 4:16-21) so Peter after his baptism with the Spirit inaugurated the church's mission by giving the keynote address of Acts. Part one, (vv. 17-21) interprets the miracle of Pentecost as the fulfillment of God's promise through Joel. Its concluding sentence, **whoever calls on the name of the Lord shall be saved** (v. 21), forms the theme of the subsequent parts of the speech. Part two (vv. 22-36 demonstrates and proclaims that Jesus is Messiah and Lord, and part three (vv. 37-40) brings the climactic conclusion in the invitation to repent, be baptized, and be saved. This structure reveals that Peter's speech about the Holy Spirit turns into a speech about God and Jesus, the Messiah and Lord who saves. In Lukan thought no one since Pentecost can speak properly about the Holy Spirit without speaking about Jesus and God's action through him and on him. But the reverse is equally true. Speech about God and Jesus must include the Holy Spirit, who on Pentecost proceeded from the Father through the Son (v. 33) to the church and its members.

17-21 (Part one)—God is the speaker in the quotation from Joel that interprets what **this** (v. 16), namely, the language miracle, is all about. Implicit in this hermeneutical use of the Old Testament is the notion of fulfillment, but its primary function is the interpretation of the Pentecost event. Luke changed the LXX text from "after these things" to **in the last days,** because Pentecost is, for him, the last great eschatological event before the parousia of Christ. The coming of the Spirit points forward to **the great and manifest day** of the End (v. 20). He also added in v. 18 the words **and they shall prophesy,** in order to indicate that the primary effect of the Spirit is prophecy, preaching which had been expressed by the disciples in a unique form (vv. 4-11). The wish in Num. 11:29 has found an initial fulfillment: "Would that all of God's people were prophets, that the Lord would put his Spirit upon them." Luke also added the pronoun **my** to maidservants and manservants (v. 18), because the disciples were not ordinary household slaves as in Joel, but servants of God equipped with his Spirit for ministry. Contrary to the RSV (and the Hebrew text) we should not translate **I will pour out my Spirit** (vv. 17 and 18b), but rather "I will pour out **from** my Spirit." The preposition indicates the difference between the Spirit endowment of Jesus and of his followers. It should also be noted that Luke did *not* hold the belief that Israel's life since the time of Malachi had been an arid desert, void of the Spirit. On the contrary, Zechariah, Elizabeth, John the Baptist, Simeon, and Anna were prophets, filled with the Holy Spirit (cf. Luke 1:41,67,76; 2:25,36). They link the Old Testament with the time of Jesus.

Jerusalem (v. 14) in Luke-Acts delineates the historical continuity between Israel and the church and attests to God's acts in *history.* The presence of the Spirit in the church expresses the theological continuity and attests to *God's* acts in history. The Spirit who had spoken through individual Old Testament prophets, including those mentioned in Luke 1–2, and who had descended upon Jesus "in bodily form" (Luke 3:22) has now been granted to the church and to each member (cf. **all** and **each one,** vv. 1-4) in consequence of Jesus' ministry (v. 33) and in fulfillment of God's promise through Joel, John the Baptist, and Jesus (cf. Luke 3:16; Acts 1:4-5). The recipients of the Spirit of God are **flesh** like all human beings. **All flesh** (v. 17) does not mean everybody in the world (cf. Isa. 44:3) but implies a contrast between many people and only a few, or between many and only one. No longer will Jesus be the sole bearer of the Spirit as he was during the time of his ministry nor will this gift be received by only a few chosen prophets and apostles. Rather, Pentecost marks the democratic outpouring of the Spirit on **all** of God's true people. All believers and only believers receive the Holy

Spirit. Joel borrowed the image of *pouring out* from his announcement that abundant rain will pour down upon the parched ground, revitalizing the land. The Pentecostal pouring out from the inexhaustible Spirit of God **upon all flesh** means that "all flesh shall see the salvation of God" (Luke 3:6).

The citation of Joel also referred to **visions** and **dreams** (v. 17) and Luke will bring examples in subsequent sections of his narrative (cf. 9:10; 10:3, 11, 17; 12:7; 16:9; 18:9; 19:20-21; 27:22-24). In vv. 19-20 the focus shifts from Pentecost to the End itself, because the Spirit is the eschatological gift and power of the future, challenging every status quo and every form of security and orienting us to **the day of the Lord.** Then it will be revealed with finality who God is and who we are. What had been one event in Joel, the outpouring of the Spirit and the day of the Lord, is distinguished in Lukan theology. Whereas in Joel the believers are saved from the terrors of the day of the Lord by calling upon his name, Luke holds that salvation "from this crooked generation" (v. 40) is possible already now through repentance, Baptism, and the gifts of forgiveness and of the Spirit. The future parousia on **the day of the Lord** will bring the final "redemption" of all believers (Luke 21:28). The **wonders in the heaven above** and **signs on the earth beneath** (vv. 19-20) are those extraordinary occurrences which, according to Luke 21, immediately precede the End (cf. Luke 21:10-12, 25-26). Therefore, vv. 19-20 should not be related to the miracles of Jesus or of the apostles nor to the storm and fire of Pentecost. Above all, we should note that Luke quotes these verses in order to get to the decisive promise and condition in v. 21. **Whoever calls on the name of the Lord shall be saved** when the End—which no one can escape—appears. Luke ended the citation from Joel at this point because the following sentence in Joel 2:32 limits salvation to Mount Zion and Jerusalem and would thus negate the universal scope of salvation which is narrated in the second part of Acts (Acts 10–28; cf. 28:28; Luke 3:6). Salvation is possible only for those who **now call upon the name of the Lord** (v. 21). The second part of Peter's address (vv. 22-36) will make clear who the Lord is upon whom we should call and the third part (vv. 37-40) will show that calling upon his name involves Baptism in the name of Jesus Christ which results in forgiveness of sins and the gift of the Holy Spirit received in the present. The future salvation becomes present already now. Moreover, to call upon the name of the Lord is possible only for those "whom the Lord our God calls" (v. 39; quoting from Joel 2:32 = LXX Joel 3:5). This final sentence from the Joel citation (v. 21), which sets forth a condition and a promise, also functions as the theme for the following parts of Peter's speech.

We may also note that the Christological interpretation of v. 21 is possible only on the basis of the Greek Bible, the LXX. In the Hebrew text of Joel the Lord who should be called upon and who saves is God himself. Luke, however, never equated Jesus with God. For him Jesus is the Lord whom God raised from the dead. Since the LXX translated *Yahweh* with *kyrios,* "Lord," the citation from Joel in v. 21 could refer to the Lord Jesus, especially since calling upon the name of the Lord Jesus Christ had already become theological terminology long before Luke wrote (cf. 1 Cor. 1:2; Rom. 10:12-13). At any rate, the equation of Lord with Jesus rather than with God means that the original language of the speech was Greek rather than Aramaic or Hebrew. One can hardly suppose that the historical Peter cited the Greek Bible in Jerusalem to a Jewish audience. Therefore, we must conclude that the Christological interpretation of v. 21 is an indication that the speech is a Lukan construction rather than a summary of an actual speech given by Peter. Other citations in this speech will reinforce this conclusion.

22-36 (Part two)—The Lord upon whom we should call and who saves is now identified, for there are "many 'gods' and many 'lords' " (1 Cor. 8:5), and by *Spirit* different people mean different things (cf. 1 John 4:1-3). Part two is structured rather carefully and has its focus in vv. 32 and 33, which proclaim that Jesus the resurrected and exalted Messiah shall reign forever at God's right hand (cf. Luke 1:33) thus fulfilling God's unconditional promise to David. But the resurrection-exaltation of Jesus also means that henceforth God shall reign through Jesus and therefore Jesus is the mediator of the Holy Spirit whose origin lies in the Father (vv. 32-33). The audience itself had seen and heard the outpouring of the Spirit in accordance with the promise (v. 33 contains a reference to Joel, cf. v. 17), just as they had seen the mighty works which God had done through the earthly Jesus **in your midst** (v. 22). But they had killed him (vv. 23 and 36). Small wonder that they **were cut to the heart** and asked, **"What shall we do?"** (v. 37). With this question begins the final part of Peter's speech. The structure of part two is as follows:

(A) The kerygma (vv. 22-24)
   (B) Proof from Scripture (vv. 25-28)
      (C) Interpretation of the Scripture (vv. 29-31)
         (D) The resurrection of Jesus and
            the witnesses (v. 32)
         (D') The exaltation of Jesus, the
            mediation of the Holy Spirit
            and the witnesses (v. 33)
      (C') Interpretation of the Scripture (v. 34a)
   (B') Proof from Scripture (vv. 34b-35)
(A') The kerygma (v. 36)

This outline shows that the kerygma forms an inclusio around this second part. Moreover, the inclusio is chiastically structured: v. 23 You killed him, but God raised him; v. 36 God made him Lord and Christ whom you crucified.

22-24 (The kerygma)—The main clause of the kerygma in the Greek of these verses can be translated, "You killed Jesus of Nazareth." In two participial clauses this action of the people of Jerusalem is contrasted with God's action on him. First, God attested the earthly Jesus with **mighty works** and **wonders and signs** (narrated in Luke's first volume) and, second, God **delivered** him **up according to** his **definite plan and foreknowledge.** His death was in accordance with the will of God. At once the main clause (you killed him) is followed by the Greek relative pronoun, which is typical in kerygmatic statements and which introduces the confession, **God raised him.** The God of the Old Testament, the God of the fathers (3:13; 5:30; 22:14), the God of the exodus and of the promises receives a new identification in the New Testament. God is the One who raised Jesus from the dead (3:15; 4:10; 5:30; 10:40; 13:30 Rom. 4:24; 8:11; 10:9; Gal. 1:1; 1 Peter 1:21). Luke would agree with Paul that if God had not raised Jesus then the Christian faith and the kerygma are false (1 Cor. 15:14).

Some details: With **men of Israel,** not just the Judeans and the Jerusalemites (v. 14), but the whole people of God is addressed. The problem with the people of God is **Jesus of Nazareth.** Luke expanded the basic kerygma (**you killed** him, **but God raised him**) by elaborating that Jesus was a man **attested to you by God** with mighty works **which God did through him in your midst** (cf. v. 11).

Peter's audience was witness to Jesus' miracles. Yet, in spite of God's authentication of Jesus **you killed** him by letting pagans from Rome, that is **lawless men** nail him to the cross (cf. 4:27; Luke 23:1-33). Even though Jesus' crucifixion seems to contradict his legitimation by God, his death occurred according to God's sovereign **plan.** Simultaneously, his death does not erase the guilt of the participants in this deed. Human guilt and divine predestination may not be balanced off against each other. That God works out all things together according to his plan is disclosed only in the encounter with God which simultaneously reveals our guilt. For Luke the death of Jesus is not a saving event in and of itself, as it is in 1 Cor. 15:3 or Rom. 3:24-25 (the exceptions are Luke 22:20 and Acts 20:28 which are pre-Lukan traditional formulations). Apart from these Luke followed another tradition which contrasted the action of the people (you killed Jesus) with the action of God (God raised him) and he expanded this contrast pattern by introducing the notion of the "divine must," or the **definite plan and foreknowledge** of God which is revealed in the Scriptures (Luke 24:25-27, 46-47). Already his Markan source had used the "divine must" in its passion predictions (cf. Mark 8:31; Luke 9:22). However, the "divine must" of God's plan does not make Jesus a pawn of a preprogrammed fate. For Luke the "divine must" does not operate with robot-like necessity but is to be obeyed and can be disobeyed (for the latter see Luke 7:30, and for Jesus' obedience toward his passion see Luke 22:37). If the servant of God does not retaliate against his opponents, his passion becomes inevitable even though Jesus could have avoided it by not setting "his face" toward Jerusalem (Luke 9:51). From this perspective the passion of Jesus continues the fate of the rejected and persecuted prophets (cf. Luke 13:33-34; Acts 7:51-52). While his passion demonstrates his obedience and faithfulness toward God, his resurrection demonstrates God's faithfulness toward him and his vindication in the face of his rejection by the **men of Israel.** God is the theological subject of this kerygma. He authenticated, **attested** Jesus, he worked miracles **through him,** he **delivered** him **up,** he **raised him up** and he **loosed the pangs of death.** The strange expression (birth-) **pangs of death** arose when the LXX mistranslated a Hebrew word which means ropes or cords (cf. Ps. 18:4-5 = LXX Ps. 17:5-6).

25-28 (Proof from Scripture)—Psalm 16:8-11 is cited to demonstrate that the resurrection is according to God's plan as set forth in the Scriptures. Originally this psalm was a prayer in which a person expressed his confidence that he will be rescued from a premature death, that he will not see the pit, the grave, but continue his earthly life in the presence of God. The LXX, which is quoted here, translated the Hebrew words "in security" with **in hope** and the Hebrew "pit" or grave with **corruption,** and it changed the singular "way" into the plural **ways.** Small as these changes are, a Greek reader of this psalm could hold that in death his **soul** would not **see** or be subject to **corruption** but live in God's presence and therefore he can now live **in hope** of eternal life after death.

How did Luke understand this psalm? First, these are words of **David . . . concerning** the Messiah; more exactly, they are David's words in which the Messiah himself is speaking. **I saw the Lord always** refers to the Messiah speaking in the words of David. This is not at once obvious but will become so in the following argumentation (vv. 29-31). Second, throughout his life and his passion, the Messiah had the **Lord always before** him, depending utterly on his God who was at his **right hand** guiding him. His **heart was glad** and his **tongue rejoiced** in God's presence. There is no cry of dereliction in the Lukan passion narrative; instead, the dying Jesus surrenders his life into the hands of his heavenly Father (Luke 23:46). His **flesh** therefore will live **in hope** in spite of death. Third, the reason for such hope lies in his confidence that God **will not abandon** his Messiah in death. The precise meaning of the text is not clear at this point. Does **not abandon . . . to Hades** mean that the dead Messiah's **soul** did not enter **Hades** but Paradise (cf. Luke 23:43; 16:22)? Or, did his **soul** enter **Hades** but was not abandoned there? Or did Luke merely mean to convey that Jesus really died and was buried but was not allowed to remain in death? In that case he understood **Hades** to be a metaphor for death. At any rate, the idea of a descent into Hades (cf. the Apostles' Creed) which the second alternative might suggest is absent in Luke. What was most important to him in this citation was that God did not let **his Holy One see corruption.** The decomposition of his body, his **flesh,** in the grave did not take place. Finally, God had made known **the ways of life** to the Messiah who had taught them to his disciples and practiced them himself, e.g., "Whoever would save his life will lose it but whoever loses his life . . . will save it" (Luke 9:24). The

Messiah had traveled the **ways of life** from Galilee to Jerusalem content to lose himself entirely in the service of the reign of God and the people of God.

29-31 (Interpretation of the Scripture)—A new address, **brothers,** not only signifies the end of the citation (there are no quotation marks in Greek) but also expresses Peter's solidarity with his audience (cf. 3:17; 13:26; 22:1; 28:17). So long as the kerygma is not explicitly rejected by different groups of Jews in Acts they are addressed as **brothers,** because the disciples as well as the Jewish audience are "sons of the family of Abraham" (13:26). Gentiles therefore are never addressed in Acts as brothers. What follows is an exposition of Psalm 16 along two lines. The negative evidence is that the psalm cannot refer to David himself. The positive evidence is that David spoke of the Messiah's resurrection in that psalm. **David,** who was **patriarch, prophet,** and king (vv. 29-30; 13:22), **died and was buried, and his tomb is with us to this day.** His body rotted in the grave, his flesh did see corruption and therefore the citation from Psalm 16 cannot possibly refer to David himself. The first person singular **I saw** (v. 25) cannot be David speaking concerning himself. Then follows the positive argumentation (vv. 30-31) which answers the question, About whom does this psalm speak? Another text from the Psalms sheds light on this question. God made an unconditional promise to David through Nathan (Ps. 132:11; 2 Sam. 7:12-13). **God had sworn with an oath** to David **that he would set one of** David's **descendants upon his throne.** Back of Ps. 132:11 lies 2 Sam. 7:13, 16 with its promise that "the throne" of the descendant of David will be "established forever." **His throne** in Peter's argumentation refers to God's and the Messiah's **throne** at the right hand of God which therefore is established "forever." Remembering God's promise and **being a prophet,** David **foresaw and spoke of the resurrection of the Christ** in Psalm 16. **The Christ** is here a title meaning "the Messiah." Psalm 16 makes it clear that the Messiah is the one who **was not abandoned to Hades nor did his flesh see corruption.** The Messiah is whoever God raised from the dead. In his interpretation of the psalm Luke made some slight changes (v. 31). Instead of the future tense ("thou wilt not abandon," v. 27) he now used the past tense ("was not abandoned") because the Messiah's resurrection lies in the past for Luke's readers as well as for Peter's audience. Instead of "your Holy One" (v. 27b) we now read **his flesh** did not see corruption (v. 31) because the resurrection of the Messiah involved not just his soul or his spirit but **his flesh** and bones (Luke 24:39).

32 (The resurrection of Jesus)—The interpretation of the psalm had demonstrated that David did not refer the words of the psalm to himself, but spoke of the Messiah who is one of David's descendants whom God raised from the dead and placed "on his throne." Now it must be shown that the Messiah is Jesus and none other. From scriptural argumentation the speech now moves to proclamation. **This Jesus God raised up, and of that we all are witnesses.** The Messiah, the promised descendant of David, is Jesus because God raised Jesus from the dead. His flesh did not see corruption. The apostles and the disciples around them **are witnesses** who testify that Jesus did not end in death but has been raised by God to new life. Just so the resurrection is not the resuscitation of a corpse returning to its former life, but the transformation into a new mode of existence (cf. Luke 24:31). As witnesses the disciples testify to the identity of the earthly Jesus with the Resurrected One and thereby guarantee the continuity between the time of Jesus and the time of the church.

33 (The exaltation of Jesus)—Nathan's promise to David had also spoken of the Messiah's **throne** (v. 30) and thus of the Messiah's reign and lordship. Peter's address now makes it clear that the throne of the resurrected Son of David is **at the right hand of God** to which he, the Messiah, is exalted. During his earthly life and in his death God had been **at the right hand** of Jesus (v. 25), but through the ascension-exaltation Jesus has become God's **right hand** man and, as such, reigns as Messiah, Son, and Lord. It is from **the Father** that the exalted One **received** the promised **Holy Spirit,** which implies that the Son of David is the Son of God (cf. 2 Sam. 7:14; Luke 20:41-44; 1:32, 35). His reign manifested itself in that **he has poured out** the Spirit which **you,** namely, Peter's audience, did **see and hear.** The Pentecost events were witnessed by the audience and are interpreted to the audience as the fulfillment of the **promise** of the gift **of the Holy Spirit.** In agreement with John's Gospel the speech of Peter holds that the Holy Spirit is granted only after Christ's exaltation (cf. John 7:39; 14:26; 15:26; Eph. 4:7-11), and that the Spirit proceeds from the Father through the Son. The speech also refers to the Joel citation in the words **poured out** (cf. vv. 17

87

and 18). Since the citation contained the title "Lord" in its concluding statement (v. 21) therefore the speech will now demonstrate that Jesus, Son of David, Messiah, and Son of God, is also the exalted *kyrios*, the Lord who saves.

34a (Interpretation of Scripture)—A demonstration of his exaltation as Lord is possible only on the basis of the Scripture. But before citing Ps. 110:1 Peter interprets it negatively. **David did not ascend into the heavens,** because he lies buried in a tomb (v. 29). Therefore the psalm to be quoted cannot refer to David any more than Psalm 16 could speak of him.

34b-35 (Proof from Scripture)—Indeed, David **himself says, The Lord said to my Lord, Sit at my right hand.** This psalm clearly distinguished between David, David's Lord, and the Lord God. It is David's **Lord** who after his ascension into heaven (v. 34a) now **sits** as Lord **at** God's **right hand,** mediates the Spirit (v. 33), and saves everyone who calls on his name (v. 21). His Lordship endures **till I make thy enemies a stool for thy feet.** The opponents of the enthroned Lord shall be defeated and their defeat will be made manifest on **the day of the Lord** (v. 20). Installed at the right hand of God, the Lord Jesus and his cause cannot be defeated. There may be persecutions of his followers, as we shall hear, and rejections of his message, but just as Jerusalem could not defeat Jesus by nailing him to a cross, so pagan Rome cannot thwart him by harassing his witnesses. His message will go forward "unhindered" (the last word of Acts!) and thereby manifest his lordship.

The ascension is mentioned by Luke three times. The first time Luke portrayed Jesus as priest blessing his people before his departure (Luke 24:50-53). The second time he used motifs from the Elijah narrative, suggesting that the disciples like Elisha will carry on the Master's work (1:1, 9-11). Finally, in this speech Jesus' ascension is interpreted as his enthronement to his Davidic-messianic Lordship, the reason why **everyone who calls on the name of the Lord shall be saved** (v. 21), and why his opponents shall become **a stool for** his **feet** (cf. 3:23).

36 (The kerygma)—The conclusion of part two of the speech is now drawn. **Let all the house of Israel therefore know assuredly that God has made him both Lord and Christ, this Jesus whom you crucified.** Peter's witness is addressed to **all** of **Israel** which must have "assurance" (Greek, *asphaleia;* Luke 1:4; Acts 2:36, *asphalos*) concerning the identity of its Messiah and Lord. This verse is probably not a pre-Lukan tradition but Luke's own summary which, together with the opening kerygma of vv. 22-24, forms an inclusio around this part of the speech. Luke does not want us to understand that Jesus became Lord and Messiah only at the time of his resurrection. Our author did not reflect upon the time when Jesus was installed but upon the contrast between his Messiahship and Lordship and the deed of the audience. He is the **Lord and Christ** whom **you crucified.** Without his resurrection-exaltation the angelic proclamation of Luke 2:11 would have ended with his death (cf. Luke 24:21a) and Psalms 16; 132:11; and 110:1 would remain unfulfilled. Jesus would not be Messiah and Lord now. His resurrection confirmed his messianic credentials which the earthly Jesus already possessed (cf. Luke 2:11; 19:31). Luke was not the first to speak of Christ's enthronement, nor the first to quote Psalm 110 in support of it (cf. Rom. 8:34). As long as believers expected his imminent return they confessed his present lordship before they reflected on its meaning. They looked forward in anticipation to his parousia and their acclamation "Maranatha," "our Lord, come" (1 Cor. 16:22), expressed their hope for his speedy appearance. But reflection on the meaning of Christ's exaltation had to come sooner or later. Does his sitting "up there" mean that he is doing nothing? He "intercedes for us," wrote Paul (Rom. 8:34). For Luke the enthronement of Christ at the right hand of God means the following: (1) Jesus mediates the Holy Spirit (v. 33). (2) He performs healing miracles through his servant-witnesses (cf. 9:34) who call on his name (3:6); he breaks demonic powers (8:9-24; 13:4-12; 16:16-18) and proclaims the light of salvation through his messengers (26:23). (3) Prayers are addressed to him (7:59-60) and he appears in visions and dreams to direct his church (e.g., 18:9). (4) As "Lord of all" (10:36) he is the appointed judge of the world (17:31), upon which he has a legitimate claim. With his parousia "the times of refreshing" come from the presence of the Lord God and then all of God's promises will be established (3:19-21). (5) He is inseparable from and subordinate to God who had worked miracles through him, was involved even in his death, resurrected and exalted him, and gave him the Spirit for transmission to his church. In all this, **God has made him both Lord and Christ.**

37-40 (Part three: Invitation to salvation)—In this soteriological conclusion the hearers are invited to participate in God's eschatological salvation. The reader of Luke's Gospel knows that Jesus had prayed for forgiveness for his opponents. "Father forgive them . . ." (Luke 23:34). This prayer finds fulfillment as repentance, Baptism, forgiveness and the gift of the Holy Spirit are offered to them "by grace alone through faith alone." The second part of Jesus' prayer from the cross, ". . . they know not what they do," was kept by Luke for Peter's next speech (cf. 3:17). For Luke, repentance, Baptism, forgiveness, and the gift of the Spirit form a unity rather than a series of three or four successive experiences, or stages of one's spiritual journey. He can therefore omit one or the other of these items and change their sequence. Here, for instance, faith is omitted whereas in 10:43 we read, "everyone who believes in him receives forgiveness of sins" (cf. 13:39). At other times Baptism is omitted (cf. 3:19; 5:31). To **repent** means to turn to God because he graciously turns to us and offers **forgiveness** in spite of our deeds. Such repentance includes faith and results in Baptism **in the name of Jesus Christ.** In turn, to be baptized means to **receive the gift of the Holy Spirit.** Water Baptism and the gift of the Spirit do not constitute two separate stages in the believer's development. They are interrelated because Baptism occurs **in the name of** him who mediates the Spirit (v. 33). The person to be baptized calls upon the name of the Lord who saves (cf. v. 21) and grants the Holy Spirit together with forgiveness of sins. "Where there is forgiveness of sins, there is life and salvation" (Luther). To be **baptized in the name of Jesus Christ** means that the act of Baptism is authorized by the exalted Christ and that the person baptized becomes the possession of Jesus Christ. For the anomalies of Acts 8:12-17 and 10:44 see comments on those passages.

The speech once more points back to its opening citation. The **promise** of God through Joel, promising the Spirit (vv. 17-18) and salvation (v. 21) is directed to Jews first, not just to Peter's present audience but also to their **children.** In distinction from earlier Christian traditions Luke expected that there will be future generations (cf. Luke 12:40; 19:11; 20:9; 21:8-9). More exactly, future generations of Jews will be confronted with the promise of Pentecost. This may imply that the mission to Jews does not end when Acts ends, in spite of 28:28 (see comments there). After the fulfilled promise has reached the Jews then the invitation to salvation will also come **to all that are far off.** Only later on will the reader learn that these are not just diaspora Jews but also Gentiles. They too will be included, not merely because of Jewish objections but because God had included them in his promise from the beginning. But to accept the promise is not merely a matter of human decision. It is first and foremost a matter of the call of God through his word (cf. Joel 2:32). **Everyone whom the Lord our God calls to him** (better, "shall call") is invited to share in the promise fulfilled and call upon the name of the Lord (v. 21). The question why some are called and not others cannot be answered abstractly. If I reject God's call I cannot blame him and if I accept it, I cannot base my acceptance on my superior religiosity, but only on his word. Peter's concluding exhortation speaks of this **crooked generation** (cf. Deut. 32:5; Ps. 78:8) and indicates the rebellious state of Israel as well as the division which the preaching of salvation introduces in Israel. The RSV at this point is incorrect. It reads, **save yourselves** (v. 40). No one can do that! It should read, "let yourselves be saved" (aorist passive imperative in Greek). The Lord Jesus Christ is the agent and God is the ultimate cause and ground (cf. v. 21) of salvation from unbelieving Israel.

41 (The result of Pentecost)—Peter's inaugural address was a tremendous success. **About three thousand** Jews **received his word and were baptized.** Numerical growth appears in Acts only with respect to Jewish Christianity. Numbers are not used to indicate the growth of the church among Gentiles. The success of Pentecost marks a difference from the Nazareth pericopes where the rejection of Jesus foreshadows his cross (Luke 4:16-30) while the result of Pentecost foreshadows the "many ten thousands" of Jews who came to faith in Jesus Christ (21:20). One should not ask how 3000 persons could be baptized in one day. Was it done by sprinkling or by immersion and, if the latter, where in Jerusalem could that be done? Such questions are beside the point. For Luke the miracle of Pentecost begins with miraculous portents from heaven, continues in miraculous speech and in Peter's prophetic interpretation and proclamation and concludes with the establishment of the true Israel that calls on the name of the Lord and lets itself be saved. Jesus in Luke-Acts is first and foremost Israel's Savior (Luke 2:11; Acts 5:31; 13:23). Conversely, baptized Jews do not form a new religion but are the true Israel under the exalted Messiah and Lord through whom the Holy Spirit is received in accordance with the promise of God.

Summary Statement: The Life of the Pentecost Community (2:42-47)

After his dramatic narrative of Pentecost Luke changes his pace and inserts the first of three summary statements (cf. 4:32-35; 5:11-16) in which he depicts the church as an alternative community within and distinct from Jewish society.

These summaries also distinguish and connect individual scenes (in this case, the Pentecost narrative and the healing of the lame man), and they create the impression that a longer period of time elapses between individual scenes. They summarize and generalize what in Luke's opinion was important in the life of the community at its beginning. For instance, Luke knew that individual Christians, like Barnabas, voluntarily had sold part of their property and contributed the proceeds of the sale to the community (4:36-37). In his summary statement Luke generalized this by writing that all sold their possessions and goods for the community's benefits (2:44-45).

This summary has an *a b a b* structure: *(a)* the life of the community (v. 42), *(b)* the effect on outsiders (v. 43), *(a)* the life of the community (vv. 44-47a), *(b)* the effect on outsiders (v. 47b-c). The messianically restored, Spirit-endowed Israel is itself a witness by its very life. Luke intended this message to be heard also by the church of his day.

42—Four basic characteristics must be present in the church of every age. **And they devoted themselves** marks the perennial issue of every Christian community. Will it remain faithful to its Lord and persevere, or was it merely a fly-by-night enthusiasm that disintegrated when the harsh winds of history began to blow? The Pentecost community of Jerusalem remained grounded in **the apostles' teaching.** This first item includes not only the traditions of "the eyewitnesses and ministers of the word" (Luke 1:2), found in Luke's Gospel, but also the apostolic teaching including the Christological interpretation of the Old Testament found in Acts. **Fellowship** (Greek, *koinōnia*) appears in Luke-Acts only in this verse. It means that **all who believed were together** (v. 44). No splits and no schisms! If difficulties arise they must be resolved in a spirit of unanimity (cf. 6:1-6; 15:1-35). The oneness of the church witnesses to the one Lord who saves and to the one Holy Spirit who created and sustains the church. Moreover fellowship, *koinōnia*, has a social dimension. It means that **all** had **all things in common** (v. 44; Greek, *koina*). There is no *koinōnia* without sharing of material goods! The **breaking of bread** in Judaism meant the act, connected with a table blessing, with which the father of the household opened a meal (cf. Mark 6:41). At Luke's time it had become the designation of the Lord's Supper (20:7; cf. 1 Cor. 10:16). Originally the Lord's Supper was celebrated in conjunction with a regular meal, in which the breaking of the bread together with the words of interpretation concerning the bread opened the meal and "the cup of blessing" followed at the end of the meal (cf. 1 Cor. 10:16; 11:25). At the next stage the Lord's Supper was celebrated at the conclusion of a regular meal. **Breaking bread in their homes** (v. 46b) refers to the celebration of the Eucharist, while **they partook of food** refers to regular meals (v. 46c). Daily celebrations of the Eucharist cannot be deduced from v. 46 because the Greek phrase **day by day** (Greek, *kath' hēmeran*) refers only to the first clause, namely, that they attended **the temple** daily, and has its correspondence in the phrase **in their homes** (Greek, *kat' oikon*) where they celebrated the Eucharist. The Eucharist was probably celebrated on Sundays (cf. 20:7). But every meal was an occasion of joyful remembrance of the meals with Jesus before and after Easter. Instead of **generous hearts** (v. 46) we should translate "simplicity of heart." Simplicity is not simplemindedness, nor stupidity, but the opposite of duplicity and doubt. The church must keep its priorities straight. In **prayers** the church responds to God's mighty acts by **praising** him (v. 47a) and Jesus. The early Christians made use of the prayers of the Psalms. But the experience of the Spirit produced new expressions—Abba! Father! (Rom. 8:15; Gal. 4:6)—even as the Lord's prayer gave new encouragement to prayer (Luke 11:2-4, 5-13). Prayer addressed to Jesus (cf. 7:59-60) probably grew out of the acclamation "Maranatha" (1 Cor. 16:22).

43-47—The presence of the Spirit-filled alternative community cannot remain unnoticed. Its effects upon outsiders is on the one hand a kind of uneasiness or **fear** which is intensified because many signs and wonders are done by **the apostles.** Later on Luke will narrate four specific miracles by Peter (3:1-11; 5:1-11; 9:32-42). On the other hand, the Pentecost community finds **favor with all the people** (v. 47a; cf. Luke 2:52). There is as yet no opposition from the people or their leaders, and therefore the church grows, which ultimately is the work of God (v. 47c). Even though the community developed new liturgical forms in the breaking of bread and in prayers (vv. 42 and 46), nevertheless it did not neglect worship in the temple. For the temple is the center of Israel's life and the place where the true Israel expresses its continuity with the past and its solidarity with the Israel that has not yet repented. In short: the Holy Spirit is manifested in the Pentecost community through miracles, bold preaching, and perseverance in the apostles' teaching, through the celebration of the Eucharist, through prayer and worship in the temple, and through growth of the people of God. Last but not least, a new social solidarity among its members manifests the presence of the Spirit of God.

The community of goods has fascinated the readers of Acts. But Luke's two summary statements (2:44-45; 4:32, 34-35) have also raised questions. For instance, if all believers had sold their houses (cf. 4:34) how could they have met in their homes (cf. 2:46; 12:12)? If no one called anything his or her own, then how could anyone give alms? Peter declared, "I have no silver," yet he was in charge of the community's funds together with the other apostles (cf. 3:6; 4:35). The two summary statements speak of a general practice while 5:1-11 speaks of a voluntary practice. Finally, nowhere else in Acts is a community of goods mentioned apart from the first two summary statements, and Paul's exhortation of "helping the weak" presupposes private property (20:33-35). These tensions suggest that Luke presented us with an idealized picture of the Jerusalem community's sharing of goods. If so, one should not speak of an early Christian communism, because historically it never existed. Voluntary sharing of possessions, as practiced by Barnabas, cannot be equated with communism. But then the question arises, What was Luke's purpose in painting this picture of a total sharing of all material goods? First, this picture reminds us of Jesus' identification with the poor (cf. Luke 1:51-53; 4:18-19; 6:20) and of his radical demands on his disciples (cf. 12:32-34; 14:33; 18:22). Therefore, Luke's picture of the community of goods illustrates the continuity between Jesus and the origins of the church. Second, Luke underscores that the church's spirituality is inseparable from social responsibility. The Spirit-filled community takes care of the material needs of its members. The presence of the Spirit liberates from preoccupation with material things and prompts the church and its members to share material possessions. What we do or do not do with our material possessions is an indicator of the Spirit's presence or absence. With this idealized picture, Luke challenged the church of his day to take responsibility for the needy (cf. 6:1-6; 11:29; 20:35; 24:17; Luke 19:8). The Holy Spirit liberates from the bourgeois quest for material security (cf. Luke 12:16-21) and he liberates for a community that expresses the Greek ideal of friendship, in which friends have all things in common (cf. Plato, *Republic* 4.424a), as well as the Hebrew hope for a community free from poverty (Deut. 15:4-5). Luke's picture of the community of goods is a criticism of the indifference of all well-to-do Christians toward their needy brothers and sisters and it is a call to find creative ways to overcome the gulf between the rich and poor in the church, which is the eschatological alternative to the communities of the world, including unrepentant Israel.

Apostolic Benefaction and Sadducean Opposition (3:1—4:31)

This section consists of four episodes: the healing of the lame man in the temple (3:1-10); Peter's speech in the temple (3:11-26); the arrest of Peter and John, their appearance before the council and their release (4:1-22) and the prayer of the community in the face of opposition (4:23-31). Common to these episodes is the reference to the **name** of Jesus (3:6, 16; 4:7, 10, 12, 18, 30) and to the miraculous healing (3:16; 4:9-10, 22, 30). The summary statement had called attention to miracles done "through the apostles" as well as to participation in temple worship (2:43, 46). Luke now narrates a particular miracle which happened in **the temple,** the place where Yahweh caused his name to dwell (Deut. 12:11). The temple was the place where Jesus taught and where his disciples praised God (Luke 2:49; 19:47; 20:1; 21:37; 22:53; 24:53; Acts 2:46). In **the temple** a lame man is healed **in the name of Jesus Christ.** Just as Yahweh's name guarantees his nearness and assures access to his heart, so the name of Jesus Christ constitutes the link between the exalted Lord in heaven and his servants on earth. His name signifies the presence of Jesus and of his saving, healing power during the time of his absence. Hence, instead of saying that Jesus' name heals, Peter in Acts 9:34 can say, "Jesus Christ heals you." The salvation of everyone is dependent on his name (4:12). In his name people are baptized

(2:38). Through it sins are forgiven (10:43); the disciples teach and preach in his name (4:17-18). It is the name of Jesus Christ which causes opposition from the leaders of Israel who warn the two apostles "to speak no more to anyone in this name" (4:17); and it is for the sake of his name that the servants of Jesus "suffer dishonor" and beatings as the opposition intensifies in the next section (5:40-41).

The Healing of the Lame Man by Peter and John in the Temple (3:1-10)

This example of the "many signs and wonders" which were done "through the apostles" (2:43) extends Jesus' program of Luke 7:22, which says, "the lame walk." Peter and John continued Jesus' healing ministry "in the name of Jesus Christ" (v. 6). The healing story follows the customary form. The exposition (vv. 1-2) pictures the tragic fate of a beggar **lame from birth.** The confrontation (vv. 3-6a) heightens the suspense. The healing (vv. 6b-7) takes place through a command and through bodily contact. The demonstration of the healing (v. 8) is followed by the effect on the people (vv. 9-10), which underscores the public nature of the miracle. Just as Pentecost was a public event with a claim on all of Israel, so the miracle in the temple was a public event which gave rise to a public speech in which all of Israel was addressed.

1-2 (Exposition)—The Christian community in Jerusalem and its leaders were faithful Jews who kept the established hours of **prayer** and attended **the temple. Peter and John** went **to the temple at the hour of prayer, the ninth hour,** that is, at 3 p.m., which is the second of three hours of daily prayer (cf. Dan. 6:10; 9:21; Jdt. 9:1). They met a beggar who was **lame from birth** asking for **alms.** Prayer and almsgiving are two equally important works of piety (cf. Matt. 6:2-6) and thus it is not surprising to find beggars gathering at the temple. This one lay at the gate **called Beautiful.** Its actual location is a matter of dispute, because this designation does not appear in ancient descriptions of the temple. Christian tradition identified it with the Shushan gate, located on the east side of the Outer Court, opposite the Mount of Olives, permitting entry from the Kidron Valley. Interpreters have pointed out that this gate would be a poor place to bring a lame beggar since the access is steep and most people would enter the temple area directly from the west side. Therefore, the Nicanor Gate, which probably led from the Court of the Women to the Court of the Men of Israel, has been suggested. However, in v. 11 Peter addressed the people in Solomon's portico, which is on the east side of the Court of the Gentiles. Thus Luke seems to have thought of a gate through which one would enter the Court of the Gentiles, or else he failed to say in v. 11 that the apostles left the inner court and went into the Court of the Gentiles to Solomon's portico. Probably Luke himself had no clear picture of the temple any longer.

3-6a (Confrontation)—Seeing Peter and John, the beggar **asked for alms.** They in turn **directed** their **gaze at him** and said, **Look at us.** And **he fixed his attention upon them.** Eye contact is established! It is so easy for religious people to stare piously into heaven (cf. 1:10 where the same Greek verb is used as in v. 4a), rather than to look at the world's misery. Equally easy it is for beggars to see people as mere means for getting something and as occasions for frequent disappointments. With the eye contact established, the expectations of the beggar are heightened, only to be disappointed by the words **I have no silver and gold.** One should not ask how Peter could say a thing like that since he together with the other apostles was in charge of the community's purse (cf. 4:35). We are dealing here with a tradition which was a self-contained unit and was transmitted apart from Luke's context. This tradition did not presuppose the Lukan picture of the community of goods but held instead that Peter had no money and therefore could not give alms. **But I give you what I have.** The reader is left to wonder what went through the beggar's mind at that moment.

6b-7 (The healing)—Without waiting for a reaction from the beggar, Peter speaks: **In the name of Jesus Christ of Nazareth, walk.** The apostles continue Jesus' ministry (cf. the command in Luke 5:23) but they do so in his name, by his saving power. By issuing the command in Jesus' name Peter placed the lame beggar under the saving power of Jesus. In the temple where Yahweh made his name dwell (cf. Deut. 14:23; 16:2, 11), the name of Jesus, exalted to Yahweh's right hand, is his saving presence among the suffering. The healing command "Walk!" is followed by physical contact (cf. 9:40-41). Grasping the beggar's **right hand** Peter **raised him up; and immediately his feet and ankles were made strong.** We may not rationalize miracles nor attach the label of "name magic" to this one. Where such ideas arise in Acts they are at once debunked (cf. 19:13).

Jesus Christ is not controlled by humans. The name formula expresses that it is not Peter, but Jesus who heals (cf. 4:10; 9:34). Peter is only one of his faithful and believing instruments (cf. 3:16). Through them the saving power of the exalted Christ becomes operative.

8 (**The demonstration**)—We have here an allusion to Isa. 35:6, which is found also in the Gospel (Luke 7:22). Isaiah promised for the time of salvation that "then shall the lame man *leap* like a hart." In the **leaping** of the healed lame man, mentioned twice in this verse, God's promise has come to fulfillment. Certain of his healing, he **entered the temple with** Peter and John, **leaping and praising God** for his deliverance from lameness.

9-10 (The effect)—And all the people saw him walking and praising God. As in the Pentecost narrative, so here **all the people** are witnesses. The public nature of God's eschatological acts through Christ and his Spirit is stressed by Luke. Moreover, these verses allude to Isa. 35:2—the people shall "see the glory of the Lord." Later on Peter will say, "Let it be known . . . to all the people of Israel that by the name of Jesus Christ . . . this man is standing before you well" (4:10). The healing is a sign that should serve the gathering of **all the people** into the community under the resurrected and exalted Messiah. Indeed the people, recognizing the identity of the lame beggar now healed, **were filled with wonder and amazement at what had happened to him.** Their amazement is not faith, but may be a first step toward faith. At any rate their amazement gives an opportunity to Peter to address the people. Only in Acts 9:35, 42 do we hear that miracles produce faith; otherwise faith is the result of hearing the Word.

Miracles in Acts are invitations to faith rather than the cause of faith. Moreover, as in the Fourth Gospel so here miracles are opportunities for proclamation. Miracles in Acts indicate the following: (1) Salvation is by grace alone and not by "our own power or piety" (3:12). (2) In them the saving power of the eschaton is at work; they are signs pointing beyond themselves to the End, to the "times of refreshing that come from the presence of the Lord" (3:19-21). (3) The gift of healing may not be separated from Christ the healer who is active through his servant witnesses (cf. Luke 17:11-19; Acts 4:10). (4) Moreover, healings are the testimony of the Holy Spirit to Jesus, the exalted Lord and Savior (5:32). (5) Salvation includes bodily wholeness—not just an "I-thou" relationship—and therefore all miracles point forward to the resurrection of the dead. After all, also the healed persons died.

Peter's Speech in the Temple (3:11-26)

The speech consists of two parts which are marked by two addresses (vv. 11-16 and 17-26). The first part is connected with the miracle (vv. 11-12 and 16) and gives an interpretation of it by means of the Christological kerygma (vv. 13-15). The second part (vv. 17-26) brings the invitation to repent with an eschatological-apocalyptic motivation followed by allusions, citations, and interpretation of Scripture. Their point is that the audience should turn, **every one of you, from your wickedness** (v. 26). A comparison between Peter's Pentecost speech and his temple speech shows similarities and differences. Both speeches are connected with a miracle and defuse a misunderstanding. Both contrast the deeds of the Jews against Jesus with God's vindication of Jesus. But whereas the Christological kerygma was unfolded broadly in the Pentecost speech and the invitation to repent received little space, it is the other way around in the temple speech, where the call to repentance is unfolded at length with the new accent on the parousia and the final judgment and with an emphasis on the present as the time of decision. Through repetition of the kerygma and through new emphases Luke hoped not only to keep the reader's attention but also to move the plot of his narrative forward. The temple speech has a more aggressive tone than Peter's inaugural address and thereby prepares the way for the first controversy with the opposition.

11-16 (Part one of the speech)—The structure of the first part is:
(*a*) The miracle was not done by Peter's powers or piety.
(*b*) God glorified his servant.
(*c*) You delivered him up . . . and denied him.
(*c*) You denied him and killed him.
(*b*) God raised him from the dead.
(*a*) In his name, by faith, the healing miracle came about.

11-12—The healing leads to Peter's speech and his speech leads to the arrest of the two apostles. The healed beggar **clung to Peter and John** and will also be present at the hearing before the council (4:14). Peter's second speech is also given in response to an amazed crowd (cf. 2:12) which **ran together to them in the portico called Solomon's** (cf. 5:12; John 10:23). This was a colonnade situated along the eastern wall of the Court of the Gentiles (cf. Josephus, *War* 5.185). The Western text seeks to overcome the tension between v. 11 on one hand and vv. 2 and 8 on the other by adding that Peter, John, and the healed person "went out of" the court to which the Beautiful Gate led. According to the Western text the Beautiful Gate lies within the temple area. However, Luke's description can be right only if that gate leads into the Court of the Gentiles. Peter, recognizing the reason why **all the people** were gathering, addressed them not as individuals, but as representatives of **all of Israel** and he began by correcting a possible misunderstanding (cf. 2:15). This lame man was healed not **by our own power or piety.** Apostles differ from magicians such as Simon who claimed to be "somebody great" and was hailed as the "power of God which is called Great" (8:9-10). Apostles are servants, instruments of their Lord. They exercise no control over him, but remain his faithful subjects who do not advertise themselves as being "somebody" (5:36). The miracle of healing did not result from divine powers inherent in them, nor from mysterious magic, nor from their own superior piety which prompted God to answer their prayers. But then what or who healed the lame man? To answer this question Peter begins with **the God of Abraham and of Isaac and of Jacob, the God of our fathers** (cf. Exod. 3:6,15; Isa. 52:13; cf. Acts 7:32). If this healing has come about through Israel's God then this healing must be of concern to all of Israel. In what sense is Israel's God the ultimate source of this healing?

13-15—An expanded kerygma contrasts God's action toward Jesus with the action of the audience and lays the foundation for answering the question concerning the source of the healing. The contrast between God's action and the deeds of the Jerusalem Jews who participated in Jesus' death and who are now addressed by Peter also serves as rationale for Peter's call to repentance (vv. 17-26). Three old and relatively rare Christological titles lend an ancient patina to the kerygma. The designation **servant** is used in Luke-Acts of the people of Israel (Luke 1:54), of David (Luke 1:69; Acts 4:25), and of Jesus (3:13,26; 4:27,30; cf. Matt. 12:18). What is surprising is that the notion of the suffering servant of Isaiah 53 is never connected with this title in the New Testament. The reason for this probably lies in the fact that the Greek word for servant (*pais*) can also mean "son," or "child." *Servant* as well as *son* designates a relationship of obedience to God and of divine authorization and commission by God. Through Jesus the servant, God fulfills his saving purpose. **The Holy and Righteous One** as a Christological title occurs only here in this combination (cf. Mark 6:20). **Holy** is that which is set apart by God for his special purpose (cf. Jer. 1:5; Sir. 45:6). As Christological title the **Holy One** is found in Peter's confession in John 6:69 (cf. 1 John 2:20; Rev. 3:7). Demons sense the powers of "the Holy One of God" who has come to destroy them (Luke 4:34). **The Righteous One** went in obedience to God on his foreordained way that included his innocent passion and death (7:52; Luke 24:47; Acts 22:14; 1 Peter 3:18; cf. Pss. Sol. 17:35). **The Author of life** or "the Prince of life" (KJV) was probably a Jewish messianic title (cf. 5:31; Heb. 2:10; 12:2). Its derivation from the Hellenistic emperor cult or from gnosticism is rather unlikely. The Lukan meaning of this title is the royal Messiah who brings about salvation because death could not keep him in its clutches (2:24-28; 26:23). Eternal life, to which Israel and—as we shall see—also Gentiles are called (13:46, 48), has been realized in him first and is now available through him. These Christological titles heighten the contrast between God and his Messiah, on the one hand, and, on the other, the deeds of the audience that acted out its sinfulness in the passion of Jesus.

God **glorified his servant** (cf. Isa. 52:13) through this miracle as well as through the servant's exaltation (Luke 24:26), which is the presupposition for this healing performed in his name. **You delivered** him **up** and denied him in the **presence of Pilate, when he had decided to release him** (Luke 23:1-5, 22-24); **you denied the Holy and Righteous One and** you **asked for** the release of Barabbas, **a murderer** (Luke 23:18-19, 25). Finally, you inflicted death, **you killed the Author of life.** The past action of the audience involves a supreme religious irony. They rejected the innocent Jesus in favor of a murderer and killed the God-appointed author of life. But God's plan was not thwarted; he vindicated Jesus by the resurrection. **God raised** him from the dead and **we are witnesses** to this. Luke laid the guilt for the crucifixion of Jesus primarily on the people of Jerusalem even though he recognized that Pilate was not innocent, but shared in the guilt (cf. 4:27). This Lukan view raises serious historical problems. Historically it was Pilate, and not the Jews, who issued orders for the execution of Jesus. But in Luke's Gospel, as well as in Acts, we find a stereotyped pattern. Initially, the people, in contrast to their leaders, respond favorably to Jesus as well as to the Christian message (cf. Luke 7:16-17; 12:1; 13:17; Acts 2:43, 47; 4:21; 5:13, 16). But eventually, at the trial of Jesus and of Stephen, the people line up with their leaders in a solid front of rejection (Luke 23; Acts 6:12—7:60). The use of this literary pattern determined Luke's passion account which is summarized in the extended kerygma of Acts 3:13-15.

Equally important is the fact that Luke never blamed the Jews as such for the crucifixion. He did not hold a doctrine of corporate guilt nor did he think that guilt can be transferred from one generation of Jews to another. On the contrary, guilt presupposes personal involvement. Hence, Jews of the diaspora are never blamed for the crucifixion of Jesus. In distinction from Peter's audience in Jerusalem the diaspora Jews did not participate in Jesus' trial and rejection and therefore they were not asked to repent because of it.

16—On the basis of the expanded kerygma Peter now deals with the healing through which God "glorified his servant" Jesus. At first sight the sentence seems to be jumbled. The Greek text contains the following *a b b a* structure:

(*a*) by **faith;**
(*b*) in his **name;**
(*b*) his **name** has made this man strong whom you see and know;
(*a*) the **faith** which is through Jesus has given him perfect health in the presence of you all.

In short, the healing took place by **faith** as well as by his **name.** This is unfolded in two clauses with proof of healing stated in each clause. First, the miracle demonstrates not the apostles' superior power or piety, but the saving presence and power of the **name** of this Jesus whom God raised from the dead. However, his name does not operate like magic. It was not a magical formula pronounced over the lame man which made him whole. The power of the "Prince of life" becomes effective through **faith.** Second, lest a new misunderstanding arise which holds that faith is a religious achievement Peter added that **faith . . . is through Jesus.** Faith is not a virtue achieved, but a gift received even though it is also a matter of our decision. The gift of faith is mediated through proclamation in his name. The saving power of the resurrected Jesus is present in the word of the apostles that calls to and mediates faith. Does v. 16 imply that the lame man had faith? He is now clinging to the apostles (cf. v. 11; 2:42) and praising God (v. 9). But the story does not speak of the faith of the healed person and Peter's following exhortation refers to repentance rather than to faith. Should we think of the apostles' faith? This would be more likely. Without faith Peter would not have called upon the name of the Lord (cf. 2:21). However, it would seem that the verse is deliberately vague at this point, for it would have been easy to introduce the person who had faith into the second clause. By not referring to the faith of either the lame man or the apostles this verse focuses attention on faith itself. **Faith** in his **name** is faith brought about by the Resurrected One himself through the apostolic word, and such faith is indispensable for wholeness in body and soul. The healing of the lame beggar becomes a sign for salvation by calling upon the name of the Lord Jesus in faith (cf. 2:21).

17-26 (Part two of the speech)—After a new address and an introduction (vv. 17-18) there comes the exhortation to repent and turn to God. This exhortation forms brackets around the second part of the speech (vv. 19 and 26). The listeners should repent and turn to God for two reasons: first, because they were responsible for Jesus' death (vv. 13-15) and second, because God invites them to turn to him since he has turned to them with blessing to **every one of you** (v. 26). Within these brackets additional reasons for the urgency and the necessity of repentance are given. (For comments on the structure, see the Introduction, §3.)

17-18—Both the people and their leaders acted **in ignorance** when they rejected Jesus. They did not know his true identity as God's Anointed One. Still their failure to recognize him constitutes guilt which requires repentance (cf. 13:27; 17:23,30) and, with it, recognition of their responsibility for Jesus' death. Readers of Luke's Gospel will recall that the disciples of Jesus also participated in the all-pervasive ignorance. Though they did not actively engage in opposition against Jesus, they did not understand his predictions concerning his passion (Luke 9:45; 18:34) and they too failed to understand the Scriptures. It was the resurrected Christ who had opened the disciples' minds and communicated a new understanding of the

Scriptures (Luke 24:25,31-32,44-47). By the authority of the resurrected Christ, Peter is now trying to liberate his audience from
their blindness and ignorance and to convey a new understanding
of Christ and the Scriptures which he himself had experienced on
and after Easter. Moreover, the crucified Messiah had prayed on
the cross, "Father, forgive them; for they know not what they do"
(Luke 23:34). This prayer now finds a partial fulfillment in the invitation to repent and turn to God. But Peter went further and made
a most surprising statement. Even their rejection of Jesus out of
ignorance had furthered the plan of God foretold by **all the prophets**
(cf. 2:23) **that his Christ should suffer.** His Christ is God's Anointed
One, the Messiah. God in his sovereign majesty fulfilled his purpose
not only in spite of, but even through the sinful deeds of Peter's
audience. The God of Israel is indeed full of surprises. He works
out his plan through the misdeeds of his people and he offers them
a chance to repent. Their repentance is not motivated by a corporate
guilt, but rather by their personal involvement in Jesus' passion.
The stakes, therefore, are high. Will the Jerusalemites and their
leaders let themselves be turned by Peter's word and thus be saved
(cf. 2:40) or will their ignorance turn into hardness of heart (cf. 28:25-
27)?

**19-21—Repent therefore and turn again, that your sins may be
blotted out.** These two imperatives result from the insight that Jesus'
passion reveals both the guilt of its perpetrators and the saving action
of God. Repentance is the negative turning away from a wrong
course while the positive action is turning to God. Both are the
conditions for forgiveness (cf. 2:38; 5:30-32; 8:22; 26:18; Luke 24:47;
Mark 1:4; 4:12). The heavenly Father is eager to accept his prodigal
children who in ignorance acted against his Messiah. If they but
turn to him their past misdeeds can be **blotted out.** Israel's repentance is related not only to their past, but also to their future and to
God's future (cf. 1 Thess. 1:9-10).

These verses are one long and difficult sentence, the interpretation of which is subject to much debate. The problem lies in the
meaning of **times of refreshing** (Greek, *kairoi*) and **time** (Greek,
chronoi) **for establishing all** of God's promises. We shall not deal
with the problem of whether Luke used a prior tradition or only
individual traditional expressions. The latter would seem to be more
probable. We begin by noting that *kairoi* and *chronoi* appear in

reverse sequence in 1:7 and the verb "restore" of 1:6 reappears as the noun "restoration" or "establishing" in 3:21. According to 1:6-8, the restoration of the kingdom to Israel occurs with finality at the God-appointed "times and seasons," the date of which the church does not know. But the restoration of the kingdom to Israel begins already in the mission to the end of the earth (1:8) and in the call to repentance, the offer of forgiveness and the gift of the Holy Spirit. Thus the Jerusalemites should repent now so that the **times of refreshing** may come also to them **from the presence** (literally, "from the face") **of the Lord** God. These times of refreshing stretch from the time of Jesus (Luke 4:18-21) and the time of the Spirit (Acts 2:17) up to and including the time of the parousia. The audience should repent so that God **may send the Christ appointed for you, Jesus.** The times of refreshing find their climactic conclusion in Christ's parousia. He remains in **heaven** (cf. 1:11) . . . **until the time(s) for establishing all** of God's promises. These times of restoration or establishing of **all** of God's promises have begun with Jesus' appearance and the coming of the Holy Spirit. But they are not yet completed, because the church's witness has not yet reached the end of the earth and the restoration of the kingdom to Israel—which has only begun—awaits its completion.

Jesus had not rejected the disciples' hope for the restoration of the kingdom to Israel (1:6-8). This hope had formed the background of Luke's narrative from the beginning of his Gospel. Mary was told by Gabriel that her son "will reign over the house of Jacob forever" (Luke 1:32-33) and Zechariah praised God "for the horn of salvation . . . in the house of David" who would save us "from our enemies" and bring political freedom to Israel (Luke 1:71-73), just as God spoke through the mouth of his holy prophets from of old (Luke 1:70; cf. Acts 3:21). The restoration of the kingdom to Israel is part of the establishing (Greek, *apokatastasis*) of all of God's promises found in the Scriptures. Luke did not dwell on this hope at length just as he mentioned the parousia only occasionally in Acts. Instead of focusing his attention on what comes after the "times of the Gentiles" when "your redemption draws near" (Luke 21:24, 28), Luke's updated biblical history is addressed to the present, and the focus of his biblical interpretation lies in what God has already fulfilled among us (Luke 1:1). Participation in the future fulfillment of Israel's hope demands turning to God and his saving activity in the present.

Otherwise, the times of refreshing and the times of establishing all of God's promises cannot become effective for Peter's audience. Through the apostolic proclamation, God grants Jerusalem a new, a second opportunity for repentance and the last opportunity for participation in the times of refreshing and restoration to come. Repentant Israel will be reunited with its God-appointed Messiah whom God will send.

The identification of the sending of the Messiah with his parousia is found in the New Testament only here and indicates the presence of pre-Lukan language. Otherwise, the sending of Jesus always refers to his first coming, to his coming in the flesh (cf. Gal. 4:4). The notion that Israel should now repent in order that the parousia can occur may also point to the use of a pre-Lukan tradition. To be sure, Peter does not say that Israel's repentance would "hasten" the parousia (cf. 2 Peter 3:12), but he does say that the time of refreshing and the parousia are linked to Israel's repentance and that without repentance and turning to God, those Jews who heard and rejected the gospel in the post-Easter period will be cut off from God's people on the day of judgment (cf. v. 23).

22-23—Peter provides an example of God's promises spoken **by the mouth of his holy prophets from of old.** This fulfilled promise serves as motivation for repentance by the audience. **Moses said, "The Lord God will raise up for you a prophet from your brethren as he raised me up. You shall listen to him in whatever he tells you"** (cf. Deut. 18:15). It now becomes clear that the **time for establishing** (v. 21) begins with the raising up of the prophet like Moses. But to whom does **as he raised me up** refer? Does it refer to the mission of the earthly Jesus? In favor of this is the parallel to Moses. However, the emphasis of vv. 22-23 lies in the demand to **listen** to the prophet like Moses. His raising therefore must also include his resurrection. If the raising were limited to the mission of the earthly Jesus, then there would be no point in preaching to Jews of Jerusalem because they did not listen to him, but rejected him. However, now in the situation after Easter when Jesus, the prophet like Moses, is preached in the power of the Spirit, **it shall be that every soul that does not listen to that prophet shall be destroyed from the people** (Deut. 18:19; Lev. 23:29). Note that Peter did not say that Israel, the people, shall be destroyed. Only individuals who have been confronted twice with the message of repentance and forgiveness in Jesus' name and have rejected it twice shall be purged **from the people** of God—at the final judgment and not before (cf. 10:42; 17:31). Those individual Jews who do not listen now to the God-appointed Messiah (v. 20) shall cease to be members of Israel at the Messiah's parousia. Their past rejection of the earthly Jesus could be **blotted out,** but their rejection of the exalted Lord who in the power of the Spirit speaks through his witnesses "will not be forgiven" (Luke 12:10). The parousia will signal their destruction rather than their participation in the restoration of the kingdom to Israel and in the fulfillment of **all** of God's promises (cf. 1:6).

With the prophet like Moses, Luke introduced another old Christological title (cf. John 6:14; 7:40; 7:52, according to Papyrus 66). Jesus like Moses was "mighty in word and deed" (Luke 24:19; Acts 7:22), functioned as instrument of salvation (4:12; 7:25), as ruler, deliverer, and judge (3:15; 5:31; 7:35; 10:42). Both were twice rejected by their own people (Luke 23:18-25; Acts 6:11—7:60). The threat of ultimate rejection in the final judgment gives urgency to Peter's call for repentance and places a clear-cut alternative before his audience.

24-26—Not only Moses, but **all the prophets . . . from Samuel** (who anointed David, the "father" of the Messiah) **and those who came afterwards also proclaimed these** present **days** as times of refreshing and of restoration which find their climactic conclusion in the future parousia. The Scriptures in their totality are united in their prophetic testimony to salvation through the Messiah who is Jesus (cf. Luke 24:25,44; Acts 10:43; 18:28; 24:14; 26:22). **You are the sons of the prophets** and thus heirs to God's promises found in the prophetic Scriptures. Upon the believing sons and daughters of the prophets the Holy Spirit is poured out in accordance with the prophetic promise (2:17-18). Moreover, the Jews are the sons **of the covenant** and of the promise attached to God's covenant with Abraham. In Luke-Acts the word *covenant* never refers to the conditional Sinai covenant (. . ."if you obey my voice . . . you shall be my own possession," Exod. 19:5) but always to God's unconditional covenant with Abraham. This covenant is unconditional because God himself pledges to fulfill its promise: **in your posterity** (literally, "in your seed") **shall all the families of the earth be blessed** (Gen. 12:3; 22:18, LXX). As in Gal. 3:16 so here the "seed" is an individual, Jesus Christ. Luke substituted **families** for "nations" in this citation, with a view to his Jewish audience. The promise and its fulfillment are directed *first* and foremost to the sons of God's covenant with Abraham. **God, having raised up his servant** Jesus from the dead **sent him to you first.** Through the call to repentance addressed to the Jews of Jerusalem, through the recital of Jesus' story by his witnesses, Jesus is now sent to them first after Easter (cf. Luke 24:47; Acts 26:23). He is sent not to condemn them for their participation in his passion, but to **bless you in turning every one of you from your wickedness.** Thus repentance and turning to God are not just conditions and tasks to be fulfilled by the audience, but also a gift, like faith (v. 16; cf. 5:31; 11:18). The gracious opportunity for a second chance after failure and ignorance (vv. 13, 17) is made possible through the servant of God who **sent** his witnesses to Israel **first** and through them turns everyone if they but "listen" to him. Jesus had been accused of "perverting the people" (Luke 23:14; the same Greek verb as in Acts 3:26), but in fact he now turns them from their perversion and grants them God's blessing. God's blessing will become effective if Israel "repents," that is, "listens" to the prophet like Moses and permits him to bless them and turn everyone around to God. Peter's listeners are personally involved in God's work through Jesus Christ—negatively in that they rejected and killed him, and positively in that God worked his purpose through their very rejection and now offers them through Jesus the fulfillment of the covenant of promise.

Arrest, Appearance before the Council, and Release (4:1-22)

This episode signals the beginning of three confrontations in Jerusalem which increased in intensity and ultimately led to the martyrdom of Stephen and the persecution of the church. At the time of the first arrest the people—in contrast to their leaders—were well disposed toward the apostles. Peter's second sermon had resulted in the further growth of the church. Though not all who heard him came to faith, still **many** did (v. 4) and the community increased to 5000 men (Greek, *andrōn*) not counting women and children. The mass movement of the people embracing the Christian message is contrasted twice with the hostility of the leaders who arrested the apostles (cf. 4:4, 21; 5:26).

The stories of the first and second arrests show many parallels (cf. 4:1-22; 5:17-42). Each arrest was preceded by a miracle or miracles; a night separated the arrests from judicial proceedings; a hearing with a speech by Peter is followed by a closed conference of the council and concluded with a verdict. Moreover, in both cases the verdict is deliberately disobeyed by the apostles. These parallels gave rise to questions: Did Luke have one or two traditions before him concerning the arrests of apostles? Did he create the second arrest himself? What is the historical value of these two narratives? How could Luke know about Gamaliel's advice given in closed session? Instead of trying to answer questions such as these we will concentrate on Luke's story itself. This story raises the question, Who are the true leaders of Israel—the established leaders of the temple and their theologians, or these "uneducated" apostles (4:13) who, irrespective of the consequences, obey God rather than men? Luke's story is also connected backward to the prior healing and to Peter's speech (cf. 4:2, 9-10, 14, 16-18, 22). Both activities were done in the name of Jesus, which is the cause of conflict (4:7, 10, 12, 16-18).

1-4 (The arrest)—**As they were speaking** in the temple, offering the blessing of God through Abraham's seed **to the people,** Peter and John were **arrested** by the Sadducees. Thus begins the tide of opposition and rejection which will continue throughout Acts. The Sadducees were **annoyed** because the apostles **were teaching the people** in the temple **and proclaiming in Jesus the resurrection from the dead.** Not only did the Sadducees—in distinction from the Pharisees—deny the resurrection of the dead in general (cf. 23:8), but they had been the prime instigators of the passion of Jesus; thus they had more than one reason for being **annoyed** with Peter and John. The defenseless apostles who had been preaching for several hours were arrested and put in custody overnight, **for it was already evening.** Yet their witness to Christ had been effective among the people and the true, believing Israel grew, even as official opposition emerged for the first time. At this point in Luke's narrative the people and their leaders are divided in their attitude toward the witnesses of Jesus.

5-12 (Witness of the apostles before the Sanhedrin)—This body consisted of 71 persons with the high priest as chairman, and the captain of the temple (cf. v. 1) ranking immediately below him. The membership was composed of three groups: the chief priests of the temple, the elders who were influential Sadducean laypersons, and the scribes, most of whom were Pharisees (cf. 5:34; 23:7). Luke mentioned the presence of the notorious former high priest **Annas,** whom the Romans had deposed in A.D. 14, but who played an influential role behind the scenes, managing to get members of his family into important positions including the high priesthood. **Caiaphas,** his son-in-law, held this office from A.D. 18 to 36. The identity of **John** and **Alexander** is unknown, though the former may be Jonathan (thus a Greek ms.), a son of Annas who became high priest in A.D. 36. Peter and John were brought before the council and asked, **By what power or by what name did you do this?** This question gave Peter an opportunity to announce the kerygma and its scriptural basis. Though the Spirit is granted to all believers they still can receive special inspiration for special occasions. Jesus had promised, "And when they bring you before . . . rulers . . . do not be anxious how or what you are to say . . .; for the Holy Spirit will teach you in that very hour what you ought to say" (Luke 12:11). This promise found fulfillment in Peter's courageous speech. Peter contrasted their **good deed** done to the lame (literally, their "benefaction") with their present situation as prisoners. The apostles are the true benefactors of the people while the rulers of Jews and Gentiles alike wish to be "called benefactors" (Luke 22:25) though most of them are selfish oppressors. The temple authorities want to know by what name the healing miracle was accomplished. With **be it known to you all, and to all the people of Israel** Peter sets out to overcome their ignorance and to recognize their own involvement with that name. He tells the council **by the name of Jesus Christ of Nazareth, whom you crucified, whom God raised from the dead, by him this** lame **man,** who was also present at this meeting, has become **well,** healed. The addition of **by him** after **the name** indicates that **the name** is interchangeable with the person. The healed man functions as a visual aid and paradigm of the power of Jesus and his name. His healing (Greek, *sōzō,* v. 9) points to something greater than temporal well-being. Announcing the kerygma in the form of an accusation is not only throwing caution to the wind, but constitutes an implicit call to repentance. The leaders should realize that they and God are aligned on opposite sides, as the two apostles boldly bear witness. Moreover, Peter points to the scriptural basis of his Christological witness by citing Ps. 118:22. The established leaders, the **builders,** had **rejected** the **stone** as being worse than useless, but the God of Israel had made it into the cornerstone, the **head of the corner.** God had vindicated Jesus from the verdict of rejection cast by the Sanhedrin so that henceforth salvation is totally dependent upon this Jesus and his name (v. 12). Note that also this conclusion does not distinguish between the name and the person. Through the name, the Lord enthroned in heaven is present on earth. Instead of speaking of forgiveness of sins (cf. 3:19) Peter speaks of salvation (cf. v. 10; 14:9). Miracles are manifestations of the future salvation in the present if received by faith (cf. Luke 17:11-19). Salvation not only from lameness, but from opposition to God and hence from being cut off from God's people (3:23) is forever dependent on Jesus. Peter forcefully concluded his response with a dogmatic statement, **and there is salvation in** (Greek, *en*) **no one else, for there is no other name under heaven given among men by which** (Greek, *en*) **we must be saved.** This statement gives the rationale for proclaiming the resurrection "in Jesus" (v. 2) which annoyed the Sadducees and for the healing in Jesus' name (v. 7), which is a sign of the salvation and wholeness that is yet to come, when "the times of refreshing" and of restoration will find their climactic conclusion.

13-14 (The reaction of the Sanhedrin)—The immediate reaction of the members of the council to Peter's speech was threefold (vv. 13-14). First, they recognized **the boldness** of the two apostles. Prior to Easter Peter had bragged that he was ready to go "with Jesus" to prison and death (Luke 22:33)—and then he had failed so badly. But now Peter has become a prisoner, and boldness has replaced his former denial. Boldness is the mark of the speech of a free man in distinction from a slave; it is a gift of the Spirit and marks the witness to the rejected but vindicated Messiah. The Sanhedrin recognized that the apostles were mere country bumpkins, **uneducated, common men** lacking rhetorical and theological education. Hence, their freedom of speech was all the more surprising and impressive. For the reader this confirms the power of the Holy Spirit and encourages him or her to bold witness. Second, the Sanhedrin recognized that the apostles **had been with Jesus,** an affiliation which Peter had denied during the night prior to Jesus' death (Luke 22:57). Their testimony as well as their healing was therefore dependent on their relationship with Jesus (Luke 8:1,35; 24:29,44; Acts 1:21-22). Third, the Sanhedrin saw the healed man **standing beside them** (literally, "with them"). He had experienced healing and had heard Peter's sermon; his health in body and soul implied that he remained **with** the apostles and held fast to their teachings (cf. 2:42). In the face of such oral and visual evidence the Sanhedrin **had nothing to say in opposition,** thus fulfilling Jesus' promise of Luke 21:15, where the same Greek verb occurs.

15-17—Peter and John are requested to step outside of the council chamber so that the Sanhedrin can discuss this matter without their presence. These Jewish leaders could now draw the consequence from what they had heard and seen and decide to stand "with" the apostles, thereby losing their power and prestige, but gaining their life and their proper place in God's saving history. But such a surrender does not occur to them at all. The question concerning the truth of the apostles' proclamation is not even raised by them. The council's concern is purely pragmatic. They cannot simply ignore this matter for a **notable sign has been performed** which they **cannot deny** because it has already become known **to all the inhabitants of Jerusalem.** Therefore all the Sanhedrin can do is confine the damage already done, so that the news **may spread no further among the people.** Thus the Sanhedrin decided: **let us warn them to speak no more to anyone in this name.**

18-22—When the Sanhedrin communicated its official verdict to the two apostles, Peter and John defiantly responded that they would disobey this injunction. They said **Whether it is right in the sight of God to listen to you rather than to God, you must judge; for we cannot but speak of what we have seen and heard.** Now the Sanhedrin found itself in a bind. On the one hand, preaching and healing in the name of Jesus did not constitute a legal offense. On the other hand, **the people** thought highly of the apostles and **praised God** for the miracle performed on a man **more than forty years old** who had been lame from birth (3:2). Hence it would not be politically feasible to take stronger measures against the two apostles except to **threaten** them **further.** Their threats reveal the powerlessness and spiritual emptiness of the Sanhedrin. In contrast to the official leaders, the true leaders of the believing people of God fulfill ideals esteemed by Greeks and Jews alike. When Socrates was offered the possibility of release from prison provided he would give up teaching philosophy, he declared: "Men of Athens . . . I shall obey God rather than you. . . . God commands me to do this," namely, point out "the truth to anyone of you whom I meet" (Plato, *Apology* 29D-E). When the king of Syria, Antiochus, tortured the seven Jewish brothers and their mother in order to induce them to eat pork, the oldest son answered, "We are ready to die rather than to transgress the laws of our fathers," and the youngest declared, "I will not obey the king's command, but I obey the commandment of the law that was given to our fathers through Moses" (2 Macc. 7; cf. 4 Macc. 5:15-21). In announcing that they would defy the council's prohibition Peter and John articulate a noble tradition that insists on freedom of conscience, of speech, and of religious conviction. The apostles whom Jesus had chosen (1:2) stand under the divine mandate to witness (1:8) and therefore declare, **we cannot but speak of what we have seen and heard** (v. 20).

The Prayer of the Community (4:23-31)

Peter and John returned and reported to **their friends.** The community responded to the Sanhedrin's threat in prayer **together** (Greek, *homothymadon;* cf. 1:14; 2:46; 5:12; 15:25). Their prayer is similar to Hezekiah's prayer at the time of Sennacherib's invasion (Isa. 37:16-20). Yet there is a notable difference in the church's prayer, namely, the absence of the petition "O Lord our God, save us" from our enemies (Isa. 37:20). Instead, the community prays for boldness to withstand the threats they experience. Moreover, the community understands itself to exist in continuity with the passion of Jesus, which also was inflicted by evil men and yet determined by God's plan.

In the prayer the unity of the community which is "of one heart and soul" (v. 32) comes to expression in its vertical dimension. In God, Christ, and the Holy Spirit lies the true strength of the community which has no power otherwise. **Sovereign Lord,** creator of **heaven and the earth and the sea** constitutes the formal address. God is not the buddy in the sky whom one invokes with sloppy informality, but the One who controls nature and history (Ps. 146:6; Exod. 20:11; Acts 14:15; 17:24). God spoke through the mediation of **the Holy Spirit** as his heavenly instrument and through the **mouth of . . . David** his **servant** as his earthly instrument. The prayer cites the opening lines of Psalm 2: **Why did the Gentiles rage and the peoples** (the Jews, in the present context) **imagine vain things? The kings of the earth** (Herod and Pilate, Caesar's representatives) **set themselves in array and the rulers** (the Sanhedrin) **were gathered together against the Lord and his Anointed.** This royal psalm was used originally on the occasion of the coronation of a Davidic king who faced hostile foreign powers. Anointed with oil during his coronation the king was adopted by God as his son. This psalm was interpreted messianically (cf. Pss. of Sol. 17:26) and applied to Jesus (cf. Mark 1:11; Acts 13:33). In this prayer the opening lines of the psalm are interpreted. They predict an alliance of Gentiles and the people of Israel who brought about the passion of Jesus, God's **holy servant** whom he anointed at his baptism and who consequently is the Messiah, **the Anointed One.** The psalm anticipated the roles played by King **Herod, Pontius Pilate** and the rulers (the Sanhedrin, in this case) together with the Roman soldiers and the Jewish mob. Yet their plot against God's servant-Messiah accomplished nothing else than what the **plan** of the sovereign God **had predestined to take place** (cf. 2:23; 3:21). God's sovereignty is full of surprises. Not only is opposition to him doomed to futility, but his opponents become his instruments, his pawns for the realization of his purposes. His opponents did not have the slightest inkling of the actual role they played in God's **plan.** The reader is confronted with divine irony and surprise at hearing again that God works out his purposes even through the blindness and misdeeds of Jews and Gentiles. The church at prayer recalls this surprise because it faces hardships and threats and must continue to believe in the sovereignty of God in spite of all outward appearances and dangers which the community experiences.

The threat to the community in the present has its antecedent in Christ's passion, which in turn was anticipated in Psalm 2. The inclusion of Israel among the Messiah's opponents alludes to a theme of Peter's prior speech, namely, that those who refuse to listen to the Messiah-servant of God shall be rooted out from God's people (3:23). The prophet like Moses and servant-Messiah became the suffering servant because of the unholy alliance of Gentiles and Jews and their rulers against him. But nowhere did Luke indicate that the suffering servant made atonement for sins or that Christ gave his life as ransom for many (Mark 10:45 is omitted in Luke).

With the interpretation of Ps. 2:1-2 completed, the prayer turns
to petitions (vv. 29-30). **And now, Lord, look upon their threats,
and grant to thy servants . . . boldness** in their proclamation. The
community does not ask for deliverance from perils but for courage
to meet them. Because the community is in the world, it will experience the pressures of the world even as Jesus experienced them.
But because the community is not "of" the world, it will receive
God's continued sustaining power and it is for this that the community prays. Moreover, petition is made that bold proclamation
be supported by miracles. Healing miracles, **signs and wonders** are
done by God's **hand,** that is, by God himself, **through the name of
thy holy servant Jesus** (cf. 3:6, 16; 4:7, 10). The earthly mediators
through whom miracles are done need not even be mentioned. This
prayer makes it clear that miracles are subordinate to boldness of
proclamation. Miracles have a supportive undergirding function and
show God's approval of the apostolic witness. They are the signs that
Christ's name is present and powerful in the church but, as such,
they are perceived only by faith. Miracles in Luke-Acts are not calls
to faith. Their purpose is not the conversion of Jews and Gentiles
(except in Acts 9:35, 42). Rather, they are occasions for preaching
and expressions of the continuity of salvation history.

The effect of the prayer was threefold. The **place** of prayer **was
shaken,** indicating that God himself was present (cf. Exod. 19:18;
Isa. 6:4). God has looked upon the threats of the enemies of the
community and grants the request of his people. Second, the people
were all filled with the Holy Spirit. While the Spirit had been
received by all believers at Pentecost, God grants additional inspiration when and where it pleases him especially in answer to prayer
and special needs (cf. Luke 11:13; 12:12). Finally, **all** continued to
speak **the word of God with boldness** in spite of the Sanhedrin's
prohibition.

The Life of the Community and Threats from Within and Without (4:32—5:42)

Two summary statements (4:32-35; 5:12-16) serve as brackets
within which two contrasting actions by members of the community
are narrated. A threat to the community's integrity arises from within
(5:1-11). New and subtler internal threats will appear in subsequent

sections of Acts (cf. 6:1; 8:14; 9:26). The two summary statements also provide links with the preceding narrative and introduce the following stories.

The second summary statement (5:12-16) shows the external effects of the apostles on people outside of the community. While the people held them in high esteem (5:13), their leaders proceeded to broaden and intensify their threats against all apostles. The Sanhedrin was no longer merely "annoyed" (4:2) but had now become enraged and was ready to kill them (5:33). But the Pharisee Gamaliel advised caution, advice which was promptly ignored, as the apostles were beaten and threatened. They in turn continued to disobey the Sanhedrin and "did not cease teaching and preaching Jesus as the Christ." Thus ends this section of heightened threats and dangers arising from within and from without.

The Life of the Apostolic Community (4:32-35)

The structure of this summary statement is *a b a;* *(a)* the community of goods (v. 32); *(b)* the power of the apostolic proclamation (v. 33); *(a)* the community of goods under the authority of the apostles (vv. 34-35). This summary statement connects with the previous verse (31) by continuing the description of the community's life in the imperfect tense and by taking up again the theme of proclamation in v. 33. The Spirit that marks the vertical dimension of the community's existence and its source of power manifests itself first of all in bold, powerful proclamation of the Word of God (vv. 31c and 33). Second, the Spirit manifests itself in a new horizontal dimension. A new relationship to one's own possessions and a new relationship to sisters and brothers in the community are the marks of **the company of those who believed.** Spirituality dare not be divorced from social responsibility, and the apostles as the true leaders of the people of God see to it that the members are of **one heart and soul** through social solidarity, the sharing of possessions. The people of God do not use their property selfishly, but for the common good. Owners voluntarily (cf. 5:4) waive their rights to personal property—which is not necessarily identical with the abolition of private possessions as found in v. 34. There all **lands or houses** were **sold** by **as many as** possessed any, and the proceeds of the sale were brought to the apostles for distribution. Verse 34 presents an unrealistic idealized picture. If all houses had been sold, then the community could not have met in the homes of its members, as in fact they did (cf. 2:46; 12:12). Yet with this idealized picture, Luke challenged his readers to look at their own possessions in a new way and to see to it that there be **not a needy person among them** in their community. To believe in God is inseparable from caring for and sharing with the members of the people of God. Thus, the community fulfills the twofold commandment of Luke 10:27-28 as well as the promise of Deut. 15:4, "that there shall be no needy person among you." It also fulfills the Greek ideal of friendship according to which friends are of one soul and have all things in common.

33—This is the center of the summary statement. The apostles gave powerful **testimony to the resurrection of the Lord Jesus** even as the community expressed the power of that witness through a new life-style of oneness in sharing possessions, thereby becoming a manifestation of the Spirit. Though all members of the community are empowered to preach the Word of God (v. 31; cf. 8:4), the apostles represent the testimony which is normative for the community and for preaching by its members. Moreover, the apostles administered the community's funds and presided over the distribution **to each as any had need** (v. 35). **Great grace was upon them all** (v. 33). **All** should not be limited to the apostles but includes the community and its members because the following Greek conjunction (omitted in the RSV) gives the reason why God's grace was on **all**. "For" **there was not a needy person among them** (v. 34). This certainly refers not just to the apostles but to the whole community of believers.

Historically, it would be false to speak of an early Christian communism of love, because such a thing never existed either in fact or in Luke's narrative. Any form of communism can work only if it organizes production. Luke merely speaks of the sale of possessions for the common good, but not of the organization of production. His idealized picture, however, is not without basis in history. To be sure, there is some tension between the summaries of 2:44 and 4:32, 34, which on the one hand indicate a general practice upheld by all members, and the individual traditions about Barnabas and Ananias on the other which refer to a voluntary practice. Yet the voluntary practice of these two individuals was apparently not exceptional. Historically, the community of Jerusalem not only expected the imminent parousia, an expectation which would relativize the importance of material possessions, but this community also contained Galilean disciples in its midst. They had given up their possessions and jobs as fishermen, farmers, and peasants and had come to the city where they could not continue their former work. Therefore, the presence of the Galilean disciples constituted a rationale for sharing possessions. Finally, the warnings about riches and the teaching concerning discipleship which from the beginning were part of the Jesus tradition also played a role in the development of the community of goods in Jerusalem. Historically, this development apparently ended in failure. At any rate, it did not become the normative practice of the church outside of Jerusalem, as Acts clearly shows. Difficulties arose rather early according to Luke's story (cf. 5:1-11; 6:1-2; 11:28). Paul's great collection among the Gentile Christians was meant to aid "the poor" (Gal. 2:10), that is, "the poor among the saints at Jerusalem" (Rom. 15:25-26; cf. 1 Cor. 16:1-4; 2 Cor. 9:12). But the historical practice of sharing possessions at the church's beginning as well as Luke's idealized picture put all modern churches and their members on the spot and asks, What is our attitude toward our possessions and toward sharing with the needy? Is our church merely society on Sunday, or God's eschatological alternative to the society around us?

Barnabas's Action as Example of Sharing (4:36-37)

Barnabas's deed is singled out not because it was the exception, but because he will play an important role later on in Acts (cf. 9:27; 11:22-30; 13:1—15:36). His name originally was **Joseph,** but the apostles had given him a new name, **Barnabas.** Luke's etymology, **Son of encouragement,** is certainly not correct but would fit Manaen, or Menachen. Could it be that Barnabas originally meant "son of prophecy" and that Luke confused the etymology of Barnabas's name with that of Manaen, because both Barnabas and Manaen were Antiochian prophets (13:1)? Be that as it may, the former Levite Joseph may have given encouragement to priests to join the community (cf. 6:7). In Luke's story, Barnabas gave encouragement to the church in Antioch (11:23). He was either born in Cyprus or else his family had come from there and settled in Jerusalem. Levites were not supposed to own land in the Holy Land (cf. Deut. 10:9) and therefore it has been suggested that the **field which belonged to him** was in Cyprus. This is possible, but it is equally possible that the particular law was no longer in force and that the field was in the surroundings of Jerusalem. After selling it Barnabas brought the money and laid it **at the apostles' feet.** This strange expression indicates that the apostles controlled the community and its funds. Barnabas's generosity was a positive example of what all believers did, according to Luke's narrative.

A Negative Example: The Threat of Hypocrisy within the Community (5:1-11)

This story strikes us as being rather odd and we might begin by reminding ourselves that we should avoid psychologizing and rationalizing when we seek to understand it. For instance, we should not argue that the couple merely died of shock at having been found out, nor that the story explains the occurrence of the first deaths in a community which still expected the imminent end. Nor was it a case of death by heart failure resulting from the superstitious beliefs of a primitive society that holds that God punishes offenders who transgress religious taboos. Nor should one ask why Peter did not help the couple to repent of their relatively small deceit. Did he not remember that he himself had denied his Lord? How could he pronounce what amounts to a death sentence on a poor widow who had just lost her husband and doesn't even know it yet? Certainly this story is not an example of pastoral care and counseling either then or now.

We should rather inquire into the theological meaning of this chilling story. What is the nature of God and of the Spirit that is expressed in this picture? What is the nature of the community and of the apostles? What is the nature of the sin of this couple that had such disastrous consequences? Does Luke suggest with this picture that the church should be free from every form of sin? Are there similar stories in Acts?

To begin with the last question, we indeed find similar stories in Luke-Acts. In the case of Judas we read that "Satan entered" into his heart (Luke 22:3). Likewise "Satan filled" Ananias's heart (Acts

5:3). At the same time both Judas and Ananias acted by personal choice; their decision was their own. Moreover, in both cases property unjustly gained or deceitfully retained was involved and both men died a sudden and ugly death (Acts 1:18-19; 5:5). Another similar story is the episode with Simon the magician which involved money as well as the Holy Spirit and a stern announcement of judgment by Peter (see comments on 8:14-24). One could also refer to Luke's version of the blasphemy against the Holy Spirit which will not be forgiven (Luke 12:10). The rejection of the apostolic word after Easter is final and cannot be forgiven (Acts 7:51; 13:40-41, 46; 28:25-27). Lastly, there are punishment miracles in Acts 13:8-11; 19:13-17; and 12:20-23 (see comments there). None of these parallels is without significant differences from Acts 5. The same is true of Old Testament analogies, e.g., Josh. 7:1, 19-26. There the same verb is used as in Acts 5:3 (cf. LXX Josh. 7:1). Ananias, like Achan, "kept back" what belongs to God and while Achan was stoned, Ananias dropped dead.

Now to the story itself. **Ananias** and **Sapphira,** his wife, sold a **piece of property, . . . kept back some of the proceeds** from the sale for their own use, and brought only a part of it to the apostles, thus intentionally trying to deceive them. The couple would have had their needs taken care of by the community and simultaneously retained money for their own use. The Spirit-filled Peter as spokesman for the apostles functioned as a prophet who recognized deceit when he met it. Three rhetorical questions followed by a statement interpret the situation theologically. (1) **Satan** had **filled** Ananias's **heart** so that he would **lie to the Holy Spirit** by keeping back part of the proceeds from the sale of the land for his own use. While the community was filled with the Holy Spirit (4:31), Ananias was filled with Satan. As in the story of the temptation of Jesus, so here the power of Satan represented in Ananias and the power of the Holy Spirit represented in Peter are engaged in a struggle (Luke 4:1-13). Since Pentecost the Holy Spirit is at work in and through the community and its leaders. Therefore a lie to Peter is a lie to the Holy Spirit and thus to God (cf. v. 4 and v. 9). This lie is all the worse because the use of possessions was a primary effect of the Spirit within the community. (2) Peter made it clear that the surrender of possessions for common use constituted a voluntary decision (v. 4), even though it was the general practice (4:34-35). While your property **remained unsold,** Peter asked, **did it not remain your own? And after it was sold** were not the proceeds from the sale **at your disposal** (v. 4)? We can see here a difference from the time of Jesus when, according to Luke, the total renunciation of all possessions was an absolute requirement for becoming a disciple who followed Jesus (cf. Luke 12:33; 14:33; 18:22, 28). Now, however, at the beginning of the time of the church the surrender of one's property is understood to be a voluntary action. Why this difference in Luke's narrative? Because he was aware that the situation had changed. The community is no longer an itinerant group wandering through Galilee, but is now settled in a city. It must take care of its members. A new situation has arisen which demands a new response. Later on Paul and Barnabas will travel by land and sea, and traveling cost money then as now. Paul will work with his own hands to pay for his and his companion's necessities. The new mission situation made the community of goods obsolete. However, what remains constant and never becomes obsolete is the relationship between spirituality and the use of material possessions. (3) Peter asked, **How** (or "why") **is it that you have contrived this deed in your heart?** Satan's entry into Ananias's **heart** was not a tragic fate which he could not escape, nor was it an excuse for his fraud. His deed resulted from his own decision **in** his **heart.** Peter declared categorically, **You have not lied to men but to God** (v. 4c; **to the Holy Spirit,** v. 3; cf. v. 9). When Ananias **heard these words** of truth and judgment **he fell down and died.**

Luke's story about Ananias and Sapphira is a solemn warning that church membership is no guarantee of salvation. On the contrary, . . . "it shall be more tolerable in the judgment for Tyre and Sidon than for you" (Luke 10:14). Our story is a judgment scene before the judgment to come and as such it is a summons telling us not to trifle with God and his Holy Spirit. The people of God are the realm and instrument of the Holy Spirit who is opposed to religious phoniness and hypocrisy. Ananias's hypocrisy was shared by his wife, who had the opportunity of speaking the truth, but chose to lie. Peter's prediction of her immediate death was forthwith fulfilled. His prediction is not a curse, but an effective judgment. Small wonder that **great fear came** not only upon **the whole church** in Jerusalem, but also on outsiders (v. 11).

121

The word *ekklesia,* church, appears for the first time in Acts (v. 11). Other terms used for the community are "the brothers" (1:15), "disciples" (9:1,10), "the believers" (4:32), "the saints" (9:32) and the "Christians" (11:26). In secular Greek, *ekklesia* can mean the assembly of citizens (so in 19:32,39). In the LXX the word is used for the assembly of the people of God. In Acts the church is always the local or regional church, with one exception where it means the church universal (20:28). When Paul was revisiting and strengthening "the churches" (plural) of the first missionary journey, then the word refers to local communities in which the people of God are gathered (16:5).

Was Luke suggesting with this story that the church is and must be free from every form of sin and imperfection? He knew of complaining in the Jerusalem church, of the neglect of widows in daily distributions (6:1), of cantankerous "believers" (15:5), of disputes (15:7), of brothers who act without authorization and unsettle the minds of fellow Christians (15:7,24), of a blowup between two leaders over a minor matter and their subsequent separation (15:39) and of unfounded slander circulating in conservative Christian circles against Paul (21:20-21). In short, the church is in need of forgiveness for real sins and therefore the church continues to pray "forgive us our sins. . ." (Luke 11:4). Deceit and hypocrisy unforgiven will be purged from the people of God in the final judgment even as the deceitful couple already was purged from the church prior to the end. With this episode Luke impressed on his readers that the real threat to the church's existence lies in the church itself, in the lies, betrayals, deceits, and hypocrisies of its members. Their apostasy from God is frequently connected with their greed for material things. The opponents of God are not just outside of the church, but are found also within it. Peter had spoken about the final judgment on unbelieving Jews who shall be "purged from the people" (3:23). The reports of the deaths of Judas, Ananias, and Sapphira tell of three final judgments on disciples before the end in order to warn the reader that God is not mocked (Gal. 6:7); he is not a heavenly grandfather who lets sleeping dogs lie and cares nothing about unforgiven deceit. Just as miracle stories are signs of the salvation that is yet to come, so the story of Ananias and Sapphira is a solemn warning of the future judgment on unforgiven sins within the people of God.

The Effect of the Apostles on the People (5:12-16)

This third and final summary statement on the church of Jerusalem (cf. 2:42-47; 4:32-35) has a rather loose structure which prompted some interpreters to transpose verses, or see the hand of a post-Lukan redactor at work making additions, or to postulate the presence of a pre-Lukan tradition. Indeed, there are some difficulties with the flow of the text. It is not clear whether **they** and **them** and **all** in vv. 12c and 13 should be limited to apostles or whether they also include the community. In other words, is Luke telling us that all 5000 members of the community (cf. 4:4) **were all together in Solomon's Portico?** If so, he had a totally wrong view of the dimensions of that portico. It is more probable that he referred to the apostles and groups of members representing the whole community who gathered together there. Moreover, the conjunction **so that** in v. 15 is awkward because it now seems that the **multitudes** of believers **carried the sick into the streets.** What Luke probably meant to say was that this was done by the people outside of the church. Finally, to whom does **the rest** in v. 13 refer? They are distinct from **all** who were together in Solomon's Portico (v. 12c). In Luke 8:10 Luke had introduced the same Greek word, translated here with **the rest** (Greek, *hoi loipoi*) into a text taken from Mark. Therefore, **the rest** means outsiders, people who have not become members of the messianic people of God around the apostles.

What did Luke wish to accomplish with this summary? First, he was able to generalize concrete individual scenes and broaden the scope of his narrative. "All" the sick were healed; "many" miracles occurred; "multitudes" became believers in Christ. The space is extended from the Portico of Solomon to the streets of Jerusalem and to the towns in the surrounding region. Different groups of people appear: the apostles and the towering figure of Peter; the Christians who are united, standing "together"; Jews who are afraid to join them but hold them in high esteem; multitudes of new believers; multitudes of sick people from inside and outside Jerusalem who are brought by people expecting healing from Peter.

Second, this summary serves as transition between two rather different traditions—the judgment on Ananias and Sapphira on the one side and the arrest of the apostles on the other. The summary states the reason which provoked the **jealousy** of the Sadducees (v.

17), which lay in the church's phenomenal growth and the high esteem of the apostles by the people. Thus, the summary prepares for the reappearance of the division between the people and their leaders (5:26; cf. 4:21).

Third, the summary connects with prior material. The prayer of the church for "signs and wonders" (4:30) found fulfillment in **the many signs and wonders** of the apostles. The awe of the people (v. 13) is also the result of the judgment on Ananias and Sapphira which became known (v. 11b).

Fourth, in distinction from the prior summary (4:32-35) which looked inward at the internal life of the community, Luke's new summary looks outward at the public effect of the apostles on the Jewish people. We hear the reasons why the leaders of the church are held in high esteem by the people. The people were filled with awe, impressed by the miracles of the apostles and by the judgment on the couple, and held the apostles in high esteem.

Finally, Luke placed his statement about the church's phenomenal growth at a strategic position in this summary (v. 14). He referred to the church's growth not after v. 16—not after he told about the success of Peter's miracles—but before. He did so for theological reasons. The church's growth, in Luke's opinion, was not the result of miracles. Faith arises through the proclamation of the Word of God, not through miracles (exception: 9:35,42). Miracles are benefactions to the world, but not means of conversion. As benefactions they may be first steps toward faith in that they aid people to listen to the testimony concerning Jesus. But then they need not have that effect (cf. 4:14,21). Only to faith do miracles become signs for the future salvation free from sickness and suffering. For faith they are signs that the Spirit of God is effective through the witnesses of Christ in the present.

12-13—Miracles were done by the hands of the apostles, not just by Peter, for the church is apostolic and not a Petrine sect, even though Peter had preeminence among them. Not just Peter, but all of the apostles will be arrested in the following episode. **By the hands of** imitates Old Testament style and means the same as "through." Apostles and church members were **all together** in **Solomon's Portico** of the temple for prayer and teaching. Their togetherness reflected the overcoming of the internal threat (5:1-11). Outsiders did not dare to associate with them, not because of enmity, but because of awe lest the same judgment befall them that had fallen on Ananias and Sapphira. Simultaneously, the apostolic miracles as well as the nature of the Christian community showed their effect in that **the people held them in high honor.** The community appeared as a closed awe-inspiring group that everyone liked, but no one **dared** to **join,** unless God himself opened the door.

14—And God did just that. **More than ever believers were added,** that is, God added new multitudes **to the Lord** of the church, Jesus Christ.

15-16—The high esteem in which the miracle-working apostles were held prompted people to carry **the sick into the streets** so that at least Peter's **shadow might fall on some of them** as he walked by. These people, like others in antiquity, believed that a miracle worker's **shadow** had healing powers. "Fall on" is the same Greek verb as "overshadow" (Luke 1:35; 9:34) and it refers to the life-giving presence of God. Whether it is a **shadow** or "aprons" or "handkerchiefs" (19:12), or "the fringes of garments" (Mark 6:56), or "spittle" (Mark 8:23), or the touch of fingers (Mark 7:33), or the grasp of the hand (Luke 4:40), in all these instances the miracle is God's work of healing through human instruments. As in the days of Jesus, so at the time of the apostles mass healings were performed, according to Luke (Luke 4:40; 6:17-19). Even **from the towns around Jerusalem** the sick were brought **and they were all healed.** The news was already spilling into the region beyond Jerusalem. The church not only has a life of its own as sketched in the previous summary (4:32-35) but it must be God's agent of benefaction to the world in distress and in need of healing. In its outreach as benefactor to the world, the church identifies with the sick and those who cannot help themselves, not in order to convert them, but in order to help them. It may well be that the healed also become able to listen to the word of life.

Arrest of the Apostles (5:17-42)

The defiance of the Sanhedrin's prohibition to preach in public together with the tremendous growth of the church led to the arrest of all the apostles who, after an angelically engineered prison escape, preached again in the temple (vv. 17-21). A subplot describes the surprise and embarrassment of the council (vv. 21b-26). Apprehended and brought before the Sanhedrin, Peter witnessed to Christ's resurrection and to the opportunity for repentance and forgiveness (vv. 27-32). In a second subplot the Pharisee Gamaliel counsels caution to an enraged Sanhedrin (vv. 33-39). The conclusion of the narrative gives the verdict of the council, which consists in beating the apostles and in a renewed prohibition to preach. The verdict is followed by the reaction of the apostles and their continued defiance of the prohibition (vv. 40-42). The similarities to the prior arrest have already been pointed out. The differences between the two narratives bring out the heightened intensity of the confrontation.

17-21 (Arrest and escape)—The popularity of the apostles among the people and the church's growth filled the **high priest** and his **party of Sadducees** with **jealousy.** In distinction from Pharisees, some of whom even became Christians (15:5), the Sadducees were and remained the sworn enemies of the church not just because of the resurrection message, but because they represented the establishment intent on preserving the status quo. They proceeded to arrest all the apostles, but **at night an angel of the Lord** (cf. Luke 1:11; 2:9; Acts 8:26; 12:7; 27:23) miraculously rescued them from prison, not for the sake of their personal well-being but for the sake of their task. Their rescue concerned their mandate to witness. The apostles were commanded by the angel to preach **in the temple . . . the words of this Life.** This is ironic because Sadducees held that angels do not exist (23:8), and the **temple** which the Sadducees believed to be their very own preserve becomes the place assigned by God for the proclamation of life and salvation (cf. 13:26). Thereby the temple fulfills its true function as the house in which the Word of God is heard.

Stories about miraculous prison escapes can also be found in the literature of antiquity. For Luke such stories exemplify the hearing of the community's prayer, God's intervention and protection of his servants on earth if he so wills, and the gospel's proclamation as a mandate from God (cf. v. 39). His word cannot be stopped by the imprisonment of preachers, then or now.

21b-26 (Surprise and embarrassment for the council)—While the reader knows what is going on, the council is unaware of it. Luke used this device several times (e.g., 5:7; 14:11-13) and he introduced subtle humor into this story. We now hear that the prison is **securely locked,** presumably by the angel himself. It is typical of Luke that he does not tell everything at once but in stages (cf. 3:2 with 4:22). Hearing that the prison was found locked, but empty inside, the authorities had every reason for being **perplexed . . . wondering**

what this would come to. At last they were told that their former prisoners were **standing in the temple and teaching the people,** doing precisely that for which they had already been arrested once before. A new arrest is made with caution, without violence, because the people were on the side of the apostles and the arresting officers were afraid of violent reactions by the people if they were to manhandle the apostles.

Luke designated the meeting which the high priest called by the terms **the council and all the senate** (v. 21). This would be historically correct only if we were to translate: "The council, namely, all the senate." But if Luke had meant only one body he would have expressed himself differently. His Greek readers certainly would think of two bodies, holding a joint meeting, analogous to the structure of the government in Rome. In short, it is probable that just as Luke did not understand Aramaic (cf. 4:36) so he had no clear picture of the government in Jerusalem.

27-32 (Peter's witness)—The high priest made two accusations: (1) Recalling the prohibition of teaching **in this name** he charged the apostles with disobedience in filling **Jerusalem with your teaching.** (2) He accused them of bringing **this man's blood** upon the authorities, that is, of seeking revenge for Jesus' death, either from the people or from God. The reader knows that the people were ready to stone the Sanhedrin's police (v. 26) and the Sanhedrin knows that God is an avenger of blood spilled innocently (cf. Judg. 9:24, LXX). By claiming that Jesus was the Messiah whose innocent death God had vindicated, the apostles appeared to be calling for God's judgment to fall down upon the heads of all responsible for that death.

The reply to the accusations is made by **Peter and the apostles.** Luke suggests that their reply was unanimous, not that they spoke in chorus. Peter, their spokesman, first addressed the charge of disobedience by agreeing with it and rejecting it bluntly: **We must obey God rather than men** (cf. 4:19-20). The lines are now drawn as sharply as possible. By prohibiting the apostles from preaching the Sanhedrin is in fact "opposing God" (cf. v. 39), whom the apostles obey. Concerning the second charge Peter speaks of **the God of our fathers** (cf. 3:13) who is the common ground between the apostles and the Jewish leaders. He **raised Jesus** from the dead **whom you killed;** this is the basic Lukan Christological pattern in speeches to

127

Jews of Jerusalem (cf. 2:23-24,36; 3:13-15; 4:10). Clearly, Peter's statement implies the accusation that knowingly or in ignorance (cf. 3:17) the authorities had indeed committed murder. However, Jesus' exaltation at God's **right hand** does not mean that the **blood** of Jesus now comes on the Sanhedrin in swift divine retribution. On the contrary, it means that also they are given the opportunity for repentance and forgiveness of sins. The exalted Jesus is Israel's **leader** (prince-Messiah; cf. 3:15) **and** Israel's **Savior.** The title *savior* is always related to Israel in Luke-Acts (cf. Luke 2:11; Acts 13:23). Through him **repentance and forgiveness of sins** are granted now to the very people responsible for **hanging him on a tree** (Deut. 21:22-23; cf. Acts 10:39; Gal. 3:13; 1 Peter 2:24). Through the apostolic proclamation God offers a second chance to Jerusalem and its leaders. If the opportunity is accepted, then repentance and forgiveness are received as God's gift mediated by the **Savior.** Peter's sermon concludes with their function as **witnesses.** The apostles are witnesses to Jesus' resurrection and exaltation (cf. 1:3,9), and **so is the Holy Spirit.** He bears witness to the exalted Christ through healings in his name (cf. 4:30). The Holy Spirit testifies to Christ through miracles and through the witness of the Spirit-filled disciples. Those who **obey** God receive the Holy Spirit as a gift from him now. Peter's closing statement links up with his opening sentence. We must **obey** God rather than men.

33-39 (Gamaliel's advice)—Peter's call to repentance did not meet an obedient response from the Sanhedrin. On the contrary, its members were no longer merely "annoyed" (4:2) but now became **enraged and wanted to kill them.** While multitudes of "the people" had become obedient to the faith, their leaders are becoming ever more hardened in their opposition. The issue of the true leadership of the true people of God comes again to the fore. The powerless but obedient disciples faced an enraged establishment ready **to kill** them. Judaism, however, is better than that and Luke knows it. The Pharisees were conspicuous by their absence in Luke's passion narrative (also in Mark's) and in Acts they make their first appearance at this point. **Gamaliel** intervened and requested the apostles to leave the council chamber. He was Gamaliel I, the elder, a grandson of the famous Rabbi Hillel, who founded a rabbinic school. Gamaliel was indeed **held in honor by all people** because he was the first to bear the honorific title "Rabban" which means "our master," instead of the conventional "rabbi." His appearance in Luke's narrative comes without preparation. His prestige calmed the hysteria of the council. As a member of the moderate school of Hillel, in contrast to the more rigorous school of Shammai, Gamaliel advised the council to use restraint and caution vis-à-vis **these men,** as he called the apostles in order to show his own neutrality. He then proceeded to narrate two historical examples to undergird his moderate approach. A certain revolutionary called **Theudas** who gave **himself out to be somebody . . . was slain** after he had raised a following of about 400 people. Once he was dead his movement **came to nothing.** Likewise, **after him Judas the Galilean arose in the days of the census** and organized the anti-Roman Zealot movement; when **he perished** his followers **were scattered** and the movement ended in failure. The implication is that if Jesus is dead then his cause will end sooner or later. Therefore, Gamaliel concluded, **Keep away from these men and let them alone,** that is, set them free and do not kill them. If this Christian movement **is of men it will fail,** like the enterprises of the former revolutionaries. However (note the change to indicative mood in Greek), **if it is of God,** no one can stop it and **you might even be found opposing God!** (Greek, *theomachoi*) whom you should love with your whole heart (Deut. 6:5) but never oppose. This was good advice, partially accepted by the council, since they did not kill the apostles. At the same time it was not fully accepted because instead of **keeping away from** the apostles and leaving them alone they had the apostles beaten. Gamaliel's student Paul did not follow his teacher's path of moderation either (22:4; 26:9-11)!

For Luke, Gamaliel's advice constitutes a welcome intervention, on the one hand, and an insufficient response, on the other. As **a teacher of the law** his advice saved the apostles from a fate worse than beating and leaves open the dialog between believers in Christ and the Pharisees. Simultaneously, his advice to wait and see misses the opportunity for repentance and faith. Gamaliel articulated for the reader the insight that the Christian movement is from God and therefore cannot be overthrown, whereas the Sadducean leaders were opposing God.

We should note at least briefly several historical difficulties which the two examples raise (vv. 36-37). First, according to Josephus (*Ant.* 20.97) **Theudas,** who called himself a prophet and promised to repeat Joshua's miracle of parting the Jordan River, was decapitated during the period when Fadus was procurator of Judea (A.D. 44–

46). Thus, the Theudas incident took place about a decade after the Lukan date of Gamaliel's speech. The conclusion is inevitable that Gamaliel did not hold this speech in this form and that Luke misplaced the Theudas incident. Second, according to v. 37 **Judas the Galilean** came **after** Theudas. Historically this is incorrect. The revolt of Judas took place in A.D. 6 or 7, almost 40 years prior to Theudas' venture. One could escape these anachronisms only by arguing that there must have been another Theudas who rebelled prior to Judas. This is possible, but extremely unlikely because Josephus is well informed about the period of Herod and the following decades. Third, **Judas's** uprising is correctly placed in the time of the census (v. 37). For Lukan readers this census can only refer to the one when Quirinius was governor of Syria (Luke 2:1-3). Indeed, the Zealot movement made its appearance at that time, but it did not come to an end with the death of Judas. It continued throughout the following decades until it engulfed the nation in the war against Rome in A.D. 66. At the time of Luke's writing, however, some decades after that war the Zealots had become thoroughly discredited and Luke's reference to Judas becomes understandable.

40-42 (Conclusion)—Instead of following Gamaliel's advice to **let them alone** (v. 38) the apostles were beaten and charged again **not to speak in the name of Jesus.** The beating probably consisted of "forty lashes less one" (Deut. 25:3; 2 Cor. 11:24) and served as a punishment and warning not to transgress the prohibition against teaching again. Then they **let them go.** In spite of pain experienced they left, **rejoicing that they were counted worthy to suffer dishonor for the name.** The theme of joy and suffering is known also in Judaism (cf. 2 Macc. 6:30). Luke connected this scene with the person of Jesus and his beatitude (Luke 6:22-23; cf. Phil. 1:29; 1 Peter 4:13). Jesus' passion is continued in the suffering of his servants. Moreover, the prohibition imposed on them is boldly rejected. **They did not cease teaching and preaching Jesus as the Christ** both publicly **in the temple** and privately **at home.** Their ministry of preaching was a public confession. Jesus can be confessed as the Christ only when one is ready to suffer for it. The first large section of Acts which began at Pentecost ends on a triumphant note. In spite of opposition, prohibition, and beatings, the witness continues in Jerusalem according to Christ's mandate (1:8; 5:28).

■ The Hellenists, Stephen's Witness, and Martyrdom (6:1—8:3)

In this central section of the first part of Acts we again hear of internal as well as external threats—just as in the previous section. The solution to the internal threat as well as endurance in persecution contributed to the church's growth. The witness in Jerusalem had resulted in a divided response. On the one hand, the church grew and it continues to grow also in this section (6:1, 7). On the other hand, an ever-growing opposition ranging from sneering at Pentecost to threats, prohibitions, and beatings reached its culmination in Stephen's martyrdom and in a general persecution of the church. In the previous section "the people" had been inclined positively toward the apostles (cf. 2:47; 4:21; 5:13, 16, 26) in contrast to their leaders. Now, however, "the people" were "stirred up" and aligned themselves with their leaders, turning into a murderous mob (6:12; 7:54, 57-58). At Stephen's martyrdom Saul made his first appearance. Thereby Luke tied this section to the next one. The general persecution which followed Stephen's death did not signal the end of the church, but became the cause for the extension of the gospel into Samaria, thereby confirming Gamaliel's statement that the opponents of the apostles would not be able to stop the Christian movement "if it is of God" (5:39). In a variety of ways this central section links up with the preceding one and serves as transition to the following narrative. But it also has its own integrity. Its focus lies in Stephen's speech, the longest speech in Acts. Through it Luke disclosed that salvation history is also a history of failure to respond to "the God of glory." Opposition to Christ and opposition to the Christian witness are but the continuation and climax of the opposition to God since the time of Moses.

The Appointment of the Seven (6:1-7)

This unit is bracketed by two notices about the community's growth (vv. 1 and 7). **In these days** when the community had just experienced threats from within and from without (4:32—5:42), a new internal problem arose which resulted from the growth of the community (vv. 1-2). **The widows** of the **Hellenists** were **neglected in the daily distribution** and the ministry of **preaching the word** was overburdened. The brackets surrounding this story show that in spite of the threats the apostles had just experienced and in spite of new internal tensions the growth of the community could not be hindered because "this plan or this undertaking" is "of God" (5:38-39). Within the brackets we hear of a threat to the solidarity of the community and of its solution. A proposal for electing auxiliary leaders with specific qualifications is made by the apostles (vv. 3-4) and accepted by the community (vv. 5-6). The solution to the problem lay in a division of labor which aided the further growth of the community (v. 7). This story presents the harmonious interaction between apostles and the community in solving an internal problem. In telling it Luke followed an Old Testament pattern for narrating the appointment of auxiliary leaders (problem: Exod. 18:14-18; Acts 6:1-2; proposal for additional subordinate leaders and their qualifications: Exod. 18:19-23; Acts 6:3-4; their appointment: Exod. 18:24-25; Acts 6:5-6). Luke also introduced the names of Stephen and Philip, who will carry the narrative of Acts further, and he suggested the institution of the new ecclesiastical office of deacon.

The word **Hellenists** in Acts 6 designates Jews whose native language was Greek. In v. 1 these Hellenists are **disciples,** Christians. Historically, it would seem probable that two Christian communities existed in Jerusalem side by side; one Aramaic-speaking under the Twelve, another Greek-speaking under the Seven. Luke presented a different picture, namely, one community with two language groups within it and the Seven as persons who served at tables. Greek-speaking Jews had settled in Jerusalem and organized themselves in Greek-speaking synagogues. Some of these Hellenists became ardent believers and others, as we shall see, became fierce opponents (6:9).

A new internal problem resulting from the church's rapid growth caused tensions within the community in Luke's story and endangered the ministry of the Word. The social solidarity which had already been threatened by Ananias's and Sapphira's betrayal is now subject to quarrels. The Christian Hellenists **murmured against the Hebrews,** that is, against their Aramaic-speaking sisters and brothers because the **widows** of the Hellenists **were neglected in the daily distribution.** The widows of Hellenists were more vulnerable because they had moved from the diaspora to Jerusalem and were without extended families who could support them. The apostles were in charge of the community's funds and therefore exercised general supervision over the daily distributions. Some breakdown occurred in this area and the harmony of the community was subjected to stress. Luke did not tell us exactly what happened, but he presupposed that the responsibilities for the social welfare of fellow believers could not be surrendered by the church to authorities outside of it.

The **twelve** took the initiative and summoned the **body of the disciples,** submitting a proposal to them for additional leaders and for a division of labor. New situations demand new forms of ministry. In the formulation of the problem and the proposed solution, the apostolic **preaching** of **the word** forms a bracket around the ministry of serving at **tables** for which **seven men** should be elected by the community and appointed by the apostles to this duty, or office. The names of the seven are all Greek names. Like the list of the names of the Twelve (1:13) so this list (v. 5) is undoubtedly a pre-Lukan tradition. In this story the Seven are appointed in order to lighten the burden borne by the apostles and in order to represent the concerns of the Hellenists who felt slighted in the church. Though the ministry of the Seven who would be in charge of the daily distribution is subordinated to **the ministry of the word,** nevertheless the qualifications for it do not consist of mere human cleverness, but in the gift of the Holy Spirit, in wisdom and faith. These are prerequisites for any ministry in the church. The Seven were chosen by the community (v. 5) and **set before** the apostles who with prayer and laying on of **hands** appointed them to their office (vv. 3, 6).

Laying on of hands occurs in healings (Luke 4:40; 13:13; Acts 9:12; 28:8), blessings (Mark 10:16), mediating the Holy Spirit (Acts 8:19; 19:6), commissioning to a task (13:3), ordination (1 Tim. 4:14; 2 Tim. 1:6), and here for induction to an office (Acts 6:6). The question whether Luke understood the laying on of hands in 6:6 as ordination requires us to consider that in 13:3 Paul and Barnabas were certainly not ordained, but commissioned for a specific task with the laying on of hands. Moreover, the task of the Seven consisted in charitable service and not in the ministry of the word for which one is ordained (cf. 20:28b; 1 Tim. 4:14; 2 Tim. 1:6). Luke did not use the noun *deacon* for the office of the Seven, but merely suggested that this office which certainly was known to him can be traced back to the activity of the Seven. The laying on of hands in 6:6 should probably not be identified as an ordination, but as a commissioning as in Acts 13:3. However, the table service of the Seven is never depicted in Acts. What Luke told of Stephen and Philip is that they functioned as preachers and evangelists. Therefore, the laying on of hands could also be understood as ordination, that is, as authorization to the ministry of the word as part of their diaconal service. The phrase **ministry of the word** (cf. Luke 1:2) characterizes the apostolic ministry of the church which later will be held by elders (cf. 20:28-32). It is a ministry which serves the word by seeing to it that the Word of God is communicated in power and in continuity with the apostles' teaching as its norm.

7—The concluding summary statement displays the success of the solution to the internal problem. **The word of God increased.** That means it yielded a hundredfold (Luke 8:4-15) and even **many priests** became **obedient to the faith.** They heard the word that calls to faith and held it fast (cf. Luke 8:15). As believing priests, Luke seems to tell us, they shared Stephen's view of the temple.

Arrest of Stephen (6:8—7:1)

A dispute between Stephen and unbelieving Greek-speaking Jews led to accusations against him, to his seizure by the people and their leaders, and to a trial before the Sanhedrin during which false witnesses testified against him.

8—Stephen is portrayed as a dynamic preacher and miracle worker, **full of grace and power** (cf. v. 15) doing **great wonders and signs** (cf. 4:30), just like the apostles. The only other member of the Seven about whom we hear something in Acts, i.e., Philip, also became known as a miracle worker and evangelist-preacher (8:4-13, 26-40). His daughters were recognized as prophets (21:8-9).

9—Stephen's opponents were members of diaspora synagogues in Jerusalem. It is not clear how many Greek-speaking synagogues were involved. Since Luke used the Greek article twice we must assume that at least two, but perhaps more, synagogues took part in the dispute with Stephen. **The synagogue of the Freedmen** to which Jews from Alexandria and Cyrene may also have belonged, could have received its name from former slaves who had been brought to Rome by Pompey in 63 B.C. but were later set free. The other synagogue had members from **Cilicia and Asia.**

10—Challenging Stephen to a public debate they **disputed with him** but **could not withstand the wisdom and the Spirit.** Once again, the promise of Jesus is being fulfilled (Luke 21:15; 12:12). However, his opponents could indeed "resist the Holy Spirit" (7:51) who was seeking to convert them through Stephen.

11-14—Their failure in debate led them to **instigate** defamations against Stephen and to incite a mob action. For the first time **the people** become active in the opposition against the church. In turn, their opposition prepares the way for the future mission to the Gentiles. The defamation **secretly** orchestrated among the people consisted in the accusation, **We have heard him speak blasphemous words against Moses and God.** A similar accusation of blasphemy had been raised against Jesus (Luke 5:21). Anyone who dares to attack the laws of Moses would automatically be thought to attack the God of Israel who was believed to dwell in Jerusalem's temple. The defamation of Stephen was successful. The people and their leaders, the **elders** and **scribes,** brought Stephen by force **before the council. False witnesses** were introduced who testified that Stephen spoke **against this holy place** (cf. 7:7; 21:28), the temple, and **the law.** These two accusations were substantiated by the false witnesses in the following manner: **We have heard him say that this Jesus of Nazareth will destroy this place, and will change the customs** of **Moses.** Note the future tense of the verbs. We must ask at this point, In what sense is their witness false? Had not Jesus prophetically predicted that the temple and its cult would cease in the end-time and that God would bring about a new form of his presence (cf. John 2:18-22)? Had Jesus not prophesied the temple's destruction (cf. Luke 21:5-6)? During Jesus' trial in Mark, false witnesses claimed "we heard him say, 'I will destroy this temple that is made with hands and in three days I will build another, not made with hands' " (Mark 14:58). Luke had omitted this Markan text in his Gospel (cf. Luke 22:66-71) but he introduced the false witnesses here at the trial of Stephen.

According to Luke the Jewish Christians of Jerusalem were faithful to the Law and to the temple. Though Jesus had prophesied the destruction of the temple and of the city of Jerusalem, he had not claimed that he himself would destroy it. Rather, the city sealed its own doom by rejecting him and he wept over it (Luke 19:41-44). The temple in Luke-Acts is the house of Jesus' Father (Luke 2:49), the place where the church gathered for prayer and teaching (Acts 2:46; 3:1, 11; 5:21, 42). It is desecrated not by Jesus and his disciples, but by those who reject both him and the witness concerning him and who then rush off to war which ends in disaster (Luke 21:20-24).

6:15—7:1—Confronted with false accusations, Stephen's **face** shone **like the face of an angel** reflecting "the glory of God" (cf. 7:55; Exod. 34:29-35). The **high priest,** presiding over the council, asked **Is this so?** What have you to say to these two accusations? In contrast to the few words Jesus spoke during his trial, Stephen presented the longest address in Acts.

Luke's narrative thus far raises several historical questions. We may assume that the Twelve and the Seven were traditional designations (cf. 21:8) which referred to the leaders of the Aramaic-speaking and the Greek-speaking Christian communities in Jerusalem. Their linguistic difference implied that they worshiped separately. Luke's text also reveals that tensions developed between them over the support of the Hellenistic widows. Luke downgraded the tension by making the Seven into waiters at table in charge of the daily distribution. However, Luke's tradition contained Stephen's martyrdom—which was not caused by his charitable care of widows, but by his aggressive preaching to Hellenistic Jews. We can also assume that Luke's tradition referred to the expulsion of the Christian Hellenists from Jerusalem, an expulsion which did not include the Aramaic-speaking community. Luke, however, could not tolerate such a distinction and therefore he tells us that the whole church of Jerusalem was scattered, "except the apostles" (8:1). This is historically most improbable. It would be the only persecution from which the church leadership was excluded. The question therefore arises: Who were these Hellenists around the Seven and why did they suffer expulsion when the community under the Twelve could remain in Jerusalem? A multitude of answers has been supplied by scholars. It has been said (1) that the historical Stephen was not a Christian, which is most unlikely; (2) that he and his group should be associated with Matthew's special traditions or with the traditions of "Q," that is, traditions common to Matthew and Luke, but absent from Mark, or with traditions behind John's Gospel; (3) that he, like Paul, taught the abrogation of the law of Moses by Christ; (4) that he had affinities with Paul's opponents in 2 Corinthians; (5) that the letter to the Hebrews should be connected with the Hellenists around Stephen; (6) that Stephen himself was a Samaritan influenced by Samaritan polemics against the temple in Jerusalem and by the Samaritan expectation of a prophet like Moses. None of these hypotheses is satisfactory. Still, the historical question remains: Who were the Hellenists and what prompted their expulsion from Jerusalem? The answers proposed here are also hypothetical. Perhaps these Hellenists took the liberal posture of Jesus toward Sabbath laws and cultic purity more seriously than the community under the Twelve (cf. Mark 2:27; 7:14-15). Perhaps they believed that the parousia of Christ would spell the end of the temple, its cult, and the ceremonial laws of Moses. This expectation would result in relativizing the temple and its cult in the present. A Jewish group in Jerusalem which would advocate views like these could not remain in the city for long. Thus, it may well be that historically more than a kernel of truth lay in the testimony of Luke's "false witnesses."

Stephen's Defense (7:2-53)

This speech is not really an explicit defense against the charges that have just been raised nor does it answer the high priest's question. Instead of a defense speech we hear a summary of Israel's history. When we lift the speech from its present context, the accusations of 6:14 connect well with the reaction of the people in 7:54. Are these indications that Luke incorporated and perhaps expanded a tradition which he had received and which he believed represented Stephen's preaching? The fact that this speech is not the defense of the historical Stephen at his trial can be seen from its content, but the question concerning the presence and extent of a possible pre-Lukan tradition is thereby not answered. Dibelius tried to show that Luke expanded a Jewish summary of Israel's history by adding those verses which underscore Israel's rejection of God's messengers, its disobedience and idolatry (vv. 35, 37, 39-43, 48-53). Luke turned this expanded summary into a speech by Stephen. Another possibility is that Luke combined two traditions, namely, vv. 2-8 with vv. 20-43, 51-53 and that he added vv. 9-19, 44-50. Still other suggestions have been advanced.

The question concerning the origin of a possible pre-Lukan tradition has also received a variety of answers. Some interpreters hold that the pre-Lukan tradition came from Hellenistic Judaism; for others it originated in Hellenistic Jewish Christianity; and still others believe that it was of Samaritan origin. Because Acts 7 as a whole does not reflect Samaritan theology—for instance, the Samaritans did not accept the prophetic writings which are cited in vv. 41-43 and 49-50—therefore the argument was advanced that the present speech is the end product of two prior stages. Stage 1 consisted of a Samaritan document (vv. 2-41, 44-45, 47-48) in which God promised Abraham that his descendants shall worship "in this place" (v. 7), namely, on Mount Gerizim = Mount Ebal (cf. Deut. 27:4, 12-13; Josh. 8:30). Nearby at Shechem the patriarchs were buried (Acts 7:16). In stage 2 the Hellenists or Stephen reworked this Samaritan document by adding not only vv. 42-43, 46, 49-53, but also by attaching a conclusion which is now lost. Stage 3: Luke incorporated this Christianized tradition into Acts, omitting the conclusion about God's judgment over disobedient Israel. Moreover, according to this theory, Luke did not really understand the radical rejection of Jerusalem's temple which the Hellenists around Stephen expressed. It would seem that the more stages one is forced to postulate the less desirable a hypothesis becomes, especially when it can be shown that Acts 7 bears the imprint of Lukan language and thought and that the variant tradition of a burial of the patriarchs at Shechem (7:16) is not present in the Samaritan Pentateuch and can therefore not be used to demonstrate the presence of a Samaritan tradition.

We shall not use a hypothetical pre-Lukan tradition as key for interpreting Stephen's speech, but listen to it as the creative work of Luke who summarized a segment of Old Testament history with several objectives in mind. First, he traced the roots of the church back to God's unconditional promise to Abraham and he showed that particular promises of God were fulfilled already in Israel's history. Second, through Stephen's speech Luke interpreted Jewish opposition against Christ and the message of salvation for his readers. This opposition has its antecedents in Israel's history, in the ignorance, disobedience, and twofold rejection of Moses by the people. Israel's opposition to God's purpose found its climax in the rejection of Christ and of the Holy Spirit working through apostles. Third, Stephen, like Paul in Rome, pronounced a prophetic indictment upon the people of Jerusalem who had heard the Christian message twice and twice rejected it. Hence the speech functions as introduction and demonstration for the indictment of vv. 51-53. Fourth, this speech marks a turn in the story of Acts. The action will move away from Jerusalem without, however, losing a connection with that city. Finally, the speech also disclosed that the two accusations against Stephen were false.

The Structure of the Speech:

God's story with Abraham (vv. 2-8)
God's story with Joseph and the patriarchs (vv. 9-16)
God's story with Moses, told in three parts of 40 years each (vv. 17-29, vv. 30-34, vv. 35-43)
The story of the tent of witness and the temple (vv. 44-50)
The indictment of the Sanhedrin and the people of Jerusalem (vv. 51-53)

Similar historical summaries are found in Deut. 6:20-24; 26:5-9; Josh. 24:2-13; Neh. 9:6-31; Pss. 78; 105; 106; 136; Wis. 10; Sir. 44–50; Jdt. 5:6-18. What distinguishes Stephen's summary from its predecessors is the perspective from which Israel's history is viewed: "As your fathers did, so do you" (Acts 7:51).

Stephen's speech is based primarily on the LXX and it uses the Old Testament in different ways. We find, first, a free rendition of particular incidents. Second, with some exceptions (cf. v. 26) the brief announcements by God or by particular persons are verbatim from the LXX. Occasionally, an announcement combines different Old Testament texts (cf. v. 7 below). Third, in vv. 22, 25, 35-38 we meet a typological use of Scripture. Moses is typologically related to Christ. Fourth, vv. 42-43 and 48-50 cite Old Testament texts using an introductory formula. Fifth, individual words or phrases such as "the God of glory" (Ps. 29:3) and ideas such as the killing of the prophets (cf. Neh. 9:26) are taken from the Old Testament. At times Luke created a biblical-sounding phrase like "the covenant of circumcision" (v. 8) which is not found in the Old Testament. Sixth, Luke made use of the Deuteronomistic contrast pattern between God's saving deeds on one hand and the stiff-neckedness of Israel on the other (cf. Neh. 9:6-30). However, the themes of the tent of witness and the temple critique do not fit into the pattern of Deuteronomistic historiography. Above all, Acts 7 lacks the Deuteronomistic announcement of God's (final) judgment over disobedient

Israel (but see vv. 42b-43). Seventh, a few times Luke picked up variant traditions—or he may have made a mistake (see below).

God's Story with Abraham (7:2-8)

Stephen addressed the council as **brothers** because they, like he, were Abraham's descendants. He shows his respect by using the honorific address **Fathers** (cf. 22:1). **The God of glory** is the theme of this speech; this phrase, unique in the New Testament, comes from Ps. 29:3 and it forms a bracket with the "glory of God" (v. 55) which Stephen saw in his vision and which is reflected in his face (cf. 6:15). As divinely inspired interpreter of the Old Testament, Stephen begins his speech with Abraham's migration and God's promises to him followed by the "covenant of circumcision." Other Old Testament items such as Abraham's faith, his relations with Lot, his sojourn in Egypt, etc., are omitted, because the focus of this Abraham subsection lies in vv. 6-7 where Gen. 15:13-14 is citied. From this citation the following parts of the speech will flow. It is therefore false to say that the Abraham subsection (vv. 2-8) is irrelevant to the speech. On the contrary, God's unconditional promises to Abraham (vv. 6-7) are the basis of the history which Stephen narrated. God speaks twice in this subsection to Abraham. His words in direct speech start the movement of the story, keep it going, and disclose the purpose of the movement: **they shall worship me in this place** (v. 7). God **appeared** (v. 2), he **said** (v. 3), he promises to **show the land,** he **removed** Abraham (v. 4), he **gave him no inheritance,** but he **promised** the land (v. 5), God **spoke** (v. 6), he decreed that Abraham's posterity shall **worship me in this place** (v. 7) and he **gave** the **covenant of circumcision** (v. 8). In short, God is the chief actor of this opening subsection.

2-3 (God's appearance to Abraham)—**Before he lived in Haran** God appeared to him and said, **Depart from your land and from your kindred and go into the land which I will show you.** According to Gen. 12:1, 4 these words were addressed to Abraham, not **before** he lived in Haran, but after he came to that city, that is, after his migration from Ur **in Mesopotamia,** the land of the Chaldeans (v. 4). This could be a simple error on Luke's part who in this subsection primarily followed Genesis 15—which does not mention Haran, but refers only to Abraham's migration from Ur to this land. But Luke could also be dependent on a variant Jewish tradition. At any rate, the call to depart from **your** land and migrate to a new **land** occurred in a pagan environment. The implication is that God who appeared to and called Abraham in a pagan land cannot be encapsulated in Jerusalem's temple (cf. vv. 48-50), but is present when and where it pleases him.

4-5 (From Haran to the promised land)—After Abraham's father died, God removed him to this land. According to Gen. 11:26,31, Terah was 70 years old when Abraham was born and he died at Haran at the age of 205. When Abraham left Haran he was 75 years old (Gen. 12:4), which means that Terah lived another 60 years after Abraham's departure from that city. Luke may have made a simple mistake here, assuming that Terah had died before Abraham left because Terah's death is narrated in Genesis prior to Abraham's departure. Only when we add the age of Terah at the time of Abraham's birth and the age when Abraham left Haran and subtract the total of 145 years from the life span of Terah can we find out that he lived another six decades after Abraham's departure. However, instead of making a mistake Luke may have been dependent on a variant tradition. According to the Samaritan Pentateuch Terah died at age 145 and according to Philo Abraham left "after his father's death" (*Migration of Abraham* 177).

The **land** to which God removed Abraham is **this land in which you are now living.** Stephen reminded his hearers that God fulfilled his promise to Abraham and that their presence in this land is living proof of it. Fulfilled promises inspire trust in promises not yet fulfilled. In contrast to the audience, Abraham at this point in the story had only the promise to hold on to.

5—With words borrowed from Deut. 5:2 and combined with Gen. 17:8 God's dealings with Abraham are told. The aim of the story now becomes apparent. Abraham is the recipient of an unconditional promise of God which determines all of Israel's history. He is presented not as the prototype of piety or of obedience or of faith but as the recipient of God's promise. Yet this promise appears to be contradicted by experience. God promised to give the land to him **yet he gave him no inheritance in it, not even a foot's length.** The land is promised **to his posterity,** yet **he had no child.** He had only God's promise to hold on to. Abraham's acquisition of the field and the cave of Machpelah from Ephron the Hittite (Genesis 23) is overlooked here because the speech apparently used a variant tradition according to which Abraham was not buried in the cave of Mach-pelah (Gen. 25:9) but at Shechem (Acts 7:16).

6-7—A preview of the future is given and God's purpose with Abraham's posterity in the land is stated. The predictions contained in these verses are developed in vv. 9-16 and 17-44. Far from becoming prosperous landowners Abraham's descendants would be slaves, **aliens in a land belonging to others** and they would be oppressed for **four hundred years.** But a promise is as good as the one who promises. In direct speech God promises Abraham: **But I will judge the nation,** the Egyptians, and lead Israel out of Egypt (cf. Gen. 15:13) in order that **they shall come out and worship me in this place.** This last climactic word of God in direct speech is a combination of Gen. 15:14 with Exod. 3:12 in which "this place," namely, the land of Israel and its temple in Jerusalem is substituted for "this mountain," namely, Mount Sinai. The text of Gen. 15:14 concluded **and after that they shall come out** "with great possessions." By omitting the last three words and substituting words borrowed from Exod. 3:12 (LXX) we hear that God's ultimate purpose with Abraham and his descendants is their **worship** of God **in this place.** This last announcement spans the time from Joshua, when the people entered the land, to Stephen's own present (vv. 44-53). The unspoken question is whether or not the audience of Stephen truly worships God **in this place.** Stephen has been accused of blaspheming against "this holy place" (6:13) and he has been quoted as saying that Jesus "will destroy this place" (6:14). Stephen's answer to this accusation is the Word of God which promises and challenges his audience to worship God in the temple. The reader of Acts knows by now that this purpose finds fulfillment at Stephen's time when those who accept God's saving deed—"the exodus" which Jesus accomplished at Jerusalem (Luke 9:31)—worship God in the temple and teach in the name of Jesus whom God exalted to his right hand (cf. v. 55).

8—God gave Abraham the **covenant of circumcision** (cf. Gen. 17:5-14) in which he unconditionally promised "to be God to you and to your descendants after you." It is "an everlasting covenant," the sign of which is **circumcision** (Gen. 17:7). Circumcision is not subjected to criticism in Acts, nor is it stated anywhere that God's **covenant** has come to an end and that the church of the Gentiles has taken the place of Israel. The purpose of the covenant has already been stated: "they shall worship me in this place" (v. 7). **And so,** in God's time, **Isaac** was born in accordance with the promise and circumcised **on the eighth day** (cf. Gen. 17:12; 21:4). A first fulfillment happened and the line continued with the births and circumcisions of Jacob and his **twelve** sons, the **patriarchs.** From this summary of God's story with Abraham the rest of Stephen's historical narration flows: the migration (vv. 9-16), the oppression (vv. 17-22), the liberation (vv. 23-38), and the worship of Israel thereafter (vv. 39-50).

God's Story with Joseph and the Patriarchs (7:9-16)

In this résumé the prediction of living in a foreign land comes to fulfillment. Like Jesus, Joseph ran afoul of his brothers. Out of "jealousy" (cf. 5:17) they **sold him into Egypt** (Gen. 37:28). Humanly speaking, he was finished, like Jesus on the cross. **But** the **God** who is full of surprises, whose presence cannot be limited to Jerusalem's temple, **was with him** in Egypt (cf. 10:28; 18:9-10; Luke 1:28) **and rescued him out of all his afflictions,** even as he raised Jesus from the dead. Moreover, Joseph was exalted to a high position in Egypt (v. 10) so that through him God could save the clan from starvation when **our fathers could find no food** (v. 11). We are reminded not only of Joseph's words to his brothers (Gen. 50:20), but also of the Lukan kerygma: you killed Jesus, but God raised him in order to offer salvation through him. The **favor and wisdom** which God gave to Joseph also point back to Luke's description of Jesus (Luke 2:52) and of his disciples (Acts 6:3, 10). Joseph, rejected by his own brothers but saved by God, became God's instrument in saving Abraham's descendants and keeping the promise from coming to naught. Finally, because **Joseph's family became known to Pharaoh** (v. 13) and the clan enjoyed Joseph's prestige they were able to carry back the bodies of the dead patriarchs and bury them in the land of promise (vv. 15-16; Gen. 47:29-31; 50:24-26). Their final resting place was the beginning of the fulfillment of v. 5.

The reference to the **seventy-five souls** of Jacob's clan who **went down into Egypt** (v. 14) agrees with the LXX, but not with the 70 people of the Hebrew text (Gen. 46:27)—which indicates Luke's use of the LXX. When **Jacob** and his 12 sons had died **they were carried back to Shechem and laid in the tomb** that Abraham had bought from the **sons of Hamor in Shechem** (v. 16).

There are several difficulties with this statement. First, Abraham did not buy a tomb in Shechem; he bought the cave and field near Hebron (Gen. 23:1-17; 25:9). Second, Jacob was also buried in the cave near Hebron (Gen. 50:13), and not at Shechem. Third, it was Jacob, not Abraham who bought a piece of land at Shechem "from the sons of Hamor" (Gen. 33:18-19). Fourth, Joseph was buried at Shechem (Josh. 24:32) on the land bought by Jacob. Later Jewish tradition held that Hebron was the burial place of the patriarchs (Jub. 46:9; Josephus, *Ant.* 2.199-200). It would appear that our author confused the two land purchases. We have no proof of a variant local tradition on the burial sites of the patriarchs at Shechem. The Samaritan Pentateuch agrees with the Greek and Hebrew Old Testament on the location of Jacob's burial near Hebron. At any rate the speech differs at this point from the Old Testament.

Slavery in Egypt and God's Story with Moses, Part 1 (7:17-29)

Verses 17-19 bring a résumé of the oppression of the people in Egypt, as predicted by God to Abraham (v. 6; cf. Exodus 1). **Another king who had not known Joseph** (v. 18 = Exod. 1:8 LXX) **forced our fathers to expose their infants** (in Exod. 1:22 only the male babies were ordered to be drowned in the Nile). The oppression which threatened their very survival through the murder of their infants was **the time** when **the promise drew near.** Yet it would be still another 80 years until the exodus (cf. vv. 23, 30) and still another 40 years of wandering in the wilderness until the people would enter the promised land (v. 36). Nevertheless, the time of the promise drew near, because the deliverer's birth had come (v. 20). The sketch of the infancy and childhood of **Moses** calls to mind Luke's description of the childhood of Jesus. Like Jesus, Moses was **beautiful before God** (Exod. 2:2 LXX). Perhaps "pleasing to God" might be better (cf. Luke 2:52, "in favor" with God). However, the phrase **before God** could also be a Semitic idiom, (cf. Jonah 3:3 LXX) and its reference to Moses would then mean that he was "extremely beautiful" (cf. Philo, *Life of Moses* 1.9.18; Josephus, *Ant.* 2.224; Heb. 11:23).

Moses was instructed in all the wisdom (Luke 2:52) **of the Egyptians and,** like Jesus, **he was mighty in his words and deeds** (cf. Luke 24:19; Acts 2:22). In Exod. 4:10 we hear of Moses' lack of eloquence (like Paul, 2 Cor. 10:10; 11:6), but already Sir. 45:3 extolled his powerful speech (cf. Josephus, *Ant.* 2.272).

23-29 (Moses and his first rejection by his brothers)—Luke followed rabbinic tradition when he divided Moses' life into three periods of 40 years each. The basis for this division was Moses' death at the age of 120 years, on the one hand, and the wilderness period of 40 years, on the other (cf. Deut. 34:7). In retelling Exod. 2:11-22 only the bare minimum is retained. It is assumed that the audience is familiar with the story of Moses, but needs to hear that Moses' first encounter with his brothers ended in his rejection by them. **When he was forty years old** Moses visited his brothers and **defended** an Israelite by **striking the Egyptian.** In Exod. 2:12 he killed him (cf. v. 28). Here he is depicted as a champion of "justice" (Greek, *ekdikēsis*) for the oppressed. The incident is but a paradigm of his quest for justice on behalf of his people. Moses thought that his people understood that **God was giving them deliverance by his hand, but they did not understand.** A disobedient, stiff-necked people does not understand God's deliverance (Greek, *sōtēria*, salvation) through his agent, be it Moses or Jesus. This picture is not drawn from the exodus narrative but from the rejection of Jesus and projected into the Moses story.

Moreover, **on the following day** Moses tried to make peace between two quarreling Israelites, only to be rebuffed by the one who **was wronging his neighbor. He thrust** Moses **aside,** rejecting him, saying, **Who made you a ruler and a judge over us?** The answer to this question, namely, that God made him **a ruler and a judge** (cf. v. 35), never occurred to this Israelite, the paradigm of ignorance encountered in the Jesus story (cf. 2:36; 3:17; 13:27). Threatened by this Israelite, **Moses fled and became an exile.** He was no longer visibly among his people as their ruler and judge and his appearance as deliverer, appointed by God, seemed to end in failure, just as Jesus' first appearance among his people. But just as God made a new beginning with Moses, so he would do later on with Jesus. His story has been anticipated in the fate of Moses, who encountered rejection and lack of understanding from his fellow Jews.

God's Story with Moses, Part 2 (7:30-34)

Forty years after his first unsuccessful attempt to bring salvation to the oppressed, Moses had an encounter with God (cf. Exod. 3:1-

145

10). **An angel appeared to him in the wilderness of Mount Sinai** (Mount Horeb, Exod. 3:1) **in a flame of fire in a bush.** The command to **take off the shoes** is given after God's self-disclosure which thereby becomes the reason for the command. **I am the God of your fathers** (v. 11), **the God of Abraham and of Isaac and of Jacob** (vv. 2-9, 15). God gives continuity to salvation history in which fulfillments are connected with new promises. God defines himself as the God of the fathers because he is the God of the promises. Because of this self-revelation **the place** on which Moses is standing is **holy ground.** The "holy ground" cannot be limited to Jerusalem's temple, but is found wherever God reveals himself and wherever his word is heard. God announced to Moses that he will **deliver** his people from oppression through Moses, his instrument. **And now come, I will send you to Egypt.** God's commission of Moses at the burning bush reaffirms Moses' self-understanding of v. 25, **that God was giving them deliverance by his hand.** So then, Moses will have a second encounter with his people.

God's Story with Moses and the People, Part 3 (7:35-43)

A change in style occurs in vv. 35-38. The narrative style is supplanted by a eulogy with demonstrative pronouns at the beginning of each sentence. The high praise of Moses intensifies the contrast with the deeds of his people. **This Moses whom they refused** (v. 35) is the theme of this subsection which is thereby connected with vv. 25 and 27 and vv. 39-43. Instead of **refused** we should translate "denied" and relate the verb to Luke 12:9; Acts 3:13-14. Denying Moses or Jesus is the opposite of acknowledging and confessing them as **ruler, judge,** and **deliverer** whom **God sent.** By repeating the words of v. 27 here (v. 35) it becomes clear that Luke was not telling about a singular refusal by one exceptional Jew, but rather about the corporate rejection of God's chosen instrument. But God's plan is not defeated. The rejected Moses was made by God ruler and judge and deliverer. Guided **by the hand of the angel** (cf. Num. 20:16), Moses led the people out of Egypt in the exodus, **having performed wonders and signs in Egypt and at the Red Sea, and in the wilderness for forty years** (cf. Exod. 7:1—17:16; Num. 14; 16; 20–22). But in spite of the exodus and in spite of the miracles performed before, during, and after the exodus, the people did not acknowledge Moses but rejected him a second time, even as signs and wonders did not spare Jesus or the apostles or Stephen from rejection. Thus, Moses is a type of Christ. This is stated explicitly in the prophecy: **This is the Moses who said to the Israelites, "God will raise up for you a prophet from your brethren as he raised me up"** (cf. 3:22; Deut. 18:15). Like Moses, Jesus is ruler, judge, and deliverer. He accomplished an exodus (Luke 9:31), performed signs and wonders, and mediated the word of life (cf. 5:20). The saving deeds of Moses which began with the exodus and continued in the announcement of an eschatological prophet like him found their culmination at Mount Sinai where he **received** the law, **living oracles** from the **angel** of the Lord for transmission **to us.** The idea that the law was received from an angel does not degrade the law (in contrast to Gal. 3:19), because the angel is God's representative and the law consists of **living,** that is, of life-giving, words which have their origin in God (cf. Heb. 4:12; 1 Peter 1:23). They demand obedience and faith toward the one true God and prohibit idolatry. At once the time span between Moses and Stephen's audience has disappeared. The law is given **to us** and Stephen counts himself among those who received it. The law has not been abrogated and the charge against Stephen that he "never ceases to speak words against . . . the law" is shown to be false (cf. 6:13).

Luke's perspective on the law differs from Paul's. For Paul, to be under the law is to be under God's judgment (Gal. 3:10; Rom. 4:15) because the law always finds us to be already sinners. For Luke, the law is the divine guide to life for Israel delivered at Mount Sinai, although Israel as a whole "did not keep it" (v. 53).

39-43 (Israel's idolatry)—The narrative style is taken up again. In spite of the exodus, the prophecy, and the giving of the law, Moses is rejected once more. The rejection of God's agent inevitably leads to idolatry, then as now, and idolatry thwarts the goal of the promise given to Abraham (v. 7). Stephen's accusers belong to a people who from their very beginning practiced idolatry, rejected Moses, and **thrust him aside** (cf. v. 27) **and in their hearts they turned to Egypt,** that is, to idolatry (cf. Num. 14:3). The making of the golden **calf in those days** (Exodus 32) was but the beginning of an ongoing idolatrous worship in which Israel rejoiced **in the works of their hands** (cf. 7:48,50). Israel's history is interpreted from the perspective of its idolatry and faithlessness toward Yahweh (cf. 1 Kings 12:28; 2 Kings 10:28; 14:4; 16:3; 17:9-19; Hos. 4:11-14; 8:4-6; 9:10; 13:2; Isa. 44:9-17; Jer. 7:18,30-31, etc.).

God's reaction to Israel's ongoing idolatry was twofold. First, according to the principle articulated in Wis. 11:16 ("one is punished by the very things by which he sins") God **gave them over to worship the host of heaven.** His answer to idolatry is to let the people be enslaved by it (cf. Rom. 1:24, 26, 28). (For the worship of the astral deities of sun, moon, and stars see Deut. 4:19; 17:3; 2 Chron. 33:2-6; Jer. 8:2; etc.). Second, God removed his idolatrous people from the land of Israel into captivity **beyond Babylon.**

The evaluation of Israel's history as a history of idolatry which began with the golden calf in the desert period is undergirded by a citation from Amos 5:25-27. Originally, these verses were probably a Deuteronomistic addition to the text of Amos and announced that during the wilderness period Israel practiced an exemplary worship without sacrifices and without idolatry, in contrast to subsequent times. The LXX which Luke used reinterpreted the text to mean that Israel worshiped astral deities already during the wilderness period.

Luke changed "beyond Damascus" to **beyond Babylon** so that the Amos citation did not refer to the fate of the Northern Kingdom but to the Babylonian exile. Grammatically, the meaning of the first line from Amos (v. 42) could be: (1) No, you did not offer sacrifices to me during the wilderness period—and this is as it should always have been, for sacrifices as such are to be condemned as idolatrous practices. This cannot be Luke's understanding, in view of Luke 1:8ff.; 2:22-24; and Acts 21:22-26. (2) An alternative interpretation would be: No, you did not offer sacrifices **to me,** as you should have done. Instead you offered them to idols. This would mean that, according to Stephen, the wilderness period consisted in unmitigated idolatry, which does not agree with the Old Testament nor with Stephen's view in Luke's account. (3) Finally, the Greek particle *mē* is used occasionally in questions expecting a positive answer (see 7:28). In that case the meaning of the first line from Amos (v. 42) would be: Yes, you offered sacrifices to me during the wilderness period—as indeed you should have done. But then, the quotation continues, you also committed idolatry during that time. You carried around **the tent of Moloch** (v. 43) when simultaneously **the tent of witness** was in your midst (v. 44). In that case Stephen does not deny that true sacrifices had been offered to God in the wilderness any more than he would deny that the tent of witness was present, but what he emphasizes is that the people also worshiped idols and continued to do so. They did not just slip once with the golden calf but, as Amos put it, **you** also **took up the tent of Moloch, and the star of the god Rephan, the figures** (Greek, *typos*) which your own hands **made** for you **to worship** (v. 43). Moloch was the Canaanite sun-god who required child sacrifices (cf. Lev. 18:21; 20:2-5; Jer. 32:35). Raiphan is the LXX equivalent to "Kaiwan," the Assyrian star-deity, Saturn.

Incidentally, the LXX differs from the Hebrew text of Amos 5:26. The Greek translators misread the Hebrew *Sakkuth*, which is the name of an Assyrian star-god, as *sukkath*, meaning "tent" and they misread the Hebrew word *melek*, meaning "king," as *Moloch* and thus the LXX has the "tent of Moloch" instead of "Sakkuth your king."

In spite of the presence of true worship and true sacrifices it was idolatry which characterized Israel's history from the wilderness period to the time of the exile. In answer to it God promised to remove the people of Jerusalem **beyond Babylon** (cf. 2 Kings 20:16-18). The Babylonian exile was God's punishment for the consistent presence of apostasy and idolatry in Israel. But it was not the End.

The Story of the Tent of Witness and of the Temple (7:44-50)

With v. 44 Stephen turns from the time of Amos and of the exile back to the time of Moses and the wilderness period and discloses that in spite of idolatry rampant among "our fathers" (vv. 39-43) God left his witness in visible form among them. **Our fathers had the tent of witness** with them during their sojourn **in the wilderness.** The phrase "tent of witness" comes from Exod. 33:7 LXX, and the context of this verse clearly indicates that the wilderness time was not exclusively a time of idolatry. The tent of witness was made according to God's design, that is, according to the pattern (Greek, *typos*) God revealed **to Moses** (v. 44; cf. Exod. 25:40). It represented the very opposite of the "tent of Moloch" and "the star of Raiphan" which are handmade "figures" (Greek, *typoi;* v. 43). In short, the tent of witness bore witness to the God of the fathers, to his law, and to the prophet like Moses whom he will raise up. It therefore represented "the place" of true worship in Israel.

Our fathers brought the tent of witness into the land when, under **Joshua,** they took possession of it (v. 45; cf. v. 5; Josh. 3:14-17). **So**

it was until the days of David who, like Joseph and Moses before him, **found favor in the sight of God** (cf. 13:22; 1 Sam. 13:14; 2 Sam. 15:25). Luke had already introduced David as prophet and patriarch (1:16; 2:25,29,34; 4:25) and he will focus his attention on him again in Acts 13:22-37. Therefore he can be very brief here and mention only David's desire **to find a habitation for** "the house of Jacob" (instead of RSV, **the God of Jacob** which is probably a scribal modification; cf. Metzger). The Old Testament background to which v. 46 alludes and which Stephen assumes that his readers know is 2 Samuel 7 (cf. Psalm 132). There, in answer to David's desire to build a house for God, we hear that God promised that he will build "a house" for David (2 Sam. 7:11) by raising up his "seed" after him (LXX) and by establishing "his throne forever." Moreover, David's son (Solomon) "shall build a house for my name." The first promise will be unfolded in Acts 13; the second is dealt with here. David did not build a permanent **habitation,** a temple, **for the house of Jacob,** for his nation, because his son would do it in accordance with God's instruction (2 Sam. 7:13). And so **it was Solomon who built a house for him** (cf. 1 Kings 6; 8:12-62, Solomon's prayer of dedication). In general, interpreters state that the building of the temple by Solomon constituted an act of idolatry. This was certainly not Luke's view, and since vv. 48-53 are redactional, not pre-Lukan, as is generally recognized, we cannot argue that we find here the views of the historical Stephen which differ from those of Luke. What Luke opposes is not the temple as such, but a false idolatrous understanding of the temple. **The Most High does not dwell in houses made with hands** (v. 48). Such a false, idolatrous understanding which limits and encapsulates God in the temple was also rejected by Solomon in his prayer of dedication: "But will God indeed dwell on earth? Behold the heaven and the highest heaven cannot contain thee; how much less this house which I have built!" "Heaven [is] thy dwelling place," but the temple is "the place where God's name dwells" (1 Kings 8:27-30; cf. 2 Sam. 7:13). It would be ludicrous to suppose that Stephen (or Luke), who quite carefully summarized Israel's history from Abraham to Solomon, would at this point reject the Deuteronomistic history by denouncing the temple as such as an idolatrous institution. What is denounced is an idolatrous relationship to the temple, a false view of the temple in which Israel's faith and hope are identified with the temple as such, when God's transcendence is ignored, when it is forgotten that God's great acts with Abraham, Joseph, and Moses happened apart from "this place," namely, in foreign lands. When people become oblivious to the message that it is not God himself who dwells in the temple but only his name (2 Sam. 7:13; 1 Kings 8:29; Deut. 12:5,11,21; etc.), then indeed idolatry takes place in the temple and through the temple. The catchword **made with hands** (v. 48) connects a certain kind of temple worship with the idolatry of the wilderness period (vv. 41, 43). But the fault does not lie with the temple as such which is meant to be "the place" where Israel should worship God (v. 7) any more than Israel's idolatry in the wilderness resulted from the tent of witness. The temple can be perverted by absolutizing it, by resisting the Holy Spirit, by rejecting the prophets and the Righteous One, and by breaking the law (vv. 51-53).

The prophet Isaiah (66:1-2) clearly stated that God's transcendence cannot be limited to a **house** and that a distinction must be maintained between the creator whose **hand** made **all these things** and **houses made with hands** (plural!)—be they Jewish or pagan temples (cf. 17:24-25). Otherwise, one does not worship God "in this place" (vv. 7, 49-50), but commits idolatry. While God and temple are not joined together inseparably, as the history from Abraham onward demonstrates, it was God's purpose for Israel that it should worship him in the temple (v. 7). This purpose is thwarted by Stephen's audience because it rejected the Righteous One who took possession of the temple and it rejected his servant-witnesses who proclaimed God's Word in the temple. Without the Word of God as announced by Moses, Peter, and Stephen, there is no worship but only idolatry "in this place." The idolatry is grounded in the illusion that the temple, built by human hands, guarantees God's presence and that he is present when the champions of the temple oppose the message proclaimed in Christ's name. Therefore Stephen concluded his speech with a climactic indictment.

The Indictment of the Sanhedrin and the People of Jerusalem (7:51-53)

Israel's history of failure to respond in faith to God's promise and fulfillment is now related to Stephen's audience. His solidarity with the audience is broken. Instead of "our fathers" (vv. 11, 19, 38, 44)

Stephen now speaks of "your fathers" (v. 51). **You stiff-necked people** (cf. Exod. 33:3, 5), **uncircumcised** (cf. v. 8) **in heart** (cf. Deut. 10:16; Jer. 4:4) **and ears** (cf. Jer. 6:10), **you always resist the Holy Spirit** (cf. Isa. 63:10). The accusation that the audience **always** resists, or blasphemes (Luke 12:10) the Holy Spirit has been demonstrated in Acts by the opposition of the Sanhedrin against the prophetic witness of the servants of Jesus (2:23; 4:8-22; 5:29-40; 6:8-15). The Sanhedrin's present opposition to the Holy Spirit is in continuity with the opposition of their **fathers** who, since Moses' time, "refused to obey," "thrust aside" (v. 39), and persecuted the Spirit-filled prophets of God.

Luke knew the Deuteronomistic tradition of the persecution and murder of the prophets. During their lifetime they were persecuted but afterwards they were honored with magnificent tombs (Luke 11:47-50; 13:34). In Jer. 2:30 we read: "your own sword devoured your prophets" and according to Neh. 9:26 the people "killed your prophets who had warned them . . . and committed great blasphemies" (cf. 2 Chron. 36:16; 1 Kings 19:10; etc.). The persecution and murder of the prophets by **your fathers** reached its culmination in **the Righteous One** whom they **announced beforehand** (cf. v. 37; 3:22-24) and **whom you have now betrayed and murdered** (cf. 3:14-15, 17). The violence against God's messengers past and present constitutes transgression of **the law as delivered** from heaven **by angels** (cf. v. 38). The audience stands guilty of the accusations leveled against Stephen (6:13).

In Conclusion

The temple in Luke-Acts is the house of Jesus' Father (Luke 2:49), a house of worship and prayer (Luke 19:46), the place where Israel is called to worship God (Acts 7:7), the place where Jesus and the apostles prayed and taught (Luke 19:47; 21:37; Acts 3:1-26; 4:1; 5:20, 42), and it remains the place to which believers continued to go also after Stephen's martyrdom (21:22-26; 22:17, 24:18). These last three texts are generally ignored by interpreters who deal with Luke's view of the temple in Acts 7. For Luke, Jewish believers who called upon the name of the Lord Jesus in the temple, who preached there "in his name," thereby fulfilled God's purpose of worship "in this place" (7:7). Conversely, when Israel rejects the prophets, as well as the Righteous One and the Spirit-filled apostles and servants of Jesus, its temple worship becomes a form of idolatry. God's promise and presence dare not be limited to the temple or the promised land. The temple can no more save Israel from idolatry than the tent of witness could save their fathers from taking up "the tent of Moloch" (v. 43).

At Luke's time the temple lay in ruins, because Israel "did not know the time" of its "visitation" by God through his Messiah (Luke 19:44). Does this mean that God's unconditional promise to Abraham that his descendants "shall worship me in this place" (7:7) also lies in ruins? Was the worship of Jewish Christians in the temple the total fulfillment of that promise, or a partial fulfillment? Luke gave no explicit answer to this question. But we should note that Stephen's indictment did not culminate in the pronouncement that God has rejected his stiff-necked, idolatrous, and murderous people with finality. In spite of the litany of the people's sin from Moses' time to Stephen's present the promise of God remains in force. The stiff-necked exclude themselves, but God's purpose is not thwarted. When "the times of the Gentiles" have come to an end (Luke 21:6, 24), then God restores the kingdom to Israel (Acts 1:6) and his promise of 7:7 will find an eschatological fulfillment. Until then, true worship takes place in those houses where the Word of God proclaimed through Moses and the prophets, through Christ and the apostles, is heard and believed and where believers call on the name of the Lord.

Martyrdom and Persecution (7:54—8:3)

Interpreters generally hold that Luke changed a tradition containing a stoning by a mob into a trial by the Sanhedrin in order to create the opportunity for Stephen's speech. Perhaps they are right. But mob scenes never stopped Luke from putting speeches into the mouths of his characters (e.g., 14:14-18; 21:35-40; 22:22). Another matter is the question of whether Luke understood what was historically involved in judicial proceedings of death by stoning (cf. Lev. 24:10-14). Did Luke think that people would pick up stones and throw them at the victim? In reality the procedure was to strip the convicted person of his clothes, cast him down a 10-foot precipice and then have the first witness throw a boulder on the victim's chest.

If this did not kill him then the next witness would repeat the same procedure until death occurred. At any rate it would not be the witnesses who would take off their clothing but the victim (cf. v. 58). However, we should note that Luke referred to the outer garment (Greek, *himation*) and not to the inner garment (Greek, *chiton*) which the executing witnesses took off. There appears to be no compelling reason to deny that the tradition which reached Luke referred to a trial of Stephen.

It may well have been Luke himself who applied the coloring of a mob scene to a trial scene, just as in other instances he interwove legal features with mob features (e.g., 16:19-23; 17:5-9; 18:12-17; 23:7-10) in order to indicate that legal justice meted out by Jews or Gentiles is frequently not much better than mob action.

Luke obviously adorned the death of the first martyr by drawing parallels to Jesus' death. He also introduced Paul into this tradition and therefore he had to repeat the reference to the stoning of Stephen in v. 59 (cf. v. 58). But was the historical Paul really present at Stephen's death and did he actually participate in the subsequent persecution of the church of Jerusalem? Frequently it is asserted that the account of Acts at this point disagrees with Paul's own statement in Gal. 1:22, according to which Paul was unknown to "the churches in Judea." True enough, but the conclusion that Paul was not involved in the persecution of Christians in Judea is not warranted. Such a conclusion ignores the context of Paul's argument in Galatians, namely, that his gospel and his apostleship are independent of the Jerusalem church. In this connection Paul wrote that the Judean churches had not even seen him (as a Christian) and, hence, they could not possibly have taught the gospel to him. They had only heard of his conversion and said, "He who once persecuted *us* is now preaching the faith" (Gal. 1:23). This surely implies that Paul was indeed persecuting "us," namely, the Judean churches, especially the church in Jerusalem, as Luke told it (Acts 8:3; 9:1). Whether the historical Paul was present at Stephen's execution is another matter. It was certainly Luke who introduced Paul into his narrative (7:58) for literary purposes, to connect this subsection with the one that begins in chap. 9. According to Luke, the church's persecutor was present at the first martyrdom and his subsequent conversion shows what God can do even with those who radically oppose him.

Luke's composition has two parts. In 7:54—8:1a he narrates two reactions by the audience: one to Stephen's speech (v. 54), the other to his vision (v. 57). We hear Stephen's final three sentences (vv. 56, 59, 60) and are told about his death by stoning. The second part (8:1b-3) refers in summary fashion to a "great persecution" and its results. Both parts are connected by the names of Stephen and of Saul. Saul's role develops from being a passive bystander (7:58) to an accomplice in the capital sentence (8:1) and finally an active persecutor (8:3).

Stephen's Martyrdom (7:54—8:1a)

The reaction of the audience to his speech was rage (cf. 5:33); literally, "they were cut in their hearts" (v. 54). "Uncircumcised in heart" as they were (v. 51), the speech did not move them to ask, What must we do to be saved (cf. 16:30; 2:37)? Instead, the revelation of their failure cut them in their heart and drove them to fury. Instead of experiencing a circumcision of the heart the audience experienced anger against Stephen and his message. They **ground their teeth** (cf. Ps. 34:16 LXX). In contrast to his opponents, Stephen, **full of the Holy Spirit** (cf. 6:3,8,10), had a vision of the **glory of God and Jesus standing at the right hand of God.** His vision is effected by the very Spirit of God whom his audience resists (v. 51) and it demonstrates that God is on Stephen's side rather than on the side of his opponents. It confirms and vindicates Stephen's preaching and shows that neither **the glory of God** nor **Jesus** at his right hand can be encapsulated, objectified, in Jerusalem's temple. **Heaven** is their abode and they are accessible where and when it pleases them. The **glory of God** is inseparable from **Jesus** at his **right hand** (cf. 2:33-36; 5:31; Ps. 110:1), for the exalted Jesus participates in God's glory and power.

Stephen communicated his vision to the court: **Behold, I see the heavens opened, and the Son of man standing at the right hand of God.** Stephen has just told them that the height of their stiff-neckedness was the murder of Jesus. Now he tells them that he sees Jesus exalted to the right hand of God as Son of man, meaning that God fulfills his purposes in spite of their stiff-neckedness.

Only here does the title **Son of man** occur outside of the Gospels and on the lips of someone other than Jesus (a few manuscripts have "Son of God" instead). In Luke 22:69 Jesus predicted, "From now on the Son of man shall be seated at the right hand of the power of God." (The Markan "you shall see" was omitted by Luke; cf. Mark 14:62.) According to Luke, not the opponents of Jesus but his faithful witness Stephen shall see Jesus as Son of man, vindicated at the right hand of God and vindicating Stephen. In Stephen's vision the Son of man is **standing** while in other texts he is sitting or seated (cf. Ps. 110:1). Does **standing** here simply mean "being" (cf. Rom. 8:34)? If so, the verb would merely illustrate Luke's fondness for variation. Or does Jesus, like the angels, "stand" before God's throne? Hardly, because according to Psalm 110 he "sits" at God's right hand. Or does he stand up because he is ready for his parousia? Unlikely, according to Acts which is free of the imminent-end expectation. Does he stand up in order to welcome the first martyr, or because he is ready to pass judgment on Israel's recalcitrance, or because he is accusing Israel before God, or because he "acknowledges" Stephen before the angels of God (Luke 12:8)? Tentatively, we might choose the last suggestion because it fits the theme of Stephen's vindication prior to his death. But the first possibility also deserves consideration. More important is the connection with the theme of worship. Ever since the ascension of Jesus the worship of God (cf. v. 7) involves calling upon the name of the Lord Jesus as Stephen shortly will do.

A screaming response constitutes the reaction of the Sanhedrin to Stephen's announcement of his vision (v. 57). Being uncircumcised in "ears" (v. 51) they now **stopped their ears.** Thus the message of the speech and of the vision is lost to them. For them Stephen is blaspheming, and the punishment for blasphemy is death by stoning (Lev. 24:10-14). In reality, however, it is they who are blaspheming the Holy Spirit, present in Stephen (cf. v. 55; Luke 12:10). **They cast him out of the city** (cf. Luke 4:29) **and stoned him.** Quite correctly Luke mentioned the presence of (two) witnesses who laid down their outer garments. At this point Saul is introduced—first as a guardian of the garments (v. 58), then as consenting to Stephen's death (8:1), and finally as active persecutor (8:3). His life illustrates that God is full of surprises and that Stephen's martyrdom did not signal the end of God's dealing with his stiff-necked and murderous people to whom Saul belonged.

As they were stoning Stephen, he prayed, "Lord Jesus, receive my spirit." Worship of God includes prayer to or through Jesus, the

Lord at the right hand of God. The correspondence to Jesus' last word from the cross is obvious (Luke 23:46; cf. Ps. 31:5 which is part of the Jewish evening prayer). Jesus' first word from the cross finds correspondence in Stephen's last word: **Lord, do not hold this sin against them** (cf. Luke 23:34). Yet there is a difference between Jesus' and Stephen's petition for forgiveness. Jesus prayed for forgiveness because of the ignorance of his opponents who did not know what they were doing. That ignorance had been dealt with through preaching since Pentecost. Nevertheless, Stephen prayed for forgiveness for his murderers. Is it merely pious rhetoric which heaps coals of fire upon the opponents? Is this final prayer put on the lips of the first martyr merely for the sake of a parallel with the martyrdom of Jesus? Or does this parallel indicate that forgiveness of sins which since Easter is granted in Jesus' name (Luke 24:47; Acts 10:43) is available to the opponents of the church until the eschaton? The last three sentences of Stephen correspond to Luke 22:69 (v. 56), to Luke 23:46 (v. 59), and to Luke 23:34 (v. 60) and suggest that Jesus has power over Israel's destiny, over life, death, and forgiveness.

And when he had said this, he fell asleep, he died (cf. Luke 23:46b). With faith, death has lost its terror and therefore faith can use the language of sleep without absolutizing it (cf. Acts 13:36; John 11:11; 1 Cor. 15:6, 51; 1 Thess. 4:13-15; Wis. 3:1). The martyrdom of Jesus found an extension in the martyrdom of Stephen. Like Jesus, Stephen was filled with the Holy Spirit. His proclamation in word and deed resulted in his arrest, and at his trial false witnesses arose. A reference to the Son of man is made. Like Jesus, Stephen prayed for his persecutors and committed his spirit to his Lord. "A disciple is not above his teacher, but every one when he is fully taught will be like his teacher" (Luke 6:40). "Blessed are you when men hate you . . . and cast out your name as evil, on account of the Son of man" (Luke 6:22; 21:16). Yet in general Luke's interest was less focused on martyrdom than on daily cross-bearing (Luke 9:23) and Stephen's primary importance lay in his message—which culminates in the prayer for forgiveness of his opponents.

The Great Persecution (8:1b-3)

On that day a great persecution arose against the church in Jerusalem. Thus far only some individuals within the church have been subjected to hostility. Now for the first time the community of believers as a whole experienced persecution. The word *persecution* covers a wide area then as well as today, from ridicule to social ostracism to occasional beatings to confiscation of property to imprisonment and to execution. The note that **all** Christians were **scattered throughout the region of Judea and Samaria, except the apostles** strikes us as being odd. Not only is a Christian community present in Jerusalem in the next chapter (9:26-30), but the leadership of any group, in this case the apostles, is usually not exempted from a general persecution. We must presume that historically the persecution was directed primarily, if not exclusively, against the Hellenists, the Greek-speaking Christian community around the Seven, while the community around the Twelve remained more or less unmolested. Sandwiched between two references to persecution (8:1 and 8:3) we read that **devout men buried Stephen, and made great lamentation over him.** In spite of persecution Christians take care of their dead brother. One should not read a public protest into these lamentations, nor should we use them as proof that Stephen was the victim of a lynch mob, even though later rabbinic law forbids lamentations for legally executed criminals. Luke's point in 8:2 is that Christians who take care of each other in life will not abandon a martyr at death in spite of persecution. The third appearance of Saul in this section reveals that he not only was unimpressed by Stephen's last words, but also that he did not follow the advice of his teacher Gamaliel (cf. 5:34-39; 22:3). On the contrary, **entering house after house he dragged off men and women[!] and committed them to prison** (cf. 1 Cor. 15:9; Gal. 1:13, 23; Phil. 3:6-7). In so doing Saul fulfilled Jesus' prediction of Luke 21:12: "They will persecute you . . . delivering you to prisons." Unwittingly, Saul aided the spread of the Word of God—as the next section will show.

■ Witness beyond Jerusalem (8:4—9:43)

The story of the restoration of the people of God through the apostolic witness in Jerusalem has been told. To be sure, the mission will continue also in Jerusalem, until "many tens of thousands" of Jews have come to faith in Jesus the Messiah of Israel (21:20). But

Luke's focus is no longer on the mission in Jerusalem. He told us that the Christian witness has met an ever-growing resistance in that city, from mocking (2:13) to threats (4:21) to beatings (5:40) to death (7:60) and persecution (8:1,3), resulting in a division among the people of Jerusalem in accordance with Jesus' word? (Luke 12:51-53). Expelled believers moved beyond Jerusalem and preached the word throughout the region of Judea and Samaria (8:1,4), the coastal plain, Damascus, and eventually Antioch (8:40; 9:10; 11:19). The church grows in spite of and through persecution. Philip's mission, the surprising conversion of Saul and his early activity, and Peter's ministry in Lydda and Joppa comprise this section.

The Mission of Philip (8:4-40)

Every persecution produces personal hardships and tragedies, and Luke's readers were quite aware of this dimension in Christian existence. But there is another dimension beyond individual and family calamities which Luke would like his readers to recognize. Faith usually perceives in retrospect that all things, even persecutions, work together for good in God's grand design. The believers, expelled from Jerusalem, **were scattered** like seed across regions and bore fruit a hundredfold by **preaching the word.** It is ironic that it took a persecution to move the church to fulfill Christ's mandate to witness in Samaria (1:8). Luke offered two examples of preaching by the scattered Hellenists, choosing Philip as their representative. He was one of the Seven and was mentioned in second place (6:5).

Philip in Samaria (8:4-25)

The story of Philip in Samaria raises some questions, e.g., what is the relationship between miracle and magic, between Baptism with water and the gift of the Spirit, between the Seven (or what is left of them) and the Twelve, between Samaria and Jerusalem? Moreover, the quest for the historical Simon, whom later church fathers denounced as the originator of gnostic heresies, begins with this narrative which contains the earliest written information about him. Yet Luke's Simon was not a gnostic teacher but a magician. We might therefore ask whether Luke debunked a gnostic philosopher-prophet by making him a converted but greedy magician, or whether Simon's later followers attached their own teachings to his name. We cannot debate this issue here, but merely indicate the scholarly consensus which seems to be emerging at present. We have no evidence that a full-blown gnostic system existed during the first half of the first century, and to that extent the second alternative seems preferable to the first. On the other hand, Luke did debunk Simon together with his claim to be **the power of God which is called Great,** which at Justin's time meant that Simon was confessed and worshiped by his followers as manifestation of "the highest God," "above every lordship authority and power" (*Apol.* 1.26; *Dial.* 120.6).

The account in Acts is bracketed by two summary statements on the expansion of the mission of the church by the Hellenists and by the apostles (vv. 4 and 25). These brackets are meant to offer the perspective from which the narrative should be viewed. This means that also the separation of Baptism from the gift of the Spirit should be perceived from the perspective of th expansion of the church's mission. We begin with a general overview of this narrative:

Bracket, v. 4: Summary statement on the expansion of mission (preaching the word, *euangelizesthai*)

Part I. *Philip, the Samaritans, and Simon (vv. 5-13)*
    A. Phillip and the Samaritans (vv. 5-8)
        1. His proclamation of the Messiah in Samaria (v. 5)
        2. His impression on the Samaritans through his word and deed (vv. 6-8; they gave heed to his words)
    B. Simon and the Samaritans (vv. 9-11)
        1. His magic and claim (v. 9; fascination)
        2. His impression on the Samaritans (vv. 10-11; "they gave heed to him"; fascination)
    C. Philip's Success with the Samaritans and with Simon (vv. 12-13)
        1. His success with the Samaritans (v. 12; *euangelizesthai*)
        2. His success with Simon (v. 13; "he continued with Philip"; because "he saw" . . . he was fascinated)

Part II. *The Apostles, the Samaritans, and Simon (vv. 14-24)*
    A. The Apostles and the Samaritans (vv. 14-17)
        1. Peter and John's visit to Samaria and its reason (vv. 14-16; Spirit)
        2. Their success with the Samaritans (v. 17; Spirit)

B. Simon and the Apostles (vv. 18-19)
　　1. Simon's reflection (v. 18; "when he saw" . . . Spirit)
　　2. Simon's offer to the apostles (v. 19; Spirit)
C. The Apostles (Peter) and Simon (vv. 20-24)
　　1. Peter's pronouncements and reasons (vv. 20-23; gift of God)
　　2. Simon's reply as indication of the apostles' success (v. 24)
Bracket, v. 25: Summary statement on the apostles' mission in Samaria ("preaching the gospel," *euangelizesthai*)

The literary center of both parts is occupied by Simon and reveals the importance of the subjects of magic in part I, and of a false notion of the Spirit in part II. The same Greek verb for preaching (*euangelizesthai*) describes the activity of the expelled Christians (v. 4), of Philip (v. 12) and of the apostles (v. 25) and indicates that it was not faulty preaching by Philip which caused the delay of the Spirit's coming upon the Samaritans.

5-13 (Philip, the Samaritans, and Simon)—Philip **went down** from Jerusalem **to** the **city of Samaria** (the article is present in the oldest manuscripts and should be retained). We are not told which city is meant. It could be Sychar (cf. John 4:5, probably ancient Shechem), or Sebaste (so named by Herod the Great for the city built on the site of ancient Samaria), or, less likely, Gitta, the birthplace of Simon. At any rate Philip preached not to pagans but to Samaritans, who had a truncated Bible (without Psalms and prophets) and had set up their own temple on Mount Gerizim (which the Jews subsequently destroyed) and were not regarded highly by Jews. Recriminations were probably mutual. Jesus had found individual Samaritans who believed (Luke 17:11-19), yet he encountered rejection also in Samaria, "because his face was set toward Jerusalem" (Luke 9:51-59). Also, for Luke salvation comes from the Jews (John 4:22) but it is through the Jew Philip that salvation is extended to the Samaritan lost sheep out of the house of Israel. Even though the Samaritans expected the coming of a prophet-deliverer, called *Ta'eb* (Deut. 18:15ff.), Philip preached to them **the Christ,** the Jewish Messiah (cf. 3:20; 5:42; 18:5,28).

The people **gave heed** to his preaching which was accompanied by **signs** (cf. 4:29-30). Luke did not say that Philip's exorcisms and healings (v. 7) created faith among the Samaritans. Luke's readers already know that the miracles of Jesus, of apostles, and of Stephen did not result in faith by all who saw them. Faith comes through preaching, not through miracles (cf. v. 12). Nevertheless, the Samaritans were impressed by Philip's miracles. **So there was much joy in that city** (v. 8), in stark contrast to the fury which had exploded in Jerusalem (7:54-58).

With a flashback Luke introduces **Simon** who had **previously practiced magic** and fascinated the people (vv. 9-11; RSV, **amazed**). According to Luke, Simon had claimed that **he himself was somebody great** (cf. 5:36) while the people **gave heed to him** (vv. 10 and 11) and confessed, **This man is that power of God which is called Great** (v. 10). We could deduce that Simon probably taught, "I am the Great Power of God," meaning, "I am God incarnate, and the proof of my claim lies in my magic." Note that whereas the people **gave heed** to Philip's preaching (v. 6), they previously had been attached to the person of Simon (vv. 10, 11) who as a magician spellbound his followers by magical tricks and outrageous personal claims. Usually magicians in the first century performed their magic for profit. Apostles and disciples healed without receiving money. For the magician his magic was his message; for Philip his message was that Jesus is the Messiah whom God raised from the dead; the miracles which accompany his message indicate that the gospel of Jesus-Messiah is indeed the power of God unto salvation. Yet the miracles themselves are ambiguous. They are not the salvation itself, but signs pointing to Christ in whose name salvation is offered already now. It is therefore misleading to say that the only difference between magic and miracles is that the latter are performed by Christians and are more impressive than the former.

The result of Philip's preaching was that the people changed their allegiance from the great magician Simon to Philip. **They believed Philip** (v. 12). But note the reason why they believed him: "because" (instead of **as**, RSV) **he preached good news about the kingdom of God** and because he preached **the name of Jesus Christ** in whom the saving rule of God is present (cf. Luke 11:20). Faith comes through hearing the good news rather than through observing miracles, which are in themselves ambiguous. While our modern view of miracles is largely oriented to the idea of the laws of nature (which during miracles are thought to be suspended), the ancient view of miracles was oriented to the question: Who is made manifest in this miracle—God or Satan? Hence, Jesus could be accused of being in league with Beelzebul, the prince of demons (Luke 11:15). In short, miracles demand an answer to the question, Is it God or demonic powers that are at work here? Christ or antichrist (cf. Mark 13:22; 2 Thess. 2:9-11)? Magic and miracles appear like identical twins to neutral observers and yet to the eye of faith they are as different as night is from day and death from life. Miracles can be a help toward faith, but they cannot be the basis of faith. Because the Samaritans' faith was based on the good news about the kingdom and the person of Jesus-Messiah, therefore **they believed Philip** and turned from Simon. Consequently **they were baptized** and in Baptism they were placed under the Lordship of Jesus. Magicians seek to control God; Christ's servants are controlled by God. Their miracles are the Spirit's witness, perceived by faith, to the resurrection of Christ in whose name miracles occur (5:32; 4:30).

Philip's success in Samaria included the conversion of Simon, who had been hailed as the great power of God himself. **Even Simon himself believed,** that is, he acknowledged Christ's Lordship, and in consequence of his confession **was baptized.** Afterwards **he continued with Philip** and remained in a state of fascination as he watched **the signs and great miracles performed by** Philip. But it is difficult to shed one's former perspectives. Simon the magician had met his match. To him Philip appeared to be a super magician and so he followed Philip just as the Samaritans had formerly followed him. Miracles can be a help toward faith—but they can also mislead, as we shall see.

14-25 (The apostles, the Samaritans and Simon)—Part two of the drama begins **in Jerusalem.** When the apostles **heard that Samaria had received the word of God** they sent two representatives, **Peter and John,** to look over the situation (v. 14). The mandate to witness in Samaria had been given by Jesus to them and the Galilean disciples on Ascension Day (1:8). Yet it had not been they but one of the Hellenists who had introduced the gospel there. In this section Luke permits the apostles to complete the mission in Samaria by means of an anomaly. **The Holy Spirit . . . had not yet fallen on any** of the Samaritan converts **but they had only been baptized** (v. 16). After prayer and the laying on of hands the apostles witnessed the Pentecost of the Samaritans. Luke's purpose here was certainly not to downgrade Baptism, nor did he propose that the gift of the

163

Spirit must be separated in principle from Baptism, or treated like two stages, nor was Luke chiding Philip for improper preaching or for forgetting to lay on his hands. Nor did our author think that only the laying on of hands can bestow the Spirit. In 2:38 the imposition of hands is not even mentioned, indicating that laying on of hands was not the necessary accompanying rite for receiving the Spirit. Equally false is the suggestion that only apostles, but not the Seven, had the power to dispense the Spirit. In 9:10-19 Ananias, who was neither an apostle nor an apostle's delegate like Philip (Acts 6:1-6) but a "disciple," laid his hands on Paul so that Paul might be healed and through Baptism receive the Holy Spirit. Finally, Luke was not suggesting that the faith of the Samaritans had been defective. If so, Peter and John would have preached to them rather than prayed (v. 15).

Luke was celebrating a breakthrough. The barrier of religious racism between Samaritans and Jews was torn down in the presence of the apostolic leaders of the true Israel to whom the Lord mandated the mission in Samaria. Through their representatives, Peter and John, the apostles were incorporating the Samaritan Spirit-filled believers into the messianically restored people of God. God granted the same gift of the Spirit to the Samaritans that he had granted to apostles and disciples in Jerusalem. The anomaly of a separation of Baptism from the gift of the Holy Spirit occurred (v. 16) so that the representatives of the apostles would experience the breakdown of the barrier between believing Jews and believing Samaritans. Instead of the threat of a new Samaritan church, there is but one church of Jews and Samaritans, created by one Spirit and attested to by the one apostolate. The apostles therefore continued the mission in Samaria (v. 25) which Philip inaugurated. The unity and inclusiveness of the church is maintained.

Now when Simon saw (cf. v. 13) **that the Spirit was given through the laying on of the apostles' hands** (v. 18): What exactly Simon saw, we are not told, but the verb "saw" makes it rather improbable that the glossolalia, something that one hears rather than sees, of 1 Corinthians 14 was involved. More important is the fact that we are not told whether Simon himself had also received the Spirit. If so, his offense would be all the worse. Perhaps Luke wanted to suggest that Simon was merely an observer, seeing and thinking that through laying on of hands the Spirit could be communicated to his fellow

Samaritans. But perhaps Luke intentionally left Simon's religious status open, because he is now confronting new issues: the pseudo-Christian, his money, and a magical understanding of the Spirit. Luke has told us that the baptized Simon was fascinated by Philip's miracles (v. 13). **Now when Simon saw** what the apostles could do he saw his chance of advancing to the position of super magician within the church. He therefore offered the apostles **money,** saying, **Give me also this power, that any one on whom I lay my hands may receive the Holy Spirit** (v. 19). What Simon wanted was control over the Holy Spirit. He aspired to be a Christian magician with the power to transmit the Spirit to others. Religious magic is man's attempt to manipulate God and usually profit by it. But it is God alone who controls the Holy Spirit and not the church, nor sacraments, nor laying on of hands, nor apostles. Apostles do not lay on hands because they can manipulate the Spirit on the basis of their "own power or piety" (3:12). By laying on their hands and praying they acknowledge that they cannot bring down the Spirit; they can only ask God to give it in accordance with his promise and God grants his Spirit "where and when it pleases him." His Spirit is his free gift, that no man controls and that money cannot buy. The power to transmit the Spirit belongs to God alone (cf. Luke 11:13).

Simon received a stern rebuke from Peter which amounted to a curse: **Your silver perish with you.** That which God alone can give cannot be acquired by bribes or tricks, but is received only as his free gift. The money-oriented pseudo-Christian Simon hears of his own destruction and of his exclusion **in this matter** from the church, its message and Spirit. The reason for these two verdicts is **because you thought you could obtain the gift of God with money,** which reveals that **your heart is not right before God** (vv. 20-21). Exclusion from the community of salvation in the present leads to future destruction. And yet, Peter offered him the possibility of repentance and, with it, a way out through forgiveness of sins; **if possible** implies that forgiveness cannot simply be taken for granted. Simon's final response was a request for intercessory prayer by Peter and John. Again, Luke does not inform us whether Simon's response was genuine or not. Time will tell.

In this narrative Luke was not only celebrating the expansion of the mission and the unity and inclusiveness of the church; he was also celebrating the defeat of a magical understanding of the gospel and the Spirit. He confronted a popular miracle-oriented piety within churches of his time, a piety which infringes upon the sovereignty of God and the primacy of his word, which is power, but not magic.

Philip and the Ethiopian Eunuch (8:26-40)

After the mass conversion of the Samaritans this section together with the next narrate the conversion of two individuals, the Ethiopian eunuch and Saul. All three conversion stories are stages in Luke's drama leading to the programmatic breakthrough in the conversion of the first Gentile (10:1—11:18).

Originally, this story circulated among Hellenists and told of the Baptism of the first Gentile by Philip, one of the Seven. The legitimacy of mission among Gentiles was found in the intervention of God who directed Philip to the eunuch. Luke, however, did not regard the Ethiopian as a Gentile, but deliberately left his religious status undefined. A eunuch could not become a member of Israel, in view of the prohibition of Deut. 23:1. Hence, in spite of his social position as the queen's treasurer and in spite of his worship in Jerusalem, he was a religious outsider living like a Samaritan in the twilight zone between Judaism and paganism. His conversion is a prelude to the conversion of the Gentile Cornelius.

Geographically, the gospel has moved beyond Jerusalem to Samaria in the north and it now moves south to Gaza. The Ethiopian, like the Jews at Pentecost who came "from every nation under heaven" (2:5), had come from "far off" (2:39). His return to his homeland partially fulfills Christ's mandate (1:8) and discloses the gospel's movement "to the end of the earth" (1:8).

This story has several similarities with the story of Jesus and the Emmaus disciples. Both tell of events on a road; Philip, like Jesus, joins the traveler(s). Both begin the conversation with a question. Central to both conversations is the interpretation of Scripture with its focus on the necessity of the death and exaltation of the Messiah-servant. The Emmaus story concludes with a sacramental meal and tells of the effect of the encounter ("Did not our hearts burn. . ."). The conversion of the eunuch concludes with his Baptism followed by his "rejoicing" on the way. Finally, both Philip and Jesus vanish miraculously. In short, Luke left his stamp on the tradition which he received (cf. also "about whom," v. 34 and Luke 24:19, 27; "beginning with," v. 35 and Luke 24:27). These similarities do not disclose Philip as successor to Jesus, but they show that Philip acted like Jesus (cf. Luke 6:40).

The structure of the story:

(A) The movement of the mission, "on the way" south from Jerusalem to Gaza, directed by God (vv. 26-28).

  (B) The Spirit's command to join the eunuch (v. 29).

    (C) The question by Philip: Do you understand what you are reading? (v. 30).

      (D) First question of the eunuch: How can I, unless someone leads the way into the scripture? (v. 31).

        (E) The scripture passage (vv. 32-33).

          (F) Second question of the eunuch (v. 34): Does the prophet speak about himself or about someone else?

        (E') The interpretation of scripture is the good news of Jesus (v. 35) as told by Philip.

      (D') Third question of the eunuch (v. 36): What is to prevent my being baptized?

    (C') Philip baptizes the eunuch (who now understands what he has read).

  (B') The Spirit separates Philip from the eunuch.

(A') The movement of the mission, preaching the gospel from Azotus to Caesarea.

The questions, Does the prophet speak about himself or about some one else? and, if the latter, About whom does he speak? are of central concern to Luke's hermeneutics (cf. 2:29-31, 34-35). Luke's particular emphasis in this conversion story in distinction from the other three of chaps. 8–10 lies in the need to understand the Scripture. Such understanding occurs only if the relevant Old Testament text is connected with the story of Jesus, with his suffering and exaltation. Then conversion can occur and is sealed with the water of Baptism.

26-28—Divine interventions at the beginning and at the end of the story (vv. 26 and 39) bracket the narrative and disclose that the mission of the church is under the guidance of God. A command by an **angel of the Lord** starts the mission movement: **Rise and go**

(cf. 9:11) **toward the south** on **the road** that leads **from Jerusalem to Gaza.** Perhaps the pre-Lukan tradition located Philip in **Jerusalem** rather than in Samaria. For Luke, Jerusalem is the church's geographic center and Philip, who had evangelized in Samaria, north of Jerusalem, is now directed southwest. On the **desert road** Philip met a traveler who is sketched thus: First, he was an **Ethiopian,** a man with black skin (cf. Philostratus, *Life of Apol.* 6.1). He belonged to an exotic country, far away, along the upper Nile in the region now called the Sudan, not the present Ethiopia. Through Philip the gospel breaks down the barrier of race. Second, the traveler **was a eunuch,** which could designate a government official (cf. Jer. 34:19 with Jer. 41:19 LXX). Here the word indicates a castrated person, because his social position is given next and because officials in the service of queens were generally eunuchs. The Ethiopian man (thus in Greek) was only half a man and as such he was not permitted to join "the assembly of the Lord" according to the law (Deut. 23:1). But through Isaiah God promised to gather at the end-time not only foreigners, but also eunuchs (Isa. 56:3-8). When Philip baptized his fellow traveler he acted without precedent but he acted in accordance with the promise of God and the logic of the gospel as taught and lived by Jesus (cf. Luke 15:7, 10). Third, the eunuch held a high social position as **minister of the Candace, queen of the Ethiopians, in charge of all her treasure.** In the first edition of the RSV **Candace** was the queen's name, but historically it was a title, meaning "queen." The second edition therefore made a correction, but it is by no means clear whether in Luke's opinion Candace was not her name. The Roman prefect Petronius had launched a military expedition against an Ethiopian Candace in 23 B.C., and another one reached the capital at Nero's time, A.D. 61-62 (Strabo, *Geography* 17.1.54; Pliny, *Nat. Hist.* 6.178-197). On the road to **Gaza** the official in charge of the queen's **treasure** (Greek, *gaza*) will receive new treasures, the good news of Jesus, understanding of the Scriptures, Baptism, and joy. Fourth, in terms of his religious association the Ethiopian eunuch lived in no-man's-land. According to Luke he was neither a proselyte nor a Gentile but a person lingering on the fringes of Judaism. He had been on a pilgrimage to **Jerusalem to worship** there. He took the religion of Judaism seriously for, returning in his chariot to his homeland, **he was reading the prophet Isaiah,** reading aloud, as was the custom of that time.

29—**The Spirit** commanded Philip, **Go up and join this chariot.** The events of the narrative are under the direction of God who brings the two people together (cf. 9:10-12; 10:3-6, 19-20).

30—Hearing him read aloud from Isaiah, Philip asked, with a play on words, **Do you understand** (Greek, *ginōskeis*) **what you are reading** (Greek, *anaginōskeis*)?

31—The unnamed Ethiopian replied with a question, **How can I** understand this Scripture passage **unless some one guides me;** literally: "unless some one shows me the way" into the Scripture. Without the Jesus story the meaning of the Old Testament remains puzzling. Jesus himself had "opened" the Scriptures for his disciples on Easter and he had "opened" their minds to understand the Scriptures (Luke 24:32, 45). The eunuch **invited** Philip to **sit with him** and guide him in the interpretation of Scripture. In so doing he presented himself as the ideal person for conversion.

32-33—**The passage** which **he was reading** came from the fourth servant song of Isaiah and is cited according to the LXX (Isa. 53:7-8). References to the vicarious suffering of the servant of God are carefully omitted in this citation (e.g., Isa. 53:6, "the Lord laid on him the iniquity of us all" or, he was "stricken for the transgression of my people," Isa. 53:8). Luke avoided speaking of Jesus' death in terms of atonement or vicarious suffering. Therefore, he omitted Mark 10:45 in his Gospel and in this story he selected only those lines from Isaiah 53 which he understood according to his Christological pattern of humiliation and exaltation. There is no evidence that first-century Judaism identified the suffering servant of Isaiah 53 with the Davidic Messiah of Isaiah 11 and Psalm 2. But this identification occurred implicitly in the New Testament. Even when Isaiah 53 is cited in the New Testament, the theme of atonement or vicarious suffering for sins is absent (Matt. 8:17; Luke 22:7; John 12:38; Rom. 10:16). This theme appears in allusions to Isaiah 53 (e.g., Mark 10:45b; Rom. 4:25; 1 Cor. 15:3), while in citations individual features are connected with the suffering servant, (e.g., the lack of response to his message, Rom. 10:16; or the miracles of Jesus as bearing our diseases, Matt. 8:17).

The LXX text cited in v. 33 differs from the Hebrew text and the difference makes the application of Luke's Christological pattern of humiliation-exaltation possible. The one who like **a sheep** was **led to the slaughter** experienced **in his humiliation** that **justice was** denied him. **Who can describe his** adulterous and murderous **generation? For his life is taken up from the earth** through his resurrection-exaltation. An alternative to the RSV translation of v. 33 would be: "In his humiliation" (which ended in his death) "the judgment" of men "was taken away" by God (through his exaltation) . . . "for his life is taken up from the earth" (into heaven). Moreover, **his generation** may refer not to opponents but to his spiritual descendants who, through the reversal of the servant's fate, become his followers.

34—Politely the eunuch asked the decisive question, **About whom, pray, does the prophet** speak? in this text which he had just read. More precisely, does the prophet **say this about himself or about some one else** (cf. 2:29-31)? While the Jews in Jerusalem became enraged at Stephen's speech, this eunuch from the very fringes of Judaism asked the right question which led directly to Philip's instruction. What irony!

35—**Then Philip opened his mouth** (cf. 10:34) . . . **he told him the good news of Jesus,** relating it to this text from Isaiah 53 and in Luke's view to other texts such as Psalm 16 (2:25-32), Psalm 110 (2:34-36), Deut. 18:15-16 (3:22; 7:37), Ps. 118:22 (4:11), Psalm 2 (4:25-26; 13:33). The telling of the good news of Jesus is the content of Luke's Gospel, a brief summary of which is found in Acts 10:34-43. It included the offer of forgiveness of sins and Baptism in his name as well as Jesus' function in the final judgment.

36—Traveling together along the same **road they came to some water** and the eunuch asked his third and last question. **What is to prevent my being baptized?** His question presupposes that he has come to faith. A Western addition (v. 37) found in the footnote of the RSV made the eunuch's confession explicit. His question regarding what might **prevent** his Baptism (cf. 10:47; Mark 10:14; Greek, *kōlyo*) probably refers to the problem of impediments for Baptism. Clearly, his biological state as a eunuch is not one of them, nor is the biological age of children one (Luke 18:15-17).

38—The journey was interrupted, as **both went down into the water** and Philip **baptized him.** Thereby he placed him under the lordship of the Servant of God and incorporated him into his church, the people of God.

39—**When they came up out of the water, the Spirit of the Lord caught up Philip; and the eunuch saw him no more.** Just as the

Spirit brought these two people together so that they could travel along "the way," so now the Spirit separates their ways. With his mission completed Philip is caught up and miraculously translated like Elijah to another place (cf. 2 Kings 2:11, 16) where the Spirit entrusts a new mission to him (v. 40). **The eunuch saw him no more** (cf. 2 Kings 2:12), but in contrast to Elisha who *rent* his clothes the eunuch **went on his way rejoicing.** The Western text added that the Holy Spirit fell on him, but Luke's readers already know that Baptism and the gift of the Holy Spirit belong together (cf. 2:38). Moreover, his new-found attitude with which he leaves the story **on his way rejoicing** is a fruit of the Spirit (Gal. 5:22).

40—**Philip was found at Azotus,** the Philistine city of Ashdod, north of Gaza. From there he traveled along the coastal road and **preached the gospel to all the towns** (cf. v. 25) till **he came to Caesarea,** where he seems to have settled down. At any rate we find him there some 20 years later with four daughters— who were prophets (21:8-9).

The Conversion of Saul and His Subsequent Activity (9:1-31)

Luke had sketched Saul's persecution activity vividly (7:58; 8:1, 3). Having "laid waste" the church in Jerusalem he now proceeds to repeat his performance in Damascus but is overwhelmed on his way, thrown to the ground, and blinded by the superior power of Christ. His encounter with Jesus, his healing through Ananias, his reception of the Holy Spirit and his Baptism constitute the conversion of this exemplary persecutor of the church (vv. 1-19). Preaching in the synagogues of Damascus to the amazement of its members and arguing with diaspora Jews in Jerusalem, the former persecutor experienced a reversal of roles as he met antagonism from fellow Jews and threats on his life (vv. 20-30). With the conversion of the persecutor the church could live in peace, at least for a while (v. 31).

The narrative of Saul's conversion is strategically placed between the mass conversion of the Samaritans and the conversion of the first Gentiles (cf. 10:45; 11:18). In contrast to the pious and open-minded Ethiopian who was an ideal candidate for conversion, Saul was furiously "opposing God" (5:39) and "breathing threats and murder against the disciples of the Lord" (9:1). This unlikely candidate for conversion would become the Lord's chosen instrument, not by his own volition but by the gracious will of Christ; he also would assume an ever-increasing role in Acts. The importance of Saul's conversion is highlighted by Luke, who tells it three times: in chap. 9 in the form of a narrative, in 22:4-16 and 26:9-18 in the form of autobiographical reports by Paul. In addition to these three accounts the letters of Paul also refer to this decisive event in his life (Gal. 1:11-16; 1 Cor. 15:8-10; Phil. 3:6-8). In his letters Paul insisted that his Damascus experience was on the same level as the Easter experiences of the other apostles (cf. 1 Cor. 9:1; 15:8; Gal. 1:1). Hence, he too was an apostle. Luke, however, distinguished between the resurrection appearances prior to the ascension and subsequent visions of the exalted Lord (1:3, 21-22). Therefore, Luke did not regard Paul's Damascus vision as the qualification for the apostolate on a par with the Twelve. Moreover, Paul could not testify to the identity of the earthly Jesus with the Resurrected One, for he had not accompanied Jesus on his journey from Galilee to the ascension (1:22; 13:28-31). When in 14:4, 14 Luke granted the title *apostle* to Barnabas and Paul, he showed that he was aware of another tradition in which Paul and Barnabas were regarded as apostles. But in none of his three conversion accounts does Paul become an apostle.

It should not be surprising that the three Lukan accounts also show differences. To begin with, the first (chap. 9) is a conversion and healing narrative, while the other two focus on the call and commission of Paul. In chap. 9 it is not Saul but Ananias who hears from "the Lord" that the former persecutor is an instrument elected by Christ to confess him before Gentiles and Jews (vv. 15-16), whereas in chap. 22 Ananias transmits a call to Paul (22:14-16) and in chap. 26 it is Christ himself who calls Paul directly on the Damascus road— Ananias does not even appear. From the perspective of Luke's composition these differences are not contradictions but accommodations to the situations in which Paul tells the story of his life. The three accounts are also meant to supplement and clarify each other. For instance, in 9:7 we read that Paul's companions heard the voice but saw no one, whereas in 22:9 they "saw the light but did not hear the voice." Usually such differences are understood to be a sign of Luke's carelessness or even an indication of the presence of different traditions or sources. But if we read his accounts in chaps. 22 and 26 from the perspective that Luke is providing additional information and clarification, then we may understand the differences in the following way. Luke did not say in 9:7 that Paul's companions saw nothing, which would indeed contradict 22:9. He said: they saw no one, no person (Greek, *oudena*), which is clarified in 22:9 where we hear that they saw "the light." They did not see Jesus (cf. 9:17; 26:15-18) but only a bright light. Moreover, the Greek word *phōnē* may indicate a noise, a sound, as in 2:6, or the voice of intelligible words, as in 9:4. Reading 9:7 one may think that Paul's companions heard Jesus' words to Saul, but we should note that Luke did not write "*his* words" or "*his* voice," and he clarifies the matter in 22:9 by stating that they did not hear the voice, the words "of the one who was speaking." Therefore, what they heard in 9:7 were not the words of Jesus, but a noise, a sound from heaven, as in 2:6 or John 12:29. Finally, on the basis of 9:4, 7, a reader may conclude that only Paul fell to the ground, whereas according to 26:14 "we had all fallen to the ground." Yet Luke actually implied just that in 9:7. By using the Greek pluperfect he left open the possibility that his companions had stood up when they heard the sound. In short, from the perspective of Luke's composition we do not have to understand these differences in terms of contradictions or Lukan carelessness or the use of different traditions. The three accounts stress the objectivity of the Christophany and exclude Paul's companions from participation in that Christophany.

The Conversion and Healing of Saul (9:1-19a)

Part I. By Christ's Direct Action the Persecutor
      Is Overpowered (vv. 1-9)
  Introduction: the persecutor Saul (vv. 1-2)
  A. Saul's vision of flashing light (v. 3)
  B. Christ's first word to Saul (v. 4)
  C. Saul's puzzled reply (v. 5a)
  D. Christ's second word: a revelation (I am) (vv. 5b-6)
                     a command (rise)
                     a disclosure about the
                     future (you will be told)
  E. The companions of Saul (v. 7)

F. The results: blind   (vv. 8-9)
                  helpless
                  fasting

Part II. By Christ's Action through Ananias Saul Is Healed and
          Converted   (vv. 10-19a)
    Introduction: a disciple, Ananias   (v. 10a)
    A. His vision of Christ   (v. 10b)
    B. Christ's first word to him concerning Saul   (vv. 11-12)
    C. Ananias's puzzled reply   (vv. 13-14)
    D. Christ's second word: a command (go)   (vv. 15-16)
                            a revelation (he is my
                            chosen instrument)
                            a disclosure about the
                            future (I will show him . . .)
    E. The agent of Christ, his mission and message   (v. 17)
    F. The results: regained sight   (vv. 18-19a)
                      was baptized
                      took food

In the first part of the narrative (vv. 1-9) Saul, **still breathing threats
and murder** against the church, is directly confronted by the power
of the exalted Christ. Thrown to the ground and blinded, the persecutor's power is broken as he is led by the hand in a pitiful state
into Damascus. The overwhelming of the oppressor is followed in
the second part by his conversion and healing through the agency
of Ananias (vv. 10-19a). Moreover, through the Lord's word, addressed to Ananias only, the reader hears about Christ's plans for
Saul (vv. 15-16).

Individual motifs of this narrative have parallels in the Heliodorus
legend (2 Maccabees 3) and the romance of Joseph and Asenath.
But the differences are equally striking. Neither Heliodorus nor
Asenath are destined to be God's chosen instrument to carry his
name before Gentiles and Jews and to suffer for the sake of his name
(vv. 15-16).

Verses 1-2 introduce Saul in his role as persecutor, and presuppose
that **the disciples** live within the context of the synagogue. Jewish-
Christian disciples called Christianity **the Way** (19:9, 23; 24:14, 22).
This self-designation was also used by the people of Qumran (1QS
9:17-19; CD 2:6). Christians are those **belonging to the Way.** Christianity was not a new religion but a way of salvation and of discipleship which Jewish Christians lived as members of the synagogue.
Therefore, they could become victims of Saul's fanaticism.

His new goal was to bring Christian **men or women** (cf. 8:3) from the **synagogues at Damascus** as prisoners to Jerusalem. In order to accomplish his goal he needed **letters** of introduction and recommendation from the Jerusalem authorities, because Damascus lay outside of the immediate jurisdiction of the Jewish high priest. Saul would have to win the good will and cooperation of the leaders of the synagogues in this city, which is one of the oldest continuously inhabited cities on our planet and which had a large Jewish population during the first century (cf. Josephus, *War* 2.561; 7.368). Occasionally, by special arrangement, a Jewish high priest could extradite Jewish criminals from beyond Palestine (1 Macc. 15:15-21). Perhaps Caiaphas, who held the office from A.D. 18 to 36, procured the cooperation of the Roman authorities in this matter. Otherwise Saul always had the option of kidnapping, a possibility which he himself apparently experienced later on (cf. 2 Cor. 11:32; Acts 9:25). The police force in the Roman empire was woefully inadequate and with the aid of the local leaders of the synagogues Saul could reasonably expect to bring to justice the leading Hellenistic Christians who had fled Jerusalem (8:1, 4). Local synagogues had the authority to inflict punishment, like flogging, on their members (cf. 2 Cor. 11:24).

3-4—As **he approached Damascus** a sudden bright **light from heaven flashed about him,** making him fall helplessly to the ground. Light, lightning, and fire from heaven are traditional theophany motifs (cf. Ezek. 1:28; Acts 2:3). The sign of the supernatural blazing light is accompanied by sound (cf. 2:2-3) and Saul hears himself addressed, **"Saul, Saul."** The repetition of his name underlines the solemnity of the moment (cf. Luke 22:31; 8:24). **Why do you persecute me?** Up to this point Luke is careful not to say that Saul saw Jesus in the blazing light. That will be brought out indirectly in v. 7 and directly in v. 17. Nor does Saul yet know who addressed him. But the reader receives an important insight, namely, that Christ identifies himself with his disciples. "He who hears you hears me, and he who rejects you rejects me" (Luke 10:16, cf. Matt. 25:34-40). Because of Christ's identification with his followers, Saul had persecuted not merely his disciples but the exalted Lord himself.

5-6—Since Saul has not yet recognized the one he is encountering, he asked, **Who are you, Lord?** The reverential address **Lord** has its equivalent in the English "Sir." It is not a Christological title in this instance, because Saul does not yet know what this is all about. But the recognition of superior power is also implied in the address. In his reply to Saul's puzzled question Jesus reveals himself with the solemn revelation formula **I am** (cf. Exod. 3:6). **I am Jesus, whom you are persecuting.** So, Jesus is not dead after all, but exalted to heaven and surrounded with blazing, blinding divine glory. Years later Paul would recall this encounter which changed his life radically (1 Cor. 9:1; 15:8; Gal. 1:16; Phil. 3:6-8). The persecutor became a "slave" of Christ (cf. Rom. 1:1, *doulos*). He who had traveled to Damascus to seize the Christians has been seized by their Lord and, like a prisoner, is commanded: **Rise and enter the city, and you will be told what you are to do.**

7-9—Paul's traveling companions were awestruck. They saw **no one,** even though they were surrounded by an inexplicable light (22:9). They heard a sound from heaven, a **voice,** but did not hear the words of Jesus to Saul (22:9, see above). They could testify to the reality of a supernatural occurrence but they were not participants in the revelation of Christ to Saul. Blind and helpless, he is led into Damascus where he spent the next **three days** fasting and praying (v. 11), thereby expressing his repentance, as well as his shock.

10-12—The focus shifts from Saul to Ananias, a Christian in Damascus whom the Lord will use as his agent to heal Saul in body and soul. He is directed **in a vision** (cf. 9:12; 2:17; 10:3; 18:9; 1 Sam. 3:4) to Saul's lodging in Judas's house in Straight Street, which was the main east-west artery of the city. In his vision Ananias is told that Saul, too, had a vision and is expecting Ananias to **lay his hands on him** to **regain his sight.** This feature of a vision within a vision is found in the New Testament only in Acts (cf. 10:10, 19). We also hear, almost as an aside, that Saul's hometown is Tarsus, information we would not know from Paul's letters.

13-14—In his reply Ananias showed himself to be a reluctant messenger (cf. Jonah). He protested, pointing out what a dangerous person Saul really was, **how much evil** he had done in Jerusalem to the church. He also knew the purpose of Saul's coming to Damascus. Four designations of the church have been used in this episode: the **disciples,** those who belong **to the Way,** the **saints,** and those who **call upon the name** of the Lord (vv. 1-2, 13-14). The church appeared as people with whom Christ identifies himself (vv. 4-5).

15-16—The Lord Jesus overcame Ananias's protest, giving him the command **Go!** But it is not blind obedience which is demanded, for a reason is given. Ananias, and in this story only Ananias, is told that Saul is an **instrument,** literally, a vessel (cf. Jer. 18:3-6) specially **chosen** by Christ for his purpose, namely, to confess Christ before **Gentiles and kings and the sons of Israel. To carry my name before** refers not to Paul's missionary journeys but to his testimony, his witness, his confession of Christ in front of these groups (cf. Luke 21:12-17; Acts 9:20, 29; 23:11; 26:2; 27:24). Such testimony will involve Saul in suffering **for the sake of my name.** Instead of further inflicting suffering on others, Saul himself will experience it because of his testimony to Christ (cf. 9:23, 29; 14:22; 20:23; 21:27—26:32). Saul is chosen by Jesus to become his suffering witness.

17-19a—Ananias now obeys, comes to Saul, and addresses him as **brother.** This designation is reserved in Acts for Jews (e.g., 2:29) and Gentile believers (e.g., 16:2, 40), not for Gentiles as such. Saul remained the passive recipient as Ananias, **laying his hands on him,** announced that **the Lord Jesus** has sent him for two purposes: that Saul may **regain** his **sight,** be healed in body, and that he **be filled with the Holy Spirit,** be healed in soul (cf. Luke 11:13). The laying on of hands is a symbolic action used in miracle stories (cf. Luke 13:13; Acts 5:12; 28:8), in blessings (Mark 10:16), and in connection with the reception of the Holy Spirit (8:17). This action was done to Saul in agreement with the commission given to Ananias in v. 12. The healing miracle took place at once without any manipulations (cf. Tob. 11:11). **Something like scales fell from his eyes.** This may be an expression of folk medicine (cf. Tob. 11:13, "the white film scaled off from the corners of his eyes"). The healed Saul **was baptized** which, in view of Rom. 6:3 ("us"!), should not have been questioned by interpreters. That he also received the Holy Spirit is implied in v. 17, and should probably be connected with Baptism rather than with the laying on of hands. We are not told how or where, whether in the river Barada by immersion or in Judas's house by pouring water over him, he was baptized, but we may note that the earliest known Christian baptistry at Dura-Europos on the Euphrates river (dating from the first half of the third century) did not allow for immersion of adults. The baptized Saul took food again, ending his three-day fast (v. 9). At the beginning of the story we saw "the old Saul" filled with a spirit of self-righteous hatred, **breathing threats** (v. 1, *em + pneō,* "I breathe"; *pneuma,* "the spirit," "the breath"). At the end a new Saul **rose** up, "filled with the Holy Spirit," his conversion complete.

From this story one may draw encouragement: Christ is in control. Saul's conversion is an invitation to all opponents of the church to reconsider; an admonition to reluctant messengers, like Ananias, to love their enemies; and it also indicates the shape of ministry in terms of testimony and of suffering. Finally, Saul's conversion shows that God has not written off **the sons of Israel** (v. 15). The risen Christ overpowered his opponent for the sake of witnessing before Gentiles and Jews.

Saul's Activity in Damascus (9:19b-25)

19b-20—In stark contrast to his original intentions (vv. 1-2), Saul entered the fellowship of the **disciples at Damascus** and spent **several days** with them. Christians do not remain in isolation from the community of believers. We may assume that Ananias introduced Saul to the disciples. Moreover, **immediately** he enacted the revelation given to Ananias that he, Saul, would carry Christ's name before "the sons of Israel" (v. 15). In the **synagogues** of Damascus **he proclaimed** Jesus, and did so repeatedly (imperfect tense). According to Gal. 1:16 the purpose of the revelation of Christ to Paul was that he "might preach him among the Gentiles." Paul also preached to Jews (e.g., Rom. 15:19), but in Acts he always preached *first* to Jews. The content of his preaching was that Jesus **is the Son of God.** This title, which in Acts occurs only twice and both times on Paul's lips (cf. 13:33), is also found in his own reference to his Damascus experience (Gal. 1:16). For Paul and Luke the title **Son of God** expressed Jesus' relation to his Father. According to Luke 1:35 Jesus is the Son of God because he was conceived by the Holy Spirit in the virgin Mary. His origin and his relationship to God are unique. Because the virginal conception is not a theme in the witness of Acts, the title *Son of God* is extremely rare. Our author may have used it here because he was aware of its prevalence in the Pauline tradition.

21-22—The reaction of the members of the synagogue to Saul's conversion and testimony was amazement, especially since they knew of his past and of the original purpose of his visit. Instead of arresting Christians he now **confounded the Jews,** demonstrating, **proving,** on the basis of the Scriptures that **Jesus was the Christ,** the Messiah. For such argumentation see 2:25-36 and 13:16-39.

23-25—A plot of the Jews against Saul forced him to leave the city, **when many days had passed.** It is not clear whether the time reference in this verse is identical with the "several days" of 19b. (Note the conjunction "and" in v. 20 together with the adverb "immediately.") The same Greek words translated here "many days" are used in 27:7 and translated "a number of days." According to Paul's own statement, his leaving Damascus and returning to Jerusalem took place three years after his conversion (Gal. 1:18) which, even with inclusive reckoning of time, would be about two years. It would appear that whereas Paul in Galatians 1 sought to demonstrate his independence from the Jerusalem authorities—also in terms of a three-year absence from the city—Luke pursued the opposite goal and moved Paul's first visit into close proximity to his conversion, so close that the Jerusalem disciples were still afraid of him when he met them (v. 26).

Another reason for this tension between Galatians 1 and Acts 9 is that Luke apparently knew nothing about Paul's journey to Arabia, the territory of the Nabataean kingdom, the northern border of which lay close to Damascus (Gal. 1:17). This journey into the realm of the Nabataeans was not a religious retreat where Paul sought the solitude of the desert but rather a journey on which he witnessed to Christ and thus annoyed some Nabataean officials. This journey must be placed between Saul's first appearance as a Christian in Damascus and his exit **over the wall,** (or through a window in the wall) **in a basket,** because he wrote that, after going to Arabia, "I again returned to Damascus" (Gal. 1:17). Paul himself blamed his undignified exit in a basket by night on a Nabataean "governor under King Aretas" (2 Cor. 11:32-33), while Luke blames it on the Jews. This may not be mutually exclusive, since Saul's testimony probably angered not only Jews but also Nabataeans who lived in and around Damascus. If, as has been suggested, the Roman emperor Gaius transferred Damascus to Aretas in A.D. 37, then Aretas's representative intended to take legal action against Saul. If Damascus was not controlled by the Nabataeans then a Nabataean sheik living in or around the city may have wanted to kidnap Saul. According to Acts the Jews sought **to kill him** and for the first time Saul experienced the burden of his commission that "he must suffer for the sake of my name" (v. 16).

Saul's First Visit to Jerusalem (9:26-30)

The reader is surprised to find that in addition to **the apostles** there were also **disciples,** a community around the Twelve, in **Jerusalem.** The reader may think that some of the scattered disciples of 8:1 had returned to the city. The historian finds evidence here that only the Greek-speaking Christians around the Seven had been expelled from Jerusalem.

According to Paul this visit took place "three years" after his conversion (Gal. 1:18). Luke is not specific but gives the impression of a shorter period (vv. 19b and 23), suggesting that Paul obviously established his contact with the leaders of the Jerusalem community as early as possible. While Paul insisted that during this 15-day visit he saw only one apostle, namely, Peter, and the Lord's brother James (Gal. 1:18-19), the account in Acts states that **he went in and out among them** (the apostles, plural; vv. 27-28), and that he was **preaching boldly in the name of the Lord** (v. 29) in Jerusalem. This contradicts Gal. 1:22 where Paul wrote that he "was not known by sight" to the Judean churches at that time. Finally, the fear of the former persecutor by the Christians in Jerusalem seems incredible in light of Gal. 1:23-24, where we read, the churches in Judea had heard that "he who once persecuted us is now preaching the faith . . . and they glorified God because of me." Writing Galatians about 20 years after his first visit, Paul gave no indication that the disciples were afraid of him after they had heard about his conversion and subsequent witness. But in Acts 9 they question the genuineness of his conversion, because Luke's time span between Paul's conversion and his first visit to Jerusalem is relatively short, and Paul's missionary journey to Arabia and subsequent return to Damascus are omitted in Acts.

In this story Luke repeated motifs from 9:13-25 in order to make two points: first, to depict and establish the genuineness of Paul's conversion; second, to connect him with the apostles who represent the tradition. From the perspective of the Lukan narrative, it is quite understandable that the Jerusalem **disciples** felt threatened when their former persecutor wished **to join** them. What does he want from us? they might have asked. Our names and addresses so that he can finish his cruel job? This fellow ought to be avoided! **They did not believe that he was a disciple,** just as Ananias had expressed misgivings about him (vv. 13-14). His own word was not good enough. **But Barnabas,** a man with impeccable credentials (cf. 4:36-37) acted as spokesperson on behalf of Saul, just as the Lord had spoken to Ananias on Saul's behalf (vv. 15-16). We are not told why Barnabas but not the apostles knew that on the Damascus road Saul had indeed encountered the Lord. But Barnabas had become convinced of the genuineness of Saul's conversion and subsequent preaching, and he narrated Saul's story **to the apostles.** They in turn let themselves be convinced by Barnabas's narrative and accepted Saul even as a reassured Ananias had made contact with him (v. 17). Moreover, just as Saul after his Baptism by Ananias "was with the disciples" at Damascus (v. 19b) so in Jerusalem after his introduction by Barnabas **he went in and out among them** (v. 28). His preaching, the plots against him, and his escapes in both cities conclude the parallels. Luke has shown that Saul's conversion as well as his call to bear witness were acknowledged by the disciples and apostles of Jerusalem. In short, Saul was not an individualistic maverick, but was received in fellowship by the apostles; and he also participated in proclamation in Jerusalem which implies that he was fully approved as missionary preacher by that church and its apostolic leaders.

29-30—Like Stephen before him, Saul, too, engaged Jewish **Hellenists,** Greek-speaking Jews, in discussion; and as with Stephen so now these people seek **to kill him.** Christ's promise that Saul "must suffer for the sake of my name" receives a new partial fulfillment (cf. v. 23). Later on we will hear additional information about this visit from Paul (22:17-21). Once again, fellow Christians were able to thwart the plot on his life (cf. v. 25). They brought him to the port of **Caesarea** (cf. 8:40; 23:23-24, 31-35) **and sent him off to Tarsus** by boat. The church in Jerusalem avoided a repetition of Stephen's fate and its consequences (cf. 7:58; 8:1) by getting Saul out of the city. Martyrdom is not to be sought. Avoidance of known troubles is not necessarily cowardice but was sanctioned by the Jerusalem **brethren** and followed on later occasions (cf. 12:17; 17:10, 14; 19:30). Paul's return to **Tarsus** agrees with Gal. 1:21. Unfortunately, we

181

hear nothing about his activity in Cilicia until Barnabas, coming to Tarsus, asked him to join the work in Antioch (11:25-26).

In view of Gal. 1:22 it is unlikely that Paul had preached to Christians in Jerusalem as implied in Acts 9:28-29a. However, the matter is different when we turn to his dispute with Hellenists (v. 29b). It is rather probable that Paul would have contacted his former colleagues after his two- or three-year absence and spoken to them about the one subject that had become most important in his life, Jesus Christ. He, as well as they, had been responsible for the persecution of Christ's followers in Jerusalem and he may well have roused their antagonism by **preaching boldly** to them so that he was forced to leave Jerusalem after only 15 days (cf. Gal. 1:18). At any rate, he did not return for some 12–14 years (Gal. 2:1) and yet he could write in Rom. 15:19 "from Jerusalem and as far round as Illyricum I have fully preached the gospel of Christ" to unbelievers who had not yet heard it. Thus Paul clearly referred to his missionary preaching in Jerusalem and it is probable that he engaged in it during his first visit just as v. 29b states.

Summary Statement (9:31)

With the conversion of the persecutor completed, the church could live in peace, even though Paul himself had just experienced threats on his life (v. 29). The persecution of the church which began in 8:1 has come to an end, and Saul has gone offstage until 11:25. The word **church** is used only here and in 20:28 in the sense of the universal church—otherwise it always refers to local communities. The whole church is no longer limited to Jerusalem, as was the case at the beginning of the persecution but is present **throughout all Judea and Galilee and Samaria.** This phrase is interesting on three counts. First, the three regions are understood as one geographic unit. Thus the first part of the mandate of Christ in 1:8 has been completed and the second part, "to the end of the earth," is about to begin. Second, note the odd sequence of the regions and compare it with Luke 17:11. It would seem that Luke's knowledge of Palestinian geography leaves something to be desired (cf. Acts 23:23, 31-32 and the distance involved). Third, Luke had no stories about witnessing in Galilee after Easter. But since Jesus had many disciples in Galilee prior to his journey to Jerusalem (Luke 6:17), Luke may not have felt any need for a Galilean account in Acts.

The preservation of the church is not the work of men and women but it is God's work; **built up** by him it grew and was **multiplied.** Two metaphors are mixed here: the church as God's temple and as God's messianically restored people. With God at work in the church, the church is **walking in the fear of the Lord,** not the fear of slaves toward their despotic master, but the reverence of believers, like Saul saved by grace, toward their ultimate judge. Moreover, the church **walking,** that is, on its journey through history to its destined goal, receives **the comfort** (Greek, *paraklēsis*) **of the Holy Spirit** through hearing the Word of God ever anew. Through preaching to the church the Holy Spirit accomplishes his work of consolation and exhortation (cf. 11:23; 14:22; 15:32).

An overview of the church's growth indicates that in spite of rejections and persecutions, the witness to Israel had been a tremendous success (2:41; 4:4; 5:14; 6:7; 8:4, 6, 12; 9:31, 35, 42). This growth will continue and eventually reach "many tens of thousands" of Jewish Christians in Judea (21:20). The evil which people inflicted on the church by persecuting its members was turned into good. The church's existence in Judea, Galilee, and Samaria testifies to the faithfulness of God and his Messiah toward his people Israel, in spite of rejection of his Word. The church's existence demonstrates the success of the Spirit-informed witness among the people of God, even as it reveals a division within Israel. The church's external growth in Judea, Samaria, and Galilee corresponds to its internal strength as it walks in **the fear of the Lord.** Now with the church living **in peace** (9:31) and with Saul, the future missionary to Jews and Gentiles incorporated into the church, Luke's story must move toward the decisive breakthrough in Acts—the witness to the Gentiles. This breakdown of the barrier between Jew and Gentile is accomplished in Luke's story not just by anybody, but by the apostle who gave the keynote address at Pentecost, Peter, the spokesman of the Twelve.

Peter's Ministry of Healing in Lydda and Joppa (9:32-43)

These two miracle stories function as transition. They reintroduce Peter, bring him via Lydda to Joppa, which is in geographic proximity to Caesarea, and set the stage for the decisive episode of the conversion of Gentiles through Peter.

32-35—The healing of **Aeneas at Lydda** has the form of a traditional miracle story in which the exposition (v. 33) gives the name
of the sick person, the nature and duration of his illness. The performance of the healing is indicated by the pronouncement of the
healing word and the statement of the cure (v. 34). Finally, the
conclusion tells about the effect of the healing (v. 35). In this case
the conclusion also reflects the use of miracle stories in early Christian mission outreach. Through the telling of miracle stories people
were converted because miracles dramatically show the power of
the exalted Lord who is active in and through members of his community. The parallels with the stories of Jesus' healing a paralytic
(Luke 5:17-26) and of Paul healing a cripple (Acts 14:8-12) show that
Christ's healing power continues to be present in his servants (cf. 2
Cor. 12:12; Rom. 15:18-19).

Peter is presented as making a tour of places already evangelized,
visiting **all** the churches of the regions mentioned in the previous
verse. Unknown Christians had established the churches in Lydda
and Joppa as well as in Damascus (9:2). **Lydda** (the Old Testament
Lod) is located about 25 miles northwest of Jerusalem. Among **the
saints,** the people of God, Peter found **a man named Aeneas, who
had been bedridden for eight years and was paralyzed.** His Greek
name does not suggest that he was not a Jew. Peter's announcement,
Aeneas, Jesus Christ heals you, is an alternate form of pronouncing
healing "in the name of Jesus" (3:6; 4:10) and it presupposes that
the Lord continues his healing ministry through his chosen servants.
The announcement of healing is followed by the command, **rise and
make your bed,** which is instantaneously obeyed, demonstrating
the reality of the cure. The miracle resulted in mass conversions in
the city and the coastal plain of **Sharon** that stretched north toward
Mount Carmel. The **Lord** to whom **they turned** (cf. 11:21) is Jesus
Christ through whom Aeneas had been healed. Gentiles, on the
other hand, must first turn to the Lord God (cf. 1 Thess. 1:9; Acts
14:15; 26:18, 20). Jews, in distinction from Gentiles, do not change
their religion when they become Christians, but obtain the fulfillment of the promises made to their fathers (cf. 2:39; 3:24-26).

36-42—**At Joppa a disciple** whose name **Tabitha** in Aramaic, **Dor-
cas** in Greek, means "gazelle," was **full of good works** (cf. 13:10 for
the opposite) and gave alms freely. In short, she had "a treasure in
heaven" (Luke 12:33; Acts 10:2, 4) but she **fell sick and died.** As was

the custom the corpse was washed, but why it was brought to an **upper room** is not immediately clear. Peter is called to Joppa, which is about 12 miles northwest of Lydda, and upon his arrival is shown by mourning **widows** the **garments** which Tabitha had made for them. These widows were not a separate order within the church, as in the Pastoral Epistles, but seem to have been needy members of the community, as in 6:1. Putting **them all outside** was an action that differed from similar Hellenistic resuscitation stories in which the public is present (cf. Luke 7:11-17; Philostratus, *Life of Apollonius* 4.45), but it is in agreement with 2 Kings 4:33 (cf. 1 Kings 17:17-24). Peter, like Elijah and Elisha before him, **prayed** alone in the room. It is not the apostle but only his Lord who raises the dead. While the two Old Testament prophets stretched themselves upon the dead persons, Peter merely turned to the body and commanded **Tabitha, rise,** which in Aramaic would be *Tabitha, cumi,* like the words spoken by Jesus (Mark 5:40). By omitting any manipulations and by stating that Peter gave her his hand only after she had come to life again, Luke placed the focus upon the power of prayer and the power of the Word (Luke 11:5-13). The reaction to the miracle is that **many believed in the Lord.** Instead of returning to Lydda, as one would expect from v. 38, Peter remained **in Joppa for many days.** (The same Greek word translated "many" is used here as in 9:23.) He lodged in the house of Simon, a tanner, a detail given in anticipation of the following story (10:6, 17). The fact that rabbis regarded the tanner's job as being unclean is not reflected upon in Luke's concluding sentence.

The New Testament resuscitation miracles presuppose faith in the resurrection of Jesus. The story of Tabitha's restoration to life expresses the faith that the resurrected Lord can work through his servants when and where it pleases him. This miracle story has similarities with 1 Kings 17:17-24 and 2 Kings 4:19-37, which means that apostles in the power of the Spirit perform the works of the prophets of old and are their successors. Finally, this story praises the piety of good works and almsgiving, a subject dear to Luke's heart (cf. 10:2, 4, 31; Luke 3:11; 6:30; 11:41; 12:33; 18:22; 19:8). The Lord identifies with the poor and exalts the lowly and he exhorts his disciples to take care of the needy.

In these two miracle stories, faith is based on the miracles. In general, Luke avoided that kind of theology as we have seen in previous stories. Luke knew that miracles were ambiguous, that they did not always produce faith in the audience or in the healed persons (4:16-17; Luke 17:11-17), and that they could provoke unbelief (Luke 11:14-15). But for Luke, miracles could be a first step toward faith (Acts 3:9-10; 4:4) and therefore he was free to tell that the impact of Peter's miracles in Lydda and Joppa was faith, even though he generally held that faith arises from hearing the Word (4:4) rather than from seeing miracles. To faith miracles are God's witness to the resurrection of Jesus (4:30; 5:32b).

Interpreters have occasionally stated that in Acts the gospel is sent to the Gentiles because the Jews rejected it. This was certainly not Luke's point of view as he prepared to tell the story of Cornelius's conversion, signaling the decisive breakthrough of the gospel to the Gentiles. On the contrary, at the end of the first part of his story Luke tells us that the church was "at peace" in Judea, Galilee, and Samaria and that its membership "multiplied" (v. 31). Moreover, through Peter "all residents of Lydda and Sharon . . . turned to the Lord" (v. 35) and also in Joppa "many believed in the Lord" (v. 42).

In short, the Jews are not pictured as rejecting the Word of God when Peter takes that Word to the Gentiles. Instead, Luke tells of the continuing and unhindered success among the people of Israel, just as in the beginning (cf. 2:41; 4:4; etc.).

Part 2: The Witness to the End of the Earth (10:1—28:28)

■ Witness Not Only to Jews but Also to Gentiles (10:1—19:41)

Inauguration of the Gentile Mission (10:1—14:28)

The Pentecost of the Gentiles in Caesarea (10:1—11:18)

The importance of this narrative which begins in Caesarea, ends in Jerusalem, and stretches over several days (10:30, 48) is seen in the amount of space our author gave to it. With 66 verses it is the longest narrative in Acts. By comparison, the three accounts of Paul's conversion take up 43 verses. In importance it can only be compared to the Pentecost story of Acts 2. In both stories it was Peter who played the leading role. At Pentecost in Jerusalem he gave the keynote address which inaugurated and summarized the witness of Acts. Now at Caesarea, Peter's apostolic ministry finds its narrative climax as God, through him, inaugurates the mission to the Gentiles. His last words spoken in Acts (15:7-11) recall this high point which is also the turning point in the witnessing story of Acts. In contrast to the Baptism of the Ethiopian, which in Acts had significance only for him as an individual, the Baptism of the Gentile Cornelius and his household serves as reason for admitting Gentiles into the church. The gift of the Holy Spirit is not limited to Jews. The conversion of Cornelius constitutes God's own legitimation of the Gentile mission. Through four interventions (10:3-6, 11-16, 19-20, 44-47), God himself directed the course of action, bringing Peter and Cornelius together in one place, overcoming Peter's reluctance **to associate with or to visit** Gentiles (10:28) and finally making it impossible for Peter not to baptize them by granting the Holy Spirit to these Gentiles (10:44-47; 11:16-18), **just as on us at the beginning** (11:15; cf. 10:47). Therefore, this narrative tells of "the Pentecost of Gentiles" at Caesarea and with it the witness moves toward "the end of the earth" (1:8).

187

In retelling this story Luke had at his disposal a tradition which told of the conversion of a Gentile, Cornelius, in Caesarea. Luke expanded the tradition (e.g., 11:1-18); he repeated Cornelius's vision three more times; he added not only two speeches by Peter, but also his vision (10:9-16, 28). His purpose was to present dramatically that it was God who broke down the barrier between Jew and Gentile in the church and overcame the resistance of the church (e.g., 10:14, 28; 11:2-3) and that it was the community in Jerusalem which, after some hesitation, gave apostolic sanction to the Gentile mission (11:1-18).

Peter's vision (vv. 9-16) was in all probability another tradition which Luke introduced into this conversion story, making the necessary connections in vv. 9a, 17a, and 19a and reinterpreting the vision in vv. 28-29. In the Lukan reinterpretation the vision no longer deals with **eating** clean and unclean **food** but rather with people, with Jews associating with Gentiles (v. 28). In Acts neither Peter nor the Jerusalem community drew the conclusion from this vision that the distinction between clean and unclean food has been abrogated by God. Such an abrogation is found in Mark 7:18-19, which, however, is omitted in Luke's Gospel. Indeed, the original meaning of Peter's vision scored the same point, for it dealt with **eating** unkosher meat and it brought out the objection of the pious Jew (v. 14) to setting aside the laws of Lev. 11:2-47 and Deut. 14:3-21. It is historically quite probable that Peter had such a vision which prompted him to eat with Gentile Christians in Antioch (Gal. 2:12-14) and which developed into the tradition used in Acts 10. Luke, however, saw the matter of eating differently. In Acts he cited the apostles' decree three times (15:20, 28-29; 21:25). This decree set forth what "is necessary" for Gentile Christians "to abstain" from. In view of that decree Luke reinterpreted Peter's vision to mean that we "should not call any *person* common or unclean" (v. 28).

Moreover, Peter's vision appears as an insertion by Luke when we recognize that the flow of the narrative is not determined by it, but by the instruction which the Spirit gives to Peter, on the one hand (vv. 19b-20), and by the vision of Cornelius, on the other. Without Peter's vision the narrative sequence is close-knit. On the basis of a vision Cornelius sent messengers to Peter. Peter is instructed by the Spirit to follow them. Entering the house of the Gentile, Peter witnessed the coming of the Holy Spirit upon those present and therefore ordered them to be baptized. This could have been the shape of the tradition which told of an isolated incident of a pious Gentile becoming a Christian. Luke expanded the tradition and made the acceptance of Gentiles a matter of principle. He composed his narrative in seven scenes.

1-8 (Scene 1)—The focus shifts from Joppa to **Caesarea,** an important seaport and seat of the Roman government. The city was rebuilt by Herod the Great and named in honor of the Roman emperor. Its population consisted of Greeks and Jews and, apart from the period A.D. 41 to 44, when Herod Agrippa ruled as client king (cf. 12:1-4, 20-23), auxiliary forces—not a Roman legion—were stationed there. **Cornelius** as a **centurion** was a Roman citizen and commanded about 100 soldiers of the **Italian Cohort,** which consisted of up to 1000 archers. An Italian cohort was stationed in Syria from about A.D. 69 into the second century. Its presence in Caesarea prior to the time of King Herod Agrippa I (A.D. 41–44, cf. Acts 12:1) is not documented. Luke may have committed an anachronism. Cornelius is identified not as a proselyte, a Gentile who had become a Jew through the rite of circumcision (cf. 2:10; 6:5, Nicolaus), but as a God-fearer, a pagan who became attracted to Judaism and practiced its requirements insofar as this was possible. Cornelius's own piety extended to **all his household,** which included his wife and children, his servants and slaves, their wives and children (cf. v. 7). His piety expressed itself in the fact that he **prayed constantly to God** at the customary hours for prayer—as an officer he also had military duties to fulfill—and in the fact that he **gave alms liberally** (cf. Luke 7:4-5). Not only that but he gave them **to the people** of Israel. He was a friend of the people of God! In short, Cornelius was not just any pagan but one "who fears [God] and produces righteousness" (10:35). His spiritual quality is reiterated in vv. 2, 4, 22, 30-31, and 35. Yet simultaneously it becomes apparent as the story unfolds that his piety did not qualify him for salvation without faith in Christ and the gift of the Holy Spirit.

About the ninth hour, that is, 3 P.M. (cf. 3:1), the hour of prayer in Jerusalem's temple, Cornelius also prayed (v. 30) and **he saw clearly,** since it was broad daylight, **in a vision an angel of God** (Acts 5:19; 8:26). **Coming in** and addressing him by name the angel assured him that God had taken cognizance of his prayers and almsgiving. They **have ascended as a memorial before God** means the same as **your prayer has been heard and your alms have been remembered before God** (v. 31, cf. Ps. 141:2; Tob. 12:12; Sir. 50:16; Phil. 4:18). At this point in the story neither Cornelius nor the reader is told what God will do. Rather, Cornelius is commanded to act in blind obedience and send messengers 30 miles to Joppa to bring Simon Peter back with them. The importance of Cornelius's vision is brought out in the fact that it is retold three times (vv. 22, 30-32 and 11:13-14). God takes the initiative in opening the community of salvation to Gentiles, and Cornelius, in obedient response to God's command, **called two of his servants**—they were actually household slaves (*oiketes*, cf. Luke 16:13; 1 Peter 2:18)—and a **soldier** who was **devout** like Cornelius himself (cf. v. 2). **Having related everything,** the vision, the statement, and the command of the angel to his three delegates, **he sent them to Joppa.** Explicit as the divine instruction is, it must be obeyed or it cannot become effective.

9-16 (Scene 2)—The focus shifts to Peter. He had been called by Jesus for "catching men" (Luke 5:10); he had seen the glory of the transfigured Christ and heard the heavenly voice say, "Listen to him" (Luke 9:28-36); he had encountered the resurrected one whose final word gave the mandate to be his witnesses from Jerusalem to the end of the earth (1:8); and he had experienced the release of the Spirit by the exalted Lord. As the messengers of Cornelius approach Joppa, Peter is portrayed as praying at noontime on the flat roof of the house and, feeling hungry, he desired something to eat. Falling into a trance, he saw a vision (vv. 10-12) and heard a voice (vv. 13 and 15). Out of the opened heaven he saw something **like a great sheet** descending and in it were **all kinds of** [four-footed] **animals and reptiles and birds** (cf. the divisions of the animal world in Gen. 1:20-25; 6:20). And **a voice** commanded him, **Rise, Peter; kill and eat.** The mixture of diverse animals descending from **heaven** meant that they all are creatures of God (cf. 1 Tim. 4:3-4, ". . . everything created by God is good . . .") and therefore the voice commanded him to eat without discriminating between clean and unclean animals. This, however, is strictly against the law (cf. Lev. 11:2-47; Deut. 14:3-21).

In short, Peter has become the recipient of a special revelation, like Cornelius, but, unlike the pagan centurion, Peter replied with **No** (by no means), **Lord** (v. 14). And he gave a reason for his refusal to obey: **I have never eaten anything that is common or unclean** according to the standard of the law of God. Peter's reply recalls the confession of Ezekiel's faithfulness in matters of food (Ezek. 4:13-14). But the heavenly **voice** admonished the apostle: **What God has cleansed,** or declared clean, **you must not call common** or unclean (cf. Rom. 14:14, *koinon;* 1 Cor. 10:25-26). Three times Peter was invited to eat. Three times he rejected the invitation and three times he was admonished by the heavenly voice. Then **the thing,** or vessel (Greek, *skeuos*) like a sheet, vanished **to heaven** and Peter was left wondering. When we ask why Peter refused to obey the heavenly voice, the answer lies in his negative reply. His past experiences as a pious Torah-abiding Jew made it unthinkable for him to eat unkosher meat, to eat without discrimination. The attitude of Mark 7:19 which is advocated by the heavenly voice was not that of Peter in this narrative. Yet it was a revelation which he had just experienced and which he acknowledged in the address "Lord." However, he did not know its meaning. In contrast to Cornelius's revelation, in which the angelic words had a literal meaning, Peter's revelation and the heavenly voice have an allegorical meaning which, however, Peter did not yet know. This contrast makes it clear that we are not dealing here with the Hellenistic notion of the double dream, or double vision. For not only are the visions not identical nor directly related to each other (cf. 9:11-12) but the message of the one is to be taken literally (10:4-8) while the other is an allegory—which suggests that Peter's vision was inserted by Luke.

17-23a (Scene 3)—The messengers of Cornelius arrived at the gate of Simon's house but before they met Peter, the omniscient narrator tells us twice about Peter's inner state of perplexity **as to what the vision . . . might mean** (vv. 17 and 19a). Did God test him because he was hungry (v. 10)? Should the heavenly command be understood literally? Then it would be contradictory to God's past message. If not, what does it mean to eat all kinds of meat without discrimination (v. 12)? With Cornelius's messengers at the gate inquiring for his whereabouts, Peter, still in a state of confusion on the flat roof, received a new revelation. **The Spirit said to him . . .** (v. 19).

Peter, like the reader, would now expect a solution to the problem of the vision. Instead he is asked by the Spirit to accompany the messengers in blind obedience **without hesitation** (v. 20a). This last phrase could also be translated "without discrimination," or "without making a distinction." In fact, all of these meanings are appropriate here. Peter is to go with them because the Spirit has **sent them** (v. 20b). So, for the immediate present, Peter has to obey and forgo a solution to the problem of his own vision (cf. John 13:7; Acts 9:16).

As he went down to meet the messengers he was already on his way to discovering the meaning of his vision, not all at once, but step by step. Asked for **the reason** for their **coming** they narrated the experience of Cornelius. This narrative provides another step for Peter to understand his own vision. Without hesitation and discrimination Peter is to accompany the messengers of this pious Gentile who is **well spoken of by the whole Jewish nation** (cf. 22:12) because the same Spirit who had spoken to him on the rooftop had also appeared in the form of an angel to Cornelius, commanding him to send these **three men** (one ms, B, ignoring the "devout soldier," has "two men"). Still, in this scene which relates three divine interventions to each other, Peter did not articulate any new insight. However, with the messengers standing before him and with the story of Cornelius's experience forging a bond with his own experiences, he had to make a decision. And **so** he extended hospitality to the messengers in the house of Simon, a tanner. This "so" is emphatic and indicates that Peter's decision is in response to the narration of Cornelius's vision. By this act he took another step toward understanding the meaning of his ambiguous experience. He **called them in to be his guests** (v. 23) which, of course, included eating a meal with them (cf. v. 10b). The meal beyond doubt was kosher for we hear that Peter was a pious Jew (cf. v. 14), but associating with Gentiles and eating with them was another matter. In one form or another Peter may have heard: "Separate thyself from the nations [the Gentiles] and eat not with them . . . and become not their associate" (Jub. 22:16; cf. Joseph and Asenath 7:1).

Peter moves and is moved one step at a time on the basis of the logic of faith and the experience of God in the present. He does not yet know what his vision is all about, but he, the first named of the apostles, has extended hospitality to Gentile outsiders and in so doing the line between "insiders" and "outsiders" has become blurred, "without hesitation," "without discrimination."

One concluding comment to this scene: the messengers told Peter that Cornelius is **to hear what you have to say** (v. 22). These words are an addition to the angel's message in vv. 4-6 which will be elaborated further in v. 33 and in 11:14. Moreover, they prepare the reader for Peter's speech in vv. 34-43.

23b-33 (Scene 4)—The next day Peter, the three messengers of Cornelius, and **brethren from Joppa** began the 30-mile journey to Caesarea which took about a day and a half (v. 24). The six-man delegation (cf. 11:12) of Jewish Christians from the church in Joppa accentuates the nature of Peter's meeting with Cornelius. It will not be a private visit of two individuals but a precedent-setting encounter between representatives of the (Jewish-Christian) church and Gentiles. The delegates of Joppa will also function as witnesses to the result of the meeting (v. 45) and of the truthfulness of Peter's report to the church of Jerusalem. Cornelius, too, had assembled **his kinsmen and close friends** in his house.

When Peter entered . . . : This verb is found twice (vv. 25 and 27; cf. 21:15b, 17a; 28:14b, 16a), in order to highlight the importance of this step of entering the home of a Gentile. By entering, Peter is blurring the distinction between Jew and Gentile (cf. vv. 15 and 20). On the other hand, Cornelius, by falling down at his feet and worshiping Peter is blurring the distinction between God and his creature (cf. 14:15; 28:6; 12:22). **Stand up; I too am a man** (v. 26), not a heavenly being, but a human being. As human beings Cornelius and Peter are equals. Both are creatures of God and stand on the same side of the dividing line that separates the creature from the creator. Now Peter has come to understand at least one part of the vision and the voice which had been troubling him. The basic issue is not meat and food but people, and Peter is now ready to give a first interpretation of his vision (vv. 10-16). **You yourselves know,** he said to the assembled group of Jews and Gentiles, **how unlawful it is for a Jew to associate with or to visit anyone of another nation.** To be sure, in actual life, contact with Gentiles was sometimes unavoidable, especially in mixed communities, but associating with them as equals without hesitation and discrimination (cf. v. 20) was a breach of the law in the eyes of a devout Jew. **But God has shown me that I should not call any** (woman or) **man common or unclean.** Equality between Jews and Gentiles on the basis of their common creaturehood is part of the revelation which God has shown him. This insight amounts to a conversion of Peter who at last can articulate the meaning of the vision and of the Spirit's command (vv.

10-15, 17, 20). He has begun to perceive the implications of the
vision. The words which he used (v. 28b) to express them were not
identical with the words of the heavenly voice (v. 15) because Peter's
words have been shaped by his subsequent experiences. He now
understood that the vision is to be taken allegorically, not literally.
The animals symbolize people who, like the diverse animal creatures
(vv. 11-12), come from God. The full meaning of the words, "What
God has cleansed" (v. 15a), has not yet dawned on him. So he asked
Cornelius why he **sent for** him (v. 29b).

Cornelius himself now narrated his experience (vv. 30-32). **Four
days ago** (v. 30) should actually be three days ago (cf. vv. 9, 23, 24),
but may be an odd way of reckoning time. Cornelius concluded his
summary by stating: **So I sent to you at once** (v. 33) which parallels
Peter's **So . . . I came without objection** (v. 29). The two men had
been brought together not only by God's intervention but also by
their obedience to God's command. **Now therefore we are all here
present in the sight of God, to hear all that you** [Peter] **have been
commanded by the Lord God** (v. 33). Thus Peter remains the focus
of the narrative (since v. 9) as the Gentiles—with high expectation—
wait for his speech.

34-43 (Scene 5)—Peter's speech came in response to Cornelius's
direct request (v. 33) and also as a result of hearing the story of the
centurion's experience. Peter has come a long way in this Lukan
narrative. He had offered hospitality to pagans and accompanied
them without hesitation and discrimination as directed by the Spirit.
He had entered the house of Cornelius and announced what God
had shown him individually (v. 28). He had come to understand that
all human beings, be they Jews or Gentiles, are first of all creatures
of God and therefore equals. Peter is now taking another step as he
moves from the area of the First Article of the Apostles' Creed into
the Second Article, so to speak, and proclaims Jesus Christ as Lord
of all and Judge of all (vv. 36, 42). Through his name **every** believer,
Jew or Gentile, receives forgiveness of sins (v. 43), be he pious like
Cornelius or wayward like the prodigal son (Luke 15:11-24). Forgiveness is not cheap grace, it is free grace. However, to be acceptable to God, forgiveness and faith are to be expressed in prayer
and "doing righteousness" (v. 35). The prodigal son, received into
his father's house, may no longer live among the swine. His conduct

must reflect and implement his acceptance by his father. In interpreting Peter's address we should pay attention to the whole speech and its structure and not merely to vv. 34-35 lest we turn Luke into a moralizer. "What God has cleansed" (v. 15) through "forgiveness of sins" (v. 43) received "by faith" (15:9; cf. v. 43) is not "unclean" (v. 15).

Three parts of the speech can be distinguished: the introduction (vv. 34-36), the kerygma (vv. 37-41), consisting of the story of Jesus, followed by the conclusion (vv. 42-43). The introduction and the conclusion show a balanced structure.

Peter opened his mouth and said: Truly I perceive that
(A) God shows no partiality, but in **every** nation **any one** who fears him . . . is acceptable to him (34-35).
   (B) God sent his word to Israel, preaching peace through Jesus Christ (36).
      (C) He (Jesus Christ) is Lord of all (36).
         He (Jesus Christ) commanded us to preach to the people and to testify (42a).
      (C') He (Jesus Christ) is to be judge of the living and the dead (42b).
   (B') To him (Jesus Christ) all the prophets bear witness (43a).
(A') Forgiveness of sins through his name (is what) **everyone** receives who believes in him (43b).

The kerygma, vv. 37-41, consisting of the story of Jesus—the only one outside of the Gospels, is introduced with **you know** (contrary to RSV which places these words prior to v. 36, see below). The life of Jesus is summarized in two parts (vv. 38 and 39b-40). Each part is followed by a reference to the apostles as witnesses (vv. 39a and 41).

34-35—Peter began his speech with the insight that **God shows no partiality.** This was a matter of general Jewish conviction. "The Lord your God . . . is not partial and takes no bribe" (Deut. 10:17). As judge God shows no favoritism. Peter's experiences during the last four days have led him to a deeper understanding of this principle. God's impartiality applies not only to the Jewish people but extends beyond them to include also the Gentiles. Because he is not some tribal deity (cf. Rom. 3:29), therefore **in every nation any one who fears him** and practices righteousness **is acceptable to him** (cf. Rom. 2:11-16). Cornelius was presented as "a God-fearing man"

195

(vv. 2, 22, 30) who therefore prayed. Fear of God is not the feeling of terror of the transcendent, but the recognition that God expects to be honored, that his will is to be fulfilled, that he remains the impartial judge, and that in prayer we may address him (vv. 2, 30). "Practicing righteousness" (rather than doing **what is right,** RSV) is Luke's equivalent to giving alms, and Cornelius had performed such works (vv. 2-4). Therefore, as a God-fearing Gentile he is just as acceptable to God as any pious Jew. But what "God-fearing" and "pious" entail in this speech are indicated in the conclusion (vv. 42-43), which is the counterpart to the introduction.

36-38—These verses are grammatically very difficult sentences, as can be seen when different translations or commentaries are compared. Without belaboring the various grammatical and textual problems which have produced varying translations, we shall follow the solution of the Swedish scholar, Harald Riesenfeld, who took v. 36 to be in apposition to the object clause of vv. 34b to 35. The text then reads as follows:

> (34) Truly I perceive that God shows no partiality, (35) but in every nation anyone who fears him and practices righteousness is acceptable to him. (36) This [namely, the statement just made] is the word which he sent to the children of Israel, preaching good news of peace through Jesus Christ—He is Lord of all. (37) You know what took place throughout all Judea. . . .

"The word which God sent to the children of Israel" is the good news that God shows no partiality, that acceptance by God and entrance into his kingdom are not dependent on race or nationality but on reverence, faith, obedience, and the practice of justice and mercy, as the proclamation of Jesus has set forth. The word which God addressed to Israel through the ministry of Jesus is **the good news of peace** brought about by Jesus Christ, God's agent. *Peace* is synonymous with *salvation* (cf. Luke 1:79; 2:14). Peace between Jew and Gentile is the horizontal implementation of the vertical dimension of the saving Word sent by God to Israel, proclaimed and established by Jesus Christ, God's eschatological agent. By establishing peace between Jew and Gentile **he is** acclaimed and confessed as **Lord of all,** Jews and Gentiles. Our outline above indicated that v. 36 has its counterpart in v. 43a: **to him** [Jesus Christ] **all the prophets bear witness.** This is brought out in our verse by allusions to Ps. 107:20 and Isa. 52:7 (LXX). The Old Testament interprets the ministry of Jesus as the gospel of peace, and thus bears witness to him.

37-41—In place of an explicit scriptural quotation we hear a summary of the story of Jesus beginning from Galilee and ending with the witnesses to his resurrection. What is its purpose within the speech? *Peace* (salvation) is dependent on the person of Jesus (cf. 4:12). Jesus' present Lordship as well as his future function as judge (v. 42) are the result of his mission and fate. Therefore, in place of an explicit scriptural quotation, Peter tells the Gentiles the story of Jesus as proof of the affirmation made in the introduction (vv. 34-36). The absence of an explicit Old Testament quotation may also be due to the audience (cf. 14:8-18).

37—"You know what took place throughout all Judea" (in place of the RSV). Luke stressed that the mission of Jesus was a public event, not something that "happened in a corner" (26:26; cf. Luke 7:17; Acts 2:22) and Cornelius could be expected to know about it. Peter, however, will be interpreting his mission in its significance. **Judea** should be taken to mean "the country of the Jews," referring to the entire land, not just the southern part. Jesus' public ministry began after his baptism (Luke 3:23; Acts 1:22).

38-39a—It was after his baptism while Jesus was praying that **God anointed Jesus of Nazareth with the Holy Spirit** (Luke 3:21-22; cf. Luke 4:18). In contrast to Mark, Luke placed a prayer between Jesus' baptism and the descent of the Spirit, thereby avoiding the notion that John's baptism mediated the Spirit and that Jesus became John's successor. The gift of the Spirit conveyed the **power** of **healing all that were oppressed by the devil** (cf. Ps. 107:20; Isa. 61:1; Luke 11:20). In his healing miracles Jesus showed himself to be a true benefactor who **went about doing good** (Greek, *euergeteō*), the very opposite of the self-styled benefactors who abounded then as now (Luke 22:25). Peter stressed the deeds of Jesus here (cf. Luke 5:12-15, 29-32; 7:36-50; 8:1-2, 26-56), since his teaching had already been included in v. 36. Both his words and deeds are interpreted as actions of God through his agent Jesus Christ in whom "God has visited his people" (Luke 7:16). The clause **for God was with him** gives the reason why Jesus was a true benefactor. Luke applied the same expression to Joseph in Egypt (7:9), Mary, the mother of Jesus (Luke 1:28), John the Baptist (Luke 1:66), unknown Christian preachers in Antioch (Acts 11:21), and to Paul (18:10). They are all benefactors in the service of God, the supreme benefactor. This first part of the kerygma closes with a reference to the witnesses who accompanied

Jesus from the beginning (cf. 1:21-22a) and who can testify to the power of God at work in him (cf. 2:22).

39b-41—In stark contrast to Jesus' benefactions among the people was his fate: **They put him to death by hanging him on a tree** (cf. 5:30). The language of Deut. 21:22 to which Luke alludes brings out the shamefulness of the crucifixion. He does not refer to the guilt of the Jews of Jerusalem because they are not being addressed here. In Gal. 3:10-14 Paul had used the next verse of Deuteronomy (21:23) in order to announce the saving significance of Christ's death. Luke generally avoided speaking about Christ's death as salvation event. Instead he used a contrast pattern: they killed him, **but God raised him on the third day.** "The good news of peace" (v. 36) between Jew and Gentile is grounded not only in Jesus' word and deed but, above all, in his resurrection. Luke would fully agree with Paul's statement "If Christ has not been raised, then our preaching is in vain" (1 Cor. 15:14), and add that without the resurrection Gentiles could never become part of the people of God. The Christ event centers in the resurrection, according to Luke, and the resurrection is guaranteed by witnesses who had been with him before and after Easter and **who ate and drank with him after he rose from the dead** (v. 41; cf. Luke 24:41-43; Acts 1:4, 21-22). Already the pre-Pauline formula which summarized the basic content of faith and of preaching connected the resurrection of Christ on the third day with witnesses to whom he appeared (1 Cor. 15:3-5). He appeared to them, and they were changed by his resurrection appearances. They **were chosen by God as witnesses** (v. 41), said Peter, their representative. In saying this he gave expression to the basic trinitarian logic of Christian language. God, Christ, and the Holy Spirit according to Luke are distinct and yet inseparable. It was Jesus who had chosen the apostles (Luke 6:13-16) and appointed them to be his witnesses after the resurrection (Luke 24:48). Yet their election took place "through the Holy Spirit" in Acts 1:2 (see comments ad loc.) while here it is **God** who elected them.

42-43—These verses bring the climactic conclusion. Because the resurrection is the focal event of God's salvation, Christ **commanded** his witnesses **to preach to the people,** the Jews. Why is there no reference to Gentiles who are now being addressed and who were certainly included in Christ's final command before the ascension

(1:8, "to the end of the earth")? Luke's answer is that salvation reaches the Gentiles through the Jews, through "the people" (cf. v. 36 "to Israel," v. 37 "throughout all Judea," v. 39 "the Jews," "Jerusalem," v. 42 "the people"). Part of the apostolic preaching is that Christ by virtue of his resurrection **is the one ordained by God to be judge of the living and the dead** (cf. 2 Tim. 4:1; 1 Peter 4:5; John 5:22, 27; Acts 17:31). Our relationship to God and our future depend on his verdict. The belief in Christ as future judge of all human beings may have grown out of the futuristic Son of man sayings of the synoptic tradition (e.g., Luke 12:8). This belief interprets the resurrection of Jesus as that eschatological verdict of God which of divine necessity must reach its culmination in a final judgment. Then it will be manifest who God is, namely, the one who raised Jesus from the dead and ordained him to be the judge of all. Luke is not interested in *when* this will happen, but *that* it will take place, and the resurrection is its pledge and promise. Between Easter and the parousia the Christian church is in mission (v. 42a), namely, God's eschatological act to unite humankind "through the good news of peace by Jesus Christ" (v. 36), which is addressed first to "the people" and through them to the Gentiles.

To Christ **all the prophets bear witness** (v. 43). This is a typically Lukan statement (cf. Luke 24:27 and 44; Acts 26:22). Moreover, **forgiveness of sins through his name** is announced not only by the chosen witnesses of Christ but already by the prophets (cf. Luke 24:45-47). Luke may be thinking of Isa. 33:24; Jer. 31:34; Isaiah 53; Joel 2:32. The judge of the last day who is "Lord of all" (v. 36) offers forgiveness to **everyone who believes,** Jew or Gentile, as promised by the prophets. All debts are canceled. The forgiveness that God had granted to Israel in the past and the forgiveness that Jesus granted during his earthly ministry (Luke 5:20) and in his death (Luke 23:34, 43) was ratified by God at his resurrection. Henceforth forgiveness is dependent on **his name,** that is, on his power as Lord of all.

This final sentence (v. 43) returns to the theme of the universality of the gospel which forms an *inclusio* with the introduction. God shows no partiality, everyone is acceptable to him, because through Christ, who is Lord of all, there is peace for all, and **everyone who believes in him** (cf. 13:39) receives the forgiveness of sins from him whom God ordained to be the judge of all. But also the scandal of particularity, highlighted in the story of Jesus (vv. 37-41) forms an *inclusio* ("to Israel," v. 36; "to the people," v. 42), which indicates not only Israel's salvation-historical priority, but also God's plan to reach the Gentiles through Israel and its Messiah. Finally, the concluding sentence helps us understand the meaning of the opening sentence: **Anyone who fears him and does what is right** is **every one who believes in him** and **receives forgiveness of sins through his name.**

When we compare Peter's speech to Cornelius with Paul's Areopagus speech (17:22-31), we recognize that both begin with an acknowledgment of the piety or religiosity of the audience and both end with a reference to Christ as future judge. But otherwise these two speeches to pagans are strikingly different. In the place of the Jesus story of Acts 10 we find an introduction to the doctrine of God in Acts 17. The reason for this difference lies in the different audiences. Cornelius was already a God-fearer, the Athenians were not.

44-48 (Scene 6)—While Peter was still speaking, a holy anomaly occurred. The **Holy Spirit fell** upon Cornelius, his relatives, and his friends before they were baptized. The Spirit took hold of **all who heard the word.** In contrast to the Pentecost in Jerusalem where the Spirit was poured out unmediatedly, Luke tells us that here it is the word which mediates the Spirit. Peter's last declaration that "everyone who believes in Christ receives forgiveness of sins through his name" (v. 43) precipitated a new experience, the Pentecost of the Gentiles in Caesarea. The sending of the Holy Spirit is the answer and gift to faith (cf. 11:17; 15:8) and faith is hearing the word. The Jewish delegates from Joppa who had accompanied Peter (v. 23) **were amazed.** What happened was unexpected. The tradition in which they had grown up held that ever since the time of the Sinai covenant Gentiles have been excluded from receiving the Holy Spirit. Moreover, many Jewish Christians believed that the church's mission should concentrate only "on the lost sheep of the house of Israel" (Matt. 10:6), because only on the Day of the Lord—and not before—would God lead the Gentiles to Mount Zion (cf. Isa. 2:2; Mic. 4:1-3). Now the Jewish Christians themselves witnessed that God is full of surprises, that **the gift of the Holy Spirit had been poured out even on the Gentiles.** They drew this conclusion because **they heard them speaking in tongues and extolling**

God. From the effect they deduced the cause. They could do so because they themselves had experienced the gift of the Spirit. Incidentally, the "speaking in tongues" of v. 46 should be distinguished from the speaking in "*other* tongues," or native languages of Acts 2:4,6,8. The Gentiles of Caesarea praised God in glossolalia (1 Corinthians 14).

Then Peter, moved by God's intervention to take another step, arrived at a still deeper understanding of his vision. "God has cleansed" the Gentiles (v. 15) through forgiveness of sins (v. 43) and the gift of the Holy Spirit (v. 44). The same God who created Jew and Gentile alike and who offers forgiveness of sins to every believer through Christ has granted his Spirit also to Gentiles; therefore they are equal to believing Jews. God has accepted them and demonstrated that he "shows no partiality" (v. 34). Peter now asked a rhetorical question which presupposed a negative answer.

Can anyone forbid . . . baptizing these people? Is there any impediment for Baptism in a case where God has made his decision (cf. 8:36)? Just as Paul generally did not baptize (cf. 1 Cor. 1:13-17) so Peter may not have baptized the household of Cornelius and his friends, but **commanded them to be baptized** by someone else. They were **baptized in the name of Jesus Christ** (cf. 2:38). Christian Baptism, whether by immersion or by pouring water over a person's head, is a rite in which the baptizer calls upon the name of Jesus, just as one calls upon his name on the occasion of healing (cf. 3:6). The candidate probably confirmed this invocation by a baptismal confession (cf. 8:37; Rom. 10:9). Baptism in the name of Jesus Christ grants forgiveness through Jesus Christ; it places the baptized person under his present Lordship, promises the gift of the Spirit, and incorporates him or her into the Christian community.

The recognition of the equality between Jewish and Gentile believers prompted Peter to take still another step. When the Gentile believers of Caesarea **asked him to remain some days** with them he accepted their invitation (cf. John 4:40), stayed, and therefore also ate with them (v. 48, cf. 11:3). For Peter, accepting the hospitality of these Gentiles was the horizontal implementation of the vertical experience narrated in vv. 44-47. One cannot preach the gospel to people, or regard them as equals, and then refuse to eat with them. The problem of food that is raised here is not solved until chap. 15, but what has been solved is the acknowledgment of equality between Jewish and Gentile believers. Equality among God's people is the basic issue here, in comparison to which the problem of food is a secondary matter, even though relating to people also involves eating with them. God has accepted the Gentiles as Gentiles without circumcision and the question now arises whether the church will follow his decision.

11:1-18 (Scene 7)—Peter's stay with the Gentile Christians in Caesarea also created the time span necessary for this news to reach Jerusalem and come to the attention of **the apostles and the brethren,** referring to the Christian community understood as brotherhood and sisterhood. **So when Peter went up to Jerusalem** his actions were challenged and he had to defend himself. The RSV reads **the circumcision party criticized him.** The Greek text, however, does not include the word "party" but simply speaks of "those who were circumcised" (cf. 10:45; Greek, *hoi ek peritomēs*) which, because all were Jews, refers to the whole Christian community of Jerusalem. With the phrase "those who were circumcised" Luke introduced their basic theological problem: May uncircumcised people, on an equal basis, belong to the church, to the messianically restored people of God whose male members have all been circumcised (cf. 7:8)? Different problems that affect the integrity and unity of the church had already appeared in 5:1-11; 6:1; 8:14-16, 18-24; and 9:26. Now the question arises, How should Jewish believers relate to Gentile believers? Luke gives a first answer in this section and a final one in chap. 15.

The mere fact that the members of the Jerusalem community were free to criticize Peter demonstrates that the apostle's relationship to them was not patterned after the model of ruler and subjects. Only because they were able freely to express their opposition could there be agreement and praise of God in the end (v. 18). They had **heard that the Gentiles also had received the word of God** (v. 1). They had understood that what had happened at Caesarea was not an isolated exception but a new direction in the church's mission. Henceforth Gentiles who receive the Word of God (cf. Luke 8:15; Acts 8:14; 17:11) are members of the church. But in what sense? Do we Jewish believers have to associate with them?

Addressing Peter directly, they raised one objection in two parts and demanded to know the reason for Peter's scandalous behavior. **Why did you go to uncircumcised men? And** why did you **eat with** them? (v. 3). They did not object to his preaching to Gentiles or even baptizing them, but did Peter have to enter their home? (cf. 10:25, 27, where the same Greek verb is used as in 11:3). Certainly he should not have eaten with them (cf. 10:23, 48). How can a ministry which leads to ritual defilement forbidden by God be in agreement with the will of God? Facing the criticism of his people, Peter did not take his stand on his apostolic authority nor did he give an extended theological discourse, but he began to narrate his own experiences **in order** (v. 4, cf. Luke 1:3 where the same Greek word is used). An orderly report of his experiences in which the sequence of events permits his audience (and the reader) to recognize God at work was what Peter presented to his critics.

He told about his vision in Joppa (vv. 5-10, cf. 10:9-16), the messengers of Cornelius, the six Christians of Joppa who accompanied him and who are now present and can verify his report (v. 12), and finally about the events in Cornelius's house. In Peter's recapitulation of his experiences we note slight variations which Luke preferred to a wooden verbatim repetition. We now hear that Cornelius in his vision was told that Peter **will declare to you a message by which you will be saved, you and all your household** (v. 14; compare 10:5 with 22, 33, and 11:14). Peter's present understanding shaped his interpretation of the past experience of Cornelius. In retrospect, that is, in light of 10:44-48, Peter understood what Cornelius's vision was all about (11:14). Moreover, **as I began to speak,** Peter said, **the Holy Spirit fell on them,** while in 10:44 the descent of the Spirit came not at the beginning but during his speech, and actually at its traditional conclusion (cf. 2:38-39). This variation illustrates that God is ahead of his servants. Moreover, the gift of the Spirit to the Gentiles is now explicitly related to the first Pentecost: it **fell on them just as on us at the beginning** (v. 15). Finally, Peter closed his report with **a word of the Lord** (v. 16) just as Paul did in his speech to the elders of Ephesus (20:35). In both instances the verb "to remember" is used to introduce it. **I remembered the word of the Lord, how he said, "John baptized with water, but you shall be baptized with the Holy Spirit"** (v. 16; cf. 1:5; Luke 3:16).

The experience of the Spirit falling on Gentiles prompted Peter to **remember** a word spoken in the past and to apply it to a new situation in the present. The resurrected Jesus had addressed this word once spoken by John the Baptist (Luke 3:16) to a group of *Jews*

(1:5). For them this promise found fulfillment on the first Pentecost. In the light of his new experience Peter came to understand that the first Pentecost was only a partial fulfillment of this promise and that the Pentecost of the Gentiles completed it. What is remembered from the past receives a new meaning through the ongoing work of the Spirit in the present. This applies not only to Luke's interpretation of the Old Testament but also to his interpretation of the words of Jesus. In v. 17 Peter drew the conclusion on the basis of his experience: **If then God gave the same gift to them as he gave to us . . . who was I that I could withstand God** and refuse to baptize them (cf. 10:47)? To do so would have been an act of defiance of God (cf. 5:39). This argument presupposes the interconnectedness of the gift of the Spirit with water Baptism.

The reaction of the Jerusalem Christians to Peter's report was praise rendered to God. Peter's narrative had changed the minds of his critics because they were open to a God who acts in the present just as Barnabas's narrative of Paul's experience had changed the minds of the apostles and disciples (9:26-27). **They glorified God,** and exclaimed, **Then to the Gentiles also God has granted repentance unto life** (v. 18). They clearly understood that the events in Caesarea had constitutive significance for the church as a whole. Just as in Luke's design, Acts 2 enabled the witness to be heard in Jerusalem, Judea, and Samaria, so Acts 10:1—11:18 opens the road of witnessing "to the end of the earth" (1:8) by legitimating mission to Gentiles. Instead of forgiveness (10:43) received by Gentiles the Jerusalem Christians speak of **repentance unto life** which God grants to Gentiles. Repentance is not a first step toward forgiveness but the turning of a person to God and Jesus Christ. This is possible only because God has turned in grace toward the Gentiles and the story of God and his Anointed has the power to turn people around. Hence **repentance,** like forgiveness, is **granted** by God (5:31; 11:18). God created the opportunity for repentance through the preaching of his word by his servants and it is his word which brings about repentance.

Finally, we should note that while a basic decision has been made in this groundbreaking narrative in which God's initiative for starting the mission to Gentiles is joyfully acknowledged by the church, it is also clear that the implications of this decision have not yet been worked out by the church in Jerusalem. In his report, Peter had not directly addressed the issue of eating with Gentiles for which he was criticized (11:3). The issue of eating is present in 10:10, 13-15, 23, 41c, 48; 11:3; but the church under the guidance of the Spirit moves one step at a time. The details of how table fellowship between Jewish and Gentile Christians ought to be regulated are left to the apostles' conference to decide (Acts 15). There once again—and for the last time—Peter will speak and give his final interpretation of the Cornelius episode, of God's breaking down the barrier between Jew and Gentile.

The Churches in Antioch and in Jerusalem (11:19—12:25)

With the admission of Gentiles ratified by the church in Jerusalem, the focus shifts to Antioch, Syria, where Christians expelled from Jerusalem had established a mixed community of Jewish and Gentile believers. This community was closely tied to Jerusalem through Barnabas, its delegate, who in turn asked Paul to join him in the work in Antioch (11:19-26). When Agabus, one of several itinerant prophets from Jerusalem, arrived in Antioch and announced the coming of "a great famine," the Antiochian community expressed its unity with the church in Jerusalem by sending relief (Greek, *diakonia*) through Barnabas and Saul. This famine relief visit forms brackets around events that impinged on the life of the Jerusalem community (11:27-30; 12:25). The benefaction by the Christians of Antioch is contrasted with the persecution of the church in Jerusalem by their ruler. King Herod Agrippa I "laid violent hands upon some" members, beheaded James the brother of John, and had Peter arrested (12:1-5). God rescued Peter from prison (12:6-17) and punished Herod, the self-idolizing oppressor (12:18-24). With two brief statements on the church's growth in spite of all afflictions, and on the return of Barnabas and Saul to Antioch (12:24-25), the stage is set for a new venture of the Spirit proceeding from Antioch. Luke has also deftly introduced two new figures, John Mark, to whose house Peter went after his release and who accompanied Barnabas and Saul to Antioch (12:12, 25), and James, the Lord's brother who, together with the elders, after Peter's departure would lead the church in Jerusalem (12:17; cf. 15:13-21; 21:17-26).

The Church in Antioch (11:19-30). Luke's report has two parts, (vv. 19-26 and 27-30), each of which contains three subsections: *(a)* the beginning of the mission to Jews and Gentiles in Antioch by unnamed disciples was blessed by God with growth (vv. 19-21); *(b)* the delegate of the church in Jerusalem, Barnabas, recognized the grace of God at work in Antioch and the community grew (vv. 22-24); *(c)* Barnabas brought Saul to Antioch and both taught **a large company** who **for the first time** were **called Christians** (vv. 25-26). In the second part Luke reported *(a)* the arrival of unnamed prophets from Jerusalem (v. 27); *(b)* the specific prophecy of Agabus (v. 28); and *(c)* the decision of the community in Antioch to send relief to the church in Jerusalem (vv. 29-30).

19-21—Luke's report returns to the effect of the persecution narrated in 8:1-4. There we heard that members of the church in Jerusalem **were** all **scattered,** except the apostles. However, a community of disciples around the apostles was present in Jerusalem during Paul's first visit (9:26-30) and during Peter's report (11:1-18). Historically, **those who were scattered** (8:4 and 11:19) were the Greek-speaking Jewish Christians of Jerusalem who had been led by the Seven and who were called Hellenists (6:1). Luke generalized the extent of the persecution and in so doing created a tension between 8:1 and 11:19 on the one hand, and 9:26-30; 11:1-18 on the other. The disciples, scattered like seed through the persecution, bore fruit by preaching the word (8:4), converting only Jews and establishing congregations **as far as Phoenicia** (modern Lebanon) **and Cyprus and Antioch** (Syria) (v. 19). We hear later on of communities in **Phoenicia** (15:3) and its cities Tyre (21:4-6), Ptolemais (21:7), and Sidon (27:3). Barnabas and Mnason were natives of **Cyprus** (4:36; 21:16). Apart from 11:19 we have no knowledge of Christian communities on Cyprus prior to the mission of Barnabas and Paul (Acts 13:4-12). However, **some** of the scattered disciples, who were natives **of Cyprus and Cyrene** preached also to Greek-speaking pagans in **Antioch.** Two of the preachers of Cyrene may have been Lucius and Simeon Niger, the Black (13:1; cf. 2:10; 6:9). One of the Seven, Nicolaus, a proselyte, came from Antioch (6:5).

While some manuscripts have **Greeks** (in v. 20, so also RSV), the better manuscripts read "Hellenists," which refers to people who use the Greek language (and customs), be they Christians (6:1), Jews (9:29), or pagans (11:20). The contrast with "Jews" (v. 19) clearly indicates that the Hellenists in Antioch were pagans who had adopted Greek language and culture in this racially mixed city.

Antioch, Syria, the third-largest city of the empire after Rome and Alexandria, had a mixed population of around 500,000—Syrians, Greeks, people from Asia Minor, and Jews. It had been the capital of the Seleucid kings, among whom the infamous Antiochus IV Epiphanes ("God manifest") became the persecutor of Judaism, desecrating the altar of the temple in Jerusalem in 167 B.C. (cf. 1 Maccabees 1). After the Roman conquest of that region in 64 B.C., it became the seat of Roman governors. From Pompey onward, the Romans lavished public buildings on Antioch and it was there that Mark Antony married Cleopatra, queen of Egypt.

It is indeed amazing that the Jesus movement which began in rural Galilee and remained a rural movement throughout his life was able to establish itself in a cosmopolitan setting within a decade of its beginnings. It was in the urban setting of Antioch that a mixed community of Jewish and Gentile Christians came into being which engaged in an aggressive mission to Gentiles, **preaching the Lord Jesus** to them.

The acclamation "Jesus is Lord" (cf. 1 Cor. 12:3; Phil. 2:11; Rom. 10:9) had two roots. One was the acclamation of the Aramaic-speaking church which in its worship cried out "maranatha," "our Lord come," referring to his parousia (1 Cor. 16:22; Rev. 22:20). The other was the Christian interpretation of Ps. 110:1 in the light of Easter (cf. 2:34-35). For Luke, Jesus is Lord of both Jews and Gentiles (cf. 10:36), and therefore the mission to the Gentiles has a Christological foundation. Even though the conversion of Cornelius constituted the decisive breakdown of the barrier for Gentile mission in Acts, it was from Antioch, and not from Jerusalem, that historically this mission was pursued with vigor. **And the hand of the Lord was with them** (v. 21) is an Old Testament expression which is synonymous with the Spirit, or the power of God (cf. Luke 1:66; 2 Sam. 3:12; Isa. 66:14). God granted success to their **preaching** so that **a great number . . . turned to the Lord,** confessing at their Baptism, "Jesus is Lord" (cf. 1 Cor. 8:5-6; 12:3). The disciples bore witness to Jesus through *preaching,* and *God,* the Holy Spirit, bore witness to him through signs and wonders (cf. 4:30; 5:32; 14:3).

22-24—News of this existence of a mixed congregation of Jews and Gentiles reached **the church in Jerusalem** which asserted its role of leadership and supervision and **sent Barnabas** as its official representative to Antioch (cf. 8:14 and 9:32; 11:1-18). He had been introduced by Luke as a Levite from Cyprus who had given the proceeds from the sale of a field to the church in Jerusalem for the care of the poor (4:36-37). Through his intervention Paul had been accepted by the apostles (9:27). **Barnabas was full of the Holy Spirit and of faith,** like Stephen (cf. 6:5), but only of Barnabas is it said in Acts that **he was a good man.** He was not one of the Hellenists but belonged to the Aramaic-speaking community under the Twelve and had the complete trust of the apostles. As a Levite he certainly knew something about cultic purity. Yet what he perceived in Antioch's Christian community was not religious chaos created by indifferent people, but **the grace of God** at work and **he was glad.** The wordplay between *charis* ("grace") and *echarē* ("he was glad") cannot be reproduced in English, but we can understand Luke's point. Seeing God's grace at work among these Gentile believers of Antioch was the reason for Barnabas's joy. This "son of exhortation" (*paraklesis*, 4:36) **exhorted them all to remain faithful,** not to rules, regulations, dietary laws, and cultic practices, but **to the Lord.** Luke's narrative presupposes that the Gentiles were not circumcised and that the relationship between Jewish and Gentile believers posed no problems in Antioch. Barnabas not only approved but actively promoted the work in Antioch and **a large company was added to the Lord,** or probably "through the Lord" (cf. Acts 2:41). The mission in Antioch implemented the principle of v. 18b which stated that "to the Gentiles also God has granted repentance unto life."

25-26—Barnabas invited **Saul** of Tarsus to join the work in Antioch and together **they met with the church.** This mixed group of Jewish Christians and uncircumcised Gentile Christians who did not observe the Torah was just as much **the church** as was the community in Jerusalem (v. 22; 5:11; 12:5). Paul and Barnabas **taught a large company** of people **for a whole year,** which refers either to evangelism or to teaching converted (i.e., baptized) members, or both. **In Antioch the disciples were for the first time called Christians.** The designation **Christians** indicates that *Christ* is no longer understood as a title, the Messiah, but has become a proper name. The ending *-ianus* in Latin and, from there, *-ianos* in Greek meant a follower, a supporter of someone. Like Herodians, which means Herod's people (Mark 3:6), Christians means Christ's followers. The verb **were called** implies that it was not a self-designation by disciples but a nickname probably given to them by the populace of

Antioch rather than by Roman officials. Originally it may have had a negative connotation, like "Christ's lackeys." In Acts it is never found in the mouth of Christians (cf. 26:28), but soon the followers of Jesus accepted this designation as a title of honor (cf. 1 Peter 4:16 and the letters of Ignatius, bishop of Antioch). Finally, this designation indicates that the Christians of Antioch were recognized as a group distinct from the synagogue. The Romans frequently misunderstood *Christus* as *Chrestus* ("Useful"), which was a common slave name (Tacitus, *Annals* 15.44; Suetonius, *Life of Claudius* (25.4).

27-30—The second part of Luke's report on the Antiochian church is loosely connected with the first by the introductory phrase **Now in these days.** Unnamed **prophets . . . from Jerusalem** arrived in Antioch. The church was born as a prophetic movement (2:17-18). Jesus himself was regarded as the eschatological "prophet like Moses" whom God promised to raise up (Acts 3:22; 7:37). His Spirit had been poured out over his church. Miracles, bold proclamation, as well as glossolalia, were signs of the Spirit's presence in the community (3:1-8; 4:31; 10:46). Prophets stood out as a distinct group within the Spirit-endowed community and Luke gives us the names of some—Agabus (11:28; 21:10), Silas, Judas Barsabas (15:22), and the daughters of Philip (21:9). In the hierarchy of charismata Paul ranked the prophets second, after the apostles (1 Cor. 12:28-29, cf. Rom. 12:6; Eph. 4:11; 3:5). The church in Antioch itself was led by prophets whose names are given in 13:1. While prophets generally revealed the will of God for the present (cf. 15:32), **Agabus** made a prediction of a future **great famine over all the world.** Luke dated the famine as occurring during the reign of emperor **Claudius** (A. D. 41–54) indicating that Agabus's prediction came true. A worldwide famine did not actually occur during Claudius's reign. However, Judea suffered hard times and food shortages during A. D. 46 to 48, when Tiberius Alexander was procurator of Judea and Queen Helena of Adiabne sent grain from Egypt to Jerusalem (cf. Josephus, *Ant.* 20.51). The reaction of the church in Antioch to Agabus's prediction was not to build larger barns for themselves (cf. Luke 12:16-21) but to express their unity of faith in terms of social solidarity. The decision was made that **every one according to** her or **his ability** (cf. 1 Cor. 16:2) would contribute to the relief (Greek, *diakonia*) for their Christian sisters and brothers in Judea. We do not know the form which the relief took, but this Antiochian community which owed its very existence to refugees from Jerusalem (vv. 19-21), which was approved and led by Barnabas—who had shared his possessions (4:36-37)—and visited by prophets from Jerusalem was able and willing to express the unity of the church and to help the mother church in its hour of material want. Spirituality in Acts is inseparable from social solidarity (cf. 20:35), and the new Jewish-Gentile community in which Barnabas had seen the grace of God at work (v. 23) expressed anew the ideal of the Jerusalem church (cf. 4:34-35) by helping to feed the hungry and needy there. This interchurch relief was sent through Barnabas and Paul **to the elders** in Jerusalem.

This is the first appearance of **elders** of the church in Acts (cf. 14:23; 15:2,4,6,22,23; 16:4; 20:17; 21:18; Titus 1:5; 1 Tim. 5:17,19). Their presence anticipates a change in the leadership of the church in Jerusalem. The twelve apostles, like the twelve patriarchs, represented the people of God who, through them, were asked to appropriate the promises fulfilled through Christ. The roots of the Twelve are embedded in salvation history. The elders, with one man presiding over them, have their origin in the synagogue. In Acts 15 apostles and elders coexist, while in 21:17-19 James appears as leader of the elders and apostles are no longer mentioned.

In 11:28 the Western text (see introduction) brings its first "we" passage in Acts; it reads: "And there was great jubilation; and when *we* had come together one of them named Agabus said, signifying through the Spirit. . . ." This "we" passage probably resulted from the desire to identify Luke with Lucius mentioned in 13:1. But this section (11:19-30) gives no indication that the author of Acts was intimately acquainted with the beginning of the church in Antioch. Therefore we must conclude that the first original "we" passage appears in 16:10, in accordance with the Alexandrian text.

The brevity of Luke's report about the origins of the church in Antioch indicates a deliberate change of pace after the detailed narration of Cornelius's conversion; it may also be the result of the paucity of traditions available to him. He did not reproduce an Antiochian source but used bits and pieces of different kinds of information to produce this report. It has been suggested that historically Barnabas was one of the Hellenists who established the church in Antioch and that Luke constructed his report on the basis of the traditional list of prophetic leaders in Antioch found in 13:1.

Therefore he had to get Barnabas from Jerusalem to Antioch and Saul from Tarsus to Antioch. This suggestion, however, is based on the unlikely assumption that historically **Barnabas** was one of the Hellenists. Though he was a diaspora Jew and came from Cyprus, he was a Levite and belonged to the community led by the Twelve, not to that led by the Seven (cf. 4:36; 9:27). Therefore, Luke's report of vv. 19-26 may well be historically trustworthy in its essentials. That Barnabas and Paul worked together in Antioch is known to us also through Gal. 2:1-16.

The prediction of a **famine** by Agabus and the subsequent relief sent to Jerusalem prior to the apostles' council (Acts 15; Gal. 2:1-10) probably also reflects a historical incident. Agabus may have spoken about an eschatological, apocalyptic famine which would precede the End (cf. Mark 13:8; Luke 21:11). In spite of that the Antiochenes may have reacted with *diakonia* for Jerusalem. If Mark's imminent-end expectation did not prevent him from writing his gospel, why should an imminent famine stop Christians from sending relief? However, three items of Luke's report (vv. 27-30; and 12:25) raise serious historical difficulties. (1) His interpretive comment that a worldwide famine took place under Claudius (v. 28b) contradicts our knowledge of that period, according to which only regional famines occurred at that time. (2) By using the famine visit (11:30; 12:25) as *inclusio* Luke dated this visit to a time prior to the death of Herod Agrippa I in A.D. 44. Yet according to Josephus there was no famine in Palestine during Herod's reign, although one did occur there between A.D. 46 and 48. (3) Paul's participation in this famine relief visit is irreconcilable with his own statements in Gal. 1:18; 2:1, where he emphatically asserted that he had visited Jerusalem only once prior to the apostles' conference (Gal. 2:1-10 = Acts 15).

In light of these difficulties it would seem that the famine relief visit may have taken place ca. A.D. 46-47, prior to the apostles' conference, and that the Antiochian collection was transmitted by Barnabas only. Luke, knowing about Paul's cooperation with Barnabas, added his name in 11:30 and 12:25. Naturally, other solutions have been proposed to the problem of the famine relief visit in relation to the autobiographical data found in Galatians. We shall briefly deal with two of them.

(1) It is widely assumed that Paul's second visit to Jerusalem in

Acts (11:30) is identical with the second visit in Galatians (Gal. 2:1-10). One would also have to assume that Luke dated this second visit incorrectly (prior to Herod's death in A.D. 44); otherwise Paul's conversion, which took place 15 to 17 years prior to his second visit (Gal. 1:18; 2:1), would have been around A.D. 27–29, which is patently absurd.

The equation of the visit of Acts 11:30 with that of Gal. 2:1-10 raises other serious difficulties. It demands, for instance, that Galatians was written prior to Paul's visit in Acts 15 and therefore it would have had to be addressed to the churches evangelized during his first missionary journey (Acts 13–14). But this "south Galatian hypothesis" does not commend itself. Paul, a native of Asia Minor, would no more address the Christians of Pisidia with "O foolish Galatians!" (Gal. 3:1) than he would address the Jews with "O you Syrians!" In addition, the whole ecclesiastical tradition has always regarded the Galatians to be the people of the northern region around ancient Ankyra (present Ankara), a region through which Paul traveled after his Jerusalem visit in Acts 15. If Galatians is not addressed to the churches of Acts 13–14 then Paul's silence about a third Jerusalem visit in his letter becomes the decisive argument against the equation of the visit of Acts 11:30 with that of Gal. 2:1.

The equation of the Acts 11:30 visit with that of Galatians 2 also demands that Barnabas and Paul engaged only in informal conversations with the apostles, and that the official decisions were made at Paul's third visit of Acts 15. However, according to Gal. 2:1-10 neither Paul and Barnabas nor the "pillars"—James, Peter, and John—acted as private individuals reaching an unofficial agreement among themselves. Rather, they functioned as the representatives of their respective communities and they reached an official agreement on the subjects of the circumcision of Gentile believers, the division of missionary labors, and the collection for the poor. Hence, the equation of the visit of Galatians 2 with that of Acts 15 would commend itself, while its equation with that of Acts 11:30 does not. Finally, had Paul during his Galatians 2 visit actually brought a collection to Jerusalem, then he would have had to formulate Gal. 2:10 differently—as most commentaries on Galatians point out. Not only is an exhortation to remember the poor strange if Paul had just done so by delivering the Antiochian collection, but Paul would also have missed a golden opportunity for strengthening his case in Galatians 2 when he failed to note the gratitude of the Jerusalem church for the gifts just received. Actually the visit of Galatians 2 has as little to do with the presentation of a collection as Acts 11:30 has to do with the issue of circumcision.

(2) Another solution to the famine relief visit of Acts 11:30 correctly recognizes that the Lukan account bears the marks of his language and of his interests in tying daughter churches to the mother church of Jerusalem and in expressing social solidarity. Some interpreters have argued that Luke composed his unified account on the basis of three traditional fragments: one, a prediction by Agabus about an eschatological famine; two, information that Barnabas and Paul had traveled together to Jerusalem (cf. Gal. 2:1); and three, Luke had heard that Paul had something to do with collecting money for the Jerusalem church. The conclusion is drawn that Luke naively placed the collection at the beginning of Paul's Antiochian ministry, when in reality it should have come at the end of his ministry (cf. Rom. 15:25-32).

However, we should take cognizance of the fact that Luke was quite aware of Paul's collection brought to Jerusalem immediately prior to his arrest (24:17) and yet he did not connect it with Antioch. It is of course possible that Luke misconstrued multiple sources of information containing references to a collection by making them into two collections (Acts 11:30 and 24:17), when in reality all of his diverse traditions referred to one and the same endeavor at the end of Paul's ministry, prior to his arrest. However, it seems more probable that Luke is essentially right with his Antiochian relief action of 11:30. Had he permitted his imagination to control his composition at this point he would certainly have had Barnabas and Paul present the collection to the apostles rather than to the elders, and at least he would have noted the gratitude or a blessing or an exhortation of the mother church to its fledgling daughter community in Antioch. Hence, we conclude that in all probability it was Barnabas alone who brought famine relief to Jerusalem prior to the apostles' conference of Acts 15 = Gal. 2:1-10.

The Church in Jerusalem (12:1-25).   Once again Luke changes his pace, shifting from a bare report about the beginnings in Antioch to a vivid, dramatic narrative about incidents in the life of the community in Jerusalem just prior to Herod's death in A.D. 44. His narrative is bracketed by the sending and the return of Barnabas and Saul, the delegates from Antioch. Luke had also used the technique of telling a story between brackets in his Gospel. (The same Greek verbs occur there as here: *apostellō* in Luke 9:2; Acts 11:30; *hypostrephō* in Luke 9:10; Acts 12:25.) Luke's brackets suggest the presence of the Antiochian delegates in Jerusalem during Herod's persecution and express solidarity in suffering between churches. The brackets also create a contrast between the church's *diakonia* and benefaction on one hand and Herod's persecution on the other.

Other contrasts which enliven his account are: James's execution by Herod and Peter's miraculous deliverance by God (vv. 2 and 6-11); the persecutor's power of judgment and his powerlessness in the face of God's judgment (vv. 1-3 and 20-23); the work of men making absolutely sure that their plans will succeed and the work of God who in sovereignty brings to naught the quests of men (vv. 4-6 and 6-11); the crisp activity of the angel of the Lord and the passiveness of a drowsy Peter (vv. 6-10); Peter, fast asleep, even though his execution was just hours away (v. 6); the precision and speed of his liberation in contrast to the slowness of the community's comprehension (vv. 12-17). The church had prayed for Peter, but found it hard to believe that its prayer had already been answered (vv. 5b and 12-17). Herod had curried the favor of the Jews and lost the favor of God (vv. 3 and 23). He wanted to celebrate in splendor, basking in the adulation of men, but his feast turned sour (vv. 20-23). He was "struck" to death by the angel of the Lord while Peter was "struck" by the angel to life and liberty (same Greek verb in vv. 7 and 23). Herod accepted deification from pagans only to be eaten by worms (vv. 22-23). Besides enlivening the narrative, the contrasts also give it theological depth.

The narrative moves briskly, yet focuses long enough on the decisive action, Peter's deliverance, to give it cohesiveness. Different groups of people make their appearance: the guards (vv. 4 and 18-19); the Jewish people (vv. 3 and 11); the citizens of Tyre and Sidon and their delegation (v. 20); the people of Caesarea (v. 22); Christians who were persecuted and others who were praying (vv. 1, 5, 12) and brothers to whom a message was to be transmitted (v. 17). Names of individuals give specificity to the story: James the brother of John, Peter, Mary, John, Mark, Rhoda, James the Lord's brother, Barnabas and Saul, Blastus and Herod, and, last but not least, the angel of the Lord.

The story keeps the reader in suspense. The persecution of some Christians and the execution of James raises the question of whether Peter's fate would be the same. Neither he nor the community were expecting his release from prison. Then the unexpected happened. The closeknit narrative of the angel's appearance, the quick falling off of the chains, the process of getting Peter dressed and moving (vv. 7b-8), passing the guards, coming up to the locked and impregnable "iron gate," and its miraculous opening by itself, all indicate Luke's endeavor to heighten suspense.

Beginning with v. 11 the reader participates in a gradual process of recognition, first by Peter himself, then by the maid and, after some confusion, by the community. In the last part of the account the negative effects of Peter's deliverance accumulate, beginning with the guards' bewilderment, continuing with their examination and ending with their execution which, like James's execution, constituted a false judgment. Luke closely related the different parts of his story, e.g., Herod who had endeavored to gain favor with the Jews of Jerusalem by executing Peter cannot find him and therefore leaves for Caesarea in dismay, seeking new honors there, only to come completely to naught. The church, which experienced its powerlessness in the face of the oppressor, came to recognize God's power in an unexpected way, while the church's opponents—Herod, the soldiers, the Jews, and the pagans of Caesarea—recognize nothing of God's work.

Luke composed his narrative on the basis of three traditions: (1) The martyrdom of James, son of Zebedee and brother of John, was in all probability more detailed than the one-sentence account given by Luke. Our author shortened it and used it merely as background for Peter's imprisonment. (2) Another tradition dealt with Peter's liberation from prison, but we are not able to determine its limits. (3) A popular story of Herod's death is similar to one used by Josephus (*Ant.* 19.345-350). Luke combined these traditions and structured his narrative in four parts: (1) persecution by Herod (vv. 1-4); (2) Peter's deliverance (vv. 5-10); (3) recognition of his deliverance by Peter and the community (vv. 11-17); (4) effect of the deliverance on the guard and on Herod (vv. 18-23). Two brief notes on the church's growth in spite of and through persecution and on the return

215

of the Antiochian delegates complete this narrative and lead to new action which will proceed from Antioch.

Peter's deliverance from prison has parallels with similar stories in Acts (5:17-22; 16:22-26), but what distinguishes it from those accounts is the narration of the process of recognition and the farewell with instructions to inform **James** and the **brothers** (vv. 11-17). In place of the confirmation of the miracle by outside spectators (cf. 5:25-26), we find a recognition of God's intervention by church members which apparently serves as an explanation of why Peter left Jerusalem (v. 17). Perhaps such an explanation became necessary to combat rumors about Peter's desertion of the community in times of trial. At any rate, the tradition remembered that Mary and John Mark had helped Peter in his flight and indicated that the leadership had passed from Peter to James the brother of the Lord, who was the head of a council of presbyters (elders) mentioned for the first time in 11:30. They are probably meant by "the brothers" in v. 17. In James, whose name appears in Acts for the first time here (v. 17), the Jerusalem church found a leader for the next two decades whose piety and fidelity toward the Torah were acknowledged by everyone, and who enabled the Jewish Christian community to survive in Jerusalem. A second-century tradition quoted by Eusebius states that James "was called the Just . . . he was holy from his mother's womb. He drank no wine . . . nor did he eat meat; he put no razor to his head; he did not anoint himself with oil, and he did not go to the baths. He alone was permitted to go into the sanctuary, for he did not wear wool but linen and he used to enter alone into the temple and be found kneeling and praying for forgiveness for the people, so that his knees grew hard like a camel's, because of his constant worship of God" (*Eccles. Hist.* 2.23.4–6). Though it is most improbable that James was permitted to enter the sanctuary like a priest, since priesthood was not a calling but an inherited status, nevertheless, what this tradition remembers is the Nazirite-like piety of James, his love of the temple as the house of God, and his intense identification with his Jewish people. The Torah, the temple, and the nation were the context in which he expressed his piety and his faith in his brother Jesus who appeared to him after Easter (1 Cor. 15:7).

The leadership of the church in Jerusalem passed from Peter, not to another apostle, but to James the brother of Jesus in A.D. 44

according to Luke. In A.D. 62, after the death of the Roman governor Festus (cf. Acts 25–26), the Sadducean high priest Ananos II, son of the infamous Annas of the passion narrative, used the interim to put James to death. Josephus, who otherwise is silent about the Christians (probably because they, in distinction from other Jewish groups, did not participate in the messianic war against the Romans), preserved the tradition of the martyrdom of James by stoning (*Ant.* 20.200-201).

1-4—A summary statement about persecution by Herod is followed by the specific reports of the execution of James, the brother of John, of Peter's subsequent imprisonment, and Herod's intentions concerning Peter. **About that time** when Barnabas and Saul brought the famine relief, the church in Jerusalem was subjected to persecution for the third time. After the Sadducean party and its high priest (5:17-42), and after the mob (6:9-14; 7:57—8:4) with the approval of at least one Pharisee, Saul (8:1,3; 26:9-11), had violently discriminated against them, a new persecution occurred through the leader of the Herodians, **King Herod** Agrippa I.

Born around 10 B.C., Agrippa had been brought up in Rome, lived the life of a playboy, gotten himself into trouble more than once, but had also made many influential friends, among them two later emperors, Gaius, called Caligula (A.D. 37–41) and Claudius (A.D. 41–54). His sister was Herodias, whose first marriage to Herod II, the half brother of her father (wrongly called Philip in Mark 6:17) produced Salome. Herodias's second marriage to her first husband's half brother, Herod Antipas, was denounced by John the Baptist, who was subsequently imprisoned and executed (Mark 6:19-29). When Caligula (Gaius) became emperor he granted the tetrarchy of Philip and also the tetrarchy of Lysanias to Herod Agrippa, together with the title of king. After Agrippa defamed his brother-in-law, Herod Antipas, in Rome, the emperor added the tetrarchy of Antipas to Agrippa's possessions. Following Gaius's assassination Agrippa helped Claudius receive confirmation by the Roman Senate and the new emperor added Judea and Samaria, which hitherto had been under the control of Roman procurators, to Agrippa's kingdom. So, from A.D. 41 to 44, Herod Agrippa I ruled over a reassembled kingdom the same in size as his grandfather Herod had ruled.

Agrippa indeed understood how to gain the favor of the Jews, for he was as much loved by them as his grandfather had been hated.

He was always meticulous in the observance of the law, which pleased the Pharisees, though outside of Judea in the half-pagan city of Caesarea he had the games celebrated in honor of Caesar and even erected statues to his daughters Drusilla (24:24) and Bernice (25:13) (Josephus, *Ant.* 19.357). His coins likewise exhibit this dual trait. Those minted for use in Judea were without images but those minted for other cities bore either his or the emperor's image.

This king exhibited his religious zeal by attacking the leadership of the church. It was not a general persecution, only **some who belonged to the church,** namely, some leading members, came to feel the king's ire. We are not told what happened to them, for the story briefly focuses on one individual, the apostle **James the brother of John** and son of Zebedee whom he killed **with the sword,** either in Roman fashion by beheading, or in Jewish fashion by blows to the body (cf. Deut. 13:12-15). Peter, James, and John had been the inner trio of Jesus' disciples (cf. Luke 8:51; 9:28; Mark 14:33) and therefore one is struck by the brevity of Luke's report. He used this first martyrdom of an apostle merely to indicate the severity of the threat facing Peter. Luke had written in detail about Stephen's death and therefore he can be brief here; nor will he narrate the deaths of any of the other apostles. When Herod saw that his action **pleased the Jews,** he wanted to follow it with an encore and **proceeded to arrest Peter** during the days of **Unleavened Bread** (cf. Luke 22:1). Like his Master, Peter was arrested during **the Passover.** This was his third imprisonment and he now was guarded with maximum security by four groups of four soldiers, each group taking a six-hour guard duty. He probably was placed in a cell in the fortress Antonia, on the north side of the temple, where Paul would be a prisoner later (cf. 21:33; 22:24; 23:10). Herod was **intending after the Passover to bring him out to the people** for public trial and execution. In his passion narrative Luke had omitted the Marcan note, "not during the [Passover] feast, lest there be a tumult of the people" (Mark 14:2), but Luke could include it here, because after the Passover comes the deliverance from oppression (Exodus 12–15). Agrippa, however, planned to execute Peter publicly after the Passover.

5-10—Surrounded by bars, walls, and guards, the imprisoned Peter was also surrounded by **earnest prayer** on his behalf (cf. v. 12). Luke more than any other evangelist emphasized the importance of prayer for Jesus (e.g., Jesus' baptism, Luke 3:21; thanksgiving and praise, 10:21-22; intercession, 22:31-32; Gethsemane,

22:42-44). He encouraged and taught his disciples to pray (cf. 11:1-13; 18:1-8). Therefore the church in Acts is also a praying community (cf. 1:14,24; 2:42; 3:1; 4:24-30; 6:6; 8:15; 9:11,40-41; 10:4,9; 13:3; 16:25; 20:36; 21:5; 22:17; 28:8). Faith cannot live without prayer and while we may ask God for anything, we should above all else pray for the Holy Spirit (Luke 11:13) and also to do God's will (Luke 22:42). The Christians prayed for Peter fervently (Greek, *ektenōs;* cf. Luke 22:44). Christians are not spared hardships, persecution, or even martyrdom. The experience of powerlessness in the face of various kinds of pressures was shared also by Christians in Luke's time. The question, Where is God? is raised by all oppressed who experience evil. Luke had portrayed Jesus' death as martyrdom, and James the brother of John followed the Master. But in this story Luke showed that already before the End God can bring about reversals when and where it pleases him, be it through divine intervention or through dramatic punishment.

And behold (v. 7) signals a new beginning. In the very night before his planned trial and execution, while Peter was sound asleep (cf. Luke 12:22), chained to his two guards in his cell, **an angel of the Lord appeared** (cf. 5:19; 8:26) and the **light** of God's glory lit up the cell (cf. 9:3). Three terse commands—the first underlined by a kick in the ribs, or a push from the angel—tell Peter to get up, get dressed, and follow. The chains had already fallen off and Peter, following the angel, did not know if what was happening was **real,** or a **vision,** a dream. Without trouble they passed the two guards posted outside the cell, and when they came to **the iron gate** leading outside it swung open by itself and, once outside, **immediately the angel left him.**

Stories of miraculous prison escapes are also found outside of the New Testament. The Roman poet Ovid (43 B.C.–A.D. 17) in his best-seller, *Metamorphoses,* tells such a tale: "The officious servants hurry him away, and the poor captive in a dungeon lay. But while the whips and tortures are prepared, the gates fly open, of themselves unbarred. At liberty the unfettered captive stands, and flings the loosened shackles from his hands" (3.965-970). Similar stories were told by Jews and Greeks, but we should not suppose a literary relationship between them and Luke's account. His purpose is not only to edify his readers, but also to make them aware of the hazards which Christ's servants face. When miracles happen they are a foretaste of the victory to come. James was executed, Peter was delivered, and both served their Master.

11-17—These verses narrate the effect of Peter's deliverance on Christians, first on Peter and then on the community. In retrospect Peter now knows that what had happened to him was not a dream but an actual deliverance. Twice Luke specified the time of Peter's arrest as Passover (vv. 3 and 4). The attentive reader can hardly miss the Passover deliverance theme in Peter's reflection: **Now I am sure that the Lord has sent his angel and rescued me from the hand of Herod,** even as he had brought out Israel from Egypt (13:17; cf. 7:36). Now the oppressor is not Pharaoh and the Egyptians, but **Herod** and **all that the Jewish people were expecting.** In this sentence (v. 11) the chief actors of the narrative are all present—the Lord, the angel, Peter, Herod, and the Jews—and Peter knows himself to be liberated from any and all threats against his life by the Jews. A separation from his own people is taking place in Peter's reflection which prepares the reader for his announcement in v. 17.

But first he must decide quickly on his course of action. He must notify the community and so he made his way **to the house of Mary,** which only since the 6th century has been identified as the house of the last supper and the first meeting place after Easter (1:13-14). At any rate, the narrator presupposes the house to be known. It is strange that Mary is identified by her son John Mark, which can only mean that her son was better known to Luke's first readers. We are told that John **Mark** was a cousin of Barnabas (Col. 4:10), which explains why he was taken along to Antioch (v. 25) and on the first missionary journey (13:5,13; 15:39). It would seem that neither Barnabas nor Mark and Mary his mother belonged to the Hellenists of Acts 6:1-6.

Mark is mentioned as Paul's fellow worker in Philemon 24 and was asked to serve Paul in his imprisonment in 2 Tim. 4:11. In 1 Peter 5:13 he appears in the company of its author (Peter) in Babylon, which is a code name for Rome (cf. Rev. 17:5). It was on the basis of 1 Peter 5:13 that Papias (ca. A.D. 150) drew the false conclusion that Mark was Peter's interpreter and wrote the Second Gospel. We should note that Mark was a common Roman name and our Gospel of Mark is based on traditions rather than on Peter's direct eyewitness account.

The house of Mary appears to have been a stately building, for it had an enclosed courtyard with a door to the street, and the household had a maid, named **Rhoda** (Rose). Her excitement at recognizing Peter's voice made her forget to open the door and let him in. Rushing into the prayer meeting of this house-church, she was confronted by the fact that those within could not believe that the answer to their prayer stood right outside of the locked door. At first they told her, **You are mad,** plain crazy; and when **she insisted** that it was indeed Peter, they brushed her off saying **It is** (only) **his angel.** In short, no one reckoned with the possibility which God had turned into reality. A guardian angel is distinct from the angel of the Lord, and may reflect popular ideas similar to Tob. 5:4-21 (cf. Matt. 18:10). We might say, You have seen his ghost. But Rhoda persisted while Peter kept on knocking. By means of this comical interlude the narrator created a time span for presenting the process of recognition. At last **when they opened** the door **they saw him and were amazed.** Their reaction is typical of miracle stories. But their excitement could not be allowed to rouse the neighbors. So, **motioning to them with his hand to be silent,** Peter gave a recital of his experiences, **how the Lord had brought him out of the prison** (the same Greek verb as in 13:17). The Passover spent in prayer and in worry ended with joyful amazement at God's deliverance.

Peter also commissioned them to **tell this** news **to James and the brothers,** for with his going underground, James, the Lord's brother, would have to assume leadership in the community. James had not been among Jesus' disciples during his lifetime, but had received a resurrection appearance (1 Cor. 15:7). Luke did not mention him by name in Acts 1:12-14 nor was he a nominee at the time when a substitute for Judas was elected (1:23-26). But he became the leader in Jerusalem at the time when Peter **departed and went to another place.** Peter went into hiding, not to Rome, because a few years later Paul and Barnabas met James, Peter, and John at the apostles' conference. The three "pillars" are mentioned in this order by Paul, an indication that the preeminence of James in Jerusalem was established at that time (Gal. 2:9). The fact that also James gave "the right hand of fellowship" to Paul and Barnabas demonstrates that he was open to accepting Gentiles without circumcision into the church, in contrast to some of his legalistic fellow members (Gal. 2:1-10), with whom he apparently kept contact (cf. 21:18-25).

18-19—The focus shifts to the morning after the escape and we hear about its effect on the bewildered guards. We are not told what happened to them during the night. Did the angel put them to sleep? Small wonder that they were confused and scared, for according to Roman law a guard who allowed a prisoner to escape was subject to the same kind of punishment as the prisoner would have received (*Code of Justinian* 9.4.4; cf. Acts 16:27; 27:42). Herod Agrippa examined the guards responsible for Peter and **ordered that they should be put to death.** Actually the Greek text merely says "He ordered them to be led away." But in the context of judicial proceedings the verb "to lead away" is synonymous with leading someone to the place of execution. For Luke, Herod once again made a terrible misjudgment, because he was blind to the mighty works of God. Herod himself **went down from Judea to Caesarea and remained there.** Actually Caesarea was part of the Roman province of Judea. It was the administrative capital when Judea was under the control of procurators (cf. 23:33), but from a Jewish point of view this semi-pagan city was not considered to be part of Judea.

20-23—The following legend of Herod's death was originally an independent tradition, of which Josephus gives us a similar version (*Ant.* 19.345-350). However, Luke's tradition also contains a reference to an economic conflict between Agrippa and the people of Tyre and Sidon (on the coast of southern Lebanon). An agricultural dependence of these two Phoenician cities on Herod's territories indeed existed for centuries (cf. 1 Kings 5:1, 6; Ezek. 27:2, 17). Agrippa probably enforced a grain embargo and brought the cities to heel, so that they sued for economic peace, not military peace. An armed confrontation would never have been tolerated by the Roman governor of Syria. **They came to him in a body** means the two cities sent a delegation which persuaded **Blastus, the king's chamberlain,** to act as mediator in order to regain Agrippa's favor. The delegation of the two cities succeeded and **on an appointed day** a public reconciliation was to be proclaimed. Both Luke and Josephus agree that during a feast Herod had **put on his royal robes** (woven of silver threads and shining radiantly in the sunlight) and had received divine honors from his flatterers which he did not reject—as any good Jew should have done. **The voice of a god, and not of a man!** the pagans shouted. He was stricken immediately by intense pain and had to be carried to his palace, where he died in agony.

It is possible that the festival on behalf of Caesar's well-being (*sōteria*) to which Josephus refers took place on August 1, A.D. 44, which was the birthday of emperor Claudius (Suetonius, *Life of Claudius* 2.1). This would mean that Barnabas stayed in Jerusalem from approximately April to August A.D. 44 (Passover in that year was very late, May 1). Yet we must also recognize that it was Luke's editorial activity which placed the famine relief notice as brackets around the persecution tradition and the tradition about Agrippa's death, and we must also note that there was no famine in Judea while Agrippa was alive. Still it is possible that the Antiochian relief action was early and that Luke's editorial arrangement agreed with the historical events in time and place.

For Luke, Herod's sudden death was the result of accepting the blasphemous adulation of pagans; it was an act of divine judgment (cf. Luke 14:11) on the persecutor of the church and a demonstration of God's power over a blasphemous king who exalted himself to the place of God. **And he was eaten by worms and died** indicates the awfulness of his death to which Josephus also refers. His death is described in language similar to the death of other persecutors such as Antiochus Epiphanes IV (2 Macc. 9:5-9) or evil or self-deifying kings (Isa. 14:13-15; Ezek. 28:6-9), or rulers like Herod the Great (*Ant.* 17.168–170). When Agrippa's death became known, then, according to Josephus, a riot broke out in Caesarea, and "the people forgetting the benefactions" which Agrippa had bestowed on them "hurled insults, too foul to mention, on the deceased," and seizing "the images of his daughters" carried them into brothels (*Ant.* 19.357). On his death, Judea, Samaria, and Galilee were placed once more under the control of procurators.

24-25—Neither persecution nor famine could stop the proclamation of God's Word and the growth of God's people (cf. 6:7; 9:31). The expression that the **word of God grew and multiplied** (strange, at first sight) is dependent on Luke's identification of the "seed" with the hearer of the word (Luke 8:4-15). The word grows as more hearers hear it. The concluding sentence refers to the return to Antioch of **Barnabas** and **Saul** who brought with them John **Mark.** A footnote in the RSV shows that some manuscripts have "to Jerusalem" instead of **from Jerusalem.** But since the better manuscripts have the preposition "to" (*eis*), which can also mean "in," the suggestion has been made that we should translate v. 25 thus: "And

223

Barnabas and Saul, having fulfilled their mission *in Jerusalem* returned, bringing with them John, whose other name was Mark." This closing statement, together with 11:30, forms brackets around the Jerusalem narrative, which begins with Herod's persecution and ends with Herod's death and has its center in Peter's deliverance and in the church's recognition of his deliverance.

Divine aid in miraculous prison escapes was part of the cultural milieu of Luke's time; his audience expected stories like ours to be told of one who was acclaimed Lord and Savior. The platform announced at the opening of Jesus' mission at Nazareth included: "to proclaim release to the captives . . . to set at liberty those who are oppressed" (Luke 4:18). Precisely this program involved Jesus himself in arrest, imprisonment, and execution. Moreover, he had clearly told his disciples that if they wanted to be benefactors, following in his footsteps, they too must be ready to take risks (Luke 9:24; 14:27; cf. Acts 14:22). Thus they, like their Master, would always be endangered benefactors as they bring in word and deed God's gift of forgiveness, salvation, deliverance, and hope to all, beginning in Jerusalem. While not a hair will fall from their heads without God's will (Luke 21:18), they may be delivered into prison and even death (Luke 21:10-17; Acts 12:2). Even there, with the instruction that has been given (Luke 12:4-12) and with the conviction that the resurrected Jesus identifies with his persecuted disciples and shares in their pain (Luke 10:16; Acts 9:4-5), they can endure (Luke 21:19). Yet already before the End God is able to put down the mighty from their thrones (Luke 1:52; Acts 12:20-23) and miraculously manifest the liberation of his servants.

Mission from Antioch (13:1—14:28)

With the return of Barnabas and Saul to Antioch we leave Jerusalem behind for the next two chapters as we listen to a new venture of the Spirit which emerges from the first interracial church. It is one thing to speak about Christ to one's neighbors, acquaintances, and associates; it is another matter for a whole community to engage in a missionary effort, sending out two of its leaders on a lengthy journey. The antecedent to this innovative program was the work of some Hellenists like Phillip who, after their expulsion from Jerusalem, became itinerant prophets and evangelists until they set-

tled somewhere. Philip stayed in Caesarea (8:40; 21:8); some others
whose birthplace had been Cyrene or Cyprus apparently remained
in Antioch (11:20). Still others continued as itinerant prophets; we
hear of them as late as the Didache (ca. A.D. 110). But in Antioch
it was the worshiping community that sent out Barnabas and Saul
and apparently called them apostles (cf. 14:4, 14).

We meet here another understanding of the apostolate, distinct
from that of the twelve apostles, which was modeled after the twelve
patriarchs. They represented Christ's claim on all of Israel and they
were connected with Jerusalem. Historically, for the Antiochian
Christians, apostles were Spirit-filled missionaries who had been
commissioned by the Holy Spirit through the church at worship to
proclaim the gospel to those who had not yet heard it. Paul's own
understanding of an apostle emphasized still another point, namely,
the encounter with the resurrected Christ and a direct commissioning by him to be a missionary and to care for the authenticity
and power of the gospel (cf. 1 Cor. 15:7-8; 9:1; Gal. 1:1). For Luke
the apostles were the Twelve (cf. 1:21-26) who could guarantee the
identity of the resurrected Christ with the earthly Jesus and represent the tradition concerning his words and deeds. But Luke was
also aware that some people had called Paul an apostle; he therefore
used this title of Barnabas and Paul in 14:4, 14.

Sent off by the church in Antioch, Barnabas and Saul, with Mark's
assistance for a time, preached on the island of Cyprus, in Antioch
in Pisidia, Iconium, Lystra, and Derbe. They revisited the last three
communities on their return journey and also preached in Perga
and probably in Attalia, from where they went by ship to their place
of departure, Antioch. Upon their arrival "they gathered the church
together and declared all that God had done with them and how he
had opened a door of faith to the Gentiles" (14:27). Riots and persecutions had been endured (13:50; 14:2, 5, 19); sermons were
preached (13:16-41: 14:15-17); miracles were performed (14:8-10);
many disciples were won who could be consoled and exhorted on
the return journey (14:22); and elders had also been appointed in
each of the newly founded churches (14:23). Yet, the very success
of this new enterprise proceeding from Antioch produced a crisis
for the whole church, a crisis with which the next chapter (Acts 15)
will deal.

Luke's geographic structuring of his narrative ties Antioch closely to Jerusalem; 11:1-18, Jerusalem; 11:19-30, Antioch; 12:1-25, Jerusalem; 13–14, mission from Antioch; 15:1-29, conference and decision in Jerusalem; 15:30—19:20, Paul's mission from Antioch with visits in Jerusalem and Antioch (18:22). Up to chap. 13 Jerusalem had been the center from which the mission proceeded. Now the spread of the Word will come from the Antiochian church.

13:1-3 (The Commissioning of Barnabas and Saul)—This section is a pre-Lukan tradition to which Luke may have added the names of Barnabas and Saul at the beginning and at the end of a traditional list of prophets and teachers in Antioch. This list of church leaders who worked in a cosmopolitan setting exhibits a remarkable diversity of backgrounds and origins. A Levite from Cyprus, a black man, a North African from Cyrene, a boyhood friend of Herod Antipas and a Pharisee educated under Gamaliel were acknowledged to be spiritual dynamos.

Now in the church at Antioch there were prophets and teachers. According to Acts 2, Christian prophecy is a possibility for every Christian (cf. 2:17-18, 38). Nevertheless, there emerged individuals in whom the gift of prophetic speech was more prominent and constant than in others and who therefore were called prophets. Although Luke did not designate Stephen as a prophet, he bore all the marks of one. He was "full of faith and of the Holy Spirit," "full of grace and power (and) did great wonders and signs among the people" (6:5, 8). Luke presented him as a prophetic speaker and miracle worker. Moreover, in the tradition reflected in Luke's presentation of Stephen we can see that the same persons could be referred to as prophets and inspired teachers. The prophet interpreted the purpose of God and the will of the exalted Lord within the context of particular situations and questions. The teacher gave an inspired interpretation of the Scriptures. Teachers transmitted and interpreted the tradition. Another of the Seven who was "full of the Spirit and (divine) wisdom" was Philip. He began the mission in Samaria and his preaching was accompanied by miracles (6:3; 8:6, 12). It is therefore not surprising that the Christian Hellenists who established a biracial congregation in Antioch were led by persons recognized as prophets, rather than by elders as in Jerusalem.

The list of names is the fourth so far in Acts (1:13; 1:23; 6:5). Its traditional nature can be seen in that neither Simeon nor Lucius nor Manaen will reappear in Luke's story. These three prophets may well have been the Christian Hellenists who took the decisive step and preached the gospel to pagans in Antioch (11:20). **Simeon who was called Niger,** the Latin word for "black," was most likely a black man from North Africa who had become a proselyte and settled in Jerusalem before becoming a Christian prophet. His importance is indicated by his position in the list. Was he the same as Simon of Cyrene, the father of Rufus and Alexander, who carried the cross (Mark 15:21)? In Rom. 16:13 Paul wrote: "Greet Rufus, eminent in the Lord, also his mother and mine." Why would Paul call her his mother? Did he stay in her house in Antioch or in Ephesus with Simeon and Rufus? Is the Simeon of 13:1 identical with the one of 15:14? Obviously, Mark mentioned Rufus and his brother because they had become important persons in the church. Unfortunately, we cannot be certain of any identification.

Lucius belonged to the group of diaspora Jews from **Cyrene** whom we have already met (2:10; 6:9; 11:20). His identification with Luke is most improbable. **Manaen** is the Greek form of the Hebrew name *Menachem*, meaning "comforter." Since the same Greek word (*paraklēsis*) can mean "exhortation," "comfort," "consolation," it could be that Luke derived his incorrect etymology of Barnabas's name in 4:36 from Manaen's. Manaen came from aristocratic Jewish circles, for he had been a foster brother of **Herod** Antipas, who ruled Galilee and Peraea as *tetrarch* from 4 B.C. until his downfall, caused by his brother-in-law Herod Agrippa I, in A.D. 39. As a boy Manaen had been brought up with the young Herod as his companion at **court. Barnabas,** a Levite of Cypriot origin (4:36) is mentioned first in the list. He was not one of the Christian Hellenists who had established the church in Antioch. His real name was Joseph, but the apostles called him Barnabas, which in Aramaic probably meant "son of prophecy" (rather than "son of encouragement"; cf. 4:36). His new name indicates that the Aramaic-speaking community already recognized his prophetic ministry within its midst. He had been sent from Jerusalem to Antioch and had asked **Saul** to join him (9:27; 11:22-30). **Saul,** listed last and separated from Barnabas by three names, is identified as prophet only here. Luke probably added him (and perhaps Barnabas) to this traditional list, because Saul had been acknowledged as an inspired prophetic preacher and because the action of Luke's story will now shift to him.

While they were worshiping the Lord refers not just to the five prophets and teachers but to the community, because it is the church which ratifies decisions (cf. 1:15; 6:2, 5; 14:27; 15:22). During a gathering of the community for worship, the Holy Spirit made known his will through the prophetic word of one of its members. In direct speech **the Holy Spirit** (speaking through a prophet) **said, "Set apart for me Barnabas and Saul for the work to which I have called them"** (cf. 9:15). This command disclosed that the decision for further mission had already been made by God and what the community now had to do was to concur with it. The church in Antioch did not act on this important outreach program without prophetic directive, but the directive would have been mere words without the community's implementation. **Fasting and praying** are the two basic postures of a church's sensitivity to the will of the Holy Spirit (cf. 14:23; Luke 5:33-35). After the community had appropriated the prophetic injunction and made it their own, then, at another worship service, after fasting and praying, **they laid their hands on them and sent them off.** The laying on of hands did not signify ordination, but a commissioning for carrying out the specific task described in chaps. 13 and 14 (of. 14:26).

By laying their hands on Barnabas and Saul, the community and its prophets blessed them and identified themselves with their work of mission and the hardships they would have to endure. The Antiochenes also equipped them, providing funds for travel by sea as well as for the assistance of John Mark (v. 5). Because the church commissioned and sent them, they are called "apostles," that is, official delegates representing the church in Antioch for the specific purpose of mission (14:4, 14). There had been itinerant prophets and missionaries before, but they had operated on their own (cf. 11:19, 28). Now, however, for the first time, a congregation, inspired by the Spirit, has sent out its own delegates on a missionary journey.

13:4-12 (Mission in Cyprus)—So, being sent out by the Holy Spirit underlines the Spirit's primacy over the church's program. By boat they went from **Seleucia,** the seaport of Antioch, to **Salamis** on the island of **Cyprus** and established there the basic missionary pattern of Acts, namely, proclaiming the Word of God first to Jews **in synagogues** and only afterwards to Gentiles. This pattern reflects not merely mission strategy, but also Israel's priority in salvation history. There had been some evangelizing of Cyprus before (11:19), but

Luke apparently knew nothing of its results, for Barnabas, a Cypriot himself (4:36), and Saul did not make contact with Christians there. Crossing the island of Cyprus from east to west they came to **Paphos,** where the news of their powerful proclamation had preceded them. **Sergius Paulus,** the proconsul of Cyprus asked them to come to him. He had a court **magician, a Jewish false prophet, named Bar-Jesus.** Here we can see once again Luke's method of composing his story. A general statement about mission activity (v. 5) is followed by a specific episode (vv. 6-12). With **Bar-Jesus,** which means "son of Jesus," we enter the world of religious con artists who practiced quackery and interpreted dreams, who called themselves prophets or philosophers and vied for the favor of the masses. **But Elymas the magician (for that is the meaning of his name)** opposed them, fearing that these preachers were unwelcome competitors who might put his job in jeopardy. **Elymas** is not a translation of **Bar-Jesus,** nor is it a second name, but means "dreamer" and interpreter of dreams and hence **magician.** It is a designation of his "profession" of oneiromancy and the transcription of an Aramaic word for "dream interpreter."

As Jesus had been confronted by the devil, so Peter and Paul were confronted by magicians. Bar-Jesus is denounced by Paul as **son of the devil,** because he is an **enemy of all righteousness, full of all deceit and villainy.** Paul as prophet **filled with the Holy Spirit** confronted and unmasked this "son of Jesus" as the devil's son and laid bare that which was hidden in his heart (cf. 1 Cor. 14:25). Every magician claimed to be the medium of divine mysterious powers and an oracle of God's unfathomable will, when in reality he engaged in religious rip-offs for his own benefit. Paul roundly condemned this magician whose specialty was the interpretation of dreams, even as Jeremiah had denounced the false prophets for their interpretation of dreams (Jer. 23:25-32). Like Jeremiah who pronounced judgment on Shemaiah the false prophet (Jer. 29:32), so Paul, a prophet **filled with the Holy Spirit** announced God's verdict: **Behold, the hand of the Lord is upon you and you shall be blind and unable to see the sun for a time.** As with the magician Simon, so here the judgment is not final but temporary, and leaves room for repentance (cf. 8:22), in contrast to the judgment of Ananias and Sapphira who had been members of the church (5:5). Elymas will be blind only for some time, even as Paul himself had been (cf. 9:9). Luke does not tell us whether the magician repented, but **the proconsul believed** when he witnessed this judgment miracle and heard **the teaching of the Lord.**

Although Luke's emphasis lies on Paul's victory over a magician, he let his readers know that Christianity has now made inroads into the high society of the empire. Incidentally, Luke correctly distinguished between imperial provinces governed by legates and senatorial provinces governed by proconsuls and assigned the proper title to **Sergius Paulus,** even though at the time of Luke's writing Cyprus had changed its status. The fact that Luke does not refer to the proconsul's Baptism does not mean that he was not baptized. Our author assumes that his readers would understand that faith, conversion, and Baptism form a unity and need not be enumerated separately each time.

In the middle of the episode we hear that **Saul . . . is also called Paul** (v. 9). This change of name does not mean that Saul was so impressed standing before the highest Roman official of the island that he adopted the name (the cognomen; Roman citizens have three names) of the proconsul. Rather, Paul followed the practice of other Jews and had two names, one Jewish and the other Graeco-Roman, like John Mark. His Hebrew name, Saul, after the first king of Israel—from the tribe of Benjamin to which Paul belonged (cf. Phil. 3:5)—gave way to the Roman name Paul as he worked among Gentiles. He probably chose Paul because it sounded similar to his original name. Luke introduced the name under which he became known at this time, because Paul and not Barnabas occupied the center of the action in this story, and would continue to do so.

One final comment: Jesus did not perform miracles of judgment in Luke's Gospel. Luke omitted the cursing of the fig tree which he found in his Markan source (Mark 11:12-14, 20-25). The parallelism between Jesus' miracles and those by his apostles is therefore not complete but broken. The struggle between Paul and Elymas was at heart a struggle between the Holy Spirit and the counterfeit spirit of the devil. It was not Paul, but **the hand of the Lord** that brought about judgment, as a foretaste of the things to come. All miracles in Luke-Acts are placed within an eschatological context and are not an end in themselves. Thus, for instance, the proconsul did not come to faith just on the basis of the judgment miracle alone, for the teaching of the Lord interpreted this miracle for him and placed it into the context where faith could arise (v. 12).

13:13-52 (Mission in Antioch, Pisidia)

13-16 (Introduction)—After the completion of their mission in Cyprus Paul and his company (note the reversal of the order in comparison to 13:1-2) went by boat to Asia Minor and came to Perga in Pamphylia, where John Mark left them and returned to Jerusalem. His reasons for leaving are not given, but that Paul was annoyed over this separation can be seen from 15:38-39. Perhaps John Mark liked his mother's cooking better or was dismayed over the prospect of crossing the Taurus Mountains that loomed to the north like a solid barrier. He probably had never seen anything like that before. Or the Jewish-Christian John Mark may have felt ill at ease participating in a Gentile mission free from the Torah. Only the two Antiochian apostles passed on from Perga (cf. 14:25) and came to Antioch of Pisidia. What an understatement! Of the hardships and dangers which they endured in crossing the Taurus mountains there is no word in Luke's account. He had already passed over several opportunities to present vivid vignettes to his readers (e.g., the gratitude of Jerusalem for the famine relief, a meeting with Cypriot Christians, 11:19,30, etc.), an indication that Luke did not simply invent stories for the sheer fun of it. When traditions available to him were silent, then so was he. As good Jews, Paul and Barnabas went into the synagogue . . . on the sabbath. After prayers had been offered and the appointed lessons from the Pentateuch and the prophetic books had been read, the rulers of the synagogue approached them. Synagogues were generally ruled by one person, occasionally by several. They were charged with the maintenance of the building and the arrangements for public worship. They asked Barnabas and Paul, Brethren, if you have any word of exhortation for the people, say it. Such an invitation for delivering a sermon was not unusual and Paul gladly accepted. Standing up (in contrast to Jesus in Luke 4:20) and motioning with his hands for silence and attention he preached about Christ on the basis of the Old Testament.

16-41 (Paul's Sermon in Antioch, Pisidia)—Luke had noted on several occasions that Paul proclaimed the Word of God in synagogues (13:5; 9:20,29), and he now introduced an example of Paul's synagogue sermons so that the reader may understand the content of his preaching. We begin by noting several parallels between Peter's Pentecost speech and Paul's speech in Antioch. (1) Both speeches begin with a lengthy reference to the Old Testament (cf. also Luke 4:18-19). Peter quoted extensively from Joel whereas Paul began with a summary of Old Testament history from the patriarchs to David. In both instances the acting subject is the God of the promise "I will pour out my Spirit" (2:17, 18). God chose our fathers, exalted the people, led them out of Egypt, nourished them in the wilderness, destroyed the nations, gave them their land, gave them judges, gave them Saul, removed Saul, and raised up David (13:16-22). (2) The Christological kerygma in the two speeches is identical. The Messiah's death was brought about by the hands of lawless men (2:23) who, though they could charge him with nothing deserving death, yet asked Pilate to have him killed (13:28). Simultaneously, this death occurred according to God's plan and foreknowledge (2:23), which means that by condemning him the Jerusalemites fulfilled the Scriptures (13:27) and acted out of ignorance (13:27; cf. 3:17). (3) Both speeches relate the Christological kerygma to the Davidic promise and to Psalm 16 (cf. Acts 2:25-36; 13:22-23, 35). (4) Peter and Paul speak of witnesses who can testify to Jesus' resurrection (2:32; 13:31) and both issue an invitation to salvation (2:38-40; 13:38-39). These parallels indicate that although Paul was not one of the 12 apostles, as Peter, he was an authentic preacher, because his message exhibited continuity in content with Peter's.

Yet Paul's sermon in Antioch was not merely a doublet of Peter's, but articulated a most important Lukan theme, namely, the continuity of salvation history. Peter's inaugural address had interpreted the Pentecost event and set the stage for what was to come. Stephen's speech, which is also similar to Acts 13, had contrasted the faithfulness of God with the faithlessness of the people ("as your fathers did, so do you," 7:51). Paul's narration of God's mighty acts in history demonstrates the unity between salvation history and the Word of God. This speech does not permit the notion of a tripartite salvation history in which the period of Israel and of Jesus has receded into the past and is superseded by the period of the church. Rather, salvation history is the proclamation of promise and fulfillment. God, in accordance with his promise, has sent Israel a Savior (v. 23) and to Israel "the message of this salvation has been sent" (v. 26). That which God promised to the fathers, "the good news, he has fulfilled to us their children" (vv. 32-33) through the resurrection of Jesus Christ, so that "in him everyone that believes is justified," receiving forgiveness of sins through him (vv. 38-39). Those who hear "the message of this salvation" (v. 26), which is the story of God's promise and fulfillment, must beware, lest as scoffers they perish (vv. 40-41; cf. 3:23). Like Deuteronomy, Paul's sermon (*logos paraklēseōs,* v. 15) ends with the announcement of blessings (vv. 38-39) and judgment (vv. 40-41) and comprises Israel's history in its past, present, and future dimensions.

The structure of the speech is indicated by the three direct addresses: part one (vv. 16-25), the story of God's promise; part two (vv. 26-37), the fulfillment of God's promise; part three (vv. 38-41), God's invitation to participate in his salvation and the announcement of judgment.

16-25 (The story of God's promise.)—The story begins with the election of our fathers and ends with the last preacher of the promise, John the Baptist, who proclaimed **a baptism of repentance to all the people of Israel.**

16-19—Paul, standing up like a Greek orator (in contrast to the customary posture of sitting down, Luke 4:20), addresses the audience: **Men of Israel, and you that fear God.** As men of Israel they have a history which began with God's election of the patriarchs and his promises to them. The question already raised by this address is whether or not the audience will remain in continuity with its history or turn into troublemakers who cause persecution (v. 50; 14:2; etc.). New in the address is that Paul also addresses the Godfearers. Whether they were proselytes, or pagans attracted to the synagogue, we do not know, but in neither case were they regarded on equal terms with born Israelites. By including the Godfearers the address already hints at the universal dimension of salvation history, articulated in v. 39 ("every one that believes"). **The God of this people Israel chose our fathers.** There is one common history which unites Paul and his audience and that history is determined by God's election of the patriarchs, Abraham, Isaac, and Jacob. As in the Magnificat and Benedictus, so here salvation history is traced back to its roots (Luke 1:54-55, 72-73; cf. Acts 7:2). Implicit in the concept of the election is the concept of God's promise to the patriarchs (cf. 7:17). And he **made the people great during their stay**

233

in the land of Egypt; literally, "he exalted" Israel during its promised sojourn in "the foreign land" (*paroikia;* cf. 7:6). **And with uplifted arm** by wonders and signs performed through Moses in Egypt and at the Red Sea (Deut. 4:34; 26:8; Exod. 6:6), God **led them out of it** in the exodus, and in so doing he fulfilled prior promises to our fathers (cf. 7:6, 17, 34, 36). **And for about forty years he bore with them in the wilderness** (Deut. 1:31, LXX). In spite of their ingratitude he put up with them when they complained and wanted to return to the fleshpots of Egypt. In all probability we should use the footnote of the RSV, because the context places the emphasis on God's saving acts rather than on the contrast between Israel's sin and God's faithfulness (so Acts 7): God **cared for** Israel. He nourished them like a mother nourishes her children. In the wilderness he provided food and drink for them in their wanderings. After the destruction of **seven nations** (Deut. 7:1), he gave them their land **as an inheritance** in accordance with his promise to Abraham (7:2, 5; Josh. 24:11-13). The time span of **about four hundred and fifty years,** which the Western text connects with the period of the judges in the following verse, refers to the time from the sojourn in Egypt to the occupation of the land (400 years in Egypt, 7:6; 40 years in the wilderness, 13:18; 10 years of conquest). God had put down the mighty nations and exalted his people by giving them their land (Luke 1:52, 54). Looking at the verbs of this first subsection (vv. 16-19) we note that all of them express God's saving activity on behalf of Israel.

20-23—The second subsection begins with **and after that** (namely, the events of vv. 17-19) and describes leaders who served as savior figures prior to Jesus. God **gave them judges,** who delivered their people in times of peril. Of Othniel and Ehud, two of the judges, we read: "The Lord raised up a deliverer (*sōtēr*) for Israel and he saved them" (Judg. 3:9, 15). At the time of **Samuel,** the first **prophet** and last judge, **they asked for a king** (note the change in subject) and **God gave them Saul** . . . **for forty years** (cf. 1 Sam. 8:5-7; 10:17-24; 12:12-14). The note about Saul's 40-year reign is not found in the Old Testament, but occurs in Josephus (*Ant.* 6.378, though a different date, 20 years, is given in 10.143). When Saul failed (1 Sam. 13:8-14; 15:10-31) God **removed him** and **raised up David to be their king.** At his enthronement God himself testified, **I have**

found in David . . . a man after my heart, who will do all my will.
This is a conflated quotation with words from several texts (Ps. 89:20;
1 Sam. 13:14; Isa. 44:28). In this solemn announcement by God,
David appears as type of the Savior, Jesus. David's obedience to
God's will (cf. v. 36) does not refer to his private affairs with Bath-
sheba but to his work as king.

Of David's **posterity** (lit., "seed") **God** has **brought to Israel a
Savior, Jesus, as he promised.** This is the climactic conclusion of
the recital of God's mighty acts. It skips over the millennium between David and Jesus. Similar recitals likewise omit centuries and
focus on the exodus or the exodus and David (Deut. 6:20-24; Josh.
24:2-13; Psalm 78). Moreover, the specific promise given to David
(2 Sam. 7:12) did not find its fulfillment during the millennium which
saw the devastation of David's kingdom and its occupation by foreign
powers. The promise to David came to realization in Jesus whom
God raised up as Savior. Yet God did not abandon his people during
that time between David and Jesus. In spite of all the turmoil, the
history from David onward was but an extension of Paul's recital of
the acts of God beginning with the election, continuing in the deliverance of the exodus, the inheritance of the land, and the rescue
mission of the judges and finding the focus in the specific promise
to David concerning his seed. Such a recital constitutes an act of
faith when catastrophes seem to nullify God's promise. Hope receives its sustenance as God's past acts and promises are remembered.

The wording of vv. 22-23 is based on several Old Testament texts.
God sought out David "to be prince over his people," because "he
is a man after [my] own heart" (1 Sam. 13:14). This text, partially
quoted in v. 22, agrees with 2 Sam. 7:8. But "the counsel of God"
concerning David (v. 36) did not end with David's status as prince
over Israel. It included also "his seed," as 2 Sam. 7:8-16 had promised: "I will raise up your seed after you. . . . I will establish his
kingdom. . . . The throne of his kingdom shall be forever. . . .I will
be his father and he shall be *my son*." This promise which underlies
vv. 22-23 also forms the background of vv. 32-37 and is elucidated
by other Old Testament texts in agreement with the interpretation
of Scripture at Paul's time. In conclusion: God **promised** that he
would give **to Israel a Savior** (v. 23) beyond the judges and kings
of the past. He will be out of "the house and lineage of David" (Luke

2:4) and be called "the Son of the Most High." As Son of David he will receive "the throne of his father David and he will reign over the house of Jacob forever" (Luke 1:32). Not only does the whole Old Testament story receive a Christological interpretation in which Christ is the fulfillment of the promise that determines this story from its very beginning, but also the Jesus story is an inseparable part of a continuous history that begins with the election of **our fathers** (v. 17).

24-25—The first part of the speech closes with the witness of **John** the Baptist, who as the last prophet was Jesus' immediate forerunner, preparing the way for him by calling **all the people of Israel,** without exception, to **repentance** (Luke 3:1-20) and sealing their repentance with the sign of **baptism** (cf. Luke 7:30). His **baptism of repentance** was the promise of "the forgiveness of sins" (Luke 3:3), which was to be realized through Jesus the Savior (Acts 13:38). Nowhere in Acts is forgiveness the result of John's baptism (cf. 10:37; 19:4), but the repentance proclaimed by him remains for all time the door to Christ and to God's fulfillment through Christ. Just so, John stands on the dividing line between the time marked by the promise and the time marked by the Savior and the message of salvation (vv. 23 and 26). His own person recedes in importance before the one who comes after him (cf. Luke 3:16; John 1:20,27). In contrast to the RSV of v. 25a, the NEB and several interpreters translate John's word "What you suppose me to be, I am not." With this statement the notion of the misunderstanding of John's true identity by the people is introduced, and this notion prepares the way for the misunderstanding of Christ and of the prophetic word concerning him in v. 27. If the people did not recognize the forerunner's identity, will they recognize the Savior who comes after him, **the sandals of whose feet** John is **not worthy to untie?** There is a subtle, implicit question addressed to the audience at the end of this first part.

26-37 (God's fulfillment of his promise). 26—The second part of Paul's speech begins with a new address, **Brethren, sons of the family of Abraham, and those among you that fear God,** be they Gentiles or proselytes. This address is already an implicit appeal in which Paul continues with the role of the Baptist. He too had spoken about our father Abraham (Luke 3:8), warning his listeners that descent from Abraham does not guarantee salvation. **To us** God has sent the message of this salvation, which means deliverance (7:25), life (3:15), and peace (10:36). The message of this salvation is the proclamation of God's fulfillment of his promise through the Savior Jesus Christ (vv. 26-37) and it extends an invitation to share in this salvation (vv. 38-39). Paul and his listeners are part of a history that begins with Abraham, a history in which God made a promise to David. This promise, fulfilled in Jesus, reaches Paul's audience as word of salvation. Paul did not accuse his audience of wrongdoing in connection with the crucifixion of Jesus. The idea of a transfer of corporate, collective guilt from the Jews of Jerusalem to Antiochian Jews was not part of Luke's theology. Yet Jesus, hanging on a Roman cross, seemed to demonstrate that he was no **Savior** (v. 23).

27-29—The subject of these sentences is the inhabitants of Jerusalem and their rulers. We should not translate: They fulfilled the Scriptures **by condemning him,** because (1) in Luke's Gospel there is no verdict of condemnation of Jesus by the Sanhedrin (Mark 14:64 as well as the reference to condemning in Mark 10:33 are omitted by Luke); (2) neither the apostles nor Paul are condemned in Acts within the context of a trial by the Sanhedrin; (3) the Greek word (*krinō*) can also mean "to decide" (e.g., Acts 21:25; 25:25); (4) the following clause clearly states that the Jews did not find a legal cause (Greek, *aitia*) for the death penalty. The meaning seems to be that the Jerusalemites fulfilled the Scriptures by their decision to bring Jesus before Pilate (Luke 23:71—24:1). **Though they could charge him with nothing deserving death** (cf. Luke 23:4,14,22,47) **yet they asked Pilate to have him killed** (24:2,18,21,23). They had done so because they failed to **recognize him** in his identity as Savior (cf. 3:17) even as they failed to **understand the utterances of the prophets which are read every sabbath** (v. 27; cf. Luke 16:29-31; Acts 15:21). Yet by their infamous deed the people of Jerusalem and especially their rulers (cf. Luke 22:66; 23:2,5,10,13,18,23) fulfilled the prophetic Scriptures even though they did not understand them (cf. 2:23; 3:18). It is an irony that religion can make persons blind and Bible reading lead to no understanding, and it is even a greater irony that by their ignorance of the Scriptures the people of Jerusale fulfilled God's purpose found in the Scriptures **which are read** to them **every sabbath.**

"It cannot be," Jesus had said, "that a prophet should perish away from Jerusalem, . . . [which is] killing the prophets and stoning those who are sent" to it by God (Luke 13:33-34). In going up to Jerusalem, the city of the Messiah, Jesus had accepted his fate that "everything that is written . . . by the prophets will be accomplished" (Luke 18:31; cf. 24:25-26). The Old Testament not only predicted the passion of the Messiah (Ps. 2:1-2; Psalm 22: Isaiah 53), but it prefigured his passion in the suffering of Joseph (Acts 7:9), in the rejection of Moses (Acts 7:25, 27, 39), in the suffering of the righteous person (e.g., Wisdom 2–5), and in the suffering servant of the Lord (Acts 8:32-33). **And when they had fulfilled all that was written of him—** Judas by betraying him (Acts 1:20; Luke 22:21-22), Peter by denying him (Luke 22:31-34), the people and their rulers by handing him over, and Pilate by crucifying him—**they took him down from the tree** (Deut. 21:23) **and laid him in a tomb.** Did Luke use a tradition in which the opponents buried Jesus (contrary to Luke 23:50-56)? Or, what is more likely, did Luke merely wish to emphasize the reality of Jesus' burial and therefore of his death, without reflecting on the agents of his burial (cf. 1 Cor. 15:4)?

30-31—But God had the final word and he **raised him from the dead; and for many days he appeared to those who came up with him from Galilee to Jerusalem.** The resurrection is God's vindication of Jesus as Savior. Without it there is no message of salvation and the recital of God's mighty acts lacks its climax (v. 23). In the resurrection God's own cause triumphed in spite of the rejection experienced by Jesus and his followers. We should also note that Jesus' resurrection is inseparable from the **witnesses** (2:32; 3:15; 5:32; 10:39, 41). No one saw the resurrection itself, but Jesus **appeared for many days**—for 40 days, according to 1:3—to those disciples who came up with him from Galilee. They guarantee the reality of the resurrection and the reliability of its proclamation. Moreover, Paul did not count himself among the church-founding witnesses to the resurrection. To be sure, Paul could witness to his visions (plural, 26:16) but not to the basic Easter kerygma which, for Luke, was grounded in the appearances of Christ to the Galileans during the unrepeatable period between Easter and the ascension.

The background of the kerygmatic statement that Christ **appeared to** some of his followers (1 Cor. 15:3-7; Luke 24:34) is found in the appearance of Yahweh to Abraham (Gen. 12:7 LXX, the same verb, *ōphthē* with dative) and to the three patriarchs (Exod. 6:3). "The angel of the Lord appeared to" Moses (Exod. 3:2) and to David (2

Chron. 3:1). Yahweh's appearance to the patriarchs, to Moses at the burning bush, and the appearance of his angel to King David became the basis for the promised future when the glory of the Lord shall "appear" (Isa. 40:5; cf. 66:18). The appearance of God, or of his anointed one, was expected for the time of salvation. With the statement that Christ "appeared to" Peter and then to the Twelve (1 Cor. 15:5) the early Christians confessed that the time of salvation had begun with the resurrection appearance of Christ.

32-33—And we [Paul and Barnabas] **bring you the good news that what God promised to the fathers, this he has fulfilled to us their children by raising Jesus** from the dead. Although the Easter gospel is dependent on the witness of the Galilean disciples (v. 31), Paul and Barnabas are the messengers of the good news as set forth in Isa. 52:7 who announce the fulfillment of God's promise to David.

In Acts, God's promise is related to the land of Israel as the place of true worship (7:4-7), to Israel's deliverance from oppression (7:17), to the coming of the Savior (13:23), to the gift of the Holy Spirit (1:4; 2:33), to forgiveness of sins and salvation (2:38-40), and to the mission to Gentiles (15:16-17) and thus includes all the major themes of Luke's theology. Here the content of **what God promised to the fathers** is the resurrection of Christ as fulfillment of the Davidic promise. The fulfillment constitutes **good news,** or **the message of this salvation** (v. 26) for **their children,** who now hear Paul's sermon. He had been asked to give a word of *paraklēsis,* of consolation (v. 15, "exhortation" RSV), which would point to and look "for the consolation of Israel" in the future (Luke 2:25). Instead, Paul announced the good news of its fulfillment in Christ's resurrection. This fulfillment must be interpreted in light of the Scriptures, and Paul does just that.

As also it is written in the second psalm: Such a precise reference is unique in the New Testament. **As also** means that already Scripture had made the fulfillment of the Davidic promise dependent on the Messiah's resurrection. Psalms 2 and 110 are the most frequently cited Old Testament texts in the Christological argumentation of the New Testament. **Thou art my Son, today I have begotten thee** is a testimony which God himself spoke at the enthronement of David as king. This word is now used to shed new light on Nathan's promise to David (2 Samuel 7) concerning his "seed" (v. 23, "posterity" RSV). While Jesus was Son of God already during his earthly life (Luke

1:35; 3:22; 9:35), he is the enthroned Son of God, to whom Psalm 2 refers, only through his resurrection. In short, Psalm 2 receives its own full meaning in the light of the resurrection and, conversely, this psalm interprets the resurrection event as the enthronement of the Son of God and Son (seed) of David. The language of the psalm gives meaning to the resurrection, but Psalm 2 also exhibits the same contrast between sinful human actions and God's sovereign action which is basic to Luke's Christological kerygma. In citing one verse of this psalm we should also note its context. The inhabitants of Jerusalem and their rulers sought to destroy the Savior sent by God (vv. 27-29), just as the nations and kings of Psalm 2 "take counsel together against the Lord and his anointed" (cf. Acts 4:25-28). But God made their plans come to naught by raising Jesus from the dead (v. 30), even as he overturned the conspiracy of his enemies in Psalm 2 through the enthronement of his Son.

34-37—After demonstrating that Christ's resurrection fulfills Psalm 2 and the promise concerning David's seed, Paul cited two other Old Testament texts which are meant to interpret each other. They are connected by a common introduction, v. 34, and by two catchwords, **give** and "holy" (*hosia*, v. 34, translated as **holy blessings**) or (*hosios*, v. 35) **the Holy One.**

Paul introduced these two citations with the words, **As for the fact that he raised him from the dead, no more to return to corruption,** that is, to the decay of the body in the grave. Here we meet the first of four occurrences of the word *decay*, **corruption,** in this brief section. The resurrection of Christ as an eschatological event must be distinguished clearly from resuscitations found in the Old Testament (1 Kings 17:17-24; 2 Kings 4:32-37) as well as the New Testament (e.g., Luke 7:11-15, 22; Acts 9:36-41). Those resuscitated would die again, but Jesus through his resurrection shall die no more (cf. Rom. 6:9). The resurrection of Christ is not merely one past event among others but has significance for all times because he does not turn to decay. Only in this way does his resurrection fulfill God's word: **I will give you** (plural) **the holy and sure blessings of David.** In this quotation from Isa. 55:3 the reference to the "eternal covenant" with David has been omitted, probably because the word *covenant* is used in Luke-Acts only with reference to the Abrahamic covenant and the new covenant (Luke 1:72-73; Acts 3:25; 7:8; Luke 22:20). The **holy and sure blessings** (Greek, *ta hosia ta pista*) are not blessings in general, but specific ones promised to David that his son "will reign over the house of Jacob forever" (Luke 1:32-33). Moreover, the audience, **you** (plural), are the recipients of the blessings of David (cf. v. 33). The rabbinic method of interpreting one difficult verse by another verse would suggest that the blessings of David include the promise that God will not let his **Holy One** (the Son and seed of David) **see corruption,** but raise him from the dead, as the final citation of Ps. 16:10 states (v. 35). God grants (**I will give you**) Christ's resurrection as blessing and not as judgment to Paul's synagogue audience. These blessings include forgiveness of sins and justification (vv. 38-39), eternal life (v. 37), and the mission to the Gentiles. The latter is also part of the context of the citation from Isaiah: "Behold, you shall call nations that you know not and nations that knew you not shall run to you" (Isa. 55:5; cf. Acts 13:47-49).

The third and last citation, Ps. 16:10, had already been used in 2:25-28, 31. David, who had **served** God's will **in his own generation,** had said to God, **Thou wilt not let** (Greek, "give") **thy Holy One see corruption.** But David died and **saw corruption.** Therefore "the Holy One" could not have been David himself, but rather his Son and seed. **He whom God raised up saw no corruption.** This fulfills Ps. 16:10 and also God's promise through Nathan to David, alluded to in v. 23. The argumentation is now complete: Through the resurrection great David's greater Son has been declared the Son of God in power (v. 33; cf. Rom. 1:4) who rules over Israel forever because he is free from decay. As Savior (v. 23), he is the content of the Christian message of salvation (vv. 26, 32). Through him God graciously bestows to his people the blessings promised to David.

The last part of the sermon issues an invitation to share in **this salvation** (v. 26) proclaimed by Paul and Barnabas (v. 32), or else to be subject to the prophetic warning (vv. 38-41).

38-39—The direct address is now simply **brothers,** be they sons of Abraham, or God-fearers. In the light of the resurrection of Jesus, the basic issue henceforth is whether or not a person believes the world's best news, be he Jew, proselyte, or Gentile sympathizer. **Through this man forgiveness of sins is proclaimed to you** (cf. 2:38; 10:43). While the tradition quoted by Paul in 1 Cor. 15:3-5 connected forgiveness of sins with Christ's death, Luke (and therefore Paul in Antioch) grounded forgiveness in the resurrection of the crucified

Jesus. Moreover, Luke identified forgiveness of sins in this speech with justification, something Paul in his authentic letters did not do except in an Old Testament quotation (Rom. 4:7-8). In letters written under his name by his students or admirers we find similar equations (Eph. 1:7; Col. 1:14). **Every one that believes is freed** (literally, "is justified"). Everyone, be he or she Jew or Gentile, clearly expresses the universality of justification as a result of Christ's resurrection (cf. Rom. 3:22, 4:11-12, 25). **Everyone that believes** emphasizes Paul's *sola fide,* by faith alone (Rom. 1:17; 3:25-26, 28; 4:5; 5:1). Our author knew that justification by faith without the works of the law was the soteriological center of Paul's preaching. His statement that every believer **is freed,** or justified **from everything from which** he or she **could not be freed** or justified **by the law of Moses** could theoretically be interpreted in two ways: (1) justification by faith is partial and supplementary to justification granted by the law of Moses; (2) justification is impossible through the law. The first interpretation, which holds that for Luke (in distinction from the Paul of Romans) justification by faith goes hand in hand with justification by works demanded by the law, is certainly false in view of Luke's total theological outlook ˙as expressed, for instance, in the parables of his Gospel. The prodigal son is not justified only partially by grace, nor is the tax collector's justification a matter of good works being supplemented by grace or faith (Luke 15:11-32; 18:9-14). Therefore, in our verse it was hardly Luke's intention to coordinate obedience to the Torah and faith in Christ as the two necessary steps in achieving justification. Luke merely introduced traditional Pauline language at this point and he, like Paul, held that justification is by faith alone. For Luke, however, it is identical with forgiveness; for Paul it embraces much more than that.

40-41—Paul's final words are a solemn warning to his audience underlining the seriousness of the prior invitation. The announcement of judgment constitutes the counterpoint to forgiveness of sins and justification (vv. 38-39) and to God's election of Israel at its beginning (v. 17). This warning is also related to the behavior of the people of Jerusalem and their rulers, who perversely fulfilled the Scriptures by rejecting God's work through Jesus (vv. 26-28). Throughout the speech the subject of the action had been God. This is true also in vv. 27-29 and 31-32 where human beings appear as knowing or unknowing instruments of God's purpose. Thus the final warning also is directed by God to **you scoffers** or cynics.

The quotation from Hab. 1:5 is also found in a Qumran writing which, similar to the LXX text, warned present and future "apostates" (1 QpHab. 2:1-10), rather than "the nations" (thus the Hebrew text). Applying the prophetic word to the audience in Antioch's synagogue Paul proclaimed that unless they accept God's salvation—forgiveness and justification through God's eschatological deed of the resurrection of Christ—they are but scoffers, cynics who **will perish** (cf. 3:23). God himself will exclude them from his people. An even greater disaster will come upon them than the one that came to those at Habakkuk's time. **For I do a deed in your days, a deed you will never believe, if one declares it to you.** This **deed** (or "work," Greek, *ergon*) in the present is forgiveness and justification **through this man** Jesus (v. 38), whom God raised from the dead (vv. 30-37). Because justification is offered "to everyone who believes" (v. 39), God's deed includes also this offer to Gentiles. For the purpose of this work of God, Paul and Barnabas had been set apart (13:2) and at the end of their mission they declared **all that God had done with them** and were commended **for the work which they had fulfilled** (14:26-27). God's present **deed** which **you will never believe** is that God justifies by grace (v. 43) through faith (v. 39) without the Torah of Moses and in so doing he invites Gentiles to share in this salvation together with Jews.

Looking at the speech as a whole we find a progressive intensification of the negative aspects of the people of God. The first part gently touches on the wilderness period (v. 18) and the necessity for Saul's removal, and closes with John's statement that he is not what the people suppose him to be. The second part (vv. 26-37) excuses their behavior toward Jesus because of their ignorance of his identity and of the Scriptures which, ironically, are read sabbath after sabbath. Moreover, their very action of rejecting Jesus was part of God's grand design, of which they were blissfully unaware (v. 27, Luke 20:17; 23:34b). But then the accusation arises, no longer covered by the motif of ignorance, that, though Jesus was innocent, they asked Pilate for his death (v. 28). The reader of Acts knows that Jesus had prayed for these very same people and that the prayer had been granted in the proclamation of salvation to them (e.g., 2:28-40; 3:26). The question now arises, will the Antiochian Jews accept this salvation offered to them (vv. 38-41), or will they reject it and perish as scoffers because they do not believe God's eschatological work? Will they maintain continuity with salvation history or with the Jerusalemites and their perverse intent?

The culmination of salvation history is the resurrection of Jesus. As an event in the past, the resurrection fulfills the Davidic promise and determines the present and the future. It inaugurated Jesus' enthronement, for whom death has been left behind and who therefore lives and reigns in all eternity. The witnesses to the resurrection are the Galilean disciples as well as the Scriptures (vv. 31-37). The Scriptures make it plain that God's eschatological work will not be the restoration of the Davidic kingdom with a king reigning in Jerusalem "at this time" (1:6) but the enthronement of the resurrected Jesus as the Son of God and Son of David (v. 33), the ruler over a community of forgiven sinners, justified by faith and upheld by God's grace (v. 43), a community of faith and joy (v. 52), hope and love, in which Jews and Gentiles can share in their pilgrimage to the end of time.

In conclusion: "the holy and sure blessings of David" (v. 34) are not a restored Davidic kingdom on earth with Jerusalem as its center, but an eschatological kingdom of universal dimensions based on Christ's resurrection and enthronement as Son of God. Israel's future is tied to the reign of the resurrected Son of David. The marks of Christ's universal reign in the present are the message of salvation (vv. 26 and 32), faith, forgiveness of sins (vv. 38-39), and the gift of the Holy Spirit (v. 52). The reign of Christ was prefigured in David, a man after God's heart who did God's will (v. 22), found favor in his sight (7:46), and served God's counsel (v. 36) as king (v. 22), prophet (2:30), servant of God (4:25), and patriarch (2:29). The promise spoken to him in Ps. 2:7 and Isa. 55:3 and articulated by him in Ps. 16:10 came to fulfillment in the Holy One, the Son of David who did not see decay. His holiness was that, like David, he fulfilled the will of God in faithful obedience, for the benefit of his people, so that everyone who believes, Jew or Gentile, is justified "in" and "through" him (v. 39).

The proclamation of God's Word by God's messengers in God's house, whether the temple or the synagogue, led to a division within God's people and to a rejection of the Word by part of his people (13:43, 45). The rejection in turn was followed by a withdrawal of the messengers and by progress and growth among the believing people of God. Thus a pattern emerges which Luke uses in his Gospel (cf. Luke 4:16-30) and in Acts: (1) *proclamation* in the temple or synagogue, 13:16-41 (cf. 3:12-26; 5:21; 18:4-5; 19:8; 28:17-23 in Paul's room); (2) *division* among Jews precedes or follows rejection, 13:43, 45 (cf. 4:1-2, 4, 21; 5:25-26; 18:4-6; 19:9a; 28:24); (3) *rejection*, 13:45, 50 (cf. 4:3, 17-18, 21, arrest and prohibition to preach; 5:18, 40, arrest and beating; 18:6; 19:9; 28:22b, 25); (4) *withdrawal*, 13:46-47, 51 (cf. 4:21, release from arrest; 5:19, 40, release from prison; 18:6b-7; 19:9b; (5) *progress*, 13:48, 52 (cf. 4:31-32; 5:42; 18:11; 19:10; 28:30-31). On each of these occasions God's messengers preached to the people or their rulers twice: 13:16-41 and 44-47 (cf. 3:17-26 and 4:8-12, 19; 5:21 and 29-32; 18:5 and 6b; 19:8, "for three months"; 28:17-20 and 23). By repeating this pattern Luke would like his readers to understand that the roots of the church lie in the Old Testament (13:16-23), that the nucleus of the true people of God consists of believing Jews (13:43), that the mission to the Jews has met and will meet with rejection (13:41, 45, 50) and that the turning to Gentiles was logical and ordained by God (13:46-48).

42-43—The aftermath of Paul's sermon shows parallels with Luke 4:22-30 and Acts 28:22-28. Interest had been aroused and **the people** asked them to make another presentation **next sabbath.** The decision was postponed and an attitude of wait and see prevailed (cf. 5:34-39). But outside of the synagogue (v. 43) a second reaction is noted. **Many Jews and devout converts to Judaism,** proselytes, **followed Paul and Barnabas,** and thereby the core group of the future church in Antioch emerges. They are urged **to continue in the grace of God** (once again Luke used Pauline language, cf. 20:24). The grace of God was manifested in Israel's history beginning with its election (v. 17), culminating in the fulfillment of the promise (vv. 29-37), and resulting in the offer to receive forgiveness through Christ (vv. 38-39). To **continue** is the challenge addressed to the people of God and each individual (cf. John 8:31). It is equivalent to remaining "faithful to the Lord" (11:23).

The core group of the church in Antioch was made up of Jews and **devout converts,** proselytes (v. 43). We would expect to hear of devout, or God-fearing Gentiles who had attached themselves to the synagogue, especially since they seem to be included in the address (vv. 16 and 26). However, from Luke's perspective the nucleus of the church consisted of Jews. Moreover, "God-fearers" in Acts is not a technical term for Gentiles who attended synagogue services. It was merely an attribute of piety that could be applied to Jews (e.g., Luke 1:50), proselytes (13:16), and Gentiles (10:2, 22, 35), whether or not the latter attended the worship services of the synagogue.

When Cornelius was characterized as "devout" (*eusebēs*) and God-fearing, or "righteous" and God-fearing (10:2, 22, 35), what is important is not his membership in a group on the fringes of the synagogue, but the quality of his piety. He may or may not have attended the synagogue, but he was highly regarded by the Jewish community because of his almsgiving "to the people" (cf. Luke 7:5), and his prayers to the God of Israel. As such, his piety bears the imprint of Luke's summary of the law—love toward God and love toward the neighbor (Luke 10:27; 11:40-42). Cornelius had practiced that double commandment through praying and almsgiving and therefore he received the attribute of God-fearer.

The fact that *God-fearers* was not a technical term in Acts for Gentiles on the fringe of the synagogue is also indicated by the change in terminology which occurs in 13:43. Instead of Godfearers, Luke henceforth speaks of "devout" persons, be they proselytes or Gentiles (*sebomenoi;* 13:43, 50; 16:14; 17:4, 17; 18:7). This change in terms corresponds to a change in the mission emphasis. When Paul turns to the Gentiles (13:46), Luke consistently uses "devout" (*sebomenoi*) in place of "God-fearers" (*phoboumenoi*). Historically, one should not deny the existence of Gentiles who had been attracted to Judaism. Josephus spoke of Greeks who "revere our customs" (*Ant.* 3.217). Some Gentiles may even have attended synagogue services, though the archaeological evidence from ancient synagogues does not indicate their presence. Luke introduced the devout Gentiles in order to narrate the continuity of the Christian mission which reached the Gentiles through Jews, proselytes (13:43) and devout Gentiles.

44-52—These verses bring the conclusion of the ministry in Antioch.

(A) The whole city gathers to hear the word of God (v. 44)
(B) Threefold reaction of the unbelieving Jews (v. 45)
    1. They are filled with jealousy

2. They contradict Paul
3. They revile him
(C) Response of Paul and Barnabas (vv. 46-47)
    1. The word must be spoken to Jews first
    2. Since you reject it we turn to Gentiles
    3. For thus the Lord commanded us to be a light to the Gentiles and to bring salvation to the uttermost parts of the earth
(D) Twofold result (v. 48)
    1. The Gentiles were glad and glorified the Word of God
    2. Those ordained to eternal life believed
(A') The word of the Lord spreads into the surrounding region (v. 49)
(B') Threefold reaction of the unbelieving Jews (v. 50)
    1. They incited devout women and leading men
    2. They stirred up a persecution
    3. They cast out Barnabas and Paul
(C') Response of Paul and Barnabas (v. 51)
(D') Twofold result: the disciples were filled with joy and with the Holy Spirit (v. 52)

44-45—The next sabbath almost the whole city gathered together to hear the word of God. The place of this mighty gathering (*synagō*) is not indicated, but the success of Paul's synagogue sermon is pictured as phenomenal. Yet this very success turned the "wait and see" attitude of the previous sabbath (v. 42) into objection. **When the Jews saw the multitudes** of Gentiles they were not merely **filled with jealousy** (cf. 5:17) that these newcomers attracted such crowds, but they realized that such an influx of Gentiles would mean the end of their religious status quo. If these crowds of Gentiles become members of the **family of Abraham** (v. 26) without circumcision and Torah obedience, then they would erase the distinction between Jew and Gentile. Therefore they **contradicted what was spoken by Paul, and reviled him.** They objected to the proclamation of the resurrection of Christ as fulfillment of the promise to David and the resultant consequences, namely, that everyone, Jew or Gentile, receives forgiveness of sins through him (v. 38) and thus becomes a member of the people of God.

By reviling (literally, "blaspheming") Paul who was set apart by the Spirit (13:2) they publicly demonstrated that they were "scoffers" (v. 41) on whom the prophetic warning was in process of realization. As scoffers they cannot hinder the mission of God's messengers but only exclude themselves from salvation and thus from the true people of God.

46-47—And Paul and Barnabas spoke out boldly, saying, "It was necessary that the word of God should be spoken first to you. Since you thrust it from you, and judge yourselves unworthy of eternal life, behold, we turn to the Gentiles." The rejection of the gospel by Jews in Antioch of Pisidia resulted in the withdrawal of Paul and Barnabas from their synagogue. From now on they will engage in mission among the Gentiles, until they reach another city. The salvation-historical priority of Israel is a divine order and not merely a matter of mission strategy. To Jews the fulfillment of the promise is to be preached first (cf. Rom. 1:16; 2:9-10) and only then to Gentiles. No one is excluded, or excommunicated (cf. 8:22-24). But by their own decision against the gospel (cf. Luke 7:30; Acts 7:39) people exclude themselves. This is true not only in Antioch of Pisidia, but in Corinth (18:6), Ephesus (19:9), and Rome as well (28:25-28). Moreover, Luke made it clear that the Gentile mission is not merely the result of Jewish rejection of the message of salvation. Paul's mission to Gentiles is grounded in Christ's command: **I have set you to be a light for the Gentiles that you may bring salvation to the uttermost parts of the earth.** The reason for Gentile mission lies in the will and purpose of the Lord Jesus (Acts 1:8; Luke 24:47). The Magna Charta of Gentile mission placed an Old Testament word (Isa. 49:6 LXX) into the mouth of the Lord and demonstrated the unity between the church's mission, the church's Lord, and the purpose of God in Isaiah 49. In Luke 2:32 Simeon called Jesus "a light for revelation to the Gentiles." Jesus' messengers who announce **the message of this salvation** (v. 26) to the Gentiles are a light for them. Through his proclamation Paul brings Christ and therefore "light" to the Gentiles, because Christ himself is present in his proclamation (cf. 26:18,23). **The uttermost parts of the earth** (cf. 1:8) does not refer to Rome, which in Luke's view was the center of the Gentile world, even as Jerusalem was the center of Judaism, but refers to the edges of the (then known) universe. "The church is mission" and in its mission the church breaks down barriers of segregation and carries out the conquest of the world in the name of the resurrected Christ who is Lord of all (10:36). What the servant of the Lord was meant to be (Isa. 49:3-6) is realized by Christ's messengers. Just as the servant of the Lord after the failure of his mission to Jacob and Israel (Isa. 49:4 LXX) was commanded to be a light to the nations (Isa. 49:6), so Barnabas and Paul bring the light of salvation through Christ to Gentiles. And just as the servant of the Lord was required to "gather together Jacob and Israel" unto the Lord even after his failure (Isa. 49:4-5), so Barnabas and Paul will time and again fulfill the divine mandate and preach to Jews first. Finally we should note Luke's deft use of Old Testament citations and their contexts. In Ps. 2:8 (cf. v. 33) God promised to his enthroned Son: "I will make the nations your heritage and the ends of the earth your possession." Isaiah 55:3-5 (cf. v. 34b) envisions the Lord's anointed as "a witness to the nations, a leader and commander for the peoples. Behold you shall call nations." This universal dimension, implicit in these citations, reaches its climax in the final quotation from Isa. 49:6 (v. 47) which is applied to Paul and Barnabas, the representatives of the church's mission. The offer of salvation to Gentiles constitutes an act of obedience to the God of the Old Testament and to the resurrected Lord (1:8). With this declaration the ministry in Antioch has attained its high point.

Verses 48-52 bring the reactions of Gentiles, Jews, missionaries, and disciples. **The Gentiles** who had come **to hear the word of God** (v. 44) rejoiced and **glorified the word of God** (v. 48), because that word offers salvation through Christ to "everyone who believes" (v. 39). **As many as were ordained to eternal life believed.** Eternal life is the effect of Christ's resurrection on believers (vv. 32-33). Faith is a person's existential decision, and so is unbelief, in which the call to faith is thrust aside (cf. v. 46c). Simultaneously, faith is the gift and election of God granted when and where it pleases him. Luke does not dissolve this paradox and neither should we. As believers we cannot say that we have come to faith because of our spiritual quality. Rather we must say that it is God who **ordained** us to inherit **eternal life.** The Gentiles ordained by God to eternal, indestructible resurrection life (cf. vv. 34-35, 46) are in continuity with the history that began with God's election of the fathers whom he "chose" (v. 17), a history which found its culmination in the resurrection of Christ and the offer of salvation to Jew and Gentile. Because the church is mission therefore **the word of the Lord spread**

throughout all the region around Antioch in Pisidia. Instead of withdrawing from the world into an apocalyptic conventicle, the newly converted Gentiles carried the Word of God into the world around them. Paul and Barnabas experienced the fulfillment of the promise that in the service of Christ they must endure suffering (cf. 9:16). **Devout women of high standing and the leading men of the city** were incited to start trouble against Paul and Barnabas **and drove them out of their district.** The world, including the "religious" world, does not remain passive when God makes his assault upon it with his Word but fights back in its own way (v. 50). The **devout women** of high social status (cf. 17:4, 12) were probably Gentile adherents of the synagogue, proselytes, or sympathizers. It was easier for women to become proselytes than for men. Josephus also refers to Gentile women who were attracted to the synagogue (*War* 2.561). They probably persuaded their husbands, "the leading men" of Antioch, to move against the two missionaries. Jews in cooperation with Gentiles **drove** the missionaries not merely **out** of Antioch, but out of the **district** of Pisidia. Paul and Barnabas suffered the same fate that Jesus had suffered in Nazareth (cf. *ekballō*, Luke 4:29; "filled with," Luke 4:28; Acts 13:45). There are other parallels between Jesus' inaugural sermon and Paul's, and the effects of each. But there are also differences. In Luke's Gospel Jesus never returned to Nazareth; Paul and Barnabas did return to Antioch (14:21). **They shook off the dust from their feet against them.** This symbolic gesture commanded by Jesus (Luke 9:5; 10:11) here symbolizes the end of any relationship with the Jewish and Gentile persecutors of the missionaries. Their violent opponents are abandoned to the judgment of God (v. 41). Luke had indicated that the response of the Jews to Paul's preaching had been divided. His concluding verses (vv. 48-50) make it plain that also the response of Gentiles was divided. A new community of Jews, proselytes, and Gentiles had been established (vv. 43, 48) whose members were no longer just Jews or Gentiles but **disciples** with a mission to fulfill, **with joy and with the Holy Spirit** enabling them to fulfill it (cf. 1 Thess. 1:6).

14:1-7 (Mission in Iconium)—After his detailed account of Paul's sermon and its aftermath in Antioch, Luke changes his tone and gives a bland summary report about the mission in Iconium before narrating the dramatic events at Lystra. In this way the two high points of this journey at Antioch and Lystra stand out in sharp relief while the connecting report about Iconium serves as transition. But also this low-key report reiterates several important points: (1) Though the two missionaries, by shaking off the dust from their feet, had given notice that they regarded the unbelieving Jews of Antioch to be on a par with unbelieving Gentiles, nevertheless, "as was their custom" (cf. 13:5; 17:2; cf. Luke 4:16) they went to the synagogue of Iconium and preached there. Lukan theology of mission demands proclamation to Jews first in each new location. Paul and Barnabas are missionaries to Gentiles (cf. 13:47; 9:15) only because they are first of all missionaries to Jews. This divine order holds true throughout Acts—including the last chapter—and to the eschaton. Acceptance as well as rejection of the gospel presupposes the hearing of the message, and according to Luke involves a personal decision one way or the other. Just because some Jews in some places had turned against the gospel and its messengers, their rejection did not excuse the messengers of Christ from confronting other Jews in other places. (2) Preaching created faith and caused division among Jews and Gentiles alike (v. 4). The great company of believers in Iconium testified to the power of the Word of God, which creates and sustains the true people of God in a particular location. (3) The "signs and wonders" (v. 3) performed by the Lord through his messengers demonstrated their continuity with the apostles (cf. 5:12) and with the Lord Jesus (cf. 14:8-11 with Luke 5:17-26 and Acts 3:1-10). Moreover, the reference to miracles in general done by Paul and Barnabas (v. 3) helps the reader to understand that specific miracle stories are not isolated cases but illustrations of one aspect of the work of these missionaries. (4) The success of preaching led to conflict with Jews and Gentiles. The continuity of the church with its Lord finds expression also in conflicts which take different forms. Luke's message, based on the resurrection, is one of hope: through persecution comes growth (vv. 6-7; cf. 8:4; 11:19-20). (5) Martyrdom is not to be sought out, but voluntary flight in extreme situations is preferred (v. 6; cf. 9:25, 30; 12:17). Luke downplayed the glamour of a martyr's death, as found, for instance, in Ignatius, bishop of Antioch, Syria, at the beginning of the second century (Ign. *Rom.* 4–6). Though the gospel promises life eternal (13:46, 48), our earthly life is the good gift of our Creator, and it should not be despised (cf. vv. 15-17).

1-2—Now at Iconium [the modern Konya], about 85 miles east-southeast from Antioch, Pisidia, on the Via Sebaste, the imperial highway from Ephesus to Syria, Paul and Barnabas entered the most important city of their journey. On arrival **they entered together** (or perhaps "in the same way as before" [at Antioch]; or "as was their custom," cf. 17:2) **into the Jewish synagogue** on the sabbath. Through their preaching **a great company believed, both of Jews and of Greeks,** and a new Christian community was established. Impressive as their success was, it did not lead all Jews to faith but rather caused a division among the members of the synagogue. **The unbelieving Jews** who rejected the gospel made propaganda among **the Gentiles . . . against the brethren.** The word *brothers* usually designates the members of the Jewish or Christian community (cf. 1:15-16; 2:37; 23:1), women included, but here it refers to the two missionaries. Bracketed by the two notices about the growing opposition (vv. 2 and 4) Luke inserted a summary of the apostles' work (v. 3).

3—In this summary Luke tells us that the apostles worked in Iconium **for a long time** in spite of more or less covert hostility. They did not run away at the first sign of difficulties, but continued **speaking boldly for the Lord** (cf. 4:13, 29, 31; 9:27, 29; 13:46; 18:26; 19:8; 28:31). Perhaps we should translate: "speaking boldly on the basis of the Lord," that is, relying on the Lord. At any rate Luke contrasted their bold witness with the defamatory activity of their opponents who poisoned the minds of the Gentiles.

Moreover, he also contrasted the agitation against them with the witness of God or Jesus on behalf of his messengers. **The Lord . . . bore witness to the word of his grace, granting signs and wonders to be done by their hands.** The miracles which the Lord enabled his messengers to perform testified that their message to Jews and Gentiles had divine approval. **The word of his grace** gives a Pauline flavor to the sentence (cf. 20:24, 32) and underlines that faith comes through the word and forgiveness is by grace alone. **The Lord who bore witness** to Paul and Barnabas is either God (in 20:32 "the word of his grace" clearly refers to God) or Christ (in Luke 4:22 "the words of grace" proceed from Jesus). In 3:6 and 9:17, 34 it is Jesus Christ who effects miracles through his chosen messengers, but on the other hand it is "the grace of God" in which the new converts are urged to continue (13:43). While either identification is possible and a choice between them difficult, I would lean toward identifying

"the Lord" with Jesus. But this difficulty also reveals the insepara-
bility of Jesus Christ from the God of Israel.

4-5—Jewish agitation on the one hand, and the activity of Paul
and Barnabas on the other, precipitated a division among **the people
of the city; some sided with the** (unbelieving) **Jews, and some with
the apostles.** The crisis reached dangerous proportions when **both
Gentiles and Jews, with their rulers,** attempted **to molest . . . and
to stone** the apostles. It is not clear whether "leaders" refers only
to Jewish leaders (cf. 13:15) or also includes the Gentile magistrates
(13:50). If Luke had the latter in mind, then we would have a repeat
performance of the persecution in Antioch. It is more likely that
Luke presented here a variation of the persecution of 13:50-51,
describing a mob action of Gentiles incited by Jews and **their rulers**
(cf. 3:17; 4:5, 8, 26; 23:5).

Finally, in this verse and in v. 14, and only in these verses, Luke
assigns the designation **apostles** to Paul and Barnabas. Besides the
concept of 12 apostles which Luke had received from his tradition
(cf. Rev. 21:14; Matt. 10:2; Mark 6:30), Luke also knew that missionaries who had been commissioned and "sent" (Greek, *apostellō*)
by churches were known as "apostles." He probably found the designation "apostles" in a tradition he used, and understood it in a
functional sense (cf. [*ex*]*apostellō* in Acts 22:21; 26:17). For Luke
Barnabas and Paul, who had been prophets and teachers, were also
"apostles," because they had been *sent* by the Holy Spirit and the
church in Antioch, Syria, to be missionaries (cf. 13:1-3). Thus the
triad of "apostles, prophets, teachers" (1 Cor. 12:28) applied to them,
and Luke gave those Pauline churches that revered Paul as the
apostle to the Gentiles their due (cf. Gal. 1:1; Rom. 11:13), even
though apart from these two verses in Acts Luke never applied this
functional title to him.

6-7—In distinction from the persecution in Antioch, the apostles
learned of the attempt on their lives and were able to flee **to Lystra
and Derbe, cities of Lycaonia, and to the surrounding country.**
There is no sense in wasting one's life on bigots and fanatics. On
the contrary, their flight produced new opportunities for witnessing
in new locations. **And there they preached the gospel.** The Greek
construction makes it clear that it was a continuous activity in which
they engaged. It is the activity of Isaiah's "evangelizer" who announces the appearance of God's sovereign rule for salvation (Isa.

253

40:9), who brings a message of "peace" and "good" (Isa. 52:7) and proclaims salvation to the poor (Isa. 61:1). Luke, like Isaiah, used the verb "to preach the gospel" (*euangelizesthai*) without an object as a technical term for the proclamation of salvation. Moreover, Paul in Acts continues Isaiah's tradition of the servant mission in Israel and among the nations (Isa. 49:6; Acts 13:47; 14:7).

Looking back over Luke's presentation of the mission in Iconium, we recognize not only the tight structure of his report which, especially in v. 3, bears the marks of his style, but we also recognize his dependence on tradition, be it in written or in oral form. Formerly, interpreters supposed that beginning with 13:1 and continuing to Acts 21:16 our author had at his disposal an itinerary which listed the places of Paul's work together with brief notes about the founding of communities. We now know that the ancient literary parallels to the supposed itinerary are not really analogous to the proposed itinerary behind Acts. Though the theory of an itinerary (into which Luke inserted speeches, e.g., 13:16-41; traditions, e.g., 14:8-14; the account of the apostles' conference, 15:1-35; and redactional comments, e.g., 20:36-38) is now out of favor, nevertheless we should not deny to our author the availability of traditions in written or oral form. In this section we find such indications of their presence as the following: (1) Luke would not have mentioned Derbe in v. 6 if it had not been in the tradition available to him. The apostles reached Derbe in v. 20 and since Luke mentioned no particular incident in that city he had no need to introduce it in v. 6. (2) Luke would hardly have used the designation *apostles* had he not found it in his tradition. (3) The words "attempt" (Greek, *hōrmē*) and "flee" (Greek, *katapheugein*) in vv. 5 and 6 are not found elsewhere in Luke-Acts. (4) For Luke, the Christian mission proceeded from cities to the countryside (cf. 13:49). Only here (v. 6) do we read that apostles preached in rural communities. (5) Finally, the persecution in Iconium was not a repeat performance of the one in Antioch, because Gentile magistrates had probably not been involved and because the apostles were able to flee prior to its outbreak. Moreover, the agitation "against the brothers" (v. 2) might indicate an underlying tradition in which the new community experienced opposition. Even though it is not possible for us to reconstruct the tradition which was at Luke's disposal, it is equally impossible to deny the existence of such traditions or argue that Luke simply made up vv. 1-7 on the basis of his imagination. It would seem that vv. 1-2 and 4-6 are based on pre-Lukan tradition.

14:8-20 (Mission in Lystra)—Lystra became a Roman colony under Augustus and belonged to the region of Lycaonia together with Derbe and Iconium, though some ancient writers assigned the latter city to Phrygia. The mission in Lystra is told in one dramatic narrative in three parts. (1) A miracle by Paul had unforeseen results when the pagans regarded Barnabas and Paul as manifestations of Zeus and Hermes, two Greek gods (vv. 8-14). The gospel encountered pagan mythology and idolatry in a city which had no synagogue. Luke's readers were familiar with the story of Zeus (Jupiter) and Hermes (Mercury) visiting a pious old couple, Philemon and Baucis, in Phrygia. The two gods had appeared in the disguise of humans and had been rejected by many people, but the poor couple offered them hospitality (cf. Gen. 18:1-16), though unaware of their identity, and were divinely rewarded (Ovid, *Metamorphoses* 8.611–724). Historically, it may seem unlikely to us that the pagans of Lystra after seeing a miracle would render divine honors to two Jewish missionaries. Yet, superstition then and now knows no boundary (cf. Lucian, *Alexander the False Prophet* 13–16, and Philostratus, *Life of Apollonius* 8.5-7, for parallels). The biblical line of demarcation between the Creator and the creature is blurred in polytheism, and Christian missionaries had to compete with pagan miracle workers who claimed to be mediums of divine powers (cf. 8:9-11). The story sets forth dramatically the misunderstanding which the gospel in word and deed encounters in the world of pagans. Luke omitted the conclusion of the traditional story and in its place substituted a brief address by Paul.

(2) This first address to pagans (vv. 15-17) is a preview of Paul's paradigmatic Areopagus speech to Gentiles (17:22-31). Sermons to Jews proclaimed Jesus Christ as the culmination of salvation history in accordance with the will of God, set forth in the Scriptures. Gentiles, however, did not share those biblical presuppositions and therefore had to be converted first to the true and living God, before the announcement of Christ's resurrection and his appointment as judge made sense. In the speech to the people in Lystra only the first part dealing with the necessity of turning to the living God was developed in order to counteract the misunderstanding of the people. The speeches to Gentiles are also based on a traditional pattern which can be recognized in 1 Thess. 1:9-10.

(3) In vv. 19-20 Luke used another tradition which focused on Paul alone. He had been left for dead by stoning and almost miraculously revived and "rose up." Suddenly we hear of **disciples** (v. 20) even though vv. 8-18 did not refer to conversions. Thus, vv. 19-20 were originally a separate tradition. Paul himself wrote of a stoning which he endured (2 Cor. 11:25, without name of place) and 2 Tim. 3:11 speaks of persecutions that befell him "at Antioch, at Iconium, and at Lystra." It was probably Luke who connected the stoning of Paul in Lystra with "Jews" from Antioch and Iconium (v. 19). It seems unlikely that they would have walked a hundred miles over mountainous terrain just to throw stones at Paul. With their introduction in v. 19, Luke intensified the hatred of the Jews against Paul (cf. 13:50; 14:5) and he also reflected the feelings of his own Christian group at his time.

8-10—Now at Lystra—the Lukan pattern of proclamation in the synagogue could not be used, because the city lacked a Jewish community. The Jews who made their appearance (v. 19) came from outside, and therefore Paul spoke to Gentiles (v. 9). In his audience was **a cripple from birth, who had never walked.** The concise miracle story shows parallels with similar healings by Peter and Jesus (3:2-10; Luke 5:18-26) and conveys to the reader the continuity of the Christian ministry in word and deed as a result of the Spirit's presence. Paul is Peter's equal in terms of ministry and both bear the likeness of Jesus. But each miracle narrative in Acts also has its peculiar emphasis, which in the present case is the reaction of the crowd, Paul's response after the miracle, and the **faith** of the lame man before the miracle. **He listened to Paul speaking.** It is assumed that the reader would understand that Paul was not speaking about the weather but about God, Christ, and the Holy Spirit, as Peter had done in the house of Cornelius. Faith comes from hearing the Word of God. Paul, the charismatic, **looking intently at him** (cf. 3:4), could perceive what others were unable to see. The lame man had **faith to be made well.** This is the only time in Acts that the faith of a person in need of healing is mentioned, in contrast to the Gospels, which frequently relate faith to healing (Luke 5:20; 7:9; 17:19; 18:42). In the Synoptic Gospels, however, faith is used in an absolute sense, e.g., "Your faith has made you well" (Luke 17:19), while here it is qualified as **faith to be made well** (Greek, *sōthēnai*). The lame man's faith was his expectation and trust that the God whom Paul proclaimed could heal him. By speaking about the lame man's faith in this story of healing, Luke deftly portrayed the promise of the mission to Gentiles (cf. Luke 7:9). The salvation which Paul was to bring to Gentiles (13:47) included healing as a sign of God's saving power. **In a loud voice** Paul said to the lame man: **Stand upright on your feet.** Paul's command, in the words God addressed to Ezekiel (Ezek. 2:1), is God's own command. The demonstration of the miracle follows in that the lame person sprang up and walked.

11-14—Miracle stories conclude with the reaction of the crowd, such as the praise of God, and the admiration of the healer and the spread of his fame. Here, however, the crowd reacted in a bizzare fashion (cf. 10:25; 12:22; 28:6). The traditional conclusion of miracle stories (cf. Luke 5:26) is greatly expanded here so that, together with Paul's response, it becomes one of the two poles of the Lukan account, in which the healing merely functions as the introduction to the attempted deification. If the faith of the lame man illustrates the promise of the Gentile mission, then the reaction of the crowd points out the problem of pagan superstition which the mission encounters. The bystanders reacted in amazement to the miracle and **lifted up their voices** (cf. 2:14; 4:22; 22:22) and spoke **in Lycaonian,** which means that they were not the Roman citizens of the colony but natives of Anatolia who, in addition to Greek, still spoke their own language. Since the apostles did not understand that dialect they were unable to interfere at this point. Simultaneously, the storyteller created the necessary time and suspense. The reader knows what these people are up to before the apostles comprehend what is going on. **The gods have come down to us in the likeness of men!** the crowd exclaimed. Behind their exclamation lay the story of Zeus and Hermes visiting Philemon and Baucis in nearby Phrygia. **Barnabas they called Zeus,** the chief Greek god, and Paul was identified with **Hermes,** the messenger of the gods, **because he was the chief speaker** (cf. v. 9). Inscriptions bearing the names of the two gods have been found in the vicinity of Lystra and attest to a joint cult of these two gods in that region. **The priest** of the **temple** of Zeus, located **in front of the city,** that is, outside the walls, was ready to sacrifice **oxen** adorned with woolen **garlands** in response to this theophany, when at last the two **apostles** (see v. 4) realized that they were the object of divine honors. Their immediate reaction was to protest against this act of idolatry by tearing **their garments**

(cf. Mark 14:63; Jer. 36:24; Jdt. 14:16). Rushing **out among the multitude,** they tried to stop them by giving a speech.

15-18—Instead of a recitation of God's acts in the Old Testament and in Jesus Christ, the idolatrous pagans must first hear about the one true God (cf. Deut. 6:4). Grammatically, the speech is given by both apostles (cf. v. 7), but since Paul is presented as the chief speaker, the speech is his. He began with the situation at hand and asked, **Why are you doing this? We also are men of like nature with you,** on the same side of the line that separates the creature from the Creator.

The visitors were not gods in human form but messengers of **good news** from God (cf. v. 7), and part of the **good news** is the command **to turn** away **from these vain things** of pagan idolatry, be they worship, temple, mythology, sacrifices, statues, or priests (cf. Jer. 2:5; 8:19; Esther 4:17, LXX; Wis. 13:1—15:19). The people of Lystra were asked to give up the context of their existence. Pagan religion was not a matter of one hour per week reserved for strange rituals, but it constituted the underpinnings of society. Turning away from **these vain things** is possible only through turning to the **living God,** the creator of **the heaven and the earth** (cf. 4:24; 17:24; Genesis 1; Exod. 20:11; Ps. 146:6). In short, Paul asked for a radical break with their religious-social culture. To the Thessalonian Christians Paul, citing a tradition, wrote: "you turned to God from idols, to serve the living and true God" (1 Thess. 1:9). **In past generations** the one true God **allowed all the nations to walk in their own ways.** But "their own ways" were not God's way (24:14; Luke 20:21). They had not heard the Word of God and therefore they walked in the ways of idolatry. They were ignorant of the identity of the true God (cf. 17:30), even as the people of Jerusalem were ignorant of Jesus' identity (cf. 13:27). No overt accusations are raised, yet the ignorance of the pagans is no more excused than that of the Jerusalemites (13:28). The pagans could have acted differently because God **did not leave himself without witness,** but showed himself to be their magnificent benefactor doing **good,** giving **rains and fruitful seasons, satisfying your hearts with food and gladness.** God's work of creation could and should have led them to revere the goodness of the living God.

Scripture is a witness of God and to God, and so are eyewitnesses to the resurrection, miracles (14:3), and the proclaimed word. Here, however, we find that also creation is the place of God's revelation. It witnesses to the goodness of the almighty Benefactor (*agathour-gōn*, v. 17, "doing good") who bestows blessings on body and soul. Food is not merely meant to fill bodies, but also to fill "hearts with gladness." This theology of the First Article of the Apostles' Creed is also firmly grounded in the Old Testament (especially the Psalms, e.g., 8:3-9; 19; 145:15-16,21; 147:8; Jer. 5:24). But this natural witness to God is now supplanted by the verbal witness of the gospel proclamation which the apostles bring. Paul, however, did not even get that far. Only with difficulty he and Barnabas **restrained the people from offering sacrifice to them.** At first this seems to be the sum total of their success in pagan Lystra (cf. v. 20; 16:2).

When the two speeches to Gentiles in Acts (14:15-17; 17:22-33) are compared with Rom. 1:18-23, different emphases become apparent. Romans 1:20 clearly states that the Gentiles "are without excuse." The two speeches in Acts do not say that. However, four points should be kept in mind: (1) Romans was written to Christians; the two speeches in Acts are addressed to pagans. (2) Romans is not a sermon but comes close to being a theological treatise. (3) Implicit in Acts 14:16-17 is the accusation that the pagans could have done better than to confuse the creature with the Creator since the latter "did not leave himself without witness." (4) Finally, it is most unlikely that Paul first softened up his audiences by telling them what inexcusable sinners they were.

19-20—The Lystra episode moves quickly from one extreme to another. Pagan religion was ready to offer them divine honors, but from attempted deification the pendulum swings to attempted murder (cf. Luke 4:22-29). Mission to Gentiles has its problems. Luke introduced **Jews from Antioch** and **Iconium** as countermissionaries and agitators against the apostles. The Jews, **having persuaded the people** of Lystra and with their approval, **stoned Paul and dragged him out of the city, supposing that he was dead.** In so doing they thought they had brought to completion their attempt on his life which had been foiled at Iconium by the flight of the apostles (14:5-6). Once again Paul experienced in his own body the fulfillment of the terms of his call (9:15-16). This stoning is recalled in 2 Cor. 11:25 (cf. Gal. 6:17) and 2 Tim. 3:11, where we also read "yet from them all the Lord rescued me." **But when the disciples gathered about him, he rose up and entered the city; and on the next day he went**

on with Barnabas to Derbe. Spared once again, Paul **rose up** when **the disciples** thought they had to bury his body, and on the following day continued "the work" for which he was set apart (13:2). Though Luke had not told us before, the mission in Lystra resulted in converting some pagans into **disciples** of Jesus and in establishing a church (cf. vv. 21-23). Among his converts in Lystra was Timothy, Paul's "beloved and faithful child in the Lord" (1 Cor. 4:17), who accompanied Paul from his second great journey onward (16:1-2).

21—Mission in Derbe: While Derbe had been mentioned twice before (vv. 6 and 20) Luke's report is exceedingly brief. The apostles **preached the gospel** (see v. 7), **made many disciples** in Derbe, and decided **to return to Lystra and to Iconium and to Antioch,** in spite of the dangers which they had experienced there. Apostles are not self-employed agents, but work under the mandate of the Spirit, and therefore must reckon with dangers. Luke paid tribute to the courage of Barnabas and Paul with his low-key report. He did not refer to a persecution in Derbe, nor did the tradition in 2 Tim. 3:11, which, like Acts, mentions sufferings "at Antioch, Iconium, and Lystra," but not at Derbe. On older maps, this city is wrongly located. Through inscriptional evidence, the site of Derbe has been identified as located at modern Kerti Hüyük, 15 miles northeast of Karaman Laranda, or about 70 miles southeast of Iconium. Paul revisited Derbe (16:1) and one of his coworkers, Gaius, came from there (20:4).

Verses 21-28 have the form of a summary report in which Luke made important theological statements at the beginning (vv. 22-23) and at the end (v. 27). Interpreters have asked why the apostles did not continue east on the road from Derbe and cross the Taurus mountains through the Cilician gates instead of the much longer and more difficult return journey in this section. Or how could they return to cities from which they had been expelled (13:50), where they had been threatened or stoned? The suggestion that the return visit of the apostles was merely a Lukan construction in the interest of his theory of missionary follow-up overlooks the fact that the apostles did not return to Cyprus on this journey for any such work.

22—Retracing their steps through Lystra, Iconium, and Antioch, they moved into the second phase of mission building. We do not hear that they preached to Gentiles or Jews, but focused their attention on **strengthening** (cf. 15:32, 41; 18:23) and **exhorting** the disciples (11:23; 15:32; 16:40; 20:1,2). In 20:18-35 Luke will bring an example of exhortation and encouragement by Paul to Christians. From his own letters we know that Paul not only "planted" and established churches but he also "watered" them, by revisiting them, writing letters, or sending delegates to them. It is therefore not surprising that the verbs "to strengthen" and "to exhort" (*parakalein*) are frequent in his letters (e.g., Rom. 1:11; 1 Thess. 3:2; Rom. 12:1,8; 1 Cor. 1:10). The exhortation on this return journey was that the new house churches should resist the various social pressures brought to bear on them and **continue in the faith**—the one faith of the one church (cf. 6:7; 13:8; 15:9; 16:5). This faith comes to expression in creedal formulas (9:20,22; 17:3b; 13:30), in worship (2:42), mission outreach (13:49), life-style (20:33-35), assistance (11:29-30), and, last but not least, in enduring suffering. In direct discourse we hear the apostles **saying that through many tribulations we must enter the kingdom of God**. **We must** indicates the divine law announced and accepted by Jesus (Luke 14:27; 24:26). This law applies not only to apostles (cf. 5:40; 14:19) but to every disciple of Jesus. Suffering is not viewed from a pedagogical perspective (Sir. 2:5; Wis. 3:6), whereby tribulations purify the soul, nor from an apocalyptic perspective where suffering signals the imminent end and the "coming" of the kingdom (Mark 13:19,24). It is viewed as the norm of Christian existence. The daily pressures, ridicule, ostracism, social defamation, occasional beatings, arrests, and confiscation of property are hardships that must be endured in order "to continue in the faith" and **enter the kingdom of God** at the time of death (Luke 23:43; Acts 7:59), or for the living at the time of the parousia. Discipleship includes the endurance of **many tribulations.** "No cross, no crown." This *theologia crucis*, which is to be lived, is bracketed by references to faith (vv. 22a and 23c), which receives the power to endure from the Lord.

23—Paul's letters refer to leaders in his communities with a variety of designations. We hear of bishops, deacons (Phil. 1:1; Rom. 16:1), and administrators (1 Thess. 5:12; Rom. 12:8, *proistamenos;* 1 Cor. 12:28, *kybernēseis*), of first converts who functioned in leadership roles (1 Cor. 16:15-18). While we cannot describe their functions adequately, their presence shows the need for structure within the community. When Luke wrote that Barnabas and Paul **appointed**

elders for them in every church, he was correct to the extent that no church can be without a leadership structure, but he committed an anachronism nevertheless. Elders were unknown in Pauline churches. They were introduced at a later time. The Pastoral Epistles, written after Paul, indicate their presence in post-Pauline communities (1 Tim. 5:17; Titus 1:5). Luke projected the council of elders which existed within his own church back into the time of Paul's first missionary journey. Their tasks are stated in 20:27-35. The manner of their appointment involves **prayer and fasting,** based on the practice at Antioch (13:1-3). The apostles **committed them,** all disciples and presbyters, to the protection of **the Lord in whom they believed.**

24-28—On their return journey **through Pisidia** and **Pamphylia** they preached at **Perga,** where Mark had parted company with them (13:13). Although Luke did not disclose the result of speaking **the word** in Perga, the reader knows that God's word will not return void, that a community of believers was established in that city and that elders were appointed there as **in every church** (v. 23). From **Attalia,** the port of Perga, they sailed back to **Antioch,** Syria. As befits delegates who were sent by the community to perform a specific task, Paul and Barnabas reported on their **work** (v. 26, cf. 13:2, 41) to a meeting of the whole church. Their missionary report to the assembled church could speak in retrospect about **all that God had done with them** (v. 27). His deeds through his heralds of good news imply that the acts of God in history continue and that his messengers are coworkers of God (1 Cor. 3:9; 2 Cor. 6:1; Phil. 2:13). They are "afflicted in every way, but not crushed; perplexed, but not driven to despair; persecuted, but not forsaken" (2 Cor. 4:8). Through their labors God **had opened a door of faith to the Gentiles,** granting them the opportunity to hear the word that calls to faith (cf. 11:18; 1 Cor. 16:9; 2 Cor. 2:12) and admits them to the believing people of God. The church in Antioch had preached to Gentiles in a random fashion from its beginning (11:20), but this first missionary journey confirmed that the systematic evangelization of Gentiles is God's own work through his church. It is his will that Gentiles, without circumcision and obedience to the Torah, enter the church. Having made their report, Paul and Barnabas **remained** with the church in Antioch for some time.

Looking at this missionary journey which began and ended in Antioch (13:1-4; 14:26-28), we see it as a step toward fulfilling **Christ's** mandate of 1:8. In contrast to 1:8, it is **the Holy Spirit** that "set apart" and "sent out" (13:2, 4) Barnabas and Paul, while it is **God** who "opened a door of faith to the Gentiles" (14:27).

Luke's language expresses the basic insight that speaking about God involves speaking about Jesus Christ and the Holy Spirit. Mission is the will of the triune God and mission involves struggle with magic (13:6-12), with Jewish objections (13:40-46), and with pagan idolatry (14:11-18). What is common to all of these is the desire to control God.

In agreement with his commission (9:15-16), Paul, in witnessing to Jews and Gentiles, had suffered for the sake of the name of Jesus Christ during this journey. Through his and Barnabas's labors, God **had opened a door of faith to the Gentiles** (14:27, cf. 11:18).

The Apostles' Conference (15:1-35)

Introduction: With the apostles' conference Luke reached the center of his second volume as he narrated the most important decision made by the early church. All the major persons and groups in Acts are represented: Peter and James, Paul and Barnabas, apostles and elders, the churches of Antioch and of Jerusalem. We also hear of other groups, the churches in Phoenicia and Samaria, Christian Pharisees who champion the necessity of circumcision and obedience to the law of Moses, and Christian prophets, Judas Barsabbas and Silas, who offer exhortation and encouragement. This chapter in the center of Acts functions as retrospect and prospect. It looks back and reaffirms the gradual movement of the Christian witness from Jerusalem via Samaria to the Gentiles, and by its decision it opens the way for the future of the Pauline mission, narrated in 15:36—19:20.

Moreover, the apostles' conference deals with the great issues that had to be confronted by the early church: What does it mean to be the people of God in the light of Easter and the Spirit's presence? What is the meaning of circumcision and of the law of Moses in view of the influx of Gentiles into the church? How are Christian Jews and Christian Gentiles to relate to each other? In Acts 10:35 Peter had declared that in every nation any one who fears God and performs righteousness is acceptable to God, and the conclusion of his speech made it clear that "fearing God" included believing in Christ in response to the Christian message, and "being acceptable" to God included forgiveness of sins through Christ (10:43). The community in Jerusalem had approved the admission of Gentiles (11:18), but the issue for which Peter had been criticized, namely, eating with Gentiles (11:3), was not settled at that time. The influx of an ever-increasing number of Gentiles into the church through the Antiochian mission outreach as well as the influx of Pharisees into the church of Jerusalem (15:5) made the reopening of the question of Gentiles in the church inevitable. The point of controversy which developed was the question whether Gentile Christians were members of the people of God even though they did not live in accordance with the whole Mosaic Law, but merely regarded the summaries of the Law as normative. Jesus had approved the summary of the Law in terms of love toward God and love toward the neighbor (Luke 10:27-28; cf. Luke 11:39-42) and Peter had spoken about fear of God and doing righteousness, giving alms, as a kind of summary of the Law. There is no doubt that Gentiles who became Christians were not "free from the Law" in terms of the Lukan or Pauline summaries (cf. also Gal. 5:14; 6:2; Rom. 13:9-10; 1 Cor. 9:21). The question which the Christian Pharisees pressed concerned the obligation to render obedience to the whole Mosaic Law, of which the two commandments were merely summaries. Some Judean Christians raised the issue of circumcision, the mark of every male member of the people of God (Genesis 17, cf. Acts 7:8), and they flatly announced that "unless you are circumcised . . . you cannot be saved" (15:1; cf. v. 5). Finally, in Luke's account of the apostles' conference the problem had to be settled as to how Jewish Christians who continued to live by the Mosaic Law could associate with Gentile Christians who did not observe the Torah and who, therefore, were ritually unclean. This problem became most pressing when the church gathered for the Eucharist, the "breaking of bread," but it was present also in the daily associations between Jewish and Gentile Christians. Were Jewish Christians to be "defiled" whenever they came to the Lord's table or ate in a Gentile Christian's house? Before proceeding with the interpretation of the Lukan report of the apostles' conference we will briefly compare it with Paul's own account.

Acts 15:1-35 and Gal. 2:1-10

The problem of relating Paul's visits to Jerusalem found in Acts (9:26; 11:30; 15:1-35; 18:22; 21:17) with the two visits mentioned in Galatians (1:18-19; 2:1-10) has produced a number of theories. His second visit in Galatians has been identified by different scholars with each of the first four found in Acts. The identification of Gal. 2:1-10 with the first visit in Acts (9:26) does not deal adequately with Pauline chronology, because the visit of Galatians 2 took place some 15 years after Paul's conversion (Gal. 1:18; 2:1—part of a year can be reckoned as a full year). By A.D. 51 Paul was in Corinth (Acts 18:12-17). The single exact date for Paul's life derives from the proconsulship of Gallio, who was governor of Achaia, Greece, from July A.D. 51 to July A.D. 52; Paul appeared before him (18:12). This theory (Acts 9:26 = Gal. 2:1) not only requires at least a 15-year period between Acts 9:19 and 9:26 but also compresses Acts 9:30—18:12 into a 3-year period—which in terms of the geographic distances covered is an impossibility.

We have already dealt with the hypothesis that the second visit in Acts (11:30) was identical with the one in Gal. 2:1-10 (see comments on 11:28) and we shall briefly comment on the suggestion that Paul's fourth visit to Jerusalem in Acts (18:22) was the same as the second in Galatians (2:1-10). According to this hypothesis, the apostles' council took place after Paul's ministry in Corinth in the fall of A.D. 51 or the summer of 52. However, Gal. 1:21 would seem to refute this hypothesis. Paul wrote that between his first visit, 3 years after his conversion (Gal. 1:18), and his second visit, 14 years later (Gal. 2:1), he "went into the regions of Syria and Cilicia." This statement, which agrees with Acts 9:30 and 11:26, makes the hypothesis before us improbable. If his second visit took place after his ministry in Corinth then Paul had traveled not just to "the regions of Syria and Cilicia," but through Phrygia, Galatia, Macedonia, and Achaia. It would seem most unlikely that "Syria and Cilicia" could be stretched to include the provinces of Greece, especially since Paul's second missionary journey was largely independent of Antioch.

Two other views should at least be mentioned. (1) Acts 15:1-19 refers to the same event as Gal. 2:1-10, an event which took place at the time of the famine relief visit, Acts 11:30, that is, *prior* to the first missionary journey (Acts 13–14). In this case the agreement between Paul and the "pillars" of Jerusalem (Gal. 2:10) has been oddly formulated by Paul. The agreement that the Antiochenes should remember the poor in Jerusalem looks to a future collection (2 Corinthians 8–9) and omits any reference to a collection that had just been delivered during the apostles' conference. (2) The same objection holds true for the variant notion that the famine relief visit of Acts (11:30) took place at the time of the apostles' conference (15:4) *after* the first missionary journey. One would have to assume that Luke had two traditions before him which referred to the same event, one dealing with famine relief, the other with the conference regarding the circumcision of Gentiles, and Luke thought two visits were indicated whereas in reality there was but one. In light of Gal. 2:10, these hypotheses do not commend themselves.

It would seem that a famine relief visit (11:30) took place without Paul some time prior to the apostles' conference and that Acts 15 refers to the same conference as Gal. 2:1-10. Historically, Paul's own account of this meeting must have priority over Luke's, because it is a first-hand account. Yet we also can see that Paul pursued a definite goal when he wrote Galatians 1–2, namely, the defense of the independence of his apostleship and of his gospel. His rather impassioned account is not an "objective" report. Setting aside for the moment the question of whether absolute historical objectivity is even possible, we can assume that the purpose of his report in defense of his apostleship led naturally to the omission of items that seemed irrelevant to him and that he placed emphasis on other items for the same reason. Such considerations do not detract from the reliability of his account and in case of disagreement between Galatians 2 and Acts 15 the Pauline account has the priority as an eyewitness account.

Luke was dependent on traditions which he may have received from Antioch, but which we can no longer reconstruct. In distinction from Galatians 2, Luke narrated the apostles' conference from the perspective of the Jerusalem community. Paul's part in that meeting is deliberately downplayed (15:12). Luke may not have wanted to portray Paul as an upstart who would argue in front of or with apostles. By assigning the decisive roles to Peter and James he may have intended to defend Paul from attacks by Jewish-Christian missionaries who objected to him. Above all, he wanted it clearly understood that the all-important decision was reached by the Jerusalem

authorities. Its apostles and elders together with the whole community endorsed once more a Gentile mission without circumcision
and issued a decree which was binding on all Gentile Christians.

Although the two reports were written from distinctly different
perspectives and for different purposes, they agree in the following:
(1) Paul and Barnabas went to Jerusalem together (Gal. 2:1; Acts
15:2-4) and reported on the success of their mission among Gentiles
(Gal. 2:2; Acts 15:12). (2) The demand for the circumcision of Gentiles was raised by radical Jewish Christians, called "false brothers"
in Galatians (Gal. 2:4) and "believers who belonged to the party of
the Pharisees" in Acts (15:5). (3) The subject of circumcision and
obedience to the whole Law of Moses formed the agenda of the
meeting. (4) Both reports agree that a hard debate ensued (15:6);
in Paul's words: "to them we did not yield in submission even for a
moment" (Gal. 2:5), even though pressure was brought to bear on
the Antiochenes. (5) The leaders of the Jerusalem community affirmed that Gentile believers did not have to be circumcised. The
opinion of the Pharisees who belonged to the church of Jerusalem
was not accepted (Acts 15:19; Gal. 2:6). (6) The unity of the church
in the diversity of Jewish and Gentile Christians was affirmed, according to Gal. 2:9, by extending "the right hand of fellowship" to
Paul and Barnabas, and, according to Acts 15:23-29, by writing a
letter ("the brothers . . . to the brothers"). (7) It is presupposed in
both Galatians and Acts that Jewish Christians continued to live in
accordance with the Law of Moses.

The different perspectives and goals, together with the fact of
Luke's dependence on traditions, also resulted in differences between the two reports—to which we now turn. (1) According to Acts
15:2 Paul and Barnabas went to this conference as delegates of the
church in Antioch, while according to Gal. 2:2 the impetus for this
journey came "by revelation." Yet the two are not mutually exclusive,
as Acts 13:2 demonstrates. Moreover, Luke correctly presented the
reasons for this journey. Jewish Christians "from Judea" had come
to Antioch and caused considerable dissension and debate. In order
to settle the controversy the church in Antioch under the guidance
of the Spirit sent its delegation to Jerusalem, where the dissension
originated. Luke's account in 15:1-3 fills out the picture sketched in
Gal. 2:1.

(2) Titus was a member of the Antiochian delegation (Gal. 2:1, 3),

but his name never occurs in Acts. This is very strange, since we find more than 100 names of persons in Acts, among them Paul's companions, e.g., Gaius, the Macedonian (19:29), Gaius of Derbe (20:4; same person?), Aristarchus of Thessalonica (19:29; Philemon 24; Col. 4:10), Tychicus (20:4; cf. Eph. 6:21; 2 Tim. 4:12; Titus 3:12), Trophimus from Ephesus (cf. 21:29; 2 Tim. 4:20). The absence in Acts of Titus who was an important coworker (2 Cor. 2:13; 7:6), like Timothy (16:1), is puzzling. The explanation that Luke omitted Titus as Paul's coworker because Titus, being a Gentile, does not fit into Luke's scheme of mission to Jews first, could apply to the apostles' conference but still leaves unanswered his absence in the section beginning with 19:21, where Paul no longer enters synagogues. The absence of John from Acts 15 is more easily explained (cf. Gal. 2:9). In Acts the son of Zebedee appears merely as the silent partner of Peter (3:1—4:22) and therefore his presence is presupposed among the "apostles and elders" (15:6, 23).

(3) According to Gal. 2:2,6,9 it seems that Paul submitted his gospel for consideration and approval to two groups—"to them" (unspecified), and "separately" in a private meeting to the three "pillars," James, Peter, and John. Acts also seems to envision two meetings (v. 4 and vv. 6-30) but it does not refer to a private or separate meeting with the three leaders of Jerusalem. The reason for this omission in Acts lies in Luke's tradition which did not refer to it. Luke completes the Pauline picture when he narrates a meeting with the apostles and elders in which the assembled congregation was also present.

(4) While both reports agree that circumcision and obedience to the whole Torah are not to be demanded of Gentile Christians, we note that Gal. 2:7-9 also mentions a division of labor. Paul was to be the leader of the mission to Gentiles, while Peter's mission was directed to Jews. If Luke knew about this division of labor then he omitted it, because it was contrary to his scheme whereby Paul always preached first to Jews. Historically, the two-pronged mission thrust soon fell into oblivion. Jewish Christians challenged Paul's mission to Gentiles in Galatia, Philippi and Corinth, and Paul himself must have also preached in synagogues of the diaspora, for otherwise he could not have been subjected to repeated punishment meted out by the synagogue. "Five times I have received at the hands of the Jews the forty lashes less one" (2 Cor. 11:24).

(5) Galatians 2:10 refers to still another agreement, not found in Acts, namely, that the Antiochenes should "remember the poor." This was the one and only additional request laid upon the delegates from Antioch, and writing a few years later to the Galatians, Paul affirmed that he had been eager to comply with this request, as the Galatians themselves knew (cf. 1 Cor. 16:1-4). Acts reports two collections, one prior to the apostles' conference, the other subsequent to it (11:28-30; 24:17), but it is silent about the request in Acts 15. Its silence seems to be deliberate, because Luke apparently knew about the request but chose not to mention it, except in a side remark (24:17). The collection, which took a great amount of Paul's time and energy (1 Cor. 16:1-4; 2 Corinthians 8–9; Rom. 15:25-32), was brought by Paul and his coworkers to Jerusalem on his last journey. Paul himself feared that his arrival in Jerusalem might cause trouble (Rom. 15:30-31). It would seem that "the saints" in Jerusalem found Paul's collection not "acceptable," as Paul feared they might (Rom. 15:31). This would explain Luke's deliberate silence about this great project, as well as the statement in 24:17 (see comments below).

(6) The most important difference between the two reports is the apostles' decree of 15:20, 29 and Paul's clear statement in Gal. 2:6 that "nothing" was added "to me." Had the apostles' decree been issued at that conference, as stated in Acts 15, the decree would have constituted an additional requirement laid upon the Pauline mission praxis. Paul's emphatic statement in Gal. 2:6 indicates that the apostles' decree was not issued at that conference and Paul's argumentation on the subject of meat sacrificed to idols (1 Corinthians 8–10; Romans 14) shows that he never accepted that decree. Whether he was aware of its existence we shall never know. In 21:25 Paul is informed once more about the decree, but this verse is meant to remind the reader, rather than Paul, that the decree had validity for all Gentile Christians and not just for those living in Antioch, Syria. If we inquire about the origin of the decree, then Acts 15 may be right when it identifies James as originator of that decree. But the promulgation of the decree could have taken place only *after* the apostles' conference and not at its concluding highpoint. The apostles' decree may have been James's answer to the controversy in Antioch to which Paul briefly refers in Gal. 2:11-14. Emissaries of James had arrived in Antioch and pressured Jewish Christians to withdraw from table fellowship with their Gentile sisters

269

and brothers. Peter (who for reasons unknown was in Antioch) and even Barnabas withdrew from fellowship with Gentile Christians in the interest of ritual purity even though earlier they had eaten with them. Paul, it seems, was the only Jewish Christian who kept solidarity with Gentile Christians and confronted Peter at a gathering of the church. The outcome of this confrontation is not stated in Galatians, but we do know that Paul left Antioch without Barnabas for his next missionary journey. Probably James issued the decree in response to this controversy in Antioch. Its purpose was the protection of Jewish Christians from ritual defilement through associating with Gentiles. Luke knew about the decree and its origin by James and he combined it with the tradition about the apostles' conference. Thereby he united two temporally separate events into one report and committed an anachronism.

The Date of the Apostles' Conference

In general, three different dates have been suggested, namely, A.D. 44, 48/49, and 51/52. Three factors must be kept in mind when we deal with Pauline chronology. (1) The relative chronology on the basis of Gal. 1:18 and 2:1 requires that the apostles' conference take place 15 to 16 years after Paul's conversion; (2) his conversion took place after the crucifixion of Jesus and not before; and (3) the absolute chronology of the proconsulship of Gallio (18:12) which extended from July A.D. 51 to July A.D. 52 means that Paul's ministry began in Corinth no later than the spring of A.D. 51 and that all of Paul's work and travel from Acts 15:41 to 18:1 must be placed into the time span between the apostles' conference and his arrival in Corinth.

The early dating of this conference in A.D. 44 presupposes that not only James but also his brother John were executed by Herod (cf. 12:2), in accordance with the prophecy of Mark 10:39. This prophecy, it is argued, would not have been transmitted by the communities if the two brothers had not been executed. However, since John was present at the apostles' conference (Gal. 2:9) and since Herod died in the autumn of A.D. 44, the conference must have taken place sometime prior to Herod's death in A.D. 44. But does Mark 10:39 really demand the *simultaneous* execution of both brothers? Luke left out this Markan pericope, and since John does not play an important role in Acts, it is difficult to see why Luke omitted John's execution had his tradition contained it. Moreover, the advocates of this hypothesis generally regard the first missionary journey either as a construction by Luke without historical basis, or else transpose it to a time after the apostles' conference (and presumably prior to the rift between Barnabas and Paul, cf. 15:36-40; Gal. 2:11-14). The advantage of this hypothesis lies in the time span it creates for the work and travel of Paul prior to his arrival in Corinth. Its disadvantage lies in its skepticism toward Luke's outline and the perilous proximity of the time of Paul's conversion (about A.D. 28) to the date of the crucifixion which, according to this hypothesis, would have to be in the spring of A.D. 27. For a variety of reasons, A.D. 27 is the earliest possible date of Jesus' death. On the basis of Gal. 1:21 we have already argued against the hypothesis that Paul attended the apostles' conference after his ministry in Corinth; therefore the late dating of this event in A.D. 51/52 would seem improbable.

The majority view, which does not guarantee correctness, places Paul's conversion in A.D. 32 and the apostles' conference in A.D. 48. Its advantage is that the Lukan outline need not be altered, but its disadvantage lies in the brief period of two years into which Paul's work and travel has to be crammed (15:41—18:1) in order to get Paul to Corinth by the spring of A.D. 51. We should keep in mind that Paul did not leave on his second missionary journey immediately after the conference, but stayed in Antioch for some months until the controversy with Peter and Barnabas prompted him to move on (cf. 15:35-40; Gal. 2:11-14). Still, among the three hypothetical dates, the one of A.D. 48 seems preferable though it remains relative, approximate, and not without difficulties, especially if the date of the crucifixion should be A.D. 33.

The Structure of Acts 15:1-35

Luke carefully structured his centerpiece. His introduction (vv. 1-5) is balanced by a conclusion (vv. 30-35); the report on the conference has two parts: deliberations (vv. 6-21) and decisions (vv. 22-29). In the section on deliberations the speeches of Peter and of James are preceded by general reports (vv. 6-7a and v. 12) which function as a bland background in order to highlight the speeches.

In the section on decisions we hear of the election of two persons from the Jerusalem community to be sent as delegates to Antioch and of a carefully structured letter to the church in Antioch.

Part I. Introduction: From Judea to Antioch and from Antioch to Jerusalem (vv. 1-5)
- (A) The problem, stated in direct discourse (v. 1)
- (B) Dissension and debate (v. 2a)
- (C) Appointment of a delegation to go to Jerusalem, report on the conversion of Gentiles resulting in joy (vv. 2b-3)
- (C') Welcome by the church and report of "all that God has done" (v. 4) resulting in
- (B') The Pharisees arising and raising (v. 5a)
- (A') The problem, stated in direct discourse (v. 5b)

Part II. Deliberations (vv. 6-21)
Introduction: Much debate (vv. 6-7a)
- (A) Peter's speech on the conversion of Cornelius and its meaning (vv. 7b-11)
- (B) The report by Barnabas and Paul on all that "God had done" through them (v. 12)
- (C) James's speech on what God had always intended to do (vv. 13-18) and the conclusions which should be drawn from it (vv. 19-21)

Part III. Decisions (vv. 22-29)
- (A) The agreement is made in unanimity (v. 22a)
- (B) The election of two representatives from Jerusalem (v. 22b)
- (C) The sending of a written message stating the position of the church in Jerusalem (vv. 23-29)

Part IV. Conclusion: From Jerusalem to Antioch and Back (vv. 30-35)
- (A) The delegation is sent off to Antioch (v. 30a)
- (B) The gathered community received the letter (v. 30b) and rejoiced at the exhortation (v. 31)
- (B') Judas and Silas exhorted them (v. 32)
- (A') The delegates are sent off in peace (v. 33) and Paul and Barnabas preached in Antioch (v. 35)

Introduction (15:1-7a)

The cause that led to the apostles' conference is narrated and the position of the opponents, stated in direct discourse, forms brackets around the introduction in which the two reports of the delegation from Antioch are central and contrasted with the position of the Judean troublemakers. We note that whereas the report about the conversion of Gentiles resulted in great joy among the churches of Phoenicia and Samaria, no such result is indicated after their report to the church in Jerusalem.

1—The glowing report of Paul and Barnabas of how God "had opened a door of faith to the Gentiles" (14:27) found its antithesis in the teaching of Judean Christians who interrupted the peaceful community life in the interracial church of Antioch. Luke carefully avoided giving the impression that these Judeans had direct connections with Jerusalem or had been sent by that church or its leaders (cf. v. 24). They are designated rather vaguely as **men . . . from Judea.** But their position is stated succinctly: **Unless you** (Gentile Christians) **are circumcised according to the custom** (the Law) **of Moses, you cannot be saved.** Hence, it would be mere illusion and fraud to hold that it was God who had "opened a door of faith to the Gentiles" (14:27). These **men . . . from Judea** not only rejected the mission of Paul and Barnabas but also the salvation of Gentile believers without circumcision in Antioch. Faith, God's grace, and the gift of the Holy Spirit are not sufficient for salvation, according to them. Small wonder that Paul and Barnabas opposed them.

2—The clash of the two perspectives produced **no small dissension and debate.** The Greek word for dissension (*stasis*), which can also mean uprising, riot, revolt (Luke 23:19), strife, discord, and disunion, indicates the seriousness of the disruption caused by these interlopers and the debilitating debate which **Paul and Barnabas** had with them. Since no agreement could be reached with them, an official delegation, headed by Paul and Barnabas, was appointed during a gathering of the community (cf. 13:2-4; 14:27). Their task was **to go up to Jerusalem to the apostles and** the **elders** and seek clarification **about this question** or problem. Through its delegate Barnabas, the mother church of Jerusalem had officially approved the community in Antioch (cf. 11:22-24) and the present clash of

273

viewpoints had to be traced to its roots and resolved before harmony could be restored.

3—**So, being sent on their way,** probably during a worship service (cf. 13:2-3), the delegation took the land route and used the opportunity to tell the Jewish Christian churches in **Phoenicia** (cf. 11:19) and **Samaria** about **the conversion of the Gentiles** through Antioch's mission outreach. Their conversion was in Luke's view a partial fulfillment of Christ's mandate: "to the end of the earth" (1:8). The **great joy** which their report elicited from **all the brethren** showed that the Antiochian delegation found agreement for its position among the sister churches outside of Judea. The dispute in Antioch was no longer just a local matter but concerned the whole church.

4—The sending of a delegation from Antioch **to Jerusalem** indicated a willingness to listen to the leaders of the mother church and also a demand that the mother church clarify its position on the question of circumcision of Gentiles The delegates **were welcomed by the church and the apostles and the elders** (cf. Did. 11:4) who extended hospitality to them. To the gathered community, the delegation declared **all that God had done with them** (cf. 14:27; 15:3, 12). They narrated the experiences of the missionary journey, as well as of life in the interracial church in Antioch. These deeds of God speak a clear message, namely, that Gentiles need not be circumcised in order to be members of God's people. God's deeds demonstrate that God has already decided this dispute in favor of the Antiochian position. However, instead of rejoicing over the report of the delegation (cf. v. 3), we hear of opposition.

5—**But some believers who belonged to the party** (cf. 26:5) **of the Pharisees rose up and said, "It is necessary to circumcise them** [Gentile believers] **and to charge them to keep the law of Moses."** Note the similarity to the declaration of the Judeans in v. 1, but also the difference. The Christian Pharisees did not say, "You . . . cannot be saved," but they formulated more carefully: "It is necessary" (Greek, *dei*), it is a divine obligation to circumcise the male members of the people of God (cf. 7:8), even as it is a divine obligation for them to keep the Law of God as set forth in the Law of Moses.

Let us briefly try to understand their position. First, we should recognize that they did not object to preaching the gospel to Gentiles. They may even have recalled God's promise to Abraham that in his seed all the families of the earth would be blessed (Gen. 12:3;

cf. Acts 3:25). This promise, however, was sealed with the "covenant of circumcision" (Acts 7:8) and fulfilled by Jesus, the Messiah, who was circumcised according to the Law (Luke 2:21-24) and who never taught the abrogation of circumcision. If Gentiles want to participate in the promise granted to Abraham and fulfilled through the Messiah, then they ought to join the descendants of Abraham through the sign and seal of circumcision. Otherwise, the blessings effected by the Messiah cannot apply to them. In short, they "cannot be saved" (v. 1). Moreover, if they really believed in Jesus, the Messiah, they would submit to circumcision as a divine obligation (v. 5). Where is it written that God changed his mind, or that the Messiah taught contrary to the revealed will of God on this matter? How can one believe in Jesus, the Messiah of the circumcised people of God and not accept the Torah which demands circumcision? Are the Gentiles superior to the Messiah, who said: "It is easier for heaven and earth to pass away, than for one dot of the law to become void" (Luke 16:17)? Does not this Antiochia delegation ultimately advocate a cheap form of proselytizing and catering to Gentiles? Finally, in addition to the theological aspect of this dispute, there is also a social aspect which deserves consideration: "We Jewish Christians do not care to be contaminated ritually by associating with Gentiles, sharing common meals with them. Must Jewish Christians be ritually defiled every time they come to the Lord's Supper? Only God knows what Gentiles serve at meals in connection with the Lord's Supper." We hear the voices of these Jewish Christian Pharisees only indirectly, and while our reconstruction of their position remains hypothetical, nevertheless, their position was theologically respectable, thoroughly grounded in the Scripture and tradition and by no means the result of legalistic nastiness, or contempt for the promises of God. As a matter of fact, their position raised questions which the Gentile church of subsequent centuries ignored at its own peril, and thereby fell into cheap anti-Judaism which has been the disgrace of the Gentile church since the time of Emperor Constantine (A.D. 312).

6-7a—Luke seems to suggest a second meeting in which the position of Christian Pharisees and the counterarguments of the Antiochian delegation were debated. In this second meeting **the apostles and elders were gathered together to consider this matter** with the community of believers as silent background (v. 12). **Much debate** occurred between the two positions. What else could the Antiochenes do but reiterate their conviction that the same God who revealed himself in the past was, through his eschatological acts in Christ's resurrection and the sending of the Holy Spirit, active in the present in a new way? God's ways in the present are not identical with our perceptions of God's ways in the past, and to imprison God in Scripture and tradition does not do justice to the blazing power of the resurrection and the Spirit. Luke, very cleverly, does not give us the details of the debate and thereby succeeds in highlighting the speech of Peter. After **much debate, Peter** who was preeminent among the apostles (cf. 1 Cor. 15:5; Luke 24:34) **rose** and gave his final speech in Acts.

Peter's Speech (15:7b-12)

Its theme is that the Law of Moses is not the ground of salvation. Verses 7-9 provide the rationale for this thesis by retelling the Cornelius episode. The story of his conversion is reduced to its barest minimum and told in such a way that **God** is the subject of every main verb. God elected Peter to be his instrument, **God made choice among you; God . . . bore witness to** Gentiles and gave **them the Holy Spirit. He made no distinction between us and them, but cleansed their hearts by faith.** These acts of God demonstrate that the absence of circumcision and the absence of the whole Torah in the life of the Gentile Cornelius did not stop God from granting salvation to him and his people. Verse 10 draws the first conclusion and adds a supporting argument. A change in subject occurs, the advocates of circumcision are asked a question which functions as a warning and the problem under discussion is also addressed from the perspective of Israel's history. The possession of circumcision and the possession of the Torah did not bring salvation to "our fathers" nor to us. **Therefore,** it is false to argue that the Torah and circumcision are necessary for salvation. To do so is to put God to the test. Verse 11 draws the final conclusion and affirms the one faith of the one church of Jews and Gentiles, who are granted salvation through grace and faith, which means that the Law of Moses is not the ground of salvation.

7-9—Unimportant as the conversion of Cornelius may have been in world history (cf. Luke 2:1-7), it was an important event in God's history with humanity whereby God gave legitimation to Gentile mission without circumcision and obedience to the whole Torah.

God who knows the heart . . . **made no distinction** between Jews
and Gentiles (cf. 10:20; 11:12) but **cleansed their hearts by faith,**
which communicated forgiveness of sins (10:43) and the gift of **the
Holy Spirit.** The fact that God cleansed their hearts was attested to
by the gift of the Spirit. The result of the gift of the Holy Spirit was
the purity of hearts and therefore the total purity of Gentile believers
(cf. 10:15). This conclusion had not yet been drawn in 10:44. Cleans-
ing **by faith** does not mean any kind of faith, but faith in Jesus Christ
(cf. 20:21), which is a gift of Jesus (3:16), even as the Holy Spirit is
his gift, granted by God to Gentiles, **just as he did to us** (cf. 11:15).
Faith and the Spirit are received through hearing **the word of the
gospel.** Circumcision and the Torah are *adiaphora,* matters of indifference, when the salvation of Gentiles is under discussion.

10—With a question which contains an implicit warning the hearers are asked, **Why do you make trial of God?** A better translation
would be: "Why are you putting God to the test?" (cf. Exod. 17:2;
Deut. 6:16), arguing and acting against God's will as manifested in
the conversion of Cornelius (cf. 11:17; 15:39). It would be an act of
disobedience and rebellion, of putting God to the test, if additional
Torah requirements were to be laid upon **the disciples** who are
Gentiles. Such requirements would be a contradiction or modification of God's will to grant salvation to Gentiles as Gentiles. God's
purpose and will toward Gentiles have been clearly demonstrated
in the acts which led to their conversion. Moreover, neither **our
fathers** in the past **nor we** in the present have in fact observed the
Law of Moses completely (cf. 7:51,53). It is not that the Law is to
be faulted. On the contrary, the Torah of Moses consists of "living
oracles" (7:38). It is we in our human sinfulness who do not measure
up to the Law's demands. Hence, the Law of Moses is not the means
of salvation. Therefore it is wrong to put **a yoke upon the neck of
the disciples** who are Gentiles.

Contrary to some interpreters, the image of "bearing the yoke of
the Law" denotes neither the carrying of an impossible, oppressive
burden, nor a multitude of commandments and prohibitions which
nobody can fulfill. "Yoke" is a positive metaphor in Judaism and in
the synoptic tradition (cf. Matt. 11:29-30), referring to an obligation
to be fulfilled. Peter's argument is that not even Jews have successfully kept the obligation laid on them by their own Law. His
point is not that the Law is an unbearable burden (in which case

Jewish Christians would have been exhorted to discard it), but rather the failure of Jews, past and present, to fulfill the Law, to carry the yoke of the Torah.

11—A second, positive conclusion is drawn, which is also the climactic ending of Peter's last speech. It expresses the same theological thought which Paul had articulated in Antioch, Pisidia (13:38-39). It is surprising that Peter did not say that Gentiles will be saved on the same basis as Jews, but turned it around: Jews shall receive salvation on the same basis **just as they will.** This is Luke's version of Gal. 3:28: In Christ Jesus, "there is neither Jew nor Greek." The salvation of Jews is no less dependent on **the grace of the Lord Jesus Christ** and on faith than is the salvation of Gentiles. Precisely the Gentiles who do not know the Torah are the paradigm of salvation by grace alone through faith alone also for Jews who do not fulfill the obligations of the Torah. Salvation in Luke-Acts begins with forgiveness of sins and the gift of the Holy Spirit; it continues through death (Luke 23:43; Acts 7:59) and looks for the resurrection of the dead (24:15, 21; 26:8). In short, salvation for Jews and Gentiles alike is not achieved by the Law (cf. 13:39) but it is granted **through the grace of the Lord Jesus** Christ. An alternate translation to the RSV, suggested by J. Nolland, deserves consideration: "But through the grace of the Lord Jesus, we believe in order to be saved." Faith and salvation are directly related in Acts 16:30-31 and Luke 17:19, and since the opponents claim that without circumcision no one can be saved, the question behind v. 11 may well be: what must Jews and Gentiles do in order to be saved? The answer: "Believe in the Lord Jesus and you shall be saved" (16:31). In this translation faith is saving faith for Jews and Gentiles through the grace of Jesus Christ. Interpreted in either way this sentence is Peter's grand finale in Acts. Gentiles are the paradigm for the salvation of Jews.

12—Peter's speech silenced the opposition (cf. 11:18). He had refuted their position stated in v. 1 and 5 concerning the necessity of circumcision and Torah-obedience for salvation. But he had not dealt with the social aspects of Jews and Gentiles living together in interracial communities. The silence of the opposition is followed by a report of Barnabas and Paul (in that order, cf. v. 25; 9:27; 11:22) on the **signs and wonders God had done through them among the Gentiles** (cf. vv. 3, 4; 14:3, 10, 27). This brief report connects the two speeches by Peter and James (cf. 12:17) and is meant to highlight and draw attention to them. While the report of Barnabas and Paul supported the position articulated by Peter, we also note that James in his speech simply ignored what the Antiochenes had to say and instead referred once more to Peter's conversion of Cornelius. If Luke's intention was to downplay the role of Paul in the apostles' conference, he succeeded admirably. Colorless as v. 12 may be, its importance is seen in its thematic repetition (cf. 14:27; 15:3, 4). God's wondrous deeds among the Gentiles play an important part in the decision of the conference and refer the reader back to chaps. 13 and 14 and beyond, to divine interventions in the conversion of Cornelius and Paul, and to the mission among the Samaritans. Through signs and wonders, God legitimated the Gentile mission of Barnabas and Paul.

James's Speech (15:13-21)

The speech of James is the high point of the chapter and articulates the decision of the conference. It is linked to Peter's address by a reference to "Simeon's" role in the conversion of Gentiles. Luke's version of the apostles' conference dealt with two problems. First, how are Gentile Christians saved (v. 1)? Peter's speech gives the answer, with which James agreed (v. 14). Second, how are Jewish and Gentile believers to relate to each other in the same community that represents the one people of God in a particular location? The declaration of the Christian Pharisees in v. 5 does not necessarily question the salvation of Gentiles. Verse 5 could refer to the necessity of circumcision and obedience to the Torah for the sake of life and social relations within the one believing people of God. To both problems James gave the final answer. His citation from Amos agrees with and gives scriptural sanction to Gentile mission and to Peter's experience (vv. 7-11). In agreement with the Scriptures God had **visited the Gentiles, to take out of them a people for his name** (v. 14). From this follows the negative conclusion that the objections voiced in vv. 1 and 5 are unacceptable. Gentiles should not become proselytes (v. 19). Just so, the second problem has not disappeared. Therefore, James announced his second decision, namely, that it is necessary for Gentile believers to keep those portions of the Law of Moses which are applicable to them as Gentiles (v. 20; cf. v. 5). The Law of Moses, which plays no role in the salvation of Jews or Gentiles (vv. 10-11), has not been abrogated for Jews or for Gentiles.

It just has to be interpreted rightly, especially with respect to Gentiles. James gave the definitive interpretation, which makes it possible for Jews and Gentiles to live and worship together in the same community as the one people of God. The decree precludes the necessity of Gentiles' becoming proselytes, and simultaneously it respects the Law of Moses which is read **in every city . . . on every sabbath** (v. 21). For Luke the apostles' decree is neither a concession on the part of Jewish Christians nor a concession of Gentile Christians, nor a compromise, nor a betrayal of *sola gratia*. This decree is the apostolic interpretation of Luke 16:17 with respect to the social function of the Torah in interracial communities. Neither the Torah nor the apostles' decree is a means of salvation. They are expressions of one's identity as Jew or Gentile within the one people of God. The Torah was never a means of gaining the favor of God. It always was the sign of one's identity as a member of God's people. Just as in Luke's Gospel we meet Zechariah and Elizabeth, Joseph and Mary, John the Baptist, and Simeon, so in Acts we meet Peter and Paul—all, without exception, are obedient to the Law of Moses, as was Jesus. The apostles' decree laid ritual requirements on Gentile believers in accordance with the Law of Moses in order to give them identity as Gentiles within the one people of God and facilitate the religious and social relations between Jewish and Gentile believers. For Luke, Christ is not "the end of the law" (Rom. 10:4) but the Law, properly interpreted, was a sign of the continuity of the people of God within history. Therefore, "it is necessary" for Gentiles "to keep the law of Moses" as Gentiles, and not as proselytes (cf. vv. 5, 20).

13-15—Brethren, listen to me. James, the authoritative voice of the church of Jerusalem is speaking. He begins at the beginning, namely, with God's visitation of the Gentiles through **Simeon.** This is the Jewish form of Simon (cf. 2 Peter 1:1, Greek text). Perhaps in Luke's tradition this name referred to Simeon the Black (13:1), but here Simon Peter is meant. Through Peter **God first visited the Gentiles** (10:1—11:18; 15:7-9), even as he visited Israel through Jesus (Luke 1:68; 7:16; 19:44) and through his witnesses (Acts 1:8; 2:32). The purpose of God's visitation of the Gentiles is **to take out of them a people for his name.** This sentence contains a deliberate contradiction of terms, **Gentiles** and **people** of God (Greek, *laos*). Gentiles are precisely those human creatures (cf. 17:24-28) from whom the people of God has been set apart (cf. Exod. 19:5; Deut. 7:6; 26:18-19). God's act of including Gentiles in his people constitutes a new eschatological deed of God which is most surprising. This insight had not yet been expressed in Acts, though it has been implicitly present since 1:8 and 10:34. Luke never says everything at once, but expands and unfolds earlier themes as he moves step by step from one episode to another. James's speech takes yet another turn. God's surprising new deed in the present is grounded in Scripture, in his Word spoken in the past. More precisely, **with this** present deed of God, incorporating Gentiles into God's people, **the words of the prophets** (plural) of the past **agree.** One might have expected James to put it the other way around (cf. v. 11) and say that the Cornelius episode agrees with the Scripture. But just as the Easter event and experience functions as hermeneutical key that opens the Scripture and the minds of the disciples (Luke 24:25-27,31-32,44-45), so the event and experience of Cornelius's conversion, as a new act of God, grants new insight into the Scripture. Just so, James joyfully announced that **the words of the prophets** from of old are in harmony with the experience of God's work of mission to Gentiles in the present.

16-18—As an example of "the prophets," by which he means the minor prophets (cf. 7:42), James cited Amos 9:11-12, LXX, introducing some variations into its text, using a phrase from Isa. 45:21 at the end ("things known from of old"), and adding an introductory sentence at the beginning ("after this I will return"). The use of the LXX in James's mouth in Jerusalem shows that also this speech, like all others in Acts, is a Lukan construction. Only the LXX scores the desired point, **that the rest of men** (Gentiles) **may seek the Lord.** The Hebrew text reads here: "that they may possess [or "conquer"] the remnant of Edom." Luke omitted the verb "I will raise up" twice from his LXX citation. This omission refutes a Christological interpretation of vv. 16-18. The citation is meant to shed light on God's visitation of Gentiles.

Originally this text, which may have been added to Amos in the postexilic period, expressed the hope for the restoration of the Davidic kingdom, its conquest of Edom and of nations around Israel. The Qumran community used parts of this text and applied it to its own belief in a Davidic Messiah who "rises with the interpreter of the Law . . . to save Israel" (4QFlor 1:11-12; CD 7:15-16). James's use of this text has no explicit reference to a "scion of David," a Davidic Messiah, nor does it express the hope for a political restoration of the Davidic kingdom in Jerusalem "at this time" (1:6). He regards the turning of the Gentiles to God as fulfillment of these "words" (cf. v. 15).

After this I will return and visit the people of Israel through Jesus the Messiah and through the apostolic witness, **and I will rebuild the dwelling of David, which has fallen; I will rebuild its ruins, and I will set it up.** Through the mass conversion of Jews narrated thus far and continuing both in the land of Israel and in the diaspora (cf. 9:31; 11:19; 13:43; 14:21; 17:12; 19:10; 21:20) God has restored the fallen "tent" (Greek; RSV, **dwelling**) of David. God has restored his people under the image of "the tent" (cf. 7:44, 46), rather than the temple (cf. 7:48-50) because God does not dwell in temples made with hands, but in a tent according to his pattern (7:44). God is present among his restored people in the power of the Spirit and it is through Israel restored by God's gracious return or visitation that God incorporates Gentiles into his people (v. 14), opening the "door of the faith" to them (14:27). God's purpose in the restoration of Israel was **that the rest of men** (Gentiles) **may seek the Lord, and all the Gentiles who are called by my name. Called by my name** may refer to Baptism or proclamation leading to conversion or to both. For **seek the Lord** see Luke 11:9-13, which culminates in the gift of the Holy Spirit granted to those who ask and seek (also Acts 8:26-40; 17:22-31).

Up to this point James had told the conference that Cornelius's conversion demonstrated (1) that believing Gentiles are part of the people of God and (2) that the promise through Amos concerning Israel is being fulfilled so that through "rebuilt Israel" Gentiles share in this promise. It was not Luke's intention to have a Gentile people of God in addition to the Jewish people of God. There can be but one true people of God which now consists of believing Jews and believing Gentiles gathered by apostles and missionaries. The incorporation of Gentiles into the people of God is the result of God's plan **made . . . known from of old** (v. 18).

19—Like Peter, so James draws a negative conclusion first and then in v. 20 presents his positive conclusion introduced with "but" (cf. v. 11). **Therefore my judgment is:** This introduction indicates his official decision which follows from the scriptural citation. Because of God's new deed of incorporating Gentiles into the people of God, **therefore . . . we should not trouble those of the Gentiles who turn to God** by requiring circumcision and obedience to the whole law (cf. v. 10). Be it in terms of their salvation (cf. v. 1) or in terms of social relations (cf. v. 5) within the one community of faith, God had laid such requirements on them neither in the Amos citation nor in the conversion of Cornelius (cf. 10:44-48); nor should Jewish Christians do so. James and Peter are in basic agreement with the position of the Antiochenes. Neither in Cornelius's conversion nor in his promise in Amos had God required Gentiles to become proselytes in order to be part of the one true people of God.

20—But (now follows his second decision) we **should write** a letter to all Christians in Antioch, requesting them (cf. v. 19) **to abstain from the pollutions of idols and from unchastity and from what is strangled and from blood.** Some brief comments on the text: (1) The oldest manuscript (Papyrus 45, 3rd century) omits "unchastity," perhaps because the copyist thought this term to be out of place in a list of food regulations. Moreover, the copyist may have felt that Christians ought to know that unchastity is a vice and therefore omitted it. The conjecture that the decree originally contained the Greek word *choreias*, "swine's flesh," in place of *porneias*, "unchastity" is clever, but as in all such cases it lacks manuscript evidence. (2) The manuscripts of the Western text omit "what is strangled" but add at the end the negative form of the golden rule: "and whatever they do not wish to be done to them, they should not do to others" (cf. Matt. 7:12; Luke 6:31). When "what is strangled" is omitted, then the decree consists of three moral rules, namely, to abstain from idolatry, from fornication, and from murder (blood), which are the three cardinal sins of Gentiles, from a Jewish perspective. However, the omission of "what is strangled" is more easily explained than its later addition, and therefore the four prohibitions minus the negative golden rule are generally regarded to be the Lukan text. The omission of "what is strangled" in some manuscripts indicates that the four ritual requirements had become irrelevant and were therefore understood to be minimalistic moral norms. Thus, with the majority of interpreters we accept the text as translated in the RSV and note the different sequence of the prohibitions in v. 29, where "blood" is in second and "unchastity" in fourth place. But then the question arises: what did Luke want to convey to his readers with these four ritual prohibitions?

To abstain from the pollutions of idols (cf. Lev. 17:8-9). This injunction prohibits not only participation in the idolatrous worship of pagan cults and temples but, as v. 29 shows, it also forbids the eating of food **sacrificed to idols.** At Luke's time much, if not most, of the meat bought in the market place had idolatrous associations insofar as the pagan butcher sacrificed part of an animal, such as a few hairs, and in so doing consecrated the whole animal to some god. Since this prohibition of the decree cannot be narrowed down to the actual participation in pagan cults, or dinner parties over which a god presided, we can conclude that for all practical purposes the decree implied that meat had to be bought in Jewish butcher shops, or it had to be butchered by oneself, or one's Christian friends, or it implied that one abstain from meat altogether. In general, meat consumption was much lower in antiquity than today. Cereals, olives, vegetables, and fish were the common foods. The all-inclusive nature of the first prohibition may be the reason why particular kinds of meat offensive to Jews, such as pork, are not singled out in the decree. It was not for sale in Jewish butcher shops. We also note that the decree ignores Paul's distinction between eating idol meat, which was "lawful" in the context of private meals, and eating such food within the context of pagan cults, which he condemned (1 Corinthians 8–10, esp. 10:21). In addition to this distinction Paul also advised forgoing the eating of certain food out of consideration for the "conscience" of a neighbor or weaker brother (1 Cor. 10:23-32; Rom. 14:1-4, 13-23). But how is one to know who is offended by what? Paul's advice easily led to confusion in this matter. The decree settles this issue by forbidding the consumption of all food sacrificed to idols. This prohibition appears in Did. 6:3: "Be sure to refrain completely from meat which has been sacrificed to idols"; it underlies the polemics against libertine Christians in Rev. 2:14, 20 and it was known to Justin, who affirmed that true Christians in contrast to Gnostics do not eat food offered to idols (*Dialogue* 34:8—35:1).

The second prohibition in v. 20 proscribes pollutions caused by **unchastity** (*porneia*). The four items listed are grammatically dependent on **pollutions.** This makes it clear that we are dealing with ritual-cultic prohibitions. The noun *unchastity* appears in Luke-Acts only in this decree, but it is found also in lists of pagan vices (e.g.,

Gal. 5:19, RSV: "immorality"; 1 Cor. 5:11; 2 Cor. 12:21). It is generally agreed that here this term refers to marriage between close relatives prohibited by Moses which may also be the meaning of *porneia* in Matt. 5:32. But Lev. 18:6-23 also includes homosexuality and buggery among its prohibitions. Perhaps these "abominations" and the general sexual license prevalent in the Hellenistic world were also covered by the term **unchastity.** Some pagan cults of Syria and Asia Minor included sacral prostitution to insure fertility as gifts from some deity. Secular prostitutes, who were frequently male or female slaves, were available for men, while in general wives were carefully guarded in the home and extramarital relations were forbidden to them. Their task was to produce legitimate offspring. If this second proscription is not limited to consanguinous marriages but includes the broader issue of sexual license, then it would also abrogate the dual sexual standards of the Hellenistic world.

The last two injunctions demand abstention **from** the pollutions of **what is strangled** (cf. Lev. 17:13-14) and from the pollutions caused by partaking of **blood** (cf. Lev. 17:10-12). The method of killing small animals and fowl by twisting their necks or by strangulation without draining the blood is probably meant by **what is strangled,** but it may refer to all meat which has not been ritually slaughtered according to Jewish custom. Again, this prohibition would direct the Christian to the Jewish butcher shop. How else could one be certain that all blood had been drained off? The partaking of **blood** is especially singled out, "for the life of the flesh is in the blood" and belongs to God (Lev. 17:11; Gen. 9:4).

21—James's concluding statement gives the reason for the decree and connects the decree with the Law of Moses, which **in every city** on **every sabbath** is being proclaimed and **read** in **the synagogues from early generations.** Just as "the words of the prophets" (v. 15) agree with the admission of Gentiles as Gentiles into the people of God, so the words of Moses require of Gentiles the abstention from meat sacrificed to idols, from unchastity, from what is strangled, and from blood. Neither the Prophets nor the Law are invalidated, but both must be rightly interpreted. For a long time **Moses** has been proclaimed and read in every city so that both Jews and Gentiles who attend synagogues know that the four injunctions just given (v. 20) are what the Law of Moses requires of Gentiles living among the people of God. The decree articulated by James is an adaptation of Leviticus 17–18 and shows that the Law of Moses is valid also for Gentile Christians (cf. Luke 16:17). They do not keep the whole Law, but are required to keep that portion which is addressed to them as summarized by James.

Unfortunately, we have no evidence apart from Luke on whether demands similar to or identical with the apostles' decree were made by diaspora synagogues on God-fearing Gentiles who participated in the worship of the synagogue. It would seem reasonable to suppose that Gentiles could exist on the fringe of synagogues only if, and so long as, they did not pose a threat of ritual contamination to Jews (cf. 10:28). If this is correct, then an antecedent to this decree may have existed in some synagogues with Gentile adherents. At any rate Luke grounded the decree in the Mosaic legislation and in the general knowledge of this legislation among Jews and those Gentiles who existed on the fringe of the synagogue. God-fearing Gentiles in Acts are those of whom Jews speak well (10:22). They would hardly find these injunctions to be offensive, or a burden. On the contrary, Luke noted that the recipients of the decree "rejoiced at the exhortation" (v. 31). Yet, Luke does not suggest that Gentile God-fearers who became believers had already abstained from the four pollutions prohibited in the decree. Luke leaves unanswered the problem posed by Peter's eating with Gentiles (11:3). Moreover, in 13:44,48 and 14:20 we hear of Gentiles who had not been God-fearers becoming disciples, and in 16:4 we hear that Paul delivered the decree to them. Luke was aware of a time prior to the apostles' conference when the decree of 15:29 was not one of the "necessary things" within the church (15:28), when Gentiles were accepted apart from their compliance with that decree. Luke knew that the church moves one step at a time and gains new insight in stages. But he also insisted that the decree, articulated by James, did not constitute a radical innovation, because its roots lay in Moses.

The decree has now been articulated not as a concession of Jewish Christians toward Gentile Christians or vice versa, but as the right interpretation of the Torah with respect to Gentile believers. The interpretation took place at the right occasion, the apostles' conference. It enabled those who as Jewish believers observed the whole Law of Moses to have fellowship with Gentile believers who observed those portions of the Torah appropriate for them. From Luke's perspective the four injunctions are part of the Gentile Christian "ethos," of its law and customs. Neither these customs nor the whole

Mosaic Law (Greek, *ta ethē:* 15:1; 21:21; 26:3) have a soteriological function (v. 10), but they establish norms within which believers, be they Jews or Gentiles, live and associate and express the unity of the church.

The argument that the decree assigned a secondary status to Gentile Christians within the people of God, which has its parallel in the secondary status of God-fearers in the synagogue, does not agree with Luke's point of view. For him Gentile Christians are full members of the one people of God, saved by faith (v. 11) and admitted according to God's plan (vv. 16-18). Equally false is the alternative which holds that the decree is apostolic rather than Mosaic. It is both, for it is the apostolic interpretation of Mosaic injunctions addressed to Gentiles. The decree may have confirmed customs already established in some synagogues, but it now constituted legal proscriptions within the church.

The introduction of these proscriptions into the church is a new step, though the proscriptions themselves are based on the Law of Moses, in existence **from early generations** (v. 21), even as the admission of Gentiles does not mean that God suddenly changed his mind, for God **has made these things known from of old** (v. 18). The decree is rooted in the Mosaic tradition, and since there is a synagogue in every city where there is or will be a church it behooves the church to keep its doors open for Jews to enter the messianic fellowship of faith without being contaminated by those items which are now clearly proscribed. The law does not have a soteriological, but rather an ecclesiological, function in Acts.

The decree in Acts has its origin in Jerusalem, not in some diaspora synagogue. It forms an *inclusio* around Paul's subsequent activity (16:4; 21:25). Its promulgation by him shows him to be in agreement with the apostles and elders and faithful to the Torah of Moses, "believing everything laid down in the law" (24:14). The multiple attestation of the decree in Acts (15:20, 29; 16:4; 21:25) reflects its importance for Luke's church, in which Jewish Christians may have demanded compliance with "these necessary things" (v. 28) from Gentile Christians for the sake of harmonious relations.

22-29—The decision of James became the decision of **the apostles and the elders, with the whole church.** The collegial nature of the conference is thus made clear. The leaders and the assembly came

to one accord (v. 25). In analogy to the Greek pattern of city governance the apostles and elders functioned like the council (Greek,
boulē) which made proposals while the assembly (Greek, *demos*)
voted on them. Note the threefold **it seemed good** (Greek, *edoxe*)
which could be translated "it was resolved" (vv. 22, 25, 28; cf. F.
Danker); but note that in v. 28 the leaders and the assembly are
included in the pronoun **us,** while **the Holy Spirit** functions as the
chief authority to which the church and its leaders give their agreement. Two practical decisions were made, with no objections raised.
One was to choose and send two delegates from Jerusalem to Antioch, namely, **Judas called Barsabbas,** who may have been a brother of Joseph Barsabbas (1:23) and **Silas,** who is also known under
the Latinized name Silvanus (cf. v. 40; 16:25; 17:10,14; 18:5; 1 Thess.
1:1; 2 Cor. 1:19). These official delegates would accompany **Paul and
Barnabas** and the other members of the Antiochian delegation, and
thereby honor the church in Antioch. Second, it was resolved to
transmit a **letter** via the Jerusalem delegates to the church in Antioch
(v. 23).

23—The epistolary prescript expresses the unity and brotherhood
of the one people of God, the church. It designates the leaders of
the church in Jerusalem as the principal senders: **The brethren,
both the apostles and the elders** and it indicates the addressees: **to
the brethren who are of the Gentiles in Antioch and Syria and
Cilicia.** This prescript is most important, for it shows that collegiality
and authority, unity in Spirit and Law are complementary and need
not be contradictory. The apostles and elders of the great church in
Jerusalem are first of all **brothers** of Gentile Christians, and vice
versa. As brothers writing to brothers they must exhibit their authority in the style of the one brotherhood in which all are equal
and in which a child can be an example (Luke 18:15-17). The inclusion of **Syria and Cilicia** attests to the ecumenical scope of the
letter beyond the local dispute in Antioch (cf. 16:4; 21:25). Paul had
worked in Cilicia before he joined Barnabas in Antioch (cf. 9:30;
11:25-26). The mission in Cilicia was therefore independent of Antioch. It is surprising that the regions of the first missionary journey
are not mentioned. This omission should not prompt us to transpose
this journey to a time after the apostles' conference because (1) this
letter, like the speeches in Acts, is in its present form a Lukan
construction, and (2) those regions are implicitly included under

Antioch, which had commissioned Barnabas and Paul for mission in those regions (cf. 16:4).

24-27—The style of the main part of the letter exhibits features of Greek official decrees (Danker). Verses 24-26 are a carefully constructed period, one of only two in Luke-Acts, the other being Luke 1:1-4. Clauses and phrases are organized artistically into a well-rounded unity. The letter must therefore be considered a Lukan construction into which he incorporated the traditional decree.

A preamble introduced with **since** or "whereas" (v. 24) is followed by two resolutions introduced by **it has seemed good,** or "be it resolved" (vv. 25, 28). The preamble states the cause of the dispute: **some persons from us have troubled you with words, unsettling your minds** (cf. vv. 1-2). Implicit is an apology for the dissension which the troublemakers caused because they came **from us.** Explicitly it is stated that they did not represent the church in Jerusalem and that their teaching was unauthorized.

The first resolution (v. 25) mentions the election of delegates from the church in Jerusalem, but before their names are given there is an expression of high praise for **our beloved Barnabas and Paul** and for their role as endangered benefactors (Danker), **men who have risked their lives for the sake of our Lord Jesus Christ** (unfortunately, the NEB tones this down by translating "men who devoted themselves"). **Beloved** is found in Acts only here and expresses the closest relationship and highest esteem toward Barnabas and Paul. With this accolade the two Antiochian leaders are clearly accepted by Jerusalem, even as its own troublemakers are disenfranchised. Now the names of the two Jerusalem delegates are introduced who will accompany the Antiochian delegation, transmit and interpret the letter, as was customary, telling **you the same things by word of mouth.** The unity of the church of Jews and Gentiles, of Jerusalemites and Antiochenes is visibly manifested in the common journey of the two official delegations. Barnabas and Paul do not return to Antioch carrying the burden of compromise. Their work has been acknowledged. Gentile believers do not have to become proselytes. The Antiochenes return in unity with the delegates from Jerusalem.

28-29—The second resolution contains the apostles' decree. Its introduction is striking: It was resolved (Greek, *edoxen*) by **the Holy Spirit and** by **us.** The first person plural pronoun refers to the assembly of believers in Jerusalem and its leaders. This is not pious rhetoric, but it points the reader back to Peter's statement that Gentiles had received the Holy Spirit just as "we" did (v. 8; cf. 11:17). This insight generated the second resolution which is placed under the authority of the same Spirit. The introduction does not equate the opinions of church leaders with the Holy Spirit. On the contrary, this decision is the work of the Holy Spirit to which the community in Jerusalem and its leaders submitted. Therefore, Jerusalem can expect that the church in Antioch, guided by the same Spirit, will agree with the resolution. **No greater burden than these necessary things** is to be laid on Gentile believers. While for Jews "the yoke" of the Law is not an oppressive burden (see comments on v. 10), it would indeed be a **burden** for Gentile believers to have to become proselytes and keep the whole Torah, which was quite foreign to them. The emphasis in v. 28 lies on the minimum requirements which are **necessary,** not for salvation (cf. v. 11), but for maintaining relations between Jewish and Gentile believers within the one people of God. The proscriptions of v. 20 are repeated with a change of order. The dietary prohibitions are grouped together; therefore *unchastity* appears at the end of the list. The letter concludes with a courteous admonition which sets forth the expectation of reciprocity. The Antiochenes are assured of the good will of the church in Jerusalem if they accept the four prohibitions stated in the decree and interpreted to them by the delegates from Jerusalem.

30-35—The concluding scene, like the opening, takes place in Antioch. During a gathering of the community **the letter** is **delivered** and **read** and the community **rejoiced at the exhortation.** Good news produces joy. The Antiochenes respond with joy to **the exhortation** from Jerusalem. Luke has a large vocabulary to indicate joy, and he refers to it frequently (e.g., cf. v. 3; 8:39; 11:23; 13:52; Luke 1:14; 2:10; 15:7; 19:6; 24:52). The apostles' decree became a cause for rejoicing. It was perceived not as burden, but as liberation from uncertainty and exhortation to a life-style appropriate for Gentile believers. Once and for all it had been decided that Gentile Christians do not need to become proselytes. The church's unity and continuity are based on faith in Jesus Christ, on the work of the Holy Spirit and on the rightly interpreted Law of Moses. **Judas and Silas, who were themselves prophets** (cf. 13:1; 1 Cor. 14:3), did not just deliver the letter and return, but after explaining the decisions of the conference (cf. v. 27b) they stayed for some time and **exhorted**

the brethren with many words and strengthened them. The twofold dissension and debate at the beginning (vv. 1-2 and 5) are balanced by the twofold *paraklēsis* (exhortation, encouragement, consolation) at the end (vv. 31 and 32). The dissension as well as the exhortation had their origin in Jerusalem and Judea. Exhortation in Luke is not merely a moral appeal but the consequence of God's saving action, of the *paraklēsis*, the consolation of Israel (Luke 2:25). The *paraklēsis* of the Holy Spirit (9:31) is made by prophets (15:32) so that the people of God remain under the word of God, in faith (14:22), faithful to the Lord (11:23) and open to the guidance of the Holy Spirit (15:28). At a farewell gathering the two delegates from Jerusalem **were sent off** with the blessing: Go **in peace.** Peace has been restored and dissension has been buried. The blessing of peace as well as the rejoicing express reciprocity by Antioch toward Jerusalem for its decision.

34 (RSV footnote)—This was added in manuscripts of the Western and Byzantine text-types in view of Silas's presence in v. 40. This addition, however, contradicts v. 33 and is absent in the best manuscripts. According to Luke, Paul stayed in Antioch long enough for Silas to return from Jerusalem.

35—The report closes with Paul and Barnabas **teaching and preaching the word of the Lord** in Antioch **with many others also.** The number of coworkers and leaders in this racially mixed community has increased, so that Paul and Barnabas can be spared. Soon they will embark on the next phase of carrying the Word into new cities and regions.

At this turning point in Luke's narrative we can look back and perceive an overall pattern in which he narrated the witness beyond Jerusalem.

The commission by Christ (1:8), the guidance by the Spirit or by an angel of the Lord (8:26, 29, 39), mandate the witness beyond Jerusalem (8:4-13; 8:26-40) which is confirmed by the apostles sent from Jerusalem (8:14-17, 25).

The commission of Paul by Christ and his witness are confirmed by the apostles in Jerusalem (9:15-30).

Peter's witness and mission to Gentiles is directed by divine interventions (10:1-48) and confirmed by the Jerusalem authorities (11:1-17).

The witness of the Hellenists to Jews and Gentiles in Antioch is empowered by "the hand of the Lord" (11:21) and confirmed by Barnabas sent from Jerusalem (11:19-26). The Antiochenes in turn manifest the church's unity by sending relief to Jerusalem (11:27-30; 12:25).

The commission of Barnabas and Paul by the Holy Spirit (13:1-3, 4a) results in witness to Jews and Gentiles (13:5—14:27) and in confirmation of their mission by the apostles, elders, and the whole church in Jerusalem (15:1-29). The acceptance of their decisions by the church in Antioch manifests the church's unity (15:30-35).

As we look ahead we note that Luke introduced a commission of Paul and Silas (15:40), told of their visit to previously established churches (16:1-6), and then told of a new commission (16:10) for witness in new mission ventures (16:11—19:41) with stopovers at Jerusalem and Antioch (18:22). The confirmation in Jerusalem is interrupted by Paul's arrest. But the unity of the church is pictured in the Gentile delegation that accompanied Paul to Jerusalem (20:4) and in their reception by "the brethren" (21:17-20a).

Extension of the Gentile Mission to Europe and Western Asia Minor (15:36—19:41)

The apostles' conference forms the centerpiece in Acts. It reconfirms God's decision "made known from of old" (v. 18) and realized in the narrative of Acts since 10:44 and 11:18. The conference also signals a turning point in Luke's narrative. Peter and the other apostles disappear from the scene and the spotlight shifts to Paul. He is the connecting link between the time of the apostles and Luke's own time. From now on he will carry on his mission independently of Barnabas, and his connection with Antioch appears to be minimal. We hear neither of a formal report by Paul upon his return, in distinction from 14:27, nor of a reaction by the community to the tremendous work which he had accomplished. Although the community of Antioch had "commended him to the grace of God" (15:40b; cf. 14:26; 20:32) and thereby approved his work, he departed without an Antiochian coworker and for the next four years he worked on his own. But in Acts he kept the connection with Jerusalem and Antioch alive by a return visit (18:22-23). His journey led him to Europe, to Macedonia and Achaia, where he established churches in Philippi, Thessalonica, Beroea, Athens, and Corinth.

In Athens he delivered his major speech, narrated in this section, a paradigm for preaching to Gentiles (17:22-31), and the counterpart to his sermon in the synagogue of Antioch, Pisidia (chap. 13). From Corinth he transferred the center of his activity to Ephesus and after a long journey of some 2000 miles via Jerusalem, Antioch, Galatia, and Phrygia, he returned to Ephesus (18:18—19:1). The mission narrated in this section took place between approximately A.D. 48/49 and A.D. 55.

According to this section, Paul, the missionary to Gentiles, always entered synagogues first! When there was none, as in Philippi, then he went to the place of prayer by the river (16:13) where Jews and God-fearing Gentiles met. Even when he merely touched Ephesus (18:19) or entered Athens, the metropolis of Hellenistic culture (17:16), Luke noted his contact with the synagogue. Israel's priority in salvation history is and must be maintained and the gospel is therefore offered to Jews first. Moreover, in spite of opposition and rejection, the success of Paul's mission among Jews is clearly emphasized by Luke. "All the residents of [the Roman province] Asia heard the word of the Lord, both Jews and Greeks" (19:10) and the section closes with the announcement of the victory of the word of God through the mission of Paul (19:20).

Opposition to the witness in the synagogue led to the separation of the true Israel from the synagogue and to mission among Gentiles in accordance with the Lord's mandate. In short, opposition resulted in further extension of the gospel and it also demonstrated the continuity of Paul's experience with the experience of opposition by Jesus, his apostles, and the prophets of old (cf. 7:27,51-52). Hardships endured also became occasions for encouragement by God. The low point of Paul's and Silas's imprisonment in Philippi turned into a high point with the conversion of the jailer and his household (16:22-34). After the severe conflict in the synagogue of Corinth, the Lord gave encouragement to Paul—and to Luke's readers: "Do not be afraid, but speak. Do not be silent, I am with you. No one will attack you and harm you. I have many people in this city" (18:10; cf. 4:24-31; 5:20-21).

What is commonly called "the third missionary journey" (18:23—21:14) does not exist in Luke's design. On the one hand, it is the continuation of the second missionary journey (15:36—19:20) and, on the other, it belongs to a new section in which Paul no longer

engages in missionary activity, and therefore no longer enters synagogues (20:1—21:14; the section 19:21-41 serves as transition).

*Introduction to the Second Missionary Journey: Moving toward
Europe (15:36—16:10)*

Some time after the apostles' conference Paul took the initiative
for a second missionary journey, but its beginning is overshadowed
by the separation from Barnabas after **a sharp contention.** Paul asked
Silas from Jerusalem to accompany him. They visited the churches
in Syria, Cilicia, and those that were established during the first
journey, found in Timothy an additional coworker, delivered the
apostles' decree to all communities, and traveled through Phrygia
and Galatia; being prohibited by the Holy Spirit from preaching in
Asia and Bithynia, they arrived at Troas, near the ancient Homeric
city of Troy. After a vision the conclusion was reached that God had
called them to preach the gospel in Macedonia, Europe. This introduction is designed to distinguish the second missionary journey
from the first, and to get Paul to Europe. The following five problems
are raised by the introduction: (1) the relationship between Luke's
and Paul's narratives about the rift between Paul and Barnabas (cf.
Gal. 2:11-14); (2) the historical question of Silas as transmitter of the
apostles' decree (15:22, 27, 32) and as coworker of Paul; (3) the circumcision of Timothy by Paul; (4) the apparent aimless wanderings
without preaching through Asia Minor and (5) the first appearance
of the "we" sections in Acts (16:10). These problems will occupy us
in the comments below.

36-38—After some days indicates an indefinite period after the
apostles' conference. The time was probably the spring of A.D. 49
when travel was possible after the winter months. Paul suggested
to Barnabas that both **visit the brethren in every city** of the first
journey, which would also include the cities of Cyprus. The purpose
of the return visit was to strengthen the churches (cf. v. 41) and **see
how they are. John Mark,** who had quit during the first journey
and returned to Jerusalem (13:13), became the bone of contention.
Barnabas wanted to give him a second chance. After all, Mark was
his cousin (cf. Col. 4:10) and Barnabas "was a good man, full of the
Holy Spirit and of faith" (11:24) whose name Luke (incorrectly) takes
to mean "son of encouragement" (4:36). So he pleaded for a little
encouragement in the case of John Mark, arguing perhaps that peo-

ple are at least as important, if not more, than tasks that have to be performed. **But Paul thought** John Mark unfit for the task because he **had withdrawn from them in Pamphylia** (13:13). Since this is Barnabas's last appearance in Acts, Luke made sure that the onus for the breakup did not fall on this "good man."

39—And there arose a sharp contention, so that they separated from each other; Barnabas took Mark with him and sailed away to Cyprus, his native island (4:36), for a follow-up visit. Behind this personality clash was the theological controversy to which Paul briefly referred in Gal. 2:11-14 (see introduction to Acts 15 above). From Luke's point of view this quarrel did not hinder the spread of the gospel. On the contrary, instead of one mission outreach there now would be two.

Historically, this controversy in which "even Barnabas was carried away by [the] insincerity" of Jewish Christians who withdrew from table fellowship with Gentile believers (Gal. 2:12-13) was the real reason behind the separation of the two Antiochian missionaries. We may suppose that John Mark also played a role in it. He was from Jerusalem (Acts 12:12) and may even have been among the "certain men from James" (Gal. 2:11) who came to Antioch and requested Peter and the Jewish Christians to uphold the cultic separation demanded by the Torah and to withdraw from eating with Gentile Christians—whether from regular meals or from the Eucharist or from both is unknown. At any rate, "even Barnabas" and presumably John Mark followed Peter's example and no longer lined up with "the truth of the gospel" as Paul saw it (Gal. 2:14; cf. 2:5). By their withdrawal from table fellowship they, in Paul's view, "compelled" (cf. 2:3) the Gentiles to Judaize, to accept Jewish dietary laws (Gal. 2:14), and live like proselytes. Paul did not report the outcome of his confrontation with Peter and the other Jewish Christians but it would seem probable that he lost in that showdown and began a new phase in his mission activity. Had an agreement been reached, Paul would surely have mentioned it in Galatians 2, for it would have strengthened his case vis-à-vis the Galatians enormously. Moreover, he owed it to Peter and others whom he denounced for playacting and taking a position out of line with "the truth of the gospel" (cf. Gal. 2:5, 14) to set the record straight, if there had been an agreement. It is also probable that James introduced the apostles' decree in response to this Antiochian controversy after Paul and

Silas had left. It is less reasonable to assume that the introduction
of that decree caused the controversy in the first place and that Paul
denounced the decree as an attempt to "compel" Gentiles "to Judaize," to live like Jews. Luke, at any rate, had combined the promulgation of the decree with his narrative of the apostles' conference. Historically, the decree did not come up at that conference,
as Paul's emphatic statement in Gal. 2:6 demonstrates, and it would
be difficult to explain the episode of Gal. 2:11-14 if the decree had
been issued at the apostles' conference.

40—In Luke's narrative **Paul chose Silas** to accompany him on his
new venture after his separation from Barnabas. Here a new problem
arises, because Silas or Silvanus, who in fact became Paul's coworker
(cf. 1 Thess. 1:1), was, according to Luke, one of the two Jerusalem
delegates who transmitted the apostles' decree. There is no doubt
that from Luke's perspective the Silas of v. 40 is identical with the
one in vv. 22, 27, 32. We may ask: if Silas in fact transmitted the
decree (v. 27) and subsequently joined Paul (v. 40) then was he not
one of the "certain men from James" mentioned in Gal. 2:11? In
that case the introduction of the decree in Antioch would have ig-
nited the controversy of Gal. 2:11-14. Moreover, we would have to
assume that Paul "converted" Silas to his own position while he
failed with Barnabas, Peter, and the other Jewish Christians. Or,
contrary to Luke, was Silas, Paul's coworker, not from Jerusalem but
from Antioch? Did then two persons bear the same name, one being
a prophet from Jerusalem who transmitted the decree presumably
after Paul's departure from Antioch, the other a Roman citizen (16:37)
from Antioch who accompanied Paul? Or was it Luke who created
the link between Silas, Paul's coworker, and the decree, just as he
linked Paul with it? Since beyond doubt Luke did create Paul's
acceptance of the decree, it would seem probable that he also made
Silas the transmitter of the decree. Thereby Luke conveyed to his
readers that Paul and Silas, on whom the spotlight will focus, had
been obedient to the decree from the beginning and introduced the
decree in the churches of the first missionary journey (16:4). But
Luke's picture does not agree with what we know from Paul's letters
which show no awareness of the decree. If Paul knew it then he
rejected it as his argumentation on meat sacrificed to idols demonstrates (1 Corinthians 8–10; Romans 14–15). Whether or not Paul's
companion Silas was from Jerusalem is a question which we cannot

answer and the possibility of two persons bearing the name Silas and combined into one person by Luke cannot be ruled out. For Luke it was important to tell that before their departure Paul and Silas were commissioned, that is, **commended by the brethren to the grace of the Lord** (cf. 13:2-3; 14:26; 20:32). In spite of the contention and separation from Barnabas they left with the blessing of the church in Antioch.

15:41—16:5—The **strengthening** of churches on the initial part of their journey (cf. v. 36) forms brackets around two brief notes which narrate the circumcision of Timothy and the introduction of the apostles' decree in all churches. From Luke's perspective these two incidents demonstrate that Paul was not an apostate who had forsaken the Law of Moses, but in obedience to the Law he circumcised Timothy, and in obedience to the Holy Spirit (15:28) he introduced the apostles' decree **for observance** by Gentile Christians. At the very beginning of the great missionary enterprise, Luke presented Paul as a Jew who was faithful to the Law. This picture remains constant to the end of his story (cf. 25:8; 26:4-5; 28:17). Only because Paul was also faithful to the Law could he **strengthen** the churches (cf. "so" in v. 5). The church keeps the Law and thereby demonstrates the permanent validity of the Torah until the eschaton. Jewish members, like Paul, observed the whole Torah and Gentile members observed the apostles' decree which summarized those portions of the Torah addressed to Gentiles (cf. 15:21). Rightly interpreted, the Law remains in the church not as means for securing forgiveness but as a sign of the life-style of the people of God in the world. In a world full of idolatry the Torah, even in its minimal form of the apostles' decree, is a sign that points to the one true God and to separation from idols.

15:41—16:2—Paul and Silas visited the churches of **Syria and Cilicia, strengthening** them, and, crossing the Taurus mountains via the Cilician gates, they visited in reverse order the churches established in Asia Minor during the first missionary journey, beginning with **Derbe** (cf. 14:20). Luke either greatly condensed his sources in order to save space and focus on two essentials (16:3-4), or he lacked more detailed information. He had indicated Paul's activity in his native **Cilicia** only indirectly in 9:30 when Paul went from Jerusalem to Tarsus. Through the address of the apostolic letter (15:23) and the notice in 15:41 we hear that his labors in that region had borne fruit. Paul himself mentioned that he "went into the regions of Syria and Cilicia" (Gal. 1:21).

In **Lystra** they met a **disciple,** named **Timothy.** Paul spoke of him as "my beloved and faithful child in the Lord" (1 Cor. 4:17), thereby indicating that Timothy had been converted by him. He was the son of a Jewish mother and a Gentile father. His mother, Eunice, and grandmother, Lois, became Christians (2 Tim. 1:5), but nothing is known about his father. Timothy's good reputation came to Paul's attention. Particular roles demand particular qualifications from leaders and assistants (cf. 1:21-22; 6:3). He was the offspring of a mixed marriage, which was frowned upon and regarded as illegal (cf. Deut. 7:3), and he should have been circumcised, following the religion of his mother, but he was not.

3—**Paul wanted Timothy to accompany him; and he took him and circumcised him because of the Jews that were in those places, for they all knew that his father was a Greek** and that Timothy had not been circumcised. In spite of his good reputation, he lacked one qualification for his role as Paul's assistant. Luke shows that this circumcision was not performed to gain salvation (cf. 15:1), but was prompted out of concern for Paul's mission strategy. His mission would inevitably bring Timothy into contact with synagogues, and the presence of an uncircumcised offspring of an illegitimate marriage would indeed have been an affront to Jews and embarrassing to Paul. In fact, Paul would have been advocating apostasy from Judaism and the Torah if Timothy had become his uncircumcised assistant. The charge of teaching apostasy was always firmly rejected by Paul in Acts (cf. 21:21; 28:17).

Scholars frequently held that Timothy's circumcision was invented by Luke, that it would be contrary to Paul's own statements on this subject (cf. Gal. 5:2-6; 1 Cor. 7:17-20) and contrary to his refusal to have Titus circumcised (Gal. 2:3). According to the "historical" Paul, anyone who was uncircumcised when God called him to faith through the gospel should not seek circumcision afterwards and vice versa (1 Cor. 7:18). True enough; however, Timothy's case was different, because he was a Jew and should have been circumcised. Precisely because Paul insisted that circumcision and uncircumcision were irrelevant for salvation (1 Cor. 7:19; Gal. 5:6; 6:15) he was free to circumcise a Jew. Paul claimed that he could function as a Jew in relation to Jews (1 Cor. 9:20). Perhaps we hear an echo caused by this, or similar actions in Gal. 5:11. Behind the rumor that Paul "still preaches circumcision" (when it suits him) probably lay the fact that he did not object to the circumcision of Jews, because he was not a legalist "in reverse" and because the circumcision of Jews was appropriate (cf. Rom. 3:1) if it did not constitute a condition for salvation.

4-5—The transmission of the apostolic **decisions** is already mentioned in manuscripts of the Western text-type at 15:41. While this addition is not original, its meaning is Lukan (cf. 15:23). Moreover, the decree had validity for all churches outside of Judea, and Luke indicated the decree's importance by repeating it verbatim three times (15:20, 29; 21:15) and referring to it also in 16:4. Its authoritative nature is indicated by Luke's choice of words. The four prohibitions are "the decrees which have been issued and are in force" (Greek, *ta dogmata ta kekrimena*). Luke used the word *dogma* also for Caesar's edicts (Luke 2:1; Acts 17:7)—which are to be obeyed, with the proviso of 5:29. In short, the apostles' decree was normative also for the churches of Luke's time. Since it was given by the Holy Spirit (15:28), its authority was binding on all Gentile believers of all regions (cf. 21:15). Therefore Paul introduced it in churches of regions (v. 4) not mentioned in the address of the apostolic letter (15:23). By transmitting the decree Paul, Silas, and their new companion Timothy **strengthened** the churches **in the faith.** Law and faith are not antithetically related in Luke, as in Paul. For Luke, the Law has no soteriological function but constitutes the norm of the church's life-style in which faith finds expression. **And** the churches **increased in numbers daily.** Just as the problem of Acts 6:1 found a solution (6:5-6) which led to growth, so the conflict about circumcision and Torah obedience (15:1, 5) found a solution (15:7-29) which led to growth (16:5). Up until now Paul's journey consisted in visiting established churches. With the next verse the last part of the introduction, in which Paul travels through new territory, begins.

6-10—The church's task is mission, and mission involves travel by land and sea. Paul's travels would eventually bring him via Jerusalem to Rome. Up to now he and his two companions had followed his proposal, which had been approved by the church in Antioch (15:36, 40) and, in spite of the separation from Barnabas, this proposal had been carried out, with Barnabas going to Cyprus and Paul to the churches in southern Asia Minor, visiting the communities in Syria and Cilicia on the way. With v. 6 Paul enters new territory beyond his original proposal. He is now on his own and totally dependent on the guidance of the **Spirit.** His plan for mission **in Asia,** of which Ephesus was the capital, in Pergamum, Smyrna, Sardis, Priene, and Miletus, some of its important cities, came to naught, because **the Holy Spirit** prohibited them from preaching the word. Therefore, instead of turning west toward "Asia" they turned north and **went through the region of Phrygia and Galatia.**

Since Luke did not indicate towns and cities through which they passed, we cannot be certain what is meant by his geographic identification. The following three hypotheses have been advanced: (1) **Phrygia** in the Greek text is an adjective, and together with the Greek adjective *Galatian* refers to that part of Phrygia which was incorporated into the Roman province of Galatia, such as the territory around Antioch, Pisidia. (2) **Phrygia and Galatia** may refer to the region in which both languages were spoken, such as the western part of the Roman province Asia, or the region which was Phrygian ethnically and Galatian administratively. These two interpretations are favored by advocates of the South-Galatian theory, which holds that Paul's letter to the Galatians was sent to the churches of the first missionary journey in Asia Minor prior to the apostles' conference. On a superficial level this hypothesis avoids any contradiction between Galatians and Acts 15. (3) Luke referred to two geographically distinct regions—**Phrygia,** which was part of the Roman provinces of Galatia and Asia, and "the Galatian region" in which Galatians who were descendants of a Celtic invasion in the third century B.C. had settled. Paul addressed them as "O foolish Galatians" (Gal. 3:1). The major cities of this region were Pessinus, Ancyra (the modern Ankara), and Tavium. The Roman province of Galatia comprised not only the geographic region around Ancyra, where the Galatians lived, but also parts of Phrygia, most of Lycaonia, and most of Pisidia. This third hypothesis has a high degree of probability, for the following reasons: *(a)* Luke clearly distinguished between "the Galatian region" and Phrygia in Acts 18:23, where the same Greek words appear in reverse order and where certainly two regions are meant and not one; *(b)* when Luke mentioned "Asia" in v. 6 he had in mind the geographic region around Ephesus (cf. 19:10) rather than the Roman province. **Mysia** (vv. 7-

8) was part of the Roman province of Asia, and yet Luke distinguished between them.

In view of 18:23 and Gal. 1:2; 3:1 we must assume that as Paul, Silas, and Timothy **went through . . . Phrygia and Galatia** they also spent considerable time in establishing churches (plural) in these two regions, even though Luke does not give us any details. This parallels his brief note in 9:30, where Paul went to Tarsus. Without receiving any details from Luke we hear in 15:41 that there were churches in Cilicia which Paul strengthened at the beginning of this journey. Luke either greatly abbreviated his sources, or, what seems more likely, he did not have at his disposal an itinerary of Paul's travels which gave the names of cities visited and persons converted. He knew about the existence of churches in Phrygia and the region of the Galatians, but that was about all. We do not know how far the missionaries ventured into the Galatian region, nor how long they stayed. They traveled from there toward **Mysia,** in a western direction and perhaps at Dorylaeum they attempted to go north into **Bithynia** to the cities of Nicea, Nicomedia, and Byzantium. But this too proved to be impossible. **The Spirit of Jesus did not allow them** and therefore they continued toward the west. **Passing by Mysia** must mean passing through Mysia, because Troas was a seaport on the coast of Mysia. They could have gone by the northern coastal road or the southern road which are at the boundaries of Mysia, or else made their way without roads. In either case Troas was a difficult place to reach, involving long detours.

What was important for Luke were the prohibitions issued by **the Holy Spirit,** the **Spirit of Jesus,** who stopped the missionaries' plans to work to **Asia** and **Bithynia.** Paul's new venture is guided by God (v. 10), Jesus (v. 7), and the Holy Spirit (v. 6). The divine interventions prevail against the intention of the missionaries, even as they prevailed against Peter in Acts 10.

The divine prohibitions also highlight the positive directive received at **Troas** which pointed them to Europe. We do not know how the prohibitions were conveyed. Perhaps it was through prophetic interpretation of obstacles encountered that the conclusion was reached not to work in Asia or Bithynia at that time. We should also note that just as with the region of Galatia, so with Troas, Luke is silent about the establishment of a congregation in this city. Yet both he and Paul presuppose the existence of a church in Troas (cf.

20:6-12; 2 Cor. 2:12). At last a commission and definitive instruction was received through a **vision,** a dream, **in the night. A man of Macedonia** appeared to Paul in a dream (cf. 2:17d,e) **saying, "Come over to Macedonia and help us."** The help which he asked of Paul is the one "that comes from God" (26:22), which Paul himself had experienced. One should not ask how Paul knew that the man was from Macedonia, rather than a Thracian or Achaean, for the man told him. God's directive is not vague, but definite. Now at last clarity concerning the geographic direction of the mission was achieved and **we sought to go on into Macedonia, concluding that God had called us to preach the gospel to them.** Paul's vision at Troas is the second of six (Damascus, 9:1-9; Troas; Corinth, 18:9; Jerusalem, 22:17-21 and 23:11, and during the storm at sea, 27:23-24). They all have the same form: (1) introduction (a vision appeared to Paul at night); (2) content (v. 9b); (3) reaction (v. 10). Paul himself referred to an "abundance of revelations" (2 Cor. 12:7), to "visions and revelations of the Lord" (2 Cor. 12:1), and to one particular experience—"fourteen years" prior to writing 2 Corinthians—in which "he heard things that cannot be told" (2 Cor. 12:4). This particular experience of Paul, when he "was caught up in the third heaven" (2 Cor. 12:2), could not be Paul's Damascus experience, which was approximately 20 years prior to the writing of 2 Corinthians, nor does it seem to be identical with any of the six mentioned in Acts. Yet the "abundance of revelations" which Paul experienced are the historical context into which the examples above belong.

However, we must also recognize that visions and revelations through dreams frequently occur in Hellenistic literature before the hero of a story reaches important decisions, e.g., Philostratus, *Life of Apollonius* 4:34; Josephus, *Ant.* 11.331–337, especially 334; Suetonius, *Julius Caesar* 32 and *Claudius* 1. Above all, God in the Old Testament gave instructions in dreams (e.g., Gen. 31:10-13,24). Thus for Luke dreams and visions were also a readily available literary device through which he could express the conviction that Paul's mission is not his own, nor is it now dependent on Antioch. It belongs to God and is controlled by God. The parallel to the commissioning at the beginning of the first missionary journey (13:2-4) is not found in 15:40b, but in the commissioning by God (16:10).

The importance of the following sea journey which brings Paul and his coworkers to Europe is underlined by the first appearance of the pronoun **we** (v. 10). Actually, we find 10 to 12 sea voyages in Acts, but only 3 use the first person plural pronouns. The voyages are: (1) 9:30; (2) perhaps 11:25-26; (3) 13:4; (4) 13:13; (5) 14:26; (6) 16:10-17, "we"; (7) 17:14; (8) 18:18; (9) 18:21; (10) perhaps 18:22, return to Antioch?; (11) 20:6—21:18, "we"; (12) 27:1—28:16, "we." In voyage 8 Paul was accompanied by Priscilla and Aquila but not by "us." This sea voyage was twice as long as that of no. 6, from Troas to Neapolis, in which the first person plural is used. The presence of first person plural narration indicates the importance of three sea voyages: to Europe, no. 6; to Jerusalem, no. 11 and to Rome, no. 12. Each opens a new phase of Paul's activity.

Does first person plural narration also indicate the presence and participation of the author in the events narrated? Three explanations of the "we sections" in Acts have been given: (1) the author of Acts indicates his temporary presence among Paul's companions by changing to first person plural narration whenever he accompanied Paul; (2) the author found the "we" in a source and reproduced it, or he introduced it whenever he felt that he had material from an eyewitness at his disposal, although the author himself was not a traveling companion of Paul; (3) the author used the first person plural as a literary device, because it was commonly used in sea voyage accounts. Of these three hypotheses the second is by far the weakest, for two reasons: (1) stylistically the "we passages" are indistinguishable from the rest of Acts; (2) even if the author should have found the "we" in a source, he was not such a mechanical copyist that he did not reflect on what he was doing when he introduced the "we" into his own narrative. Concerning the third hypothesis, Vernon Robbins has demonstrated that authors in antiquity employed first person plural narration in sea voyage stories also when they were not present. We must note, however, that our author used "we" in only 3 of 10–12 sea voyages.

Moreover, as everyone knows, sea voyages begin and end on land, unless. . . . At any rate those in Acts do, and the "we" begins and ends on land. At the end of each "we section" Paul is distinguished from "us," namely, as soon as the focus shifts to him (16:17; 20:13-14; 21:18; 28:15-16). When we ask what the persons included in the "we" experienced in connection with the three important journeys which inaugurated new phases in Paul's ministry we find (1) a summary of the Lukan picture of Paul, (2) a summary of the Lukan theology of mission guided by God, and of Paul's predestined path to witness in Jerusalem and Rome, and (3) a summary of what leadership in the church should be (20:18-35, bracketed by "we": 20:15; 21:1). In the "we sections" Paul appears as: missionary (16:11-15), exorcist (16:18), resuscitator of a dead person (20:7-12), an example of Christian conduct and leadership, an example of preaching to Christians (20:18-35), a beloved pastor (21:5-6), a fearless witness who gives primacy to the will of the Lord and not to his own wellbeing (21:10-14), a faithful Torah-obedient Jew who followed the advice of James and the elders (21:18), a fearless benefactor of 276 people on the high seas and at the shipwreck (27:9-44), a man twice miraculously protected by God (27:24; 28:1-5), and a healer of the sick (28:7-10). This Lukan picture of Paul is undergirded by the "we" through which the author indicated to the reader his presence with Paul on these three important sea journeys and witnessed the incidents on land which surrounded them. How else could Luke's readers understand this first person plural narration, though without doubt it was used frequently in sea voyage stories of that time?

If the author of Acts did not accompany Paul, then the first person plural narration functions as a device of pseudonymity used by post-Pauline writers. Our author did not claim to be Paul himself, as did the writer of the Pastoral Epistles, nor did he bolster his own authority in the manner of the author of 2 Peter, who emphatically claimed: "We were with him [Christ] on the holy mountain [of his transfiguration], we heard this [God's] voice from heaven . . . we have the prophetic word." No, the author of Acts is much more modest than the one who penned 2 Peter. With his "we" Luke tucks himself away among Paul's companions and merely suggests participation in three journeys that were turning points in Paul's witness. If the "we" in Acts is pseudonymous, it represents the beginning stage of a pseudonymity which is radically different from the romances of the apocryphal Acts of later centuries and their first person plural narration. Luke's "we" in Acts grew out of his identification with the story which God accomplished among **us** (Luke 1:1), a story which begins with the announcement of the birth of John the Baptist and ends with Luke's "hero" in Rome. This is "our" story and we were there, not at the beginning, but at the end. For the story did not come to us through John the Baptist, Jesus, or Peter, but through Paul. Through the three important turning points in his ministry the story that began in Jerusalem came to us (in Rome?).

Paul's Mission in Macedonia (16:11—17:15)

The first of three sections describes Paul's evangelism in Philippi, Thessalonica, and Beroea, cities in Macedonia. The gospel finds a foothold in Europe, and the divine request to come over and help, made in the vision (v. 9), was being realized. In each of the three cities contact was made first with the synagogue, or its equivalent (v. 13). Difficulties were encountered which forced the missionaries to leave, but communities of faith were also established.

Philippi (16:11-40). Luke told his story of the first inroads of the gospel on European soil by selecting three different individuals whose lives were changed, and by narrating Paul's first confrontation with Roman justice, or the lack of it. The accusation of causing civil disturbance and advocating illegitimate Jewish customs (vv. 20-21) may sound familiar to Luke's readers. The public authorities of the Roman colony Philippi are sketched as brutal, incompetent, and cowardly bureaucrats, a foreboding of things to come. Not without some irony the reader learns that Paul and Silas made the magistrates apologize; yet he knows that had the missionaries not been Roman citizens there would have been no apology for injustice endured. The three persons whose lives were radically changed are so strikingly different that they demonstrate the gospel's inclusiveness. Two are women, one a man. One woman is a respectable God-fearing merchant with a house large enough to offer hospitality to the missionaries, the other a slave girl with no social standing, the object of ruthless exploitation by her owners. Moreover, she was possessed by a "spirit of divination," a slave twice over. And then there was the man in charge of the jail, an official, who in one terrifying night asked the religious question of the Hellenistic age: "What must I do to be saved?" Personal religious experience within a cosmic frame of redemption that includes the defeat of demonic powers is what the missionaries bring, and in so doing "help" these three Macedonians (v. 9).

11-12—From Troas the ship sailed in one day to the island of **Samothrace.** Its mountains rise 5000 feet out of the sea and its temple was the center of a famous mystery cult in antiquity. After an overnight stay on the island the ship reached **Neapolis,** the modern Kavalla, on the following day. (In 20:6 the same crossing in the opposite direction took five days.) From Neapolis they walked some 10 miles on the famous Via Egnatia which connected Byzantium (Istanbul) in the East with Apollonia and Dyrrachium on the Adriatic coast (Vlore and Durres in Albania). The missionaries came to **Philippi,** named after Alexander's father, Philip, and settled by Roman veterans after Anthony and Octavian defeated the murderers of Caesar, Brutus and Cassius, in a battle nearby in 42 B.C. After the sea battle of Actium when Octavian (Caesar Augustus) defeated the forces of Anthony and Cleopatra, Octavian settled some of Anthony's defeated soldiers there after confiscating their land in Italy and giving it to his own troops. So Philippi was a little Italy in Macedonia. Its full name, Colonia Iulia Augusta Philippensis, testified to its status as **a Roman colony** with a constitution modeled after Rome's, with autonomy and freedom from taxation, with praetors (Latin, *duumviri,* "magistrates," v. 20) and lictors (v. 38, "police"). Luke's knowledge of Roman administration would be enhanced if we were to render Philippi "a city of the first district of Macedonia," rather than "the leading city of the district of Macedonia" (so RSV). Macedonia was not a district but a senatorial province divided into four districts. Thessalonica was its leading city or capital, whereas Philippi belonged to the first district, the capital of which was Amphipolis (17:1).

13-15—On the following **sabbath day we,** that is, Paul and his friends, sought out the local Jewish community and went along the river Gangites until they found **a place of prayer.** This could refer to a synagogue, but synagogue service demands the presence of at least 10 men, and the group which the missionaries addressed consisted of women only. Jewish and God-fearing Gentile women apparently met for prayer under the open sky each Sabbath. The first European convert may have been typical of the background of these God-fearers. **Lydia** came from the region bearing the same name on the western coast of Asia Minor. Her native city, **Thyatira** (cf. Rev. 2:18-29), was known for its production of purple dye; Lydia had come to Philippi as a merchant of that product. Thyatira had some Jewish families and it may have been through one of them that she became attracted by the God of Israel. **We sat down and spoke to the women who had come together,** telling them God's story in history culminating in Jesus and continuing in the mission of his servants to the end of the earth. **The Lord opened her heart.**

God reaches out through the words of his faithful servants. Faith is not only a personal decision, but also God's work. Faith is followed by the act of incorporation into the people of God through Baptism. She, **with her household,** were **baptized,** including servants, slaves, and their offspring.

Whether any of the households that were baptized had children is unknown (cf. 11:14; 16:15,31,33; 18:8; 1 Cor. 1:16), though it would be extraordinary if all had been without children. Therefore, one cannot categorically deny that small children were also baptized. But this likelihood cannot serve as the basis for infant baptism. If that practice had been important to Luke he would have inserted a paradigmatic scene to this effect into his narrative. He had enough opportunities to do so, but he did not. Just as Cornelius had invited Peter to stay with him for some time (10:48), so Lydia asked the whole group to **come to my house and stay,** which presupposes that it was large enough and she was sufficiently affluent to be hostess to three (or four) guests. Her house became the center of the first Christian community in Philippi (cf. v. 40).

The relationship between Paul and the church in Philippi remained one of deep mutual affection, as his letter to the Philippians shows. Only from the Philippians did Paul accept financial aid, brought to him by Epaphroditus (Phil. 2:25-30; 4:18). We do not hear of Lydia in this letter. Therefore, some have suggested that Lydia was not her name, but simply meant "the Lydian woman" and that she may have been identical with either of the two courageous women, Euodia or Syntyche, whom Paul admonished to agree with each other (Phil. 4:2). Or was Lydia the "true yokefellow," the true comrade of Paul (Phil. 4:3)? Still others have ventured to guess that she was his wife! Without identifying her as Lydia, Clement of Alexandria (*Stromateis* 3.53:1) thought that in Phil. 4:3, Paul was addressing his wife, in spite of the fact that the Greek adjective "true" is in the masculine and not the feminine gender, as it should be if the word *yokefellow* referred to a woman. (Against this notion of a married Paul see 1 Cor. 7:7-8,32-35,38-40.) Be that as it may, Lydia was the head of the first household church in Europe established by Paul.

16-18—The second scene is connected with the first by the introduction, **As we were going to the place of prayer, we were met by a slave girl who had a spirit of divination.** Here we meet a

307

woman twice enslaved. In addition to her social status as a slave she was exploited **and brought her owners** (plural!) **much gain by sooth-saying,** that is, by fortune telling, because she was possessed (literally) by a **spirit** of "Python"; she was a Pythoness (Greek, *pneuma pythōna,* the second word is in apposition to the first). In Greek mythology Python was the name of the snake which guarded the oracle of Delphi and which was killed by the god Apollo. Later the word *Python* was used for ventriloquists who either by chicanery and fraud or by "inspiration" uttered mysterious oracles which were believed to be the voice of Apollo. Luke saw in the Pythoness of Philippi a demon-possessed person, since the gods of the pagans are nothing but demons (cf. 1 Cor. 10:20-21). Plutarch wrote of this popular belief: "the god himself after the manner of ventriloquists, . . . called . . . now Pythoness, enters the bodies of his prophets and prompts their utterances" (*Obsolesc. of Oracles* 414e). Just as the demon-possessed persons revealed Jesus' true identity (cf. Luke 4:34; 8:28), so the slave girl of Philippi possessed by the pythonic spirit of Apollo, speaking through her ventriloquism, revealed the true identity of the missionaries. **These men are servants of the Most High God, who proclaim to you the way of salvation.** Following **Paul and us** (note the transition to third person narration) she repeated her unwanted advertisement **for many days** until **Paul was annoyed.** Her proclamation, true as it was, proceeded not from faith but from demon possession and therefore constituted a provocation. At last Paul commanded: **I charge you in the name of Jesus Christ to come out of her.** And she was liberated **that very hour.** All healings performed in Jesus' name manifest not only his superior power but the all-encompassing purpose of God, articulated in the words of Isaiah by Jesus in his inaugural address and continued by his servants in his name: "to proclaim release to the captives" by word and deed and "to set at liberty those who are oppressed" (Luke 4:18). The defeat of evil powers is essential to the establishment of the rule of God and his Anointed One. While miracles do not persuade those who lack the eyes of faith, and certainly this one did not, as v. 19 shows, nevertheless they are signs that the future kingdom is already at work in our midst (Luke 17:20-21), that salvation is proclaimed and enacted already now (v. 17). The readers understand that the liberated girl, her psychic health restored, will be part of Lydia's house church, even though Luke does not say so explicitly.

19-24—At the close of miracle stories we generally find an acclamation by the crowd (cf. 3:9-10). Here, however, an anomaly occurred which was typical of Gentile greed. **But when her owners
saw that their hope of** (future) **gain was gone, they seized Paul and
Silas and dragged them into the market place,** the agora, accusing
them before the magistrates of creating social unrest and propagating
foreign Jewish religious **customs which it is not lawful for us Romans
to accept or practice.** Luke's readers would at once understand that
(1) the accusation is a phony cover-up. Paul and Silas were not
accused of liberating a young woman from a psychic disorder, but
of preaching the message of the one true God. Social unrest, **disturbing our city,** was not the real issue, but rather the exploitation
of a human being through quasi-religious commercialism in this
pagan culture. (2) Paul and his friends were benefactors of women
and men, and as such the very opposite of their hypocritical accusers
and of the pagan crowd which **joined in attacking them.** (3) There
is typical Roman anti-Semitism behind the charges leveled against
Paul and Silas. The Roman proconsul of Cyprus became a Christian
as did the Roman centurion Cornelius (10:48; 13:12). What is **lawful**
in the last analysis is determined not by Caesar, but God (cf. 5:29).
   The two **magistrates** (v. 22, identical with "the rulers" of v. 19)
are the praetors who were charged to uphold law, order, and justice,
but instead behaved in an incompetent and cruel manner. Instead
of giving the accused a chance to explain, they tore **the garments
off them and gave orders to beat them with rods.** The punishment
was administered by the lictors who served under these magistrates.
The representatives of Roman law and order became the instruments
of a hysterical mob. Writing a year or so later, Paul recalled: "We
had already suffered and been shamefully treated at Philippi" (1
Thess. 2:2; cf. 2 Cor. 11:23-25). In his suffering Paul endured his
own principle of 14:22 and in so doing he followed Peter, the apostles
(5:40), and the Master (Luke 23). After being beaten with rods by
the lictors, they were thrown into the inner prison with **their feet**
fastened **in the stocks.** Twice in vv. 22 and 23 Luke used words to
indicate the desire for human security (Greek, *asphalōs, asphalizō*).
The authorities wanted to make sure that the two missionaries were
securely tucked away in prison. But were earthly authorities really
in control? Could they really thwart the beginning movement of the
gospel in Europe by putting Paul's and Silas's feet in stocks? Rulers

always have the illusion that they are the ones in charge, when in reality they are but instruments in the unfolding of God's plan for salvation to the end of the earth.

When the gospel impinged upon the profit motive, Gentiles reacted in anger. Both here and in 19:24-27, they camouflaged their financial interest under the cloak of patriotism and patriotic religion. The accusation that Paul and Silas were **disturbing our city,** is a repetition of the one leveled against Jesus (cf. Luke 23:5). The second accusation of advocating Jewish **customs which it is not lawful** for Romans to accept (cf. 10:28) seems to uphold the old republican principle according to which participation in foreign cults was prohibited for Roman citizens (Cicero, *Laws* 2.8.19). Yet Roman pragmatism granted citizenship to foreigners and the Roman civil and penal laws did not contain sections dealing with membership of Roman citizens in foreign cults. Incidentally, Rome did not have a department of religious affairs which licensed foreign cults, but it tolerated them so long as they did not cause civil disturbance or engage in immoral practices. Excavations in Philippi revealed the presence not only of Roman cult centers but also of gods from Thrace, Asia Minor, and Egypt, which was typical of just about all Hellenistic cities. In short, the old republican principle was no longer enforced during this period, and Luke knew that.

We hear of the execution of Flavius Clemens and the banishment of his wife, Domitilla, on grounds of "atheism," which refers to conversion either to Judaism or Christianity (Dio Cassius, *History* 67.14). Two considerations indicate that this does not constitute a counterargument to Roman religious pragmatism and toleration: (1) that particular execution took place during the latter part of emperor Domitian's reign when he crushed all sorts of imagined and real enemies on all kinds of pretense; (2) Suetonius, writing a century prior to Dio, did not refer to Clemens's practice of "a foreign superstition," even though he despised Clemens as much as he despised Judaism and Christianity (*Domitian* 15). In Luke's view the phrase **it is not lawful for us Romans to accept** is parallel to Peter's statement in 10:28. Both statements reflect a popular but false notion. Nowhere in the Old Testament is it stated that it is prohibited by God's law to speak to a Gentile or associate with one. But for scrupulously Law-abiding Jews like Peter (10:14), association with Gentiles was improper—it contradicted his original understanding of the Law. Likewise here, those Romans in Philippi who played the role of superpatriots proudly state that it would **not** be **lawful** to turn from the good old Roman religion to Jewish practices. Unfortunately, we cannot be certain that the jailer in Philippi was a Roman citizen, though we can assume that in a Roman colony of veterans the chief guardian of the jail would be a citizen. If he was, his citizenship played no role in Luke's account when he embraced the faith, any more than it mattered to Sergius Paulus (13:12) who, as proconsul of Cyprus, was a Roman citizen with knowledge of the law. According to Luke, the Philippian accusers expressed a notion in v. 21 which was false, even though it was held in some circles, just as Peter's notion in 10:28 was in need of correction, even though it was widespread among Jews.

25-34—The tone changes. Prayer and hymn singing by Paul and Silas at the beginning and rejoicing by the jailer and his household at the end form brackets around the fourth episode, which takes place **about midnight.** With their feet in stocks they cannot move, turn or sleep. "Fear not, little flock, for it is your Father's good pleasure to give you the kingdom," Jesus had said (only in Luke—12:32). God's saving, powerful reign is manifested in their innocent suffering as their spirits rise in prayer and praise to God (cf. 5:41; T. Jos. 8:5; Rom. 5:3; 1 Peter 1:6; 4:13). Joy in the midst of suffering is not a form of masochism but the realization of one's identity as servant of God in a world of sin. Even the prison becomes a place for witnessing in the form of prayer and praise **and the prisoners were listening to them.** There is no indication that the two missionaries prayed for an early release. History is controlled by God, also when human eyes perceive only the impotence of prisoners in stocks.

26—**Suddenly** a **great earthquake** shook the prison, announcing the nearness of God, as in 4:31. **Doors** open (cf. 5:19), **fetters** fall off (cf. 12:7). These are standard motifs of prison-escape stories. Here they designate not only a Peter-Paul parallel, but also show that God's purpose of mission and witness cannot be thwarted by Roman injustice. This miracle is told in praise of God who saves and the presence of rational impossibilities is irrelevant to a miracle story. Why would a jailer commit suicide without first checking on the prisoners? Did it not occur to him that an earthquake would excuse a jailbreak? How would Paul know what he was about to do? How was it that all the prisoners remained inside with doors wide open and all fetters gone?—All these are the wrong questions, which miss the point that the story attests to the saving power of God.

27-30—What is different in this story is that the miracle serves merely as an introduction to the conversion of the jailer. Paul miraculously knew that the jailer was about to commit suicide and saved his life by calling to him: **Do not harm yourself, for we are all here.** Thus, Paul is presented as benefactor toward the very person who had put his feet in the stocks (cf. Luke 6:27-29, 31). With double entendre we hear that the jailer called for **lights.** The reader knows that Paul's calling is "to be a light to the Gentiles," that "they may turn from darkness to light" (13:47; 26:18). Trembling with fear in the presence of God's power, **he fell down before** God's messengers, doing obeisance to them and addressing them as "lords" (Greek, *kyrioi*, not "men" as in the RSV). In his trembling obeisance and in his address he acknowledged Paul and Silas as divine messengers. The security of his existence had been shattered and he asked how to escape the wrath of God and **be saved.** His question was no longer "What must we do to insure the safety of the city, province, or empire?" Individual salvation had become a prominent issue at Luke's time; his Gospel is also an answer to the quest for self-realization that emerged in the last decades of the first century. **What must I do to be saved?** This is a question raised not just by the jailer in Acts, but a theme that has been present since Pentecost (2:37; 9:6; 10:4, in connection with 11:14). It also lies behind Paul's climactic speech in chap. 26.

31—The answer to the inquiry about the conditions of salvation is: **Believe in the Lord Jesus, and you will be saved.** The reader remembers that Peter had at once corrected Cornelius's obeisance (10:26). Paul does not do that, but instead focuses on the one **Lord Jesus,** quietly correcting the jailer's address. "Jesus is Lord" is the basic Christian confession (1 Cor. 12:3; Rom. 10:9), and this confession presupposes faith "that God raised him from the dead" (Rom. 10:9). God saves those who believe in the Lord Jesus, and this salvation is available on the same terms to the jailer's **household** (2:21; 4:12; 10:43; 11:14; 15:11).

32-34—The conclusion of this episode is artfully constructed:

(*a*) speaking the word of the Lord to the jailer (32)

(*b*) bodily help from the jailer (33a)

(*a'*) his Baptism (33b)
(*b'*) his hospitality (34a)
(*c'*) rejoicing in his faith in God (34b)

The center of the conclusion is the Baptism of the jailer and his household. But before he and his people are washed from their sins and even before he, like a good Samaritan, could wash the wounds of Paul and Silas, there comes first the speaking of the word of the Lord. First things first; faith comes through hearing God's story (cf. Rom. 10:14). It is through his word that God opens hearts and leads to faith in Jesus the Lord (v. 14), to Baptism, and to eschatological joy: **he rejoiced with all his household that he** had **believed in God.** He believed "in God" by believing "in the Lord Jesus." In his joy he could not have cared less if some or all of his fellow citizens thought that it was "not lawful for us Romans to accept" Jesus as Lord (cf. v. 21). But there are two more items in this conclusion that must be mentioned, bodily help and hospitality. The jailer **washed their wounds** and **he brought them up into his house, and set food before them.** While his joy expresses a vertical dimension of faith, effected by the saving word of God, his help and hospitality is a horizontal dimension of faith.

In bodily help and hospitality the unity of the church, the brotherhood and sisterhood of the community, becomes visible. Every shared meal is a foretaste of the consummation to come (Luke 14:16-24) when the disciples, gathered from the four corners of the earth, shall eat and drink with Jesus in the kingdom of God, sitting at table with Abraham, Isaac, and Jacob and all the prophets (Luke 22:30; 13:28-29). Finally, hospitality was the prerequisite for the success of the Pauline mission. In Acts the messianic banquet is grounded in the meals of the resurrected Jesus with his disciples (1:4; 10:41; Luke 24:30-31, 35) who broke bread in their homes with eschatological praise (2:46-47; 20:7, 11). They offered their homes in hospitality to itinerant missionaries (9:43; 10:48; 16:15, 34; 17:5-7; 18:3, 7, 27; 21:8, 16, 17). Even under house arrest Paul extended hospitality, welcoming "all who came to him" and witnessing to them (28:30-31). The apostles' decree regulates the conditions under which Gentile Christians extend and accept hospitality (15:20, 29; 21:15). There is no evidence that the meal which the jailer set **before them** was a Eucharist, because only Paul and Silas seem to have eaten. Yet, every meal in Luke-Acts has sacramental overtones, and this meal was marked by the joy of the jailer's household that they had been transferred out of darkness into the light of faith in God.

35-40—The concluding episode links up directly with v. 24, continuing the narrative without reference to the miraculous events of the previous night. The Western text tried to improve the transition from the prior episode by adding that "the magistrates gathered together in the agora and, remembering the earthquake which had taken place, they were afraid" and therefore decided to let Paul and Silas go. But this is a later addition to the text. It seems that the earthquake was not even noticed in town. Our author has been criticized for this literary unevenness, but he had his own reasons for omitting the miraculous aspect of the gospel when he dealt with the issue of Roman-Christian relations. Already the previous day, the accusation had been formulated, not in terms of the miraculous exorcism, but in terms of legality and urban peace (vv. 20-21). Because these issues are taken up once more, the miraculous events of the previous night do not come to the fore. They would only muddle the problem.

35-36—**When it was day, the magistrates,** having realized that their legal procedures against Paul and Silas had been improper, **sent the police,** the lictors, to the jailer who in turn told the two imprisoned missionaries that they were released. The jailer added the Jewish-Christian farewell greeting: **go in peace** (cf. Judg. 18:6; 2 Kings 5:19; Luke 7:50; Acts 15:33). Clearly the magistrates wanted to be rid of a nuisance, from their point of view, and forget the shabby treatment which they had given the two.

37-40—Now a surprising turn occurs. Far from being glad to be free, the two prisoners insisted on an official escort by none other than the magistrates themselves as a sign of public rehabilitation. They underlined their request by pointing out that they were **Roman citizens** who had been treated in a grossly illegal manner. Indeed the Roman citizen was protected from public flogging under the *Lex Porcia de provocatione* which threatened severe penalty for flogging a citizen. Luke's point in this scene is quite clear. Roman law itself is not directed against the activity of Christian missionaries, but the administration of the law in the hands of officials like Pilate or the magistrates in Philippi is another matter. Interpreters are wrong when they state that Luke's intention was to picture Roman officials as just, fair, and tolerant. For Luke, Pilate and the Philippian magistrates perverted the law (cf. 4:27; 13:28). For Luke, the problem was not Roman law as such, but its frequently intolerant and unjust administration, caused by incompetent or corrupt officials (cf. 24:26-27).

By insisting on their legal rights, Paul and Silas demonstrated the legal vindication of Christianity under Roman law. To this end two chastened magistrates **came and apologized to them** and escorted them out of jail and into town. This public escort by the magistrates constituted a public admission that they had done wrong the previous day and that Christianity posed no threat to Roman law. They also asked Paul and Silas **to leave the city.** This the missionaries were willing to do, because they did not wish to disturb the peace. From Luke's point of view this request was not an expulsion, for in 20:6 the missionaries returned. But now, before leaving Philippi, they **visited Lydia; and when they had seen the brethren** who belonged to her house church **they exhorted them;** only then did they depart.

Three persons with different backgrounds were changed by the power of the all-inclusive gospel. Luke could not tell us that the slave girl was baptized, because Baptism presupposes instruction (v. 32) and there was no time for that. But Lydia's household church could reach out to her now. Luke's message concerning the relationship to the secular powers is twofold. Christian communities should insist on fair treatment by the authorities, who frequently received defamations and half-truths about Christians from pagans. But Christians must also be prepared to suffer unjustly because officials are frequently swayed by mob hysteria (v. 22), greed (24:26), cowardice (Luke 23:24-25), and favoritism (24:27). Not only in pagan Lystra but also in the Roman colony of Philippi the missionaries were subjected to innocent suffering, linking them to the passion of Jesus. Like the Master, so his servants were arrested without offering resistance (Luke 22:52-53), were subjected to the same kind of accusation (v. 21; Luke 23:2, 5), functioned as benefactors, (v. 28; Luke 22:51), were beaten (v. 22; Luke 22:63), did not liberate themselves (vv. 26-28; Luke 23:37, 39) and brought salvation to a fellow human being (v. 31; Luke 23:43). According to Luke the passion of Jesus is reenacted in his servants, Peter, Stephen, and Paul. They, like the Master, serve as examples for the church of Luke's time, that "through trials and tribulations we must enter the kingdom of

God," according to his all-embracing plan (14:22). In the midst of suffering, prayer and praise, confession and witness are to be offered to God (vv. 25, 31; Luke 22:68-70; 12:8-12). Some months later Paul referred to his suffering and shameful treatment in Philippi (1 Thess. 2:2), but his letter to the Philippians is testimony that his suffering had not been in vain.

Thessalonica (17:1-9). Luke's narration of the founding of churches is condensed and stylized. Many details, important to us, are omitted and only what is significant to him is briefly sketched. As always, Paul enters a synagogue and, as always, conflict arises and forces him to leave. Yet rejection and opposition take the gospel from place to place. There are, of course, variations in his narrative. Miracles are absent in the story of Paul's mission in Thessalonica, Beroea, Athens, and Corinth. The shape of persecution as well as the composition of his converts varies. The report of the mission in Thessalonica is told in two parts. Verses 1-4 contain the success of Paul's work, vv. 5-9 tell of the persecution.

1-4—From Philippi via Amphipolis, the capital of the first district, and Apollonia, Paul, Silas, and Timothy traveled about 100 miles on the Via Egnatia until they reached Thessalonica, capital of the second district and residence of the Roman proconsul. There is no indication that the three missionaries traveled on horseback or that they established communities in the cities through which they passed. On the contrary, Paul's own note in 1 Thess. 2:1-2 seems to suggest that his next field of mission after Philippi was Thessalonica, just as Luke tells us.

Thessalonica was "a free city" and Luke correctly identified the magistrates by their proper title, "politarchs" (17:6), in distinction from those of Philippi who were praetors (Greek, *strategoi*). The economic welfare of Thessalonica was due to its seaport, its location on the Via Egnatia, and its seat as the capital of a district and a province. Moreover, it had a large Jewish community and Paul could easily find a point of contact. A church once established in this important city would have the responsibility for mission in the region. In such a city Paul could find work as tentmaker or leatherworker. Mission is also dependent on financial resources (cf. 18:3; 20:34). After all, even frugal persons must eat and sleep, and both require money (1 Thess. 2:9). On **three** consecutive sabbaths Paul spoke in the **synagogue.** The RSV is misleading when it translates **for three weeks,** giving the impression that he also spoke during the week (see the RSV footnote). During the week Paul earned his livelihood, which also gave him opportunities for witnessing. Luke's condensed report focused on the beginning and on the end of Paul's stay in this city. Just as with Philippi, so here Luke did not deal with the time in between, when the church grew in depth and in breadth. Therefore, the reader could gain the impression that Paul stayed in Thessalonica only three weeks. This was not Luke's intention. His report emphasized what was important to him—Paul's initial contact with the synagogue, **as was his custom** (cf. Luke 4:16), and the reasons for his departure. Moreover, from Phil. 4:16 we know that his first European community, at Philippi, sent aid to its impoverished apostle in Thessalonica several times. In view of the length of the journey, this demands that Paul's stay was longer than three weeks.

Luke summarized the content of Paul's preaching in the synagogue along the pattern of the creedal formula of 1 Cor. 15:3-5, omitting, however, any reference that Christ's death was "for our sins." This omission is typically Lukan. The basis of Paul's presentation is **the scriptures,** meaning the Old Testament (cf. "according to the scriptures," 1 Cor. 15:3). Scripture speaks of the suffering (that is, the death) and the resurrection of **the Christ,** the Messiah. This Messiah is none other than **Jesus, whom I proclaim to you.**

Paul **argued with them.** This does not mean a quarrelsome, abusive confrontation. The verb, as used by Luke, is synonymous with discussing, teaching, dialoging, reasoning (cf. 19:8-9; 20:7-9; 24:25, where the same Greek verb is used). Moreover, he was **explaining** the content of the kerygma on the basis of the Scripture. The same Greek verb (*dianoigein*) is used in Luke 24:31; Jesus "opened" the eyes of the Emmaus disciples through the breaking of the bread, revealing himself; in Luke 24:32, he "opened" the Scriptures, revealing their true purpose and intent; in Luke 24:45, "he opened their minds to understand the scriptures." In short, the **explaining** Paul did in the synagogue was a revelatory discourse in which the truth and purpose of the Scripture, which is hidden to the eye and to unaided reason, is disclosed. This disclosure is grounded in the resurrection of Jesus, which grants a new perspective for understanding the Scriptures. Without this new perspective the Scriptures lead to the Talmud rather than to faith in Jesus the Messiah. In short, Paul's "hermeneutical key" that opens the Scripture is the resurrection of Christ and the identification of the Messiah with Jesus.

Luke's readers know that the abbreviated argumentation (v. 3) has already been presented in greater detail by Peter (2:22-26; 3:18-26), and by Paul (13:26-41). Among the Jewish people of the synagogue Paul's success is relatively small; only **some of them were persuaded and joined Paul and Silas.** Yet, though they be few in numbers, if the word falls on "good soil" they are the ones who "hold it fast in an honest and good heart and bring forth fruit with patience" (Luke 8:15). Numbers are relative in the kingdom of God, and that applies also to the success story that **a great many of the devout Greeks and not a few of the leading women** joined the first church in Thessalonica. Just so, the success among Gentiles is contrasted with the small number of Jews who accept the gospel. The report in Acts concerning the makeup of the membership of the church in Thessalonica seems to be confirmed by 1 Thessalonians, which is addressed to a primarily Gentile-Christian church (cf. 1 Thess. 1:9). The loss of upper-class women from the circle of God-fearers attached to the synagogue motivated the jealousy of the Jews (cf. 5:17). Their departure meant a loss of influence on the part of the synagogue. Simultaneously, their resources helped the struggling young church and perhaps their influence resulted in the lenient treatment which Jason received from the magistrates. Luke remembers them as pillars of the community, probably because they functioned as such in his own day also.

5-9—The center of the action is Jason, not Paul. This points to the presence of a tradition which Luke compressed and stylized (e.g., jealousy, 5:17; 13:45) and into which he introduced part of the accusation in direct discourse. The Jews incited some local Gentile **rabble** who gathered a mob and surrounded **the house of Jason.** Luke's story presupposes that Paul stayed in Jason's house but that he was absent at that moment. It also presupposes that Jason was a Christian, perhaps one of the few Jews who were persuaded by Paul, perhaps a member of the guild of tentmakers (cf. 1 Thess. 2:9) who was converted and offered hospitality to Paul and his companions. The intention of the mob was **to bring them** (Paul, Silas, Timothy) **out to the people.** It is not clear what is meant by **the people**

(Greek, *demos*). It could refer to the **crowd** surrounding Jason's house (cf. 12:22) or it could refer to the "popular assembly" which existed in the free city of Thessalonica (cf. 19:30, 33). **When they could not find** the missionaries there, **they dragged Jason and some of the brethren,** members of the church, **before the city authorities.** Was it accidental that other Christians had come to Jason's house? Had they gathered for worship in his house-church? We do not know. If "the people" in v. 5 refers to the popular assembly, then the crowd changed its mind, for it brought Jason and the brothers before the magistrates. The accusation is given in direct discourse (cf. 16:20-21) and has three parts. (1) **These men who have turned the world upside down have come here also.** The subject, **these men,** cannot refer to Jason and the brothers, because they lived in Thessalonica and were distinguished from "these men" in v. 7a. It is Paul and his two companions who are accused, literally, of "disturbing the whole civilized world" (Greek, *oikoumenē*), to Greeks and Romans identical with the empire, in distinction from the lands of the barbarians beyond. This charge reflects the feelings of pagans at Luke's time when the church was rapidly spreading across the empire. It hardly reflects the situation in A.D. 50 when only the second church had been established by Paul in Europe. Luke placed accusations and problems of his own day back into the time of Paul's mission and in so doing made his story relevant for his readers who were only too familiar with charges like these. (2) **And Jason has received them.** Here we have a genuine historical reminiscence. Jason is accused of providing lodging and hospitality to Paul and his friends who have caused trouble in Thessalonica rather than in the whole civilized world. (3) **They are all acting against the decrees of Caesar.** The subject seems to be the three missionaries, Jason and the brothers, "all" Christians. It is not clear which specific **decrees** (Greek, *dogmata*) **of Caesar** are meant. An imperial decree against astrologers, magicians, and practitioners of divination had been issued by Tiberius in A.D. 16. There is also evidence for the administration of an oath of loyalty to Caesar's house and for the necessity of reporting persons suspected of disloyalty. At any rate **the decrees of Caesar** cannot refer to Roman public law (cf. 16:21). However, the accusation receives specificity here in that the Christians are accused of saying: **there is another king, Jesus.** Their message exhibits political disloyalty. The word **king** is to be understood as synonymous

319

with *emperor.* These Christians act against Caesar's decrees by proclaiming a counteremperor, Jesus. Since, with the exception of this
verse, Luke always calls the emperor "Caesar" and never **king,** it
is probably right to conclude that v. 7c, like 7a, is a pre-Lukan
tradition (cf. Luke 2:1; 23:2; Acts 25:8). While the second accusation
was directed only against Jason, charging him with sheltering troublemakers, the third accusation was directed to "all," charging all
Christians with plotting Caesar's overthrow. The Christian proclamation is an act of disloyalty, because it promotes a rival to Caesar,
Jesus, as ruler of the world. Luke's readers know that this accusation
is false, that it had already been leveled in similar form against Jesus
(Luke 23:2) and that it was being heard in their own day also, even
as it had been raised at the beginning in Thessalonica. We do not
know how Jason and the brothers defended themselves, but to our
surprise, we hear that they merely had to post security bond and
the city authorities **let them go,** even though the civic rulers **were
disturbed** by the accusations against the Christians. In the face of
unsubstantiated charges, made by a mob led by disreputable **rabble,**
the politarchs acted justly and wisely, justly in letting Jason and his
people go, wisely in insuring the tranquility of the city by means of
posted security. Should further disturbance arise, the bond would
be forfeited. Hence, it was necessary that Paul and his friends leave
immediately and they did so **by night** (v. 10a; cf. 9:25, 30; 14:6).

In 1 Thess. 1:6 Paul, some months later, wrote, "You became
imitators of us and of the Lord, for you received the word in much
affliction," and in 2:2 he refers to "great opposition" which his
preaching encountered in Thessalonica (cf. 1 Thess. 3:3-4). In 2:14
the persecutors are identified as "your own countrymen," which
means that they were Gentiles and not Jews. In light of Acts 17:1-
9, how can this be understood? The following explanations are possible, though none is certain. (1) 1 Thessalonians 2:14 refers to the
Gentile "rabble" and "crowd," not to the Jewish instigators of Acts
working behind the scene. In short, both Acts and 1 Thessalonians
reflect what actually happened. (2) There were no Jewish instigators,
but the persecution was a purely Gentile affair and Luke introduced
them, perhaps because of his anti-Jewish bias, or because he read
the experience of the church of his own day back into the mission
of Paul, thereby making his story relevant for his reader. In short,
historically, Paul was forced to flee because of Gentile opposition

in which Jews played no role. (3) The case of Jason was taken up again by Gentiles and pursued further, resulting in the suffering caused by Gentiles to which 1 Thess. 2:14 refers. (4) Finally, we must note that quite a few scholars regard 1 Thess. 2:13-16 as an interpolation into the text of 1 Thessalonians, which means that it did not come from Paul's pen, but was added by someone else later. Yet, even if this hypothesis is correct, and I think it is, even as an interpolation this text reflects a tradition which held that the persecution in Thessalonica was not caused by Jews, but by Gentiles. Among the possibilities outlined, it would seem best to choose the last and the second, but add that Luke was not an anti-Semite. This text of Acts brings us the following historical data: (1) There was a tumult, the center of which was Jason, who was dragged out of his house together with some Christian brothers and brought before the magistrates. (2) The accusation against them was that of harboring troublemakers who engaged in treason by proclaiming Jesus as Lord and emperor of the world, in opposition to Caesar. (3) The case was settled by the posting of a security bond, because the accusers could not make their charges stick. (4) The whole affair was probably Gentile inspired.

Mission in Beroea (17:10-15). Luke's account gives the impression that Paul and his friends, after walking 45 miles, went directly into the synagogue of Beroea, the modern Véroia. His account is condensed and stylized. Therefore, it follows the same pattern found in the previous episode: preaching in the synagogue, acceptance of the word, resistance through mob action incited by Jews, flight of the missionaries. But we also find variations, namely: **these Jews were more noble than those of Thessalonica.** They **received the word with all eagerness, examining the scriptures daily,** in order to understand Paul's hermeneutics, which approached the Old Testament from the vantage point of the resurrection of Jesus. In Beroea Paul met with his fellow Jews **daily** in the synagogue, not just on the Sabbath. **Many of them** came to faith in Jesus the Messiah, as did many socially prominent Gentile women and men. The third church in Macedonia had been founded. But at last the opposition also became active. **Jews of Thessalonica** heard of Paul's success, came to Beroea (cf. 14:19) and did what they had done before, namely, incited Gentile **crowds** (plural!). This development alarmed the brothers of the church of Beroea and they **immediately sent Paul off on his way to the sea, but Silas and Timothy remained** in Beroea. Probably at Pydna, Paul and some members of the new church of Beroea took a boat that brought them to **Athens.** The Beroeans returned with Paul's request that Silas and Timothy should join **him as soon as possible.** Thus ends the mission in Macedonia: three churches, three enforced departures, and many a cup of bitter woe.

When we look at Paul's career thus far we realize that the prediction made at his call is in the process of fulfillment. Jesus had announced to Ananias, "I will show him how much he must suffer for the sake of my name." Just so, Paul's journey as witness for Christ was marked by plots in Damascus and Jerusalem (9:23, 29), an expulsion from Antioch (13:50), flight from Iconium, a stoning which left him for dead in Lystra (14:6, 19), a public flogging and imprisonment in Philippi and forced escapes from Thessalonica and Beroea (16:23; 17:10, 14). Paul, the suffering witness, follows in the footsteps of his Lord (Luke 14:27) as he carries the gospel across the empire, an instrument through whom Jesus fulfills his mandate "to the end of the earth" (1:8). As such Paul's career is a sermon of encouragement to Luke's church. Undoubtedly, when leaving Thessalonica for Beroea, Paul must have planned to make his way south to Athens by way of Thessaly, but the new opposition in Beroea convinced him to move at once by sea to the great metropolis of Greek culture. The mission continues, and Paul's success in Beroea is reflected in Sopater's participation on the last journey to Jerusalem, where he transmitted the collection (20:4).

According to Acts 18:5, "Silas and Timothy arrived from Macedonia" while Paul was in Corinth, whereas according to 1 Thess. 3:1-2 Paul sent Timothy from Athens to Thessalonica. Naturally, one can harmonize the two accounts by postulating that Silas and Timothy met Paul in Athens (omitted in Acts) and that the apostle then sent Timothy to Thessalonica (omitted in Acts but stated in 1 Thessalonians) and Silas to Philippi, or some other place in Macedonia (omitted in Acts and in Paul's letters). Later, they both joined Paul in Corinth, as stated in 18:5. But there is a simpler explanation. Luke is wrong and Paul is right. Both companions traveled with Paul to Athens, from whence he sent Timothy to Thessalonica. He later rejoined Paul and Silas in Corinth. Nevertheless, we should recognize that Luke knew of a temporary separation of Timothy from Paul at this stage.

Paul's Mission in Achaia (17:16—18:11)

The mission in Achaia is Luke's centerpiece in Paul's great missionary enterprise which began in Antioch (15:36) and ended in Ephesus (19:20). Paul had planted the gospel in Macedonia. In Achaia, he established churches in Athens and Corinth, and from there he went to Ephesus in the province of Asia. It comes to us as a surprise to hear that according to Luke the Ephesian ministry marks the end of Paul's missionary activity. Afterward, with his eyes fixed on Jerusalem and Rome (19:21), Paul will still be a witness to Christ, but not as a missionary. He will give encouragement to established congregations (20:1—21:14), and bear witness as a prisoner (21:27—28:31), but he will no longer enter synagogues or establish new churches. His mission in Achaia is the center of his missionary activity and for this reason alone it is important in Luke's design. Its importance is highlighted by Paul's famous Areopagus speech, the only extended speech in this whole mission section (15:36—19:20), delivered at midpoint after the mission in Macedonia and prior to the mission in Asia. It is addressed to Gentiles (cf. 14:15-18) and has its counterpart in Paul's great speech to Jews in the synagogue of Antioch in Pisidia (13:16-41). With these two paradigmatic speeches Luke tells us what "the whole counsel of God" for humanity, for Jew and Gentile, is all about (20:27).

Mission in Athens (17:16-34).   Athens is located midway between Jerusalem and Rome. Though at Paul's time Athens had been overtaken by Corinth in size and in political and economic importance, it remained the symbol of Greek philosophy, religion, and culture. Tourists then as now flocked to see the places where Socrates and Plato, Epicurus and the early Stoics had taught, marveled at the Parthenon and the many temples that adorned the city, and sat in the theater of Dionysius, the birthplace of western drama. Luke wisely chose the stage for Paul's paradigmatic address to Gentiles. Just as Jerusalem is the center of the church and the symbol of the continuity of salvation history, and just as Rome is the center and symbol of imperial power, so Athens is the citadel of pagan thought and symbol of Hellenistic religiosity.

How is one to speak the gospel to people who are ignorant of the God of Israel, his promise and Law, the prophets and the Scriptures, the Messiah and the resurrection? This is the question which the Athens episode addresses. In the context of the synagogue, Paul and his hearers shared a common background, but in the Agora and the Areopagus he had to face the problem of communication as he spoke to people who were neither Jews nor God-fearers, but religious pagans. Yet, there is a common ground which enabled Paul to make contact, and that is our common humanity within our common world. Both are gifts of the benevolent Creator. Just so, Paul sought to make contact with his hearers by unfolding to them the meaning of the First Article of the Apostles' Creed and doing it in language understandable to them.

16-21—The introduction sets the stage for the following speech and indicates that the reaction to Paul's speaking in the Agora, the marketplace, prompted his Areopagus address.

16-17—**While Paul was waiting** for Silas and Timothy to join him, he too wandered like a tourist through Athens. Far from being impressed by the glory that was Greece, **his spirit was provoked** because he saw a **city full of idols.** The sheer beauty of Athens receded from his mind's eye as he saw nothing but idolatry. Indeed, the Athenians prided themselves on the superabundance of temples, statues, and altars dedicated to gods, godlets, and half-gods—male, female, and hermaphrodite. With this opening verse Luke disclosed his perception of the relationship between Christianity and Greek culture. This perception must be kept in mind when we hear Paul say that the Athenians are "very religious" (v. 22). On the Sabbath Paul preached **in the synagogue,** because the missionary to Gentiles must speak the word first to **Jews,** even though in Athens Luke's focus shifts at once from the **synagogue** to the Agora, the **market place.** We do not hear of conflicts with or conversions of Athenian **Jews and the devout persons.** With the verb **he argued** (Greek, *dialegesthai*) Luke begins to use Socratic coloring in depicting this scene (Plato, *Apol.* 19d). Socrates argued, dialoged, with those who would listen. But for Luke the verb still retains the meaning of "preaching" (cf. 20:7). **Every day** Paul engaged people in dialog in the Agora, among them some **Epicurean and Stoic philosophers.**

18—Epicurus (342–271 B.C.) and the schools named after him sought to attain happiness by natural reasoning and philosophical discussion and to free people from the fear of death, from irrational belief in gods and from ensnarement in vices. His philosophy was primarily a system of ethics in which gods played no role. Gods did exist, but in infinite realms far removed from mortals. They lived a life of blissful tranquility and were unconcerned about humans, bestowing neither blessing nor revenge. Their undisturbed tranquility was what humans should seek to attain in this life, but gods cannot and will not help them attain that goal. Tranquility is the state where one cannot be shaken by poverty, pain, fear, or the desire for material or sexual gratification. At death the soul disintegrated, and that was the end.

The Stoics traced their origin to Zeno (ca. 320 B.C.) and their name to the beautiful colonnaded hall (Greek, *stoa*) located in the Agora where Zeno taught. In New Testament times Stoic philosophy had spread throughout the empire and was embraced by slaves and emperors alike. The fundamental belief of this philosophy was that virtue is the only good and vice the only evil. To be virtuous was to live in conformity with nature, our own and the nature of the cosmos. The cosmos was ruled by reason, also present in humans. But in humans, passions, ignorance, superstitions, fears, and bondage to customs resulted in a life not lived according to reason, the law of the universe, which could be called "God," "Zeus," or other names. The Stoic gospel was therefore an appeal to change from a life of passions to a life in accordance with reason, the law that pervades the cosmos. Since reason is universal, Stoics upheld the unity of all human beings and believed in the pantheistic idea of God's (or Zeus's) indwelling in nature and in people.

The result of this initial meeting between the philosophers and Paul was that **some** attached the epithet **babbler** to him. By this colorful term (Greek, *spermologos*) they characterized him as a dilettante who picks up bits of wisdom, slogans, and scraps of learning like a bird picking up seeds, and then tries to show off by mouthing half-baked ideas. **Others,** echoing the charges leveled against Socrates, said: **He seems to be a preacher of foreign divinities. He seems** implies that this is only an opinion and not a formal charge, but as opinion it is in need of further investigation. The reason for their opinion is also stated: Paul **preached Jesus and the resurrection** (Greek, *anastasis*). It is quite possible that the philosophers thought that Paul was proselytizing on behalf of two oriental **foreign** divinities (plural), one called Jesus and the other, his female consort, called Anastasis. If this were the case, Paul was not even understood. He said one thing and his audience in the Agora heard something quite different, a situation not unfamiliar to the modern preacher. It is equally possible that their opinion resulted from Paul's preaching of the God of Abraham, Isaac, and Jacob and his eschatological deed in the resurrection of Jesus. Be this as it may, the reader knows that Jesus' resurrection was the topic of Paul's preaching in the Agora, and this topic connects Luke's introduction with the following speech (cf. vv. 30-31).

19-20—The interpretation of these verses is disputed. **They took hold of him** (Paul) can be understood in a friendly sense (9:27), meaning "they accompanied him," but it can also have a more or less hostile sense (cf. 16:19). Moreover, the phrase **to the Areopagus** is also debated. It could refer to the hill of the god Ares, god of war (Latin, *Mars*, hence Mars' Hill). The preposition "to" (Greek, *epi*) can mean "upon." If so, the Areopagus must be the rocky hill of Ares, northwest of and at the foot of the Acropolis, overlooking the Agora. In ancient times the council of Athens conducted its trials on that hill, but in New Testament times that council, called the Areopagus, conducted its meetings in the city, frequently in the Royal Colonnade, or in the Hall of Zeus Eleutherios. Finally, the Greek preposition translated "to" (the Areopagus) is also used by Luke in the sense of "before" (e.g., 16:19, where the same Greek participle occurs as in 17:19). If that should be Luke's meaning, then Paul was not led to that rocky Areopagus hill, but before the council by that name. In favor of this interpretation are the following: (1) Luke reports the conversion of an Areopagite (v. 34), that is, a member of the Areopagus. (2) The statement that Paul "went out from among them" (v. 33) fits a council meeting better than a steep descent from the Areopagus hill. Also the phrase **Paul, standing in the midst of the Areopagus** seems to envision a council meeting rather than a hilltop (v. 22). (3) Paul was asked about **this new teaching** and about **some strange** (foreign) **things** that he brought to their attention. The suggestion had been raised that he might be introducing "foreign divinities." All of this could point to an appearance of Paul before the Areopagus council, which apparently in New Testament times had oversight not only over religious matters but also over education and visiting teachers. While we cannot be certain whether

Luke referred to the hill or to the council, we lean toward the latter. We should understand that the council did not act as a court but as a gathering of leading citizens who investigated out of curiosity, seeking an explanation from this preacher of foreign divinities. Unlike Socrates, Paul was not on trial. His speech was not a defense speech, an apologia, but a proclamation of the Creator. It was an informal inquiry which gave Paul the setting for his famous speech. Having been declared innocent by Roman magistrates in Philippi, he was free to leave the highest council in Athens after preaching to it (v. 33). This would seem to be one of Luke's minor points in this episode.

21—Luke directs an aside to the reader, referring to the proverbial curiosity of the Athenians who **spent their time in nothing except telling or hearing something new.** This curiosity, rather than a formal judicial charge, was the reason for Paul's appearance before the Areopagus. Hence his response is not the apology of one accused of wrongdoing, but the proclamation of a missionary. Simultaneously Luke suggests that among these supercilious Athenians the gospel will have a hard time. For as much as they liked to hear "new" gossipy things, a truly new approach to and from God which would undercut the status quo of popular religion and philosophical sophistication would be threatening indeed. The defense mechanism of the Athenians when confronted with something really new was ridicule, as Luke aptly indicated (vv. 18 and 32).

22-31 (The Areopagus Speech)—This climactic speech of Paul's missionary career to Gentiles has become the subject of much debate. M. Dibelius, whose brilliant study of this speech has greatly advanced our understanding, concluded that "the Areopagus speech is absolutely foreign to Paul's own theology, that it is, in fact, foreign to the entire New Testament" (p. 71). Now, it ought to be clear that the speeches in Acts are Lukan compositions, even though Luke incorporated traditional patterns and traditional motifs. We should also keep in mind that all of Paul's letters are addressed to believers and churches that have broken with their pagan past. We do not know how the historical Paul preached to Gentiles. However, in 1 Thess. 1:9-10 Paul reminded the Thessalonians who had been converted only months before what the content of the gospel as preached by him was: (1) "How you turned to God from idols, to serve a living and true God, (2) and to wait for his Son from heaven,

(3) whom he raised from the dead, (4) Jesus [Christ] who delivers us from the wrath to come." There are good reasons to believe that Paul here summarized a traditional pattern of Christian preaching to Gentiles. To be sure, only the first part is fully unfolded by Luke (vv. 24-29)—for two reasons. One, because Luke wanted to show how Paul proclaimed the true and living God to Greeks. The other items, 2-4 above, had been heard already in prior speeches. Two, Paul was interrupted at the point when he would unfold the Christological kerygma. But he still managed to refer briefly to it in vv. 30-31, which constitute the high point of the speech.

Turning to the differences between Romans and Acts 17, we should be aware of the different audiences. Romans was addressed to Christians who had turned from idols; in Luke's design Acts 17 was addressed to pagans. Moreover, it is unlikely that in his missionary preaching to Gentiles the historical Paul first painted the darkest possible picture of human existence under the wrath of God—as found in Romans 1—in order to tell them about the solution to the human problem through Christ. He rather worked the other way around. Only in the light of God's solution in Christ does the human problem of sin become apparent in its fullness. It is true that in Acts 17 the problems of sin and ignorance are treated rather lightly, whereas Romans 1:18—3:20 interprets human existence in terms of bondage to sin and subjection to God's judgment from which none can free themselves by their own efforts. Romans is addressed to Christians, and we should not expect its theology to be present in a Lukan speech addressed to Gentiles.

Secondly, there are differences of perspective. For instance, Acts 17:28-29 holds that kinship with God is an innate characteristic of all humanity, whereas divine sonship in Romans is the gift of God accepted through faith in Christ. According to Paul we are not sons of God by nature; by nature we are sons of Adam (Rom. 5:12-21; 8:14-17). The difference between Luke and Paul at this point is to some degree a matter of semantics. For Luke, Adam is the son of God (Luke 3:38) and his descendants are depicted in the parable (Luke 15) either as the prodigal son who wasted his father's substance in riotous living, or as the self-righteous elder brother. But the father in the parable remains constant throughout and he welcomes the repentant son, because his fatherly love "abounded all the more" in the face of his son's sins (cf. Rom. 5:20b). In Luke's parable the son remains "the offspring" of the father (cf. Acts 17:28) even when he lives among the swine or engages in idolatry. Just so in Paul the sinner enslaved by law and sin and subject to judgment remains God's creature. Both Luke and Paul held that acceptance by God is an undeserved gift and not the result of merit. The difference between them is a matter of perspective, of different concepts, and of a different mood. Luke showed little interest in presenting the peculiarities of Pauline theology, provided that he knew them. For him, Paul was the representative of the beginnings of the Gentile mission, a mission inaugurated by Peter, but carried by Paul across Asia Minor and Greece, and ending in Rome. The Areopagus speech was Luke's endeavor to show how Paul preached to Gentiles and in his composition he used a traditional missionary pattern.

The theme of the speech might be: Knowledge of the one true God demands repentance that is based on Christ's resurrection and oriented to the final judgment. Its individual parts are: Introduction (vv. 22-23); part 1, God is the creator and Lord of the world who objects to temples and religious cults (vv. 24-25); part 2, all people are created by God "from one" in order that they should seek him (vv. 26-27); part 3, their relationship to God prohibits idolatry in its crass and sophisticated forms (vv. 28-29); part 4, the time for repentance is now, in view of the judgment to come which will be executed by him whom God raised from the dead (vv. 30-31).

The whole speech is carefully balanced and its parts interrelated; e.g., "the times of ignorance" (v. 30) relate to the introduction; "the man appointed judge" (v. 31) is the counterpart to the "one" (v. 26). There are two infinitives in the second as well as in the fourth part, and a total of three negative statements expressing divine objection in parts 1 and 3. The universal scope of God's creation and purpose expressed through the sixfold appearance of "all," "everything," "every," "each" (Greek, *pas, panta*) in parts 1 and 2 finds its counterpart in part 4 in that "all men everywhere" are asked to repent. No one will be excluded from the judgment to come and the resurrection of Christ is God's assurance "to all" (v. 31).

22-23—Introduction: **Paul, standing in the middle of the Areopagus,** that is, in the midst of the council, is given the opportunity to deliver his message to the representatives of Greek religion and culture. Instead of denouncing their idolatry he praises their reli-

giosity. **Men of Athens,** he begins, **I perceive that in every way you
are very religious.** The Greek word translated "religious" (*desidai-
mon*, lit., "demon-fearing") can have a positive or a pejorative meaning, such as "superstitious." Here, undoubtedly, it has a double
meaning. The reader should remember that while he strolled
through the city Paul's spirit was provoked, for he saw a city full of
idols (v. 16), and in his opening address he did not claim that the
Athenians were "God-fearing" or "devout" (cf. 10:2; 17:4). Thus
there is tongue-in-cheek irony in the words **in every way very religious** (cf. 25:19). Yet it is not just sarcasm that comes to expression,
as the next sentence clearly shows. While the Athenians were famous
in antiquity for their curiosity as well as their religiosity, for Paul
they are religious in a complimentary sense for one reason only. **For
as I passed along, and observed the objects of your worship, I found
also an altar with this inscription, "To an unknown god."** Not the
multitude of glorious temples, altars, and statues prompted Paul's
captatio benevolentiae (currying favor). His compliment at the beginning of his speech resulted from seeing one lonely altar with this
inscription. Paul's attitude toward idolatry, found in v. 16, is not
reversed. The Athenians are superstitious idolaters without knowledge of God. But this altar inscription enabled Paul to make contact
with his audience and to use the adjective "religious" in a positive
sense. Further, it refuted the suggestion that he imported new divinities (v. 17).

Two questions arise at this point. First, did such an inscription
exist? There is neither literary nor archaeological evidence for an
inscription in the singular "to an unknown god." Pausanias (2nd cent.
A.D.) mentioned altars to unknown gods (plural) near Athens and in
Olympia (1.1.4; 5.14.8). They were erected out of fear lest by overlooking some unknown gods, one would invite their envy or fury.
It is therefore probable that Luke changed the plural into singular
to create a point of contact between Paul and his audience.

Second, what did Luke wish to convey to the reader with this
inscription? Did he mean to suggest that the Athenians had always,
though unknowingly, worshiped the one true God? Certainly not.
The inscription according to Luke did not say "To *the* unknown god,"
but **To an unknown god,** and Paul did not say "Him whom you
worship," but **What you worship** (neuter, as if unknown), **this** (neu-

ter) **I proclaim to you.** With this formulation Paul indicates that it is not just ignorance about the person and name of God, but ignorance about his "deity" (v. 29). Paul suggests that by erecting this altar with this inscription the Athenians themselves announced the failure of polytheism and its cults to come to terms with the deity of God. Simultaneously this inscription expresses a hunch, a vague notion that the reality of God, his deity, is to be found beyond all pagan cults, temples, and religious efforts. Thus the inscription marks the place where the Athenians are open for knowledge of the true God, where they are truly "religious." Open, but not more than that! Since they worship an unknown god in ignorance, their worship is noncommittal and without any obligations.

Paul now proclaims the unknown God in his deity not by linking up with the monotheistic beliefs of Stoicism but by linking up with the biblical message of the Creator. God is not a new or foreign divinity, but the one who has always been Creator and Ruler and who has always been near. The Athenians did not know God, but they had a vague hunch about him, as their altar with its inscription attests. The altar shows that they worship something beyond the gods; the inscription shows that they do not know God.

24-25—Part 1: The true God is the Creator of all that exists, the Lord of the world and the giver of life: **The God who made the world and everything in it, being Lord of heaven and earth.** Whereas the Stoics compromised their monotheistic beliefs about God's essence by connecting them with polytheistic notions, Paul uncompromisingly announced the biblical doctrine of the Creator by using words from Isa. 42:5. In contrast to Aristotle's transcendent unmoved Mover, and in contrast to the pantheism of the Stoics according to which God was completely merged in the world and the world simultaneously filled with a host of higher and lower mediating gods representing natural forces, Paul implicitly stated that God as Creator and Lord is not identical with natural necessity or forces of nature. Creation is God's sovereign act and in this action God's deity is hidden. One cannot see God in nature, and the attempt to make God visible in images, temples, and cults constitutes idolatry, the ultimate sin. Therefore Paul at once raised a twofold objection: the Creator and Lord on whose power the world and all that is in it are dependent at all times and without whose will nothing can take place—this God **does not live in shrines made by man nor is he**

served by human hands. The structure of Paul's argumentation is *a b b a*, with *a* forming the basis for the two negative conclusions, *b b*. The Creator does not live in temples, "made by hands" (cf. 7:48-50). On the contrary, it is God who provides living space for humanity (v. 26). Heaven is God's throne and the earth is God's footstool (7:49). No temple can encapsulate the Deity and subject him to manipulations. God's presence cannot be objectified (Jer. 7:1-12). On the basis of Stoic pantheism, Plutarch reached the same conclusion: "It is a doctrine of Zeno: 'one should not build temples for gods!' " (*Moralia* 1034B). Paul would agree with this conclusion, but not with its pantheistic premise. Also, his second objection against the cult would fall on sympathetic ears among the Athenian intelligentsia. God is not **served by human hands, as though he needed anything.** This notion of God's self-sufficiency arose in the Greek philosophical tradition (e.g., Plutarch, *Moralia* 1052D). It is foolish to think that God is in need of sacrifices and the cult.

This objection is limited to the sacrificial cult. Paul echoes ideas common to Greek philosophers. The Old Testament can also speak about the impropriety of the sacrificial cult: "If I were hungry [says Yahweh], I would not tell you; for the world and all that is in it is mine. Do I eat the flesh of bulls, or drink the blood of goats? Offer to God a sacrifice of thanksgiving . . . and call upon me in the day of trouble; I will deliver you and you shall glorify me" (Ps. 50:12-15; cf. Amos 5:21-23). Paul rejects temples and sacrificial cults in one specific regard, namely, when temples result in the illusion that God has to live in them and when sacrifices are offered under the illusion that God needs them and can be manipulated with them. Where God dwells is his free choice and if God chose to dwell in Jerusalem's temple in the past, that past choice does not guarantee the future of the temple or its cult. God is not confined to a building, and "has need of nothing" (2 Macc. 14:35). On the contrary, it is God who **gives to all men life and breath and everything.** Again Paul used language from Isa. 42:5, but he substituted "life" for "spirit," thereby creating a wordplay (*zōēn kai pnoēn*) lest anyone conclude that the Holy Spirit is a person's endowment by nature. The Creator is the great benefactor of every human being. The biblical creation narrative has formed the basis of Paul's proclamation thus far, but the presence of Hellenistic motifs, abundant in vv. 27b-28, can also be detected in this first part (vv. 24-25). Probably Hellenistic

Judaism of the diaspora functioned as a channel through which Greek ideas, such as God's self-sufficiency, flowed into early Christianity. What is more important than the occasional use of Hellenistic language and thought-forms is the insight that our author did not discuss God as he is in himself, but only as he relates to his creation. God's deity can be articulated not in terms of essence but only in terms of God's action and its meaning for us. The implication is clear: as the giver of life and "everything" we are and have, we should love, trust, and obey God.

26-27—Part 2: God's relation to human beings: In these verses we face problems of translation. Should we translate, **He made . . . humanity to live,** meaning "He caused people to live" (so RSV), or are both Greek infinitives dependent on the main verb? Then we could translate, "He made [or created] . . . that they should live . . . [and] that they should seek God." It would seem that in view of the use of the verb *made* in the sense of "created" in v. 24 we cannot assign a different meaning to it at the beginning of v. 26 and treat it as if it were the causative form of "to dwell." In short, the second translation is preferable. Therefore, "from one" does not mean from one principle, blood, or stock, but from Adam. Instead of **every nation of men,** Luke probably thought of "all of humanity," picking up the Stoic notion of the unity of all human beings. (The absence of the Greek article would be irregular, but not impossible, for this translation.)

The meaning of **allotted periods and the boundaries of their habitation** is also disputed. Do the "periods" (Greek, *kairoi*) refer to the seasons of the year, as in 14:17? But there, in the speech at Lystra, the word is specified by the adjective "fruitful" which makes the meaning "season" (of the year) definite. Such an adjective is absent here. Hence, other interpreters have thought that "the times" means "epochs," or "periods" of growth or decline in the history of "every nation" (cf. Job 2:23); "boundaries" then would mean national boundaries (cf. Deut. 32:8). The meaning of this clause would be that God determines the history of each nation, assigning periods to its rise and fall (cf. Dan. 2:21), marking the expanding or contracting national borders. The clause would then express the ethnic differentiation of nations which came about in spite of the fact that they all came "from one."

There is still another possibility, namely, that we understand "the times" in terms of Lukan usage. He knew of the time of the Law and the Prophets "until John" (Luke 16:16). In the 15th year of Tiberius Caesar the time came for John to preach a baptism of repentance (Luke 3:1,3). When Jesus came to Jerusalem, it was "the time" of its "visitation" (Luke 19:44). After the ascension there followed the time for witnessing to the end of the earth (Acts 1:8) and "the times of the Gentiles" (Luke 21:24). For Athens "the times of ignorance" are past and the time for repentance is "now" (v. 30). At the end comes the time of judgment (v. 31; Luke 21:25-28). In short, God has determined times for his actions in history.

The meaning of **boundaries** is not clear. It may refer to national boundaries, or to natural boundaries between the raging sea and the dry inhabitable land (cf. Ps. 74:13, 16-17). In favor of the latter are three observations: (1) National boundaries are ever fluctuating. Luke, it would seem, wanted to communicate the stability which God granted to humanity as his gift. (2) Clearly, the emphasis of v. 26 lies on the final clause **that they should seek God** (v. 27). The ground of this divine purpose is not the differentiations between nations with different national boundaries, but rather the unity of all of humanity from one Adam. (3) The interpretation "national boundaries" would seem to presuppose that we translate with the RSV, **He made from one every nation,** but this translation runs into difficulty, because **every** nation does not live on **all the face of the earth** (v. 26a), especially not when national boundaries limit its space.

It would seem that Luke is telling us in v. 26 the following: (1) God created the whole human race from one, namely, from Adam. This affirmation of the creation of all human beings who stem from Adam undercuts all racist and nationalistic ideologies and agrees with the best insight of Stoic philosophy which also affirmed the unity of humanity. (2) One divine purpose was that all of humanity should live **upon all the face of the earth** created by God for all people (Gen. 1:28). (3) God determined the periods of human history (e.g., that the "times of ignorance" are now over, v. 30), and created boundaries between land and sea. In terms of time and of space God cared for his human creatures. (4) While the first infinitive expresses the horizontal dimension of God's purpose, namely, that humanity should expand across the face of the earth, the second infinitive expresses the vertical dimension of his purpose. Each and every one **should seek God,** which is possible because God is not removed at infinite distance beyond the sky, unreachable and unapproachable by mortals. On the contrary, **he is not far from each one of us.** (5) Whether this quest for God, which is the destiny of all humans, is successful or not is left open by Paul, though he indicates in a rare Greek construction (*ei* plus optative) that the end result is rather uncertain. Seeking God is like blind people groping in the dark, hoping to find what they seek (Isa. 59:10). Note that to grope or **feel after** precedes **find him,** and probably indicates a human condition comparable to the blind. Such a notion sharply modifies the Stoic belief which held that the Deity could clearly be inferred from nature. In the Greek tradition, seeking truth is a process of rational inquiry and deduction, the outcome of which cannot be uncertain, or merely hypothetical, as it is in this speech. Paul did not indicate at this point the conditions under which God may be found (but see v. 30). For him the goal of finding God is not a matter of accumulating theoretical knowledge about God, but true worship within a relationship of faith and love, trust, and hope. For his part God has done everything in order that he may be found. Moreover, God is near to **each one of us,** which includes Paul and his audience.

The nearness of God is also a topic of popular Greek philosophy, and the Old Testament psalmist said: "Whither shall I flee from thy presence? If I ascend to heaven, thou art there! If I make my bed in Sheol, thou art there! If I take the wings of the morning and dwell in the uttermost parts of the sea, even there thy hand shall lead me" (Ps. 139:7-10). For the Stoics God is near because he is immanent, for Luke and the psalmist the transcendent God is near, because "he holds the whole world in his hand," and surrounds it.

28-29—Part 3: The human's relation to God: Old Testament allusions are absent in v. 28 but reappear in the polemics against idols in v. 29. According to the structure of the speech, the previous verse (v. 27) indicated that God's nearness is the ground for the possibility of finding God. The troublesome v. 28 explicates in what sense God is near to "each one of us," and v. 29 draws the conclusion with respect to idolatry. God is near to every one, **for in him we live and move and have our being.** We do not know whether Luke is citing a Greek pantheistic statement.

Stoics generally would speak of the Deity permeating the cosmos and human reason, rather than humans living "in" God. How did Luke understand the preposition *in?* God is near because he surrounds us. We live in God's presence whether we know it or not (cf. Rom. 11:36). Moreover, the preposition *in* may have been understood in the sense of "through," as in v. 31 where it is said that God will judge the world through a man (Greek, *en*). We live through God, because God has given us life and everything we are and have (v. 25). Finally, this statement is further interpreted by a sample quotation, **even some of your poets have said, "For we are indeed his offspring."** We belong to God's family whether we know it or not, whether we worship or commit idolatry, whether we stay at home or run away like the prodigal son (cf. Luke 3:38 where Adam is God's son because God created him). For Luke, being God's offspring does not imply that we have a divine spark within us, be it an immortal soul or a divine logos. But to him it means that we are dependent on God. Even when the prodigal son wasted his substance in riotous living he depended on his father's wealth. Just as our globe is dependent on the gravitational pull of the sun in its travel through interstellar space, so we are dependent on God. To be **his offspring** means we are related to God and dependent on him, whether we recognize it or not.

The quotation cited by Paul comes from a poem by Aratus of Soli, who also had lived in Tarsus (3rd cent. B.C.). It had already been used by the Hellenistic Jewish author Aristobulus to interpret the biblical creation story (Eusebius, *Preparat. Evang.* 13.12.3). Since we hear of **poets,** plural, the author may have also thought of a line from the hymn to Zeus by the Stoic Cleanthes: "To call upon you is proper for all mortals, for we are your offspring" (*Fragment* 537). It strikes us as odd that we find a quotation from a pagan "poet" at the place where synagogue sermons would cite the Old Testament. Within the context of his biblical-theological presuppositions Luke could acknowledge that truth exists also outside of the Bible, without accepting the pantheistic content in which the Aratus citation originated.

It is clear that Paul is accommodating his language to his audience, especially in v. 28. His point is twofold: (1) v. 28 explains why God "is not far from each one of us" (v. 27), and (2) v. 28 serves as ground for the conclusion that idols in any form ought to be rejected (v. 29).

It is not obvious how **being God's offspring** demonstrates why idols are objectionable. The idea probably is that our relationship to God should lead us to the insight that anything created by us cannot possibly represent our Creator. An idol is our product to be manipulated as we please and so we reject **the Deity** and confuse him with created things. Perhaps the notion in the background is that human beings are created in God's image and therefore are called to live in accord with that image, to live in an obedient relationship with their Creator, a relationship which would preclude the making of idols and images as substitutes for the living God.

In the objection to idols, the Areopagus speech converges with philosophical criticism raised by Stoicism (e.g., Plutarch, *Moralia* 167 D-F) and with the monotheistic polemics of Hellenistic Judaism (cf. Wisdom of Solomon 13–15). Yet it is not just idolatrous representations made by artisans which are rejected by Paul but also **a representation by. . .the imagination of man.** Here the speech objects not only to popular Hellenistic folk religion (cf. 14:11) but to the idolatry of pantheistic Stoicism and other philosophies as well. They too are products of the reflection and thought of man. Only if Luke, in spite of his efforts to make contact with his audience, included his audience among those engaged in idolatry, does his call for repentance to "all" people "everywhere" follow logically (v. 30). Otherwise, the concluding part of the speech would be unconnected. Incidentally, the making of idols was also defended by Hellenistic writers on the basis of the human desire to be near the gods (Dio of Prusa, 12.60–62).

30-31—Part 4: The command to repent: Up to this point the speech dealt with the topics of the Creator in relation to human beings and their relation to God. Three negative conclusions were drawn which rejected temples, sacrificial cults, and idolatry in any form. The speech thus far stands in continuity with the missionary preaching in Hellenistic synagogues. Before the church can proclaim Jesus Christ to Gentiles, they must hear about God, who gave them life in the past and preserves it in the present. They must be able to confess: "There is one God, the Father, from whom are all things and for whom we exist"; only then can Gentiles confess: "And [there is] one Lord, Jesus Christ, through whom are all things and through whom we exist" (1 Cor. 8:6). Therefore, the pattern of missionary preaching dealt first with the doctrine of God in opposition to idolatry and then with the Christological kerygma (1 Thess. 1:9). In this last and climactic part "the world" and human beings are related to God's future eschatological activity in light of which the command for repentance is issued in the present. History has a beginning with creation and it comes to an end in the final judgment. In between, there are **the times of ignorance of** the Gentiles when knowledge and worship of the Creator and Preserver are replaced by idolatry and illusions. This epoch of Gentile ignorance is followed by the time **to repent,** which is the time of proclamation to "all nations" (Luke 24:47). Paul's audience, philosophers and Areopagites, have been part of "the times of ignorance," and the appeal to repent is addressed also to them. No one is excluded.

This concluding high point brings a brief summary of the Lukan kerygma. **God overlooked** the ignorance of Gentiles, even as he did the ignorance of the Jerusalem Jews in their rejection of Jesus (cf. 3:13; 13:27). **But now** God issues the call for repentance (2:38; 3:19; Luke 24:47), a call addressed to **all** people **everywhere** (1:8; 2:39: Luke 24:47), in view of God's future judgment over all forms of idolatry, a judgment which is to be executed **in righteousness by one man,** Jesus Christ, the representative of God (3:21, 23; 4:12; 10:42; Luke 3:16-17; 21:27-28). To this end God **has given assurance to all men by raising him from the dead** (4:33; 5:30; 10:40-42; 13:31-33). The resurrection is the guarantee of the judgment to come, which in turn is the final reason for repentance.

But now (v. 30b) signals a change in God's attitude toward idolatry. God is not the timeless being of Greek philosophy in which past, present, and future are all the same, but God is involved in history and there is a time before the resurrection and a time after, a time of ignorance and the end of it. **To repent** includes two movements here; one, to turn from idols made with hands or the imagination of humans; two, to turn to the living God who raised Jesus from the dead and appointed him to be the judge of all forms of idolatry.

According to Luke, Paul's concluding kerygma is in continuity with the preaching of the apostles, even as the preceding three parts of the speech are in continuity with the Old Testament and the preaching of the synagogue.

Paul avoided the word *sin* in Athens, and in general his negative statements about temples, cults, and idols are cast in a subdued mood. Instead, he spoke of ignorance of the true God. The Athenians themselves testified to it by their altar inscription as well as by their religious practices. Yet, their ignorance of, as well as their hunch about, God was not just a little deficiency in their knowledge of God which could be made up either by further "groping" (v. 27) or by some additional information. Knowledge of God does not consist in the right kind of information nor in a process of rational deduction. Rather, knowledge of God consists in a right relationship to God and in worship of him. Our proximity to God (vv. 27-28) needs to be lived in faith, obedience, and hope and needs to find expression in worship. God, who related all human beings to himself from the beginning, wills that all relate "rightly" to him and to this end God calls **all men everywhere to repent.** Luke did not speak about faith, obedience, and hope, because repentance is an aspect of each and the entry to all. The urgency of God's call to repentance is undergirded by the judgment to come which will be executed **by one man** (Greek, *en*, "in," as in 28a). His resurrection is God's pledge to all people that the judgment will come, no matter how long it may seem to be delayed (cf. Luke 12:45; 19:11) But the resurrection also marks the beginning of the eschatological proclamation of repentance to all nations (Luke 24:46-47). Where the gospel is being proclaimed, there the times of ignorance are past and the hearers face the **now** of the decision to repent or be rejected. At the beginning there was **one** man from whom the whole human race spread across the face of the earth (v. 26). At the end there shall be another **man** who will hold judgment over all descendants of Adam. The resurrection of Jesus Christ has the same universal dimension as the creation of Adam had.

32-34—Now when they heard of the resurrection of the dead, some mocked. Who needs a resurrection when we already have immortal souls? Others dismissed Paul more politely: **we will hear you again about this** (cf. 24:25). The time for repentance can be missed. But as always, so here, Paul's preaching created faith among members of his audience, **among them Dionysius the Areopagite and a woman named Damaris and others with them.** The response in Athens was divided, but a new church was formed and placed under the leadership of a member of the Areopagus. This poses a historical problem, because Paul wrote that his first converts in Achaia were the household of Stephanas (1 Cor. 16:15). Perhaps when writing to the Corinthians he forgot about Dionysius of Athens.

He almost forgot that he had baptized Stephanas (1 Cor. 1:14-16)! At any rate, from Luke's perspective Paul's stay in Athens was not a failure, even if it did not result in a mass conversion, but only in winning a few people for Christ. In the Areopagus speech Luke gave us an example, not of how his readers should preach, but of how the great missionary Paul spoke to the representatives of Greek culture and philosophy. It was not he who failed that day; it was they who missed their chance for repentance and faith. Luke's readers can take comfort from this. If Paul could not convert the pagan philosophers, then they should not be surprised when their message of the resurrected Lord is also greeted by ridicule. These philosophers are a prime example of seeking God without finding him. Even though God is near to them, they do not achieve knowledge of God and when it is offered to them it is rejected. When Gentiles repent upon hearing the message of God, the Creator of all and of Jesus Christ, the Lord and Judge of all, then in retrospect they realize that they should have known God all along. They should have known that God is the one who gave them life, sustains and surrounds them. In retrospect they know that God has always been near.

Paul's address endeavored to make contact with the wisdom and idolatry of the Greeks through the message of the First Article of the Creed. However, on the crucial matter of the Second Article, the resurrection of Jesus Christ, the contact broke down. Yet the dialog with the wisdom of the world must continue and Luke's Areopagus speech, which followed similar endeavors of Hellenistic Judaism, also remains a call to the church not to overlook the philosophers of their own day.

Mission in Corinth (18:1-17)

He left Athens and went to Corinth. The Corinth of classical times had been destroyed by the Romans in 146 B.C., but Julius Caesar had founded a Roman colony in 46 B.C. in which Italian freedmen, Greeks, people from Asia Minor, and Jews settled. It became the capital of the Roman province Achaia which in A.D. 44 was changed into a senatorial province. Corinth's strategic location on the narrow isthmus which connects the mainland with the Peloponnesian peninsula also gave it access to two seaports. Cenchreae (v. 18) on the

Saronic Gulf received shipping from the Aegean Sea; Lechaeum, on the Gulf of Corinth led to the Ionian Sea and the Adriatic. Since sea voyages around the Peloponnesus were feared in antiquity, cargoes would frequently be unloaded in one port, transported over land, and picked up by a sister ship in the other, or else whole vessels would be dragged on ramps across the three-mile isthmus. Thus, Corinth lay at the center of a north-south and an east-west axis. Its location brought not only trade and affluence, but also a measure of decadence. Its immorality became proverbial: "The voyage to Corinth is not for every man," so the saying went (Strabo 8.6.20). Strabo (early first century A.D.) even claimed that more than 1000 sacred prostitutes had been connected with the temple of Aphrodite. However, Strabo's statement did not refer to the city founded by Julius Caesar, but to classical Corinth. At any rate, there is no evidence that sacred prostitution was practiced in Corinth at Paul's time. Poverty and affluence, cleverness and crude behavior existed side by side. A Greek writer of the late second century A.D., explaining why he did not enter Corinth, said: "I learned in a short time the nauseating behavior of the rich and the misery of the poor" (Alciphron, *Epistles* 3.60). An inscription of a Jewish synagogue and sanctuaries dedicated to Isis, Serapis, and the Mother of the gods have been identified; they testify to the city's cosmopolitan population.

Luke's account of Paul's labors in Corinth differs from the one given for Athens, in which we have a carefully structured single unit with an introduction, a conclusion and a speech in the center. In his report on Corinth Luke merely connected four pieces of information: vv. 1-4, Paul's beginnings in Corinth; vv. 5-8, preaching and separation from the synagogue; vv. 9-11, Paul's vision and decision to remain and teach; vv. 12-17, Gallio's refusal to interfere. These four incidents contain quite a few historical facts, such as the reference to Aquila and Priscilla as coworkers, the edict of Claudius, Paul as artisan gaining his own livelihood, the arrival of Timothy and Silas from Macedonia, the conversion of Crispus, ruler of the synagogue, the duration of the mission, the appearance before Gallio, the beating of Sosthenes, and even the tribunal in the Agora where the proconsul held a hearing. Luke worked over the material available to him, probably cutting it and shaping it in such a way that the Gallio episode and with it the vindication of Christianity become the high point of his story of Paul's mission in Corinth.

341

1-4—Paul stayed with a Jewish couple, **Aquila, a native of Pontus** (a province on the Black Sea coast of Asia Minor) and **his wife Priscilla,** called Prisca in Paul's letters (Rom. 16:3; 1 Cor. 16:19; 2 Tim. 4:19). Their names form an inclusion around Luke's report (cf. v. 18 and, regarding Lydia, 16:14, 40). They had **come from Italy** to Corinth, because the emperor **Claudius** had expelled some Jews from Rome, a fact attested to by Suetonius. Luke exaggerated when he wrote that **all the Jews** had to leave Rome. Acts 28:17 presupposes the existence of a Jewish community in the capital. It would seem that only the "troublemakers" (from the Roman viewpoint) were expelled by Claudius. According to Suetonius, the reason for the expulsion was "disturbances at the instigation of Chrestus" (*Claudius* 25). It has been suggested that Suetonius mistook "Chrestus" for "Christus," Christ, and that the disturbances involved riots between Christians and Jews. Tacitus also called the Christians "Chrestians." The expulsion from Rome probably took place in A.D. 49 and Paul arrived in Corinth some time later, but hardly later than the spring of A.D. 51. **Because he was of the same trade he stayed with** Aquila and Priscilla. **By trade they were tentmakers.** Since neither Acts nor 1 Corinthians mentions that Paul converted Aquila and Priscilla, we can safely suppose that the couple had been Christians actively engaged in mission among Jews before they were forced to leave Rome. Paul's first converts in Corinth were "the household of Stephanas" (1 Cor. 16:15).

Because Paul refused to engage in "charismatic beggin," that is, living off the wealth or charity of his converts, he probably spent most of the week working, from sunrise to sunset and sometimes even longer hours (1 Thess. 2:9), with the exception of the Sabbath. Moreover, he worked as **tentmaker,** a leatherworker, specializing in making tents from leather. There is no evidence that he had followed the later rabbinic ideal, that rabbis should learn a trade and combine the study of the Torah with the practice of a trade. This ideal probably did not exist at Paul's time. Moreover, Paul's profession according to Acts and his letters was not that of a rabbi, though as a Pharisee he had studied under Gamaliel, according to Luke (Acts 22:3). His profession was leatherworker, tentmaker, which like all artisan professions was stigmatized in the Hellenistic world. Paul had no social status. Moreover, since he traveled, he frequently experienced "toil and hardship, . . . hunger and thirst, often without food, in cold and exposure," insufficiently dressed (2 Cor. 11:27) because of lack of funds. He tried to find lodging in houses of church members (e.g., 16:18; 17:5-6) but he contributed from his wages lest he be a burden to anyone and thus a hindrance to the gospel. The apostle to the Gentiles was—in terms of money—a very poor man! He had to save enough to travel only to face anew the problem of finding work and lodging. In Corinth he struck up a friendship with the Jewish-Christian couple in whose home he stayed and to whom he paid a lasting tribute in Rom. 16:3-4. With Aquila he worked day by day cutting leather, stitching seams in some workshop and, as occasions arose, speaking to fellow workers or to customers about God, Christ, and the Holy Spirit. Even in Corinth Paul "was in want" (2 Cor. 11:9). **And he argued in the synagogue every sabbath, and persuaded Jews and Greeks.** The last clause could also be translated: "he tried to persuade" both groups, without indicating success or failure. At any rate, he preached to them for a period of several Sabbaths.

5-8—When Silas and Timothy arrived from Macedonia the evangelization of the Jews was intensified, and Paul became wholly **occupied with preaching** to Jews. Financial contributions from Macedonia transmitted by his coworkers enabled him temporarily to leave the workshop and preach full-time. Luke did not tell us the reason for this change, but on the basis of Phil. 4:15 and 2 Cor. 11:8-9 we may conclude that for a limited period the monetary needs of Paul and his coworkers were met by the gift from the Macedonian churches. Still, 1 Cor. 4:12 shows that normally he toiled in a workshop, "working with [his] own hands." The content of his preaching to Jews is summarized with the statement: the Messiah, **the Christ was** (and is) **Jesus** (cf. 17:3; 18:28; 9:20, 22; 13:16-41). Although Luke kept the spotlight on Paul, the reader knows that by now five persons, including Priscilla (v. 26), are engaged in mission.

The intensified proclamation met resistance from the Jews who **opposed and reviled** Paul. In response to their negative reaction he performed a symbolic act and **shook out his garments,** which signified the breaking off of fellowship (cf. Neh. 5:13; Acts 13:51), and he interpreted his action saying, **Your blood be upon your heads!** He had fulfilled his responsibility as servant of the Lord and therefore is **innocent** of their unbelief. **Blood** here is a metaphor for guilt (Matt. 27:25) and it is up to God to pass judgment. **From now on**

I will go to the Gentiles. The separation from the synagogue meant that he would no longer preach there. Therefore, he went next door **to the house of a man named Titius Justus.** This Gentile **worshiper of God** offered space for the first house church in Corinth and that is why Luke remembered his name. Contrary to the Western text, Paul did not leave his lodging with Aquila and Priscilla, but continued to stay with them. Surprisingly, we now hear of the conversion of the ruler of the synagogue, named **Crispus,** and of **all his household** (cf. 16:15, 33-34). From 1 Cor. 1:14 we know that Crispus was one of the few Corinthian Christians whom Paul himself had baptized. Crispus's conversion in turn affected **many of the Corinthians,** that is, many Jews and Gentiles who had some relations with the synagogue. They also **believed and were baptized.**

It is possible that Luke transposed the conversion of Crispus to the end of this brief scene in order to highlight the break with the synagogue (v. 6). If so, the historical sequence might have been as follows: (1) Crispus gave permission for Paul to speak on each Sabbath for a longer period. (2) Crispus himself was converted by Paul, which in turn affected many God-fearing Gentiles. (3) The growing opposition forced Paul and the Jewish and Gentile believers to move to the house of Titius Justus.

9-10—This scene comes quite unexpectedly after the note about the success. **The Lord** Jesus appeared to Paul **one night in a vision,** and said in a stereotyped formula typical of epiphanies and commissionings: **Do not be afraid.** Paul himself later wrote: "I was with you in weakness and in much fear and trembling" (1 Cor. 2:3). Instead of indulging in fear, Paul is commanded **to speak and . . . not be silent** (cf. 4:29; 5:20). The reason for such boldness which overcomes fear is: **I am with you** (cf. Josh. 1:9; Isa. 41:10; 43:5; Jer. 1:8; Matt. 28:20; Luke 1:28, 66; Acts 7:9; 10:38). This last phrase places Paul in continuity with the Old Testament servants of God, with Mary, and with Jesus, the Servant. The consequence of Christ's presence with Paul is that **no man shall attack you to harm you.** Therefore, speak and continue speaking! A second reason for bold proclamation is: **I have many people in this city.** The structure of this commission is: *a b a b a b,* with *b* giving the positive command and the reasons: **Speak . . . for I am with you,** for "the people in this city that belongs to me is large." Instead of **many people** (RSV), where one would think of individuals, the Greek text has the singular (*laos*). The exalted Lord has decided to gather a large people in Corinth. As in 15:14, so here the **people** means the people of God, the church, which God or Christ gathers for his name from among the Gentiles. Having received this divine directive, Paul knows that he has to stay longer than usual and **he stayed a year and six months, teaching.**

The purpose of the vision is (1) to give personal encouragement to Paul; (2) to highlight the importance of the church in Corinth; (3) to prepare for the next scene; (4) to indicate a divine mandate for the unusual duration of Paul's mission in that city and (5) to confirm Christ's promise at Paul's call (cf. 9:15; 13:47). Paul's mission is under the direction of the Lord who called him and chose him to be his instrument, and nothing on earth can thwart that mission, as the following episode illustrates. It was not necessary for Luke to report further mission success, for the reader knows that the Lord fulfilled his promise. **Preaching** aims at conversion, faith, and Baptism. **Teaching** is the instruction of the people of God in Scripture and the apostolic tradition.

12-17—The danger to which the Lord indirectly referred in the night vision also came true, when **Jews made a united attack upon Paul and brought him before the tribunal** of the proconsul. Paul's preservation in the proceedings before Gallio appears as fulfillment of the Lord's promise that no harm shall befall him (v. 10). But this scene contains two additional points: (1) The repudiation of Paul and his mission by Corinthian Jews (v. 6) now intensifies as the synagogue calls upon the secular authorities to suppress the Christian movement. (2) The authority of Rome represented by its proconsul refused to be drawn into a religious dispute and by rejecting the Jewish complaint it granted a legal victory to Paul and his cause. Since **Gallio's** action constituted the high point of the mission story in Corinth, Luke moved the episode toward the end of the period of Paul's stay in that city, though the incident may have happened shortly after his separation from the synagogue. The topic of Roman-Christian relations will be taken up in the defense speeches of the last part of Acts, but the reader already knows that in Achaia Paul was not viewed as a menace to Roman law and order.

12—**But when Gallio was proconsul of Achaia**—when was that? Nine fragments of a stone bearing a rescript of Emperor Claudius were found in Delphi, Greece, and are located in its museum. The inscription mentions Gallio's name and proconsulship and the 26th acclamation of Claudius as emperor. On the basis of other inscriptions and available data of Claudius's history, scholars have deduced that the 26th acclamation fell between January 25 and August 1, A.D. 52. Consequently, the inscription itself falls within that period. Therefore, the latest possible date for Gallio's entry into his one-year office as proconsul of Achaia would be July 1, A.D. 52. However, dating Gallio's entry into office on July 1, A.D. 52 would leave only one month for Gallio to hear the case involving the city of Delphi, make his decision, and report to Claudius, and for the emperor to send his rescript before his 27th acclamation occurred. The time span is too short for the time it takes bureaucratic wheels to turn. Therefore, the general consensus has opted for Gallio's assumption of the office of proconsul on or shortly prior to July 1, A.D. 51 and his holding it for one year, till June A.D. 52.

Gallio's tenure provides the most important date for a chronology of Paul's life. Paul appeared before the tribunal in Corinth during his proconsulship. Unfortunately, Acts gives no indication whether the hearing before Gallio occurred at the beginning, the middle, or the end of his one-year term of office. Luke reported that Paul was not forced to leave Corinth, but stayed "many days longer" (v. 18a), but we still do not know how the 18 months of Paul's mission in Corinth relate to Gallio's tenure. Two observations help us to arrive at an approximate date. (1) Travel by sea was not possible from late October to mid-March. Thus, for instance, Paul could not have arrived in Corinth in the summer, stayed 18 months, and left by boat for Ephesus (v. 18a). (2) In all probability Aquila and Priscilla were expelled from Rome in A.D. 49 (cf. v. 2). They had to move to Corinth, settle, and find work—all of which takes time. It would seem most likely that Paul arrived in Corinth in the fall of A.D. 50 and left for Ephesus in the spring of A.D. 52, or else that he arrived in the spring of A.D. 51 and left in the fall of 52. A later date for the Corinthian ministry forces us to press too many subsequent events into too short a time span and an earlier date, such as Paul's arrival in Corinth in the spring of A.D. 50, demands that we press the second mission journey into a period of one year or less. In the light of Gal. 2:11-14 and Acts 15:35,39 it would seem that Paul left

Antioch at the earliest in the spring of A.D. 49, and in the light of
Acts 16–18 it would seem that he came to Corinth at the earliest in
the fall of A.D. 50.

Who was **Gallio**? His name originally was Marcus Annaeus No-
vatus. He was born in Cordova, Spain, the son of the Spanish orator
Marcus Annaeus Seneca, who moved to Rome with his sons. Our
proconsul was adopted by a wealthy benefactor by the name of
Lucius Junius Gallio, whose name he thereafter bore. His full name
was Junius Annaeus Gallio. When his younger brother, the philos-
opher Seneca, was asked by Nero's mother, Agrippina, to take charge
of Nero's education, he was most eager to comply. Seneca, in turn,
was influential in getting Gallio the office of consul in Rome in A.D.
50, and of proconsul of Achaia, probably in A.D. 51. When Nero
became emperor (A.D. 54) Seneca was one of the most influential
persons in the empire, until Nero ordered him to commit suicide
(ca. A.D. 65), a fate which also befell Gallio a little later.

13-16—At some time between the summers of A.D. 51 and 52
Paul was brought before Gallio's **tribunal** in Corinth, which has been
excavated by the American School of Classical Studies, Athens. Set
on the south side of the Agora, the tribunal was a raised marble
platform that served as the proconsul's judgment seat for official
hearings. The Jews accused Paul, **saying, "This man is persuading
men to worship God contrary to the law."** The accusation itself is
ambiguous. Does it refer to the Roman law or to the Jewish law?
Obviously, the accusers hoped that Gallio would pass judgment on
Paul because of violations of Roman law. But Rome did not have a
law proscribing Christianity, and Gallio knew that. Just when Paul
was ready to speak in his own defense, Gallio cut him short and
addressed the Jews. In direct discourse we hear him say what is all-
important to Luke and his readers: **If it were a matter of wrongdoing
or vicious crime, I should have reason to bear with you, O Jews;
but since it is a matter of questions about words and names and
your own law, see to it yourselves; I refuse to be a judge of these
things.** Caesar's representative has openly confessed that he is incompetent to serve as judge in theological disputes between Christians and Jews. How much Luke would have liked all imperial magistrates to act according to Gallio's example! Religious questions do
not fall into the sphere of competence of secular powers. Similarly,
Luke would also have liked Jews to refrain from accusing Christians

347

before pagan courts. Not all Jews in Acts are depicted as are those of Corinth or Thessalonica. In Philippi, Beroea, and Athens the difficulties Paul experienced were not caused by Jews or sympathizers. Finally, Luke did not claim for the church any of the privileges which Rome had granted to Judaism (quite a few Lukan interpreters would disagree with this observation). There is not a sentence in Luke-Acts which supports the notion that the aim of the author was to gain Roman recognition at the expense of Judaism. The idea of *religio licita*, of a licensed religion, did not exist in the first-century Roman empire, no matter how often it is repeated in books and articles. Luke hoped for toleration of the church by the empire, that is, for a general acceptance of the verdict and attitude represented by Gallio. Wrongdoings and crimes were subject to Roman law, matters of faith were not. **And he drove them from the tribunal,** that is, Gallio dismissed the Jews.

17—The concluding verse strikes a bizarre note. **And they all seized Sosthenes, the ruler of the synagogue, and beat him in front of the tribunal. But Gallio paid no attention to this.** There was a principle in Roman law that the false accuser would be punished with the punishment that would have fallen on the accused if the accusation had been proven to be true. But this principle does not apply here, since a mob action occurred. Did Luke merely wish to indicate that Paul's Jewish opponents in Corinth suffered total humiliation when their spokesman Sosthenes, leader of the synagogue, colleague or successor to Crispus (v. 8), was beaten by a pagan mob? While Luke commended Gallio for his indifference to religious matters, does he also commend him for his indifference to the breakdown of law and order right **in front of the tribunal?** Or does not Luke also indicate that what happened to Sosthenes today can happen to Christians tomorrow? Law and order are imperfect, even with the best of Roman magistrates!

Other interpreters have supposed that Sosthenes was beaten up by Jews, because he, being a sympathizer of Paul and identical with the person so named in 1 Cor. 1:1, did not present the Jewish case against Paul effectively. But this was hardly Luke's view! If the pre-Lukan tradition regarded Sosthenes as a Christian, then it would have been he and not Paul who was brought in front of Gallio's tribunal. In that case it was Luke who substituted Paul for Sosthenes, because Luke wanted to keep the spotlight on Paul. In short, the tradition would have told of Sosthenes' appearance before Gallio, and this episode would have taken place after Paul's departure from Corinth, making the tenure of Gallio less important for Pauline chronology. In view of the other historical data in this section, which are verifiable, it would appear that Luke did not substitute Paul's name for that of Sosthenes in vv. 12-16.

Mission in Ephesus (18:18—19:41)

The last part of the story of Paul as missionary is located in Ephesus and covers a period of three years (cf. 20:31). Paul reached Ephesus by boat, and, according to Acts, he returned to it after his fourth visit to Jerusalem and a lengthy journey via Antioch, Galatia, and Phrygia. In this section we meet religious oddities—Apollos who lacked Christian Baptism but taught accurately, yet needed further instruction; disciples of John the Baptist who had never heard of the Holy Spirit; Jewish exorcists who pronounced the name of Jesus, but were not believers; and believers who practiced magical arts and had not really broken with their pagan past. But through Paul "the word of the Lord grew and prevailed mightily" (19:20) and "all the residents of Asia heard the word of the Lord, both Jews and Greeks" (19:10). The Ephesian ministry concludes with the riot of Demetrius. Just before the riot broke out, Paul announced that he must travel to Jerusalem and then to Rome (19:21). This decision determined the events of the two remaining parts of Acts (20:1—21:14; 21:15—28:28) and tied them to the narrative of his mission.

Luke told the story of Paul's mission in western Asia Minor and Ephesus, not by producing a tightly structured unified account, but by connecting a conglomeration of colorful incidents and by using travel summaries and progress-report summaries. Traditional material which Luke worked over included the preaching of Apollos, the Baptism of the disciples of John, Paul's teaching in the hall of Tyrannus, the Jewish exorcists, and the riot at Ephesus.

18-23—This brief travel summary bristles with problems, which we shall discuss one at a time. Luke's opening sentence indicates that Paul was not expelled from Corinth, which is also a point of his Gallio story. The note that Paul stayed **many days longer** may give the reader the impression that the hearing before Gallio took place some months before Paul left Corinth, that is, toward the end of Paul's stay. After all, it is the last episode of Paul in Corinth. But on the other hand, v. 12 might suggest that the hearing took place

349

shortly after Gallio's arrival. With a change of administration Paul's opponents might have hoped they could further their cause.

Paul sailed for Syria (v. 18), but in fact he landed in **Ephesus,** Asia Minor, and later in Caesarea Maritima. To be sure, Judea belonged to the Roman province of Syria, but the geographic designation **Syria** is still odd and has given rise to all sorts of speculations, e.g., that Paul wanted to visit Antioch, Syria, but could not find a boat, or that the northerly wind prevented the ship from reaching Seleucia, the port of Antioch.

Paul sailed from Corinth in the company of **Priscilla** and her husband. She is mentioned first also in v. 26 (Rom. 16:3) because she was the more active church worker (cf. Phoebe, a woman deacon [Greek, *diakonos*], in nearby Cenchreae, Rom. 16:1). This couple put themselves at the disposal of the gospel mission and of Paul. It is frequently stated that they were financially independent and well off. This, however, is probably false, for otherwise Paul could not have referred to his want during his stay in Corinth (2 Cor. 11:9a). They shared their poverty with Paul, and he and Aquila worked as tentmakers during the week. Though Luke does not tell us, we may assume that Paul also lodged with them in Ephesus. Neither is it stated whether Silas and Timothy accompanied Paul. The last we heard of them was their return from Macedonia (v. 5). Timothy probably went with them, for we find him later in Paul's company (20:4). Perhaps Silas remained in Corinth. Before sailing to Ephesus Paul **cut his hair** at Cenchreae, Corinth's eastern seaport (cf. Rom. 16:1) because **he had a vow.** Some Latin manuscripts have Aquila as subject and still others read that Aquila and Priscilla cut their hair. Undoubtedly, only Paul was involved! But which vow was meant? Only a Nazirite vow involved the cutting of hair. Thus, the cutting of Paul's hair might have suggested to Luke that Paul had made a temporary Nazirite vow. But the ceremony of shaving one's head and offering the hair as a sacrifice to God was permitted only in the temple of Jerusalem—and not in Cenchreae (21:23-26; Num. 6:1-12; tractate *Nazir* in the Mishnah). In short, Luke probably made a mistake, because he no longer knew the details of a Nazirite vow. If Paul had made a Nazirite vow in Cenchreae in thanksgiving to God, he would not have shaved his head, but refrained from cutting his hair and abstained from alcoholic drink and other items until he had spent 30 days in Jerusalem and presented himself for the completion of his vow in the temple. While Luke shows some confusion in this matter, his point is that Paul was a pious Jew who observed the customs of the fathers also as a Christian missionary.

19-21—The note that Paul **left them** (Priscilla and her husband) **there** in Ephesus, while **he himself went into the synagogue** is also odd, for we find the couple in the Ephesian synagogue later (v. 26). But Luke's purpose was to indicate that (1) the first Christian preacher in Ephesus was Paul, not Apollos or someone else; and that (2) whenever Paul entered a city as missionary, he, the "light for the Gentiles," must first preach to Jews. Paul's preaching (in dialog form; RSV, he **argued**) in the Ephesian synagogue clearly demonstrates that his dramatic separation and pronouncement in Corinth (vv. 6-7) were not directed against Judaism as a whole but only against the synagogue in Corinth. In Acts Paul does not turn his back on Judaism! Therefore, immediately after Corinth he entered the synagogue in Ephesus and received a favorable reception. **They asked him to stay for a longer period.** Thus "a door was opened" in this city (cf. 14:27), famous for its temple of Artemis (Latin, *Diana*), one of the seven wonders of the ancient world, famous also for its commerce and wealth. It was the most important city of Asia Minor and its ruins are impressive still today. In Luke's narrative, Paul, however, had other plans and, promising to return **if God wills** (Plato, *Alcibiades* 1.135 D; James 4:15; 1 Cor. 16:7), **sailing from Ephesus.**

22-23—The travel summary in these two verses describes a journey of more than 2000 miles, and raises two questions: (1) What was Luke's purpose in telling it? (2) Did this journey actually take place? Regarding the first question we note that every major section in Acts is connected with Jerusalem, the church's place of origin and symbol of its salvation historical continuity. According to Luke Paul's great mission has to be connected with Jerusalem, and therefore upon landing in **Caesarea, he went up and greeted the church** in Jerusalem. Luke did not even have to mention its name. **The church** and **went up** can refer only to Jerusalem's Christian community, which had preeminence over all churches. To be related to this church was to be part of the people of God. Then he touched base with the church in **Antioch,** for Luke did not wish to suggest that Paul's quarrel with Barnabas (15:36-40; Gal. 2:11-14) had led to a permanent separation. After some time there he revisited the churches in Asia Minor **from place to place through the region of**

Galatia and Phrygia. Clearly Luke thought of two different regions, not of one (see 16:6), and meant by Galatia probably the "north Galatian" region. Even though Paul did not engage in extensive mission there (16:6) we now hear of **disciples** and thus of churches which he strengthened on this return visit. Apparently, Luke knew of Galatian churches, but either he was not well informed about them, or did not want to write more than this brief reference.

Turning to the second question, concerning the historicity of this journey, we face several options. (1) We can conclude on the basis of Paul's letters that as apostle he did not make five visits to Jerusalem, as Acts tells us, but only three (Gal. 1:18 = Acts 9:26; Gal. 2:1 = Acts 15; Rom. 15:25 = Acts 21:17). This summary statement in Acts 18:22-23 would then appear to be a Lukan construction, made to assure Paul's Jerusalem connection, but without any basis in history. Perhaps Luke had two traditions referring to the same visit, namely, Paul's last (Acts 21:17), and thought that two visits to Jerusalem were involved. If so, Luke had to get Paul back from Jerusalem to Ephesus. A stop at Antioch would be appreciated by Luke's reader, and 16:6 provided the language for 18:23b.

(2) Another option would be to connect the apostles' conference of Gal. 2:1-10 with the visit of Acts 18:22 (see above, Introduction to Acts 15). This hypothesis creates more problems than it solves. Contrary to Acts, Paul's great mission without Barnabas would have taken place prior to the apostles' conference, and the story of Acts 15 would have to be transposed to 18:22. Moreover, we would have to suppose that Paul forgot to mention that he "went" also into the regions of Galatia, Macedonia, and Achaia when he wrote Gal. 1:21. Finally, there is the matter of Barnabas and Gal. 2:1, which clearly states that Paul and Barnabas went up to Jerusalem together, taking Titus along. However, Paul's ship in 18:22 did not land in Seleucia/ Antioch, but in Caesarea. Of course, one could suppose that Barnabas and Titus somehow knew that and met him there.

(3) Finally, we could also accept the Lukan report as it stands, realizing that our knowledge of Paul's mission and movements contains large gaps, e.g., when and where he worked in Illyricum (Rom. 15:19). However, it would be difficult to fit this lengthy, time-consuming journey of Acts 18:21-23 into our chronology of Paul, remembering that travel by sea or crossing the Taurus mountains was not possible from November to mid-March, and dangerous in the

month before or after. It would be equally difficult to find a reason for a visit of Paul to Jerusalem. The collection had not yet been completed and Paul was eager to go to Rome (Rom. 1:13; 15:22). Nevertheless, this third option cannot simply be dismissed. Some commentators support it by a reference to Gal. 4:13, where Paul wrote: "You know that it was because of a bodily ailment that I preached the gospel to you at first." "At first" (Greek, *to proteron*) could imply that Paul was with the Galatians twice before writing his letter (e.g., Acts 16:6 and 18:23). But Betz in his commentary on Galatians has shown that only one visit by Paul can be inferred from Gal. 4:13. So, among the three options, this interpreter would choose the first. Luke, it would seem, created this journey to Jerusalem in order to tell the reader that Paul always had a good relationship with the great church in Jerusalem.

24-28—Apollos: Luke bridged the absence of Paul from Ephesus with notes about Apollos and the beginnings of the Ephesian church. Some interpreters thought that the pre-Lukan tradition told of Apollos's conversion through Priscilla and Aquila, because Apollos is designated "a Jew" and not a brother. However, in 10:28; 18:2; 21:39; and 22:3 the word *Jew* refers to Christian Jews, even as the word *brother* can refer to fellow Jews who are not yet members of the church, but are confronted with the gospel (e.g., 2:29; 3:17; 7:2; 13:26; etc.). Luke probably had a report about a Jewish-Christian missionary, Apollos, who worked on Paul's turf. Luke added to the report the last clause of v. 25 ("though he knew only the baptism of John") and all of v. 26. Through these additions the Lukan Apollos became an anomaly, a "sectarian" Christian who needed further instruction. Paul's good friends, Priscilla and her husband, obliged, and taught him **more accurately.** Now, as a good Paulinist, Apollos received a letter of recommendation from the church and went to Achaia. Indeed, Apollos came to Corinth (1 Cor. 1:12; 3:4-9, 22), but at the time of the writing of 1 Corinthians he was apparently back in Ephesus (1 Cor. 16:12).

24-25—During Paul's absence from Ephesus **a Jew named Apollos, a native of Alexandria,** began a Christian mission in the synagogue of Ephesus. He is characterized as **an eloquent man,** or learned person (the opposite of 4:13), **well versed in the scriptures.** Alexandria in Egypt was the home of the great Jewish philosopher-theologian and Bible interpreter Philo. Whether Apollos became a

Christian in Alexandria is unknown. In addition to his eloquence and knowledge of the Scripture we hear that he **had been instructed in the way of the Lord** (cf. Deut. 5:33; Jer. 7:23; 1QS viii.13-14; Acts 16:17), he was **fervent in spirit** (cf. Rom. 12:7; Acts 6:3), **and taught accurately the things concerning Jesus.** In short, Apollos is presented as a model Christian teacher. Unexpectedly, we hear that **he knew only the baptism of John.** What kind of a Christian was this Apollos—from Luke's point of view? What did Luke think Apollos was teaching "accurately" **concerning Jesus?** Luke knew the "Q" material (material common to Matthew and Luke but absent in Mark) which may have circulated in and been transmitted by distinct early Christian communities. If so, Luke may have pictured Apollos as a missionary of the "Q" communities, transmitting the teachings of Jesus as found in "Q." Like "Q" he would have emphasized the baptism of John and the Holy Spirit (Luke 3:7-9; 15-17; 7:24-30; 12:10-12) and the ethical and eschatological sayings of Jesus. Like "Q" he may have lacked the kerygma of the death, resurrection, and exaltation of Jesus, the Messiah. The title *Messiah* does not occur in "Q." At any rate, according to Luke his teaching as a whole was deficient, even though what he taught about Jesus was accurate, as far as it went.

26-28—When Priscilla and her husband **heard him** in the synagogue, they took him and privately instructed him. They **expounded to him the way of God more accurately.** They taught him "the whole counsel of God" (20:27), as they had heard it from Paul. Thus they helped him overcome his lopsided, deficient content of preaching. In short, Apollos entered the mainstream of Christianity which had its foundation in and its tradition originating from Jerusalem. Oddly, Luke does not say that Apollos was subsequently baptized in the name of Jesus (cf. 19:5; 10:44-48). Did Luke want the reader to conclude that Apollos was baptized because he had now been instructed fully and "more accurately"? Or did Luke think that because Apollos had received the Spirit he did not need to be baptized with water (but see 10:44-48)? Were the Lukan apostles and Easter disciples, who apparently underwent John's baptism, baptized in the name of Jesus after they received the Spirit at Pentecost? Perhaps Luke himself did not know the answer to this question and therefore left the matter as is. Should we assume that Apollos lacked not only Christian Baptism but also the gift of the Holy Spirit mediated by it (2:38)? Then "fervent in spirit" would not indicate the effect of the Holy Spirit but merely his vivaciousness. In that case it would be incomprehensible why Luke omitted a reference to Apollos's Baptism in the name of Jesus (cf. 19:1-7). In an aside we learn that a Christian community existed within the context of the synagogue of Ephesus. **The brethren encouraged** Apollos (so RSV), or probably they encouraged the disciples in Achaia to receive him, and to this end wrote a letter of recommendation on his behalf (cf. 2 Cor. 3:1; Rom. 16:1). On his arrival in Corinth he showed his eloquence and skill by thoroughly refuting **Jews in public.** After the separation from the synagogue in Corinth (v. 6), Christians could no longer preach there. But outside of the synagogue Apollos found ample opportunity to speak and argue with Jews, **showing by the scriptures that the Christ was Jesus** (cf. v. 5; 17:3; 9:22; Luke 24:44-46). In so doing **he greatly helped those who through grace had believed.** Faith and salvation are related to grace (cf. 15:11). In short, Apollos now preaches the same message as Paul and Peter. Priscilla did a good job, and we will hear no more of this in Acts (but see Rom. 16:3-4).

According to Luke's point of view Apollos was an independent Jewish-Christian missionary who proclaimed a defective message. But through Paul's friends he received further instruction, which he accepted. Thereby he is incorporated into the Pauline mission and enters Corinth (19:1) with the blessing of Paul's coworkers. The doctrinal unity of the church is preserved. When we turn to the historical question concerning Apollos's identity and message we enter the realm of conjecture. Luther suggested that the Epistle to the Hebrews might have been written by Apollos. That is not a bad suggestion, considering its proximity to Philo's hermeneutics. Luke may have heard that there was something wrong with Apollos and, on the basis of 1 Cor. 1:12; 3:4, we can at least conclude that Apollos, who entered a Pauline congregation without Paul's permission, contributed to the party strife in Corinth. In 1 Corinthians Paul leans over backwards in acknowledging the validity of Apollos's ministry (1 Cor. 3:6, 22) and Apollos's independence from the apostle. Yet Paul's guarded attitude toward Apollos cannot be missed either, especially if 1 Cor. 2:1-5 contrasts Paul's style and message with that of Apollos. Acts 18:24-27 would permit us to conclude that it was Apollos, and not Paul, who established the first Christian community within the context of the synagogue in Ephesus.

19:1-7 (The disciples of John at Ephesus)—A period of about two years would have intervened before Paul returned to Ephesus, provided the journey of 18:22-23 took place at all (see above). In Ephesus he remained a minimum of two years (v. 10) and three months (v. 8; cf. 20:31, perhaps three years, but part of a year may be counted as a year). In Acts the Ephesian ministry marks the glorious conclusion of Paul's missionary activity. Luke did not tell us that Paul wrote several letters from Ephesus: probably Galatians and Philippians, certainly the "previous" letter which is lost (1 Cor. 5:9), 1 Corinthians, and parts of what is now 2 Corinthians. He also omitted a description of Paul's difficulties with the church in Corinth which necessitated a brief return visit (2 Cor. 2:1-2) and the sending of Timothy and Titus (1 Cor. 16:10; 2 Cor. 12:18). Moreover, Paul experienced severe affliction and dangers during his stay in Ephesus. Reflecting on them, he wrote: "we were so utterly, unbearably crushed that we despaired of life itself" (2 Cor. 1:8). "I fought with beasts at Ephesus" (1 Cor. 15:32; cf. 16:9). This should not be understood literally, for Paul would have lost his Roman citizenship had he been condemned to fight with beasts in the theater (see Acts 22:25). Luke, however, is silent about the grave internal and external difficulties of Paul's Ephesian ministry. Instead, his story sets the church off from syncretism, magic, and folk religion (vv. 13-20), the synagogue, and from deficient forms of Christianity (vv. 1-7, 18). Apollos, as well as the Ephesian disciples, knew only the baptism of John.

In Luke's composition, John's baptism connects this story with the previous one (v. 3; cf. 18:25) and enables Luke to speak about two forms of Christianity that manifest deficiencies—one in terms of knowledge of tradition (Apollos) and the other, in addition to lack of knowledge, lack of experience of the Holy Spirit (the Ephesian disciples).

1-3—Luke connected the following episode with Paul's journey (18:23), with his promise to return (18:21), and with Apollos's departure (18:27). In Ephesus **he found some disciples.** The reader would naturally think that these disciples were Christians (cf. 6:1, 2, 7; 9:1, 10, 25, 26, 38; 11:26, 29), but this designation merely represents a first impression. They appear to be disciples and may even call themselves disciples, but Paul will find out what kind of disciples they really were. He asked them: **Did you receive the**

Holy Spirit when you believed? "Any one who does not have the Spirit of Christ, does not belong to him" (Rom. 8:9; 1 Cor. 12:3). Luke and Paul wholeheartedly agree on this point. In place of **when you believed** Luke could have written "when you became disciples," or "when you were baptized," or "when you first confessed the faith that Jesus is Lord." It expresses the objective act of becoming a Christian, not the subjective state of an individual's faith (cf. 2:44; 4:32; 15:5). The disciples in turn replied to Paul: **No, we have never even heard that there is a Holy Spirit.** With this answer they revealed that Paul's and the reader's first impression, the outsider's view, and their own self-designation were false. These "disciples" never came to faith. They were ignorant about the Holy Spirit, not just about the Spirit's coming on Pentecost, but about the Spirit's existence. Yet, although John the Baptist had announced the Spirit's coming (Luke 3:16), these "disciples" had never heard of it because they had lost their roots. In short, they were not disciples of Jesus, and their deficiency was far more serious than Apollos's had been. Since Christian Baptism and the gift of the Holy Spirit are interrelated (2:38) Paul now asked the decisive question: **Into what then were you baptized?** Notice: "into what," not "into whom." Paul realized that since they were without the Spirit there must be something wrong with their baptism.

For a disciple of Jesus, Baptism can only be "in the name of Jesus" (2:38). With an odd formulation these Ephesian "disciples" answer that they were baptized **into John's baptism.** They avoid saying that their baptism was "in the name of John," but it becomes obvious that they no longer understood the meaning of John's baptism either. By their answers they demonstrated that they were not Christian disciples but syncretists, people who swallowed a concoction of diverse beliefs. They thought that they were disciples of the Baptist but they were no longer in continuity with the tradition of the Baptist. They missed the mission and message of John, "the prophet of the Most High," who was destined to "go before the Lord to prepare his way" (Luke 1:76). Had they preserved the message of John they would have been baptized in the name of Jesus and received the gift of the Spirit.

4-7—Paul now proclaims what they should have known as disciples of John, but did not, because they had forgotten their tradition and become syncretistic. Paul's instruction elaborates the relation-

ship between John and Jesus which Luke had delineated in his first
volume (cf. Acts 13:24-25). It was **John** who told the people **to believe
in the one who was to come after him, that is, Jesus.** That was the
meaning of his **baptism of repentance.** Repentance sealed by baptism should lead to faith in the coming one, whom Paul proclaims
is **Jesus.** The reader knows that at this point Paul will bring a summary of the life, death, and resurrection of Jesus (cf. 13:26-35). After
hearing Paul, the Ephesian disciples **were baptized in the name of
the Lord Jesus.** It was not a rebaptism, for after Easter and Pentecost
there is but one Baptism and one faith in one Lord (Eph. 4:5). The
imposition of hands in connection with Baptism reflects the liturgical
practice of Luke's church. Baptism mediates the gift of the Holy
Spirit, whose manifestation in this episode was speaking in **tongues**
and in prophecy (cf. 2:17-18). Speaking in (or with) tongues does
not refer to the miracle of speaking in foreign intelligible languages
(cf. 2:6-11), but to glossolalia (cf. 10:46). The miracle of the first
Pentecost in Jerusalem can no more be repeated than the incarnation
and the resurrection. For the sake of the reader Luke depicts the
reality of the Spirit's coming in the audible force of glossolalia. But
he also adds that these disciples **prophesied.** They were not only
incorporated into the eschatological people of God through Baptism
and the gift of the Spirit, but they would also function as preachers,
missionaries, and coworkers of Paul. That **there were about twelve
of them in all** indicates a tremendous growth of additional participants in mission. Finally, Luke also draws a parallel between Peter
and Paul. Just as Peter and John were the human instruments
through which God incorporated the Samaritans, semi-Jews, into
the one people of God through the gift of the Holy Spirit (8:14-17),
so Paul led syncretistic followers of the Baptist into the people of
God in Ephesus.

Thus far Luke's point of view. Now we turn briefly to some historical matters. It is hard to imagine that at Paul's time there existed
a Baptist group which did not claim to possess the Spirit of God,
as, for instance, the Qumran community had claimed, and it is even
harder to imagine that such a group had never heard about the
existence of the Holy Spirit. Whatever information about this group
was available to Luke he thoroughly rewrote to fit his purposes.
What was it? In addition to items already mentioned (e.g., the Peter-
Paul parallel) we note that the church in the province of Asia was

threatened by heresy at Luke's time (20:29-30; Revelation 1–3; Pastoral Epistles, letters of Ignatius). With his account of Apollos, Luke showed his church how to deal with deficient forms of Christianity, namely, not to shout "heresy!" every time one encounters doctrinal deficiencies, but to offer private instruction, as Paul's coworkers had done in the case of Apollos. Moreover, the Lukan church should also engage sectarian, syncretistic groups which have the outward appearance of being Christian but have lost the Christian substance, the tradition. (1) They should be "found," and their identity should be uncovered by asking questions. (2) They should receive further instruction in accordance with the Lukan tradition contained in his two-volume mini-canon. (3) Their baptism is invalid, for it does not mediate the Spirit which controls the one church and its tradition. (4) They should be incorporated into the church through Baptism, and simultaneously their specific gifts of the Spirit, including prophecy, should be acknowledged. There are no second-rate members in the church. (5) Should syncretists reject and continue to "speak evil" of the Christian message, in contrast to the Ephesian disciples, Luke's subsequent pericope supplies the direction which the church's response should take, that is, separation from them, even as Paul separated from the synagogue in Ephesus.

An inquiry into the "historical" disciples of John inevitably leads into the realm of hypotheses, of which some are more plausible than others, though all are relative. It would indeed appear that followers of John lived in western Asia Minor. If the Fourth Gospel had been written in Ephesus, it would corroborate the existence of such groups in that region, because one of its thrusts is directed against an overevaluation of John the Baptist by his disciples. They may have moved to Asia Minor at or shortly before the outbreak of war in A.D. 66, and were probably led by 12 prophets, the leaders of the true Israel. They probably practiced an eschatological sacrament of baptism and transmitted apocalyptic traditions originating with the Baptist. These traditions may have been similar to or even identical with those found in Revelation 4–11, where the name *Jesus* does not even occur. They awaited the apocalyptic judgment of God and a baptism "with fire" by the coming one, of whom John had spoken. A relationship between "converted" followers of John the Baptist in Asia Minor and the Book of Revelation which originated in geographic proximity is quite possible, but also remains hypothetical.

8-10—Into this and the following scene Luke brings the climactic conclusion of Paul's missionary activity and shows Paul's tremendous success. Through Paul, the church in Ephesus, and therefore Christianity itself, has withstood Jewish rejection, overcome religious competitors and become a threat to the economic greed connected with pagan cults. The lessons which Luke wished his readers to learn will be summarized when we reach the end of chap. 19.

For the last time in Acts Paul **entered the synagogue** and carried on his ministry to Jews **for three months,** which is quite a long time compared with his work in other cities (cf. 17:2; 18:19-20). Three Greek verbs describe his activity in the Ephesian synagogue. The main verb indicates he **spoke boldly.** Boldness of speech, saying all that needs to be said, is an effect of the Holy Spirit (cf. 4:29-31). The form of his bold speech was **arguing.** A better translation would be "discussing, lecturing and answering questions" (cf. 17:2, 17; 18:4, 19; 19:8, 9; 20:7, 9; 24:12, 25). The aim of his bold speech was **pleading** with (better: "trying to convince") the Jews **about the kingdom of God,** his eschatological reign present in Jesus (8:12; 20:25; 28:23; Luke 17:20-21). Up to this point the Christian community in Ephesus existed within the context of the synagogue, but it celebrated the Lord's Supper in homes, even as the community in Jerusalem had done (cf. 2:42-46). Now we hear of **some** Jews who opposed Paul's message. The word *some* does not permit us to conclude that there were just a few who did not believe. "Some people" is a typical expression used in polemics and frequently veils an actual majority. With the word *some* Luke indicates here that the others who believed were the true Jews of Ephesus. But when **some** Jews were **stubborn** (better: "became hardened," cf. 28:26-27; Rom. 11:7) **and disbelieved** (or "remained unconvinced") **speaking evil of the Way** (the Way = the Christian faith and life, 9:2; 19:9, 23; 22:4; 24:14, 22), Paul took the decisive step and **withdrew from** the synagogue in Ephesus, **taking the disciples with him.** The typical Lukan pattern is repeated in which only the data concerning time (vv. 8 and 10) and place (v. 9) are pre-Lukan tradition. Having separated from the synagogue Paul found a new location for his activity **in the hall of Tyrannus,** a name referring to its owner or to a teacher who normally taught there. Instead of witnessing just once a week on the Sabbath, Paul now lectured **daily,** for **two years.** The Western text added "from the fifth to the tenth hour," that is, between 11 a.m. and 4 p.m., during siesta time, when the affluent would be indoors and the rent for Tyrannus's hall would be cheap. The result of Paul's labor was **that all the residents of Asia** had the opportunity to hear **the word of the Lord, both Jews and Greeks.** The Pauline mission spread from urban centers into the surrounding region and Christian communities were established by Paul's coworkers in the province of Asia and as far to the east as Colossae, Laodicea, and Hierapolis (cf. Col. 4:13). Luke did not speak of a mass conversion of the people of the province of Asia, but that they **heard the word of the Lord.** The word had been "sown" across the province of Asia and it will "bring forth fruit with patience" (Luke 8:11-15). To the **two years** of v. 10 should be added the **three months** of v. 8 and perhaps the indefinite period after the riot (20:1), so that Luke could arrive at a total of "three years" (20:31).

11-19—Luke placed two summaries back to back. Paul's ministry of the word (vv. 8-10) is followed by a summary of his extraordinary deeds of power in Ephesus (vv. 11-12). Word and deed were integral parts of the public ministry of Jesus (10:36-38) and of his messengers (cf. Luke 9:2; 10:9). The work of preaching and healing begun by Jesus in Galilee was continued by Peter in Jerusalem and Philip in Samaria and was extended by Paul to Jews and Gentiles beyond the Holy Land. This summary not only indicates a Paul-Peter parallel (cf. 5:12-16). It also introduces the following episode (vv. 13-19), dealing with the topic of syncretistic magic outside and inside the church. Ephesus was famous for magic in antiquity, and magical books were known as "Ephesian writings" (Plutarch, *Moralia* 706E). It is not surprising that it was in Ephesus that Luke narrated Paul's encounter with syncretistic magic. Whereas Peter's encounter with Simon emphasized the aspect of greed (cf. 8:18-24), Luke's story of Paul in Ephesus raised the subject of syncretism.

11-12—When we hear that Paul's **handkerchiefs** for wiping perspiration and his **aprons** worn during his hours of tentmaking **were carried away** by people and laid on **the sick** with the result that **diseases left them and the evil spirits came out of them,** such notions strike us as being indistinguishable from magic. It is precisely Luke's point that, to the naked eye, magic and miracle are in fact indistinguishable. Many a Lukan interpreter has squirmed in discomfort when dealing with these verses (e.g., Marshall), or else flatly stated that Christian miracles according to Luke are merely superior magic (e.g., Hull). However, there is a line of demarcation between magic and apostolic miracle, a line that is invisible but decisive theologically. Miracles are performed by God through "the hands of" his servants, be they Peter, Philip, or Paul. Magic is what humans do when they create a syncretistic mixture of divine names with the goal of manipulating God. The servants of God are nothing in themselves. As servants they are instruments of that God who raised Jesus from the dead and who manifests his power through his servants when and where and in whatever manner it pleases him. The magician uses God and God's name as means to an end. God's servant, however, is God's means for accomplishing his will.

Frequently, interpreters contrast Luke's portrait of the miracle-working missionary in Ephesus with Paul's own self-understanding as found in his letters. For the historical Paul, it is said, his apostolic ministry is genuine and legitimate only because it reflects the humiliation, the weakness, the cross of Jesus Christ. True enough, yet he did not deny that he too, performed miracles, perhaps tangentially (2 Cor. 12:12; Rom. 15:19). His opponents in Corinth may not have thought much of his miracles. For Paul himself they certainly were not the basis of his apostleship nor the focus of his preaching. What was central in his understanding of the gospel was "Jesus Christ, and him crucified" (1 Cor. 2:2). So, there is indeed a difference between Paul's portrait in Acts and the Paul who speaks to us through his letters. The tangential miracles of the historical Paul have become an integral part of his missionary work in Acts. Yet, caution is needed at this point to avoid overstatements. Commenting on vv. 11-12. Haenchen concluded: Paul "lives no longer in the sphere of the cross, but in that glory." This is false on two accounts: (1) These verses serve primarily as introduction to the following episode and as contrast to the theme of magic. (2) The theme of Paul's suffering in accordance with the will of God is Luke's longest section in Acts (chaps. 21–28). Paul's suffering, predicted at his conversion (9:16), had also been depicted by Luke in the persecutions which Paul had endured thus far.

13-16—This burlesque episode reveals what is otherwise hidden, namely, the difference between miracle and magic. God did exorcisms through Paul. In contrast, Jewish magicians become the object of a miracle in reverse and Paul does not even have to lift a finger. The use of the name of Jesus by syncretistic exorcists is found in the great magical papyrus of Paris, where the formula occurs, "I adjure you by Jesus, the God of the Hebrews" (PGM 4, 3019). For magicians, God, or in this case the name of Jesus, is the means to an end. They do not believe in Jesus but would like to use him. **A Jewish high priest named Sceva** is not known to have existed. Perhaps Luke was aware of this and gave these charlatans phony credentials. However, the word can also designate a person within the group of "chief priests" (cf. 9:14). The high point of the episode is the response of the demon to the exorcism formula of the magicians: **Jesus I know, and Paul I know; but who are you?**

The demon had supernatural knowledge (cf. Luke 4:31-37) and was aware that God, Jesus Christ, and his servant Paul could expel him, but these charlatans had no power. This he demonstrated by turning on the seven exorcists, tearing off their garments and beating them up, **so that they fled that house naked and wounded** in utter defeat. The name of Jesus is effective only in the mouth of those who are his legitimate instruments through whom God accomplishes his will.

17-20—Every miracle story closes with a reference to the reaction of the crowd. The effect of the attempted exorcism which boomeranged is narrated at great length. Among the Jewish and Gentile public of Ephesus it resulted in holy awe, and **the name of the Lord Jesus was extolled** (cf. 2:43).

Even more important was the effect within the Christian community. The demonstration of the phoniness of syncretistic magic caused **many** who **were now believers** to come forward **confessing and divulging their practices.** Syncretism in the form of magic also existed secretly within the church. Three different types of syncretists are brought to the reader's attention in this chapter: (1) "Disciples" who have lost their roots and no longer understand their own tradition (vv. 1-7); (2) Jews who, contrary to their tradition, practiced pagan magic, incorporating the name of Jesus into their exorcism formula (vv. 11-17), and (3) Christian "believers" who had embroidered their pagan ways of thought and **practices** on the language and ritual of the church (v. 18). In each instance a reformation was called for which resulted in Baptism, in a beating and book burning. The radical nature of the reform in Ephesus is highlighted

363

by a voluntary burning of magical texts, worth **fifty thousand pieces of silver.** The amount also shows the magnitude of this religious underground movement. (On book burnings see Lucian, *Alexander* 47; Suetonius, *Augustus* 31.)

So the word of the Lord grew and prevailed mightily. This sums up Paul's great work of mission. Internally the church has been cleansed of magic and syncretism; externally it has grown and spread across Asia Minor and Greece. The very existence of the church demonstrates the power of the word of God. Luke had no interest at this point in recalling the afflictions which Paul had to endure in Ephesus, afflictions caused by pagans and also by diverse Christian opponents. Rather, he ends the missionary section of his book on a triumphant note, present also in Paul's letters (cf. 2 Cor. 2:14-16), especially in his definition of the gospel as "the power of God for salvation" for Jews and Gentiles alike (Rom. 1:16-17). Like Paul, Luke affirmed that the word of God is victorious in every strife, for through it God establishes his claim over this world from Jerusalem to Rome and "to the end of the earth." That the triumph of God's word includes confrontation and division, rejection and suffering for God's chosen agents, be they Moses (7:25b, 27, 35, 39-43), Jesus, Peter, or Paul, had been told already (cf. 7:51-52) and will be a theme in the last two parts (chaps. 20–28).

21-22 (To Jerusalem and to Rome)—Before Luke described the riot in Ephesus he set forth Paul's programmatic decision. Thereby he connected Paul's mission with his journey to Jerusalem and Rome (chaps. 20–28). Luke made it clear that Paul's decision to leave Ephesus was not forced on him by the riot—he reached it prior to the riot—but his decision was prompted by **the Spirit** of God and by Paul's insight into the will of God. In direct discourse we hear Paul announce his plan. **After I have been there,** namely, in Jerusalem, **I must also see Rome.** It was not Paul's whim but God's will, expressed in the divine **must** (cf. 1:21-22; 3:21; 5:29; 9:16; 23:11; 27:24) which determined the events in chaps. 20–28. Yet it was not blind fate that governed Paul's life, for the "must" includes a challenge that is to be obeyed but can be rejected. Paul will no longer appear in the role of the missionary, evangelizing Jews and Gentiles and entering synagogues in each city. Luke will depict him as chief pastor who strengthened his churches and their leaders (20:1— 21:14). In **Jerusalem** he will take on a new role, to which Luke allotted the largest amount of space. He will become the imprisoned suffering witness and defender of the gospel in accordance with the promise made at the time of his conversion (9:16). **Rome,** which had been in view since Christ's mandate before his ascension (1:8), is now explicitly mentioned for the first time. It will be Paul's ultimate God-appointed goal and the many obstacles that he will experience on his way (chaps. 21–27) cannot stop him from reaching Rome.

Now after these events: better, "when God brought these events [of Paul's great mission] to completion." This introductory clause underlines the importance of the hour and signals the completion of Paul's missionary period in the story of Acts. It may remind the reader of Luke 9:51, "When the days were completed," Jesus "set his face to go to Jerusalem and he sent messengers ahead of him." Paul will also **go to Jerusalem** and to his passion, and his journey will lead him **through Macedonia and Achaia.** He, too, sent **two of his helpers, Timothy and Erastus,** ahead of him while **he himself stayed in Asia for a while.**

Acts and the Pauline letters agree that (1) Paul left Ephesus and revisited the churches in Greece; (2) he sent helpers ahead of him to do advance work (cf. 2 Cor. 2:12-13); (3) he intended to go to Jerusalem and from there to Rome (Rom. 15:25, 28, 32). Luke failed to mention the twofold reason for Paul's journey to Greece, namely, reconciliation with the Corinthian community and, above all, the gathering of the collection for Jerusalem on which he had worked so long and so hard (cf. Gal. 2:10; 1 Cor. 16:1-4; 2 Corinthians 8–9; Rom. 15:25-33). Finally, Paul hoped that Rome would become not his ultimate goal, as in Acts, but his base for evangelizing the western part of the empire, including Spain (Rom. 15:24). Titus, as always, is omitted from the group of Paul's **helpers** in Acts even though he was sent to Macedonia ahead of Paul (2 Cor. 2:13; 7:6). For **Timothy** see 16:1; 17:14-15; 18:5; 1 Cor. 4:17; 16:10. Of **Erastus** we know nothing. A person by that name was apparently city treasurer of Corinth (Rom. 16:23), and therefore hardly identical with the Erastus of Paul's advance team into Macedonia.

23-41 (The riot in Ephesus)—Luke saved the longest story for the end of Paul's stay in that city. Contrary to Haenchen, Luke's account is based on a tradition. This can be seen from the following: (1) the use of the Greek word *ekklēsia* for a political assembly (vv. 32, 39,

41; the word elsewhere means church, the people of God, the assembly of believers); (2) the subdued role played by Paul in this lengthy account; (3) the reference to Aristarchus (see Philemon 24); and (4) the odd appearance of the Jew, Alexander (vv. 33-34). These were hardly invented by Luke.

In Philippi as well as in Ephesus the opposition to Christianity was generated exclusively by pagans and motivated by a variety of forces. Luke dramatically portrayed the unholy alliance of pagan religion, vested financial self-interest, patriotism, and mob-hysteria, creating a contrast with the competent conduct of the chief executive officer of Ephesus. The worry of **Demetrius** and his fellow craftsmen about their business and their religion summarizes Paul's success as "light to the Gentiles" (13:47). Not only magicians but the very heart of pagan religion felt threatened by the power of the gospel present in Paul's witness. Luke's narrative also discloses the presence of some decent pagans (cf. Rom. 2:14-15, 26). The Asiarchs are concerned about Paul's welfare and the town clerk diffuses a mob by insisting on due legal process. These public representatives are quite aware that Christianity poses no threat to public order and their presence is a comfort to Luke's readers (cf. 18:12-17). The church's stance against polytheism does not transgress the law (v. 37) (see Josephus, *Ant.* 4.207).

23-27—Demetrius, a silversmith . . . made silver shrines of Artemis. The Greek virgin goddess Artemis, protectress of wild animals and patron of hunting, was worshiped as the mother of gods and humans in Ephesus. Her temple, one of the seven wonders of the ancient world, contained her image of which copies have survived (e.g., Rome, Musei Capitolini). The top of her high crown is a replica of her temple. Her fertility is indicated by 28 breasts or eggs or bulls' testicles in several rows. Lions, rams, and bulls in relief cover her lower torso, legs, and arms. Two lions sit on her shoulders and the disk of the moon forms a halo around her head. The temple of the Ephesian Artemis was not only the center of her cult but also a financial institution, a bank in which cities and rich individuals stored their funds under the goddess's protection. Tourists and pilgrims from the Hellenistic Roman world flocked to Ephesus to worship in and admire this beautiful Hellenistic temple. In turn, the cult of the Ephesian Artemis was brought into dozens of cities of the Mediterranean world. Miniature terra cotta models of the temple have been found, but not silver copies. They were used as devotional objects or brought home as souvenirs. The alarm of Demetrius and his guild members about the future of their lucrative business demonstrates the spread of the gospel through **this Paul** who **has persuaded and turned away a considerable company of people** not only in Ephesus **but almost throughout all Asia.** His teaching that **gods made with hands are not gods** (cf. 17:24, 29) not only hurts our business but is above all an affront to the **magnificence** of our great goddess, **she whom all Asia and the world worship.**

28-32—When economic self-interest, patriotism, and religious loyalty feel threatened simultaneously the result is collective anger. The guild of silversmiths was **enraged** and, chanting the cultic acclamation, **Great is Artemis of the Ephesians,** they marched through the city, drawing crowds after them on their way **into the theater.** They were able to seize two of Paul's traveling companions, **Gaius and Aristarchus** (20:4; 27:2; Philemon 24; Col. 4:10), here identified as **Macedonians,** though Gaius, we are told in 20:4 came from Derbe ("Doberus" in Macedonia, according to ms. D). Perhaps two persons by that name were in Paul's company, or perhaps an early copyist changed the singular *Macedonian* into the present plural, or else Gaius of Derbe was known also as Gaius the Macedonian, but this is unlikely.

30-31—The focus briefly shifts to Paul who wished to join the "civic assembly" (rather than **crowd;** Greek, *demos*) and support his endangered companions. He was restrained by fellow Christians and by the counsel of concerned **Asiarchs.** We hear that **some of the Asiarchs** who as elected officials belonged to the prominent families of the province of Asia were **friends of** Paul. Christianity already had sympathizers in the highest social-political circles of the province. Unfortunately, we do not know the precise functions of these officials. The term may designate the elected city representatives to the provincial assembly which met in Ephesus; it may designate the annual presiding officers of that assembly; or it may refer to the chief priests (Greek, *archiereus*) of the imperial cult chosen from the representatives of the provincial assembly. In *Mart. Pol.* 12:2 we hear of an Asiarch, Philip, of the city of Tralles who was also high priest. What is certain is that Asiarchs dealt with internal political and religious issues of the province, that Asia was a hotbed of the emperor cult and the goddess Roma, and that Asiarchs by virtue of their position were involved in the emperor cult. The contrast between two approaches to the problem of church and state becomes apparent when we compare Luke's friendly Asiarchs with the beast of Revelation 13 and the great harlot of Revelation 17. Both authors wrote within a decade and included the same province in their writings. For the exiled prophet John, the imperial power of Rome manifested in the emperor cult was a monstrosity, an extension of Satan, a manifestation of anti-Christ who cannot but wage war on God's elect. "All who dwell on earth will worship" the beast in the emperor cult. A peaceful coexistence between emperor worshipers and the saints of God is impossible (Revelation 13). The goddess Roma is but a great harlot bedecked with unbelievable wealth, and the rulers of the earth commit fornication with her. She is the incarnation of Roman oppression and idolatry and "drunk with the blood of the saints and the martyrs of Jesus" (Rev. 17:1—18:24). Luke's approach to the church-state problem differs. Was Luke projecting his own wishful thinking for coexistence between church and the imperial cult onto the past? Or was he reflecting and exaggerating a past period when Asiarchs were indifferent to and ignorant of the church? Luke would agree with Josephus, who interpreted Deut. 7:25 to mean: "Let none blaspheme the gods which other cities revere, nor rob foreign temples . . ." (*Ant.* 4.207). At any rate, the reader hears that Paul had **friends** in highest places who were concerned about his well-being.

One final point: Paul is portrayed here as one who let himself be persuaded to remain incognito in an hour of adversity that overtook coworkers. He did not rush "bravely" into the theater and into almost certain martyrdom. If there were some Christians at Luke's time who clamored for a martyr's death and voluntarily gave themselves up, his picture of a cautious, reasonable Paul would warn them not to surrender voluntarily to magistrates for the sake of martyrdom. Both Paul and, later, Polycarp (bishop of Smyrna, martyred ca. A.D. 155) were genuine martyrs who also went into hiding (*Mart. Pol.* 5.1—6.11).

32-34—Back in the open-air theater, which according to estimates could seat up to 24,000 people, the ad hoc meeting was unable to constitute itself into a formal assembly of citizens that could have passed resolutions. Ephesus was a free Greek city with its own senate and citizens' assembly. Instead, disarray reigned, which Luke sketched with masterful irony: **Now some cried one thing, some**

another; for the assembly [*ekklēsia*] was in confusion and most of them did not know why they had come together. Jews were also present and apparently thought it necessary to disassociate themselves from the Christians. **Alexander** was **put forward** as their spokesman. But when the people recognized him to be a Jew, and therefore not a worshiper of Artemis, they shouted him down and began to chant their acclamation in unison: **Great is Artemis of the Ephesians,** and continued it **for about two hours.** There is satire in Luke's portrayal of a hysterical mob and its mindless chanting, and irony in the description of a pagan anti-Judaism which kept Jewish hostility against Christianity from succeeding.

35-41—At last, **the town clerk** took charge and **quieted the crowd.** He was not a secretary who took dictation but held the position of either the clerk of the council or, more likely, he was "the clerk of the people" which in Ephesus was the position of the chief magistrate. Like a smooth politician, he appealed to the patriotic instincts of his fellow citizens and their civic pride. The fact that Ephesus was **temple keeper** referred to a special privilege which was by no means granted to every city with temples, not even to major ones. Coins attest to the fact that Ephesus was **temple keeper** of the emperor cult. Our text, together with a later inscription, attests to this rare privilege. The honor was extended so that Ephesus was also designated **temple keeper of the great Artemis.** Moreover, Ephesus possessed **the sacred stone that fell from the sky.** The Greek text does not contain the word "stone" and probably refers to the original cult image in the temple, of which copies have been found, rather than to a meteorite. Because the image was believed to have fallen from heaven, it was considered to be of divine origin and not made by human hands (cf. v. 26).

Since Ephesus's honor is established beyond doubt and **cannot be contradicted,** therefore, the town clerk concluded, **you ought to be quiet and do nothing rash.** Now follows his first reason for keeping civic peace. These men, Gaius and Aristarchus (cf. v. 29), and implicitly all other Christians, including Paul, **are neither sacrilegious nor blasphemers of our goddess.** Sacrilege is the crime, punishable by law, of robbing temples, (which also served as banks) or of descecrating a temple (cf. 2 Macc. 4:39-42). To blaspheme, for instance, would be to denounce the goddess publicly as a harlot who is drunk and fornicating, etc. (cf. Revelation 17, which, how-

369

ever, used apocalyptic code words and was not meant for public consumption but for Christian apocalyptic conventicles). Does Luke suggest that the town clerk's declaration about the innocence of Paul's companions was merely a clever political trick designed to cool a heated mob? Or was it Luke's view that Christians, in spite of their rejection of polytheism and idolatry, do not commit the crime of public blasphemy? Undoubtedly, the latter alternative expresses his point of view. If so, Luke would demand that Christians refrain from publicly insulting the religion of their pagan neighbors. The Christian faith is not a punishable offense, Luke held. Offensive public behavior is another matter.

Having declared that no criminal offense had occurred which would demand the attention of magistrates, the town clerk now turns to the private concerns of Demetrius and the craftsmen of his guild and he lectures to them on what is obvious to every adult. There are established legal procedures which must be followed in complaints against individuals. **Courts** and **proconsuls** (two generic plurals) will hear charges and bring about justice. If, however, anyone should wish to bring up matters other than private complaints, matters that concern the city as a whole, then **it shall be settled in the regular assembly** (Greek, *ennomos ekklēsia*), not in an ad hoc assembly such as the present one. The regular assembly met in the theater at certain fixed intervals, and all adult males of Ephesus had access.

The town clerk closed with a subtle warning, typical of politicians. One of his functions was to serve as connecting link between the civic Greek administration and the Roman provincial administration, also located in Ephesus. Now if there was one matter the Romans disliked greatly it was civil disturbance. **We are in danger,** he said, **of being charged with rioting** (Greek, *stasis*) and that, as anyone knows, would hurt our image, impair our excellent reputation and have unpleasant consequences for us all. With this **he dismissed the assembly.** In so doing, this chief municipal officer publicly vindicated the Christians and tactfully censured those who were disturbing urban tranquility. Since we find Gaius and Aristarchus among Paul's company (20:4), we must assume that the town clerk permitted them to leave. A victory for the Way (cf. 19:23) occurred on the eve of Paul's departure, because law and order prevailed.

Of course, we recall that historically Paul's tribulations in Ephesus were most severe (cf. 1 Cor. 15:32; 16:9; 2 Cor. 1:8), that he was probably imprisoned (certainly so, if Philippians and Philemon were written from there) and probably expelled (see comments on 20:16). These hardships and trials were either unknown to Luke, or he set them aside.

In telling the story of Paul's mission, Luke used a stereotype pattern, giving Paul's activity in each city unique, individual features. The general pattern in which Luke told of Paul's mission in Philippi, Beroea, Athens, Corinth, and Ephesus includes (1) movement, (2) proclamation/confrontation, (3) success/division, (4) reaction or danger to Paul, (5) rescue/resolution. Parts of the pattern may be repeated in the mission story of a city (e.g., proclamation in Athens, 17:17, 22-31). Some parts may be indicated only indirectly (e.g., proclamation in Philippi, 16:13; its success, 16:15, 40c). Some parts are told at length (e.g., Paul's travels at the beginning of this section, 15:41—16:10, and at the end, 18:18-23; his preaching in Athens, 17:22-31; the hostile reaction in Philippi at the beginning of this section and in Ephesus at the end). Individual stories of Paul's missionary activity become unique not merely through a variation of a stereotyped pattern, but through delineating peculiar characters and groups, times and places. In addition to Paul, Silas, and Timothy, we meet believers such as Lydia, a slave girl, a jailer, Jason, Dionysius and Damaris, Aquila and Priscilla, Titius Justus, Crispus, nameless "devout Greeks" and "leading women" of Thessalonica, "women of high standing" from Beroea, and others (e.g., 19:9) who became Christians. In distinction from the "jealous" Jews of Thessalonica, we meet "more noble" Jews in Beroea, and a ruler of a synagogue in Corinth, who accepted Paul's testimony. The Jew, Alexander of Ephesus, did not receive a hearing and the Jew, Sosthenes of Corinth, was given a beating. The three mob actions in Philippi, Thessalonica, and Ephesus are told with striking differences, as are the actions of the magistrates in Philippi, of Gallio in Corinth, and the town clerk in Ephesus.

The places referred to in Luke's story include regions through which Paul traveled in Asia Minor, Macedonia, and Achaia, as well as several cities and specific locales such as a riverside (16:13), a jail, Lydia's house, the house of Titius Justus in Corinth, synagogues in Thessalonica, Beroea, Athens, Corinth, Ephesus, the Athenian Agora, the Areopagus, the tribunal in Corinth, the hall of Tyrannus, and the theater of Ephesus. Paul's mission, covered in this section of Luke's story comprises two and one-half years in Corinth, two years and three months in Ephesus, plus the time after the riot (cf. 20:1,31). If we add the time spent from Paul's departure from Antioch to his arrival in Corinth, we come to something like seven years. If Paul left Antioch in the spring of A.D. 49, then he left Ephesus in A.D. 56.

Beside the theme of the gospel's encounter with secular and religious pagan patriotism (16:20-21; 17:7,18; 19:27-40; cf. 18:13), and the theme of the encounter with Christian and Jewish oddities (18:24-28; 19:1-7,13-18), we find the theme of the growth of the church in the face of persecution and rejection. Moreover, there are in this section two scenes of separation from the synagogue—at Corinth and at Ephesus. Yet in both instances we hear that also *after* the separation from the synagogue, Jews did come to faith, or heard the word or deed of the Lord (18:8,28; 19:10,17). In short, the church's mission to the Jews did not come to an end with Paul's separation from synagogues, nor does the conclusion of this section signal the end of mission to Jews. The response of diaspora Judaism to Paul's preaching was divided, just as Jerusalem's response had been.

■ Witness to and Encouragement of Christian Communities (20:1— 21:14)

Introduction: This section serves as a transition in Luke's overall design. The missionary activity of Paul in Acts has been completed. On his way to Jerusalem in accordance with his programmatic statement (19:21), we find Paul encouraging his churches. He no longer entered synagogues nor preached to Jews and Gentiles. Previously we had heard that Paul "strengthed," "admonished," or "encouraged" Christian communities (14:22; 16:5,40; 18:23; cf. 15:32). Faith lives and draws its vitality from the Word. As a missionary Paul could not ignore the fact that believers remain the people of God only so long as they continue to hear the Word of God. This theme of Christian nurture which up until now had only been touched upon is broadly unfolded in this section and given prominence through the centrally located farewell speech to the elders of Ephesus in Miletus. The opening verses of this section twice accent the theme of exhortation-encouragement (Greek, *parakalein;* 20:1-2). Moreover, this section offers a retrospect of Paul's achievement as a model missionary and the prospect of his imminent passion in Jerusalem. Just as the theme of encouragement ties this section to the one preceding, so three passion predictions on his way to Jerusalem connect this section to the following story of his imprisonment (20:23, 25; 21:4, 11-13).

Finally, Paul's farewell gift in Troas consisted in the miraculous deed of bringing a dead young man back to life, a deed enclosed by the breaking of bread, by God's visible and enacted Word. Wherever the Eucharist is celebrated, the same Lord who through Paul raised a dead young man is present as the giver and the gift, uniting all across space and time in his church. In Miletus Paul's farewell gift was his last will and testament, his legacy for his communities and their leaders. The response to Paul was the love of his people toward their chief pastor, a love which is pictured in ever more vivid scenes the closer Paul gets to Jerusalem. The reader knows that Paul's work was not in vain. While his people wept and begged him "not to go on to Jerusalem" (20:37-38; 21:4-5, 12-14), in the end they were able to affirm: **The will of the Lord be done** (21:14; cf. Luke 22:42), and with this submission to the Lord Jesus our section closes.

From Philippi onward (20:6) Luke's story returns to first person plural narration (cf. 16:16) and continues so until Jerusalem, except for the two scenes where the focus shifts to Paul in Troas and Miletus (20:7-12, 17-38). The "we" form underlines the importance of this particular sea voyage through which the gospel came to "us" (Luke 1:1; cf. comments on 16:10). The gospel, our author stated, came to "us" through Paul—because Paul traveled to Jerusalem and as prisoner to Rome. Since ancient sea voyage narratives frequently employed first person plural narration, and since Luke knew that coworkers and friends accompanied Paul in his travels, he tucked himself away anonymously among their company. Geographic details and specific time references greatly increase in this "we" section, which suggests either the author's presence, or his diligent research (Luke 1:3). The first missionary journey, we recall, contained no time references, and the second was also silent on the longest and most compressed journey (18:22-23; but see 16:11; 17:2;

18:11; 19:8,10). Now Luke specifies different time periods on this journey, beginning with Paul's three months' stay in Achaia (20:3). Correspondingly, the list of places on this journey increases, so that it can easily be traced on a map.

Yet Luke also streamlined and simplified his account. He used only two verses to get Paul from Ephesus to Corinth (20:1-2), and he omitted Paul's mission "as far as Illyricum" (Rom. 15:19). This mission took place, not during his first journey in Greece (cf. 17:10,14), but prior to his three months' stay in Corinth (20:3). From Thessalonica (20:2) he traveled west on the Via Egnatia, establishing congregations in western Macedonia as far as Illyricum on the Adriatic coast. Then he traveled—most likely by boat—to Corinth, from where he wrote Romans, stating: "at present" (Greek, *nyni de*) "I am going to Jerusalem" (Rom. 15:25). This would hardly permit us to move Paul's mission in western Macedonia–Illyricum into the period after his departure from Corinth. If Luke was ignorant of Paul's mission to Illyricum, then he certainly was not a traveling companion of Paul. He could have known about this mission and deliberately omitted it, because the Lukan Paul in this section does not function as a missionary, but as an "enabler," an encourager of established Christian communities.

In addition to omitting Paul's mission as far as Illyricum, Luke also omitted the collection "for the saints" in Jerusalem (Rom. 15:25), which was the primary reason for Paul's journey from Corinth via Macedonia and the coastal cities of Asia Minor to Jerusalem. Once more we would argue that if Luke had been ignorant of the collection, he could not possibly have been a traveling companion of Paul. But he did know about the collection, as 24:17 clearly shows. Hence Luke deliberately omitted all other references to the collection, because for him the story of Paul's journey to his passion and his subsequent imprisonment held primacy over a collection which proved to be unsuccessful (see comments on 21:19; 24:17; see also Rom. 15:31-32).

Luke's streamlining becomes apparent even in his reworking of a traditional list of delegates (v. 4). Historically, together with Paul, they brought the collection of Gentile churches to the center of Jewish Christianity in Jerusalem. The collection was meant to be a visible, tangible expression of the unity of faith, a thankoffering of Gentiles, an acknowledgment of the salvation-historical priority of

Jewish Christianity and the fulfillment of a promise made by Paul at the apostles' conference (Gal. 2:10). However, Luke omitted the names of the delegates from Corinth and Philippi, because he did not wish to present a list of community delegates transmitting the collection of their respective churches. Instead he presented a list of Paul's traveling companions. Seven of them (v. 4) would indeed be sufficient for that purpose. There was no need to mention them at all, because the collection has been relegated to a footnote in Luke's narrative. We have argued that Luke's omission was deliberate at this point, rather than accidental or due to lack of information. This conclusion is undergirded by the minutiae of details which show that Luke was better informed about this journey than any other.

To Macedonia and Achaia and Return to Troas (20:1-12)

1-6 (Travel report)—The theme of this whole section is introduced by the twofold occurrence of the Greek verb *parakalein*, which is translated once in the RSV "exhort" (v. 1) and once "give encouragement" (v. 2). Paul in Acts left Ephesus not because he was banished following imprisonment, but by his own decision (probably in A.D. 56). He would see the Ephesian community no more but meet only its leaders, on his return trip in Miletus (vv. 17-38). Thus it was indeed important that he would give one final exhortation to the Ephesian believers before he **took leave of them and departed for Macedonia.** There he also gave **much encouragement.** From Macedonia he wrote 2 Corinthians, or, if it is a composite letter, 2 Cor. 1:3—2:13; 7:5-16. This letter was his response to the good news about the Corinthian situation, brought to him by Titus (cf. 2 Cor. 2:12; 7:5-16). Historically, the mission to western Macedonia–Illyricum followed, omitted in Acts. Then Paul came to Greece, that is, Achaia, probably in the late fall of A.D. 56. He spent the three (winter) **months** in Corinth in the house of Gaius (Rom. 16:23), who may be identical with Titius Justus (18:7; cf. 1 Cor. 1:14; his full Roman name would then be Gaius Titius Justus). From Corinth he wrote Romans. In Corinth some representatives of the congregations which participated in the collection for Jerusalem had also gathered. Paul's plan had been to sail directly via **Syria** to Caesarea Maritima, perhaps on a pilgrim ship, and arrive in Jerusalem. In Rom. 15:25

he wrote: "But *now* I am going to Jerusalem" with the collection, which agrees with his travel plans in Acts. However, these plans had to be changed when it was discovered that **a plot was made against him by the Jews as he was about to set sail.** Perhaps some rowdies wanted to start a fight on board. With the collection at stake, the decision was reached to make a detour via **Macedonia,** to which they returned, perhaps by boat. He now hoped to arrive in Jerusalem in time for Pentecost **if possible** (v. 16). The list of names of seven community representatives, who in Acts are traveling companions, is artistically arranged. **Sopater of Beroea** (17:10; he was probably Sosipater who sent greetings to Rome and is identified as a Jew, Rom. 16:21), **and of the Thessalonians, Aristarchus** (19:29; 27:2; Philemon 24; Col. 4:10) **and Secundus** (he is not mentioned otherwise); **and Gaius of Derbe** (see the comment on 19:29; the "Western text" reads "of Doberus," which is a city in Macedonia; it may be a substitution made in view of 19:29, where Gaius is called a Macedonian) **and Timothy** (of Lystra, 16:1; 17:14; 18:5; 19:22; Rom. 16:21; 1 Cor. 4:17; 16:10; 2 Cor. 1:1, 19; Phil. 1:1; 2:19; 1 Thess. 1:1; 3:2,6; Philemon 1; 1 Tim. 1:2; etc.) **and the Asians, Tychicus** (Eph. 6:21; Col. 4:7; 2 Tim. 4:12; Titus 3:12) **and Trophimus** (21:28-29; 2 Tim. 4:20). Titus is again absent from the list. Some hold that he represented Corinth, because Paul had sent him there as his representative and he had worked hard for the success of the collection in Corinth. Historically this may be true, but in Acts he is never mentioned.

These seven had met Paul in Corinth and traveled with him to Macedonia, where the party split into two groups. One remained with Paul. The other group, consisting either of the seven or of some of them, left Philippi as an advance party and sailed to Troas, probably in order to make arrangements for travel by ship. Paul celebrated the days of Unleavened Bread, the Passover, in Philippi. Even on Hellenistic soil and among Gentile believers Paul remained a pious, Law-abiding Jew. God's act in Christ does not abrogate that which it fulfills but retains its continuity with it. Therefore, Jewish Christians observed the Torah and celebrated Jewish feasts. After Passover **we sailed away.** If all seven had left for Troas beforehand, then the appearance of this "we" would tell the reader that our anonymous author and Paul traveled together to Troas, a trip which took **five days,** due to the prevailing winds (cf. 16:11). In Troas Paul and his companions stayed another **seven days.**

7-12 (Encouragement at Troas)—In summary fashion Luke had reported Paul's exhortation and encouragement in Ephesus and to the churches of Macedonia (vv. 1-2). Now he introduces an example into his travel report which shows us what Paul's exhortation-en-couragement was like. Luke enclosed a traditional miracle story in brackets (vv. 7 and 11). The tradition told of Paul's bringing Eutychus back to life, for Luke a parallel to the story of Peter's raising of Tabitha (9:36-42). But Luke subsumed the resuscitation of Eutychus under the primary thrust found in the brackets. These contain three elements: (1) the breaking of bread, which was the purpose of the gathering of the community and which, due to Paul's lengthy ser-mon, was postponed until after midnight, after the miracle of the raising (vv. 7 and 11); (2) Paul's preaching, which was interrupted by the accident and the miracle, and continued after the eucharistic celebration; (3) the imminent departure of Paul, the context within which this encouragement took place (vv. 7 and 11). This bracketing determines the nature of Paul's encouragement at Troas and down-plays the miracle by making it one element of Paul's farewell en-couragement.

The worshiping community, gathered to hear Paul's final exhor-tation and to celebrate the Eucharist, was interrupted by an accident which resulted in the death of a young man, who had ceased hearing Paul's words and **sank into a deep sleep.** Falling three stories to the ground he **was taken up dead,** but Paul brought him back to life. The interruption of the community's worship due to deep sleep, death, and resuscitation was not permanent. At once Paul returned and continued the worship by breaking bread, speaking, and ad-monishing till dawn. His final encouragement at Troas included preaching, a miracle, a Eucharist, and more preaching. The same Lord whose Word he spoke, whose meal he celebrated, and whose power he manifested in the miracle is with his church also after Paul's departure. **And so** [he] departed and they **were not a little comforted** (v. 12; Greek, *parakalein*, to admonish, exhort, encour-age, and comfort). The verb relates to all elements of Paul's farewell, not just to the miracle. Indeed Paul, the chief pastor of his churches, spent his time and strength fully **in the ministry which** he **received**

from the Lord Jesus (v. 24b) and spared no efforts "night or day to admonish every one" of you (v. 31).

7—The first day of the week is the day after the Sabbath, the day of the Lord (Rev. 1:10; Luke 24:1; 1 Cor. 16:2; Did. 14:1) when Jesus Christ was raised from the dead and appeared to his disciples (Luke 24:1, 13-52). Our text is one of the earliest references to Christian worship on Sunday. However, what is not clear is whether Luke used a Roman or Jewish method of reckoning time. Since the verse is a Lukan redactional addition it would be idle to ask when the believers of Troas gathered together in A.D. 56, Paul's time. Rather, our question should be: according to Luke, did the community gather for worship on Saturday evening after sunset, listen to Paul till midnight and then witness a miracle of raising followed by a Eucharist and more preaching until daybreak on Sunday? Or did Luke presuppose a Roman timetable, for which Sunday began after midnight Saturday? In that case, the meeting took place Sunday evening and the miracle and Eucharist would have occurred in the early hours on Monday. Luke stressed the anomaly of Paul's lengthy sermon **until midnight.** Normally, a Sunday evening Eucharist would surely end before midnight. It seems that Luke used the Roman timetable (cf. 4:3, 5; 23:31-32), even when he was aware of the Jewish reckoning of time (cf. Luke 23:54—24:1). If so, the worship in Troas took place on Sunday evening. Incidentally, a Sunday evening Eucharist is also attested for Bithynia in Pliny's letter to Trajan (around A.D. 112, *Epistles* 10.96). The worship, called "the breaking of bread," began with Paul's lengthy sermon. Word and sacrament belong together. The Greek verb (*dialegesthai*), translated **he talked with them,** also means to discuss, argue, preach (17:2, 17; 18:4, 19; 19:8). No effort was too great for Paul to fulfill his ministry of exhortation and encouragement.

8-9—There were many lights (literally, "lamps") **in the upper chamber.** Why this detail? Three possible interpretations have been offered: (1) The many lights made the room smoky and stuffy, and so the young man fell asleep. But we note that **he was sitting in the window,** where the air was fresh and cool. Therefore, a contrast may be intended: in spite of the many lights Eutychus fell asleep. (2) Perhaps the **many lights** were intended to indicate that Christian gatherings did not take place in dark rooms where all kinds of unsavory things were said to happen during their love-feast (see Jude

12-13). Luke's emphasis on the public nature of the Christian faith may have prompted this detail (cf. 26:26). There is nothing secret or subversive in the worship of Christians. (3) Luke gave this miracle story an additional symbolic turn, by describing it as an interruption within a worship service. The many lights, like Paul's lengthy sermon, denote that Christian worship is the sphere of life and light where the Word of God is heard (cf. 26:18). The person who ceased to hear **sank into** the darkness of **a deep sleep** and fell, not into the room of the assembled believers, but outside into the depths of death. By tying a miracle story into Paul's farewell, Luke's story took on some symbolic coloring.

10-12—Like Elijah and Elisha (1 Kings 17:21; 2 Kings 4:34-35) Paul **bent over him** (literally, "fell upon," or "threw himself upon"), the dead young man, **embracing him.** Then he announced, **Do not be alarmed, for his life is in him.** This does not mean that Eutychus had not died, but only appeared to be dead. Rather, life returned to him who in fact was dead (cf. v. 9). At once Paul went back to the upper room and the interrupted worship continued with the eucharistic breaking of the bread. It is not clear whether Luke thought that the sacramental breaking of bread was still connected with a regular meal. One could argue that it was not, since waiting until after midnight would spoil dinner and keep empty stomachs growling far too long (cf. 1 Cor. 11:22a, 33). On the other hand, it might have been a regular fellowship meal in the course of which the Lord's Supper was celebrated. We do not know. Luke's point lies in Paul's continuing to preach even after the sacramental meal **until daybreak.** As an afterthought we hear of the corroboration of the miracle. **They took the lad away alive.** And they **were not a little comforted** (Greek, *parakalein*). **Not a little** is a typical Lukan idiom, meaning greatly (cf. 14:28; 19:23, 24). Their consolation and encouragement resulted not just from the miraculous restoration of Eutychus but from the total event of Paul's farewell, which can be seen from the adverb **so** (Greek, *houtos*, "in this manner," "thus," v. 11): in this manner, after giving exhortation and encouragement. After restoring a dead man to life, after celebrating the sacred meal followed by more preaching, Paul **departed** at dawn. The reaction of his people is registered in the concluding clause: and they were greatly **comforted.**

To Miletus, Exhortation and Farewell (20:13-38)

Report of travel from Troas to Miletus (13-16)—For this report Luke did not use an itinerary, nor did he construct it out of the blue. An itinerary which merely listed the names of places where Paul and his company stopped would have been an irrelevant product without precedent in ancient writings (see Plümacher). Simultaneously, it would seem improbable that Luke simply invented the route of the journey on the basis of his general knowledge of the geography of the coast of Asia Minor. Had he done so, he probably would have given a reason why Paul walked from Troas to Assos (about 18 miles) while **we set sail for Assos** (v. 13). It would appear that Luke himself did not know the reason for this detail, but mentioned it because it was based on fact. Perhaps the ship's departure was delayed and perhaps Paul simply preferred walking to sailing in the choppy waters off Cape Lecton; perhaps he wanted briefly to visit some friends on the way, since he had traveled that road at least once before (cf. 16:8), perhaps twice (cf. 20:1). At any rate, the shortcut over land enabled him to arrive ahead of the ship, and **he met us at Assos** where he went on board. From there the ship sailed to **Mitylene,** the capital of the island of Lesbos, home of Sappho, the Greek poet. The following day **we came** . . . **opposite Chios,** the island where Homer was born, **and the next day we touched at** the island of **Samos,** birthplace of Pythagoras, the father of mathematics and geometry. These names designate places where the ship anchored overnight. It would have been easy to send a messenger from Samos to nearby Ephesus and save time (cf. v. 17). The next stop was **Miletus,** which is now five miles from the coast, due to the accumulation of silt carried by the Meander river. At Paul's time the harbor was still active and the city with its large theater, public buildings, and two market places was quite impressive. The reason for sailing **past Ephesus** to Miletus was Paul's decision **not to spend time in Asia** but to reach **Jerusalem, if possible** for **Pentecost.** However, in the following verse we hear that Paul sent messengers from Miletus back to Ephesus and asked the Ephesian elders to meet him in Miletus. This does not make sense, if Paul's purpose was to save time. The trip to and from Ephesus, including gathering the elders would take about four to six days. From Samos Paul could easily have reached Ephesus by boat in one day, met the elders in the evening, and left the following morning. We should also note that in Luke's story it is Paul who **decided** the route of the ship's journey. It would appear that Paul avoided Ephesus, because of "the affliction we experienced in Asia, for we were so utterly, unbearably crushed that we despaired of life itself . . . we felt that we had received the sentence of death; . . . [but God] who raises the dead . . . delivered us from so deadly a peril" (2 Cor. 1:8-10). Historically, Paul had probably been imprisoned and banished from Ephesus and therefore could not return. Luke omitted this detail, provided he knew of it, for apologetic reasons and for reasons of design. He will deal with Paul's passion extensively in the final part of Acts.

Exhortation and Farewell in Miletus (17-36)

Introduction: Paul's ministry in Acts has three distinct phases, (1) as missionary to Jews and Gentiles; (2) as chief pastor visiting churches on his way to Jerusalem; and (3) as imprisoned witness defending the gospel in Jerusalem, Caesarea, and Rome. For his missionary phase Paul gave two major speeches, one to Jews (13:16-41, 46-47) and the other to Gentiles (17:22-31). For his second phase Paul's speech to the Ephesian elders at Miletus is the great example of his hortatory preaching to Christians and the only example of its kind in Acts. To be sure, Peter and James had also spoken to Christians (1:16-22; 15:7-11, 13-21), but their speeches related to particular historical problems which called for particular decisions. Paul's exhortation of the Ephesian elders connects the past with Luke's own present and deals with the style and the content of the ministerial office, with heresies confronting the church, and with the social responsibility of the church toward its socially "weak" members. The speech is an exhortation of Christians within the context of Paul's farewell. As farewell speech, it summarizes his achievement which is meant to serve as a permanent example for the church. His legacy is what the Ephesian elders should keep before their eyes as they face new situations after Paul's departure.

The literary genre of the farewell speech is found in the Old Testament (e.g., Gen. 47:29—50:14; all of Deuteronomy; Josh. 23:1—24:30; 1 Sam. 12:1-25; 2 Kings 2:1-10), in the literature of the intertestamental period (1 Macc. 2:49-70; The Testaments of the Twelve Patriarchs; etc.), and in the New Testament (e.g., Luke

22:14-38; John 13–17; 2 Timothy; 2 Peter). Though the Miletus address is not directly dependent on any one of them, it shares basic motifs with all of them, such as: in view of his impending death, God's servant gathers his followers, his offspring, or successors and gives an account of his life and work; he obligates them to carry out his legacy, gives exhortations and warnings; he makes prophetic predictions; he appoints successors and grants blessings or commends them to the faithfulness of God.

There are striking parallels between this speech and Luke 22:14-38. Just as Jesus immediately before his passion prepared his followers for the time after his departure, so did Paul with respect to the elders. Both look back to the past (Luke 22:35; Acts 20:18-21, 26-27, 31) and forward to difficult times that lie ahead (Luke 22:35-38; Acts 20:29-30); both give exhortations and warnings (Luke 22:24-27; Acts 20:28-31, 35), and both use their own ministry as normative example (Luke 22:27; Acts 20:18-21, 24, 27, 31, 33-35). Jesus prayed for Peter (Luke 22:32) and Paul commended the Ephesian elders **to God and to the word of his grace** (Luke 22:35-38; Acts 20:32). As the apostles were destined by Jesus to "judge," that is to rule "the twelve tribes of Israel" (Luke 22:30), so likewise the elders are "to feed the church of God" by declaring to them "the whole counsel of God" and doing so in a style that has its norm in Paul's service (Acts 20:27-28; cf. vv. 18-26 and Luke 22:24-27). Finally, Paul's declaration that God obtained the church for himself **with the blood of his own Son** has its parallel in Jesus' declaration concerning the "new covenant in my blood," "poured out for you" (Luke 22:20).

In addition to these parallels we note Luke's conscious endeavor to use Pauline language in his farewell at Miletus. Luke's tradition probably referred to a meeting with Ephesian Christians in Miletus. He certainly knew and used the tradition that Paul gained his livelihood through manual labor as tentmaker and leatherworker (cf. vv. 33-34; cf. 18:1-3). He incorporated the tradition concerning the atoning death of Jesus, a tradition which he otherwise strictly avoided (cf. Rom. 3:25). Pauline language appears in words and phrases such as "to serve the Lord" (v. 19; cf. Rom. 12:11), "the ministry (*diakonia*) which I received from the Lord" (v. 24, cf. 2 Cor. 5:18-20). His inclusive ministry is directed to "Jews and Gentiles" (v. 21; cf. Rom. 1:16). Its content is the "gospel" (v. 24, cf. Rom. 1:1, 9, 16, etc.). Only here and in 15:7 is the noun *gospel (to euangelion)* used in

Acts. The Pauline word *grace* appears twice (vv. 24 and 32) and the Greek verb for "admonish" (*nouthetein*) appears only in Pauline letters and here (v. 31). However, the imitation of Pauline language is insufficient for us to conclude that this speech is a condensation of what the historical Paul actually said on this occasion. On the contrary, the speech is a Lukan construction, written in Lukan style and, with the exceptions just noted, its vocabulary is also Lukan. It presupposes a post-Pauline situation in which churches were under the leadership of elders. The churches established by Paul himself did not have elders as their leaders. Moreover, the speech presupposes Paul's death (vv. 25, 37-38) and summarizes his total life's work as legacy and example for ministry in the future, namely, in Luke's own day. In retrospect, Paul appears as the ideal pastor and shepherd, an exhortation for Luke's own present. This Lukan perspective differs from Paul's own injunction: "be imitators of me" (1 Cor. 4:16, cf. 11:1; Gal. 4:12; Phil. 3:17), given in response to specific problems that arose in his churches. In the farewell at Miletus the style and content of Paul's ministry is a timeless example which has validity for all churches and their leaders.

Different proposals concerning *the structure of the speech* have been submitted. We suggest a modification of Michel's conclusion.

Theme: Exhortation of Christians within the Context of Paul's Farewell.

Narrative Introduction (vv. 17-18a)

Part I. Paul's Ministry as Example and Exhortation (vv. 18b-27)

(a) Retrospect, Paul as example (vv. 18b-21)

(b) Prospect, Paul as example (vv. 22-26)

(a') Retrospect, Paul as example (v. 27)

Part II. Exhortations and Commendation (vv. 28-35)

(a) Exhortation to watchfulness, "remembering" Paul's example (vv. 28-31)

(b) Paul's farewell commendation (v. 32)

(a') Paul's example as exhortation to help the weak (vv. 33-35)

Narrative Conclusion (vv. 36-38)

(a) "*He* knelt down and prayed with *them*" (v. 36)

(b) Their response: "*they* all wept . . . and kissed *him*, sorrowing" (vv. 37-38a)

(a') "Because . . . *he* had spoken, that *they* should see his face no more" (v. 38b)

(b') Their response: "And *they* brought *him* to the ship" (v. 38c)

Note the careful balancing of motifs, e.g., Part Ia and a', "I did not shrink," etc. (vv. 20 and 27); Paul's "tears" in Ia are repeated in IIa (vv. 19 and 31); "declaring" what is "profitable" in Ia has its counterpart in the heretics' "speaking perverse things" in IIa (vv. 20 and 30); the public nature of Paul's teaching (v. 20 and, implicitly, v. 27) has its counterpart in the esoteric teaching of the heretics (v. 30). The declaration of what is profitable "from house (church) to house (church)" (v. 20) is taken up in IIa in his ceaseless admonishing "night and day," "everyone" for "three years" (v. 31). In view of his impending affliction, imprisonment, and death (Ib), Paul commends them "to God and the word of his grace" (IIb; cf. "gospel of grace" or "word of grace" in vv. 24 and 32). As Paul's ministry looks to its future completion (Ib), so the Ephesians also have a future (IIb, v. 32) because the Word of God will build up the Ephesian believers and give them "the inheritance among all those who are consecrated." One last sample of parallel structure: Just as IIa contains an explicit exhortation which is connected with Paul's example, so does IIa'. (Additional parallels can easily be recognized, e.g., "and now" in Ib and IIb; "remembering" in IIa and a', etc.) Formal features serve to organize the content of this farewell exhortation and reveal the speech to be a Lukan construction.

17-18a—From Miletus Paul sent a messenger to Ephesus and asked **the elders of the church** to come to him. They obeyed. From 14:23 the reader knows that Paul appointed elders "in every church." This Lukan statement and similar statements in the Pastoral Epistles (e.g., Titus 1:5-9) reflect the situation of post-Pauline churches rather than the Pauline churches during the apostle's lifetime. Paul waited in Miletus a minimum of four days until the elders arrived. We are not told that this delay (cf. v. 16) was due to his changing ships. On the contrary, the narrator assumes that the same vessel that brought him to Miletus was used for the journey to Patara (21:1). Luke probably knew that Paul had met Ephesian Christians in Miletus on this journey and he made that meeting the occasion for Paul's great speech to Christian leaders.

18b-21—Paul summarizes his work **in Asia** in such a way that it can function as example and norm for ministry in the future. Ministry in the church is **serving the Lord with all humility and with tears and with trials,** as Paul had done. Paul had identified himself as a "slave" of Christ (Rom. 1:1). As a slave he is unreservedly at the call of his Lord, who determines his total existence. From this it follows that his style of ministry may not exhibit presumptuousness or pomposity, acting as if one were lord and master of the church. The appropriate ministerial style is **humility,** the opposite of domineering based on religious egocentricity (cf. 2 Cor. 4:5; 11:7; Phil. 2:3; 1 Thess. 2:5-8). Humility as style of ministry was described by the historical Paul in this way: "I know how to be abased, and . . . how to abound; in any and all circumstances I have learned the secret of facing plenty and hunger, abundance and want. I can do all things in him who strengthens me" (Phil. 4:12-13). Paul's service as pastor had been rendered with **tears** (cf. 2 Cor. 2:4; Phil. 3:18). He had known the sorrow of rejected love when all earnest pleading fell on deaf ears (cf. Rom. 9:2). To the style of Paul's ministry also belonged the endurance of **trials which befell me through the plots of the Jews.** To be sure, according to Acts it was Gentiles and not Jews in Ephesus who instigated difficulties. But the narrator was thinking of Paul's whole ministry, beginning with plots by Jews in Damascus (9:23), continuing with troubles in Jerusalem (9:29), Antioch (13:50), Iconium (14:5), Lystra (14:19), Thessalonica (17:5), Beroea (17:13), and Corinth (18:12; 20:3), and ending with the trials that awaited him in Jerusalem (21:28-31; 23:12). References to Paul's afflictions and sufferings also abound in his letters (e.g., 1 Thess. 3:3-4; 1 Cor. 4:9-13; 15:32; 2 Cor. 1:8-10; 4:8-12; 6:4-10; 11:23-29; Phil. 1:12-18), but he does not single out the Jews (cf. 2 Cor. 12:24, 26). Acts, on the other hand, reflects the situation of the church at Luke's time, which felt threatened by Jews more than by Gentiles. The Greek word for "trials" (*peirasmoi*) can also mean "temptations" (cf. 1 Peter 1:6: 4:12). By enduring trials, which function as temptations to lose faith, Paul became an example (cf. 2 Tim. 3:10-12).

From the style of his ministry Paul turned to its central content, its witness. He reminded the elders: **I did not shrink from declaring to you anything that was profitable, and teaching you in public and from house** church **to house** church. With these words Paul claimed that he fulfilled the ideal of a good citizen. "Since we are free men," Plutarch wrote, "we must speak with boldness and may conceal nothing nor pass over in silence what is profitable" (*Moralia* 60C). Paul's **public** ministry (cf. 19:9) is in contrast to the secret teachings of heretics. While he **did not shrink from declaring . . . anything**

that was profitable for salvation, the false teachers are **men speaking perverse things** (v. 30). While he witnessed **to the whole council of God** (v. 27), they peddled a reductionist message. Moreover, Paul testified **both to Jews and to Greeks** that **repentance** in relation to God **and faith in our Lord Jesus Christ** are necessary for salvation— no more and no less (cf. 1 Thess. 1:9). Readers are referred to Paul's sermons to Jews and Gentiles (Acts 13; 14; 17). In general, what is **profitable** is to be found in Luke-Acts. Luke's mini-canon enables the reader to confront those who are **speaking perverse things** (v. 30).

22-26—And now, behold introduces the prospect that lies ahead of Paul and functions as a bracket with the identical phrase in v. 25. The following verse (v. 26) draws a conclusion which in turn serves as basis for the retrospect (v. 27). Paul is **going to Jerusalem,** he hopes for Pentecost (v. 16), to celebrate the outpouring of the Spirit in the city of God (cf. 2:1). He must go there, for he is **bound in the Spirit.** His journey is guided and determined by the Holy Spirit who made him an obedient servant of the Lord (cf. v. 19; 13:2; 16:6-10; 19:21). He is on the one hand uncertain of his future, **not knowing what shall befall me there,** and simultaneously he has a premonition that what lies ahead will not be a joyous celebration but new tribulations. **The Holy Spirit testifies** to him **in every city** through Christian prophets that **imprisonment and afflictions await him** in Jerusalem (cf. 21:4, 10-12 for concrete examples). The exemplary willingness of Paul to face new suffering is made evident in his statement: **I do not count my life of any value, nor as precious to myself, if only I may accomplish** (or "complete") **my course** (or "race") **and the ministry** (Greek, *diakonia*) **which I received from the Lord Jesus.** The word of Jesus forms the background: "Whoever would save his life will lose it; and whoever loses his life for my sake he will save it." Paul's concern lies with the goal and end of his life and service, not with the scaffolding of life, its trappings, or its length. The quality of one's life is revealed at its end (cf. Phil. 2:16; 2 Tim. 4:6-8). To Gentile sinners, life is the most **precious** possession, jealously and selfishly guarded and developed in accordance with the principle of self-fulfillment. To the exemplary minister of the Lord, life is the energy and the vitality that is to be expended in service. Paul compared ministry to running a race toward the finish line, expending one's strength in the course (Phil. 3:14; 1 Cor.

9:24-26). The exemplary style of Paul's ministry facing the future is characterized by (1) his guidance by the Holy Spirit, (2) his ability to live with uncertainty, (3) his willingness to bear suffering, and (4) his determination to finish his course and spend his life in faithful service. The content of his ministry shall always be to **testify to the gospel of the grace of God,** which is synonymous with **preaching the kingdom** of God (cf. 28:23-31; Luke 15:11-24). The **gospel** (only here and 15:7) is the unconditional promise of God that he in his **grace** opens **the kingdom** to all believers, be they Jews or Gentiles. **And now, behold** (v. 25) introduces Paul's solemn announcement of his impending death. You **will see my face no more** (cf. v. 38). According to Acts, Paul did not return to Asia Minor again. This holds true even if he should have been released after his two-year Roman imprisonment (cf. 28:30-31; 1 Clem. 5:7). To argue that Paul did return once more to Ephesus and Macedonia (as the Pastoral Epistles would presuppose) would in fact demand that Acts was written prior to Paul's hypothetical release from his Roman imprisonment. This is a most improbable assumption, especially in view of Luke's use of the Gospel of Mark. We hold that the Pastorals are pseudonymous writings, that Acts 20:25, 38 precludes a return visit of Paul to Ephesus, that Paul was not released from his Roman imprisonment, and that Luke did not place a false prediction into Paul's mouth in his farewell.

Moreover, Paul is taking leave not just of the Ephesian elders, but from **all you among whom I have gone preaching,** that is, from all his churches. They will not see him anymore, because he will suffer martyrdom. The announcement of his final departure leads him to affirm his innocence. **I am innocent of the blood of all of you** (cf. Ezek. 18:13). Similar affirmations appear in farewell speeches (e.g., 1 Sam. 12:2-5; Jub. 21:2-3; T. 12 Patr., Jos. 1). Paul bears no guilt for their **blood,** that is, for their ultimate condemnation by God if they lose faith and fall into unbelief or follow the **perverse** teachings of the heretics (cf. v. 30; 18:6).

27—The reason why Paul is innocent of future failures among his churches and their members lies in the fact that in retrospect he can claim: **I did not shrink from declaring to you the whole council of God** (cf. vv. 20 and 24c). Not a reductionistic, one-sided message consisting, for instance, in a new gnostic self-understanding), but God's revealed will and plan of salvation constituted the content and burden of his ministry, for the sake of which he was willing to suffer imprisonment and martyrdom.

28-31—Thus far Paul's farewell speech contained implicit exhortations to his hearers. The style and content of his ministry are to be an example and normative pattern for ministry in the church after his time. Now in the second part of his speech Paul turned to direct exhortation and addressed his audience in imperatives.

The elders are called **overseers** (Greek, *episkopoi*), which may also be translated "bishops" or "guardians" (first ed. RSV). Elders and bishops are not two different groups of church leaders—they are identical (cf. v. 17). At Luke's time the local community was led by a presbytery whose members were called bishops (plural, cf. Phil. 1:1). This structure differs markedly from the later notion of one monarchical bishop in each Christian community and from the still later development of diocesan bishops with presbyters as local representatives of episcopal authority. Even more significant is the fact that in this farewell speech to elders-bishops Paul did not introduce a theory of succession (Greek, *diadochē*), which was known in Rabbinic Judaism as well as in Hellenistic philosophical schools. Nor did he introduce the notion of delegating the community's authority to leaders elected by the community. Rather, he affirmed that the ministerial office of elders-bishops is instituted by God and that it is God, **the Holy Spirit,** who **has made you overseers,** bishops, in the local community. The ministerial office belongs to the essence of the church, without which the church cannot exist because the church also must hear the Word of God ever anew. To be sure, according to Acts Paul had appointed elders (14:23), but he did not deduce the presbyterial office from his own (apostolic) office (as later ecclesiastical theory would have it). Rather he grounded the presbyterial office directly in the will of God. A theory of apostolic succession is not a part of Luke's view of ministry, or he would have had to introduce it in this section. Yet the elders function as Paul's successors, because the Holy Spirit who "set apart" Paul (13:2) has made them overseers who will work after Paul.

28—The responsibilities of the elders-bishops are, first, to **take heed to yourselves.** Pay attention to your own spiritual life. Only if the leaders themselves are faithful to the Lord can they fulfill their ministerial function and set an example for their people. Second, **Take heed . . . to all the flock, . . . to care for the church of God.**

The metaphor of God's people as a flock is found in the Old Testament (Isa. 40:11; Ezekiel 34; Psalms 23; 100:3; etc.) and in the New Testament (Luke 15:3-7; 12:32; John 10:1-16, 27-30). Under Jesus, the Shepherd and Guardian (*episkopos*, 1 Peter 2:25), church leaders are called by God to function as "shepherds," or "pastors" (Eph. 4:11), giving spiritual oversight and pastoral care (1 Peter 5:2) by preaching and teaching rightly. Their local community is the church of God in a particular place. The church belongs to God (1 Cor. 1:2; 10:32; 15:9) because he has "purchased" or obtained it with the blood of his own Son. This translation of v. 28 in the second edition of the RSV is better than that found in the first edition. The Greek text does not contain the word *Son*, but reads "his own." Like "the Beloved" (Eph. 1:6), so "his own" refers to the Son of God. Only once in Acts does Luke speak of the saving efficacy of the death of Jesus (cf. Rom. 3:25; 1 Cor. 15:3; 1 Peter 2:24; 3:18) by using a traditional formulation. God redeemed his people, the church, through the atoning death of his Son. Therefore the church is God's possession.

29-31—With the pastoral responsibility of shepherding and taking care of God's flock firmly established, Paul now turns to the future. I know that after my departure fierce wolves will come in among you. A transition in pastoral authority occurs. After Paul's departure the elders, as good shepherds, were to guard God's flock against dangers from outside the church. Fierce wolves, without camouflage—in distinction from wolves in sheep's clothing (Matt. 7:15)—will try to rip the church apart. Luke did not specify the characteristics of the church's outside opponents. The danger envisioned might come from persecutors, Jewish countermissionaries, pagan preachers, or magicians. And from within the church, from among your own selves (that is, from the ranks of the leaders of the church) will arise men speaking perverse things; and their heresies will shatter the unity of the people of God as they draw away the disciples after them and into heresy (cf. 1 Tim. 1:19-20; 4:1-3; 2 Tim. 1:15; 2:15-18, which reflect the growth of heresy in the post-Pauline church of Ephesus and the province of Asia).

It is quite possible that Luke used Mark 13:21-23 as the basis for his formulation of vv. 29-31. He had omitted this Markan text in his Gospel. But just as he reproduced Mark 13:10 (omitted in Luke 21) in a new Lukan form in Luke 24:47, and just as he reproduced Mark

13:32 (omitted in Luke 21) in Acts 1:7, so it is quite possible that he had saved Mark 13:21-23 for the occasion of Paul's Miletus speech and rewrote it drastically. According to Luke the time for false prophets within the church is the time after Paul, a time predicted by Paul. He bears no blame for the damage they caused.

Because of dangers from outside and inside the church, watchfulness is mandated to all church leaders. **Therefore be alert** (cf. 1 Cor. 16:13: Phil. 3:2; 2 Cor. 11:12-15). Paul's own example serves as the model for ministry. **For three years** he **did not cease night or day** (cf. v. 11) **to admonish every one with tears.** His example is an exhortation and encouragement for all leaders in the church and must therefore be remembered. For the phrase "night and day" see 26:7; Luke 2:37; 1 Thess. 2:9; 3:10. No time was inconvenient for Paul to admonish and shepherd individual believers, lest they go astray. Church leaders were to remember that and offer individual pastoral care. His intense personal involvement in pastoral admonition of individuals is indicated by his **tears** (v. 19; cf. 2 Cor. 2:4).

32—**And now** signals the introduction of a new thought. Solemnly, Paul announces and enacts his farewell commendation. Just as his own future does not lie in his own hands, so likewise the future of the church and its leaders will be determined by God. Paul will depart from them, but **God** and his Word shall be with them. And **to God and to the word of his grace** Paul committed his churches and their leaders in his farewell act (cf. 14:23). The problem of the church's continuity forms the agenda behind this farewell discourse. According to Luke the continuity of the church is guaranteed by the Word of God and by the ministerial office which is to serve the Word of God. But elders can serve the Word only when they themselves live under it, and not above it or apart from it. Therefore, Paul **commended** the elders **to God and the word of his grace.** That he **commended** means that he entrusted them to the care and protection of God's Word. This Word "has power" (RSV, **is able**) to build **you up.** The church is God's eschatological temple (cf. 1 Cor. 3:16-17) and body of Christ (Eph. 4:16), built **up** by the Word of grace in which the Holy Spirit is active. That Word of grace is powerfully able to bestow **the inheritance among all those who are sanctified** (cf. 26:18; Col. 1:12; Wis. 5:5; Deut. 33:3). **Those who are sanctified** are the people who are separated from the world of idolatry and unbelief and incorporated into the people of God through the Word of grace. They live in faith, obedience, and love (cf. Paul's example in this speech) and hope for the **inheritance,** for their final salvation on the last day, promised by the Word of grace.

How then did Luke relate the ministerial office to the Word of God? For Luke pastors, like apostles, are "ministers of the word" (Luke 1:2, genitive of object!), serving the Lord (v. 19) by testifying to the gospel (v. 24). They are challenged to minister to the Word, as Paul and Peter before him had done, so that the Word of God is heard and becomes lively and powerful in the church and the world. When the Word of God interacts with the world it will stir up controversy, challenging established assumptions and breaking down entrenched positions and barriers. This in turn frequently causes afflictions for ministers of the Word, as can be seen from Paul's example.

Finally, how did Luke relate the Word of God to the "apostolic" traditions which he gathered in his two volumes? Are the two simply identical, as in the Pastorals (e.g., 1 Tim. 6:20; 2 Tim. 1:14)? No, not for Luke. Tradition is what pastors must *guard;* the Word of God is what *guards them* and builds them up. The tradition, like the ministerial office, exists for the service of the Word of God. The tradition serves as norm and guide for teaching and preaching and thus grants reliability and authenticity to the church's teaching (Greek, *asphaleia,* Luke 1:4). Tradition does not become Word of God through mere repetition but through reinterpretation and proclamation (as Paul, for instance, had done in his Areopagus speech) and through the Holy Spirit using human words as his vehicle.

33-35—The center of the second part is Paul's farewell act, contained in the previous verse, in which he committed the elders to God and placed them under the power of his Word of grace. This center is flanked by two exhortations (vv. 28-31 and 33-35). (1) Vigilance against opponents without and heretics within demands that elders be faithful to the tradition and the example of Paul. (2) Obedience to the divine injunction to help the weak, exemplified in Paul, demonstrates that the church's leaders have been liberated from greed and covetousness by the power of the Word of grace. It is a basic Lukan insight that the spirituality of the people of God finds expression in a new attitude toward material possessions (cf. 2:43-47) and toward the poor, the needy, and the sick. Church leaders themselves, then as now, could cover up their greed with religious slogans, while engaging in a rip-off of the people of God. The compensation package, the bigger the better, becomes the measure of pastoral success and self-esteem. Over against that "clergy" phenomenon (cf. 2 Cor. 11:20; Titus 1:11; 2 Peter 2:3; Did. 11:5-6, 9, 12) Luke held up the example of Paul, even though he was aware of the Lord's saying that "the laborer deserves his wages" (Luke 10:7). Paul not only had not coveted the status symbols of his day, **silver or gold or apparel** (cf. James 5:2-3) but also had waived his right for compensation and earned his livelihood with his own hands (1 Thess. 2:9; 1 Cor. 4:12; 2 Cor. 11:7-9; Acts 18:3; 2 Thess. 3:8). **These hands ministered to my necessities, and to those who were with me.** Luke generalized and exaggerated when he described Paul as supporting his companions also. But his point is clear. Church leaders ought not to be a financial burden to their congregations nor be possessed by greed, but rather work for their livelihood and set an example **that by so toiling one must help the weak.** The word "must" (Greek, *dei*) expresses a divine obligation. The fulfillment of the obligation toward the "weak," the sick, the aging, and those who cannot work characterizes existence under the Word of grace. This insight is now undergirded by a concluding word of **the Lord Jesus: It is more blessed to give than to receive.** This saying is not meant to put down the weak who "receive" help. Rather it is meant to challenge church leaders who want to receive compensation for services rendered rather than give to the needy (cf. Did. 1:5; 4:5; Sir. 4:31). It is probable that the background of this saying was a Hellenistic proverb (Thucydides 2.97.4, Plutarch, *Moralia* 173D) which became Christianized and which Luke understood in analogy to Jesus' injunctions concerning almsgiving (Luke 6:30, 34-35, 38). The leaders of the church and its well-to-do members should be **remembering** this concluding word of Jesus, which Paul had followed in exemplary fashion. Indeed, the historical Paul had voluntarily forgone his right for compensation, lest he be a burden to his churches and a hindrance to the gospel proclamation.

In this speech Paul declared three times that he had instructed them fully (vv. 20, 27, 31). Like the faithful steward in Jesus' parable, he had given to God's household its food at the right time (Luke 12:43). Paul had alerted the elders to watchfulness (vv. 29-30), as Jesus had alerted his disciples (Luke 12:35-40; 21:34-36), and finally he had called them to social responsibility in their ministry by citing a word of Jesus (v. 35). In short, Paul's ministry was grounded in Jesus' word.

36-38—And when he had spoken thus, he knelt down and prayed with them all. And they all wept and embraced Paul and kissed him, showing their emotions unashamedly (cf. 21:5, 12-14) and **sorrowing most** that they should **see his face no more.** The concluding farewell narrative not only indicates the finality of Paul's departure from his churches in Asia, but also vividly portrays the love of his people which surrounded Paul, their chief pastor, as he moved toward his passion in Jerusalem.

Warnings and Farewell at Tyre and Caesarea (21:1-14)

1-6—Farewell at Tyre: The coastal ship sailed to the islands of **Cos** and **Rhodes,** anchoring overnight, and then reached the port of **Patara** near the southern tip of western Asia Minor. There Paul boarded a larger vessel which cut across the open sea, sailing also by night, and after some days reached the city of **Tyre** on the coast of Phoenicia. A delay of **seven days** gave Paul and his companions the opportunity to visit with the Christians of Tyre. Actually, if speed had been his foremost concern (cf. 20:16) he could have walked from Tyre to Caesarea (v. 8) in about four days. But perhaps in the interest of the security of the collection which his party was carrying he may have preferred to wait and travel by boat. In Tyre some Christians **through the Spirit** urged Paul **not to go on to Jerusalem** (v. 4). Luke saw no contradiction between this warning in Tyre and Paul's declaration in Miletus that he was under divine obligation, "bound in the Spirit," to go to Jerusalem (20:22). The warning in Tyre was not a divine command but a conclusion reached on the basis of a revelation concerning Paul's future in Jerusalem. Foreseeing **through the Spirit** what would happen to Paul, Christians of Tyre urged him not to go there, out of concern for his well-being. Paul, on the other hand knew that he was under the Spirit's mandate to complete this journey and he obeyed, even though he could have decided otherwise. An emotional farewell, similar to the departure scene in Miletus, highlights the esteem in which Paul was held by a church which he had not established, but which he had visited once before (cf. 11:19; 15:3).

7-14—Farewell at Caesarea: The "we" group arrived by boat at **Ptolemais,** the ancient Acco (cf. Judg. 1:31), modern Acre, and stayed for one day with Christians, whom Luke calls **brethren** (v. 7) or "disciples" (v. 4). The former expresses the horizontal dimension of the faith, the latter asserts the continuity with the first disciples. Either by boat or on foot the party arrived at **Caesarea** and stayed in **the house of Philip the evangelist, who was one of the seven** (cf. 6:5; 8:4-14, 26-40). He had been an itinerant preacher-missionary in Samaria and the coastal plain and eventually settled in Caesarea (8:40). The designation **evangelist** occurs only here in Acts (cf. Eph. 4:11; 2 Tim. 4:5) and refers to his missionary activity, distinguishing him from the apostle Philip (1:13). The brief note, that Philip had **four unmarried daughters, who prophesied** is just as interesting as the reference to the Christian **children** of Tyre (v. 5) who with their mothers accompanied Paul to the beach. It is the only occasion where real children appear in Acts, in distinction from the theological use of the word (e.g., 13:33). The promise of Pentecost that "your daughters shall prophesy" receives concrete form through the note about Philip's prophesying daughters. Luke did not elaborate his tradition by placing a prophecy into the mouth of Philip's daughters, but he used the tradition as an introduction to the climactic Agabus prophecy. Agabus is identified as **a prophet** coming **from Judea,** as if the reader did not already know that (cf. 11:28). This may point to Luke's use of an originally separate tradition. **Coming to us** in Philip's house, he took no notice of the four prophets present, but performed a symbolic act, as many an Old Testament prophet had done, and then spoke an interpretive word (cf. Isa. 8:1-4; 20:2; Jer. 13:1-11; 27:1-7; Ezekiel 4; etc.). **He took Paul's girdle,** consisting of a rope or a long strip of cloth, **and bound his own feet and hands,** and he interpreted his action, saying: **Thus says the Holy Spirit, "So shall the Jews at Jerusalem bind the man who owns this girdle and deliver him into the hands of the Gentiles."** Old Testament prophets introduced their oracles with "Thus says the Lord." Jesus used the sovereign "Truly, truly I say to you." The post-Pentecost prophet is God's messenger through Jesus in the power of the Holy Spirit and he expresses the trinitarian foundation of the faith in unreflected language by announcing: "Thus says the Holy Spirit." The Spirit given by God through Jesus (2:22) anticipated the fate of Paul and guaranteed its realization. Agabus did not tell Paul what he ought to do, he merely foretold his destiny. Simultaneously, Paul was free to disobey his mandate to journey to

Jerusalem (cf. 20:22). The wording of Agabus's announcement, that the Jews shall **deliver** Paul **into the hands of the Gentiles,** is a clear parallel to the third passion prediction of Jesus (Luke 18:32). Paul's fate parallels to some degree that of his Lord, and it was probably Luke who inserted the reference to Paul's deliverance into the hands of Gentiles here, just as he did in 28:17, in order to underline that parallel. Strictly speaking, Paul was not delivered by Jews into the hands of Gentiles. He was rescued by the Romans from a Jewish mob (vv. 31-36), and it was the Romans, not the Jews, who bound him in chains (v. 33). But from Luke's perspective it was the Jews who caused Paul's imprisonment in Jerusalem and hindered his possible release by the Romans.

The effect of Agabus's announcement was that Paul's companions as well as the Christians in Caesarea **begged him not to go up to Jerusalem.** Their reaction is as normal and natural as Peter's had been at Caesarea Philippi (Mark 8:32), a reaction which Luke had omitted in his Gospel and now brought in a new setting. Neither Jesus' disciples nor Paul's friends understood and accepted "the divine must" of the respective passions (cf. Luke 9:45; 18:34). Paul, on the other hand, recognized God's will in this prophecy and submitted to it. He accepted his fate, willed by God and his Messiah (cf. 9:16) and foretold by the Holy Spirit. To be sure, Paul, like Jesus, could have saved his life only to lose it (Luke 9:24; 12:4-12). The **weeping** and lamenting of his friends and fellow Christians was **breaking** his **heart.** But like Jesus he was **ready not only to be imprisoned but even to die** in Jerusalem. His forthcoming passion, now predicted three times (cf. 20:23, 25; 21:4, 11) will be **for the name of the Lord Jesus.**

In the end Paul's companions and the members of the church in Caesarea affirmed what is and must be the goal of every exhortation: **The will of the Lord be done,** "not my will, but thine, be done" (Luke 22:42). And with this affirmation the section which portrayed Paul as pastor in retrospect and prospect is completed. Paul was an example, a living exhortation, who not merely repeated with his mouth "Thy will be done, on earth as it is in heaven" (Matt. 6:10) but lived it at whatever cost to himself, walking in the way of the Lord (cf. Luke 14:27). While Luke's primary purpose in this section was hortatory preaching to and encouragement of Christians, we may also recognize an apologetic interest. If in Luke's time there were Jewish Christians, or heretical Gentile Christians to whom Paul was unacceptable, then Luke held up his picture of Paul the pastor who proclaimed "the whole council of God" and unreservedly submitted to the will of his Lord Jesus (cf. 20:24), which led him into a passion, like that of his Lord. This picture, together with such details as Paul's gaining his livelihood with his own hands, would surely put detractors to shame.

■ Witness in Jerusalem, Caesarea, and Rome (21:15—28:28)

Introduction: This concluding section is the high point of Luke-Acts. It presents Paul as the suffering witness of Jesus Christ and defender of himself and the gospel in Jerusalem, Caesarea, and Rome. Paul's divine mandate, "I must also see Rome." (19:21), is articulated twice more (23:11; 27:23-24). But this mandate is endangered by the hatred of the Jews of Jerusalem, the conniving of the Sanhedrin, the dishonesty of two Roman procurators, as well as by a ferocious storm at sea, a shipwreck, and a snakebite. When Paul reaches Rome at last, the reader knows that God's cause has triumphed against incredible odds. It has triumphed through Paul's suffering, in which the word of Jesus spoken at Paul's conversion found its fulfillment (9:16; cf. 14:22). The parallels between Paul's suffering and the passion of Jesus show that history repeats itself and that the Christian takes up his cross daily (Luke 9:23) and is shaped into the pattern of the Master (Luke 6:40). Moreover, in Paul's journey from Jerusalem to Rome the mandate of Christ given to his disciples before his ascension (1:8) has found an open-ended fulfillment. Rome will be the symbol of the unhindered gospel proclamation (28:31), while Jerusalem has become the symbol of the opposition to Christ and his Word.

Acts 21–28 does not tell of conversions nor the spread of Christianity through mission work (13:1—14:23; 16:1—19:20), nor does it deal with encouragement given to churches (20:1—21:14). Its subject is the defense of Paul and of the gospel primarily over against Jews and in a secondary way over against Gentiles. The importance of this concluding section can be seen from its length—eight chapters, in comparison with six dealing with Paul's missionary enterprise, and 66 verses of defense speeches, in comparison with 42 verses of his missionary speeches to Jews and Gentiles. For Luke, Paul the imprisoned, suffering witness and defender of the faith is even more important than Paul the missionary. By portraying Paul as defender of the faith this section functions also as a defense of Paul. But in what sense is he being defended? Some older interpretations suggested that Luke-Acts was written in order to defend Paul at his trial before Caesar's court. This view is unacceptable once we realize that Luke did not write during Paul's lifetime, but some 20 to 30 years after his death. Another theory holds that Luke wanted Christianity to become a *religio licita* in the eyes of the Roman government and share in the privileges granted to Judaism by Rome. Therefore in this section Paul tries to prove that Christianity is the genuine form of Judaism, in order to gain Roman recognition for the church.

However, a legal category of "permitted" and "forbidden" religions did not exist in the first century Roman empire. Precisely this concluding section shows that Paul did not submit to the judgment of the Sanhedrin (25:6-12), and that the distance between Christianity and Judaism grows ever wider. From the Jewish viewpoint this Christian "sect" is "everywhere spoken against," while from Luke's perspective Judaism has become obdurate (28:22, 25-27). Paul turns to the Gentiles (28:28), separating himself from the Jews and their leaders. Hence it is not possible to hold that Luke's aim was to gain political toleration from the Romans by sailing the ship of the church under the Jewish flag. The church of Luke exists in discontinuity with empirical Judaism, but in continuity with the Old Testament (cf. 24:14-15; 26:22-23; cf. Luke 24:25, 32, 44-45). However, the theological continuity cannot be used as a tool for political apologetics. "No Roman official would ever have filtered out so much of what to him would be theological and ecclesiastical rubbish in order to reach so tiny a grain of relevant (political) apology" (Barrett).

But was not Luke's picture of the fair-minded Roman officials, as well as his emphasis on the political innocence of Jesus and of Paul designed to gain the favor of the Roman government? Let us briefly consider these two items. (1) To be sure, there are fair-minded Roman officials in Acts, e.g., the tribune Claudius Lysias (Acts 21–23), or the proconsul Sergius Paulus (13:7, 12), even as there are fair-minded Jews, e.g., the Pharisees of the Sanhedrin (23:9) or Gamaliel (5:33-39). However, this is only half of Luke's picture.

Pilate, Caesar's representative, knew very well that Jesus was innocent and yet he subverted Roman justice (Luke 23:22-25) and became a conspirator in the murder of Jesus (Acts 4:27). The procurator Felix kept Paul in prison because he did not receive the expected bribe (24:26), and his successor Festus was ready to send Paul to certain death because he was eager to do the Jews "a favor" (25:7-11). All three procurators were a disgrace to the ideals of Roman justice. Even the picture of Gallio, proconsul of Achaia, shows a stain, because he tolerated the beating of Sosthenes right in front of his tribunal (18:17). Last, but not least, the Roman magistrates of Philippi are pictured as brutal cowards (16:22,39). Luke's presentation of Roman officialdom was hardly designed to win favor for the church in its eyes. (2) The innocence of Jesus and of Paul of all charges leveled against them is repeatedly stressed by Luke (cf. Luke 23; Acts 18:14-15; 24:22; 25:18-19; 26:32). Nevertheless, in Luke's story Jesus was executed and Paul remained a prisoner.

The religious charges against Paul (cf. 21:21,28a) would be of no interest to the Romans (cf. 25:19). However, Paul was also accused by Jews of creating civil disturbances and profaning the temple (24:5-6; 21:28b). Likewise, the Romans of Philippi accused him of "disturbing our city" (16:20). Yet in Luke's story Paul did not defile the temple nor cause civil strife. He was innocent of political subversion or conspiracy but became the victim of Jewish hatred and Roman lack of integrity. Again we must ask, is this Lukan picture meant to convince the Romans that the Christians are politically harmless? Or is not Luke's message of Paul's innocence rather directed to the members of his own church, to the Christian reader? It is the reader who ought to understand that Christian testimony will frequently result in false accusations, among them the charge of causing civil unrest. It is the reader who must learn to behave in an inoffensive manner, and avoid provocations and simultaneously be prepared to endure innocent suffering. In Acts the Roman government is not the beast and Antichrist of apocalypticism (cf. Revelation 13 and 17–18) but an institution to which Paul appealed for justice (25:6-12) when it became obvious that the Sanhedrin of Jerusalem was bent on destroying him by any means (25:2-3,10-11). Though Roman justice was marred, as Luke repeatedly had shown, still in his opinion it was better than what Paul could expect from the highest Jewish tribunal. Since Paul made an appeal to Caesar it is also obvious that he did not seek martyrdom. The fact of Paul's martyrdom in Rome was known to Luke (cf. 20:25,38), but he did not end his second volume on this note because he did not wish to encourage a fanatical seeking of martyrdom which would prompt Christians to behave in an obnoxious manner and defy the government. Christians must be objectively innocent when charges are brought against them, even though their ultimate allegiance is to God, rather than to Caesar (cf. 4:19; 5:29). They may at times receive justice from Roman courts and have charges against them dismissed, as with Gallio in Corinth (18:14-15). But Gallio could do so only because Paul in fact was innocent of political or civil wrongdoings. In short, Luke's concluding section is not a political apology directed to outsiders, to Roman officialdom, but it is a message for his church and his readers.

In Luke's narrative Paul is not just an example of innocent suffering, bravely borne. Rather Paul, the former persecutor, had been called to suffering (9:15-16). He was destined to carry Christ's name, to bear witness to his Lord as the persecuted and imprisoned servant of Jesus Christ. The high point of his career is therefore not his missionary activity, nor his pastoral encouragement, but his witness as the imprisoned and suffering servant of Jesus. As such he bears witness almost exclusively to Jews, even though as missionary he was to be "a light to Gentiles" (13:47; 26:17-20). The focus of his witness to Jews is the resurrection of his Lord which constitutes "the hope of Israel" (cf. 23:6; 24:15; 26:22-23; 28:20). It is the resurrection of Jesus, not obedience to the Law, which separates the church from Judaism (23:6; 24:21; 26:6-7). As far as the Law is concerned Paul was, is, and shall be a pious Pharisee, who believes and practices "everything laid down by the law or written in the prophets" (23:6; 24:14; 26:5). Ever since his conversion Paul had endeavored to lead Judaism to faith in Jesus the Messiah, whom God raised from the dead (26:22-23). When Jews in particular cities rejected his message, Paul turned to Gentiles, e.g., in Antioch (13:46-47), Corinth (18:6), Ephesus (19:9), and finally also in Rom? (28:28). The separation of Christianity from Judaism resulted not from Paul's disobedience to the Law of Moses (cf. 21:22-26; 25:8) but from the Jewish rejection of the ground of Israel's hope which is the resurrection of Jesus. The inclusion of Gentiles into the people of God was not the work of Paul either, nor was it merely the result of Jewish rejection of Paul's resurrection message. The inclusion of

Gentiles had been foretold by Old Testament prophets (plural, cf. 15:15-18), envisioned by Simeon (Luke 2:31-32), announced by John the Baptist in the words of Isaiah (Luke 3:6), mandated by Jesus (Luke 24:47), enacted by God (Acts 10:1—11:18), and ratified by the church under the leadership of Peter and James and under the guidance of the Holy Spirit (Acts 15). The Gentile mission which was envisioned at the beginning of Luke's first volume is reaffirmed at the conclusion of volume two (28:28). Likewise Jewish rejection of Jesus, noted by the aged Simeon (Luke 2:34-35) and apparent since Jesus' inaugural sermon at Nazareth (Luke 4:17-40) is present at the conclusion of Luke's story (28:25-27). Nevertheless, the imprisoned Paul in Rome continued to witness to *all*, Jews and Gentiles (28:30-31), and he could do so because he "had done nothing against the people or the customs of our fathers" (28:17). He was not an apostate Jew, but a faithful and pious Jew, innocent of the charges against him (25:8). When Paul preached in Rome about "this salvation of God" (28:28), which is "the kingdom of God," his eschatological saving rule, inextricably connected with "the Lord Jesus" (28:30-31), then the commission of Jesus to be his "witnesses . . . to the end of the earth" reached a new phase (1:8). This commission and mandate is not yet completed, but it is in the process of completion. Luke's church is part of that process and so are Luke's readers. From Rome, the center of the empire, all roads lead to "the end of the earth."

The opponents of Paul in these last chapters are the Jews, not Roman officials. In spite of the shabby behavior of the two procurators, Festus at the end declares Paul to be innocent of crimes punishable by law (26:31; cf. 25:18; 24:22-26). The Jewish charges stated at the beginning, the middle, and the end of this section are shown to be false (21:21, 28; 24:5-6; 28:17). Paul has turned neither against the Law nor against the people, nor did he defile the temple. Neither he nor the Christians of Luke's day were apostates or heretics, no matter what their Jewish contemporaries might have said. Jewish Christians obey the whole Law, as can be seen in Paul (21:23-26; 26:5). Gentile Christians observe those portions appropriate to them. Hence Luke once more reminded his readers of the validity of the apostles' decree (21:25).

Why should all of this be important to Luke and his church? Because the problem of the relationship of Christianity to Judaism had become a burning issue in Luke's day. This can also be seen from the Jewish perspective if, as is probable, the 12th benediction was inserted into the synagogue prayers during the 80s of the first century A.D. It reads: "For apostates may there be no hope and may the Nazarenes and the heretics suddenly perish." It is commonly assumed in New Testament scholarship that Luke's church was primarily a Gentile church. But this assumption may well be false and the Lukan church may have had a significant portion of Jewish-Christian members. The theological issue would then be: In what sense is our church, made up of Jews and Gentiles, the people of God, when official Judaism has now repudiated the church, its message and faith? Luke's answer through these last chapters is: (1) "Many ten thousands" of Jews have become believers (21:20) whose roots are embedded in the Old Testament promises which God fulfilled among us through the resurrection and exaltation of the Messiah Jesus and the gift of the Holy Spirit. In accordance with his promise God incorporated Gentiles into his people, and among them the kingdom of God, "this salvation of God," is present already now in a hidden manner (Luke 17:21; Acts 28:23, 28, 31). (2) Political accusations instigated by Jews using mob actions or manipulating pagan magistrates are false. Should Christians commit crimes, however, then they should be punished accordingly (25:8, 11). The religious charges raised against the church are equally false (25:8; 28:17). In contrast to unbelieving Jews it is Christian Jews and Gentiles who believe God's promise and its fulfillment through Jesus, the Messiah and Savior of Jews and Gentiles whom God raised from the dead. With respect to Torah-obedience Jewish Christians can hold their own vis-à-vis the unbelieving Jews. (3) Jewish rejection of the gospel does not invalidate the promises of God, nor their fulfillment for those who believe in Jesus. Jewish rejection demonstrates that "this people's heart has grown dull, their ears are heavy of hearing and their eyes they have closed" (28:27). Utmost caution is needed at this point. Luke did not say that God has rejected the unbelieving Jews prior to the eschaton nor that he has predestined them for damnation. No, until the eschaton "they have Moses and the prophets; let them hear them" (Luke 16:29, 31) and "Moses is read" and preached in the synagogue "every sabbath" (Acts 15:21). While it is true that the Christian church is "everywhere" in Judaism "spoken against" (28:22), it is equally true that "the hope of Israel"

401

(28:20) is not taken away. On the contrary, "God exalted [Jesus] at his right hand as Leader and Savior, to give repentance to Israel and forgiveness of sins" (5:31). So long as they have Moses and the prophets and so long as the mission to Jews continues as Luke indicates (28:23, 30-31), so long the possibility remains that God will open their hearts, ears, and eyes. A final rejection by God comes only at the End (3:23, future tense!) and not during the time of the church's mission. (4) Luke challenges his church to be the people of God to whom God has sent his salvation and who have listened in faith (28:28). It may have to endure unjust suffering, but it has an identity grounded in the past, a hope for the future consummation, and the present experience of God's saving action in history. It is summoned to witness to Jews and Gentiles to the end of the earth.

Paul and the Christians in Jerusalem (21:15-26)

From Caesarea to Jerusalem (15-16)

Disciples from Caesarea accompanied Paul and his party on the 65-mile journey to Jerusalem. The Western text expands the journey and describes Paul and his companions as staying the first night in Mnason's home in a village on the way to Jerusalem. However, **the house of Mnason of Cyprus** which offered hospitality to Paul's extended party should be located in **Jerusalem.** The note that he was **an early disciple** indicates that, like the Cypriot Barnabas (4:36), Mnason did not belong to the community led by the Seven, which subsequent to Stephen's martyrdom was expelled from Jerusalem (see comments on 8:1 and 12:12). Both belonged to the community led by the Twelve, and both Cypriots were open to receiving and living with Gentile Christians. It is clear that Gentile Christians were in Paul's company (cf. v. 29). Not every Jewish Christian in Jerusalem was prepared to offer hospitality to such a mixed group, and therefore Mnason is remembered in Luke's story.

Paul's meeting with James and the elders and his participation in a vow (17-26)—Paul's arrival in Jerusalem and in Rome is noted twice (cf. vv. 15 and 17; cf. 28:14, 16), which may indicate the importance of the city, or distinguish the urban area from the city itself. If the latter is the case, then Mnason's house would have been on the outskirts of Jerusalem. Upon the arrival of Paul's party **the brethren received us gladly,** presumably in Mnason's house, where some representatives of the Jerusalem community waited for them. **On the following day Paul went in with us to James; and all the elders were present** (cf. 11:30; 15:2, 23; 12:17). This is the end of the "we" account that began in 20:5. The focus now shifts to Paul, who told in orderly fashion what **God had done among the Gentiles through his ministry** (cf. 15:4; 20:24). It was God himself who worked through Paul's preaching and teaching and brought Gentiles to faith. Faith is not a pious work but a gift and work of God (cf. 14:27; 18:27; 11:18; 5:31; 3:16b). The response to Paul's missionary success was that James and the elders **glorified God.** Addressing Paul as **brother,** they tell him of the **many thousands** (literally, "the many ten thousands") of Jews who have come to faith, and who, like Paul, **are all zealous for the law.** Jewish Christianity appears not as an insignificant minority, but as an exceedingly large group within Judaism. However, and now comes an embarrassing matter, Jewish Christians, presumably of Jerusalem, Judea, and Galilee, had been told that Paul preached apostasy from Judaism. The defamation of Paul which had been circulating was **that you teach all the Jews who are among the Gentiles to forsake Moses, telling them not to circumcise their children or observe the customs.** The reader of Acts knows that Paul circumcised Timothy (16:3) and kept the Law. (Greek, *ta ethē,* "the customs," refers to the injunctions of the Torah, cf. 6:14; 26:3; 28:17.) The accusation is false, though we can easily see how these rumors could have arisen in the light of statements like Gal. 5:6. How can the Jewish-Christian leaders of Jerusalem prove that the accusation is in fact a defamation? **What then is to be done?** Paul's presence will certainly become known in Jerusalem, and it would take more than mere verbal assurances to persuade the tens of thousands of Jewish believers that Paul was not an apostate Jew. There was, however, one way in which Paul could demonstrate his Torah-loyalty. **We have four men** who are Jewish Christians and who have taken a Nazirite **vow** (see 18:18). If Paul were to **purify** himself **along with them and pay their expenses, so that they may shave their heads,** then all will know that the accusations against you are mere defamations and **that you yourself live in observance of the law.** By undertaking a rite of purification and by paying the considerable expenses for the termination of four Nazirite vows, Paul demonstrated in Jerusalem his loyalty as a Jew to the Torah, even as

403

James and the elders testified that Gentile believers were obligated to keep the apostles' decree in accordance with the Law of Moses (v. 25).

Since the vow of the four men involved shaving their hair, it was clearly a Nazirite vow undertaken by the four Christian Jews. But what does it mean that Paul was **to purify** himself **along with them** (cf. v. 26)? Does Luke mean that the four men as well as Paul had taken a Nazirite vow abroad in Gentile lands (cf. 18:18) and had come to Jerusalem for the termination of the vow (cf. Stolle)? All five of them would then be required to undertake a seven-day ritual to remove Levitical impurity (cf. v. 27). The ritual consisted in reporting to the priest and being sprinkled with the water of atonement on the third and the seventh day (Num. 19:9, 12). These 7 days of purification would then be followed by a minimum of another 30 days in the Nazirate, at the end of which the vow would be terminated in the temple with cutting and burning of the hair and offering of sacrifices, namely, one male lamb, one female lamb, one ram plus cereal and drink offerings for each Nazirite. The **expenses** for the termination of a Nazirite vow were therefore considerable, and it was considered an act of piety to pay the cost of someone else's offerings (cf. Josephus, *Ant.* 19.294). The difficulty with Luke's text is that it assumes that the offerings would be presented after the completion of the seven days' purification (v. 27). This was not possible, because (1) Paul would have had to remain in the Nazirate for another 30 days and so would the other four if they came from abroad, which, however, Luke does not say. (2) But if they were Nazirites from the land of Israel and required Levitical purification, they would still have to complete the remaining days of their Nazirate before they became ritually pure. If the four did not become impure at the same time, their Nazirate could not be terminated at the same time either. (3) If Paul had entered a Nazirate during his time as missionary, he could not have drunk wine, nor celebrated the Eucharist. Therefore, another interpretation would seem more likely.

Luke brought together two separate rituals (cf. Haenchen). We must assume that Paul did not enter a Nazirate but that he was willing to pay the expenses for the termination of the Nazirite vows of four poor Jewish Christians. These four did not participate in the seven-day purification ritual, which Paul took upon himself in order to participate in the termination ceremonies of those four in the temple. Paul, after accepting the request of James and the elders (v. 24), went with the four Nazirites into the temple to arrange for his own purification and to report when the Nazirate of the four would be completed, and made the appropriate **offerings for every one of them** (v. 27). By combining a purification ritual with a termination of a Nazirate Luke produced an account that makes little sense when compared with Jewish practices of his day.

Two questions must be raised. (1) Would the historical Paul have undertaken a purification ritual? Would he have paid the expenses for the termination of four Nazirite vows? (2) What happened to the collection of Paul (cf. Rom. 15:25)? Beginning with the second question we note Luke's silence about the collection at this point in the story. Yet historically when Paul and his company met James and the elders we must assume that Paul, after reporting about God's work among the Gentiles, did in fact endeavor to hand over the collection from the Gentile churches. It was meant to be a sign of the unity of the people of God, the church of Jews and Gentiles. We know that Paul had entered upon his journey to Jerusalem with trepidation. Not that he envisioned being imprisoned there. On the contrary, he had hoped to come to Rome and from there proceed to Spain, but he was not certain whether his collection, this ministry of love on behalf of the Jerusalem community, would be accepted. Therefore he implored the Roman Christians "to strive together with me in your prayers to God on my behalf, that I may be delivered from unbelievers in Judea, and that my service [Greek, *diakonia*] for Jerusalem may be acceptable to the saints" (Rom. 15:30-31). It would seem that in response to Paul's attempt to solemnly transmit the collection to James and the elders, he heard from them a litany of rumors that were circulating about him (v. 21). No, the Jerusalem authorities could not accept money from the uncircumcised with rumors of apostasy flying around about the author of the collection. The growing Jewish nationalism and its rejection of everything Greek (Josephus, *Ant.* 20.159-161) made life for the Jewish Christians in Jerusalem ever more difficult. The real problem consisted in Jewish Christians who belonged to mixed congregations, and who no longer felt obligated to keep the Torah. While the historical Paul did not teach that Jewish believers in Gentile-Christian churches should "forsake Moses" (v. 21), he certainly did not obligate them

405

to live as Jews (cf. 1 Corinthians 8–10). It was the life-style of Jewish Christians in mixed congregations of the diaspora that scandalized Jews in Jerusalem and caused rumors about Paul teaching apostasy.

Historically, it would seem that James and the elders made a twofold request: Would Paul demonstrate the falsity of these rumors by undergoing a Levitical purification rite in the temple, and would he use part of the collection money to pay the expenses for the offering which would terminate the vows of our poor Christian Nazirites? Through such a demonstration of obedience to the Torah Paul would unmask the rumors about him (v. 21)—so James thought. This in turn would enable the Jerusalem Christians to accept Paul's collection.

Did the historical Paul comply with James's request? It has been said that it would be more credible for the dying Calvin to bequeath a golden dress to the Holy Virgin than for the historical Paul to submit to a Levitical purification rite. But this glib answer may merely show how little we know about Paul. It is obvious that Luke did not invent this incident, but found it in his tradition. Moreover, Paul was prepared to live as a Jew among Jews (1 Cor. 9:20) and the unity of the church was most important for him (1 Cor. 12:12-27). Should he not have been willing to submit to a purification ritual in the interest of the unity of the church and in the interest of the collection which was to demonstrate this unity? Finally, why should he not have used part of the collection for the benefit of the poor Nazirites, since the collection was meant for "the poor" in the first place (Gal. 2:10)? Since for Paul the Law of Moses had no soteriological function, he was indeed free to submit to it!

However, before Paul could complete his purification ritual or pay for the offerings of four Nazirites he was almost killed in a mob action and became a Roman prisoner. A new accusation of defiling the temple was added to the old charges of teaching apostasy in the diaspora (v. 28, cf. v. 21). It is most improbable that after this tumult, with hatred of Paul aglow in Jerusalem, the elders and James would accept the collection which they had not accepted before. Luke therefore omitted mentioning the collection at this point. He did so, not because he did not know about it (cf. 24:17), nor because he thought it to be unimportant. Charity, almsgiving, and helping the weak are a major subject in Luke-Acts (cf. Luke 6:30,34-36;

11:41; 12:33; 14:12-14, 33; 18:22; 19:8-9; Acts 2:44; 4:34; 6:1-6; 9:36; 10:2; 11:29-30; 20:33-35). The word *almsgiving* is found, with the exception of Matt. 6:2-4, only in Luke-Acts. Luke probably omitted the collection because he was aware that it had not been accepted by James and the elders. Paul may even have brought it to the temple (see 24:17). Luke was silent about this spectacular failure to demonstrate the unity of the church of Jews and Gentiles, a failure which was one of the great tragedies of the earliest church, and which in turn contributed to the ever-growing alienation between Jewish and Gentile Christianity (in spite of Rom. 11:17-24 and in spite of Luke-Acts and Ephesians). Had he narrated the rejection of the Gentile-Christian collection he would have hopelessly marred his picture of the unity of the believing people of God, which is basic to Luke-Acts. It is a bitter irony that the collection for which Paul had worked hard since the apostles' council (Gal. 2:10; 1 Cor. 16:1-4; 2 Corinthians 8–9; Rom. 15:22-32), a collection that he hoped would forge the bond between his churches and Jerusalem, now became the cause of his imprisonment and eventual martyrdom.

Riot in the Temple, Arrest, and Witness of Paul (21:27—23:11)

27-28—In contrast to the RSV, which suggests that the riot started toward the end of the seven-day period of purification, the Greek text implies that Paul went into the temple on the seventh and last day in order to complete the purification ritual. At this time, when one of James's two conditions was almost fulfilled **Jews from Asia,** that is, the region around Ephesus (cf. 19:9-10) recognized Paul in the temple and started a riot crying out: **Men of Israel, help! This is the man who is teaching men everywhere against the people and the law and this place** (the temple, cf. 6:13); **moreover he has also brought Greeks into the temple and he has defiled this holy place.** These accusations will be repeated during Paul's subsequent hearings (cf. 24:5-6). It is bitter irony that the charge of defiling the temple should be raised at the very moment Paul was ready to complete the Levitical purification ritual. The accusation of defiling the temple would indeed constitute a capital offense. Gentiles could enter into the "court of the Gentiles," but not into "the court of the women" or "the court of the men" of Israel. A barrier with Greek and Latin inscriptions warned Gentiles not to go beyond this point, and if anyone did so he would be subject to the death penalty. Such an ancient inscription has been found and it indicates not only Roman sensitivity to Jewish customs, but the importance for Jews of keeping the inner courts of the temple free from Gentiles. Their presence beyond the low barrier would automatically defile the temple.

28-30—Luke assures the reader that the accusation of defiling the temple resulted from an error. The Asian Jews had previously seen Paul in the company of the Gentile **Trophimus** from Ephesus (cf. 20:4), and reached the false conclusion that he had brought Trophimus into the temple beyond the court of the Gentiles. Hysterical people are usually wrong. In the subsequent riot **they seized Paul and dragged him out of the temple, and at once the gates were shut.** The closing of the gates probably refers to the gates leading to the inner courts; they were closed so that Paul would be unable to flee there, or worse, be killed there, which would also defile the temple.

31-36—As the mob was beating Paul, Roman soldiers stationed in the fortress of Antonia, located northwest of the court of the Gentiles and connected with it by stairs (cf. v. 35), intervened and saved Paul's life. Luke's message here is that God works also through Gentiles, but his work is perceived frequently only in retrospect. Then the Roman **tribune** Claudius Lysias, commander of the cohort stationed in the Antonia fortress, formally **arrested** Paul **and ordered him to be bound with two chains** (cf. 21:11). His immediate inquiry as to **who** his prisoner was **and what he had done** yielded no certain facts (Greek, *asphales*, v. 34; cf. 22:30; 25:26; Luke 1:4), **because of the uproar,** with **some in the crowd shouting one thing and some another** (cf. 19:32). Therefore the tribune **ordered him to be brought into the barracks** of the Antonia fortress with the mob screaming: **Away with him,** just as another Jerusalem mob had done in Luke's narrative some quarter of a century earlier (cf. Luke 23:18; Acts 22:22). With this mob scene Luke indicates that for the third time Jerusalem has rejected God's invitation represented by his messengers, Jesus, Stephen, and Paul. Henceforth it will function in the remaining story of Acts as the symbol of opposition to the gospel.

Paul's Defense before the Crowd (21:37—22:21)

Introduction: Paul's speech is framed by two scenes in which Paul clears up two misunderstandings in the mind of the tribune Claudius

Lysias. Paul is not an Egyptian but a Jew. He is not a revolutionary, but a citizen of Tarsus. The first subsection is not a realistic report. One should not ask: how did Paul find the strength to stand and speak to the mob without a loudspeaker when he had to be carried away by the soldiers half-dead because of the beating he had received? Or, how would an enraged crowd suddenly turn into a quiet audience, listening to the man they wanted to kill? Luke created a scene for Paul's defense before the people of Jerusalem, and he introduced Paul in his new role as the public defender of Christianity.

The three chief actors in this and the following episodes are the Jews, the Romans, and Paul. We shall look at them briefly as they appear in the concluding drama of Acts. The Jews are the accusers who more than once want to kill Paul (21:31, 36; 22:22; 23:10, 12-15; 25:2-3). For them Paul is the despicable "ringleader of the sect of the Nazarenes." Yet important distinctions are made between the mob, Jewish leaders, and fanatics on the one hand, and the Pharisees and King Agrippa on the other. The Pharisees in Jerusalem could "find nothing wrong in this man," and in Caesarea the Jewish king declared Paul innocent (23:9; 26:31-32). Moreover, the Roman Jews received no official word of Paul's condemnation from the authorities in Jerusalem (28:21). In short, Judaism as a whole does not share in the role of Paul's accuser.

The Romans play the role of judges in this concluding part of Acts. At first they were bewildered and confused about Paul's identity. Was he the leader of a band of assassins (21:38)? They put chains on Paul and were ready to flog him, but they could be persuaded to desist and listen (21:39; 22:25-29), and eventually they understood that the whole commotion was "about questions of their law" and disputes "about their own superstition" (23:29; 25:19). In short they were ready to acknowledge that Paul committed "nothing deserving death or imprisonment" (23:29; cf. 26:31-32). Yet Paul remained a Roman prisoner because of the connivings of two procurators (24:26; 25:9). Roman justice was a mixed bag. It was Festus who forced Paul to appeal to Caesar, thereby prolonging his imprisonment (25:10-11). But simultaneously it was the Romans who through the irony of misunderstanding (thinking Paul to be an Egyptian assassin) saved him from certain death (21:31-39). In general the Romans treated their prisoner with leniency (cf. 25:23; 27:3; 28:16, 30).

Paul is cast in the role of defender under arrest. Yet he retains the initiative throughout his imprisonment and hearings by witnessing to Christ and by disrupting the plans of both Romans and Jews (22:25; 23:6, 12-22; 24:26; 25:2-3, 9-10). In his defense speeches the Old Testament promises recede into the background while his own life story, told twice, exemplifies the fulfillment of "the hope of Israel" (23:6; 26:6-8; 28:20). He deals with Jewish accusations only indirectly, or in summary fashion (25:8). But in his witness to the resurrected Christ he turns the tables on his accusers and demonstrates that not he but they are unfaithful to "the hope of Israel." In so doing he is not just his own defender, but functions as the public defender of the church and its message.

The words and deeds of the three chief actors are enclosed by the One who in heaven directs the drama that is being played out on the stage of history and who wills that Paul should "see Rome" (19:21; 23:11; 27:24). In so directing the closing drama of Acts, God fulfills in Paul what Jesus had predicted: "They will lay their hands on you and persecute you, delivering you up to . . . prisons, and you will be brought before kings and governors for my name's sake. This will be the time for you to bear witness" (Luke 21:12-13; Acts 9:15-16).

37-40 (Paul and the Tribune)—Paul, carried up the stairs that led from the court of the Gentiles into the Antonia fortress, was able to address **the tribune** in polite Greek. This surprised the tribune who thought that he had captured an **Egyptian** Jew who had recently led an unsuccessful revolt and then disappeared mysteriously. According to Josephus (*Ant.* 20.169; *War* 2.261-264) the Egyptian Jew had claimed to be a prophet, led a band of his followers first into the desert and then to the Mount of Olives, where he promised them that at his word the walls of Jerusalem would come tumbling down (as did Jericho's at Joshua's time), whereupon they would liberate the holy city from the Roman oppressor. The procurator Felix did not look kindly on this undertaking and his troops dispersed the revolutionaries, killing some and taking some prisoners, but their leader escaped. Naturally, the tribune thought, the people were venting their rage on this Egyptian. God works in mysterious ways. Through the misunderstanding of a Roman officer, Paul is saved from death by his fellow Jews. I thought you were **the Egyptian . . . who led the four thousand men of the Assassins out into the**

wilderness. The word *assassins* (the Greek, *sikarioi*—a loanword from Latin, *sica*, "dagger"—means "daggermen") refers to Jewish terrorists who killed pro-Roman Jews, such as the high priest Jonathan, son of Annas (Josephus, *War* 2.255-257). According to Josephus the number of the followers of the Egyptian was 30,000 instead of **four thousand.** The difference resulted perhaps from confusing the Greek capital letter Delta (Δ), which equals 4000, with the similar capital letter Lambda (Λ), which equals 30,000. The centurion's question gave Paul the opportunity to identify himself. **I am a Jew, from Tarsus in Cilicia, a citizen of no mean city.** As a Jew Paul had every right to enter the inner court of the temple and hence he did not defile the temple. Moreover, he was not a revolutionary nor terrorist, but a citizen of a respected Cilician city. It is only through Acts that we know that Paul came from **Tarsus.** It is typical of Luke that he never told everything at once, and so he left Paul's Roman citizenship for the episode after Paul's speech (22:22-29). Typical also is that Luke does not explain everything. Why would Paul's elegant Greek prove to the tribune that he was not the Egyptian? Greek was spoken in Egypt too! Or, why would the tribune give him permission to speak? For our author, such questions would be beside the point. The point is that Paul is standing in the temple for the last time, and this occasion calls for a speech. With the tribune's permission, Paul, standing at the top of the stairs facing the temple and surrounded by Jews and Romans, **motioned with his hands,** the sign for silence (cf. 13:16; 26:1), **and when there was a great hush he spoke to them in Hebrew,** which means Aramaic, the common language of the near East, and then **they were the more quiet** (22:2).

Defense Speeches, Acts 22–26.

Neyrey has shown that elements of secular defense speeches, as discussed in rhetorical handbooks, are found in the speeches of Acts 22–26. We modify his insights slightly.

1. Paul's opening statements are designed to show his good reputation (22:3; 23:1,6a; 24:10-11; 26:4-5; even his authorization by the Sanhedrin, 22:5; 26:10,12).

2. Defense speeches must deal with the basic issue. The charges leveled against Paul by his opponents (21:28; 24:5-8) are not the basic issue and are therefore refuted in summary fashion (24:12-

411

13, 19-20; 25:8). Paul's good reputation and background already function as an implicit refutation of the false charges by his opponents. However, the basic issue between him and them is the resurrection of Jesus and its agreement with Scripture. This basic issue is clearly articulated by Paul (23:6b; 24:14-21; 26:6-8, 16-23), and it was also known to Felix (as Luke tells his readers in an aside [24:22, 24-25]) and to Festus (25:18-19).

3. Defense speeches must offer proof and additional corroboration. Paul's Damascus experience is his proof of the correctness of his belief and witness regarding the basic issue, the resurrection of Jesus. This proof can be corroborated (a) by his traveling companions, (b) by Ananias, and (c) by his subsequent obedience to "the heavenly vision" (22:9, 12-16; 26:14, 19-23).

One cannot speak of a "new literary form . . . of the forensic defense speech" (so Neyrey), because the sequence of the parts is not identical in the defense speeches of Acts (in contrast to the sequence of the parts of miracle stories). Nevertheless Luke was aware of *some* of the elements that belong to a defense speech. But he used the defense speeches primarily for the reader's edification, for his or her understanding of the basic issue between church and synagogue. He also gave to each of Paul's defense speeches its own peculiar accent; e.g., in the first it is the mandate for mission among Gentiles issued to Paul by the resurrected Christ in Jerusalem's temple (22:17-21; cf. 1:8).

1-21 (Paul's defense speech to the people of Jerusalem)—Like Stephen before him, Paul addressed the people of Jerusalem as **brethren and fathers** (cf. 7:2), which expressed his respect for older people present as well as his solidarity with his audience. He characterized his speech as **defense** (Greek, *apologia*, cf. 25:16; and the verb in 24:10; 25:8; 26:1, 2, 24; Luke 12:11-12; 21:12-15). His defense is not a rebuttal of each of the charges against him but a witness to his Lord in the light of his own experience.

Jesus had admonished his followers: "When they bring you before the synagogues and the rulers and the authorities, do not be anxious how or what you are to answer or what you are to say; for the Holy Spirit will teach you in that very hour what you ought to say" (Luke 12:11-12). Now Paul is ready to defend his cause before "the people" (cf. 21:39). His defense is an autobiographical recital in three parts: (1) his background, persecution of Christians, and Damascus experience, vv. 3-11; (2) his call to be a witness "to all men" (vv. 12-16); (3) his temple vision in which Christ sent him "far away to the Gentiles" (vv. 17-21). His defense moves from a declaration of solidarity with his audience to an ever more intensive challenge to his hearers. When all is said that need be said, the audience reacts with fury (vv. 22-23).

3 **(His background)—I am a Jew.** This opening statement is a theme of the whole speech. He is not an apostate but a Jew and he remained a faithful Jew also as a Christian. In sketching his vita he follows a Hellenistic pattern that uses three phases to indicate a man's development, namely, **born, brought up,** and **educated** (cf. 7:20-22 for the same pattern). He was **born in Tarsus,** which is mentioned only in Acts (cf. 9:11, 30; 21:39). Later we will hear that Tarsus was the place where his Roman citizenship originated (cf. v. 28). He was **brought up in this city,** Jerusalem, which implies that he left Tarsus in early childhood and spent practically all his life (prior to Damascus) in Jerusalem. Thus he did not learn his trade as leather worker/tentmaker in Tarsus, but in Jerusalem. He was **educated at the feet of Gamaliel** (the RSV misplaced the comma, which should be after "city"). Rabban Gamaliel I, mentioned in 5:34, was the grandson of the great Hillel who founded the rabbinic school of Hillel. Many interpreters have rejected the notion of Paul's education under Gamaliel. However, Paul himself asserted that he was a Pharisee, blameless according to the Law (Phil. 3:5). Since we have no evidence of the existence of Pharisaic schools outside of Palestine prior to A.D. 70, Luke may well be correct about Paul's education. But we may not conclude that Paul became an ordained rabbi, a notion which neither his letters nor Acts support. The study of the Torah was also undertaken by persons other than future rabbis. What is important here in v. 3 is that Paul did not repudiate his education under Gamaliel. Thus the accusation that he is "teaching . . . against the people and the law and this place" is implicitly rejected. With the following clause Paul articulates the abiding result of his education. (Again the punctuation of the RSV should be changed. Place a comma before "according" and omit the comma after "fathers.") **According to the strict manner of the law of our fathers** Paul was and is **zealous for God as you all are this day.** He not only *was* but *is* a Pharisee also as a Christian (cf. 23:6; 26:5). Beginning with the direct address ("brothers and fathers," v. 1) and

ending with "the law of our fathers" and their common zeal for God, we can hear that in every phrase Paul expresses his solidarity with his Jewish audience. He readily grants that they **all are zealous for God,** just as he was and still is.

4-5 (The persecutor of the Way)—Zeal for God, however, can be misguided (Rom. 10:2; Gal. 1:14; Phil. 3:6). The zeal of religious fanatics has caused as many deaths and tears as the brutality of a despot like Nero. With zeal for God crusades were fought, infidels slaughtered, heretics burned, and Jews exterminated. Paul now proceeds to give an example of his zeal for God which still expresses his solidarity with his people but which simultaneously places a large question mark behind their present zeal for God. Though he narrates his activity as persecutor objectively, there can be no doubt that from Luke's perspective his former zeal for God was misguided. Paul had gone further than most if not all of his audience in his religious zeal and **persecuted this Way,** the church, even to the point of **death, binding and delivering to prison both men and women** (cf. 8:3; 9:1-2; 1 Cor. 15:9; Gal. 1:13; Phil. 3:6). His narration of his persecution of Christians, including his journey to Damascus, can be confirmed by the Sanhedrin.

6-11 (His Damascus experience)—Paul did not become a Christian by his own volition, but an encounter with **Jesus of Nazareth** ended his activity as persecutor once and for all. He recounts in his own words what happened to him on his way to **Damascus** (cf. 9:1-9). For variations between the first and the second account, see comments on 9:3-9. Additional information includes the note that the experience took place **about noon,** that the light from heaven was **great,** that Jesus is **of Nazareth** and that Paul's blindness resulted from **the brightness of that light,** rather than from a temporary punishment (cf. 9:8-9; 13:11). This first part of Paul's autobiographical recitation has portrayed him as a strict, Law-obedient Jew who would not voluntarily have become a Christian had it not been for a personal encounter with Jesus. He had been officially authorized to punish Christians and in so doing was in fact persecuting Jesus who identifies himself with them (vv. 7-8). His misguided zeal for God came to an end, not by a process of rational investigation but through an unexpected encounter which changed him from a zealous persecutor into a blind man who had to be **led by the hand** into Damascus. Henceforth his zeal for God would have its orientation in Jesus, who did not heap suffering on others but endured it himself. No less important is the fact that Jesus on the Damascus road did not tell him to forsake "the law of our fathers." Faithfulness to the "law of our fathers" is not incompatible with faith in Jesus Christ, because the Law does not have a soteriological function in Acts or the Pauline letters (15:10-11; Gal. 3:21).

Identification with his people and challenge to his people continue throughout this speech. In Acts Paul does not reject zeal for the Law (contrary to Phil. 3:4-6). What is rejected are the false consequences drawn from zeal for God and his Torah. False consequences led him to persecute Christians. His audience, who had almost killed him, is now challenged to recognize that hatred and persecution manifest misdirected zeal for God and his Law. Paul realized his misdirected zeal when he encountered the living, exalted Jesus who identifies himself with the persecuted. The implicit challenge and question with which the first part closes is this: Will Paul's witness to the living Jesus persuade his audience that their zeal, like Paul's prior to Damascus, is misdirected and that they are drawing wrong consequences from their zeal by persecuting Paul?

12-16 (The call of Paul)—The second part functions as transition by interpreting the Damascus vision and paving the way for the temple vision. The double vision of 9:10-12 is omitted, for it would contribute little to the present situation. Omitted also is the reference to Ananias as a Christian. The reader knows this already and the audience does not need to know. What is emphasized instead is Ananias's publicly acknowledged piety, because it serves the purpose of identification with the zeal of the audience. **A devout man according to the law, well spoken of by all the Jews** of Damascus healed Paul's blindness. The miracle of receiving sight corroborates his Damascus experience. Ananias here does not mediate Paul's call and election (cf. Gal. 1:1, 11-12, 16), but he interprets the Damascus event. In contrast to 9:15-17 it is not "the Lord" Jesus, but **the God of our fathers** who is the subject of an announcement. In 9:15-16 we heard what Jesus said to Ananias, but now we hear what Ananias spoke to Paul. In comparison with 9:10-16 Ananias's role diminishes in this speech (22:12-16) and disappears completely in chap. 26. In chap. 9 Ananias was the recipient of a vision, commission, and explanation from Jesus through which he is "converted" to go, heal, baptize, and incorporate Paul into the church. Thus he played the role of Paul's spiritual father. Here (chap. 22) Ananias's role is that of an interpreting and corroborating messenger on the one hand and a link between the Damascus vision and the temple vision on the other. His importance is overshadowed by the climactic vision of Jesus in the temple, a vision which would have been out of place in chap. 9.

Ananias said to Paul, **The God of our fathers** (cf. "the law of our fathers," v. 3) **appointed you** (or "chose" or "destined you," cf. 3:20) **to know his will,** God's plan in salvation history (cf. 20:27). God's election is prior to Paul's response; God has chosen Paul **to see the Just One** (3:14; 7:52) **and to hear a voice from his mouth.** The reader knows that **the Just** (or Righteous) **One** is none other than Jesus of Nazareth who appeared to Paul as a great bright light and spoke to him (vv. 7b, 8b, 10b). The challenge for the audience is to relate to the Just One who appeared to Paul in accordance with the will of "the God of our fathers." The purpose of Paul's election is to be **a witness for him to all men of what you have seen and heard.** The Lukan concept of **witness** has its focus in Jesus' resurrection and exaltation and it presupposes "seeing" and "hearing" Jesus (see comments to 1:21-22; 13:31). In Acts, Paul cannot be a resurrection witness, testifying to the identity of the earthly Jesus with the Resurrected One, because Paul had not been a disciple during Jesus' earthly life and during the 40 days between Easter and the ascension. But he, as well as Stephen, can testify to the exalted Christ, to what he has **seen and heard** (cf. v. 15; 26:16; 7:55-56; 22:20)!

Paul is not the 13th apostle in Acts, but the one who in theological continuity with the apostles and their church-founding witness has been chosen to testify to Christ from Jerusalem to Rome, including Asia Minor and Greece. His witness bridges the time between the apostles and "us," the Lukan church. Moreover his witness must be **to all men.** The reader understands this to mean Jews and Gentiles. At this point Paul's audience thinks it refers to Jews only (cf. vv. 21-23). The Damascus experience does not mean that the Law of our fathers is abrogated, but that a new relationship to the God of our fathers is initiated. He revealed the Just One to Paul and elected Paul to be his witness. This new relationship is sealed by Baptism through which God bestows forgiveness of **sins** (v. 16) in response to **calling on** the **name** of the Lord Jesus (cf. 2:21). Paul who was and remains a Jew (v. 3), through Baptism becomes a member of the community that acclaims Jesus as Lord. The implicit challenge to the audience is unmistakable. Through his witness to them they are invited to draw some far-reaching conclusions, such as: (1) to recognize that the "law of our fathers" is not the whole revelation for all of salvation history; (2) to consider that the Just One is Jesus of Nazareth who appeared to Paul; (3) to take seriously Paul's calling to witness to "all men," a calling issued by "the God of our fathers."

This second part of the speech serves not only as interpretation of the preceding Damascus experience, but also functions as transition to the concluding highpoint. **To see the Just One and to hear** a word from him are taken up in vv. 18 and 21, which also clarify for the audience the meaning of witnessing to "all men." As transition, Ananias's words to Paul point to the future. God, who has appointed Paul, will reveal to him his will and the Just One, who in turn will speak to Paul.

17-21 (The commission of Paul)—The interpretation of the Damascus vision finds its confirmation in a new scene. Jesus appeared to Paul in the temple and commissioned him to leave Jerusalem and preach to the Gentiles. Speaking in the temple area, Paul told his audience that upon his return from Damascus he was **praying in the temple,** like any pious Jew, and then he **saw him** (v. 18). Jesus thereby manifested himself as Lord of the temple (cf. Luke 2:41-45; 19:45-48). Paul again identified with the audience through the prayer and temple motif, and he challenged his hearers to gain a new perspective. Jesus had been condemned as one "perverting our nation" (Luke 23:2). Moreover, the command of Jesus and its underlying reason pose a challenge for his audience. **Make haste,** Jesus commanded Paul, **get quickly out of Jerusalem, because they will not accept your testimony about me.**

Luke had deliberately omitted the temple vision and commission in chap. 9, because the reader should understand that it was Peter and not Paul who inaugurated the Gentile mission. In 9:29 Luke gave the attempted murder of Paul as the reason for his sudden departure from Jerusalem. Had he brought the temple vision at that point in his narrative, Paul would have appeared to start the Gentile mission while Peter was still in Jerusalem or in Joppa, where he stayed "for many days" (9:43). Now in his defense speech we also hear why Paul was ordered to leave Jerusalem quickly. His witness would not be accepted. This prediction finds an ironic fulfillment in the Jerusalemites' subsequent behavior (vv. 22-23). Paul objected to the commission, just as Peter and others had done (cf. 9:10-16; 10:12-16; Jer. 1:4-10). Objections are a standard feature of commission narratives. However, Paul's commission is odd, since he is commanded not to preach in Jerusalem, but to get out quickly. To this he objected, because as a converted persecutor he thought his witness would be all the more effective. If anyone could persuade Jews that Jesus is the Messiah, then it would be a Jew who had been "zealous for God," and in his zeal had gone so far as to be present and **approving** when **the blood of Stephen thy witness was shed** (7:58; 8:1,3). Stephen is identified here as Jesus' "witness," in view of his vision and testimony (7:55-56). But the reference to the shedding of his blood gives to Stephen's witness some coloring from the "martyr witness" of later Christian usage. (The RSV translation "in every synagogue" should be changed to "in the synagogues," v. 19.)

Paul's objection is rejected by Jesus, who definitively commands: **Depart** from Jerusalem; **for I will send you far away to the Gentiles.** Thus Paul is one who is sent by Jesus himself. While Luke generally avoided the title "apostle" for Paul (except 14:4,14) in the interest of his periodization of salvation history, the commission of Paul in the temple makes it nonetheless clear that he functions as apostle to the Gentiles, because he is "sent" (Greek, *exapostellō*) by Jesus himself. Furthermore, the commission enables the audience to understand what witnessing "to all men" means (v. 15). For **far away** see 2:39, where Peter's Pentecost speech alludes to the Gentile mission. The challenge of Paul's commission is not lost on his audience (cf. vv. 22-23). The speech began with Paul's first person singular, "I am a Jew," and it ended with Jesus' first person singular, **I will send you far away to the Gentiles.** In his zeal for God, Paul the persecutor was stopped on the Damascus road and in the temple vision Jesus pointed him in a new direction. A strict Jew, zealous for God, can be a Christian, sent to the Gentiles by his Lord, because neither on the Damascus road, nor in the temple was Paul told to turn against the Law of the fathers (v. 3).

22-29 (The reaction of Jews and Romans)—The literary device of interrupting the speech indicates the issue as an unbearable provocation of the audience. The issue is mission to Gentiles and their incorporation as Gentiles into the people of God. **Up to this word they listened;** then they cried, **"Away with such a fellow from the**

earth! For he ought not to live" (cf. 21:36). They lent emphasis to their screaming by either waving, or shaking out, or throwing off, or perhaps even tearing their outer **garments** (the Greek is not clear) and throwing **dust into the air.** With this symbolic action of utter disgust they separate Paul from the community of Israel and themselves from him. In their view Paul is no longer "a Jew," much less zealous for "the God of our fathers." From Luke's perspective the Jerusalemites confirm that they cannot hear the word of Jesus, the truth of which they demonstrate by their action (cf. vv. 18 and 22).

The Roman **tribune,** by now bewildered, had to find out **why they shouted thus against him.** He brought his prisoner into the barracks of the fortress Antonia and **ordered him to be examined by scourging.** This procedure was quite legal when applied to slaves and non-Romans. It was also quite painful, worse than being beaten with the rods of lictors (16:22), for the scourge consisted of leather thongs with pieces of metal or wood tied into them and attached to a wooden handle. Paul, already tied up for this interrogation by torture, asked the centurion in charge: **Is it lawful for you to scourge a man who is a Roman citizen, and uncondemned?** The answer was clearly no. Citizens were exempt from this method of examination prior to trials, according to the Lex Julia. Roman law also forbade that uncondemned citizens be put into chains. The centurion reported to the tribune and the tribune came to Paul and asked: **"Tell me, are you a Roman citizen?" And he said, "Yes."** Whereupon the Roman replied: **I bought this citizenship for a large sum** by bribing officials in the imperial bureaucracy—probably at the time of Emperor Claudius and for the purpose of placing his name on the list of candidates. New citizens usually adopted the name of the reigning emperor, hence Claudius Lysias (23:26). Paul could practice one-upmanship. **But I was born a citizen.** The examination by scourging was canceled and the scene closes with the **tribune** being **afraid.** He had acted against the law, because **Paul was a Roman citizen and . . . he had bound him.**

A difficulty arises at this point. (1) Luke is quite aware that it was illegal to put Roman citizens in chains prior to a judicial verdict. Yet v. 30 seems to suggest that Paul was kept in chains overnight even though the tribune was afraid because of this illegal action (v. 29). Why did he not unfasten the chains at once? Or did Luke mean to say in v. 30 that the next morning the tribune "released him" from his cell rather than **unbound** his chains? (2) The matter is complicated because 26:29 and 28:20 seem to indicate that Paul did wear hand-chains. Or are the chains in these two texts to be understood as metaphor for imprisonment (cf. Eph. 6:20; 2 Tim. 1:16)? In some Western manuscripts the tribune releases Paul at once from his chains in v. 29, but this is a later improvement of the text. Frankly, we can only point out the problem, but not a solution.

Some concluding comments: (1) Geographically, every major section in Acts is connected with **Jerusalem,** from the ascension via the apostles' witness through the inauguration of the Gentile mission (11:2) and the Pauline mission (18:22) to Paul's destiny (20:22; 21:13). Though there are many believers in Jerusalem, even "a great many priests" (6:7), the city since Stephen's martyrdom has become the symbol of opposition to the gospel. The heart of the city is its temple, in which Paul made his defense. The climax of this witness is that the Lord of the temple appeared to him in the temple and sent him **far away** because Jerusalem would not receive his witness. Nevertheless, Jerusalem and its temple are not rejected in Paul's defense speech—which is all the more surprising since at Luke's time the city had been conquered and its temple lay in ruins. But in contrast to the post-Pauline interpolator of 2 Thess. 2:13-15 Luke does not gloat over Jerusalem's destruction. On the contrary, Jesus wept over it (Luke 19:41-44), and the temple remained God's house (Luke 19:46) in which Jesus appeared to Paul. Paul had traveled to Damascus to oppose Jesus' followers with authorization from the Jerusalem leaders. His mission was not only not accomplished but turned into the very opposite of what the authorities had commissioned him to do. Damascus becomes the great turning point in his life, where he forsakes the authority of the Sanhedrin and becomes subject to the Lord Jesus. Instead of commissioning a converted Paul to remain in Jerusalem, Jesus sent him into the lands of the Gentiles to preach to Jews and Gentiles. Now upon his return to the city he has witnessed to Jerusalemites for the last time (cf. 9:27-29).

(2) Paul did not announce that God has already cut them off from the people of God, or is going to cut them off prior to the eschaton. In his defense speech Paul represents one part of the divided people of God, namely, those who believe that God raised Jesus from the dead and who admit Gentiles into the people of God on the basis

of Jesus' word and their repentance and faith. The division within the people of God becomes painfully visible (21:31; 22:22). Yet Paul also knows that his accusers are believers in God and zealous for the God of the fathers, even though they cannot believe that Jesus is the resurrected Messiah and that Gentile mission is willed by God. In the last defense speech Agrippa functions as representative of the Jews (26:2) who do not believe in Jesus, but who "believe the prophets," as Paul is aware (26:27). Also, the non-Christian Jews are and remain "sons of the prophets and of the covenant" and heirs to God's promises (3:25; 13:32-33). Paul identified with them by addressing them as "my brothers and fathers" (22:1). They had "Moses and the prophets," and he could speak to them on the basis of the Scriptures (cf. 24:14). Paul's own story shows that it took a miracle of grace to change him from a persecutor zealous for God into a witness of Christ. His biography is an invitation to change, and simultaneously an indication that his own change resulted from divine intervention, not from his own decision. His own experience shows what is possible and what is impossible for zealous Jews who believe in God, and simultaneously his life story shows what is possible for God and his Anointed One. God's future with Israel can no more be controlled by zealous men than Christ's intervention in Paul's life could be controlled.

(3) The story thus far does not justify the conclusion that Luke endeavored to present a political apology of Christianity to the officialdom of the empire. If Luke sought to influence any outside group at all, then it would be the Jews. They ought to see some of the ugly results of their zeal for God in the mirror of Luke's narrative and stop engaging in mob action (cf. 17:5) and using pagan magistrates in their confrontation with the church. But this would at most be a minor aim of Luke, provided that his church and the synagogue were still on speaking terms (see below and 28:17-31). For Luke a Christian could be a good citizen of Rome, or a zealous Jew, and Paul was both.

22:30—23:11 (Paul before the Sanhedrin)—This scene contains a number of historical improbabilities, such as:

• The failure of the tribune to cross-examine Paul after learning that he was a Roman citizen.

• Luke's statement that the tribune **commanded the chief priests and all the council to meet** (22:30). For this he had no authority.

- The presence of the tribune and soldiers, unclean pagans, at the meeting of the Sanhedrin.
- The assumption that the tribune understood Aramaic, the language of the meeting. If he did not, he hardly could find out **the real reason why the Jews accused Paul** (v. 30) by attending that meeting.
- The high priest's order to have Paul struck on the mouth.
- The failure of the tribune to protect a Roman citizen from illegal punishment by the high priest.
- The unlikelihood of Paul's cursing the high priest because he failed to recognize him, the chairman of the meeting.
- The unlikelihood that Paul could divide the members of the council by referring to longstanding theological differences between the Sadducees and the Pharisees.
- The disappearance of the reason for the meeting, namely, clarification about the cause of the tumult in the temple on the day before.
- The description of the meeting as a hearing (22:30) and Paul's reference to a "trial" (23:6).

Interpreters have dealt with these improbabilities in several ways. One, by arguing that the text is a Lukan invention from beginning to end. However, the name of the high priest **Ananias** should caution us against this conclusion. It would not have been easy for Luke to find out the name of the high priest who functioned at the time when Felix was procurator. We can safely assume that Luke's story is based on information received by him. A second approach, with considerable imagination, changes the Lukan text. For instance, "command" (22:30) would mean "invited," or "asked for" a meeting. In that case, the meeting would have to be an unofficial consultation with no one presiding; the high priest would be indistinguishable from the other Sanhedrin members; the presence of unclean Gentiles posed no problems because the council members were eager to shift the blame for the riot to Paul; the tribune had an interpreter; Paul lost his temper momentarily and apologized for it; the tribune did not mind that Paul was struck on the mouth, etc. There is a third approach, namely, that we recognize the historical difficulties present in this episode, but instead of trying to reconstruct what actually happened, we inquire about Luke's point of view. What was he telling the reader?

22:30 (Introduction of the scene)—Since the agitated mob could give the tribune no intelligible reason for its demand for the death penalty, and since Paul's Roman citizenship prevented him from getting to the truth by an examination with torture, therefore the tribune **desiring to know the real reason why the Jews accused** Paul **commanded** that a meeting of the Sanhedrin be held. He **unbound** Paul, which means either he freed him from his handchains (cf. 21:33), or he let him out of his cell (cf. 22:29). The charge of causing a riot in the temple was a serious matter on which the temple authorities ought to shed light. So he **brought** Paul **down** to the council and he also attended the meeting.

1-5 (Confrontation with the high priest)—A fearless Paul, **looking intently at the council** began to speak without being asked. Before any charges were formulated he took the initiative. Indicating his equality with the members of the Sanhedrin, he addressed them as "brothers," not with the more respectful "fathers," (cf. 22:1) and he told them that he had **lived before God in all good conscience up to this day.** Naturally, the reader should not argue that this declaration is contradicted by his participation in Stephen's murder. His present statement summarizes his autobiography which had already been presented to the people in the temple (22:1-21). Even the historical Paul could say of himself that he was "blameless" with respect to "righteousness under the law" (Phil. 3:6), in spite of his painful awareness of having persecuted the church (Phil. 3:6; cf. 1 Cor. 15:9). As summary of his life's story, his declaration of a **good conscience** (cf. 24:16; 1 Tim. 1:5,19; 1 Peter 3:16,21) refers in the present context to his zeal for God and his Law as well as to his obedience toward the resurrected and exalted Christ who sent him to the Gentiles. Small wonder that the high priest reacts vehemently, for if Paul's declaration should be accepted, then Judaism as represented by the Sanhedrin would be disobedient toward God and "the Just One" (22:14-15).

Ananias became high priest around A.D. 48 and was dismissed around A.D. 59, during the tenure of the procurator Felix. According to Josephus he was a greedy, corrupt person who had been cited at Rome in A.D. 52 and had successfully defended himself against the suspicion of having fomented riots. He was also present at the hearing before Felix (24:1) and in A.D. 66 he was assassinated by Jewish revolutionaries as a friend of the Romans (Josephus, *Ant*. 20.103,180; *War* 2.441-442).

When Ananias realized the implications of Paul's declaration he ordered someone **to strike** Paul **on his mouth.** Instead of engaging Paul in a discussion, the high priest employs violence. Fearlessly and prophetically Paul proclaimed to him: **God shall strike you, you whitewashed wall!** Luke does not mean to convey that Paul lost his temper or acted contrary to Luke 6:27-29a. He exercised his prophetic ministry as did Stephen (cf. 7:51-56) and foretold God's judgment on the high priest. Paul's prediction may also refer to the high priest's assassination by a terrorist. The metaphor of the **whitewashed wall** recalls Ezek. 13:10-11 and suggests a fragile wall, the cracks of which have been hidden by whitewash. Thus the metaphor is synonymous with hypocrite. Fearlessly Paul presses his point of the hiatus between being and appearance. **Are you sitting to judge me according to the law, and yet contrary to the law you order me to be struck?** Indeed, Paul is more faithful to the Law than the high priest who wants to appear as judge according to the Law, but who has just demonstrated that he is a lawbreaker himself. When it is pointed out to Paul that he was speaking to **God's high priest,** he at once said: **I did not know, brethren, that he was the high priest; for it is written, You shall not speak evil of a ruler of your people** (Exod. 22:28). This can be understood in two ways. As an apology it shows Paul's superior piety, his knowledge of and submission to the Law. But there could be some bitter irony in his words, such as: "I did not think that a man like this who flaunts the Law in front of the Sanhedrin could be the high priest. Nevertheless, the law of Exod. 22:28 remains in force, to which I submit obediently." That law guards the office, but does not preclude God's judgment on the person holding it.

6-10 (Division within the Sanhedrin)—Paul took the initiative once more and revealed the fact that there is not only a division between Christians and Jews, but also within Judaism. Paul realized that two parties were represented in the Sanhedrin, the Pharisees, who were the minority, and the Sadducean majority. Rather cleverly he provoked a controversy between them, aligning himself firmly with the Pharisees as he called out: **Brethren, I am a Pharisee, a son of Pharisees; with respect to the hope and the resurrection of the dead I am on trial.** Not only was the Paul of Acts a Pharisee in the past, but he remained one also as a Christian (contrary to Phil. 3:5-8). The Lukan Paul could affirm this because the hope of the **resurrection** of the dead constitutes the common ground between Christianity and Pharisaic Judaism. The phrase **hope and the resurrection** does not refer to two different items, such as messianic hope and future eschatological hope. The two items are equivalent to one, namely, the hope of the resurrection of the dead. Moralizers are offended that Paul engaged not only in cursing and name-calling (v. 3), but also in using the cheap trick of dividing his opponents on the basis of an insignificant issue. In so interpreting this scene they totally miss Luke's point, that the belief in the future resurrection of the dead is indeed the bridge and common ground between Pharisaic Judaism and Christianity. Even the historical Paul connected the resurrection of Christ with the belief in the general resurrection of the dead, similar to Luke: "But if there is no resurrection of the dead, then Christ has not been raised" (1 Cor. 15:13,16). The importance which Luke attaches to the theme of future eschatology can be seen from its recurrence in the defense scenes: (1) here, and before Felix (24:15,21); (2) in Festus's comment to Agrippa (25:18-19); (3) in the speech to Agrippa (26:6-8,22-23); and (4) in Paul's statement to the Jews in Rome (28:20). From Luke's perspective the Sadduccees are infidels who do not share "the hope of Israel" (28:20), whereas the Christian proclamation is nothing but the fulfillment of the Pharisaic eschatological expectation. Hence, there would seem to be a basis for Christian-Jewish dialog in Luke's time. It is not just the apostles' witness, or the witness of the Scriptures, or the witness of the Holy Spirit, or signs, wonders, and visions of Jesus, but also the Pharisaic hope of the resurrection of the dead which should enable Luke's church to make contact with Pharisaic Judaism. In addition to their eschatology, the Pharisees in Luke are noted for their faithfulness to the Law, but so are the "many ten thousands" of Jewish Christians, including Paul (21:20-26). He can therefore rightly claim: **I am a Pharisee** and my ancestors have been **Pharisees.** In the Gospel of Luke the Pharisees are absent in the passion narrative, and in Acts "a Pharisee in the council named Gamaliel" advised that the truth-claim of the Christian resurrection message be left an open question (5:34-39). Thus it is not surprising to find that some **scribes of the Pharisees' party** defended Paul at the meeting of the Sanhedrin saying: **We find nothing wrong in this man.**

What if a spirit or an angel spoke to him on the road to Damascus or in the temple? In v. 8 Luke had explained the difference between Sadducees and Pharisees for his readers. The **Pharisees acknowledge** a future resurrection of the dead, as well as the existence of angels and spirits; the Sadducees do not. In their defense of Paul the Pharisees are not (yet) ready to accept that it was Jesus who spoke to him on the Damascus road and in the temple, but why could it not have been an angel of God who appeared to him? From Luke's perspective it would seem that the bridge between Christianity and Pharisaic Judaism might still be intact, though it may be under severe strain.

The **dissension** (Greek, *stasis;* cf. 15:2; 23:7, 10; 24:5) between Pharisees and Sadducees eventually **became violent** (v. 10). This was the point when the tribune intervened, being **afraid that** in the tug-of-war **Paul would be torn in pieces,** and he brought his prisoner back to the safety of the barracks.

In addition to his main point, the resurrection as the common ground between Pharisaic Judaism and Christianity, what was Luke telling his readers? We suggest the following: (1) The scene made it obvious that from a Sanhedrin controlled by Sadducees and chaired by a person like Ananias, Paul could not expect to receive justice. This august body even turned into a mob. This insight prepares the reader for Paul's appeal to Rome (25:1-12). (2) Not all Jews were like Ananias and his party, or like the plotters who were out to get Paul by any means (23:14; 25:2-3). There are Pharisaic Jews who are zealous for the Law of God, brave enough to speak up, defend Paul and declare him innocent (23:9). Judaism is not a monolithic anti-Christian block and the church dare never forget that (though unfortunately it did forget it)! (3) Had the council agreed that there was no case for Paul's instigation of a riot, the tribune would have let this Roman citizen go free. The fact that the council did not agree on Paul's innocence with respect to causing a tumult meant that the tribune could keep him in custody. This in turn paved the way for Paul's statement in Rome that he "was delivered . . . into the hands of the Romans" (28:17), even as it fulfills Agabus's prophecy (Acts 21:11). (4) The consultation (or was it a trial? v. 6) gave the tribune the basis for his subsequent letter, in which he cleared Paul of crimes, but noted that he "was accused about questions of their law," which, as the reader knows, was not a subject for Roman judicial proceedings (23:29; cf. 18:15; 25:18-19). Nevertheless, the tribune felt that he should protect himself and not release Paul at once, but rather urge his superior officer, the procurator Felix, to make a decision. Even the best of the Romans had to "look out for number one"! After all, the high priest was a powerful figure. (5) Soon, namely, the night after the following day, Paul would leave Jerusalem once and for all, and leave behind a hopelessly divided Judaism engaging in irrelevant discussions while missing the fulfillment of Israel's hope, the resurrection of Jesus, the Messiah. (6) Luke mentions no aid from the Christian community of Jerusalem. The reason for its absence lies in Luke's aim in this section. He has already shown that Paul, James, and the elders agreed that Jewish Christians are and ought to be "zealous for the law" of Moses (21:20-26). In Luke's design, however, the public defender of Christianity is the imprisoned Paul, and not James and the elders. Therefore, the latter do not appear in the trial scenes, nor do the Christians of Caesarea later on.

(7) Paul identified himself as:

(a) a citizen of Tarsus (21:39) who was not the Egyptian revolutionary;

(b) a Jew who was born, brought up and educated as a Jew (22:3) and who was not an apostate;

(a′) a Roman citizen (22:27-28) who was not a Greek, though he could speak the language (21:37);

(b′) a Pharisee (23:6) who held the hope of the resurrection of the dead in distinction from Sadducees.

Two religious identifications are interspersed with two secular ones. In each case the *b* heightens the *a*. Being a Christian is compatible with being a Tarsian citizen, a Jew, a Roman, and a Pharisee. Negatively, neither Greek, Roman, nor Jewish laws are means of gaining salvation. Positively, these diverse laws can be obeyed by Christians with the proviso of Peter's clause (5:29; 4:19). However, being a Jew and a Pharisee involves more than obedience to laws; it involves the hope of the resurrection of the dead (23:6). With this Jewish Pharisaic hope Paul links two identifications: (*a*) He was chosen by God and sent by Jesus "far away" into Gentile lands to preach Jesus' resurrection to both Jews and Gentiles (22:14, 21). (*b*) He is the person who "must" witness publicly to the resurrected Jesus both in Jerusalem and Rome and in so doing defend Christianity (23:11).

(8) The reader can hardly miss parallels between the passion of Jesus and the sufferings of his apostles, of Stephen and of Paul. To be sure, Jesus could say: "When I was with you, day after day in the temple, you did not lay hands on me" (Luke 23:53), while in Paul's case Asian Jews "laid hands on him" precisely in the temple (Acts 21:27). Yet the occurrence of the verb "to lay hands on" in both passion stories, the occurrence of other identical verbs (such as "to be delivered into the hands of," Luke 9:44; 24:7; Acts 21:11; 28:17), the emphasis on the divine necessity of both passions, the presence of identical opponents (chief priests, elders, etc.), the appearance of Jesus and Paul before the Sanhedrin, procurator(s) and a Jewish king, Herod, together with the emphasis on the innocence of Jesus and Paul would suggest that Luke was quite deliberate in drawing parallels between the two passions. What was his purpose? To show that history repeats itself, because God is ultimately in control and continues his saving history, initiated in the Old Testament, inaugurated eschatologically in and through Jesus and carried forward in time and space through the disciples of Jesus, the church and its chosen and faithful leaders. History repeats itself, because sin finds expression in repeated rejections of God's messengers (cf. Luke 11:49-51; Acts 7:35,39). Because Jesus works through his servant-witnesses, they too are subject to rejection and innocent suffering. Of course, there are differences between the passion of Jesus and of Paul, because both passion accounts depend on traditions and because Paul is not Jesus, but the servant and witness of Jesus. Hence Paul made speeches at his trials while Jesus spoke only a few words (Luke 22:67-70).

11 (**Paul's vision at night**)—That night, the second in Roman custody, **the Lord stood by him** (cf. 18:9-10) **and said, "Take courage, for as you have testified about me at Jerusalem, so you must** (Greek, *dei*) **bear witness also at Rome."** This is the second time that **Rome** is mentioned explicitly in Acts (cf. 19:21; 27:24), and in Rome Luke's story will end. Paul is the only person in this scene who is certain about what is to be, not about the details of his future but about his goal and end. God's hands shall guide him to Rome, the Lord Jesus assured him after a disappointing day when he had faced the highest religious authority of Judaism and had not been cleared of the charge

of defiling the temple (21:28). His speeches to the people and the Sanhedrin of Jerusalem are called by Jesus a testimony, a **witness** to Jesus, and as such the reader should understand what Paul had said (22:1-21; 23:3-5,6). His defense is to be a public witness to his Lord and not just a personal apology in answer to specific charges. The divine **must** of God's great plan will not be stopped by human plots, human weaknesses, or the forces of nature (23:12-33; 24:26-27; 25:2-3,9; 27:14—28:6). Paul shall reach Rome because Jesus wills it. Jesus' word to Paul not only sheds light on the diverse events that follow, but it is the force behind the scenes that moves Paul away from Jerusalem.

Transfer to Caesarea and Witness before Felix, Festus, and Agrippa (23:12—26:32)

This section narrates the first stage of Paul's journey from Jerusalem to Rome. Two years he will spend in custody in Caesarea (24:27) and bear witness before two procurators, Felix (chap. 24) and Festus (chaps. 25–26). He appealed to Caesar when Festus wanted him returned to Jerusalem (25:6-12). The high point of the section is the climactic defense speech before Agrippa, representing Judaism, and Festus, representing Rome. Their final statements in turn speak of Paul's innocence of crimes (26:31-32), which forms an *inclusio* with the appraisal by the tribune Claudius Lysias (23:29). Within these brackets Paul once more fulfills his mandate as imprisoned witness to Christ.

12-25 (Paul's transfer to Caesarea)—His future had been revealed to him during his second night in Roman custody (v. 11). In the morning there began a tug-of-war about his future which was threatened by assassins who in turn were outwitted by Paul, his nephew, the tribune, and his soldiers. They led Paul out of murderous Jerusalem to the safety of Caesarea and in so doing they unknowingly accomplished the first stage of his God-appointed journey to Rome. Each of the players in this drama retains his freedom and all serve the purpose of God, ignorant though they be of it, except for Paul. Almost nothing is done or spoken by him and yet he remains the center of everyone's intense actions.

12-15 (The plot)—The Jews plotted to kill Paul the morning after his night vision. This general identification reflects the narrator's conviction that in contrast to the early times of the apostles, when "the people" of Jerusalem esteemed the Christian leaders (cf. 5:13, 16, 20, 26), now "the people" joined their anti-Christian leaders in repudiating the gospel. This situation continued even though many "myriads" of Jews had become Christians (21:20). **The Jews** who plotted against Paul's life symbolized Jerusalem as the center of opposition to the gospel and its appointed witnesses. Though there were Christians (still) in Jerusalem, as well as fair-minded Jews (23:6-10), the dominant attitude of its leaders and people is anti-Christian. Next, the conspirators are specified. They are **more than forty** who have **bound themselves by an oath neither to eat nor drink till they had killed Paul.** The narrator gives this information a total of three times (vv. 12, 14, 21) and alludes to it twice more (vv. 16 and 30), to convey the seriousness of the threat to Paul's life and to God's plan, and also to amuse the reader, at least in retrospect. What are these fanatics going to do when they find out that their plans have come to naught? Break their oaths, or starve! Did Luke know that Judaism had ways of absolving people from unfulfilled vows? The narrative gives no indication. The conspirators went to the **chief priests and elders,** told them of their plan and requested: **You therefore, along with the council,** ask the tribune to have Paul brought down to the council **to determine his case more exactly** and we will **kill him** on the way. Note: (1) the chief priests and elders are distinguished from the council. Luke is quite aware that the Pharisaic minority of the council would never have agreed to such a lawless plot (cf. vv. 6-10). The terrorists therefore approached the council's Sadducean power structure, which of course kept the Pharisees in the dark. (2) The phrase **more exactly** links up with the consultation before the council on the previous day (22:30). That hearing did not really establish Paul's guilt or innocence, or possible charges against him. Hence the tribune should be interested in a second consultation. "More exactly" is a Lukan phrase (cf. 18:26; 24:22) and the tribune in Luke's view would welcome the council's help in establishing more precisely the Jewish and the Roman case against Paul. Historically, this scene fits well into the situation of Felix's procuratorship, when the Zealot liberation movement and the appearance of "sicarii" ("assassins," see comments on 21:38) were on the upswing. These people fought for Israel's purity and took the law into their own hands in accordance with the example of Phinehas (Num.

25:7-8). Since they were aware of the hatred of the Sadducees against Paul, they made a temporary alliance of convenience with some of the leaders whom they otherwise detested as friends of Rome.

16-22 (The plot becomes known to Paul and the tribune)—In a new scene we hear of **the son of Paul's sister** visiting his uncle in the barracks and telling him about the plot on his life. A mass of intriguing questions remains unanswered. Were the nephew and his mother Christians? If so, why did not Paul stay with them rather than with Mnason (21:16)? Did Paul's sister live in Jerusalem also, or did she remain in Tarsus while her son was educated in Jerusalem (cf. 22:3; 23:6)? What were Paul's relationships with his family after he became a Christian? Does Phil. 3:8 ("I count everything as loss") perhaps include his family's having disinherited him after his conversion? How did the nephew find out about the plot? Did the conspirators talk too much, or was he himself related to the Zealot movement, but found blood thicker than ideology? Questions, but no answers! This scene has been declared unhistorical by some interpreters—for insufficient reasons. As an uncondemned Roman citizen, Paul could certainly receive a visitor. Nor is it strange that the centurion accepted Paul's request and led the young man to the tribune. In a quiet corner Paul's nephew tells the tribune about the conspiracy, adding that it was planned for **tomorrow** (v. 20), and pleading with him: **But do not yield to them,** or "do not trust them," namely, the Saducean members of the council and their request (cf. v. 15). They are part of the conspiracy. The tension generated by the narration is heightened. Will the tribune believe the young man and protect Paul or shrug his shoulders and do nothing? As the conspirators made their final preparations, the tribune made his. First he told Paul's nephew to **tell no one that you have informed me.**

23-30 (The tribune's countermeasures)—Next he made preparations for Paul's immediate transfer to Caesarea and, last, he wrote a letter to **Felix the governor.** The tribune, who was in charge of about 1000 soldiers, ordered **two centurions, two hundred** footsoldiers, **seventy** calvary men and **two hundred spearmen to get ready at the third hour of the night,** that is, between 9 and 10 p.m. and to bring Paul to Caesarea. For the sake of safety and speed Paul was also to be mounted. Half of the tribune's military might was to be employed for Paul's protection from his assassins, which indicates the greatness of the danger, the importance of this prisoner, and a little exaggeration on Luke's part. (Incidentally, **spearmen** is borrowed from the Latin version; the meaning of the Greek word is uncertain.) The tribune lacked the necessary legal powers to dispose of this particular case involving a Roman citizen, and would have had to send Paul to the procurator in Caesarea, unless Felix came to Jerusalem in the near future. The information about the assassins speeded up the process and hardened his resolution to foil their plans by using maximum Roman power. There also needed to be a message to the procurator summarizing the basic facts of the case, and so **he wrote a letter to this effect.**

The letters in Acts, just as the speeches, are Lukan constructions in which the author tells what was appropriate to write in a particular situation (cf. 15:23-29; 25:26). The tribune's letter conforms in style and form to Hellenistic-Roman letters, except that the final "farewell" is missing (which some copyists later supplied). At last we hear that the tribune's name was **Claudius Lysias** (see 22:28). For the procurator's benefit he stated the basic facts of the case: (1) At the beginning and at the end of the letter we read that it was the tribune with his soldiers who **rescued** Paul when he was about to be killed by Jews (v. 27) and when subsequently they plotted aqainst his life (v. 30). (2) Paul, whose name is not given in the letter, was a **Roman citizen** who therefore, the letter implied, must be judged by a Roman court. (3) The tribune's investigation showed that while Paul was **accused about questions of their law,** he was innocent of charges **deserving death or imprisonment** by Roman law. (4) His accusers were ordered to state their charges against him before the procurator (cf. 24:1). The last item would be taken care of, once Paul was safely out of Jerusalem. The first time a Roman official voiced his verdict regarding Paul the defender of Christianity it read: **Nothing deserving death or imprisonment.** Here lies the importance of the tribune's letter for Luke's readers. Paul, like his master, was found innocent of crimes by the Romans (cf. Luke 23:4, 14-15, 20, 22, 47) from the very beginning, though Jews wanted both killed. The viewpoint of Claudius Lysias is identical with the one expressed by Gallio (18:14-15). But note: the Romans did not pass the verdict that Christianity is "really nothing but a legitimate Jewish sect." Rather both Roman officials state that whatever differences there are between Jews and Christians, they do not concern us so long as crimes against

Roman law do not occur. This is Luke's primary message to his readers through the tribune's letter.

In addition to stating this main point clearly, the letter is also an amusing masterpiece of self-protection on the part of a good Roman official. Cleverly, the tribune omitted that he "rescued" Paul because of a case of mistaken identity (21:38), that he put a Roman citizen in two chains (21:33), and that he ordered his examination by torture (22:24). The letter also contains the little white lie that he saved Paul from the mob, **having learned that he was a Roman citizen.** Of course, that is not quite true. He "learned" this, not at the time of Paul's arrest in the temple court, but later, after he had ordered Paul's examination by scourging in the fortress (22:26-28). The best of us are imperfect and even Claudius Lysias has to put himself in a good light (cf. 25:9-21).

31-35 (Journey to and arrival in Caesarea)—The armed escort of 470 soldiers brought Paul **by night to Antipatris,** which is 37 miles from Jerusalem, between Lydda and Caesarea. From there the foot soldiers **on the morrow returned to the barracks,** while the horsemen brought Paul to **Caesarea.** Luke's knowledge of the geography of Palestine was not very good (cf. Luke 17:11, "between"; Acts 9:31, the sequence of the regions). The infantry simply could not have marched in one night from Jerusalem to Antipatris. Moreover, its protection was not needed once Paul was outside of Jerusalem and its immediate environment, and its presence would only have slowed down the cavalry. Either Luke's timing was off, or the infantry did not continue all the way to Antipatris but **returned to the barracks,** in the morning after escorting the cavalry through the narrow streets of Jerusalem and some miles beyond. Then the cavalry proceeded at a brisker pace to **Antipatris.** Paul was also mounted (cf. v. 24). After a rest, the party rode 25 miles to **Caesarea.** The tribune's **letter** was delivered to the procurator (frequently called **governor**) and **Paul** was presented before him. Upon reading the letter he held a brief preliminary interrogation and quite properly asked Paul **to what province he belonged.** Normally, the governor of the province in which a crime was committed or a legal accusation raised was responsible for investigating charges and reaching a verdict. However, the governor could legally extradite a prisoner to the governor of the province in which the accused was born, for trial there. In cases where the accused came from client kingdoms such extraditions would spare the Romans later recriminations. Felix heard that Paul came from **Cilicia,** which at that time had not yet become a full Roman province but was still part of the Roman province Syria, just as Judea. Felix may have thought that the Roman legate of Syria would hardly welcome the transfer of a minor case involving religious nuisance into his jurisdiction. Nor would the Jews of Jerusalem welcome such a move. So he decided to **hear** the case himself **when your accusers arrive** (cf. v. 30c) In the meantime Paul should be **guarded** in the palace built by Herod the Great which now served as Felix's official residence or **praetorium.**

On another level the inquiry about Paul's province of origin suggests a parallel to Jesus' passion (Luke 23:6-7). In both cases the question is connected with the possibility of getting rid of the accused, or with the desire not to get involved. In both cases the desire is thwarted. Herod returned Jesus, and Felix's insight into the political situation prevented him from sending Paul away. Jesus must die in Jerusalem (Luke 9:51; 13:33) and Paul must see not Tarsus but Rome (Acts 19:21).

Excursus: Felix. Felix and his brother, Pallas, were freedmen, former slaves who had been released by Antonia, the mother of emperor Claudius. Hence his name, Antonius Felix. Pallas served as financial secretary and confidant of the emperor Claudius and helped advance his brother's rise to power. Felix's first wife was the granddaughter of Cleopatra and Anthony; his second is unknown, and his third wife was Drusilla (cf. 24:24), the daughter of Herod Agrippa I (cf. 12:1), and sister of Herod Agrippa II (25:23). Naturally, high Roman society was envious of this freedman's attaining the position of procurator, normally reserved for members of the equestrian order. Tacitus reflects the jealousy of Roman nobility when he writes that Felix "exercised the power of a king with the mind of a slave" and that he believed he could commit all kinds of evil with impunity (*History* 5.9; *Annals* 12.54). Felix's tenure saw the rise of the Zealot movement which he ruthlessly opposed (see 21:38). Josephus blamed him for the outbreak of the Jewish war. He became procurator of Judea in A.D. 52 or 53. The end of his term is disputed. Josephus wrote that when Festus succeeded Felix (cf. Acts 24:27) a delegation of Jews from Caesarea accused Felix in Rome. However, his brother Pallas entreated emperor Nero to dismiss the charges (*Ant.* 20.182). Since Pallas fell from Nero's favor in the latter part of A.D. 55, one can assume that he could not have helped his brother against Jewish accusations after he had lost his office. Thus Felix's term would have ended in A.D. 55 and not later. In that case the sequence of events and the data found in Acts as well as in our suggested chronology are wrong. However, the majority of scholars hold that Felix remained in office until A.D. 59 or perhaps 60, because Josephus's *Jewish War* reports too many activities while Nero was emperor (A.D. 54–68) and Felix governor. These activities cannot be pressed into a one-year period between A.D. 54 and A.D. 55 (Josephus, *War* 2.250–270). Moreover, Pallas's influence with the emperor did not cease after his dismissal, because he was exceedingly rich. He could have helped his brother against Jewish accusations also after A.D. 55, until Nero had him poisoned in A.D. 62, because he wanted Pallas's money. Finally, in Acts 24:10 we hear that Felix had been in office "for many years" when Paul made his defense before him, and Acts 24:27 tells us that Paul was "two years" in Caesarea when Felix was succeeded by Festus. It would therefore seem that Felix was procurator of Judea probably from A.D. 52 or 53 to A.D. 59 or 60, with Paul appearing before him in A.D. 57 or 58.

Accusation against Paul and His Defense before Felix (24:1-23)

Five days after Paul's arrival, a delegation of the Sanhedrin led by the high priest Ananias appeared before Felix in Caesarea, and Paul's trial began. The spokesman for the prosecution, **Tertullus,** skilled in legal rhetoric, presented the charges against Paul, which Paul answered point by point, while the procurator sat and listened in stony silence. In contrast to the mob scenes in Jerusalem generated by the people and the Sanhedrin, we find a different atmosphere in Paul's trial at Caesarea. Roman law determines the legal proceedings and Roman compromise delays a final decision.

The scene is carefully structured. An introduction (vv. 1-2) is followed by two speeches in parallel, one by Tertullus for the prosecution (vv. 2-8), the other by Paul in his defense (vv. 10-21). The conclusion brings Felix's preliminary verdict (vv. 22-23). While the spokesman for the Jewish delegation shifted the religious issue to the political sphere, as in Jesus' trial (Luke 23:2), Paul cited the resurrection as the basic issue between him and his accusers (vv. 15 and 21).

Each of the two speeches begins with a *captatio benevolentiae,* a rhetorical device for currying favor (vv. 2b-4 and 10b), and each speech ends with a confession from Paul (vv. 8 and 21c-d, "except this one thing . . .") and a reference to the Jerusalem delegates as supporting witnesses (vv. 9 and 20a-b). Paul's speech answers the two charges against him: he is (1a) a pest and agitator (vv. 11-13), and (1b) a ringleader of the sect (vv. 14-16), and (2) that he attempted to profane the temple (vv. 17-19). Grammatically, two, not three, charges are made against Paul though the first can be divided into two parts. Note also that Paul's opening statement, "as you [Felix] may ascertain" (v. 11), links up with Tertullus's closing sentence, ". . . you [Felix] will be able to learn from him . . ." (v. 8).

2-9 (The accusation against Paul)—Tertullus begins with an elaborate adulation, which was customary, and in which he praises Felix as benefactor **of this nation.** The reader will remember Jesus' words about earthly rulers who are called "benefactors" (Luke 22:25-27, see Danker). The **most excellent Felix** was being flattered with catchwords such as **much peace . . . your provision,** or "your providence" (Greek, *pronoia*) . . . **reforms . . . on behalf of this nation, in every way and everywhere** . . . our **gratitude,** your **kindness.** This kind of language is part of the conventional style of opening speeches before rulers and judges. The harsh reality of Felix's rule can be read in Josephus (*War* 2.253–263).

Historically, the peace-keeping and reforms of this "benefactor" consisted in executions, oppression (cf. 21:38), and taxation of Jews. But Tertullus could hardly bring up such matters in this situation. Also, in traditional style he promised to state his case briefly. Tertullus was quite aware that religious charges against Paul, such as those of 21:21, would be thrown out of a Roman court. Therefore, he had to translate them into political charges. Hence, he first of all accused Paul of fomenting social unrest and sedition. **We have found this man a pestilent fellow,** literally "a plague" (Greek, *loimos*). Like a plague he infects people and is therefore a most dangerous threat to society. The emperor Claudius had written a letter in A.D. 41 to the people of Alexandria in which he referred to Jewish troublemakers who were instigating "a universal plague [Greek, *loimos*] infecting the entire world." Around A.D. 111 Pliny, the governor of Pontus and Bithynia, wrote in a letter to emperor Trajan that Christianity was a contagious disease by now infecting even the countryside. Tertullus places the Jews firmly on the side of Roman law and order, social health, and communal well-being. The common enemy of Jews and Romans is Paul, "the plague." Unless he is stopped, the health of the life of the empire will be destroyed. Indirectly, Tertullus confirmed the tremendous effect of Paul's mission. Next, he specified in what way Paul functioned as plague among

Jews. He is **an agitator among all the Jews throughout the world.**
The word translated "agitator" can be translated "one who stirs up
sedition or rioting" (Greek, *stasis*). Sedition and riots were threats
to the *pax Romana,* the peace of Rome which every governor must
uphold. All riots found in Acts are blamed on Paul and receive a
political twist in terms of sedition. The allusion to Luke 23:2 is
obvious. Like the Master, so Paul is accused of being a threat to the
political order. But how could Paul have such power? Because he
is the **ringleader of the sect of the Nazarenes.** Not Peter, who at
that time was still alive, but who last appeared in chap. 15, nor
James, who presided in Jerusalem, but Paul is the **ringleader**
(Greek, *prōtostatēs*), the chief troublemaker of the dangerous "sect
of the Nazoreans" (Greek). Only here are the followers of Jesus called
"Nazoreans"; otherwise the term refers to Jesus (2:22; 3:6; 6:14; etc.).
Together with Paul, the Christian church is to be condemned as the
cause of political unrest and sedition. What is objectionable is not
that the church is a "sect" or party (Greek, *hairesis*). The Sadducees
as well as the Pharisees are different sects or parties (cf. 5:17; 15:5).
What is objectionable is that the church is "the Nazorean sect." It,
like its founder, is an enemy of society and of the empire (cf. 17:6-
7).

There is also a second, more specific accusation, for which this
man (Paul), whose name is left unspoken, should be condemned by
the procurator. **He even tried to profane the temple, but we seized
him** in the very act (cf. 21:28). His attempt at desecration is presented as fact and not merely as something which "we have found"
out (v. 5). His attempt at desecration did not succeed, because we
caught him flagrante delicto, in the very act. This crime certainly
demanded capital punishment, for Rome was the protector of Jerusalem's temple, as the procurator knows (cf. Josephus, *War* 6.124-
128).

The prosecution rests its case, but suggests that the procurator
by examining Paul himself **will be able to learn from him about
everything of which we accuse him.** In short, Paul's own confession
is to support the accusations articulated by Tertullus. The Western
text and some other late manuscripts add after v. 6: "and we would
have judged him according to our law (v. 7). But the chief captain
Lysias came and with great violence took him out of our hands,
commanding his accusers to come before you." This is clearly a later
addition, because in v. 8 the first and second "him" would refer to

Lysias while the third must refer to Paul—an impossibility according to Lukan style (see the footnote in the RSV). Moreover, the Jewish delegation led by the high priest Ananias (v. 1) also supported the accusations and **joined in the charge, affirming that all this was so.** In short the accusations are supported by the delegation of the Sanhedrin, and will be supported by Paul when the procurator examines him. But the procurator does nothing of the kind. He keeps silent throughout and merely nods, or motions with his hand for Paul to speak.

10-21 (Paul's defense)—Paul too had listened in silence to the accusation that he was a pest, a seditionist, a leader of the politically dangerous Nazorean sect. Before the Jews he had already been accused as an enemy of "the people," and as a false teacher who opposes the Law of Moses (21:21, 28; 28:17). Before the Romans he is now presented as being a Jewish seditionist (revolutionary) who acts against Roman law. In front of both Jews and Romans he is accused of actual or attempted desecration of the temple (21:28; 24:6). Yet Paul loves his people, obeys the Law of Moses, and worships in the temple. How should he defend himself (Luke 12:11-12; 21:12-14)? **Cheerfully,** and not hysterically.

Thus he spoke, beginning with a modest *captatio benevolentiae* in which he omitted the direct address, but pointed to the **many years** in which Felix had been **judge over this nation.** These (five to seven) years (from A.D. 52/53 to 58/59) ought to have given him expertise and competence in seeing through the phoniness of the accusation and evaluating Paul's defense and witness—all the more so, since his wife was a Jewess (v. 24). Paul begins the body of his defense by stating: **As you may ascertain** for yourself by your inquiry, **it is not more than twelve** days that I spent in Jerusalem between my arrival and my arrest. In contrast to Tertullus who speaks of Paul's worldwide agitation and conspiracy, Paul limits his comment respecting time to a 12-day period, and respecting space, to Jerusalem. Felix held the power of pronouncing judgment only for the area of Judea and therefore only for the 12-day period prior to Paul's arrest. After his arrest Paul could hardly have fomented sedition. (Hence the 12-day period is not the result of Luke's stupidly adding the 7 days of 21:27 and the 5 days of 24:1, as some interpreters think. Luke would have had to forget his time references in 22:30; 23:11; 23:23, 32.) Because of the limitation in time and space the procurator can find out for himself that the two accusations of Paul's opponents are trumped up.

12-16—Precisely as to the charge of fomenting riots, Paul declared: **they did not find me disputing with any one** (Greek, *dialegesthai,* cf. 17:2, 17; 18:4, 19; 19:8-9) or **stirring up a crowd either in the temple or in the synagogues, or in the city.** Paul had not come to Jerusalem for the purpose of evangelism and mission, but for the purpose of **worship** in the temple (cf. 20:16). Hence he did not enter the synagogues of Jerusalem, speak in the temple or on the streets of the city, nor seek to convert anyone; much less had he incited anyone to riot (vv. 11-12). The burden of proof must lie with his accusers, Paul asserted. They must prove their accusations, not he his innocence. This principle of Roman law, though frequently disregarded, is to be upheld (v. 13). With it Paul placed his opponents on the defensive, for they cannot **prove to you what they now bring up against me.** Concerning his position in the Nazorean sect he did not deny his leadership role in the church, but he did deny that the church was a Jewish sect, and politically suspect. Far from being a Jewish sect, Christianity is the fulfillment of Judaism. As such, it is **the Way** to which Paul bears witness as prisoner in accordance with the divine mandate (23:11). He bears witness to the **worship,** the beliefs, and the **hope** of **the Way** which he represents. **According to the Way . . . I worship the God of our fathers.** Implicit in this statement is that **the Way** worships the God of Israel by calling upon the name of the resurrected Lord Jesus in the power of the Holy Spirit. The church's worship no more endangers society than the church's belief and hope pose a threat. Paul, the spokesman of the church, accepted the entire **law** of Moses as binding for himself as a Jew, believing it to be God's revelation of his will to Israel. In like manner he believed the promises of God spoken through the **prophets** (cf. 26:22; Luke 24:44-45), promises which include **a hope in God . . . that there will be a resurrection of both the just and the unjust** and a final judgment (Dan. 12:2; Acts 23:6; 26:5-8). The future hope is something **which these themselves accept.** Thereby Paul put the Jerusalem delegation on the spot. Let his accusers deny Israel's future hope and just so reveal themselves as infidels who do not believe the prophetic promises. In his life-style both before and after his conversion Paul **always** took **pains to have a clear conscience toward God and toward men** in view of God's judgment to

439

come (cf. 23:1; 24:25). Therefore he did not engage in hurling reckless accusations against others, as his opponents had just been doing.

17-19—Now the second accusation of desecrating the temple must be dealt with. Paul has already stated that belonging to the Way has ethical implications, namely, of striving to have a good conscience before God and man (v. 16). He has to answer an implicit question: what was he doing in the temple at the time when the riot broke out? He had already pointed out that he "went up to worship at Jerusalem" (v. 11). Now he added: **I came to bring to my nation alms and offerings.** By **offerings** Paul refers to the Nazirite sacrifices of 21:26. **Alms** to **my nation** comes as a surprise for the reader but indicates that true worship is inseparable from acts of charity; Paul, being a pious Jew, identified not only with the church but also with the poor in his **nation.** Consequently he had a clear conscience toward people. Instead of desecrating the temple, he actually brought alms to the temple.

The reader would not understand **alms** for **my nation** as referring to Paul's great collection (see above 21:20-26). For Luke as well as Paul, interchurch aid is not called "almsgiving" but *diakonia* (11:29, RSV "relief"; Rom. 15:31, RSV "service"). Almsgiving is directed to the poor outside the Christian community, e.g., **to my nation,** while *diakonia* in Luke-Acts is service within the Christian community and to members of the community (cf. 6:1,4; 11:29). *Diakonia* also refers to the ministry of the Word (cf. 20:24). The conclusion is warranted that Paul's *diakonia* for the Jerusalem church was not accepted (cf. Rom. 15:31), and therefore he presented the collection to the temple as **alms** for **my nation.** Luke certainly knew more about the collection than he lets the reader know!

What is important for Luke in this verse is to heighten the contrast between the accusation of desecrating the temple and Paul's own acts of almsgiving for the benefit of his nation. **As I was doing this,** namely, bringing alms and offerings to the temple, **they found me . . . in the temple.** In short, the alms were also brought to the temple. Now comes a second contrast. Far from being surrounded by a **crowd** whom he sought to incite, far from causing any **tumult** and, above all, far from desecrating the temple, Paul was found consecrated or **purified in the temple** (cf. 21:26-27). Those who found him were **some Jews from Asia.** They created the riot and **they ought to be here . . . and to make an accusation** against him.

This is the third time Paul puts the delegation led by the high priest on the spot. The delegation could not function as eyewitnesses, for it was not they but Asian Jews who had found him. But the Asian Jews are not present. Their absence demonstrates that they have no accusations against Paul. If it were otherwise why are they not here? The reader of course knows why they are not present. These hysterical Asian Jews had drawn the wrong conclusion (cf. 21:29), realized it in the meantime, and therefore just melted away.

20-21—With lightning speed Paul put members of the delegation on the spot once more, reminding them of the embarrassing scene they had made at the consultation before the Sanhedrin (cf. 23:1-10). Abruptly he asked his accusers to tell **what wrongdoing they found when I stood before the council** (cf. 23:6). None! Thus they are witnesses for the defense—or just plain liars! **Except**—there is one "offense" of Paul to which the representatives of the Sanhedrin can point, namely, his confession of the resurrection, **which I cried out while standing among them, "With respect to the resurrection of the dead I am on trial before you this day."** However, this confession was hardly a crime under Roman law. Rather, it was part of Jewish orthodoxy in contrast to the beliefs of Sadducean infidels (23:8). The irony of Paul's confession is apparent. Tertullus suggested to Felix that Paul's own confession would support the accusations of the plaintiff (v. 8). Paul now confesses his "offense," which has nothing to do with sedition against Rome nor desecration of Jerusalem's temple, but which reveals the fundamental issue which unites (Pharisaic) Judaism and Christianity and divides non-Christian Judaism. That issue is **the resurrection of the dead,** for which Paul is on trial and to which he witnesses as prisoner. In this first trial before a Roman procurator, the resurrection of Jesus is deliberately kept in the background, because it will be a theme in the climactic witness before King Agrippa, and because the Lukan Paul is challenging non-Christian Judaism to discuss the one issue it is competent to discuss before Felix—the resurrection of the dead.

22-23 (Felix's decision)—With Paul resting his case, the judge must now speak. Up to this point the procurator has clothed himself in silence, merely nodding to Paul to begin his defense. Now he must announce his decision. He does not decide in favor of the accusers, because he has **a rather accurate knowledge of the Way,** perhaps through his wife (v. 24). Luke's interpretive comment comes as a surprise. Apparently Felix knew from the beginning that the accusations were untenable and that Christianity was not a seditious movement constituting a threat to public order. Therefore, he should have announced a verdict of acquittal, declared Paul innocent, and released him from custody. Instead, Felix announced an indefinite adjournment of the case. The outcome of the trial was not a complete victory for Paul, for he continued in custody, but at the same time the procurator had found no criminal action for which Paul deserved to be condemned. Postponing his final decision, the procurator announced at the close of the trial: **When Lysias the tribune comes down, I will decide your case.** The plaintiffs as well as Paul did not know what the reader already knows, namely, that the tribune had expressed his opinion on Paul's innocence (23:29). The reader therefore knows that this adjournment is a compromise of truth and justice. Felix was not quite the weakling that Pilate showed himself to be (Luke 23:23-24), but his image begins to suffer, as self-interest prevails against better judgment with this compromising politician. The best Felix could do under the circumstances was to grant Paul **some liberty** during his custody and order that **none of his friends should be prevented from attending to his needs.** His travel companions of the last "we" section (cf. 20:4-5) or, less likely, Christians from Caesarea (cf. 21:7-14), were permitted to visit him and bring him food (cf. Josephus, *Ant.* 18.204). Indirectly this concession attests to Paul's innocence in the eyes of Felix.

23-27 (Felix and Paul)—Felix not only considered Paul to be innocent, but he was attracted to Paul on two different levels (vv. 23 and 26). First, he and his **wife Drusilla who was a Jewess . . . sent for Paul and heard him speak upon faith in Christ Jesus . . . justice and self-control and future judgment.** Some scholars thought that Luke created this episode out of a Markan scene which he had omitted in his Gospel. In Mark 6:20, Luke read that King Herod "feared John [the Baptist], knowing that he was a righteous and holy man, and kept him safe. When he heard him, he was much perplexed; and yet he heard him gladly." But it is doubtful that this Markan verse served as the basis for this episode in Acts. Luke was interested in showing that high society took notice of and was even attracted to Christianity (cf. 13:7,50; 17:4,12,34; 19:31). Moreover, the motif of the persecuted prophet or holy man who strikes awe into a ruler's heart was so widespread (e.g., Jer. 38:14-15; Sir.

48:6, 12) that the hypothesis of a literary dependence of this episode on Mark 6 becomes unnecessary. The different behavior of the women in the two scenes points in the same direction.

Felix, in his 50s at that time, was in his third marriage, this time with the beautiful and young **Drusilla,** daughter of Herod Agrippa I (cf. 12:1) and sister of Bernice and Agrippa II (cf. 25:23). Drusilla was born in A.D. 38, and had been engaged as a child to Antiochus Epiphanes of Comagene, but, probably in A.D. 53, had married King Azizus of Emesa of Syria. Shortly thereafter Felix wooed her away, employing a Cypriot magician, and married her when she was still 16 (Josephus, *Ant.* 20.141–144). The odd couple was attracted to Paul, a holy man, and showed a superficial interest in Christianity (cf. 26:28). They heard him speak, not about interesting anecdotes in the life of Jesus, but about **faith in Christ Jesus** and its ethical and eschatological consequences, **justice and self-control and the future judgment,** over which God has appointed Jesus Christ (cf. 17:31; 10:42). Paul's witness did not provide religious entertainment, but had an existential thrust. He spoke about unpleasant subjects, and Felix was **alarmed** (like Herod Antipas, Mark 6:20); so he put off making a decision in terms of repentance, faith, and future hope, just as he had postponed his decision concerning Paul's future. Quite politely but firmly he told Paul: **Go away for the present; when I have an opportunity I will summon you.** The Greek word for "opportunity" (*kairos*) means "time—right, opportune time." The procurator hid his fear behind a busy schedule. While the imprisoned Paul had witnessed to "the hope in God" (v. 15), Felix, in spite of his "very accurate" knowledge of the Way (v. 22), held out for another hope. **He hoped that money would be given him by Paul.** He hoped for a bribe with which Paul would buy his freedom and in so doing relieve him of a decision (cf. v. 22). So Felix **sent for him often and conversed with him,** but his hope for a bribe remained unfulfilled. Paul gave him no tangible reason to take action. After two years (cf. 28:30) of Paul's custody in Caesarea, Felix **was succeeded by Porcius Festus; and desiring to do the Jews a favor, Felix left Paul in prison.** Behind the official facade of objectivity (v. 10b), knowledge (v. 22), and generosity (v. 23) hides a corrupt and fearful heart (vv. 24-27). Thus Luke explains why the innocent Paul remained in custody.

Paul before Festus, Appeal to Caesar (25:1-12)

1-6b (Introduction)—Porcius Festus probably became governor of Judea in A.D. 59 or 60 and died in 62. He was succeeded by Albinus. In the interim after Festus's death and prior to the arrival of his successor, the Jewish high priest Ananos executed James, the brother of Jesus (Josephus, *Ant.* 20.200). Little is known about Festus except that during his rule the rising tide of Zealots devastated villages in Judea by setting them on fire, and sicarii assassinated pro-Roman Jews in Jerusalem. He successfully employed his forces against a revolutionary leader who promised his followers "salvation and rest from troubles" and who led them into the wilderness where the Romans destroyed them (*Ant.* 20.182–188).

Like the proverbial new broom, the new governor moved with speed and determination. Only **three days** after his arrival in Caesarea **he went up to Jerusalem,** where members of the Sanhedrin brought up the case against Paul and asked him **a favor** (Greek, *charis,* 24:27; 25:3,9,11, *charizesthai*). The favor was to have Paul returned **to Jerusalem.** In an explanatory note Luke tells the reader that members of the Sanhedrin planned to ambush and kill Paul **on the way.** An attempt on his life was to be repeated (cf. 23:12-15), but this time members of the Sanhedrin were the originators of the plan and not merely the accomplices. Festus, however, did not grant the favor, but pointed out that **Paul was being kept at Caesarea,** and if Jewish leaders felt the case to be urgent they should accompany him and state their accusations in a formal manner before his court there. After **not more than eight or ten days** Festus left Jerusalem for Caesarea and **the next day** Paul's trial before Festus took place. This introduction to Paul's trial contains references to time and place (Jerusalem–Caesarea–on the way) and contrasts (favor/murder; deceit/correct behavior of Festus; hatred/judicial proceedings; etc.). Jerusalem was ready to destroy Paul by illegal or legal means (cf. Luke 13:34-35). For Paul it will be the fourth time that he makes his defense, after his witness to the people (22:1-21), to the Sanhedrin (23:1-10), and before Felix (24:1-21).

6c-12 (Trial before Festus and appeal)—Luke merely sketched the trial scene and summarized the speeches because the reader already knows the accusations of the Jews (24:5) as well as Paul's defense (24:11-21). Nothing new could be added, apart from Paul's appeal. Luke structured his scene carefully:

(*a*) Festus on the tribunal (v. 6c);

(*b*) Accusations by Jews (v. 7);

(*c*) Paul's defense (v. 8);

(*d*) Festus's favor to the Jews and preliminary decision (v. 9);

(*a'*) Paul's insistence on remaining before Caesar's tribunal (v. 10);

(*b'*) Paul's acceptance of the legal consequences, provided the Jewish accusations are true (v. 11a-b);

(*c'*) His appeal to Caesar (v. 11c);

(*d'*) Festus's decision: To Caesar you shall go (v. 12).

6c-8—Festus ascended the tribunal the day after his arrival in Caesarea and arraigned Paul before him. In summary fashion Luke reported that Jews from Jerusalem brought **many serious charges** against him **which they could not prove** (cf. 24:5, 13, 19-20; Luke 23:1-5, 13-16). The summary of Paul's threefold defense was: **Neither against the law of the Jews, nor against the temple, nor against Caesar have I offended at all.** An offense **against the law** of the Jews would be of no interest to the Roman procurator (cf. 18:14-15; 23:29; 25:19). Nevertheless, Paul insisted that he and the Christians were obedient to the Law of Moses. Jewish Christians, like Paul, kept the whole Mosaic Law (21:20-26) and Gentile Christians kept those portions that pertained to them as Gentiles (cf. 15:29; 21:25). Jewish accusations to the contrary were false. Paul's rejection of the accusation of offending against the Law of Moses is not meant to imply that he sought political toleration for Christianity as a Jewish sect. He made a religious, not a political, claim. If he and the Christians are obedient to the Torah, then they are the obedient and true Israel, and his accusers, who cannot substantiate their accusations, are in fact offending against "the law of the Jews." Second, Paul did not desecrate **the temple** (cf. 24:17-18). Since the temple of Jerusalem was under the protection of the Roman empire, the charge of its desecration would fall under the jurisdiction not only of the Sanhedrin but also of the Roman procurator. Out of this dual jurisdiction grew Festus's decision to move the trial to Jerusalem (v. 9). The Sanhedrin had been granted the power to pass capital sentences in cases involving the desecration of the temple, and that power may have extended also to Roman citizens. Third, Paul claimed he had not offended **against Caesar** and his laws. Thereby he rejected the accusation of inciting people to riots and sedition (cf. 24:5, 11-13). To foment sedition was a crime against the emperor's majesty (*crimen laesae majestatis*), subject to capital punishment under Roman law. From Paul's defense we can infer the three charges against him. The first was purely religious; the second was religious and political, since the procurator also had to uphold the temple's integrity; the third charge was purely political. The weakness of all three charges was the lack of substantiation. The plaintiffs and the defense have stated their case and the time has come for the judge to announce his verdict. Under the circumstances one would expect Festus to acquit Paul of all charges.

9 (**Festus's preliminary decision**)—The expectation that Paul would finally be acquitted comes to naught because of the conniving of the procurator. **But Festus, wishing to do the Jews a favor,** is now ready to do what formerly he had rejected (v. 4), namely, return Paul to Jerusalem. From Luke's point of view Festus now moves into the same league as his predecessor in a desire to ingratiate himself with the Jewish establishment (cf. 24:27). But while Felix indefinitely adjourned the trial, Festus set a trap for Paul. Quite deceitfully the procurator asked his prisoner: **Do you wish to go up to Jerusalem and there be tried on these charges before me?** As if the governor needed the consent of a prisoner for a change in venue! Festus could hold a trial in Jerusalem as well as in Caesarea as he saw fit, and needed nobody's agreement, unless he was after something else, namely, to surrender Paul to the Sanhedrin. Very cleverly, Festus concealed his intention behind verbiage. Paul is to be tried **before him** (Greek, *epi* with genitive), which was designed to give Paul the impression that he would be tried before a Roman tribunal in Jerusalem with Festus sitting on the judgment seat. According to Luke however, that was not Festus's intention. Paul was to be tried by the Sanhedrin "in the presence of" the Roman procurator and as a favor to the Jews. Only if we understand the apparently harmless question of v. 9 as an expression of deliberate deceit does Paul's response make sense.

10-11 (**Paul's response and appeal**)—As a prophet, Paul penetrated the mask of treachery and realized what Festus had in store for him: a trial by the Sanhedrin (cf. v. 20), with accusers acting as judges (and executioners, cf. 6:12-13; 7:57-60), and with Festus's presence giving legality to this judicial farce. Boldly, Paul put the procurator on the spot. **I am standing before Caesar's tribunal,** of which the procurator is a representative. If Festus did not acquit him but continued the proceedings by using the Jews not only as accusers but also as co-judges, then the procurator was acting against his better judgment. For, addressing Festus directly, **you know very well** that **to the Jews I have done no wrong.** Paul went on to acknowledge the government's right to inflict capital punishment also on him, provided he had **committed** a capital crime. On the other hand, **if there is nothing in their charges against me, no one can give me up to them** (literally, "hand me over as a favor to them"). Paul, the accused, has turned the tables and openly and politely accused his judge of favoritism and subversion of Roman law. Festus who was called as procurator to uphold law and justice has failed miserably; the accused now becomes the upholder of Roman law. Therefore, Paul ends by speaking two far-reaching words (in English, four words): **I appeal to Caesar.** As a Roman citizen (cf. 16:37) he had the right of appeal and he made use of this right because Caesar's law was being subverted by Caesar's representative. Festus had not interrupted Paul nor stated that the accused had drawn the wrong conclusion from his "friendly" question (v. 9). No, Paul had correctly interpreted the procurator's question, which camouflaged his intention. He had seen through Festus's little scheme and with his appeal had thwarted the procurator's plan.

His appeal to the tribunal in Rome was also an appeal against the Sanhedrin in Jerusalem. Rome may have had deceitful representatives like Felix and Festus, but its legal system was preferable to the unmitigated defamation from Jerusalem, that is, from official Judaism. With his appeal Paul was liberated from the juridical realm of Judaism represented by the Sanhedrin. Luke also knew of Jewish leaders who did not belong to the category of accusers and defamers of Christianity, but exhibited courage in their defense of Christianity, that is, of Paul (23:6-10), but they were not part of the delegation.

12 (Festus's final decision)—With his cleverly concealed plan unmasked Festus must now regain his dignity and restore his image as a fairminded bureaucrat, who would think twice before double-crossing Paul again. The procurator conferred with his council of legal experts (Latin, *consilium*) as to whether the type of accusation applied to the right of appeal, and he granted the request: **You have appealed to Caesar; to Caesar you shall go.** That Caesar was Nero. Luke never mentioned his name, probably because after Nero's suicide on June 9, A.D. 68, the Roman senate declared him an enemy of the state. Not the person, but the imperial tribunal in Rome was important to Luke. The appeal to Caesar's tribunal in Rome was an important turning point. The plan of the Jews and of Festus to have Paul returned to Jerusalem had been thwarted. The accused Paul retained the initiative and "the divine must" had proceeded one step further on its way to Rome (cf. v. 10, literally, I "must" be tried; cf. 19:21; 23:11). From now on the Jews will no longer play the role of Paul's accusers. When he meets Jews again he will be in Rome, and he will speak of his past tribulations "on account of the hope of Israel," but they do not raise accusations against him (28:17-28).

We have tried to understand this episode from Luke's point of view. We shall touch briefly on three historical questions: (1) Some scholars have denied that Paul held Roman citizenship, because he never referred to it in his letters and because he stated that he had been "beaten with rods" by Roman lictors three times (cf. 2 Cor. 11:25; see Acts 16:22, 37). However, his Roman citizenship probably did not mean much to the apostle whose citizenship was grounded "in heaven" (Phil. 3:20). For the sake of his mission he may have found it advantageous not to refer to his Roman citizenship. For instance, when his Christian fellow prisoners lacked this status he could hardly break solidarity with them by claiming his status as Roman citizen. It would also take time to verify his Roman citizenship before local magistrates, time in custody away from his calling. However, his appeal to Caesar's tribunal presupposes his Roman citizenship, and to argue that Luke invented both the appeal and the citizenship would seem rather absurd. After all, Paul did reach Rome and, according to 1 Clement, he died a martyr's death in Rome and not in Antioch, Caesarea, or Jerusalem. The most probable explanation of how he got to Rome is Luke's. He appealed to Caesar. (2) The appeal process which Acts presupposes was called *provocatio;* by it during the first century A.D. a citizen could appeal to the emperor even before a provincial governor had sentenced him. This process must be distinguished from the right of *appellatio* which was developed in the second century A.D., and in which the appeal could be made only after sentencing. (For information see Sherwin-White.) (3) Judicial proceedings which began before a Roman tribunal also had to be completed there and Paul's case would be no exception. Festus could not possibly hand Paul over to the

Sanhedrin and let the Sanhedrin pass the final verdict which would close the case. However, provincial governors had broad discretionary powers in defining guilt and arriving at a verdict. The charge that Paul had desecrated the temple also lay within the jurisdiction of the Sanhedrin, and Festus had the legal right to move the trial to Jerusalem. Moreover, he could ask the pro-Roman Sanhedrin to act as his *consilium*, his body of legal advisors. "In his presence" (v. 9) the Sanhedrin could then examine Paul and communicate its verdict to the procurator. Festus himself would have to pass sentence. According to Acts Paul foresaw the outcome of any proceedings which would involve the Sanhedrin beyond its status as plaintiffs. He objected to the excessive influence of the Sanhedrin on Festus if, in accordance with the Sanhedrin's wishes (cf. v. 3), the trial were to be moved to Jerusalem and the Sanhedrin become Festus's *consilium*. Therefore he made his appeal. In short, there is nothing in Luke's narrative of 25:6-12 which is historically improbable, so long as Paul's final statement, **no one can give me up to them,** is not interpreted to mean that the final sentencing of Paul would be done by the Sanhedrin.

Agrippa, Festus, and Paul (25:13—26:32)

With the ratification of Paul's appeal by Festus the trial before the procurator is concluded and Paul will shortly—but not at once—be on his way to Rome. One last grand show will (1) testify to Paul's innocence, (2) interpret his trial, (3) complete his witness and defense on Jewish soil, (4) serve as the basis for Festus's report to Caesar, and (5) illustrate that Christianity is a public affair. The whole section is arranged in such a way that Paul's climactic speech is at its center.

1) Festus informs Agrippa about Paul in private (25:13-22)
2) Introduction to the public meeting with Paul (25:23-27)
3) Speech by Paul (26:1-23)
4) Dialog between Festus and Paul, Agrippa and Paul (26:24-29)
5) Reaction of Agrippa and Festus to Paul (26:30-32)

13-22 (Festus informs Agrippa)—One is tempted to call this and the following subsection "Festus's defense," because the procurator explains his actions to other persons, and he does so twice. Luke, however, restricted the use of the verb and the noun *defend* and *defense* in this section to Paul, the witnessing prisoner (25:16; cf. 22:1; 26:1,2,24; cf. 24:10; 25:8), and simply permitted Festus to justify himself before Agrippa, and the next day before a larger crowd. Luke's reader cannot help but notice the shabbiness of Festus's twofold rehearsal of his deeds, as he hears Festus's declarations of Paul's innocence (25:18-19,25; 26:31; cf. Luke 23:4,14,22). The three declarations of innocence are tightly connected with Paul's appeal in such a way that it appears to be Paul's own fault that he is not free (25:21,25b; 26:32). What an irony! If only Paul had trusted honest Festus and not appealed he "could have been set free" (26:32). Of course, Luke and his readers know that the governor has the right and the power to set his prisoner free also after an appeal (see Sherwin-White, 65). But such a bold action would of course alienate the Sanhedrin.

13-14a—King **Agrippa** II and his widowed sister **Bernice** made a state visit to **Caesarea** to welcome the new procurator **Festus.** Agrippa II, son of Herod Agrippa I, brother of Felix's wife, Drusilla, was the last Jewish king on Palestinian soil. He ruled from about A.D. 53 to 100 over a territory northeast of Palestine together with portions of Galilee and Perea. Much of his territory had at one time belonged to Philip, son of Herod the Great. Agrippa was fiercely pro-Roman, and his troops participated in the assault on Jerusalem in the war of A.D. 66. His sister **Bernice** had first married a commoner called Oraneus, and then her uncle, Herod II, king of Chalcis. After his death in A.D. 48 she lived with her brother in an incestuous relationship, as Roman and Jewish gossip would have it (Juvenal, *Satires* 6.156–158; Josephus, *Ant.* 20.145). Later she married King Polemon of Cilicia but quickly left him and returned to her brother's court. Finally, she became the mistress of Titus, conqueror of Jerusalem and later Roman emperor (A.D. 79–81). Their love affair was widely known. Luke did not reflect on the morality of the royal visitors but on their social prominence. Sometime during the VIP visit **Festus laid Paul's case before the king** in private conversation. In direct discourse Luke permits Festus to explain this case to his visitor (vv. 14b-21). In so doing Luke presents the Roman point of view and expects his readers to see through it.

14b-15—Festus recounted his visit to Jerusalem (cf. 25:1-3). He added that the Sanhedrin requested Paul's condemnation, **asking for sentence against him.** This is something new, which throws light on 25:2. But Festus conveniently omitted mentioning that at his visit members of the Sanhedrin had asked him to do them "a favor" and return Paul to Jerusalem.

16—Festus now expressed his displeasure with the Sanhedrin's request, citing a basic and widely quoted principle of Roman law: **it was not the custom of the Romans to give up anyone** (Greek, *charizesthai;* cf. 25:11) **before the accused met the accusers face to face and had opportunity to make his defense concerning the charge laid against him.** But, so the reader will ask, did not Festus himself subvert his own principle when he was ready to use Paul's accusers as his concilium and thus in fact "give up" Paul as a favor to his accusers (v. 11)? There was nothing wrong with the principle of the Roman law. Its execution, however, left something to be desired, and so does Felix's self-justification.

17-19—Paul's **accusers** at his trial **brought no charge in his case of such evils as I supposed.** Yet they had requested his condemnation (cf. v. 15)! What their accusations really amounted to were **certain points of dispute with him about their own superstition** (better, "religion"; Festus would hardly wish to offend his Jewish visitor by referring to Jewish "superstition"). The points of disagreement between Paul and his accusers dealt with **one Jesus, who was dead, but whom Paul asserted to be alive.** Surprisingly, Festus has in focus the basic disagreement between Judaism and Christianity, which is the resurrection of Jesus. Before the Lukan Paul ever mentioned the resurrection of Jesus explicitly in his defense speeches, the Roman procurator understood the basic issue, which was the religious issue of Jesus' resurrection and which had nothing to do with the desecration of the temple or with fomenting riots and sedition. These latter were phony issues designed to have Paul condemned without evidence. But equally surprising was Festus's failure to set Paul free at once, which would have been merely to draw the conclusion from his own insight and his legal principle (cf. v. 16).

20-21—Luke is at his most brilliant in sketching the hypocrisy of Festus without any overt polemics. **Being at a loss how to investigate these questions,** the procurator continues with audible self-pity. "I, a Roman and not a Jew, am just perplexed by these theological questions!" He speaks as if he had not articulated the theological issue perfectly, an issue that is not and cannot be of concern to Roman law. The hypocritical procurator continues by telling Agrippa that he had asked Paul **whether he wished to go to Jerusalem and be tried there,** blissfully omitting that he had no business to ask that question and drag out the trial, because he already knew of Paul's innocence of crimes (v. 18). Furthermore, the procurator omitted telling his guest that he had posed that question to Paul because he, the procurator, wanted to do "a favor" for Paul's accusers (cf. v. 9a). To Agrippa, Festus justified his wish to transfer the trial to Jerusalem on the basis of his own ignorance of Jewish theological teaching, as if that constituted a case for criminal proceedings under Roman law (cf. 18:15). Luke's reader is asked to understand the duplicity of magistrates they may have to face. On the one hand, Roman law is not directed against Christianity. On the other, the actual practice of that law is something else and in the mouth of magistrates such as Festus, that practice even sounds "honest," to a point—honest in the open admission that Christians are not common criminals but, like Paul, innocent of crimes (cf. Pliny's letter to Trajan, in which the governor of Bithynia admitted that Christians had not committed crimes—though he still executed them!). What Festus suggested to his royal visitor was that since he, as Roman procurator, could not possibly be expected to pass judgment in religious matters between Jews and Christians, he referred Paul's case to the Sanhedrin for judgment. Then, of all things, Paul **appealed to be kept in custody for the decision of the emperor** (literally, "of the Augustus" or "of his Majesty"). It is really Paul's fault that he is not yet free. He **appealed to be kept in custody.** If only he had not appealed! The reader knows, unless he or she is blind and deaf, that Festus is telling a half-truth, typical of all non-Christian officials in Luke-Acts. The marvel of the Lukan composition of Festus's speech is that Festus's words are without overt polemics and almost believable. Now, since Paul has taken the decision out of Festus's hands, the procurator cannot but hold Paul in custody until such time when he can **send him to Caesar.** Again a half-truth! After the appeal, Festus did not have to "command" that Paul remain a prisoner. Festus could have let him free on the basis of his insight into Paul's innocence (v. 18).

22—With Festus's speech completed, the interest of his royal visitor **Agrippa** has been aroused, and he says: **I should like to hear the man myself. Tomorrow,** Festus replies. The stage of the great show in Caesarea has now been prepared. Historically, it is not inconceivable that Agrippa paid a courtesy visit to the new procurator shortly after his arrival. As client king of Rome he had to be careful to cultivate good relations with Caesar's representative in Judea. Nor is it inconceivable that Festus would bring up the matter of Paul and present Paul to Agrippa. At any rate, Luke correctly placed Felix and Drusilla, Agrippa and Bernice in terms of time and place. Naturally, the speeches of Festus, Paul, and Agrippa are Lukan compositions.

23-27 (Introduction to the public meeting with Paul)—Paul's great speech is framed by this introductory narrative and by a concluding narrative (26:30-32). Even though Paul makes his final defense (26:1,2,24), the scene is not meant to be a trial scene, because his appeal precluded a trial by the procurator. Moreover, no accusers are present who meet Paul "face to face" (v. 16). The meeting resulted from Agrippa's curiosity to hear this man Paul (v. 22), and from Festus's need for "definite" information on Paul to be included in his letter to the emperor (vv. 26-27). Luke did not write another trial scene, but presents a hearing to satisfy the king's curiosity and the procurator's need for writing his report which would accompany Paul to Rome. Yet, this hearing before the two highest officials of the land, one a Jew, the other a Gentile, will give Paul the opportunity to function as public defender of Christianity in a grand setting (cf. 9:15).

23—So on the morrow Agrippa and Bernice came with great pomp and pageantry (Greek, *phantasia*), processing into the **audience hall,** accompanied by the **military tribunes** and the **prominent** citizens of Caesarea. Then a lone prisoner was **brought** in before this illustrious assembly (Luke 21:12-13).

24-25—Festus began his introductory speech by pointing to Paul. **You see this man about whom the whole Jewish people petitioned me, both at Jerusalem and here,** to have him executed, **shouting that he ought not to live any longer** (cf. 22:22). Festus alludes to 25:1-3,7. He regarded the delegation of the Sanhedrin as representative of **the whole Jewish people,** according to the *pars pro toto* principle. The Sanhedrin, or its official delegation, spoke for the whole Jewish nation. Yet the procurator's own judgment is in total contrast to the Jewish request for Paul's execution. **But I found that he had done nothing deserving death.** This contradiction is embarrassing. On the one hand, the whole Jewish people want him condemned; on the other hand, Roman law judges him innocent. Since the historical Paul was not acquitted at his trial before Festus, it was important for Luke to tell his readers that in the judgment of the tribune Claudius Lysias (23:29), of Felix (24:22-23), and of Festus, Paul was innocent, and that Festus himself stated it three times (25:18, 25; 26:31). Paul's innocence, however, poses a problem. Why was he not released? Luke's answer has already been given (25:9a). But Festus would have to be "a good man" (cf. 11:24) to confess publicly why he did not release Paul. Instead of confessing, he covered up his failure and indirectly blamed Paul. Had he not **appealed** he could have been released (see. v. 21). Since he himself **appealed to the emperor I decided to send him to Rome** (cf. 26:32). Like all non-Christian Roman officials in Luke-Acts, Festus is a divided person. He can witness to Paul's innocence, but must cover up his own failings.

26-27—Next, Festus turned to the purpose of this illustrious gathering and told his audience that he needed additional enlightenment so that he could **write** a report about Paul and send it **to my lord** (Greek, *tō kyriō*). "The lord" was Nero, during whose reign this title became more common among divine emperor titles. At Luke's time the emperor Domitian (A.D. 81–96) was called "Lord and God." Eventually the confession "Jesus is Lord" (1 Cor. 12:3) became antithetical to the acclamation in the emperor cult (*kyrios Kaisar*), but such polemics are not present in Acts.

Even though legal terminology appears in vv. 26-27 ("bring before," "examine," "indicate charges"), the gathering is not a judicial proceeding but an informal hearing for the purpose of securing information. This purpose seems odd at first, for obviously Festus has ample materials from the accusers and the defendant, in addition to his own perception, to enable him to write his report for Caesar. He has twice announced Paul's innocence and the reader knows how Festus will talk himself out of his embarrassment at not freeing this prisoner in spite of his innocence under Roman law. So what is the point of gathering more information? Festus had admitted that he was "at a loss how to investigate" the religious charges which he had clearly perceived to be the basis of the Jewish political charges against Paul (vv. 18-20). But the presence of King Agrippa who was an expert in Jewish religious affairs offered an opportunity for understanding the religious charges more definitely. **For it seems to**

me unreasonable, concluded Festus, **in sending a prisoner, not to
indicate the charges against him.** Luke suggests that Paul's great
climactic speech will be part of Festus's report sent to the emperor.

Paul before Agrippa (26:1-32)

Introduction. Paul's speech will be his answer "to the whole Jewish
people," whose verdict was that "he ought not to live any longer"
(25:24). Even though the hearing before Agrippa was not a trial in
the legal sense, because the accusers did not meet Paul "face to
face" (25:16), nevertheless Paul could say, "I stand here on trial" (v.
6), because the hearing was part of the trial which was to be concluded before the emperor's tribunal. With his speech Paul made
his defense "against all the accusations of the Jews" (v. 2), but simultaneously his defense is so constructed that it transcended Paul's
own unique situation and became a defense of Christianity and witness for Christ "to all people" (22:15). Its purpose was not to seek
toleration from the empire. Festus, Caesar's representative, was not
even addressed by Paul, even though the procurator was the host
of the grand show. When he interrupted Paul, Paul said that he was
speaking to Agrippa and, by implication, not to Festus (vv. 24-26).
Paul's defense is directed to Judaism rather than to Rome, though
the procurator hears it and may use it in his report to Caesar.

The form of Paul's defense is an autobiographical recital of his
hope, belief, and actions as a Pharisee, a persecutor of the church,
a person called and sent by the resurrected Jesus, a servant-witness
obedient to his call. There is general agreement on the structure of
the chapter, with the exception of the speech. Some prefer a two-
part structure (vv. 4-8 and 9-23). One weakness of this episode is
that it ignores Luke's signal in v. 19, which consists in the direct
address, "O, King Agrippa." Hence, a threefold structure of the
speech is preferable, especially when we recognize the pivotal significance of the call and commission of Paul.

I.   Paul's defense speech (vv. 1-23)
     Introduction (vv. 1-3)
     Agrippa gives Paul permission to speak (v. 1)
     Paul's *captatio benevolentiae* (vv. 2-3)
     A. Paul's life as a Pharisee and God's promise of the resurrection
        (vv. 4-8)

1. His life as Pharisee (vv. 4-5)
2. God's promise of the resurrection (vv. 6-8)
B. His life as persecutor and his call by Jesus (vv. 9-18)
1. His life as persecutor (vv. 9-11)
2. His call by Jesus (vv. 12-18)
C. His life as servant and his resurrection witness (vv. 19-23)
1. His life as servant (vv. 19-21)
2. His resurrection witness (vv. 22-23)

II. Dialog of Festus, Paul, and Agrippa (vv. 24-29)
A. Festus and Paul (vv. 24-25)
B. Paul about Agrippa (v. 26)
C. Paul and Agrippa (vv. 27-29)

III. Concluding reactions (vv. 30-32)
A. Collective verdict (v. 31)
B. Verdict of Agrippa (v. 32)

Parts I.A and I.B of the speech are introduced by the same Greek conjunction (*men oun*); part C is introduced by a new direct address to Agrippa. The first as well as the second sections of each part relate to each other. For instance, the second sections relate the theme of the Jewish resurrection hope (vv. 6-8) to Paul's call by the resurrected Jesus (vv. 12-18), and to Paul's resurrection witness (vv. 22-23). Paul's vision of Christ and his call by Christ (vv. 12-18) connect Israel's resurrection hope (vv. 6-8) with Paul's resurrection message (vv. 22-23). Part I.B (vv. 9-18) also narrates the basic disagreement between Judaism and Christianity. Prior to Damascus, Paul persecuted Christians "in raging fury" (v. 11) because in spite of his future resurrection hope (part I.A) he "was convinced" that "opposing the name of Jesus of Nazareth" was the right thing to do (v. 9). But then he was confronted by the resurrected Jesus who "appeared to" him (v. 16) and a radical change occurred in Paul from persecutor to servant-witness. While parts I.A and I.C maintain the continuity between Paul's Pharisaic hope and his present activity as servant-witness of the resurrected Jesus, this continuity has its counterpoint in the discontinuity which comes to the fore in part I.B. Paul's life-story also functions as an invitation to Judaism to reconsider its opposition to Christianity in the light of its hope (part I.A) and in the light of Paul's experience (parts I.B and I.C). Paul's life is an invitation to consider that "God raises the dead" (present tense, v. 8), and that Jesus who appeared to Paul (vv. 12-18) is "the first to rise from the dead" (v. 23). Equally important is that the readers gain an understanding of Paul's unique position in God's grand design (vv. 15-18 and 22-23). Moreover, Paul's defense fulfills Christ's promise and mandate of 9:15; Luke 12:4,8-12; 21:12-15,19 and draws parallels to Jesus' passion. At the conclusion of the scene Paul is declared innocent by a Herodian king and a Roman procurator, just as was Jesus (vv. 30-32; cf. Luke 23:4,14,15,22) and, just as with Jesus, his passion continues. "Everyone who is fully taught shall be like his teacher" (Luke 6:40), "a light" for revelation to Jew and Gentile (Luke 2:32; Acts 26:17,23) and an obedient servant of God in suffering.

1-3 (Introduction to Paul's defense)—Agrippa grants permission to Paul to speak **for yourself** or, better, "about yourself," thus already suggesting that Paul's **defense** will be autobiographical. Paul will speak about himself, but beginning with v. 12 he will also speak about Jesus. In the manner of an orator he **stretched out his hand.** Did Luke forget that Paul wore chains (cf. v. 29)—or are the chains a metaphor for imprisonment?

Neither in the *captatio benevolentiae* nor in the following speech is Festus addressed. Paul speaks to Agrippa, the representative of Judaism and pays him a compliment concerning his "great expertise" (the RSV **familiar** is too weak) in matters of **all customs and controversies of the Jews. Customs** in Acts is synonymous with *law,* and **controversies** refers primarily to the disagreement between Pharisees and Sadducees concerning the resurrection (cf. 23:6-10; 25:19). Paul's speech before Agrippa is to be his fifth and climactic **defense,** after his defense before the people (22:1), the Sanhedrin (23:1), Felix (24:10), and Festus (25:8). In Luke's Gospel the verb *to defend* (RSV, "to answer") occurs only twice (Luke 12:11; 21:14). In the face of Paul's "wisdom" Festus will reveal his lack of it (cf. v. 24). Paul wants to defend himself against **all charges** in the presence of Agrippa, the expert of **all customs and controversies.** Paul will answer them by focusing on the basic controversy between Judaism and Christianity as he tells his life's story. The reader already knows that the political charge of sedition has been found groundless by Claudius Lysias (23:29), by Felix (24:22-26), and by Festus (25:18-19,25). The accusation of profaning the temple had also been answered already in 21:29 (cf. 24:17). That leaves the charges of teaching against the people and the law (21:28). Paul will deal with them indirectly by rehearsing his own story. At any rate, Paul expressed his pleasure at being able to make his defense before Agrippa, this "outstanding expert" of Jewish affairs, which implies that Paul was glad not to have to talk again to Festus—who is and remains an ignoramus (v. 24). Of course, Festus can correctly repeat words and ideas, but he lacks understanding (cf. 25:19-20). Paul asked the king **to listen** to him **patiently.**

4-5 (Paul's life as a Pharisee)—Three phrases, **From my youth, from the beginning, for a long time,** indicate the constancy of Paul's orthodox **manner of life.** He spent his life **among** his **own nation,** the heart and center of which is **Jerusalem** (vv. 4, 10, 20). He belonged **to the strictest party of our religion** and he has lived all his life, past and present, **as a Pharisee** (cf. 23:6). So how could anyone accuse him of speaking against the people, the Law, or the temple? **All the Jews** of Jerusalem can **testify** to his orthodox manner of life. As a Pharisee Paul believes the Law and the Prophets (24:14-15; 26:6), is "zealous for God" and "the law of our fathers" (22:3), and appears for purification in the temple (21:26; 24:18).

6-8 (The hope in God's promise)—However, Pharisees are not only strict observers of the Law, they are also earnest believers in the **promise made by God to our fathers,** and **hope** for the fulfillment of God's promise. Note that *hope* (as noun and verb) occurs three times in these verses. Thus it is indeed odd that Paul presently stands **on trial** and is **accused by Jews** for **this hope** in the fulfillment of God's **promise** (cf. 1:6; Luke 24:21). This is all the more odd because it is not just he, but **our twelve tribes** who **hope to attain** the fulfillment of the promise and therefore **worship** God **night and day.** In its worship Israel testifies to its hope by praying, for instance, the second of the Eighteen Benedictions: "Thou, O Lord, art mighty forever, thou raisest up [or "quickenest"] the dead, thou art mighty to save. . . ." Note the first person pronouns in Paul's speech ("my nation," "our religion," "our fathers," "our tribes") by which he identifies himself with the people of Israel and its king, its Law, promise, and worship. Agrippa is addressed, not Festus or other Gentiles! These pronouns draw a line of separation between Jews and Gentiles. In v. 8 the pronoun changes to the second person plural and draws a dividing line between Paul and his non-Christian audience, be it Jewish or Gentile, when he asks the question: **Why is it thought**

incredible by any of you that God raises the dead? The point of
"controversy" between Judaism and Christianity has emerged.
Agrippa as well as the reader know the Christian claim, that God
has raised Jesus from the dead in accordance with his promise.
Through Jesus Israel's corporate hope for resurrection and redemption is in process of realization. A Pharisee ought therefore become
a Christian, as should Agrippa, the expert on Jewish affairs (cf. vv.
27-29). The following section (vv. 9-11) will show that becoming a
Christian is not quite as self-evident as it appears from vv. 4-8. In
these verses we heard that the surface reason for Paul's trial lay in
Israel's **hope,** shared by all twelve tribes (vv. 6-7). Yet the deeper
reason for his situation is the resurrection (v. 8), not as the object
of hope, but as present reality, inaugurated through Jesus' resurrection and proclaimed by preachers like Paul. When he is on trial
because of his **hope in the promise,** then he is on trial because he
believes and proclaims that in Jesus' resurrection God's **promise** is
fulfilled and Israel's **hope** is in process of realization. Verses 22-23
shed additional light on vv. 6-8.

9-11 (Paul as persecutor)—The autobiographical sketch of vv. 4-
5 comprises not only Paul's past but also his present (cf. 23:6). This
new section, however, radically contrasts his past activity as persecutor with his present calling as servant-witness of Jesus. The
reader is now made aware that a Pharisee who holds the "hope in
the promise" does not inevitably become a Christian. On the contrary, Paul held that hope, and yet he **was convinced that** he **ought
to do many things in opposing the name of Jesus of Nazareth,** by
persecuting his followers who had been "baptized in the name of
Jesus Christ" (2:38; cf. 19:5). Before Damascus Paul was no more
willing to acknowledge the resurrection of Jesus than were his contemporaries at the time of his trial. He was no more able to believe
in God's eschatological deed which brings Israel's hope to realization
than was his Jewish audience. The path from holding Israel's hope
to accepting the fulfillment of that hope is not a matter of logical
deduction, but a decision of faith grounded in "the light" of the
gospel generating faith. The sketch of Paul as persecutor is drawn
in sharper, darker colors in comparison with previous reports. We
hear of the divine **ought** (v. 9, Greek, *dei*). Paul believed that his
persecution of Christians was the will of God. His ultimate objective

459

was to oppose **the name of Jesus.** His opposition to Jesus (v. 15) included all who were baptized in his name and therefore believed that Israel's hope was dependent on his resurrection (cf. v. 8). **In Jerusalem** he operated **by authority from the chief priests,** functioning as cojudge when Christians (plural) were put to death. He punished them **often in all the synagogues,** trying **to make them blaspheme,** that is, deny that Jesus is the fulfillment of Israel's hope. His persecutions extended even **to foreign cities. In raging fury** he acted against **the saints,** just as the Jews of Jerusalem acted against him (cf. 21:30-31a; 22:22; 25:24). The pre-Christian Paul had no intention that the name of Jesus and his community, the resurrection faith and message should continue in the heart of Judaism (cf. v. 4)—much less prevail there. Thus Paul's pre-Christian life as an opponent of Jesus' name is a mirror in which Judaism can perceive its own opposition to the faith and witness of the church.

12-18 (His call by Jesus)—The decisive break in Paul's life is underlined by a new address to the king (v. 13). The Christophany was followed by the call and commissioning of Paul by Jesus, who appeared to him in divine glory. This third account of Paul's Damascus experience differs from the others. Ananias has disappeared, together with his vision and Christ's words to him (cf. 9:10-17; 22:12-16). Paul's blindness and healing are therefore also omitted (9:7, 18). Nor is there any longer a need for a temple vision (22:17-21), because in this report Christ commissioned Paul immediately on the Damascus road (cf. Gal. 1:15-16). Now the emphasis lies on the call rather than on the conversion of Paul. The differences noted, to which some minor ones will be added below, reflect Luke's literary freedom which enabled him to vary the narrative to suit the occasion. Moreover, Luke was also aware of a tradition in which Paul was commissioned directly by Christ himself. We do not know the form of this tradition, except to say that it differed from that used in chap. 9, which enabled him to telescope and condense the narrative so that the speech of Jesus to Paul (vv. 16-18) became its climax.

12-14—Thus, or "at that time" (cf. Luke 12:1), when he operated in foreign cities (v. 11), he also went **to Damascus with the authority and commission of the chief priests** (cf. 9:1-3; 22:6). At noon on the way to that city he **saw a light from heaven, brighter than the sun,** shining around him and his travel companions. Note the intensification in the description of the Christophany. The light is brighter than the sun at midday (cf. 22:6). Not just Paul, but **all** fall to the ground (in contrast to 9:4; 22:7; but see comments on 9:4-7). Yet in this third report Paul is not blinded by the brightness of the heavenly light. Rather, he is illuminated by the light. The light brighter than the sun is the manifestation of the resurrected Jesus who reveals himself to Paul in the divine splendor of his exaltation. Light is also used as a metaphor for salvation and revelation. "The Lord is my light and my salvation" (Ps. 27:1). The Messiah is "a light for revelation to the Gentiles" (Luke 2:32). The light brighter than the sun here signifies the revelation which enlightens Paul (cf. "light" in vv. 18 and 23). Through the revelation he can perceive the identity of Jesus whom he had persecuted. The question whether he saw Jesus or only a light poses a false alternative. He saw both (cf. v. 16, "I have appeared to you"). The question of how Paul saw Jesus cannot be answered except by saying: he saw him as a light, brighter than the sun. Only Paul heard a **voice** speaking **in . . . Hebrew,** that is, in Aramaic, addressing him by his original name, **Saul, Saul, why do you persecute me?** Opposition to the church is opposition to the resurrected Jesus himself who identifies himself with the church and who is in unity with God the Father. Paul's opponents might remember this in their persecution of him. The heavenly voice added a Greek proverb, which can be traced back to Euripides, but which had become quite popular at Luke's time. **It hurts you to kick against the goads.** In the present context it means: "It is hopeless for you, Paul, to struggle against your God-ordained destiny, just as it is hopeless for an animal to struggle against the goad of its master." Jesus placed Paul under his dominion to use him as the instrument of his divine will.

15-18—To the question "Why are you persecuting me?" Paul answered, **Who are you, Lord? And the Lord** replied, **I am Jesus whom you are persecuting** (cf. 9:5; 22:8). Then follows Paul's commission, which is without parallel in the two prior accounts. Jesus now calls him directly and without intermediary. His address to Paul (vv. 16-18) is filled with allusions to Old Testament texts from the prophets and from the call of prophets. **Stand upon your feet** is language from Ezek. 2:1. In direct discourse Paul hears: **I have appeared to you** (Greek, *ōphthēn,* cf. 1 Cor. 15:5-8; Luke 24:34). With this verb Paul's vision is placed in proximity to the Easter

461

appearances of Jesus to his disciples and apostles. In Acts this verb form is applied only to Paul in the time after Pentecost. The purpose of the Christophany was to **appoint you,** or "select you." Note that in 22:14 it is God who appointed Paul, while here it is Jesus **the Lord.** If the subject of the appointing can be either "the God of our fathers" or the exalted Lord Jesus, then such change of subject indicates the unity of purpose between God and Jesus, who is exalted at God's right hand (cf. 2:33). His election also places Paul in proximity to the apostles whom Jesus had elected (1:2), and the same holds true for the dual function of "servant and witness" to which Jesus appointed him (the RSV correctly translates the Greek nouns as verbs: **to serve and bear witness).** Luke 1:2 refers to "eyewitnesses and ministers of the word." The apostolic eyewitnesses guarantee the normative tradition concerning the earthly Jesus up to the ascension (cf. Acts 1:21-22). While Paul cannot be an eyewitness of the words, deeds, and passion of the earthly Jesus, he too can function as witness of the resurrected and exalted Christ, because Jesus **appeared** to him. Paul is to be a witness **to the things in which you have seen me and to those in which I will appear to you.**

He is an authorized witness of the Resurrected One. Moreover, the appearance of Christ outside of Damascus initiates Paul's function as witness but is not limited to the initiation. There will be future appearances and visions (cf. 16:9-10; 18:9; 22:17-18; 23:11: 27:23-24) through which Christ shall guide his chosen witness. Furthermore, Paul is appointed to be a "servant" or minister (Greek, *hypēretēs*). He serves Christ by being "a minister of the word" (Luke 1:2, where the same word is used). A minister of the Word (genitive of object!) serves the Word by seeing to it that the Word of God is proclaimed truthfully and boldly so that Christ himself speaks through the Word or, to use Paul's phrase, that Christ himself "would proclaim light" to Jew and Gentile (v. 23) through the words of his servant. The servant who serves the Word will speak it so that "the hope in the promise" (v. 6) finds its realization in the fulfillment brought about by the resurrection of Jesus. As servant, Paul was given the task of prophet-preacher. As witness, he had to testify to the reality of the resurrection which he encountered in the Damascus vision and subsequent visions.

17—His appointment is followed by a promise of protection, which alludes to Jer. 1:8. Christ will be **delivering** (that is, saving the life of) Paul **from the** Jewish **people and from the Gentiles** (cf. 9:23,29; 13:50; 14:2,5,19; 16:25-40; 17:1-15; 21:27-39; 23:11-33; 25:3-4), only to **send** Paul to them again as his servant-witness. The protection promised applies to the task to which he is called, a task which, for Jeremiah as well as for Paul, included suffering (cf. 9:16). Also the verb *send* (Greek, *apostellō*, in distinction from *pempō*) in Luke-Acts places Paul in the proximity of the apostles. Since Paul's function was similar to that of the apostles, Luke on rare occasions could apply this designation to him (14:4,14). But generally he did not refer to Paul as an apostle, because in Acts Paul is the connecting link between the twelve apostles and Luke's own church. Why Paul was not called an apostle more often is not a matter of rank but a matter of time. Paul became a Christian after the ascension, yet he received the singular honor in Acts of being the only one elected and sent by Christ directly. The scope of Paul's commission, of his being sent by Christ, is universal. He is sent not just to Gentiles (cf. Gal. 1:16), but to Jews *and* Gentiles.

18—The purpose of Paul's commission is threefold. First, he is **to open their eyes,** so that Jews and Gentiles perceive what God has accomplished through Jesus. When the eyes of the two Emmaus disciples "were opened," then "they recognized" Jesus who had "opened" the Scriptures to them. Their hope that "he was the one to redeem Israel" found fulfillment only through the opening of their eyes (Luke 24:21,31-32). Paul's own eyes had been opened, his perception of Jesus had been radically changed and illuminated. Now he is sent to perform the task of Isaiah's servant of the Lord (Isa. 42:7; 61:1).

Second, the reason why he should open the eyes of Jews and Gentiles is **that they may turn . . . to God.** This involves turning away **from** the **darkness** of pagan idolatry (cf. 1 Thess. 1:9; Acts 14:15; 15:19), or of Jewish unbelief and hatred of Christianity (cf. vv. 9-11; 22:22). It involves a turning **from the power of Satan** who operates in the realm of infirmities, idolatry, magic, unbelief, deceit, and hatred (cf. Luke 8:12; 13:16; Acts 10:38; Luke 22:3,31,53; Acts 5:3; 8:23; 13:10). But Jesus and, after him, his servant-witnesses bring God's revelation, which is **light** "to those who sit in darkness and in the shadow of death" (Luke 1:79; 2:32; Acts 13:47; 26:23).

Third, the consequence of turning to God is to **receive forgiveness of sins** in the present **and a place among those who are sanctified** both now and in the future resurrection of the just (cf. 3:19; 24:15; cf. Col. 1:12-14). Such turning to God takes place **by faith;** not by any kind of faith, but **by faith in** Jesus Christ. This phrase, **by faith,** should probably be related to each clause in v. 18, rather than to the last one only.

Forgiveness of sins means to have a place or share among the saints (Col. 1:12) who are sanctified by forgiveness of their sins and the gift of the Holy Spirit (cf. 2:38; 10:43; 13:38-39). Paul's appointment as servant-witness by the resurrected Lord himself indicates the uniqueness of his position in God's design. But his task of leading people to faith, forgiveness, and a place among the saints is not limited to him.

19-23—The beginning of the third part is marked by a new address which also marks the end of Jesus' speech to Paul. Just as vv. 9-11 continue the autobiographical report of vv. 4-5, so v. 19 continues Paul's story after his call. However, v. 19 draws a contrast to v. 9. Whereas Paul was convinced that his opposition to Jesus and his community expressed God's will (v. 9, *dei*), so now after his encounter with the resurrected Lord he is convinced that he had been wrong in opposing Jesus, that in spite of his "hope in the promise" he too had lived in the realm of darkness and under the dominion of Satan (v. 18). After the appearance of the resurrected Jesus he not only gave up opposing Jesus, but became obedient **to the heavenly vision** and in accordance with his call he preached in **Damascus, Jerusalem** (cf. 9:20-30) **and throughout all the country of Judea.** This last phrase poses difficulties: (1) It is not in the dative case, as is the noun *Jerusalem.* (2) Acts knows nothing about Paul's preaching throughout Judea. (3) Galatians 1:22 precludes such preaching. Therefore, some interpreters regard this phrase as a later interpolation into the text of Acts (which it may well be); others try to emend the text. On the basis of textual variants one might translate: "and in every land where Jews live and to Gentiles" (papyrus 74 has "Jews" in place of "Judea"). (4) Perhaps Luke formulated on the basis of Luke 4:44 and Acts 10:39, suggesting a Jesus-Paul parallel. At any rate, Paul preached not only to Jews but also to **Gentiles** and both are invited on the same terms **to repent and turn to God** (cf. 3:19), the giver and fulfiller of the promise (vv. 6-8). Repentance may perhaps accentuate a change in vision and outlook, while "turning" may also place the accent on change in life-style. Both are related to "faith in" the resurrected Christ (v. 18). Repentance, turning to God, and faith in Christ are different aspects of the new reality of having one's eyes opened (v. 18). Such change produces good works, **deeds worthy of . . . repentance** (cf. Luke 3:8). These are not conditions which must be met prior to receiving "forgiveness of sins," as Paul's biography illustrates. Good deeds are the necessary consequence of repentance, faith, and turning to God, and without them faith is illusion and repentance is sham.

Having sketched his missionary activity among Jews and Gentiles, Paul has arrived at his immediate past (v. 21). Because of his missionary activity the Jews had **seized** Paul **in the temple and tried to kill him** (21:27-32). The Greek verb for "kill" (*diacheirizomai*) is also used of Jesus (5:30). There is no need to rehearse the details of the tumult or the trial scenes (21:27—25:22), which the reader already knows.

22-23—**To this day I have had the help that comes from God,** who works through people like a Roman tribune, or Paul's own nephew (21:31-33; 23:16-22). In retrospect, Paul can speak of God's helping hand through which Jesus' promise of protection (v. 17) found fulfillment. **So I stand here** as servant-witness of the resurrected Christ in whom Israel's hope finds its realization, a person on trial for preaching the fulfillment of the resurrection hope. **I stand here testifying both to small** people by the world's standards (cf. Luke 6:20-22) **and great,** such as the king, the procurator, and high society (cf. 8:10; 9:15). Once more Paul reiterates a summary of his message. It is based on the promises of **the prophets and Moses,** promises concerning the future (cf. 24:14-15) and promises which have already been fulfilled, namely, **that the Christ must suffer** (3:18; 17:3; 8:32-33) and that he was destined to be **the first to rise from the dead** (2:25-27; 3:22-24; Luke 24:44-47; cf. 1 Cor. 15:20; Acts 3:15, "the Author" or "the Prince" of life; 5:31). Because of his resurrection **he,** the Resurrected One proclaims **light** to Jews **and to the Gentiles** through his servant-witnesses. Paul's proclamation is in continuity with the prophetic promises and with the message of the resurrected Christ (Luke 24:44-47). But even more important is the insight that through his servants Christ himself proclaims **light** (cf. vv. 13 and 18) and salvation to all. He as well as Paul are a **light** for Gentiles (Luke 2:32; Acts 13:47). The content of Paul's witness in vv. 22-23 also indicates the two points of conflict between Judaism and Christianity, namely, Christology and ecclesiology. First, Judaism cannot "see" that a suffering and resurrected Jesus is the fulfillment of Israel's hope in God's promise (vv. 6-8). Second, the universal dimension of the Christian witness and therefore of the church is likewise unacceptable and becomes the reason for Paul's arrest (v. 21). On the other hand, Paul's missionary activity was the result of Israel's resurrection hope fulfilled in Christ's resurrection and inaugurated by Christ's appearance and call (vv. 12-18). The universal mission and message was not a Pauline innovation but the mandate of the resurrected Christ (v. 17). If Paul is on trial because of "the hope and the resurrection of the dead" (23:6; 26:6), then he is accused because of his missionary activity in which he proclaims the fulfillment of that hope, and proclaims it not only to Jews but also to Gentiles. Paul is and remains a Pharisee, but he has become and continues to be a servant-witness of Jesus. His new activity stands in radical contrast to his old activity as persecutor. In his present state he himself experiences persecution. Yet his new activity can also be viewed as a logical consequence of his hope and piety as a Pharisee. He remains in continuity with his past and with the Old Testament hope. The path from Pharisaic hope to Christian faith need not involve a radical break nor an existential change but could be a continuous development. The person who believes Moses and the prophets merely needs to take the step of faith in the fulfillment of the promise. Christianity is authentic, repentant, and believing Judaism. In combining the two possibilities of Jews' becoming Christians (from persecutor to servant of Christ, or from pious Pharisee to believer in the fulfillment through Christ) Luke viewed the resurrection of Jesus as the pivotal point in this grand defense of Christianity vis-à-vis Judaism.

Dialog between Festus, Paul, and Agrippa (24-30)

24—With the key term "resurrection from the dead" Paul's defense has reached its concluding high point, and Luke used the literary device of interruption (cf. 17:32; 24:25) to move on to the dialog. For Festus, the talk about resurrection of the dead was sheer nonsense. Dead people do not rise and then proclaim (v. 23); we all know that. Rudely, he interrupted and declared with a loud voice: **Paul, you are mad; your great learning is turning you mad.** Thus the procurator demonstrated that: (1) his eyes and his mind remained closed (cf. v. 18; 25:20); (2) he recognized Paul's great book learning (Greek, *grammata*), his exceptional biblical scholarship of the Mosaic and prophetic books (cf. vv. 22 and 27); (3) he believed Paul's studies were driving him crazy; (4) he knew that, crazy as Paul may be, he was not a criminal and that the crazy stuff he talked about was not subject to criminal proceedings.

25—Festus's rudeness is met by Paul with politeness. Only here does he address a procurator with "Excellency" (cf. 24:2-3 with 24:10). Coolly and politely, he disagrees with the procurator. **I am not mad.** The opposite of madness is sobermindedness (Greek, *sōphrosynē;* Plato, *Protagoras* 323B), one of the great Greek virtues (Plato, *Republic* 4.430E; 4 Macc. 1:3,31). "In my defense speech," Paul said, "I spoke **the sober truth**" (literally, "words of truth and sobermindedness"), that is, true and rational words. Having rejected the governor's slur, Paul had nothing more to say to him.

26—His next sentence serves as transition in which he speaks about Agrippa and indirectly about Festus. **The king knows about these things,** while Festus by implication understands nothing about the relationship of Christianity to Judaism. Moreover, Paul's speech had not been addressed to the Roman procurator but to the Jewish king, and Festus might remember that. To Agrippa Paul said, **I speak freely;** Paul was confident he understood the Christian message, for that message is a matter of public knowledge. Festus would not know this, since he had come to the province only recently. Using a Greek proverb, Paul said, **This was not done in a corner.** "This" is the content of the proclamation, beginning with the life of Jesus and ending with the spread of the church. The church is not a secret and sinister society and its proclamation is not some esoteric teaching, but a public phenomenon in every respect. Every Jew in Judea and certainly the king knew about Jesus' public ministry and the church's message, which relates to the prophetic promises.

27—Turning to Agrippa, Paul pointedly asked, **Do you believe the prophets?** Thereby he put the king momentarily on the spot, and the prisoner showed himself to be the one super-VIP in this illustrious gathering. But Paul let him off politely by answering his own question: **I know that you believe.** It is implied that if Agrippa believes the prophets who express Israel's hope in God's promise (vv. 6-7) then he ought to believe the fulfillment of that hope and promise brought about by God through the resurrection of Jesus.

28—Now Agrippa must answer. **In a short time you think to make me a Christian,** or: "Soon you persuade me to play the role of a Christian." Agrippa's reply should not be interpreted as sarcasm, but rather as his attempt to get out of a tight spot. He seeks distance between himself and the implications of Paul's confident assertion: "I know that you believe." (For the Greek verb "to make" in the sense of "to play" see LXX 1 Kings 20:7.) There is, of course, some irony in his reference to "playing" the Christian. He acknowledged the persuasive power of Paul's speech and yet he did not want to submit to its claim.

29—Paul's reply to Agrippa is cast in elegant language. Picking up the king's expression, he turns his slightly ironical exclamation into a real wish. (This is the only verse in the New Testament where a Greek verb in the optative mood followed by *an* occurs in the main clause—in contrast to the interrogative sentences of 8:31; 17:18.) **Whether** in a **short** time **or** in a **long** time **I would** pray **to God that not only you but also all who hear me this day might become such as I am—except for these chains.** The Greek construction leaves no doubt that his wish is a realistic one, capable of being fulfilled. The importance of this sentence should not be overlooked, though generally it is. (1) This is Paul's last sentence on Judean-Palestinian soil and it expresses his trust and hope, his wish and prayer, that Christian proclamation will continue among Jews "small and great" (v. 22). The sentence is addressed to the Jewish king! (2) This last word of Paul in Caesarea will become important for our understanding of the last word spoken in direct discourse to the Jews in Rome (28:28). (3) The reader may be confident that God's Word will continue in Palestine also after Paul's departure, and through it Jews will become Christians like Paul.

The phrase **except for these chains** may be understood metaphorically, as in 20:23; 23:29; 26:31 where the RSV translates the same word (Greek, *desmos*) as "imprisonment." But we should also note that the word may refer to actual chains. The second decree of Caesar Augustus found on an inscription in the agora of Cyrene, North Africa, indicates that even Roman citizens could be put in chains during their transport to Rome (Supplem. Epigr. Graec. 9, 1944, no. 8). In 21:33 and 28:20 "the chains" (Greek, *halysis*) are indeed metal—and not metaphorical—chains.

30-32 (Concluding reactions)—Either we translate, "**When Agrippa, Festus, Bernice, and their entourage **had withdrawn,**" or, "As they withdrew," they could be heard by the larger audience saying **to one another, "This man is doing nothing to deserve death or imprisonment"** (literally, "chains"). No one disagreed. Agrippa, the expert on Jewish affairs (v. 3), gave his personal verdict to Festus: **This man could have been released if he had not appealed to Caesar.** The reader would expect that Festus would communicate this unanimous verdict in his report to Caesar (25:26). The two highest officials in Palestine, the Jewish king and the Gentile procurator, together with their entourage, which functioned as an unofficial *consilium,* agreed on Paul's innocence before he ever reached Rome. Though historically Paul was condemned by Caesar's tribunal, this does not count, in Luke's opinion, because the Caesar was Nero and even Nero's memory was condemned by the Roman senate after his suicide. His verdict need not concern Luke (who never mentioned Nero by name, in contrast to Claudius [18:2; 11:28], Tiberius [Luke 3:1], and Augustus [Luke 2:1]). What counted was Paul's innocence in the eyes of the highest officials in Palestine. Incidentally, king Agrippa had the authority to despose and appoint Jewish high priests (Josephus, *Ant.* 20.179,203,213). The fact that Paul, though innocent, is not freed is parallel to Jesus' fate. In this case, it was Festus's failure (see 25:8-12). He should and could have freed Paul even after his appeal, but in so doing he would have alienated the pro-Roman Sadducees of the Sanhedrin. Agrippa almost bemoans Paul's appeal, since otherwise his release would have been a foregone conclusion. Yet, to release him did not enter Agrippa's mind. Luke, of course, knew that Paul had been sent to Rome and that Paul, like Jesus, was innocent.

Sea Voyage to Italy and Witness in Rome (27:1—28:28)

To Malta (27:1-44)

Luke had portrayed Paul as persecutor (8:1-3; 9:1), as chosen missionary to Jews and Gentiles (13:1—19:41), as miracle worker (13:6-12; 14:8-18; 16:16-24; 19:8-12; 20:7-12), as chief pastor who brings consolation and exhortation to his churches (20:1—21:14), and as accused witness to Christ's resurrection who must testify before Caesar's tribunal. On this sea journey Luke portrayed Paul not just as a calm nautical expert, but also as beneficent hero at sea.

As man of God he foresees and warns of coming danger, and when all hope is gone he promises deliverance to all passengers, prevents the treachery of the sailors' flight, urges his fellow passengers to take food and gain strength, and sets an example by taking bread and giving thanks, breaking it, and beginning to eat (v. 35). The God to whom he belongs (v. 23) is the supreme benefactor. The sea is his and he made it (Ps. 95:5), and in life and death we are in his hands (Luke 23:46). Though Paul was merely another prisoner on board, he became the benefactor of sailors and soldiers, passengers and fellow prisoners, all of whom "escaped to land," saved from the raging sea. Paul's promise of deliverance (vv. 21-24), which he received from God, is contrasted with the hopelessness of the situation (cf. v. 20). Moreover, his promise was threatened twice (vv. 27-32 and 39-42). To Luke's readers the miraculous rescue from the sea and from the treachery of sailors and soldiers points to an even greater benefaction, the salvation promised by the Christian message but threatened by life experiences. To be sure, Paul did not function as a missionary seeking to convert sailors, soldiers, fellow travelers, and prisoners, but he is depicted by Luke as the endangered benefactor (Danker) who brought strength (Greek, *sōtēria*, v. 34) and encouragement (Greek, *parakalein*, vv. 33-34) to people in despair.

Though prior to his last journey to Jerusalem the historical Paul could write: "Three times I have been shipwrecked; a night and a day I have been adrift at sea" (2 Cor. 11:25), Luke has told nothing about disasters at sea thus far. But for the final sea journey in Acts he wrote a dramatic story, the greatest sea voyage story in the Bible and one of the best in Greek and Roman literature. Divine destiny is in control when ships and mortals are tossed to and fro by the raging fury of a storm at sea. But Christ's mandate to witness in Rome (23:11; 19:21) appeared to be in jeopardy once more. It had already been threatened by a Jewish mob (21:31; 22:22), by fanatics (23:14), the chief priests (25:3), and a conniving procurator (25:9), and it is now being threatened by the chaotic forces of nature. The end of Luke's story shows that Christ's mandate and promise cannot be thwarted. When Paul reached Malta, its fulfillment had come one step closer. Paul shall testify before Caesar (v. 24). God's promises, which often appear to be in jeopardy, move toward fulfillment step by step. Past fulfillments are cause for consolation and encouragement to a church that experiences perils and waits for the final fulfillment to come. The journey from Troas to Caesarea had been a tearful voyage of parting and farewell (20:6—21:14). The predictions made on this journey by "the Holy Spirit" concerning Paul's future have already been fulfilled (20:23; 21:11). His future would be imprisonment.

As a prisoner he now travels by ship to his final destiny in Rome and he twice receives divine vindication on this journey. Deliverance from the raging storm and the shipwreck and deliverance from the poisonous snakebite (28:4) represent Paul's vindication by God. According to this point of view, had he been a criminal he would not have escaped divine retribution. No matter what the outcome of the trial before Caesar, God, the supreme Judge, the Lord of the sea, has already given his verdict and twice declared Paul innocent, before he ever reached Rome. Thus as prisoner vindicated by God, he will bear witness before Caesar (v. 24).

Some interpreters have suggested that the sea voyage parallels Jesus' passion and resurrection. It is true that discipleship involves suffering and taking up one's "cross each day" (Luke 9:23; cf. Acts 9:16; 14:22), and that the sea voyage subjected Paul to suffering and granted him vindication by God. Nevertheless, the differences between Jesus' passion and Paul's may not be ignored. Jesus spoke only twice and only very briefly during his trial, while Paul witnessed continuously (Luke 22:67-70; 23:3; Acts 22–26). Jesus' death on the cross is narrated. Paul's death is not even mentioned. Paul's deliverance by God at Malta is only a foretaste of, but not a parallel to, the resurrection of the Messiah. The differences between Jesus and Paul indicate the uniqueness of each story and the distinction between the Lord and his servant, while parallels between Jesus and Paul (and other disciples) show that the work begun by Jesus is continued by his disciples, apostles, and servant-witnesses.

Paul is the benefactor and main actor in Luke's sea voyage narrative (vv. 9-11, 21-26, 31, 33-36). In v. 3b and v. 43a ("wishing to save Paul") he is the recipient of kindness from the Roman centurion Julius. One can take the verses just cited out of their present context and still retain a complete story, which would also free it from the tensions in Luke's present account. For instance, in the present account the decision to proceed with the voyage is explained twice, the first time because the centurion paid more attention to the captain and the ship's owner than to Paul (vv. 9-11). But v. 12 offers a different explanation. "The majority" of the persons responsible for the ship decided in favor of proceeding with the journey. It would seem reasonable to suppose that neither the centurion (an infantry officer) nor Paul (a prisoner) belonged to the decision-making group. In short, if we omit the verses which focus attention on Paul, we would still have a complete—and to some degree more plausible— story. Some scholars (e.g., Dibelius) suggested that Luke found a secular sea voyage story and inserted the "Pauline" verses. If so, Luke was extraordinarily lucky to find a ready-made sea voyage story in which prisoners were transported (vv. 1 and 42) from Palestine to Rome, a story which subsequently was lost without a trace. Even less likely is Conzelmann's suggestion that Luke created his story on the basis of available sea travel and adventure stories from which he took individual bits and pieces and wove them together. If so, why did he not "weave" his Pauline material into it instead of merely adding it to his otherwise unified account?

It would seem probable that our author received an eyewitness report, perhaps by **Aristarchus** from Thessalonica (v. 2), who had shared Paul's Ephesian imprisonment (Philemon 24; Col. 4:10), had accompanied Paul to Jerusalem (20:4), and continued to stay with him through the perils of the journey by sea. Aristarchus's report surely contained references to Paul, such as v. 3, but it was the author of Acts who added the verses cited above in order to improve the picture of Paul as benefactor of his fellow human beings during perils at sea. Note also that the report contained both "we" and "they" narration in vv. 13-20. But the third person is also retained in vv. 21, 33, 35 ("all," instead of "all of us") and in v. 38, revealing Lukan redaction. It would seem that Aristarchus's report contained both first and third person plural narration (vv. 13-20). In this story Luke's additions (vv. 9-11, 21-26, 31, 33-36, 38) avoid first person plural narration (cf. v. 31, "you" cannot be saved, instead of "we").

1-5 (Journey to Myra)—The Roman provincial administration **delivered Paul and some other prisoners to a centurion of the Augustan Cohort, named Julius.** The first person plural narration, typical of sea voyage stories, is used again (see 16:10; 20:5). Paul and other prisoners (plural), a few soldiers of an auxiliary cohort that had received the honorary title **Augustan** and had been stationed in Syria at Augustus's time, the officer in charge of the prisoners, paying passengers (among them **Aristarchus**), as well as cargo **put to sea . . . in a ship of Adramyttium,** a port southeast of Troas. After one day of sailing, **Sidon** was reached, and during the unloading and loading of cargo the centurion **Julius treated Paul kindly, and gave him leave to go to his friends and be cared for.** There were Christians in Sidon as well as in Tyre (cf. 11:19; 15:3; 21:3-6) who might offer hospitality and give him a meal and food for his journey. They are called **friends** (Greek, *philoi,* 3 John 15; Luke 12:4; the "friends" in 24:23 [Greek, *hoi idioi*] were probably Paul's travel companions). Paul is the recipient of kindness not only from the Christian community represented by Aristarchus and the friends in Sidon but also from the broader human community, represented by the centurion. God works benefactions through believers and through pagans. **Putting to sea** from Sidon, the ship laboriously and slowly moved north **under the lee of Cyprus, because the winds were against us.** A ship's company is a community and the story of a sea voyage draws the writer and the reader into that community by use of first person plural narration. The prevailing winds in early autumn were west-northwest, and therefore it was easier to sail around the east coast of Cyprus, always keeping close to shore and taking advantage of the night breeze from off shore. Near the coast of Asia Minor the ship turned west where, close to land, a western current and the night breeze enabled the ship slowly to reach the port of **Myra,** the city in which almost three centuries later Saint Nicholas was bishop.

6-8 (From Myra to Fair Havens)—Ships transporting grain from Egypt to Italy to feed the vast population of Rome frequently stopped at Myra. The centurion, his soldiers, and prisoners left the vessel from Adramyttium and boarded a grain ship (cf. v. 38) from **Alexandria,** which sailed for Italy. **We sailed slowly for a number of days** against the prevailing westerly winds and **arrived with difficulty off Cnidus** on the southern tip of the west coast of Asia Minor. Beyond Cnidus the ship would have no more land breeze to help in sailing west and, since ancient ships were not well designed for sailing against the wind, the Alexandrian ship headed southwest until it sighted Cape **Salmone** on the eastern tip of **Crete.** They sailed **under the lee of Crete** around the east side of the island, picked up some offshore breeze close to land and, **coasting along it with difficulty, we came to a place called Fair Havens,** near the city of **Lasea,** where the ship found shelter in an open bay. The location of these places is not certain. They may have been situated some miles east of Cape Matala.

9-12 (A benefaction rejected)—Much time had been lost, and the voyage was already dangerous. From the beginning of November to the first week of March, the sea was generally closed to shipping. **The fast had already gone by,** the Jewish Day of Atonement, which, according to the lunar calendar, could have been anywhere between September and October. In A.D. 59 the Day of Atonement was on October 5, and the feast of Tabernacles five days later was regarded by Jews as the end of the season for safe sailing. At any rate, the Day of Atonement already lay in the past and the autumn storms were therefore imminent. Paul, the prisoner, offered unsolicited advice and warned of dangers ahead for ship, cargo, and passengers. **But the centurion paid more attention to the captain and to the owner of the ship than to what Paul said.** The story seems to assume that the centurion, a landlubber, was in charge of the vessel—a questionable assumption. Next we hear why it was decided to proceed with the journey: **Because the harbor was not suitable to winter in** and protect the ship against the winter storms. **The majority advised,** with Paul obviously disagreeing, to try to reach the harbor of **Phoenix . . . looking northeast and southeast.** Note: (1) In the pre-Lukan account "the majority" would include neither the centurion nor Paul, but would consist of those responsible for the vessel—the owner, the captain, and the sailors. (2) The harbor of Phoenix is probably identical with the modern Phineka bay, which preserves its ancient name. Since Paul's time the bay has become silted and is now no longer suitable as a harbor. (3) A footnote in the RSV reads that the harbor was open toward **southwest and northwest.** This is undoubtedly the correct translation and would also fit Phineka bay (see the Bauer-Danker lexicon: *lips* and *chōros*). While the KJV correctly translated this statement, the RSV, under the impact of the delightful books by Smith and Ramsay, who favored the present Lutro as the site of ancient Phoenix, made a mistake, but gave its readers the correct translation in the footnote. (4) In Luke's story, the majority opinion proved to be wrong. The question of whether Paul's advice was given on the basis of common sense or by prophetic inspiration poses a false alternative, because from Luke's perspective it was both, as the introduction (v. 9) and Paul's **I perceive** show. Common sense is often a rare commodity. Moreover, the majority opinion at that time appeared to be rather reasonable. After all, Phoenix was less than 50 miles away from Fair Havens, and the latter was unsuitable for anchoring the ship during the winter months.

13-20 (The storm strikes)—A gentle **south wind** promised good sailing. **So they weighed anchor and sailed along Crete, close inshore.** But as soon as they had sailed around Cape Matala they lost the protection of the mountains and suddenly the **northeaster** wind **struck down from the land.** This tempestuous wind was called "Euraquilōn," a hybrid term, from Greek *euros,* "east wind," and Latin *aquilo,* "north wind." The ship was unable to turn into the wind and was therefore driven out to sea, running before the wind. In the shelter of the small island **Cauda,** about 35 miles south of Phoenix, they managed to haul up the auxiliary **boat,** which normally was towed off the stern but which, with the ship running before the wind, could easily smash into it. For the ordeal that lay ahead the sailors strengthened the ship with cables, either passing them under the hull to hold the planks together, or stretching them lengthwise over the ship from stem to stern to keep the keel from breaking, or tying ropes across the inside of the boat. Finally **they lowered the gear.** The meaning of the Greek words is uncertain. Probably the main sail was lowered and storm sails were set. Perhaps some sea anchor was thrown out to slow down the speed **and so** the ship was **driven.** They had feared they would be blown onto the sandbanks and shoals of the **Syrtis** off the coast of modern Libya; their countermeasures sought to avoid that. **As we were violently storm-tossed** and probably taking on water, the decision was made the next day to begin to jettison some cargo (cf. Jonah 1:5). On **the third day,** with the storm continuing, they threw **the tackle** overboard, the spare gear, perhaps also the main sail. Because the compass had not yet been invented, orientation and the ship's course could be determined only by sighting the sun or stars. But **neither sun nor stars appeared for many a day** because a great **tempest** continued to engulf us, so that **all hope of our being saved was at last abandoned** and a spirit of gloom took hold of passengers and crew.

21-26 (Promise by Paul)—Luke's second insertion does not fit well into the context. With the storm howling, how could Paul be heard by the passengers? But Luke is not interested in questions such as these. His point is that at the moment of greatest despair, when all

hope was abandoned, Paul gave a divine promise and encouragement to seasick and despondent fellow human beings. He told them:
You should have listened to me, which was rather obvious under
the circumstances, but faith means listening with an open mind.
His prophetic-commonsense prediction had come true (cf. v. 10).
But he had more to say to them than "I told you so." In the hour
of despair he unconditionally promised them certain deliverance, a
promise that was anything but an expression of common sense.
There will be no loss of life among you, he categorically declared,
and added that merely **the ship** will be lost. Moreover, Paul told
them the reason for his unconditional promise. **This very night there
stood by me an angel of the God to whom I belong and whom I
worship.** Paul is giving encouragement to polytheistic pagans, who
are fellow human beings. Therefore he uses appropriate language.
He does not give a lecture about the one true, but unknown, God
(cf. 17:22-31) nor does he speak about Jesus Christ, God's messenger
(Greek, *angelos*), the Messiah of Israel and Savior-Lord of Gentiles
who appeared at night to him (cf. 23:11). A reference to Jesus would
have required a detailed recital of his words, works, and fate, which
would have been inappropriate to the situation and to Luke's intent.
Paul therefore speaks of the **God** whom he worships and of **an angel**
of that God. A knowledgeable reader would understand this as a
reference to an "angel-Christology." A pagan would take it to refer
to a divine messenger of Paul's God. The message which Paul had
received at night was: **Do not be afraid** (cf. 18:9); **you must** (Greek,
dei), in accordance with God's will, **stand before Caesar; and lo,
God has granted you all those who sail with you.** For Paul's sake
all will be rescued. He is the reason why all on board will be saved
from the raging sea. **You must stand before Caesar** is part of the
last vision in Acts and therefore it is important. In 19:21 Paul had
resolved to go to Jerusalem and afterwards he "must also **see** Rome";
in 23:11 Jesus told him: "you must bear witness" in Rome. This is
now specified: **You must stand before Caesar.** No doubt Paul did
appear before Nero's tribunal, though Luke does not tell us about
it. He could omit it also because Paul's unconditional promise, mediated by the angel of God, was fulfilled (cf. v. 44). What is important
in Luke's story is that the reader realizes that God's promises, mediated by his servants, seem to be contradicted by storms and the
hopelessness of the situation of the people to whom those promises

are addressed. Contrary to the prevailing despair, Paul boldly announced: **I have faith in God** that, no matter what, **it will be exactly as I have been told.** Paul cannot ask the pagans to trust in the one true God who has not yet been proclaimed to them, but they can take courage from Paul's trust in God. Finally he predicted that the ship will **run on some island.**

27-32 (Paul averted the threat of the sailors' escape)—For two weeks the ship drifted **across the sea of Adria,** not the Adriatic between present-day Yugoslavia and Italy, but the sea between Greece and Sicily. **About midnight the sailors suspected that they were nearing land** and began to take soundings in order to determine the depth of the water beneath the ship. When their soundings confirmed that they were getting close to land **they let out four anchors from the stern,** lest they run onto the rocks. Had they thrown out the anchors from the ship's stem, or bow, the ship would have swung around and its bow would have pointed into the wind, not toward the island. Since it was night, nothing could be seen and all **prayed for day to come.** At this point (v. 30) a problem arises which demands that we distinguish between the pre-Lukan report and Luke's own account in Acts. In the pre-Lukan report the sailors may have wanted to lower the lifeboat (cf. v. 16) in order to drop anchors some distance from the bow. The soldiers, misinterpreting their action as desertion, cut the ropes and let the lifeboat drift away. In Luke's account it is Paul who perceived that the sailors were about to abandon the ship **under the pretense of laying out anchors from the bow,** and he intervened for the third time, telling the centurion: **Unless these men** (the sailors) **stay in the ship, you cannot be saved.** This time the centurion paid attention to Paul's words, and his soldiers cut the ropes of the lifeboat. It is therefore false to say that Paul "was responsible not for the rescue but rather for the shipwreck" (Haenchen, p. 710). In the pre-Lukan account Paul did not appear at all at this point. The soldiers' reaction expressed their panic. Sailors abandoning the passengers were popular in stories. However, in Luke's narrative Paul prevented the sailors' desertion and hence contributed not to shipwreck (cf. v. 22), but to the rescue. In v. 31 Paul appears as benefactor of all people aboard.

33-38 (Paul's final encouragement and example)—Paul appears as benefactor in the final scene as well. After two weeks of seasickness the passengers were weak in body and spirit. Only if they eat and gain strength will they be able to endure the next hours. Near dawn Paul went among the desolate passengers and **urged them all to take some food. . . .** "**It will give you strength,**" literally, "it will be in the interest of your deliverance" (Greek, *pros* with genitive; *sōtēria*, "salvation," as deliverance from drowning at sea). **Not a hair is to perish from the head of any of you** (cf. Luke 21:18). But you must eat! The encouragement is followed by his own example. **He took bread, and giving thanks to God** (Greek, *eucharistēsen*, cf. Luke 22:19; in Acts only here and 28:15) **in the presence of all he broke it and began to eat.** Some manuscripts add, "after he gave [bread] also to us," that is, to his fellow Christian travel companions, thus indicating the celebration of a Eucharist at night amidst the storm. The context makes it clear that Paul's eating was meant to be an example, the result of which was that all passengers **were encouraged and ate some food.** Yet Luke's wording does remind the reader of the Eucharist. Jesus, who was present with Paul in the desolation of the storm, is present with us in hopeless situations when we celebrate the Eucharist. The number of the persons on board was **two hundred and seventy-six,** which is considerably fewer than the 600 persons on board to which Josephus refers (*Life* 15). The number 276 is a triangular number, the sum of all numbers from 1 to 24, and as such as mysterious and perfect number. The number 76, found in the footnote of the RSV, is not original, but the result of scribal misreading. When all the passengers had eaten, they jettisoned the remaining ballast (cf. v. 18), **throwing out the wheat into the sea** so that the ship would draw as little water as possible and come close to the beach before running aground.

39-44 (Shipwreck and rescue at Malta)—At daybreak **they noticed a bay with a beach and** decided to **bring the ship** to land there. The probable site was what became known as St. Paul's bay, on the northeast coast of Malta. At its entry lies a submerged shoal which in ancient times was closer to the surface than it is now. **They cast off the anchors and left them in the sea,** untied the **rudders,** that is, the steering paddles, and hoisted a small foresail, so that the ship could move toward the beach, but they ran into the **shoal** (the Greek text reads: "a place of two seas"). **The bow stuck and remained immovable** and the stern, being pounded by the surf, began to break up. Now **the soldiers** panicked and were ready to **kill the prisoners**

for whose escape they would be held responsible (cf. 12:19). The soldiers' intention indicates that the prisoners had not been chained to the ship during the storm, but could move around the vessel; otherwise the soldiers could have just left them there. **But the centurion, wishing to save Paul, kept them from carrying out their purpose.** "Wishing to save Paul" is probably a Lukan addition. He ordered those who could **swim** to make for the beach **first. The rest** held **on** to **planks or . . . pieces of the ship,** or were aided by swimmers to reach land. **And so it was that all escaped to land,** and Paul's promise (v. 22) came to fulfillment.

In Malta (28:1-10)

1-6 (Paul vindicated)—After the escape **we then learned that the island was called Malta.** The **natives** (Greek, *barbaroi*, non-Greek-speaking people; cf. Rom. 1:14) were of Phoenician descent and spoke a Punic dialect. These islanders showed **us unusual kindness** (Greek, *philanthrōpia*). Human kindness is not limited to the people of God, for the benefactions of the Creator enclose all of his creatures, satisfying their "hearts with food and gladness" (14:17). Human **kindness** expressed by the centurion (27:3, 43) and the natives of Malta is a reflection of God's kindness and a bond of our common humanity. The islanders had **kindled a fire** because it was **cold** and the survivors were wet. The focus shifts to **Paul,** who had made himself useful by gathering **a bundle of sticks.** When he threw it on the fire **a viper** bit him **on his hand** (Luke 10:19; Mark 16:18). Since Malta is free from poisonous snakes today some interpreters concluded that none existed at Paul's time, a rash conclusion in view of the disappearance of many animal species, including snakes, from regions in which they lived only a century ago. When the natives saw the viper on Paul's hand they said: **No doubt this man is a murderer. Though he has escaped from the sea, justice** (the goddess *Dikē*) **has not allowed him to live.** The people interpreted the snake-bite on the basis of their religious context. The retribution of the goddess of justice had caught up with him at last. Unperturbed, Paul **shook off the creature into the fire** and the expected effect of the poison did not occur. When the islanders **had waited a long time and saw no misfortune come to him, they changed their minds and said that he was a god** filled with the power of immortality.

479

Whereas in Lystra the natives first acclaimed Paul as a god and then almost killed him (14:11-19), at Malta they first expected him to be killed by poison and then they regarded him as a god. Both episodes, according to Luke's point of view, indicate the ambiguity of miracles. But the two episodes exhibit a marked difference. Paul's miracle in Lystra served the purpose of mission and the acclamation of Paul as a god was corrected in the missionary speech (14:8-18). In Malta, however, we find no missionary speech to correct the distorted views of the natives. Luke did not report Paul's mission to Malta, nor did he refer to any conversions. The missionary section in Acts ended with 19:20. Luke's point in the present story was that God gave a verdict concerning Paul's innocence. Even pagans understood that and expressed it in their own, obviously pagan, way. Had Paul been guilty in the eyes of divine justice, the wrath of divine retribution would have struck him down.

7-10 (Paul is a benefactor on Malta) —In this second story also the miracle is unconnected with the message of salvation. It does not function as a sign of the saving power of Jesus nor as a call to faith in his name. There is not a word about Paul preaching the gospel. Why? Being a benefactor to people in distress is an end in itself and needs no other justification. Human kindness (Greek, *philanthrōpia*) is not limited to Christians (27:3, 43; 28:2, 7, 10), although it is also to be shown by Christians who ought to "do good" on the basis of need without regarding the needy as objects of conversion (cf. Luke 10:29-37). To be sure, Luke had portrayed Jesus as benefactor "who went about doing good, healing" the demon-possessed (10:38). Likewise, Peter in doing "a good deed" (4:9) to a lame man (3:1-15) fulfilled the role of benefactor. Their miracles, however, functioned in the broader context of mission and proclamation. This broader context is absent in the healings at Malta. Luke's portrayal of Paul's benefaction is not grounded in the Second Article of the Creed, and for good reason. Luke wanted to show that doing good *may* have an explicitly Christological basis, but it *need* not have one, for it can also be grounded in the First Article of the Creed and our common creaturehood. To help people in distress without preaching Christ to them is what Paul did in Malta, and that needs no apology. Moreover, Paul's last miracle in Acts has its counterpart in Jesus' first miracle in the Gospel (Luke 4:38-39).

The chief man of the island, named Publius, extended hospitality to Paul and his friends **for three days. Chief man** in Malta is a title known from an inscription and probably refers to an honorary position. When Paul heard that Publius's father lay **sick with fever and dysentery** he visited him and **prayed.** In contrast to Jesus' miracle (Luke 4:38-39), Paul prayed because he could not heal by his "own power or piety" (3:12). Moreover, by praying he also demonstrated that he was not a god, but totally dependent on God. Praying and **putting his hands** on the sick father, he **healed him.** As God was with Jesus (10:38) and worked miracles through him (2:22), so he was with Paul, continuing his healing benefaction. News of the cure spread and in a summary we hear that **the rest of the people on the island who had diseases also came and were cured.** They showed their gratitude by presenting **many gifts to us** (literally, "they honored us with many honors," perhaps dedicating an inscription to their benefactor). When the time of departure came **they put on board** a new vessel **whatever we needed** for the last stretch of the journey.

To Rome (28:11-16)

11-13—**And so we came to Rome,** from Malta to Puteoli by ship, and from there by foot to Rome. **After three months we set sail.** Note the different use of the first person plural "we." In most of chap. 27 and in 28:1, 11-13 it refers to the ship's company, while in 28:7, 14-15 it refers to the group of Christians who accompanied Paul (cf. 27:1, 6). A departure from Malta after only **three months** presents some minor difficulty if we take this time reference seriously. In 27:9 the discussion at Fair Havens took place sometime after the Day of Atonement, which in A.D. 59 was on October 5. Unfortunately, we do not know how many days after the Day of Atonement the decision was made to leave, nor how many days the ship had to wait for favorable winds before it actually sailed out of Fair Havens (27:13). If the ship left around the first of November, then the shipwreck occurred around the middle of November, and if **after three months** includes a timespan of three and a half months, then the date of departure from Malta would have been the first week in March A.D. 60. The Egyptian ship which had spent the winter months in Malta was, of course, eager to get an early start and leave the island as soon as possible. This vessel from **Alexandria** had the

Twin Brothers, Castor and Pollux, **as figurehead,** either on the bow of the ship or painted on its sides. The twin sons of Zeus were regarded as patrons of navigation and their stars, Gemini, were signs of good luck when they could be seen during a storm. The ship docked in **Syracuse,** Sicily, **for three days,** then in **Rhegium,** and from there it sailed about 230 miles in only two days, with a **south wind** blowing, to **Puteoli,** the chief Italian port for overseas shipping at that time.

14-16—Thus far we have had a straightforward travel account. Now the first person plural is used to refer to the Christians around Paul, and the impression is given that Paul is no longer a prisoner but could freely decide where to spend his time. In Puteoli **we found brethren, and were invited to stay with them for seven days** (cf. 27:3). Julius, the soldiers, and the other prisoners have disappeared from the narrative since the shipwreck, and Luke gives the reader no reason why this delay in the prisoner transport occurred. The suggestion has therefore been made that Luke added vv. 14a, 15 and 16, and created the week-long visit in Puteoli to allow time for news to reach the Roman Christians. This may well be, but Luke scores still another point. Hospitality is extended to fellow believers who come from other parts of the church, and in hospitality the unity of the church finds visible expression. Moreover, two delegations of Christians from Rome came out of the city and walked toward Paul to meet and greet him at the **Forum of Appius,** about 40 miles from the city, and at **Three Taverns,** about 30 miles from Rome on the Via Appia. **On seeing them Paul thanked God and took courage.** Their coming to greet him and his prayer of thanks also exhibit the unity of the church. That he was encouraged by the welcome does not mean that he was distraught before. Rather, the welcome by the Roman Christians, the favorable impression they made on Paul, the realization that they were with him, leading him in a humble and yet triumphant procession to Rome, became a source for renewed courage (cf. 23:11). The promise of the Lord to witness in Rome has now been fulfilled, and the unity of the church has been made manifest once more. It would be false to say that only Christians, but not the church in Rome welcomed him. Disciples, or brothers and sisters, are believers in community united by the apostles' doctrine, the breaking of bread, and prayer (2:42). The church existed in the form of house churches, and the Lukan

Christians knew that they belonged to the one church. Each house church is the church in the full sense of the word, though not in an exclusive sense. It is equally false to argue that Luke was embarrassed by the presence of Christians in Rome before Paul's arrival, or that in Luke's opinion Paul was to be the first preacher of the gospel in Rome (so Haenchen). Far from being embarrassed that there already existed a church in Rome, and to which the historical Paul had written a letter, the Lukan Paul rejoiced in the fellowship which his Roman brothers and sisters extended to him. Peter and Paul function as authoritative, normative witnesses in Acts and not just as church founders. Hence, Luke tells us that Peter found disciples in Lydda and Joppa when he went there (9:32,36), and Paul encouraged disciples in Galatia and Phrygia (18:23), even though Luke did not tell us that Paul had established churches there. Had the existence of the Ephesian church prior to Paul been an embarrassment to Luke he could have easily moved the Apollos story to the next chapter. He did something similar in Acts 11 where he positioned the Antiochian Gentile mission after Peter's inaugural act in the conversion of the Gentile Cornelius. Before Luke narrated the concluding high point of his story he remembered Paul's thanksgiving to God for the church in Rome. **And so we came to Rome.** Luke used this sentence twice (vv. 14 and 16), just as he mentioned Paul's coming to Jerusalem twice (21:15, 17). This may be an indication of Luke's use of a source—it surely shows the importance of the city to the reader by means of repetition, and it may distinguish the larger urban area from the city itself. The note that **Paul was allowed to stay by himself** is also found twice (vv. 16 and 30) and forms brackets around the two meetings with Jewish leaders of Rome. Paul was guarded by one soldier only, probably connected to him by a chain (cf. v. 20; for the Western text of 28:16 see Metzger). He was allowed to live in rented quarters (v. 30) and receive visitors. Perhaps the Roman church saw to it that the rent was paid. With the arrival in Rome, the "we" section comes to an end. Luke has told the story of how the normative apostolic witness, carried by Paul, the chosen servant-witness (26:16), has come to Rome.

Paul's Witness in Rome (17-31). This is the conclusion of Luke's updated history of the people of God, and it bristles with difficulties. We shall briefly deal with three problems.

1. *Paul and the Roman Christian communities.* The reader would expect a scene with Paul and the church(es) in Rome. Such a scene would balance Luke's pictures of the Jerusalem community at the beginning of Acts. Yet our author paid little attention to the church in Rome, even though he knew of its existence (cf. v. 15). If he had regarded Rome as the new center of Gentile Christianity, in place of Jerusalem, or if he had viewed Rome as the symbol of the institutional separation of the church from Judaism we would expect him to present a picture of the Roman church with Paul in its midst.

Luke did, however, relate Rome to Jerusalem. Paul's journey to Rome, like Jesus' journey to Jerusalem, was undertaken in obedience to "the divine must" (19:21; 23:11; 27:24; cf. Luke 9:31,51; 13:33). Jerusalem and Rome are the only two cities in Luke-Acts that are expressly connected with God's plan. Jerusalem is the center of the people of God and the symbol of the rejection of the messengers of God by the people of God (cf. Luke 11:47-54; 13:33-34; 23:18; Acts 7:51-53; 22:22). Therefore destruction comes to it (Luke 19:41-44; 21:20-24). Rome is the center of the world of the Gentiles and the symbol of the unhindered proclamation of the gospel (28:31). However, "the times of the Gentiles" who trampled down Jerusalem will also come to an end (Luke 21:24). Rome is not the eternal city of God. Its importance in Acts lies in the fact that it was in Rome that Paul bore witness to the representatives of Judaism from that city (vv. 17-24). He interpreted with finality why Christianity is "everywhere" in Judaism "spoken against" (v. 22b; vv. 25-27). Moreover, in Rome Paul let it be known once more that the rejection of God's salvation by Jews will be offset by the inclusion of Gentiles within the people of God (v. 28). God has sent (past tense!) his salvation to Gentiles (v. 28) in fulfillment of his promise (Isa. 42:6; Ezek. 3:6; Ps. 67:2). The inclusion of Gentiles as well as the obduracy of Jews are both in accordance with the Scriptures.

Paul's witness in Rome is also related to Christ's mandate at the beginning of Acts (1:7). By **testifying to the kingdom of God** and **teaching about the Lord Jesus Christ** on the basis of the Scriptures (vv. 23, 31), the mandate of Jesus to witness "to the end of the earth" found a partial fulfillment. Rome is not the end of the earth, but the heart of the empire. Because Paul, in obedience to the will of God and in spite of numerous obstacles, reached Rome, the reader of Acts can draw the assurance that the gospel will reach the end of the earth. Moreover, the reader is implicitly challenged to enter that journey of witnessing. The process of fulfilling Christ's mandate continues, and Luke's church was part of that process. Thus Acts closes in an open-ended way. Rome is an important way station on the church's witnessing journey, but only a way station.

2. *Paul's martyrdom.* Even more surprising than Luke's slight attention paid to the church in Rome is his omission of Paul's trial and his subsequent fate. Paul had come to Rome to bear witness "before Caesar" (27:24; cf. 9:15-16), yet Luke tells us nothing about it. Small wonder that interpreters have proposed a variety of explanations for this omission. Some suggest that Luke died a martyr's death together with Paul (cf. 2 Tim. 4:11), or that he wrote Acts for the purpose of Paul's defense before the imperial tribunal, or that he planned to write a third volume in which he would narrate not only Paul's trial and martyrdom, but also the acts of the other apostles, who apparently had left Jerusalem after the apostles' conference (cf. 21:17-18). Still others hypothesize that the abrupt ending of Acts is due to a lack of information about Paul's trial and death, or that Paul was released after two years without trial because his accusers from Jerusalem failed to appear in Rome. In response to these diverse opinions it has rightly been pointed out that Luke-Acts was not written prior to Paul's death, because Luke's Gospel depends on Mark, and this dependence places the time of the composition of Luke-Acts into the decades after Paul's death, e.g., A.D. 80–90. It is also unlikely that Luke was ignorant of Paul's martyrdom, in view of the hints in 20:23-25, 38. A release from Roman imprisonment would have furthered Luke's political apologetics and therefore he would probably have noted it. Paul's release from his Roman imprisonment is postulated by those scholars who hold that the Pastoral Epistles were written by Paul himself. Indeed, the geographic data found in the Pastorals would demand that Paul returned to the Eastern parts of the Mediterranean (Ephesus and Crete) once more, if these letters are authentic Pauline writings. But their pseudonymous character is widely recognized today and Acts 20:25, 38 precludes Paul's return to Ephesus, as far as Luke is concerned.

According to Acts 28:30 it would seem that Paul's two-year imprisonment in Rome was followed by his martyrdom and not by his release. Answers to the question of why Luke did not narrate Paul's martyrdom are necessarily hypothetical. Was it because Luke's re-

485

peated insistence on Paul's innocence would be jeopardized if Paul had been executed after a verdict of guilty by Caesar's court? Hardly, because that very Caesar was Nero, whose infamy was widely acknowledged at the time of Luke's writing. As a matter of fact, Luke could have completed his Jesus/Paul parallels. Jesus, like Paul, was pronounced innocent three times and yet he was surrendered for execution by Caesar's inept representative. Just so, we may ask why Luke did not narrate Paul's execution and thereby complete the Jesus/Paul parallelism.

Several answers suggest themselves: *(a)* Luke did not wish to narrate Paul's martyrdom because, unlike Jesus, his death was not followed by his resurrection. Paul was called to suffering (9:16) and stands in a long line of suffering prophets and servants of God (Luke 11:49; 13:34; Acts 7:52). Yet, in distinction from Jesus, the suffering of Paul in Acts is not part of the salvation event (cf. Luke 24:26, 46). His suffering is a by-product of his witness and the occasion for God's intervention in one form or another. Moreover, all Christians have to bear their cross "daily" (Luke 9:23) and enter the kingdom "through many tribulations" (Acts 14:22), which demand endurance, watchfulness, and prayer (Luke 21:19, 36). In short, Luke may also have omitted the story of Paul's martyrdom because he downplayed a martyr ethos and replaced it by emphasizing the daily endurance of difficulties encountered by all Christians, most of whom do not meet a martyr's death.

(b) For Luke, it is not the person and fate of Paul, but his message that is of ultimate importance, and that message continues "unhindered" in spite of his martyrdom (28:31). Rome and its Caesar can no more destroy the Word of God by executing Paul, than Jerusalem and its Sanhedrin could by crucifying Jesus.

(c) Luke may have omitted the story of Paul's martyrdom because Jewish Christians at Rome played an ugly role in it (thus Cullmann, *Peter*). A letter from the last decade of the first century (1 Clem. 5:2) locates the cause of Paul's martyrdom in "jealousy and envy," apparently of Christians (cf. Phil. 1:15, 17). The post-Pauline Pastoral Epistles may also reflect the memory that it was fellow Christians who turned against Paul (cf. 2 Tim. 1:15; 4:9-10; for the earlier period see 2 Cor. 11:26, "danger from false brothers"). If Christians had been instrumental in or contributed to Paul's martyrdom, then Luke had reason enough to omit it (cf. his handling of Paul's collection).

Luke had stressed the church's unity in the power of the Spirit from the beginning to the end of his story, and he had shown that when problems arose they were solved in a spirit of unanimity (cf. 6:1-6; 15:5, 22-29). He would not possibly mar this story at its conclusion.

(*d*) Perhaps he omitted Paul's martyrdom in the interest of his political apology. We should not suppose that his aim was to convince the authorities of the empire of the political harmlessness of the church. His book is not directed to outsiders but to his church for internal consumption. To all church members who sympathized with an apocalyptic hatred of the Roman empire (cf. Rev. 13; 17–18) Luke held up a series of pictures which show that in spite of occasional lapses, moral imperfections, greed, favoritism, and misjudgments Roman officials could also be just. Roman law did protect Paul, and officials such as Claudius Lysias and several centurions did save Paul's life on more than one occasion (cf. 21:31; 22:25-26; 23:23-24; 27:43). Christians must be blameless before the laws of Judaism and of the empire, and the church has no reason to engage in political provocation and agitation against the state. While miscarriages of justice existed in the empire, as demonstrated by the imprisoned but innocent Paul, still the same Paul acknowledged the emperor's court and therefore appealed to Caesar. Luke's political apologetics, directed to his church, may have contributed to his omission of Paul's martyrdom.

3. *Christianity and Judaism.* By ignoring the life of the Roman church and its relation to Paul and by omitting Paul's trial and martyrdom, Luke made room for his chief concern and was able to produce a startling conclusion in which he summarized his two-volume work and laid the ground for subsequent development. Just as Luke 24 had marked the result of the story of his first book and simultaneously indicated the future development of preaching in Christ's name to "all nations, beginning from Jerusalem" (Luke 24:47), so Paul's witness in Rome is both a summary of Acts and a foundation for the future. Acts closes in an open-ended way. The end of the biblical history of God and his people did not come with Paul's arrival in Rome, but it will come when the Messiah of God arrives from heaven (1:11). Then Luke's story will need to be updated again. Then and only then will the message of salvation no longer meet rejection, as it was rejected all the way from Jesus' inaugural

address in Nazareth (Luke 4:16-30) to Paul's concluding speech in Rome.

These two speeches form one set of brackets around Luke's story and both contain extended citations from Isaiah indicating the fulfillment of prophecy. But whereas in Nazareth Jesus, in the words of Isaiah, announced "good news," "recovering of sight to the blind," freedom for the "oppressed" and "the acceptable year of the Lord," Paul, quoting Isaiah in Rome, announced the bad news of the blindness of the people whose eyes, ears, and hearts are closed. They lack the freedom to hear and understand and the time of their visitation seems once more to be missed (cf. Luke 19:44). "This salvation" has been sent to the Gentiles. In Nazareth as well as in Rome the audience exhibited polite curiosity (Acts 28:22a, 23; Luke 4:22) and in Rome some were even persuaded by Paul (v. 24a). Yet Jesus as well as Paul aggressively confronted the people, denounced their unbelief, and referred to salvation among Gentiles (Luke 4:23-27; Acts 28:25-28).

Even though Jesus in Nazareth predicted that his mission would meet with rejection from his people (cf. Luke 8:10), nevertheless he did not simply write them off. On the contrary, in spite of opposition he opened the eyes and ears and hearts of some, even as he met rejection from others. Likewise, Paul's commission had been to "open the eyes" of Jews and Gentiles that they may "turn from darkness to light" (26:18), and in spite of the rejection by some or by most of the leaders of the Roman Jews he did not establish a new ecclesiastical particularism that would exclude Jews and thereby deny the universal scope of God's salvation. Rather, he welcomed "all" and preached to all (28:30, 31), which—as we shall see—can only mean Jews and Gentiles.

However, at the end of his story Luke did not deal thematically with the End, but rather he interpreted the time before the End. He merely referred to the End by means of two concepts, namely, "the hope of Israel" (v. 20) and "the kingdom of God" (v. 23) in which that hope will find its ultimate realization. Luke did thematically interpret the time before the End. He absolved the Jews for the outcome of Paul's trial, but he also indicated that the time before the End is the time of Israel's obduracy, a time of testifying to all people and therefore a time of decision. But does Israel's obstinacy mean that God has rejected his people with finality? No, not according to Luke, To be sure, at the End "every soul that does not listen" to Jesus, the prophet like Moses "shall be destroyed from the people" (3:23), but Israel as a whole shall not be destroyed. Only individuals shall be cast out "from the people," because God's unconditional promise is "to Abraham and his posterity *forever*" (Luke 1:55).

Luke left his story open-ended for several reasons. (1) Luke's aim was to write about what God had fulfilled among us (Luke 1:1). Luke had updated Israel's history and incorporated teaching concerning the End, but he had not written an apocalypse. His focus, especially in Acts, had been on what God, Jesus Christ, and the Holy Spirit had accomplished through his chosen servants. (2) Luke knew only too well that God is full of surprises, as his narrative—from the announcement of the birth of John the Baptist to Paul's preaching in Rome—shows. The future is controlled by this surprising God who can open the eyes of the blind and make the deaf hear. (3) At the End there will be a final judgment, which underlines the seriousness of the decision for Christ in the time before the End (cf. 3:23), as well as the seriousness of obduracy which can only decide against him. So, at the end of his story Luke leaves it up to God as to how he will fulfill "the hope of Israel" (v. 20) and all prophetic promises which have not yet been fulfilled. Instead, he focuses the reader's attention on the great problem before the End, which is the church, represented by Paul on the one side and Judaism, represented by Roman Jews, on the other.

Through Paul, the missionary to Jews and Gentiles, Luke assures his church of its legitimacy within and continuity with the people of God. The Lukan church of believing Jews and Gentiles has not left the people of God, but official Judaism represented by the Sanhedrin of Jerusalem and the Jewish leaders of Rome have become blind, deaf, and stiff-necked, even as Paul had been prior to his conversion and call. Paul as persecutor of the church had represented official Judaism (26:10), and had exhibited the same obstinacy with which official Judaism in Rome "disbelieved" (v. 25) the message of God's salvation through the Messiah Jesus. Paul's witness in Rome on behalf of the kingdom of God and the Lord Jesus therefore constitutes God's own refutation of official Judaism in its rejection of the gospel. But just as Paul was able to turn from persecutor to witness only by means of the miraculous appearance of Christ, so likewise official Judaism, represented by the leaders of Rome, cannot come to faith by their own reason or strength. To be sure, the eyes of some Jews were opened by Paul in Rome (v. 24a), but the rest will need a miraculous intervention, even as Paul needed it, and as the disciples of Jesus before Paul needed it (Luke 9:45; 18:34; 24:31-32, 45). Thus, the end of Acts, with official Judaism remaining obdurate like the fathers of old (cf. Luke 11:47; Acts 7:51-53), points forward to the future of God and his Messiah who can open eyes and change hardened hearts.

The climactic confrontation of Paul with Judaism in Rome answered several questions. In the aftermath of the destruction of Jerusalem by Rome, *Jewish* Christians may have wondered how Jesus could be the Savior and Messiah of Israel if such a calamity could befall the nation. Luke's answer is that many in Israel did not know "the time of [their] visitation" by God's Messiah, but rejected him (Luke 19:44) and continued to reject the Messiah's witnesses from Jerusalem to Rome. Hence Jesus indeed "was set for the fall . . . of many in Israel" (Luke 2:34). Yet the surprising turn of events was that God's visitation of Israel brought about a visitation of the Gentiles (Acts 15:14; 28:28) in accordance with God's promise. *Gentile* Christians may have wondered about their legitimacy within the people of God since official Judaism "everywhere" (v. 22) objected to Christianity. Luke's answer is that God has sent (past tense) this message of salvation to Gentiles (v. 28; cf. 13:46-47). The presence of Gentiles within the believing people of God was, on the one hand, the result of Jewish rejection of the gospel; on the other hand, their presence resulted from the fulfillment of God's promise found in Scripture (15:15-18).

Luke's conclusion may also answer the question, "How did we get to where we are now, with ever more Gentiles entering the church, and where do we go from here?" Since some Jews were persuaded by Paul also in Rome (v. 24), it is obvious that the mission to Jews has not come to an end. To be sure, this interpretation is contrary to the majority opinion of Lukan interpreters, and we shall consider this question once more below.

The Structure of the Narrative.   Luke's open-ended conclusion contains three scenes. In the first (vv. 17-22) we hear about a friendly meeting of Paul with the leaders of various synagogues in Rome.

The attitude of these Roman Jewish leaders (Greek, *prōtoi*) was in stark contrast to the leaders of Jerusalem (Luke 19:47; Acts 25:2). Paul explained the reason why he came to Rome as a prisoner. **The hope of Israel** was the ultimate reason for his imprisonment. The Roman Jewish leaders indicated an interest in Paul's views in spite of the fact that they already knew that Christianity was opposed "everywhere" within Judaism. Thus a second meeting of Paul with Roman Jews took place (vv. 23-28). While in the first scene Paul offered an apology, defending himself, insisting on his innocence, and confessing "the hope of Israel," in the second he functioned as missionary who was seeking to win the Roman Jews for **the kingdom of God . . . and Jesus.** The reaction of his audience was, as always, divided. Therefore, Paul made a prophetic interpretation of unbelieving Judaism: Isaiah 6:9-10 had come to fulfillment in them, and Paul concluded that God had sent his salvation to Gentiles (v. 28)—the climax of the second scene.

Verses 30-31 contain the third scene, which also functions as epilog. It is connected with the second scene by the word *all*, that is, Jews and Gentiles (cf. vv. 23 and 28); by the subject of Paul's preaching and teaching, namely, "the kingdom of God" and "the Lord Jesus Christ" (v. 31, cf. v. 23b); and by the reference to Paul's lodging (vv. 23, 30). The epilog places the message of Paul above his person and notes that this message is proclaimed **openly** (literally, "with all boldness," cf. 4:31) and **unhindered.** These last words are the triumphant conclusion of Luke-Acts. Neither Jewish obduracy nor Roman villainy can hinder the spread of the good news of "this salvation of God" (v. 28).

Witness in Rome (28:17-28)

17-22 (The first meeting with Jews at Rome)—As in every new city so also in Rome Paul first turned to the Jews, and he did so twice. Since his house arrest made it impossible for him to enter synagogues he took the initiative and called a meeting with the local **leaders of the Jews.** What is surprising is that they came at his request, especially since they already knew of the widespread opposition to the church in Judaism (v. 22). With this scene Luke clearly shows that Judaism was not a mass of unmitigated hostility toward the church, and that Paul's authority was so imposing that the official representatives of Judaism in Rome were willing to listen to him. At the first meeting Paul presented a concise summary of his defense speeches and in so doing he also functioned as defender of Christianity in its relation to Judaism. The speech should therefore be read in terms of Paul's personal biography and in terms of the relation of church and synagogue. He addressed them as **brothers** (cf. 2:29; 7:2; 13:26). In spite of the numerous rejections which Paul, the servant-witness of Christ, had suffered from Jews on his mission fields and in Jerusalem, the Roman Jews are his "brothers" because they have not yet refused to listen to his message, and because the Lukan Paul did not hold a doctrine of the transfer of sin and guilt. Hence, Roman Jews were not blamed for Christ's rejection and death in Jerusalem, or for Paul's rejections in Corinth, Ephesus, or Jerusalem, even as Gentiles were not blamed because of Pilate's deed (cf. 4:27; Luke 23:25). Each person must make his or her decision, and Jews who have not yet decided against the hope of Israel and its Messiah are brothers of Paul and of his church.

The following speech is chiastically structured (in reverse order, X-shaped sequence), as Miesner has shown. Paul had **done nothing against the people of Israel** or **the customs of our fathers,** the laws of Moses, even though at one time he had done "many things" against Christians in "opposing the name of Jesus of Nazareth" (26:9). Paul had been a loyal Jew (21:22-26). Moreover, in spite of what Jews in Jerusalem did to Paul he did not and would not retaliate. At his past trials before procurators **he had no charge to bring against** his **nation** (v. 19), nor will he bring charges against his nation before the court of Caesar. Neither he nor his churches may retaliate against Judaism, even when they are falsely accused and persecuted by segments of Judaism. This chiastically structured twofold statement of Paul ("had done nothing against the people"; "I had no charges to bring against my nation" before Roman courts) should express the church's posture in relation to the synagogue, according to Luke's concluding narrative.

Like Jesus, so his servant-witness Paul **was delivered prisoner from Jerusalem into the hands of the Romans** (21:31). Luke may have thought that had it not been for the attempted lynching by the Jerusalem mob Paul would not have become a prisoner of the Romans. Moreover, the words "delivered into the hands of" connect Paul's fate with Jesus' passion (cf. 3:13; 21:11; Luke 9:44; 18:32; 24:7).

Paul the servant of Jesus was called to suffer for the sake of his master (9:16), share in his fate, and, like him, be delivered by his own people into the hands of Gentiles. The fate of the prophets was rejection by their own people, because as representatives of God they became the object of sin within the people of God (cf. 7:35, 39-40, 52; Luke 11:47-49; 13:34). Paul's solidarity with his nation is contrasted with the hostile action of the Jews of Jerusalem (v. 17), and their action in turn is contrasted with Roman judicial procedure (v. 18). The Romans examined Paul and found that there existed **no reason for the death penalty in** his **case,** just as in the case of Jesus (13:28). Therefore, **they wished to set** him **at liberty.** Paul had not offended against the laws of Caesar (25:8). According to Luke, Roman officialdom clearly recognized that the conflict between Paul and his accusers was a theological matter in which Rome was incompetent to function as judge (cf. 18:14-15; 25:18-19, 25). Luke's reader should remember that Roman law and order is not the enemy of the church and that Christians can and must be found innocent of crimes against Caesar's law, even as they can and must uphold the Law of Moses. The just procedure of the Romans is now contrasted with Jewish hostility (v. 19a). **The Jews objected** to Paul's release by the Romans. The verb *object* (Greek, *antilegomai*) will reappear in v. 22 and refer to Judaism's worldwide objection to the church and its message. The basic issue for Judaism is not the person of Paul but the Christian gospel which Paul proclaimed. Again, Luke intentionally draws a parallel to Jesus' passion. Just as Pilate found Jesus innocent and wished to release him, but the Jews objected, so it was with Paul (cf. 13:28; Luke 23:4, 16, 22). Their objection in turn motivated his **appeal to Caesar,** which breaks the parallel to Jesus' passion. The appeal to Caesar demonstrates to Luke's church that Paul had some confidence in Rome's legal system. We should also note that Luke's prior account did not state that the appeal to Caesar resulted from Jewish objections to Festus's desire to set Paul free (cf. 25:8-11). On the contrary, Festus wanted to do the Jews a favor and give them Paul as a present (25:9, 11). Luke once again telescoped his account in vv. 18, 19 and drew a parallel to Jesus' passion. It was important for Luke to emphasize that in spite of rejection by Jews in Jerusalem Paul was and remained faithful to his people and would not use his appeal to **bring charges against** his **nation** (19b). He will not accuse his people of fomenting anti-Roman riots or plotting rebellion. Luke wrote after the Jewish rebellion of A.D. 66, and knew about Jerusalem's destruction (Luke 21:20-24), but found no delight in this calamity. On the contrary, Jesus wept over it (Luke 19:41-44) and the apostles, including Paul, never refer to it, even though they had ample occasion to do so.

20—The ultimate reason for Paul's imprisonment and suffering is **the hope of Israel** with which he identifies. This hope refers to the resurrection of the dead (cf. 23:6; 24:15; 26:6-7), grounded in God's surprising deed of Christ's resurrection (26:23). Easter is the world's best news, because death and destruction, including Jerusalem's destruction, are no longer the ultimate reality.

Paul's "hope of Israel" forms brackets with Anna's hope "for the redemption of Jerusalem" (Luke 2:38), with Simeon's hope "for the consolation of Israel" (Luke 2:25), with the Emmaus disciples who had hoped that Jesus would "redeem Israel" (Luke 24:21), and with the apostles, who on ascension day asked, "Will you at this time restore the kingdom to Israel?" (Acts 1:6). It is important for us to recognize that neither the apostles nor the Emmaus disciples were criticized for expressing Israel's special "nationalistic" hope for a corporate redemption. The disciples were upbraided only for failing to understand the necessity for the Messiah's death and resurrection (Luke 24:25-26). The apostles were instructed on ascension day that it was not for them to know the time of the End when God, or the Messiah, would restore the kingdom to Israel with finality. Their hope (Acts 1:6) did not express a nationalistic misunderstanding because they articulated it after Jesus had "opened their minds to understand the scriptures" (Luke 24:45), and after Jesus "during forty days" following Easter had spoken to them about the "kingdom of God" (1:3; cf. 28:23). The hope which Israel holds (24:15; 26:6-7) is therefore a **hope for Israel,** for the redemption, consolation, restoration of the kingdom to, and the resurrection of, Israel. This hope is grounded in God's unconditional promises "to Abraham and to his posterity forever" (Luke 1:55, 73; Acts 22–26). In Luke-Acts Abraham is the father of the Jews and not of Gentiles (in contrast to Romans 4). This hope is also grounded in God's unconditional promise to David (Acts 2:30; 13:23, 32-35) whose son "will be called the Son of the Most High and the Lord God will give him the throne of his father David (cf. Acts 2:33-36) and he will reign over the house of Jacob forever" (Luke 1:32-33).

This hope of Israel has found a preliminary fulfillment in Jesus' resurrection. He is "the first" to rise from the dead (26:23). But only his second coming will bring Israel's special "nationalistic" hope to its full realization. Then "the times of the Gentiles," when Jerusalem is trodden down, will have come to an end (Luke 21:24). Then and only then when God sends his Messiah from heaven, "all" of God's promises made to Israel shall be established (Acts 3:19-21). Then with the coming of the Son of man "in a cloud with power and great glory," then "your redemption is drawing near" (Luke 21:28).

In the time between Pentecost and parousia, the hope for Israel is in process of realization through the church's mission. Already now, Jesus is Israel's "Savior," a title which Luke always connected with the Jewish people (Luke 2:11; Acts 5:31; 13:23). Between Pentecost and parousia, God is rebuilding "the dwelling of David which has fallen" (15:16). Through mission and witness the people of the kingdom are being restored, on the condition of repentance, faith, and baptism, and the Gentiles are incorporated into this people on the same condition. But the resurrection of the dead is still to come. Meanwhile, Israel's redemption, consolation, and messianic restoration have already begun, but still await ultimate completion, the future resurrection and the future kingdom (23:6; 24:15; 26:6; 28:23).

The future resurrection expresses not only an individualistic hope for individuals' rising from the dead. According to Luke and the Old Testament, it also expresses a corporate hope for a corporate resurrection-salvation of Israel (cf. Ezek. 37:11-14; Hos. 6:1-2; Isa. 25:6-8; 26:19-21; T. Ben. 10:6-11). Also for Luke hope in the future resurrection is a corporate hope held by "our twelve tribes." The future resurrection does not eliminate the corporate people of God, because the twelve tribes "hope to attain" it and therefore they, like Anna, "earnestly worship night and day" (Luke 2:37-38; Acts 26:6-7). In the Eighteen Benedictions Israel prays to God who "raises the dead" and causes salvation to spring forth (Bened. 2); "look upon our affliction . . . and redeem us speedily" (Bened. 7); "sound the great horn for our freedom; lift up the ensign to gather our exiles" (Bened. 10); "and to Jerusalem, thy city, return in mercy . . . and set up there in the throne of David" (Bened. 14). In short, the hope of and for Israel which the Lukan Paul holds is in close proximity to the historical Paul who wrote Romans 11. Both look toward a stunning reversal of Israel's fate at the resurrection.

To be sure, both Luke and Paul also know of a final future judgment (cf. Acts 3:23; 24:15; 10:42; 2 Cor. 5:10; Rom. 14:10). But it may just be that then Israel may hail its Savior. Jesus had addressed a twofold prediction to Jerusalem: (1) A dire prediction of a penultimate judgment: Jerusalem will experience desolation for its obstinacy. "Its house," its temple, will be "forsaken" (Luke 13:34-35a); "the blood" guilt of Israel's history will be required "of this generation" (Luke 11:49-51); a penultimate judgment will descend upon Jerusalem when "the days of vengeance" and divine retribution come upon the city in accordance with "all that is written" (Luke 21:22-24; cf. 19:41-44).

(2) Jesus, however, had also promised to recalcitrant Jerusalem "And I tell you, you will not see me until you say, 'Blessed is he who comes in the name of the Lord' " (Luke 13:35b). This promise was only partially fulfilled by the disciples at Jesus' entry into Jerusalem (Luke 19:38), because Jesus did not address them, but those that had killed the prophets and rejected him (Luke 13:34). This promise awaits a future fulfillment. When "the times of refreshing come from the presence of the Lord" (God) (Acts 3:19-21), when he will send "the Messiah appointed for you," then perhaps Israel will break out in jubilation, "Blessed is he that comes in the name of the Lord."

21-22—If Paul came as a prisoner to Rome because of **the hope of Israel,** then the leaders of the Jewish synagogues in Rome owed him a response. Their reaction to Paul's defense was polite, in contrast to the mob scene in Jerusalem (23:7-10). First, they assured Paul that they had not received **letters from Judea.** No official communications from Jerusalem concerning him had reached them. With this Luke indicated that Jerusalem was not directly responsible for the outcome of Paul's trial in Rome. Second, the Jewish leaders told Paul that none of the **brothers** from Judea or elsewhere who had come to Rome had spread calumnies about him. With the word **brothers** the Roman leaders express their solidarity with Paul's opponents. He had addressed the Roman leaders as "brothers," but spoken of his opponents as "Jews" (v. 19), because, in contrast to the Roman Jews, they had already rejected the hope of Israel, as promised in Scripture, fulfilled in the resurrection of the Messiah, and proclaimed by his servant-witnesses.

Yet Luke also seems to imply that the outcome of Paul's trial before Caesar was not the result of Jewish calumnies, perpetrated by influential Roman Jews such as Aliturus, Nero's favorite Jewish actor, or Poppaea Sabina, Nero's mistress and later wife, who favored Judaism (cf. Josephus, *Life* 13–16). The politeness of the Jewish leaders of Rome during their meeting with Paul would seem to suggest that Luke absolved the Jews for any evil that befell Paul in Rome. In turn, this would lend support to the hypothesis that on the historical level, it was the "jealousy and envy" of Christians which brought him to grief (1 Clem. 5:2-4).

Third, the Roman Jewish leaders expressed their desire **to hear** Paul's **views** again, and they cast their request in polite language (Greek, *axioumen*). The verb **to hear** (v. 22) will reappear in vv. 26, 27b, and 28. Lastly, the Jewish leaders in Rome state the reason why they want to hear Paul again: **For with regard to this sect we know that everywhere it is spoken against.** It is false to conclude from this last sentence that the Roman Jews knew nothing of the existence of Christian churches in Rome, or were ignorant of the church's basic doctrines. Rather, Luke tells us that in spite of the fact that these leaders had already been aware of the universal objection to Christianity by Judaism, they nevertheless desired to hear Paul again, because he was the leader of a Jewish sect (cf. 24:5). The word **sect** (Greek, *hairesis*) refers to a group or "party" with a particular teaching (e.g., the sect, party, or group of the Sadducees, 5:17; and of the Pharisees, 15:5; 26:5). The leader of such a group can present the group's normative teaching. Yet with their last statement these Roman Jewish leaders fulfilled unknowingly and once again Simeon's prophecy that Jesus would be a sign that is **spoken against** (Luke 2:24), for Jesus is the content of the Christian teaching. Moreover, they affirmed that "wherever" the Christian message has been heard within Judaism it met with objection. Nevertheless, the Roman Jewish leaders are willing to continue the discussion and listen to Paul's views.

23-28 (The second meeting with Jews at Rome)—At a time mutually agreed upon an even greater number of Jews arrived at Paul's **lodging.** There was indeed interest among Roman Jews in hearing Paul. Questions such as how Paul could have packed **great numbers** of Jews into his lodging do not concern Luke, who wrote both scenes for his climactic conclusion. Paul's lodging becomes transformed into a kind of synagogue with Paul functioning not as defender but as witnessing missionary. Two interrelated subjects comprise the content of his witness, which lasts **from morning till evening.** The missionary made a day-long concentrated effort (cf. 20:11, 20) **testifying to the kingdom of God and trying to convince them about Jesus both from the law of Moses and from the prophets.** Paul's witness is a concise summary of the total teaching of Luke-Acts. The subject of the **kingdom of God** forms brackets around the book of Acts. It is what Jesus taught after Easter (1:3, cf. 1:6) and before Easter (Luke 4:43), and what Paul taught in Rome at the end of Luke's story (28:23, 31; cf. 8:12; 14:22; 19:8; 20:25; Luke 9:2). Preaching or **testifying to the kingdom of God** refers to the Christian message which is in continuity with the apostles, with Jesus, and with the Old Testament. The center of this message is Jesus Christ, in whom God's eschatological reign, his kingdom, has already come for eyes of faith to see (cf. Luke 11:20; 17:21). To speak to Jews about the kingdom of God means **to convince them** on the basis of **Moses and the prophets** that Jesus is the one through whom God inaugurated his saving reign with a climactic future yet to come. This entails interpretation of the Scriptures in the light of the cross and of Easter (cf. Luke 24:25-27, 32, 44-45). Paul had affirmed that he believed "all" that is written (24:14-15) and that he could expect his Jewish hearers to examine the Scriptures "to see if these things were so" (17:11), and investigate the Christ event in the light of the Scriptures and understand the Scriptures in the light of the Christ event. The uniform messianic testimony of the Scripture demands a uniform corporate response from Israel.

For Luke, to speak of **Jesus** on the basis of the Scripture is to proclaim him as the prophet like Moses (Deut. 18:15-16), whom God has raised up and to whom Israel should "listen" (3:22; 7:37; Luke 9:30-31, 35). He is the "Messiah-Savior," promised to David (2:25-36; 13:22-23, 32-37), the humiliated servant of Isaiah 53 (8:32-33), "the Lord," exalted to God's right hand according to Psalm 110 (2:24-36). Through him God gives repentance and forgiveness to Israel (5:31) and grants a share in his Holy Spirit (2:33; 5:32), and in so doing God establishes his saving reign in the present among all who "listen."

To speak about **the kingdom of God** against the background of the Old Testament story also implies speaking about the faithful God and his dealings with a faithless people who rejected the messengers of God, beginning with Moses and the wilderness generation, continuing with the rejection of Jesus, the Messiah, and ending with the rejection of his servant-witnesses. However, to speak about the kingdom of God also entails speaking about Israel's hope, the resurrection of the Messiah and the future resurrection (cf. 26:6-7; 1:6; Luke 13:28-30; Luke 22:28-30).

24—The reaction of the Roman Jews to Paul's witness was divided. **Some were convinced** by his teaching, while **others disbelieved.** Some interpreters hold that those who were convinced (Greek, *peithō*, cf. 13:43; 18:4; 19:8, 26; 26:28) merely exhibited sympathetic curiosity about Paul's teaching. Yet the immediate context clarifies the meaning of the verb. Paul had been **trying to convince** the Roman Jews (v. 23) and he succeeded with **some,** but not with **others** who **disbelieved** (v. 24). In short, the sentence **some were convinced** is synonymous with "some believed" or "were converted." The reader already knows that believers will be baptized. The division between believing and unbelieving Jews represented the typical response of Judaism. When it confronted the message of Israel's hope already fulfilled in Jesus, albeit in a hidden way and only for eyes of faith to see, its response was divided. While Israel's Scriptures are in agreement (Greek, *symphōnousin*, 15:15), the people of Israel as a corporate entity is divided in its response and in disagreement (Greek, *asymphōnoi*, v. 25). However, "the hope of Israel" demanded a corporate affirmative response. Instead, there was disagreement all the way from Jesus' first sermon in Nazareth (Luke 4:16-30) to Paul's last speech in Rome. It is this disagreement within corporate Israel which is placed under prophetic indictment and interpreted for the reader. And this is not a new development. On three prior occasions Paul had reacted in a similar vein to Jewish opposition (13:40-41, 46-47; 18:6; 19:9; cf. 7:51-53).

25-28—The Jews departed in disagreement **after Paul had made one statement** in which he interpreted the unbelief that caused the division within Judaism. This **one statement** has three parts: An introduction (v. 25b) followed by the citation of Isa. 6:9-10 (vv. 26-27), which serves as the basis for a solemn conclusion (v. 28). The center of Paul's tripartite statement is one of three extended citations from the Old Testament found in Acts (cf. 2:17-21; 15:16-18). Coming at the end of Luke's story the message of this citation cannot be overlooked. It summarizes all prior rejection scenes in Luke-Acts, beginning with Jesus' sermon in Nazareth (Luke 4), and sets the stage for future developments. The extended Joel citation in Acts 2 proclaimed and interpreted the new stage of the Spirit's coming upon the messianic community; the Amos citation of Acts 15 interpreted and guaranteed the legitimacy of this community made up of believing Jews and Gentiles. The Isaiah citation of Acts 28 makes clear why antimessianic Jews excluded themselves from the messianic community, and why the one people of God is divided into church and synagogue.

The audience of this **one statement** consists of the Roman Jews who had already heard the gospel, but the statement does not apply to all of them. Believers and unbelievers must hear it, but the citation from Isaiah applies only to the latter and not to the myriads of Jews in Jerusalem or in the diaspora who had come to faith (21:20), nor to those Roman Jews who were persuaded by Paul (v. 24). **The Holy Spirit was right in saying to your fathers through Isaiah the prophet.** . . . In v. 17 Paul had spoken of **our** fathers and had expressed his solidarity with the Roman Jews. The fathers, or our fathers, were the recipients of God's promises (cf. 13:32-33; 26:6), which are the basis of "the hope of Israel" (v. 20). Yet there is also a division among the fathers. By speaking of **your** fathers (v. 25) Paul breaks his solidarity with those Roman Jews who have responded in unbelief to his testimony. Their obduracy is in continuity with the stiffneckedness of their fathers of the wilderness generation and with the unbelief and rejection of the prophetic word at the time of Isaiah and the prophets of old (cf. 7:25, 27, 35, 39-43, 51-53; Luke 11:47-48; etc.) The Lukan interpreter should note that even though the rejection of the Word of God evoked God's judgment upon his people (cf. 7:42-43; Luke 13:34-35a), it did not result in God rejecting them with finality. On the contrary, the Old Testament story and Luke's updated version presuppose that God kept faith with his faithless people and only for this reason was and is the story of God's dealings with his people not just a story of failure and judgment but also of salvation and gracious fulfillment. **Through** his earthly instrument, **Isaiah, the Holy Spirit,** predicted the stubbornness of the unbelieving part of the divided people of God and interpreted the cause and nature of their unbelief.

Go to this people and say . . . (v. 26). Note that in spite of their recalcitrance they are still called the **people** (Greek, *laos*) of God.

Like Isaiah, Paul must announce to this unbelieving people a prediction with an interpretation. The LXX version of Isa. 6:9 used by the synoptic writers, changed the commands of the Hebrew text ("make" their hearts fat and "shut" their eyes) into predictions. Hence, in the LXX version, the obstinacy of the people is not the God-intended result of the prophet's proclamation. Rather, their obduracy constitutes their guilt, because they do not respond in faithful obedience to the Word of God. The words **You shall indeed hear but never understand, and you shall indeed see but never perceive** are a divine prediction which in the Lukan context found its fulfillment in the rejection of the Christian message by Jews. What Isaiah spoke to the unbelieving fathers is not limited just to them but applies also to their unbelieving children in the present and, coming at the end of Luke's story, it applies also to the future unbelief of **this people.**

The rest of the citation (v. 27) is an interpretation of Jewish obduracy and its result. Its result is **lest they should perceive . . . and turn for me to heal them.** Grammatically it is possible to translate: "Whether perhaps they perceive . . . and turn and I shall heal them." If so, the clause would express Luke's hope that the corporate obduracy of "this people" might come to an end before the End. But it is doubtful that Luke intended such a meaning here. For him, those who twice heard the Word of God but rejected it, as some Roman Jews had done, are obdurate. The hearts, ears, and eyes of the unbelieving part of the people of God are closed. They do not and cannot hear the Word of God who through Jesus has visited them and through his messengers announced salvation to them. Therefore God does not **heal them.** God's saving and healing word through Jesus must be heard. Precisely such hearing—together with repentance, faith, and opening of ears, hearts, and eyes—is the gift and work of God through his Word (Luke 24:31, 45; Acts 3:16; 5:31b; 16:14; 26:18), while unbelief after hearing the Word constitutes culpable obduracy. This tension may not be resolved. I cannot blame God for my unbelief, and I cannot claim credit for any faith. The unbelieving part of the people of God represented by Roman Jews heard only objectionable words when confronted with the message of "this salvation of God." They did not and could not respond in faith. Therefore, God does not **heal them,** by granting them forgiveness of sins and life related to God, Christ, and the Holy Spirit in the present. **This** unbelieving **people** of God has excluded itself from "this salvation of God" (cf. v. 28), because they did not listen.

However, the Isaiah citation does not state that God has rejected his stiffnecked people, nor does it say that the church has taken the place of Israel. If we were to interpret this citation in terms of God's rejecting his people with finality, then we would produce the absurdity that the whole biblical story beginning with God's unconditional promise to Abraham (cf. 7:1-8) and ending with Paul's arrival at Rome (v. 16) would function merely as prolog to the final rejection of Israel by God in Rome through Paul in vv. 25-27. Theologically, that would mean that there are no unconditional promises of God, but only conditional ones (If you do, believe, etc., . . . then God will . . .). In terms of literary composition it would mean that the end of Luke's story would disagree with its beginning. We should note that the citation does not pronounce God's ultimate judgment on his people, but it interprets and denounces Israel's attitude before the End.

According to Luke, the recalcitrance of the Roman Jews does not express a new development, but it expresses the attitude of much of God's people throughout their history (7:39-43, 51-53). Hence, more than once, penultimate judgments fell on them (cf. 7:42-43; Luke 13:34; 19:41-44; 21:20-24). According to Luke there is a division and disagreement between this obstinate people of God, on one hand, and the church, the believing people of God, on the other, and this division may last until the eschaton. What God who raises the dead and who can open hearts, ears, and eyes will do with his recalcitrant people collectively at the End is not stated here. The story of Acts is open-ended. It does not conclude on the note that God has already now rejected his stubborn people.

Just as the Holy Spirit predicted the rejection of Jesus by Jews and Gentiles (4:25-28), so he predicted the rejection of the apostolic witness by osbstinate Judaism. Those who refuse to hear and see shall neither hear nor see! The message of salvation through Jesus Christ either draws into the gravitational pull of the kingdom of God or else it reveals the culpability of hardened hearts, deaf ears, and closed eyes. Israel, insofar as it is afflicted with obduracy, has rejected not only the earthly Jesus but also the message about the Resurrected One and thereby it has excluded itself from "this salvation of God" (cf. v. 28). However, God has not finally excluded it. The end of Acts is not the End—and Luke knows that. God, who is faithful to all his promises, will see to it that those promises which have only partially been fulfilled or have not yet been fulfilled at the end of Luke's story will in God's time and in his surprising ways come to fulfillment (cf. Isa. 11:6-9; 26:19-21; 61:5-9; Acts 3:21). Moreover, besides the rejection of the Christian message by obdurate Judaism there was also an acceptance of Jesus and, later, of the apostolic testimony in Judaism from the beginning to the end of Luke's story (cf. Luke 1:38, 43, 67; 2:25-38; 6:13; 10:1; 12:1; 23:49; 24:31-32, 45; Acts 1:13-15; 2:41; 4:4; 5:14; 6:7; 9:31; 13:43; 14:1; 17:4, 12; 18:7; 19:9-10; 21:20; 28:24). Believing Judaism is the faithful remnant with a mission that has not yet ended.

28—Let it be known to you then that this salvation of God has been sent to the Gentiles; they will listen. This last word of Paul in direct speech indicates the end of the hope that corporate Israel would accept the gospel, and it discloses that the church's future lies in its mission to Gentiles rather than to Jews. One phase in the church's history has come to an end, and a new one begins. No longer will Christian missionaries have to make contact with synagogues first before preaching to Gentiles. A shift in mission emphasis occurs in this verse.

Paul's concluding word is almost identical with his announcement in the synagogue at Antioch, where he said: "To us [Jews] has been sent the message of this salvation" (13:26). Yet this announcement at Antioch did not preclude his preaching to Gentiles, envisioned since Luke 2:32; 3:6, and inaugurated in Acts 10, just as Paul's last announcement in Rome does not preclude preaching to Jews. This can be concluded from the three prior rejection scenes which lead up to the final scene in Rome. After Paul had encountered opposition from the Jews at Antioch he said: "It was necessary that the word of God should be spoken first to you. Since you thrust it from you . . . behold, we turn to the Gentiles" (13:46). Yet, after the mission at Antioch, he preached in the synagogue of every other city, provided there was one. When he met rejection from Jews at Corinth he declared: "Your blood be upon your heads! I am innocent. From now on I will go to the Gentiles" (18:6). But immediately after his break with the Corinthian Jews we hear of conversions of Jews in Corinth (18:7-8), which means that Paul continued preaching to Jews even after his break with the synagogue. The same holds true in

Ephesus. "When some [Ephesian Jews] were stubborn [literally, "hardened," "obdurate"] and disbelieved, speaking evil of the Way before the congregation," Paul simply "withdrew from them, taking the disciples with him" (19:9). However, his withdrawal from the synagogue did not signal the end of his preaching to Jews in that region, because some verses later we hear that during his two-year mission in Ephesus "all the residents of Asia heard the word of the Lord, both Jews and Greeks" (19:10). These rejection scenes demonstrate that according to Luke preaching to individual Jews in a particular city continued even after Paul had broken with the synagogue of that city.

The situation at Rome is hardly different, and for four reasons. First, though Paul's concluding statement (vv. 25-28) focuses upon the unbelieving Jews, nevertheless Luke had deliberately told us that in Rome "some [Jews] were convinced" by Paul's message (v. 24). Preaching to Jews was not a total waste of time, even at the end of Luke's story. For that reason alone we conclude that v. 28 cannot signal the end of preaching to Jews, but v. 28 should be interpreted in the light of the three prior rejection scenes and their aftermath. Second, the epilog of Acts (vv. 30-31) clearly states that for two years Paul "welcomed all," which can only mean that he welcomed and preached to Gentiles *and* Jews "who came to him." He excluded no one. Third, the theme of his preaching during that period was identical with the theme of his testimony to the Roman Jews (vv. 23 and 31). He did not preach on the subject of the unknown God who is near, a subject appropriate for a purely Gentile audience (cf. Acts 14:15-17; 17:22-31), but on the "kingdom of God" and "the Lord Jesus" (v. 31). Fourth, preaching to Jews could end in Rome only if Luke regarded Rome to be "the end of the earth" (1:8). However, Rome is but a way station and a pledge that the witness to Jews and Gentiles **will** reach the end of the earth. Therefore, Paul did not stop preaching in Rome, but continued to do so for two whole years (vv. 30-31).

In short, Paul's concluding announcement to the Roman Jews (v. 28) means that henceforth the world of the Gentiles rather than corporate Judaism will be the primary object of the church's witness and mission according to God's design. However, v. 28 does not preclude proclamation to, and conversion of, individual Jews.

One might ask how Luke envisioned that preaching to Jews could be accomplished in his own time, when Christian missionaries were probably no longer able to enter synagogues, and Christian teaching was "spoken against everywhere" in official Judaism (v. 22). Luke's answer would be that these obstacles did not prevent Paul from inviting Jews and meeting them repeatedly and welcoming **all,** when for various reasons he was unable to enter the synagogues of Rome (vv. 17, 23, 30). Extending hospitality to Jews was possible even when Christian preaching in synagogues had become impossible.

A fairly common interpretation of v. 28 holds that in response to the division among and the obduracy of some Roman Jews, God will send the gospel to the Gentiles. But we should note that the verb is **has been sent** (past tense, not future tense), and that the conjunction **then** or "therefore" is connected with **let it be known,** and not with "has been sent." This means that the division within and obduracy among Roman Jews is the reason why Paul **let it be known** that God has sent the gospel to Gentiles. The division and obduracy themselves are not the reason for Gentile mission. Rather, they are the reason for Paul's announcement in v. 28. Their recalcitrance prompts him to tell them that God has already inaugurated the Gentile mission. The sending of **this salvation of God** to Gentiles has already occurred in the past (cf. Acts 10–11). It had been mandated by Jesus (1:8), envisioned by Simeon, announced by John the Baptist (Luke 2:32; 3:6), and promised by God through the prophets (Acts 15:15). Since Acts 10, Luke has described in different episodes how God has **sent** to Gentiles **this salvation.** The sending of God's salvation occurs whenever God's messengers preach "the kingdom of God" and teach "about the Lord Jesus Christ" (vv. 22, 31). **They will listen.** Faith, above all else, is listening to the unconditional promise of salvation (e.g., "All flesh shall see *the salvation* of God." Luke 3:6; Greek, *sōtērion*, as in Acts 28:28). Faith is listening to the message of and about Jesus Christ. Because death is behind him he guarantees the validity of God's unconditional salvation promise, which also includes Gentiles. Faith is not a virtue nor a pious work, nor an attitudinal state which requires introspection and self-examination. Faith is first of all listening to that Word which draws us into the saving rule of God. Faith is "the way" of life that is determined by listening to the unconditional promise of God fulfilled in Christ.

The sending of the gospel to the Gentiles which was inaugurated in the past will direct the future course of the church's mission. At the end of Luke's story Paul once again announces the Gentile mission. A shift in mission emphasis, Luke suggests, will occur, and ever more Gentiles will enter the church and **listen** with open ears. The past encounters with Gentiles narrated in Acts do not imply that all Gentiles will **listen,** but that more Gentiles than Jews will do so. The vision of a corporate response in faith of Judaism as a whole has faded. Yet "some" Jews can still be reached at Luke's time, just as they were reached by Paul in Rome (v. 24).

Finally, just as the obduracy of Judaism fulfills the prediction of Isaiah 6, so the mission to Gentiles in v. 28 fulfills Acts 1:8; Luke 24:47; 2:32; 3:6, as well as Isa. 42:6 (the servant is to be "a light to the nations, to open the eyes that are blind . . ."), Ezek. 3:6 ("surely if I send you to such [Gentiles] they would *listen* to you"), and Ps. 67:2 ("that thy way may be known upon earth, thy saving power among all nations").

Epilog (28:30-31)

Some manuscripts contain v. 29 (see the RSV footnote, which is a later addition to the text of Acts. This verse is missing in the oldest manuscripts). The epilog in vv. 30-31 concludes Luke's story, and tells us that for **two whole years** Paul had the privilege of living "in his own hired dwelling" (see the RSV text and footnote). The Greek word (*misthōma*) can mean "payment for hiring," or "that which is hired." The Greek preposition (*en*) in this sentence would suggest the latter, namely, a hired dwelling rather than **at his own expense.** His rented quarters (vv. 16 and 23) imply that Roman Christians paid the rent for Paul's housing. The imperial authorities granted him this privilege for **two whole years.** With this time reference, Luke also indicates that after two years a change in the apostle's fortune took place. We may assume that Luke's readers knew that Paul suffered martyrdom after that period. In the epilog, however, his fate was not Luke's concern. What was important to Luke was that Paul **welcomed all,** namely, Jews and Gentiles. Since Luke did not write "all Gentiles," we must assume that the meaning of **all** is inclusive of Jews rather than exclusive. In the epilog Luke did not establish a new Gentile particularism at the expense of Jews—something which would run counter to his whole narrative. Some later copyist correctly interpreted **all** by adding "Jews and Greeks" to the text. A limitation of preaching to Gentiles only would also contradict Paul's mandate (26:16-18). Though the hope of a conversion of Israel as a whole has faded at the end of Acts, individual Jews were nevertheless welcomed by Paul even at the end of his ministry. Paul's message had been designated "the hope of Israel" (v. 20) or "this salvation of God" (v. 28; cf. Luke 2:30). In the epilog his message is summarized under two aspects, as in v. 23: **Preaching the kingdom**

of God and **teaching about the Lord Jesus Christ.** It is through Jesus that God's saving reign is in the process of realization, fulfilling Israel's hope, and it is Jesus who through his servant-witnesses proclaims and enacts salvation or "light both to the people [of Israel] and to the Gentiles" (26:23). The theme of **the kingdom of God** also expresses the continuity between the proclamation of Paul and of Jesus (cf. Acts 1:3-6).

However, the emphasis of the epilog is not on the content of Paul's preaching, on the *what*, but rather on the *how*, on the manner in which he carried out his mission as prisoner in Rome. Paul preached with all boldness **and unhindered.** "With all boldness" is a better translation than **quite openly** (RSV). **Boldness** is the confidence and fearlessness of the Christian who is empowered by the Holy Spirit, in answer to prayer (cf. 2:29; 4:13, 29-31). **Unhindered** refers first of all to the magnanimity of the Roman government that permitted Paul to carry out his mission even as a prisoner for two whole years. Second, it contains an implicit question. Will the Roman government of Luke's own present and future time pursue a policy of noninterference in the affairs of the church, or will it act as it did after Paul's two years were up? The Neronian persecution took place some two decades before Luke wrote, and the question which is left unanswered at the end of Acts is not whether the church would receive official toleration from the empire, but rather whether the church's proclamation would go on **unhindered** by imperial authorities. Luke's narrative is open-ended also with regard to his political apologetics. Finally, the phrase "with all boldness" is a fulfillment of Jesus' promise (Luke 21:15-19), and the last word of Acts, **unhindered,** also expresses Luke's own faith. The Word of God will continue unhindered, come what may. Neither Roman chains (cf. 2 Tim. 2:9) nor Roman persecutions can thwart the will and purpose of God. "With all boldness **and unhindered**" is Luke's bugle call of victory for God's cause in the midst of the church's ongoing history. Luke invites his readers to participate in this history.

The term *open-ended* has been used rather frequently in this final section; there is, however, one task that has been completed at the end of Acts, namely, the normative witness of the chosen witnesses. Their witness is enclosed in Luke-Acts. Luke's literary achievement was meant to serve also as a norm for his church, a compass to guide the churches on their way through history in the task of preaching, teaching, and mission to Gentiles and Jews. The readers of Luke-Acts can draw guidance and strength, consolation and joy from Luke's work and retain continuity with Paul, Peter, the teachings of Jesus, and the Old Testament as they participate in the church's mission "with all boldness **and unhindered.**"

SELECTED BIBLIOGRAPHY

I. Research Reports and Bibiographies

Kümmel, W. G. "Das Urchristentum." *ThR* 14 (1942): 81-95, 155-173; 17 (1948): 3-50, 103-142; 18 (1950): 1-53; 22 (1954): 138-170, 191-211.

Grässer, E. "Die Apostelgeschichte in der Forschung der Gegenwart." *ThR* 26 (1960): 93-167.

————. "Acta Forschung seit 1960." *ThR* 41 (1976): 141-194, 259-290; 42 (1977): 1-68.

Plümacher, E. "Acta Forschung 1974–1982." *ThR* 48 (1983): 1-56; 49 (1984): 105-169.

Mattill, A. J., and Mattill, M. B. *A Classified Bibliography of Literature on the Acts of the Apostles.* Leiden: Brill, 1966.

Wagner, G. *Bibliographical Aids No. 7, An Exegetical Bibliography on the Acts of the Apostles.* Rüschlikon-Zurich: Baptist Theological Seminary, 1975.

II. Commentaries

Rackham, R. B. *The Acts of the Apostles: An Exposition.* London: Methuen, 1901.

Foakes-Jackson, F. J., and Lake, K. *The Beginnings of Christianity.* 5 vols. London: Macmillan, 1920–1933.

Hanson, R. P. C. *The Acts.* The New Clarendon Bible. Oxford: Clarendon, 1967.

Haenchen, E. *The Acts of the Apostles: A Commentary.* Translated by B. Noble and G. Shinn. Philadelphia: Westminster, 1971.

Conzelmann, H. *Die Apostelgeschichte.* Tübingen: Mohr, 1963.

Marshall, I. H. *The Acts of the Apostles: An Introduction and Commentary.* Grand Rapids: Eerdmans, 1980.

Selected Bibliography

III. Studies

Barrett, C. K. *Luke the Historian in Recent Study*. London: Epworth, 1979.

Betz, H. D. *Galatians: A Commentary. . . .* Hermeneia. Philadelphia: Fortress, 1979.

Black, M. *An Aramaic Approach to the Gospels and Acts*. 3rd ed. Oxford: Clarendon, 1967.

Bowker, J. W. "Speeches in Acts: A Study in Proem and Yellammedenu Form." *NTS* 14 (1967): 96-110.

Cadbury, H. J. *The Making of Luke-Acts*. New York: Macmillan, 1927
———. *The Book of Acts in History*. London: Black, 1955.

Cassidy, R. J., and Scharper, P. J., eds. *Political Issues in Luke-Acts*. New York: Maryknoll, 1983.

Cochrane, C. N. *Christianity and Classical Culture*. New York: Galaxy, 1957.

Conzelmann, H. *The Theology of St. Luke*. Translated by G. Buswell. New York: Harper and Row, 1960.

Cosgrove, C. H. "The Divine 'dei' (Must) in Luke-Acts." *NovTest* 26 (1984): 168-190.

Crook, J. *Law and Life of Rome*. Ithaca: Cornell University Press, 1967.

Danker, F. W. *Benefactor: Epigraphic Study of a Graeco-Roman and New Testament Semantic Field*. St. Louis: Clayton, 1982.

———. Luke. Proclamation Commentaries. Philadelphia: Fortress, 1976.

———. "Graeco-Roman Cultural Accommodations in the Christology of Luke-Acts." In *SBL 1983 Seminar Papers*, edited by K. H. Richards, pp. 391-414. Chico, Calif.: Scholars Press, 1983.

Dibelius M. *Studies in the Acts of the Apostles*. Translated by M. Ling. New York: Scribner, 1985.

Dumais, M. *Le Lange de l'évangélisation (Actes 13:16-41)*. Montreal: Bellarmin, 1976.

Dupont, J. *The Sources of Acts*. Translated by K. Pond. New York: Herder and Herder, 1964.

———. *The Salvation of the Gentiles: Studies in the Acts of the Apostles*. Translated by J. R. Keating. New York: Paulist, 1979.

Goulder, M. D. *Type and History in Acts*. London: SPCK, 1964.

Franklin, E. *Christ the Lord: A Study in the Purpose and Theology of Luke-Acts*. Philadelphia: Westminster, 1975.

Hengel, M. *Acts and the History of Earliest Christianity*. Translated by J. Bowden. Philadelphia: Fortress, 1979.

Jervell, J. *Luke and the People of God: A New Look at Luke-Acts*. Minneapolis: Augsburg, 1972.

Selected Bibliography

Jewett, R. *A Chronology of Paul's Life*. Philadelphia: Fortress, 1979.

Johnson, L. T. *The Literary Function of Possessions in Luke-Acts*. SBLDS 39. Missoula, Mont.: Scholars Press, 1977.

Juel, D. *Luke-Acts: The Promise of History*. Atlanta: John Knox, 1983.

Karris, R. J. "Missionary Communities: A New Paradigm for the Study of Luke-Acts." *CBQ* 41 (1979): 80-97.

_____ . *What Are They Saying about Luke-Acts? A Theology of the Faithful God*. New York: Paulist, 1979.

_____ . "Poor and Rich: The Lukan Sitz-im-Leben." In *Perspectives . . .*, edited by C. Talbert, pp. 112-125 (cited below).

Keck, L. E., and Martyn, J. L., editors. *Studies in Luke-Acts*. 1966. Reprint. Philadelphia: Fortress, 1980.

Kingsbury, J. D. *Jesus Christ in Matthew, Mark, and Luke*. Proclamation Commentaries. Philadelphia: Fortress, 1981.

Kraabel, A. T. "The Roman Diaspora: Six Questionable Assumptions." In *Essays in Honour of Yigael Yadin*, edited by G. Vermes and J. Neusner, pp. 445-464. Publications of the Oxford Centre for Postgraduate Hebrew Studies 6. Oxford: Allanheld, 1983.

Kremer, J., ed. *Les Actes des Apôtres: Traditions, redaction, théologie*. Bibliotheca Ephemeridum Theologicarum Lovaniensium 48. Leuven: University Press, 1979.

Kümmel, W. G. *Introduction to the New Testament*. Revised edition. Translated by H. C. Kee. New York: Abingdon, 1975.

Maddox, R. *The Purpose of Luke-Acts*. Studies of the New Testament and Its World. Edinburgh: T. & T. Clark, 1982.

Marshall, H. I. *Luke: Historian and Theologian*. Grand Rapids: Zondervan, 1971.

Martin, R. A. "Syntactical Evidence of Aramaic Sources in Acts 1–10." *NTS* 11 (1964): 38-59.

Mattill, A. J. "The Jesus-Paul Parallels and the Purpose of Luke-Acts: H. H. Evans Reconsidered." *NovTest* 17 (1975): 15-46.

Metzger, B. M. *A Textual Commentary on the Greek New Testament*. 3rd ed. New York: United Bible Societies, 1971.

Moessner, D. P. "Jesus and the Wilderness Generation: The Death of the Prophet like Moses according to Luke." In *SBL 1982 Seminar Papers*, edited by K. H. Richards, pp. 319-340. Chico, Calif.: Scholars Press, 1982.

Nock, A. D. "Soter and Euergetes" (Savior and Benefactor). In *The Joy of Study*, edited by Sherman E. Johnson, pp. 127-148. New York: Macmillan, 1951.

_____ . *Essays on Religion and the Ancient World*. 2 vols. Edited by Z. Stewart. Oxford: Clarendon, 1972.

Selected Bibliography

Norden, E. *Agnostos Theos.* Reprint. Stuttgart: Teubner, 1956.

O'Neill, J. C. *The Theology of Acts in Its Historical Setting.* 2nd ed. London: SPCK, 1970.

O'Toole, R. F. *The Unity of Luke's Theology: An Analysis of Luke-Acts.* Wilmington, Del.: M. Glazier, 1984.

Plümacher, E. "Wirklichkeitserfahrung und Geschichtsschreibung bei Lukas." *ZNW* 69 (1977): 2-22.

Praeder, S. M. "Miracle Worker and Missionary: Paul in the Acts of the Apostles." In *SBL 1983 Seminar Papers,* edited by K. H. Richards, pp. 87-106. Chico, Calif.: Scholars Press, 1983.

Sherwin-White, A. N. *Roman Society and Roman Law in the New Testament.* Oxford: Clarendon, 1969; Grand Rapids: Baker, 1978.

Smalley, S. S. "Spirit, Kingdom and Prayer in Luke-Acts." *NovTest* 15 (1973): 59-71.

Talbert, C. H. *Literary Patterns, Theological Themes, and the Genre of Luke-Acts.* SBLMS 20. Missoula, Mont.: Scholars Press, 1974.

————— , ed. *Perspectives on Luke-Acts.* Special Studies Series 5. Danville, Va.: Assoc. of Baptist Professors, 1978.

————— . "Again: Paul's Visits to Jerusalem." *NovTest* 9 (1967): 26-40.

————— , ed. *Luke-Acts: New Perspectives from the SBL Seminar.* New York: Crossroad, 1984.

Tannehill, R. C. "Israel in Luke-Acts: A Tragic Story." *JBL* 104 (1985): 69-85.

Tiede, D. L. *Prophecy and History in Luke-Acts.* Philadelphia: Fortress, 1980.

Turner, C. H. "The Chronology of the New Testament." *Hastings Dictionary of the Bible* 1:421.

Tyson, J. B. "The Jewish Public in Luke-Acts." *NTS* 30 (1984): 574-583.

Unnik, W. C., van. "The Book of Acts, the Confirmation of the Gospel." *NovTest* 4 (1962): 26-59.

Walaskay, P. W. *"And So We Came to Rome". The Political Perspective of St. Luke.* SNTSMS 49. Cambridge: Cambridge University Press, 1983.

Wilckens, U. *Die Missionsreden der Apostelgeschichte.* 3rd ed. WMANT 5, Neukirchen-Vluyn, 1974.

Wilcox, M. *The Semitisms of Acts.* Oxford: Clarendon, 1965.

————— . "The Promise of the 'Seed' in the New Testament." *JSNT* 5 (1979): 2-20.

Wilson, S. G. *The Gentiles and the Gentile Mission in Luke-Acts.* SNTSMS 23. Cambridge: Cambridge University Press, 1973.

————— . *Luke and the Law.* SNTSMS 50. Cambridge: Cambridge University Press, 1983.

Selected Bibliography

Ziesler, J. "Luke and the Pharisees." *NTS* 25 (1979): 146-157.

IV. Bibliographical Additions by Chapters

Introduction:

Chatman, S. *Story and Discourse*. Ithaca: Cornell University Press, 1978.

Goodspeed, E. J. *An Introduction to the New Testament*. Chicago: University of Chicago Press, 1937.

Johnson, L. T. "On Finding the Lukan Community: A Cautious Cautionary Essay." In *SBL 1979 Seminar Papers*, vol. 1, edited by P. J. Achtemeier. Missoula, Mont.: Scholars Press, 1979.

Mosley, A. W. "Historical Reporting in the Ancient World." *NTS* 12 (1965): 10-26.

Petersen, N. R. *Literary Criticism for New Testament Critics*. Guides to Biblical Scholarship. Philadelphia: Fortress, 1978.

Praeder, S. M. "Luke-Acts and the Ancient Novel." In *SBL 1981 Seminar Papers*, edited by K. H. Richards, pp. 269-292. Chico, Cal.: Scholars Press, 1981.

Rhoads, D. "Narrative Criticism and the Gospel of Mark." *JAAR* 50 (1982): 411-434.

Unnik, W. C. van. "Luke's Second Book and the Rules of Hellenistic Historiography." In *Les Actes . . .* , edited by J. Kremer, pp. 21-35 (see §III above).

Wilcox, M. "Luke and the Bezan Text of Acts." In *Les Actes . . .*, edited by J. Kremer, pp. 447-455 (see §III above).

Chapter 1:

Fuller, R. H. "The Choice of Matthias." In *Studia Evangelica VI = TU* 112, edited by E. A. Livingstone, pp. 140-146. Berlin: Akademie-verlag, 1973.

Wilcox, M. "The Judas-Tradition in Acts 1:15-26." *NTS* 19 (1972–73): 438-452.

Chapter 2:

Fitzmyer, J. A. "David, 'Being Therefore a Prophet,' Acts 2:30." *CBQ* 34 (1972): 332-339.

Lohse, E. "Pentecoste." In *TDNT* 6:44-53.

Schweizer, E. "Concerning the Speeches in Acts." In *Studies in Luke-Acts*, edited by L. Keck and J. L. Martyn, pp. 208-216 (see §III above).

―――――― . "Pneuma." In *TDNT* 6:396-444.

Selected Bibliography

Zehnle, R. F. *Peter's Pentecost Discourse: Tradition and Lukan Reinter-pretation in Peter's Speeches of Acts 2 and 3*. SBLMS 15. Nashville: Abingdon, 1971.

Chapter 3:

Dahl, N. A. "The Story of Abraham in Luke-Acts." In *Studies in Luke-Acts*, edited by L. Keck and J. L. Martyn, pp. 139-158 (see §III above).

Hahn, F. "Das Problem alter christologischer Überlieferungen in der Apostelgeschichte unter besonderer Berücksichtigung von Act 13:19-21." In *Les Actes . . .*, edited by J. Kremer, pp. 129-154 (see §III above).

Hardon, J. A. "The Miracle Narratives in the Acts of the Apostles." *CBQ* 16 (1954): 303-318.

Johnston, G. "Christ as Archegos (3:15, 5:31)." *NTS* 27 (1981): 381-385.

Kurz, W. S. "Acts 3:19-26 as a Test of the Role of Eschatology in Lukan Christology." In *SBL 1977 Seminar Papers*, edited by P. J. Achtemeier, pp. 309-324. Missoula, Mont.: Scholars Press, 1977.

McRae, G. W. "Whom Heaven Must Receive until the Time." *Interpretation* 27 (1973): 151-165.

Neirynk, F. "The Miracle Stories in the Acts of the Apostles: An Introduction." In *Les Actes . . .*, edited by J. Kremer, pp. 169-213 (see §III above).

Tannehill, R. C. "The Composition of Acts 3–5: Narrative Development and Composition Effect." In *SBL 1984 Seminar Papers*, edited by K. H. Richards. Chico, Calif.: Scholars Press, 1984.

Chapters 4–5:

Black, M. "Judas of Galilee and Josephus' Fourth Philosophy." In *Josephus Studien,* edited by O. Betz, K. Haaker, and M. Hengel, pp. 45-54. Göttingen: Vandenhoeck and Ruprecht, 1974.

Brown, S. *Apostasy and Perseverance in the Theology of Luke.* Analecta Biblica 36, pp. 98-109. Rome: Pontifical Biblical Institute, 1969.

Dodd, C. H. *According to the Scriptures.* New York: Scribner, 1953.

Horst, P. W. van der. "Peter's Shadow: The Religio-Historical Background to Acts 5:15." *NTS* 23 (1977): 204-212.

Lampe, G. W. H. "Miracles in the Acts of the Apostles." In *Miracles: Cambridge Studies in Philosophy and History*, edited by C. F. D. Moule. London, 1965.

Noorda, S. J. "Scene and Summary. A Proposal for Reading Acts 4:32—5:16." In J. Kremer, *Les Actes . . .*, pp. 475-483 (see §III above).

516

Selected Bibliography

Chapter 6:

Hengel, M. *Between Jesus and Paul: Studies in the Earliest History of Christianity.* Translated by J. Bowden. Philadelphia: Fortress, 1983.

Richard, E. *Acts 6:1—8:4, The Author's Method of Composition.* SBLDS 14. Missoula, Mont.: Scholars Press, 1978.

Schneider, G. "Stephanus, die Hellenisten und Samaria." In *Les Actes* . . . , edited by J. Kremer, pp. 215-240 (see §III above).

Chapter 7:

Barrett, C. K. "Stephen and the Son of Man." In *Apophoreta, BZNW* 30, edited by W. Eltester and F. Kettler, pp. 32-38. Berlin: Topelmann, 1964.

Dibelius, M. "The Speeches in Acts and Ancient Historiography." In *Studies in the Acts of the Apostles.* New York: Scribner, 1956.

Donaldson, T. L. "Moses Typology and the Sectarian Nature of Early Christian Anti-Judaism: A Study in Acts 7." *JSNT* 12 (1981): 27-52.

Kilgallen, J. *The Stephen Speech: A Literary and Redactional Study of Acts 7:2-53.* Analecta Biblica 67. Rome: Pontifical Biblical Institute, 1976.

Pummer, R. "The Samaritan Pentateuch and the New Testament." *NTS* 22 (1975-76): 441-443.

Richard, E. "Acts 7: An Investigation of the Samaritan Evidence." *CBQ* 39 (1977): 190-208.

—————— . "The Polemical Character of the Joseph Episode in Acts 7." *JBL* 98 (1979): 255-267.

Wilson, S. G. *Luke and the Law,* chap. 3 (see §III above).

Chapter 8:

Barrett, C. K. "Light on the Holy Spirit from Simon Magus, Acts 8:4-25." In *Les Actes* . . . , edited by J. Kremer, pp. 281-295 (see §III above).

Kraabel, A. T. "New Evidence of the Samaritan Diaspora Has Been Found on Delos." *Biblical Archaeologist,* March 1984, pp. 44-46.

O'Toole, R. F. "Philip and the Ethiopian Eunuch, Acts 8:25-40." *JSNT* 17 (1983): 25-34.

Wilson, R. McL. "Simon and the Gnostic Origins." In *Les Actes* . . ., edited by J. Kremer, pp. 485-491 (see §III above).

Chapter 9:

Hedrick, C. W. "Paul's Conversion/Call: A Comparative Analysis of the Three Reports in Acts." *JBL* 100 (1981): 415-432.

Selected Bibliography

Hubbard, B. J. "The Role of Commissioning Accounts in Acts." In *Perspectives . . .* , edited by C. Talbert, pp. 187-198 (see §III above).

Parker, P. "Once More, Acts and Galatians."*JBL* 86 (1967): 175-182.

Schüssler-Fiorenza, E. "Miracles, Mission and Apologetics: An Introduction." In *Aspects of Religious Propaganda in Judaism and Early Christianity.* Notre Dame and London: University of Notre Dame Press, 1976, pp. 1-25.

Wainwright, A. W. "The Historical Value of Acts 9:19b-30," In *Studia Evangelica* 6, edited by E. A. Livingstone, pp. 589-594. Berlin: Akademieverlag, 1973.

Chapter 10:

Broughton, T. R. S. "The Roman Army." In Foakes-Jackson, *Beginnings . . .* , 5:427-445 (see §II above).

Jervell, J. *Luke and the People of God*, pp. 41-74 (see §III above).

Kraabel, A. T. "The Disappearance of the 'God-Fearers.' " *Numen* 28 (1981): 113-126.

Riesenfeld, H. "The Text of Acts 10:36." In *Text and Interpretation: Studies in the New Testament Presented to Matthew Black*, edited by E. Best and R. McL. Wilson, pp. 191-194. Cambridge: Cambridge University Press, 1979.

Chapter 11:

Cadbury, H. J. "Names for Christians and Christianity in Acts." In Foakes-Jackson, *Beginnings . . .* , 5:354-374 (see §II above).

Lacey, D. R. de. "Paul in Jerusalem." *NTS* 20 (1973): 82-86.

Neirynk, F. "The Miracle Stories of the Acts of the Apostles: An Introduction." In *Les Actes . . .*, edited by J. Kremer, pp. 169-213 (see §III above).

Robinson, D. F. "A Note on Acts 11:27-30." *JBL* 63 (1974): 169-172.

Talbert, C. H. "Again, Paul's Visits to Jerusalem." (see §III above).

Chapter 12:

Lake, K. "The Death of Herod Agrippa I." In Foakes-Jackson, *Beginnings . . .* , 5: 446-452 (see §II above).

Chapter 13:

Bowker, J. W. "Speeches in Acts: A Study of Proem and Yellammedenu Form." *NTS* 14 (1967): 96-110.

Dumais, M. *Le Lange . . .* (see §III above).

Selected Bibliography

Ellis, E. E. "The Role of the Christian Prophet in Acts." In *Prophecy and Hermeneutic in Early Christianity*, pp. 129-144. WUNT 18. Tübingen: Mohr, 1978.

———. "Midrashic Features in the Speeches of Acts." In Ellis, *Prophecy . . .* (see preceding item).

Goldsmith, D. "Acts 13:33-37: A Pesher on 2 Samuel 7." *JBL* 87 (1968): 321-324.

Gordon, R. P. "Targumic Parallels to Acts 13:18 and Didache 14:3." *NovTest* 16 (1974): 285-289.

Harvey, A. E. *Jesus and the Constraints of History*. Philadelphia: Westminster, 1982.

O'Toole, R. F. "Christ's Resurrection in Acts 13:13-52." *Biblica* 60 (1979): 361-372.

Pillai, C. A. J. *Apostolic Interpretation of History: A Commentary on Acts 13:16-41*. Hicksville, N.Y.: Exposition, 1980.

Townsend, J. T. "The Speeches in Acts." *Anglican Theological Review* 42 (1960): 150-160.

Unger, M. F. "Archaeology and Paul's Visit to Iconium, Lystra and Derbe." *BS* 118 (1961): 107-112.

———. "Pisidian Antioch and Gospel Penetration of the Ancient World." *BS* 118 (1961): 46-53.

Wilcox, M. *The Semitisms. . .*, pp. 161-164 (see §III above).

Yaure, L. "Elymas-Nehelamite-Pethor." *JBL* 79 (1960): 297-314.

Chapter 14:

Ballance, M. "The Site of Derbe: A New Inscription." *Anatolian Studies: British Institute of Archaeology at Ankara* 7 (1957): 145-151.

Fenton, J. "The Order of the Miracles Performed by Peter and Paul in Acts." *Expository Times* 77 (1965-1966): 381-383.

Hengel, M. *Acts and. . .*, pp. 108-110 (see §III above).

O'Neill, J. C. *The Theology. . .*, pp. 143-145 (see §III above).

Wilson, S. G. *The Gentiles. . .*, pp. 116-120 (see §III above).

Chapter 15:

Catchpole, D. R. "Paul, James and the Apostolic Decree." *NTS* 23 (1977): 428-444.

Danker, F. W. "Reciprocity in the Ancient World and in Acts 15:23-29." In *Political Issues in Luke-Acts*, edited by Cassidy and Scharper, pp. 49-58. New York: Maryknoll, 1983.

Jervell, J. "James, the Defender of Paul." In *Luke and the People of God*, pp. 185-207 (see §III above).

Selected Bibliography

Johnson, L. *Decision Making in the Church: A Biblical Model.* Philadelphia: Fortress, 1983.

Kaiser, W. C. "The Davidic Promise and the Inclusion of the Gentiles (Amos 9:9-15 and Acts 15:13-18)." In *Journal of the Evangelical Theological Society* 20 (1977): 97-111.

Nolland, J. L. "A Fresh Look at Acts 15:10." *NTS* 27 (1980): 105-114.

O'Neill, J. C. *The Theology. . .*, pp. 66-68, 125-131 (see §III above).

Richard, E. "The Divine Purpose: Jews and the Gentile Mission (Acts 15)." In *Luke-Acts. . .*, edited by C. Talbert, pp. 188-209 (see §III above).

_____ . "The Old Testament in Acts: Wilcox's Semitism in Retrospect." *CBQ* 42 (1980): 339.

Ropes, J. H. "The Text of Acts." In Foakes-Jackson, *Beginnings. . .*, 3:265-270 (see §II above).

Wilson, S. G. *Luke and the Law,* chap. 3 (see §III above).

Chapter 16:

Bowers, W. P. "Paul's Route through Mysia. A Note on Acts 16:8." *JThS* 30 (1979): 507-511.

Dibelius, M. "Style Criticism of the Book of Acts" (on the proposed "itinerary"). In M. Dibelius, *Studies. . .*, pp. 4-8, 125-126 (see §III above).

Hemer, C. J. "Phrygia: A Further Note." *JThS* 28 (1977): 99-101.

Kratz, R. *Rettungswunder: Motiv-, traditions- und formkritische Aufarbeitung einer biblischen Gattung,* pp. 474-492. Frankfurt, Bern, Las Vegas, 1979.

Lake, K. "Paul's Route in Asia Minor." In Foakes-Jackson, *Beginnings. . .*, 5:224-240 (see §II above).

Plümacher, E. "Wirklichkeitserfahrung. . ." (see §III above).

Ramsay, W. M. "Antiquities of Southern Phrygia and the Border Lands" (Acts 16:6; 18:23). *American Journal of Archaeology* 3 (1897): 344-368; 4 (1888): 263-283.

Robbins, V. K. "By Land and By Sea: The 'We' Passages and Ancient Sea Voyages." In *Perspectives. . .*, edited by C. Talbert, pp. 215-242 (see §III above).

Chapter 17:

Cadbury, H. J. *The Book of Acts in History,* pp. 44-53. London: Black, 1955.

Conzelmann, H. "The Address of Paul on the Aereopagus." In *Studies. . .*, edited by L. Keck and J. L. Martyn, pp. 217-230 (see §III above).

Selected Bibliography

Dibelius, M. "Paul on the Aereopagus," and "Paul in Athens." In Dibelius, *Studies. . .*, pp. 26-77, 78-83 (see §III above).

Hemer, C. J. "Paul at Athens: A Topographical Note." *NTS* 20 (1974): 341-350.

Judge, E. A. "The Decrees of Caesar at Thessalonica." *Reformed Theological Review* 30 (1971): 1-7.

Kurz, W. S. "Hellenistic Rhetoric in the Christological Proof of Luke-Acts." *CBQ* 42 (1980): 171-195.

O'Neill, J. C. *The Theology. . .*, pp. 160-171 (see §III above).

Chapter 18:

Boyd, D. A. "Ephesus." In *IDB Supplement*, pp. 269-271.

Deissmann, A. *Paul: A Study in Social and Religious History*, pp. 261-286 (Appendix 1, "The Proconsulate of L. Junius Gallio," and Plate I in front of book). New York: Harper Torchbooks, 1957.

Goodspeed, E. J. "Gaius Titius Justus." *JBL* 69 (1950): 382-383.

Greeven, H. "Euchomai." In *TDNT*, 2:777.

Hock, R. F. "The Workshop as a Social Setting for Paul's Missionary Preaching." *CBQ* 41 (1979): 438-450.

Rylaardam, J. C. "Nazirite." *IDB*, pp. 526-527.

Thompson, C. L. "Corinth." *IDB Supplement* (1976), pp. 179-180.

Chapter 19:

Hull, J. M. *Hellenistic Magic and the Synoptic Tradition*. SBT, second series, 28. Naperville: Allenson, 1974.

Käsemann, E. "The Disciples of John the Baptist in Ephesus." In *Essays on New Testament Themes* 41, pp. 136-148. London: SCM, 1964.

Kaiser, C. B. "The 'Rebaptism' of the Ephesian Twelve: Exegetical Study on Acts 19:1-7." *The Reformed Review* 31 (1977–1978): 57-61.

Mastin, B. A. "A Note on Acts 19:14." *Biblica* 59 (1978): 97-99.

————— . "Sceva the Chief Priest." *JThS* 27 (1976): 405-412.

Moessner, D. P. "Paul and the Pattern of the Prophet like Moses." In *SBL 1983 Seminar Papers*, edited by K. H. Richards, pp. 203-212. Chico, Calif.: Scholars Press.

Schüssler-Fiorenza, E. "Miracles, Mission and Apologetics: An Introduction," pp. 1-125 (see above).

Chapter 20:

Lambrecht, J. "Paul's Farewell Address at Miletus (Acts 20:17-38)." In *Les Actes. . .*, edited by J. Kremer, pp. 307-337 (see §III above).

Selected Bibliography

Lampe, G. W. "Grievous Wolves, Acts 20:29." In *Christ and Spirit in the New Testament*, edited by B. Lindars and S. Smalley, pp. 253-268. Cambridge: Cambridge University Press, 1973.

Michel, H. J. *Die Abschiedsrede des Paulus an die Kirche, Apg. 20:17-38.* StANT 35. Munich: Kösel, 1973.

Chapters 22–26:

Cadbury, H. J. "Roman Law and the Trial of Paul." In Foakes-Jackson, *Beginnings.* . ., 5:297-338, 172-185 (see §II above).

Jervell, J. "Paul: The Teacher of Israel, The Apologetic Speeches of Paul in Acts." In Jervell, *Luke and the People of God*, pp. 153-183 (see §III above).

Neyrey, J. "The Forensic Defense Speech and Paul's Trial Speeches in Acts 22-26." In *Luke-Acts.* . ., edited by C. Talbert, pp. 210-224 (see §III above).

O'Toole, R. F. *Acts 26, The Christological Climax of Paul's Defense.* Analecta Biblica 78. Rome: Biblical Institute, 1978.

Schubert, P. "The Final Cycle of Speeches in the Book of Acts." *JBL* 87 (1968): 1-16.

Sherwin-White, A. N. *Roman Society.* . ., pp. 48-70 (see §III above).

Stolle, V. *Der Zeuge als Angeklagten.* BWANT 102. Stuttgart: Kohlhammer, 1973.

Trites, A. A. "The Introduction of Legal Scenes and Language in the Book of Acts." *NovTest* 16 (1974): 278-284.

Chapters 27–28:

Conzelmann, H. *The Theology* . . . (see §III above).

Cullmann, O. *Peter: Disciple, Apostle, Martyr*, pp. 100-104. Translated by F. Filson. Philadelphia: Westminster, 1962.

Dibelius, M. "The Acts of the Apostles in the Setting of the History of Early Christian Literature." In Dibelius, *Studies.* . ., pp. 204-206 (see §III above).

Hauser, H. J. *Strukturen der Abschlusserzählung der Apostelgeschichte (Apg. 28:16-31).* Analecta Biblica 86. Rome: Pontifical Biblical Institute, 1979.

Katz, S. T. "Issues in the Separation of Judaism and Christianity after 70 C.E.: A Reconsideration." *JBL* 103 (1984): 43-76.

Ladouceur, D. "Hellenistic Preconceptions of Shipwreck and Pollution as a Context for Acts 27–28." *HTR* 73 (1980): 435-449.

Miesner, D. R. "The Circumferential Speeches of Luke-Acts: Pattern and Purpose." In *SBL 1978 Seminar Papers*, edited by P. J. Achtemeier. Missoula, Mont.: Scholars Press, 1978.

Selected Bibliography

Miles, G., and Trompf, G. "Luke and Antiphon: The Theology of Acts 27–28 in the Light of Pagan Beliefs about Divine Retribution." *HTR* 69 (1976): 259-267.

Ramsay, W. *St. Paul the Traveller and the Roman Citizen.* 14th ed. London: Hodder and Stoughton, 1920. Reprint, Grand Rapids: Baker, 1949.

Sanders, J. "The Salvation of the Jews in Luke-Acts." In *Luke-Acts. . .,* edited by C. Talbert, pp. 104-128 (see §III above).

Smith, J. *The Voyage and Shipwreck of St. Paul.* 4th ed., 1880. Reprint, Grand Rapids: Baker, 1978.

Walaskay, P. W. *"And So We Came to Rome," The Political Perspective of St. Luke.* SNTSMS 49. Cambridge: Cambridge University Press, 1983.

ABOUT THE AUTHOR

Dr. Gerhard Krodel has been dean of Gettysburg Seminary and professor of New Testament since 1977. His professional education took place at the Universities of Erlangen (Ph.D., 1950) and Tübingen. He also attended Concordia Seminary, St. Louis (1950–1951) and took courses at Union Theological Seminary, New York. He served as pastor (1951–1955), taught classical languages at Capital University (1955–1958), and was professor of New Testament at Wartburg Theological Seminary (1958–1964) and at the Lutheran Theological Seminary at Philadelphia (1964–1977). He has served on the Commission on Faith and Order of the National Council of Churches and on its Executive Committee, on the Task Force on Theology of the New Lutheran Church (1983), and, since 1978, on the International Orthodox-Lutheran Dialog. He is the editor of Proclamation Commentaries (Fortress Press).

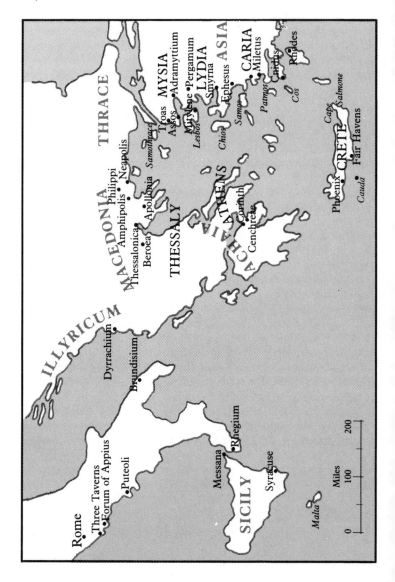

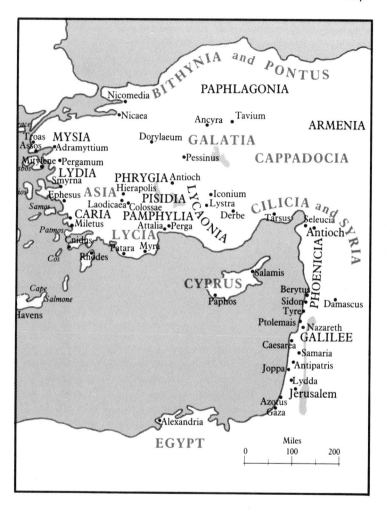

DATE DUE
